WEBSTER'S
WORLD FACTFINDER

WEBSTER'S

WORLD
FACTFINDER

OVER 5000 ENTRIES
INCLUDING GEOGRAPHICAL, ECONOMIC AND POLITICAL FACTS AND FIGURES

MORE THAN 500 MAPS

CHANCELLOR
PRESS

First published in 1990 by
Random Century Group Ltd

This 1992 edition published by Cresset Press

ISBN 0 09177 194 3

Set in Century Old Style

Data prepared on Telos and typeset
by Falcon Typographic Art Ltd, Edinburgh

Automatic Page Make-up
Digital Publications Ltd, Edinburgh

Printed and bound by
Thomson Press, India

Editors

Editor
Michael Upshall

Associate Editor
David Munro BSc, PhD

Project Editor
Jane Dickins

Database Editors
Claire Debenham
Gian Douglas Home
Claire Jenkins
Pamela Sharpe

Text Editor
Ingrid von Essen

Art Editor
Penny Hext

Office Administration
Anne von Broen

Designed by
Tek Art Ltd

Administration & Production
Edna A Moore, Tek Art

Cartography
Cedric Robson
Malcolm Ward

Database Software
BRS Software Products Ltd

Computers
Radstone Technology

Page Make-Up
Alex N Watson

Contributors

Ian D Derbyshire MA, PhD
J Denis Derbyshire BSc, PhD, FBIM
Bob Moore PhD
David Munro BSc, PhD

Aachen (French *Aix-la-Chapelle*) German cathedral city and spa in the *Land* of North Rhine–Westphalia, 72 km/45 mi SW of Cologne; population (1988) 239,000. It has thriving electronics, glass, and rubber industries, and is one of Germany's principal railway junctions.

Aachen was the Roman Aquisgranum, and from the time of Charlemagne until 1531 the German emperors were crowned there. Charlemagne was born and buried in Aachen, and founded the cathedral 796. The 14th-century town hall, containing the hall of the emperors, is built on the site of Charlemagne's palace.

Aalborg (Danish *Ålborg*) port in Denmark 32 km/20 mi inland from the Kattegat, on the south shore of the Limfjord; population (1988) 155,000. One of Denmark's oldest towns, it has a castle and the fine Budolfi church. It is the capital of Nordjylland county in Jylland (Jutland); the port is linked to Nørresundby on the north side of the fjord by a tunnel built 1969.

Aalst (French *Alost*) industrial town (brewing, textiles) in East Flanders, Belgium, on the river Dender 24 km/15 mi NW of Brussels; population (1982) 78,700.

Aarhus (Danish *Århus*) second city of Denmark, on the east coast overlooking the Kattegat; population (1988) 258,000. It is the capital of Aarhus county in Jylland (Jutland), and a shipping and commercial centre.

Abadan Iranian oil port on the east side of the Shatt-al-Arab; population (1986) 294,000. Abadan is the chief refinery and shipping centre for Iran's oil industry, nationalized 1951. This measure was the beginning of the worldwide movement by oil-producing countries to assume control of profits from their own resources.

Abakan coalmining city and capital of Khakass Autonomous Region, Krasnoyarsk Territory, in S USSR; population (1987) 181,000.

Abbeville town in N France in the Somme *département*, 19 km/12 mi inland from the mouth of the Somme; population (1982) 26,000. During World War I it was an important base for the British armies.

Abeokuta agricultural trade centre in Nigeria, W Africa, on the Ogun River, 103 km/64 mi north of Lagos; population (1983) 309,000.

Aberbrothock another name for ◊Arbroath, town in Scotland.

Aberdare town in Mid Glamorgan, Wales, formerly producing high-grade coal, and now with electrical and light engineering industries; population (1981) 36,600.

Aberdeen city and seaport on the E coast of Scotland, administrative headquarters of Grampian region; population (1986) 214,082. Shore-based maintenance and service depots for the North Sea oil rigs.

It is Scotland's third largest city, and is rich in historical interest and fine buildings, including the Municipal Buildings (1867); King's College (1494) and Marischal College (founded 1593; housed in one of the largest granite buildings in the world, 1836) which together form Aberdeen University; St Machar Cathedral (1378), and the Auld Brig o'Balgownie (1320). Industries include agricultural machinery, paper, and textiles; fishing, ship-building, granite-quarrying, and engineering. Oil discoveries in the North Sea in the 1960s–70s transformed Aberdeen into the European 'offshore capital', with an airport and heliport linking the mainland to the rigs.

Aberdeenshire former county in E Scotland, merged in 1975 in Grampian region.

Aberystwyth resort town in Wales; population (1981) 8,500. It is the unofficial capital of the Welsh-speaking area of Wales. The University College of Wales 1872, Welsh Plant Breeding Station, and National Library of Wales are here.

Abidja'n port and capital of the Republic of Ivory Coast, W Africa; population (1982) 1,850,000. Products include coffee, palm oil, cocoa, and timber (mahogany). To be replaced as capital by Yamoussoukro.

Abilene town in Kansas, USA, on the Smoky Hill River; population (1980) 98,500. A western railway terminus, Abilene was a shipping point for cattle in the 1860s. Its economy includes the manufacture of aircraft and missile components and oil-field equipment.

Abingdon town in Oxfordshire, England, on the Thames 10 km/6 mi S of Oxford; population (1981) 22,500. The remains of the 7th-century abbey include Checker Hall, restored as an Elizabethan-type theatre. The 15th-century bridge was reconstructed 1929. There are light industries.

Abkhazia Autonomous Soviet Socialist Republic within Georgia, USSR, situated on the Black Sea; area 8,600 sq km/3,320 sq mi; population (1989) 526,000. Abkhazia, a Georgian kingdom from the 4th century, was inhabited traditionally by Abhkazis, an ethnic group converted from Christianity to Islam in the 17th century. By the 1980s some 17% were Muslims and two-thirds were of Georgian origin. In Mar–Apr and July 1989, Abkhazis demanded secession from Georgia and reinstatement as a full union republic; violent inter-ethnic clashes erupted in which at least 20 people died. Georgian nationalists want instead the republic to be incorporated as part of Georgia.

Åbo Swedish name for ◊Turku in Finland.

Abomey town and port of Benin, W Africa; population (1982) 54,500. It was once the capital of the kingdom of Dahomey, which flourished in the 17th–19th centuries, and had a mud-built defence wall 10 km/6 mi in circumference.

Abruzzi mountainous region of S central Italy, comprising the provinces of L'Aquila, Chieti, Pescara, and Teramo; area 10,800 sq km/4,169 sq mi; population (1988) 1,258,000; capital L'Aquila. Gran Sasso d'Italia, 2,914 m/9,564 ft, is the highest point of the ◊Apennines.

Abu Dhabi sheikdom in SW Asia, on the Arabian Gulf, capital of the United Arab Emirates. Formerly under British protection, it has been ruled since 1971 by Sheik Zayed Bin al-Nahayan, who is also president of the Supreme Council of Rulers of the United Arab Emirates.

Abuja city in Nigeria, under contruction from 1976, planned to replace Lagos as capital. Shaped like a crescent, it was designed by the Japanese architect Kenzo Tange.

Abu Musa a small island in the Persian Gulf. Formerly owned by the ruler of Sharjah, it was forcibly occupied by Iran in 1971.

Abu Simbel former site of two ancient temples in S Egypt, built during the reign of Ramses II and commemorating him and his wife Nefertari; before the site was flooded by the Aswan High Dam, the temples were moved, in sections, 1966–67.

Abydos ancient city in Upper Egypt; the Great Temple of Seti I dates from about 1300 BC.

Abyssinia former name of ◊Ethiopia.

Acadia (French *Acadie*) name given to ◊Nova Scotia by French settlers 1604, from which the term Cajun derives.

Acapulco or *Acapulco de Juarez* port and holiday resort in Mexico; population (1985) 638,000.

Accra capital and port of Ghana; population of greater Accra region (1984) 1,420,000. The port trades in cacao, gold, and timber. Industries include engineering, brewing, and food processing. Osu (Christiansborg) Castle is the presidential residence.

Accrington industrial town (textiles, engineering) in Lancashire, England; population (1981) 36,000.

Achaea in ancient Greece, and also today, an area of the N Peloponnese; the *Achaeans* were the predominant society during the Mycenaean period and are said by Homer to have taken part in the siege of Troy.

Achill Island or *Eagle Island* largest of the Irish islands, off County Mayo; area 148 sq km/57 sq mi.

Aconcagua an extinct volcano in the Argentine Andes, the highest peak in the Americas. Height 6960 m/22,834 ft. It was first climbed by Vines and Zeebruggen in 1897.

Acre or *'Akko* seaport in Israel; population (1983) 37,000. Taken by the Crusaders 1104, it was captured by Saladin 1187 and retaken by Richard I (the Lionheart) 1191. Napoleon failed in a siege 1799; Gen Allenby captured it 1918; and it became part of Israel 1948.

ACT abbreviation for ◊*Australian Capital Territory*.

Adana capital of Adana (Seyhan) province, S Turkey; population (1985) 776,000. It is a major cotton-growing centre and Turkey's fourth largest city.

Addis Ababa or *Adis Abeba* capital of Ethiopia; population (1984) 1,413,000. It was founded 1887 by Menelik, chief of Shoa, who ascended the throne of Ethiopia 1889. His former residence, Menelik Palace, is now occupied by the government; the city is the headquarters of the Organization of African Unity.

Adelaide capital and industrial city of South Australia; population (1986) 993,100. Industries include oil refining, shipbuilding, and the manufacture of electrical goods and cars. Grain, wool, fruit, and wine are exported. Founded in 1836, Adelaide was named after William IV's queen.

It is a fine example of town planning, with residential districts separated from the commercial area by the river Torrens, dammed to form a lake. Impressive streets include King William Street and North Terrace, and fine buildings include Parliament House, Government House, the Anglican cathedral of St Peter, the Roman Catholic cathedral, two universities, the State observatory, and the museum and art gallery.

Adélie Land (French *Terre Adélie*) region of Antarctica claimed by France; about 140 km/87 mi long, mountainous, covered in snow and ice, and inhabited only by a research team. It was claimed for France 1840.

Aden (Arabic *'Adan*) capital of South Yemen, on a rocky peninsula at the SW corner of Arabia, commanding the entrance to the Red Sea; population (1984) 318,000. It comprises the new administrative centre Madinet al-Sha'ab; the commercial and business quarters of Crater and Tawahi, and the harbour area of Ma'alla. The city's economy is based on oil refining, fishing, and shipping. A British territory from 1839, Aden became part of independent South Yemen 1967.

history After annexation by Britain, Aden and its immediately surrounding area (121 sq km/ 47 sq mi) were developed as a ship-refuelling station following the opening of the Suez Canal 1869.

It was a colony 1937–63, and then, after a period of transitional violence between rival nationalist groups and British forces, was combined with the former Aden protectorate (290,000 sq km/112,000 sq mi) to create the Southern Yemen People's Republic 1967, later renamed the People's Democratic Republic of Yemen.

Adige the second longest river (after the Po) in Italy, 410 km/255 mi in length. It crosses the Lombardy Plain and enters the Adriatic just north of the Po delta.

Adirondacks mountainous area in NE New York State, USA; rising to 1,629 m/5,344 ft at Mount Marcy; the source of the Hudson and Ausable rivers; named after a Native American people. It is noted for its scenery and sports facilities.

Admiralty Islands group of small islands in the SW Pacific, part of Papua New Guinea; population (1980) 25,000. The main island is Manus. The islands became a German protectorate 1884 and an Australian mandate 1920.

Adowa alternative form of ◊Aduwa, Ethiopia.

Adriatic Sea large arm of the Mediterranean Sea, lying NW to SE between the Italian and the Balkan peninsulas. The western shore is Italian; the eastern Yugoslav and Albanian. The sea is about 805 km/500 mi long, and its area is 135,250 sq km/52,220 sq mi.

Aduwa or *Adwa, Adowa* former capital of Ethiopia, about 180 km/110 mi SW of Massawa at an altitude of 1,910 m/6,270 ft; population (1982) 27,000.

Aegean Islands the islands of the Aegean Sea, but more specifically a region of Greece comprising the Dodecanese islands, the Cyclades islands, Lesvos, Samos, and Chios; population (1981) 428,500; area 9,122 sq km/3,523 sq mi.

Aegean Sea branch of the Mediterranean between Greece and Turkey; the Dardanelles connect it with the Sea of Marmara. The numerous islands in the Aegean Sea include Crete, the Cyclades, the Sporades, and the Dodecanese. There is political tension between Greece and Turkey over sea limits claimed by Greece around such islands as Lesvos, Chios, Samos, and Kos.

The Aegean Sea is named after the legendary Aegeus, who drowned himself in the belief that Theseus, his son, had been killed.

Aegina (Greek *Aíyna* or *Aíyina*) Greek island in the Gulf of Aegina about 32 km/20 mi SW of Piraeus; area 83 sq km/32 sq mi; population about 11,100. In 1811 remarkable sculptures were recovered from a Doric temple in the

northeast (restored by Thorwaldsen) and taken to Munich, Germany.

Aeolian Islands another name for the ◊Lipari Islands.

Afars and the Issas, French Territory of the former French territory which became the Republic of ◊Djibouti 1977.

Afghanistan mountainous, landlocked country in S central Asia, bounded to the N by the USSR, to the W by Iran, and to the S and E by Pakistan.

Africa second largest of the continents, three times the area of Europe.

area 30,097,000 sq km/11,620,451 sq mi

largest cities Cairo, Algiers, Lagos, Kinshasa, Abidjan, Tunis, Cape Town, Nairobi

physical dominated by a central plateau, which includes the world's largest desert (Sahara); Nile and Zaïre rivers, but generally there is a lack of rivers, and also of other inlets, so that Africa has proportionately the shortest coastline of all the continents; comparatively few offshore islands; 75% is within the tropics

features Great Rift Valley; immensely rich fauna and flora

exports has 30% of the world's minerals; crops include coffee (Kenya), cocoa (Ghana, Nigeria), cotton (Egypt, Uganda); but many countries (Zaïre, Uganda, Ethiopia, Zambia, Mozambique) produce less than 50% of their own food needs

population (1984) 537,000,000; annual growth rate 3%

language Hamito-Semitic in the north; Bantu below the Sahara; Khosan languages with 'click' consonants in the far south

religion Islam in the north; animism below the Sahara, which survives alongside Christianity (both Catholic and Protestant) in many central and southern areas.

Africa, Horn of the projection constituted by Somalia and adjacent territories.

Agadir resort and seaport in S Morocco, near the mouth of the river Sus. Population (1984) 110,500. It was rebuilt after being destroyed by an earthquake in 1960.

Agaña capital of Guam, in the W Pacific; population (1981) 110,000. It is a US naval base.

Agincourt site of battle in which Henry V of England defeated the French on 24 Oct 1415, St Crispin's Day. The village of Agincourt (modern *Azincourt*) is south of Calais, in N France.

Agra city of Uttar Pradesh, republic of India, on the river Jumna, 160 km/100 mi SE of Delhi; population (1981) 747,318. A commercial and university centre, it was the capital of the Mogul empire 1527–1628, from which period dates the Taj Mahal.

history Zahir ud-din Mohammed (known as 'Babur'), the first great Mogul ruler, made Agra his capital in 1527. His grandson Akbar rebuilt

Afghanistan
Republic of
(Jamhuria Afghanistan)

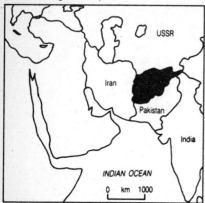

area 652,090 sq km/251,707 sq mi
capital Kábul
towns Kandahár, Herát
physical mountainous, with rivers and desert areas
features Hindu Kush mountain range (Khyber and Salang passes and Panjshir Valley)
head of state Najibullah Ahmadzai (president) from 1986
head of government Sultan Ali Keshtmand (prime minister) from 1989
political system military emergency republic
political parties People's Democratic Party of Afghanistan (PDPA), Marxist-Leninist; Hesb-i-Islami and Jamiat-i-Islami, Islamic fundament alist mujahaddin; National Liberation Front, moderate mujahaddin
exports dried fruit, rare minerals, natural gas (piped to USSR), karakul lamb skins, Afghan coats
currency afgháni (99.25 = £1 Feb 1990)
population (1988) 10,000,000–12,000,000 (more than 5 million have become refugees since 1979); annual growth rate 0.6%
life expectancy men 37, women 37
language Pushtu
religion Muslim: 80% Sunni, 20% Shi'ite
literacy 39% male/8% female (1985 est)
GNP $3.3 bn (1985); $275 per head of population
chronology
1747 Afghanistan became an independent emirate.
1838–1919 Afghan Wars waged between Afghanistan and Britain to counter the threat to British India from expanding Russian influence in Afghanistan.
1919 Afghanistan recovered full independence following Third Afghan War.
1953 Lt-Gen Daud Khan became prime minister and introduced reform programme.
1963 Daud Khan forced to resign and constitutional monarchy established.
1973 Monarchy overthrown in coup by Daud Khan.
1978 Daud Khan ousted by Taraki and the PDPA
1979 Soviet Union entered country to prop up government; they installed Babrak Karmal in power.
1986 Replacement of Karmal as leader by Dr Najibullah Ahmadzai. Partial Soviet troop withdrawal.
1988 New non-Marxist constitution adopted.
1989 Withdrawal of Soviet troops; state of emergency imposed in response to intensification of civil war.

---

the Red Fort of Salim Shah (1566), and is buried outside the city in the splendid tomb at Sikandra. In the 17th century the buildings of Shah-Jehan made Agra one of the most beautiful cities in the world. The Taj Mahal, erected as a tomb for the emperor's wife Mumtaz Mahal, was completed in 1650. Agra's political importance dwindled from 1658, when Aurangzeb moved the capital back to Delhi.

Agrigento town in Sicily, noted for Greek temples; population (1981) 51,300. The Roman *Agrigentum*, it was long called *Girgenti* until renamed Agrigento 1927.

Aguascalientes city in central Mexico, and capital of a state of the same name; population (1980) 359,454. It has hot mineral springs.

Agulhas southernmost cape in Africa. In 1852 the troopship *Birkenhead* sank off the cape with the loss of over 400 lives.

Ahaggar or *Hoggar* mountainous plateau of the central Sahara, Algeria, whose highest point, Tahat, at 2,918 m/9,850 ft, lies between Algiers and the mouth of the Niger. It is the home of the formerly nomadic Tuaregs.

Ahmadnagar city in Maharashtra, India, 195 km/120 mi E of Bombay, on the left bank of the river Sina; population (1981) 181,000. It is a centre of cotton trade and manufacture.

Ahmedabad or *Ahmadabad* capital of Gujarat, India; population (1981) 2,515,195. It is a cotton-manufacturing centre, and has many edifices of the Hindu, Muslim, and Jain faiths.

Ahmedabad was founded in the reign of Ahmad Shah 1412, and came under the control of the East India Company 1818. In 1930 Mahatma Gandhi marched to the sea from here to protest against the government salt monopoly.

Ahváz industrial capital of the province of Khuzestan, W Iran; population (1986) 590,000.

Ahvenanmaa Island island in the Gulf of Bothnia, Finland; largest of the ◊Åland Islands.

Ailsa Craig rocky islet in the Firth of Clyde, Scotland, about 16 km/10 mi off the coast of Strathclyde, opposite Girvan. Ailsa Craig rock is used in the manufacture of curling stones. It is a breeding ground for birds.

Aïn French river giving its name to a *département* (administrative region); length 190 km/118 mi; it is a right-bank tributary of the Rhône.

Aïntab Syrian name of ◊Gaziantep, city in Turkey.

Aisne river of N France, giving its name to a *département*; length 282 km/175 mi.

Aix-en-Provence town in the *département* of Bouches-du-Rhône, France, 29 km/18 mi north of Marseille; population (1982) 127,000. It is the capital of Provence, and dates from Roman times, when it was known as *Aquae Sextiae*. It has a Gothic cathedral and a university 1409. The painter Cézanne was born here.

Aix-la-Chapelle French name of ◊Aachen, ancient city in Germany.

Aix-les-Bains spa with hot springs in the *département* of Savoie, France, near Lake Bourget, 13 km/8 mi north of Chambéry; population (1982) 22,534.

Ajaccio capital and second largest port of Corsica; population (1982) 55,279. Founded by the Genoese in 1492, it was the birthplace of Napoleon; it has been French since 1768.

Ajman smallest of the seven states that make up the United Arab Emirates; area 250 sq km/96 sq mi; population (1980) 36,000.

Ajmer town in Rajasthan state, India; population (1981) 376,000. Situated in a deep valley in the Aravalli mountains, it is a commercial and industrial centre, notably of cotton manufacture. It has many ancient remains, including a Jain temple. It was formerly the capital of the small state of Ajmer, which was merged with Rajasthan 1956.

AK abbreviation for ◊*Alaska*.

Akaba alternative transliteration of ◊Aqaba, gulf of the Red Sea.

Akko Israeli name for the port of ◊Acre.

Akola town in Maharashtra state, India, near the Purnar; population (1981) 176,000. It is an important cotton and grain centre.

Akron (Greek 'summit') city in Ohio, USA, on the Cuyahoga River, 56 km/35 mi SE of Cleveland; population (1980) 660,000. Almost half the world supply of rubber is processed here.
history Akron was first settled 1807. Dr B F Goodrich established a rubber factory 1870, and the industry grew immensely with the rising demand for car tyres from about 1910.

Akrotiri peninsula on the south coast of Cyprus; it has a British military base.

Aksai Chin part of Himalayan Kashmir lying to the east of the Karakoram range. Occupied by China but claimed by India.

Aktyubinsk industrial city in the republic of Kazakh, USSR; population (1987) 248,000. Established 1869, it expanded after the opening of the Trans-Caspian railway 1905.

AL abbreviation for ◊*Alabama*.

Alabama state of S USA; nickname Heart of Dixie/Camellia State
area 134,700 sq km/51,994 sq mi
capital Montgomery
towns Birmingham, Mobile, Huntsville, Tuscaloosa
physical the state comprises the Cumberland Plateau in the north; the Black Belt, or Canebrake, which is excellent cotton-growing country, in the centre; and south of this, the coastal plain of Piny Woods. The main river is the river Alabama
features Alabama and Tennessee rivers; Appalachian mountains; George Washington Carver Museum at the Tuskegee Institute (a college founded for blacks by Booker T Washington)
products cotton still important though no longer prime crop; soybeans, peanuts, wood products, coal, iron, chemicals, textiles, paper
population (1987) 4,149,000
famous people Nat King Cole, Helen Keller, Joe Louis, Jesse Owens, Booker T Washington
history first settled by the French in the early 18th century, it was ceded to Britain 1763, passed to the USA 1783, and became a state 1819. It was one of the Confederate States in the American Civil War.

Åland Islands (Finnish *Ahvenanmaa* 'land of waters') group of some 6,000 islands in the Baltic Sea, at the southern extremity of the Gulf of Bothnia; area 1,481 sq km/572 sq mi; population (1988) 23,900. Only 80 are inhabited; the largest island has a small town, Mariehamn. When Finland became independent 1917, the Swedish-speaking

Alabama

islanders claimed the right of self-determination and were granted autonomous status 1920. The main sectors of the island economy are tourism, agriculture, and shipping.

Alaska largest state of the USA, on the NW extremity of North America, separated from the lower 48 states by British Columbia
area 1,531,100 sq km/591,005 sq mi
capital Juneau
towns Anchorage, Fairbanks, Fort Yukon, Holy Cross, Nome
physical much of Alaska is mountainous and includes Mount McKinley, 6,194 m/20,329 ft, the highest peak in North America, surrounded by a national park. Reindeer thrive in the Arctic tundra and elsewhere there are extensive forests
features Yukon river; Rocky Mountains, including Mount McKinley, Mount Katmai, a volcano which erupted 1912 and formed the Valley of Ten Thousand Smokes (the smoke and steam still escaping from fissures in the floor) now a national monument; Arctic Wild Life Range, with the only large herd of North American caribou; Little Diomede Island, which is only 4 km/2.5 mi from Big Diomede/Ratmanov Island in the USSR; reindeer herds on the tundra; an act of 1980 gave environmental protection to 42 million ha/104 million acres. The chief railway line runs from Seward to Fairbanks, which is linked by road (via Canada) with Seattle. Near Fairbanks is the University of Alaska
products oil, natural gas, coal, copper, iron, gold, tin, fur, salmon fisheries and canneries, lumber
population (1987) 538,000, including about 50,000 American Indians, Aleuts, and Inuits
history the first European to visit Alaska was Vitus Bering 1741. Alaska was a Russian colony from 1744 until purchased by the USA 1867 for $7,200,000; it became a state 1959. Exploited from 1968, especially in the Prudhoe Bay area to the SE of Point Barrow, are the most valuable mineral resources. An oil pipeline (1977) runs from Prudhoe Bay to the port of Valdez.

Oilspill from a tanker caused great environmental damage 1989. An underground natural-gas pipeline is under construction to Chicago and San Francisco.

Alaska Highway road that runs from Fort St John, British Columbia, to Fairbanks, Alaska (2,450 km/1,522 mi). It was built 1942 as a supply route for US forces in Alaska.

Alba Celtic name for Scotland.

Albacete market town in the province of the same name, SE Spain; population (1986) 127,000. Once famous for cutlery, it now produces clothes and footwear.

Alba Iulia (German *Karlsburg*) a city on the river Mures, W central Romania, founded by the Romans in the 2nd century AD. The Romanian kings were crowned here. Population (1985) 64,300.

Albania country in SE Europe, bounded to the W and SW by the Mediterranean sea, to the N and E by Yugoslavia, and to the SE by Greece.

Albany capital of New York State, USA, situated on the river Hudson, about 225 km/140 mi north of New York City. With Schenectady and Troy it forms a metropolitan area, population (1980) 794,298.

Albany port in Western Australia, population (1986) 14,100. It suffered from the initial development of ◊Fremantle, but has grown with the greater exploitation of the surrounding area. The Albany Doctor is a cooling breeze from the sea, rising in the afternoon.

Alberta province of W Canada
area 661,200 sq km/255,223 sq mi
capital Edmonton
towns Calgary, Lethbridge, Medicine Hat, Red Deer
physical the Rocky Mountains; dry, treeless prairie in the centre and south; towards the north this merges into a zone of poplar, then mixed forest. The valley of the Peace River is the most northerly farming land in Canada (except for

Alaska

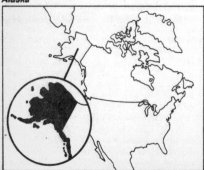

Alberta

Albania
Socialist People's Republic of
(Republika Popullore Socialiste e Shqipërisë)

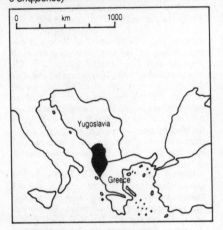

area 28,748 sq km/11,097 sq mi
capital Tirana
towns Shkodër, Vlorë, chief port Durrës
physical mainly mountainous, with rivers flowing E–W, and a small coastal plain
features Dinaric Alps, with wild boar and wolves
head of state Ramiz Alia from 1982
head of government Adil Carcani from 1982. Enver Hoxha remained premier as first secretary of Albanian Party of Labour until his death 1985

political system one-party socialist republic
political parties Party of Labour of Albania (PLA), Marxist-Leninist; Committee for the Democratic Movement in Albania (based in Yugoslavia)
exports crude oil, bitumen, chrome, iron ore, nickel, coal, copper wire, tobacco, fruit
currency lek (10.19 = £1 Feb 1990)
population (1987) 3,080,000; annual growth rate 2.1%
life expectancy men 69, women 73
language Albanian
religion Muslim 70%, although since 1967 Albania is officially a secular state
literacy 75% (1986)
GNP $2.8 bn (1986 est); $900 per head of population
chronology
1912 Albania achieved independence from Turkey.
1925 Republic proclaimed.
1928–39 Monarchy of King Zog.
1939–44 Under Italian and then German rule.
1946 Communist republic proclaimed under the leadership of Enver Hoxha.
1949 Admitted into Comecon.
1961 Break with Khrushchev's USSR.
1978 Break with 'revisionist' China.
1985 Death of Hoxha.
1987 Normal diplomatic relations restored with Canada, Greece, and West Germany.
1988 Attendance of conference of Balkan states for the first time since the 1930s.
1990 State of emergency imposed around border town of Shkoder.

Inuit pastures), and there are good grazing lands in the foothills of the Rockies
features Banff, Jasper, and Waterton Lake national parks; annual Calgary stampede, extensive dinosaur finds near Drumheller
products coal; wheat, barley, oats, sugar beet in the south; more than a million head of cattle; oil and natural gas
population (1986) 2,375,000
history in the 17th century much of its area was part of a grant to the Hudson's Bay Company for the fur trade. It became a province in 1905.
Albert Canal canal designed as part of Belgium's frontier defences; it also links the industrial basin of Liège with the port of Antwerp. It was built 1930–39 and named after King Albert I.
Albert, Lake former name of Lake ◊Mobutu in central Africa.
Albi chief town in Tarn *département*, Midi-Pyrénées, SW France, on the river Tarn, 72 km/45 mi NE of Toulouse; population (1983) 45,000. It was

the centre of the Albigensian heresy and the birthplace of the artist Toulouse-Lautrec. It has a 13th-century cathedral.
Ålborg alternative form of ◊Aalborg, Denmark.
Albuquerque largest city of New Mexico, USA, situated east of the Rio Grande, in the Pueblo district; population (1982) 342,000. Founded 1706, it was named after Alfonso de Albuquerque. It is a resort and industrial centre, specializing in electronics.
Albury-Wodonga twin town on the New South Wales/Victoria border, Australia; population (1981) 54,214. It was planned to relieve overspill from Melbourne and Sydney, and produces car components.
Alcatraz small island in San Francisco Bay, California, USA. Its fortress was a military prison 1886–1934, and then a federal penitentiary until closed 1963. The dangerous currents meant few successful escapes. Inmates included the gangster Al Capone and the 'Birdman of Alcatraz', a prisoner who used

his time in solitary confinement to become an authority on cage birds. American Indian 'nationalists' took over the island 1970 as a symbol of their lost heritage.

Aldabra high limestone island group in the Seychelles, some 400 km/260 mi NW of Madagascar; area 154 sq km/59 sq mi. A nature reserve since 1976, it has rare plants and animals, including the giant tortoise.

Aldeburgh small town and coastal resort in Suffolk, England; site of an annual music festival founded by the composer Benjamin Britten. Also the home of the Britten-Pears School for Advanced Studies.

Aldermaston village in Berkshire, England; site of an atomic and biological weapons research establishment. In 1958–63 the Campaign for Nuclear Disarmament made it the focus of an annual Easter protest march.

Alderney third largest of the UK Channel Islands, with its capital at St Anne's; area 8 sq km/3 sq mi; population (1980) 2,000. It gives its name to a breed of cattle, better known as the Guernsey.

Aldershot town in Hampshire, England, SW of London; population (1981) 32,500. It has a military camp and barracks dating from 1854.

Alençon capital of the Orne *département* of France, situated in a rich agricultural plain to the SE of Caen; population (1983) 33,000. Lace, now a declining industry, was once an important product.

Alentejo a region of E central Portugal divided into the districts of Alto Alentejo and Baixo Alentejo. The chief towns are Evora, Neja, and Portalegre.

Aleppo (Syrian *Halab*) ancient city in NW Syria; population (1981) 977,000. There has been a settlement on the site for at least 4,000 years.

Alessandria town in N Italy on the river Tanaro; population (1981) 100,500. It was founded 1168 by Pope Alexander III as a defence against Frederick Barbarossa. There is an annual motorcyclists' rally at the shrine of their patroness, the Madonna of the Centaurs.

Aletsch most extensive glacier in Europe, 23.6 km/14.7 mi long, beginning on the southern slopes of the Jungfrau in the Bernese Alps, Switzerland.

Aleutian Islands volcanic island chain in the N Pacific, stretching 1,900 km/1,200 mi SW of Alaska, of which it forms part. Population 5,000 Inuit (Eskimo), most of whom belong to the Greek Orthodox Church, 1,600 Aleuts, plus a large US military establishment. There are 14 large and over 100 small islands, running along the Aleutian Trench. The islands are mountainous, barren, and treeless; they are ice-free all the year round, but are often foggy.

Alexandretta former name of ◊Iskenderun, a port in S Turkey.

Alexandria or *El Iskandariya* city, chief port, and second largest city of Egypt, situated between the Mediterranean and Lake Maryut; population (1986) 5,000,000. It is linked by canal with the Nile and is an industrial city (oil refining, gas processing, and cotton and grain trading). Founded 331 BC by Alexander the Great, Alexandria was for over 1,000 years the capital of Egypt.

history The principal centre of Hellenistic culture, Alexandria has since the 4th century AD been the seat of a Christian patriarch. In 641 it was captured by the Muslim Arabs, and after the opening of the Cape route its trade rapidly declined. Early in the 19th century it began to recover its prosperity, and its growth was encouraged by its use as the main British naval base in the Mediterranean during both world wars. Of the large European community, most were expelled after the Suez Crisis 1956 and their property confiscated.

Few relics of antiquity remain. The Pharos, the first lighthouse and one of the seven wonders of the ancient world, has long since disappeared. The library, said to have contained 700,000 volumes, was destroyed by the caliph Omar in 642. Pompey's Pillar is a column erected, as a landmark from the sea, by the emperor Diocletian. Two obelisks that once stood before the Caesarum temple are now in London (Cleopatra's Needle) and New York respectively.

Alexandrovsk older name of ◊Zaporozhya, city in the USSR.

Algarve ancient kingdom in S Portugal, the modern district of Faro, a popular holiday resort; population (1981) 323,500.

The Algarve began to be wrested from the Moors in the 12th century and was united with Portugal as a kingdom in 1253. It incudes the SW extremity of Europe, Cape St Vincent, where the British fleet defeated the Spanish in 1797.

Algeciras port in S Spain, to the W of Gibraltar across the Bay of Algeciras; population (1986) 97,000. Founded by the Moors 713, it was taken from them by Alfonso XI of Castile 1344. Virtually destroyed in a fresh attack by the Moors, it was re-founded 1704 by Spanish refugees who had fled from Gibraltar after it had been captured by the British.

Algeria country in N Africa, bounded to the E by Tunisia and Libya, to the SE by Niger, to the SW by Mali, to the NW by Morocco, and to the N by the Mediterranean Sea.

Algiers (Arabic *al-Jazair*, French *Alger*) capital of Algeria, situated on the narrow coastal plain between.the Atlas mountains and the Mediterranean; population (1984) 2,442,300.

Founded by the Arabs AD 935, Algiers was taken by the Turks 1518, and by the French 1830. The old town is dominated by the Kasbah, the palace and prison of the Turkish rulers. The

Algeria
Democratic and Popular Republic of
(al-Jumhuriya al-Jazairiya ad-Dimuqratiya ash-Shàbiya)

area 2,381,741 sq km/919,352 sq mi
capital al-Jazair (Algiers)
towns Qacentina/Constantine; ports are Ouahran/Oran, Annaba
physical coastal plains, mountain plateau, desert
features Atlas mountains, Barbary Coast
head of state Benjedid Chadli from 1979
political system one-party socialist republic
political parties National Liberation Front (FLN), nationalist socialist
exports oil, natural gas, iron, wine, olive oil
currency dinar (13.51 = £1 Mar 1989)
population (1988 est) 23,850,000 (83% Arab, 17% Berber); annual growth rate 3.0%
life expectancy men 59, women 62
language Arabic (official); Berber, French
religion Sunni Muslim
literacy 63% male/37% female (1985 est)
GDP $58.0 bn (1986); $2,645 per head of population
chronology
1954 War for independence from France led by the FLN
1963 Independence achieved. Ben Bella elected president.
1965 Ben Bella deposed by military, led by Col Houari Boumédienne.
1976 New constitution approved.
1978 Death of Boumédienne.
1979 Bendjedid Chadli elected president. Ben Bella released from house arrest. FLN adopted new party structure.
1981 Algeria helped in securing release of US prisoners in Iran.
1983 Chadli re-elected.
1988 Riots in protest at government policies; 170 killed. Reform programme introduced. Diplomatic relations with Egypt restored.
1989 Constitutional changes proposed, leading to limited political pluralism.

---

new town, constructed under French rule, is in European style.

Algoa Bay broad and shallow inlet in Cape Province, South Africa, where Diaz landed after rounding the Cape 1488.

Alicante seaport and tourist resort in Valencia, SE Spain; population (1986) 266,000. The wine and fruit trade passes through the port.

al-Khalil Arabic name for ◊Hebron in the Israeli-occupied West Bank.

al Kût alternative term for ◊Kût al Imâra.

Allahabad ('city of god') historic city in Uttar Pradesh state, NE India, on the Yamuna River where it meets the Ganges and the mythical Saraswati River; population (1981) 642,000. A Hindu religious festival is held here every 12 years, the participants washing away sin and sickness by bathing in the rivers. 15 million people attended the festival of the jar of nectar of immortality, Khumbha-mela, Jan–Mar 1989.

Allegheny Mountains range over 800 km/500 mi long extending from Pennsylvania to Virginia, USA, rising to more than 1,500 m/4,900 ft and averaging 750 m/2,500 ft. The mountains are an important source of timber, coal, iron, and limestone. They initially hindered western migration, the first settlement to the west being Marietta 1788.

Allen, Lough lake in county Leitrim, Republic of Ireland, on the upper course of the river Shannon. It is 11 km/7 mi long and 5 km/3 mi broad.

Allen, Bog of morasses east of the river Shannon in the Republic of Ireland, comprising some 96,000 ha/240,000 acres of the counties of Offaly, Leix, and Kildare, the country's main source of peat fuel.

Allier river in central France, a tributary of the Loire; it is 565 km/350 mi long, and gives its name to a *département*. Vichy is the chief town on it.

Alma-Ata formerly (to 1921) *Vernyi* capital of the Republic of Kazakh, USSR; population (1987) 1,108,000. Industries include engineering, printing, tobacco processing, textile manufacturing, and leather products.

Established 1854 as a military fortress and trading centre, the town was totally destroyed by an earthquake 1887.

Almadan mining town in Ciudad Real province, Castilla-La Mancha, central Spain. It has the world's largest supply of mercury, worked since the 4th century BC. Population (1981) 9,700.

Almería Spanish city, chief town of a province of the same name on the Mediterranean; population (1986) 157,000. The province is famous for its white grapes, and in the Sierra Nevada are rich mineral deposits.

Alost French name for the Belgian town of ◊Aalst.

Alps mountain chain, the barrier between N Italy and France, Germany and Austria.

famous peaks include *Mont Blanc* the highest at 4,807 m/15,777 ft, first climbed by Jacques Balmat and Michel Paccard 1786;

Matterhorn in the Pennine Alps 4,477 m/14,694 ft, first climbed by Edward Whymper 1865 (four of the party of seven were killed when the rope broke during their descent);

Eiger in the Bernese Alps/Oberland, 3,970 m/13,030 ft, with a near-vertical rock wall on the north face, first climbed 1858;

Jungfrau 4,166 m/13,673 ft, and *Finsteraarhorn* 4,274 m/14,027 ft.

famous passes include *Brenner* the lowest, Austria/Italy;

Great St Bernard the highest, 2,472 m/8,113 ft, Italy/Switzerland (by which Napoleon marched into Italy 1800);

Little St Bernard Italy/France (which Hannibal is thought to have used), and *St Gotthard* S Switzerland, which Suvorov used when ordered by the tsar to withdraw his troops from Italy. All have been superseded by all-weather road/rail tunnels. The Alps extend into Yugoslavia with the Julian and Dinaric Alps.

Alps, Australian highest area of the E Highlands in Victoria/New South Wales, Australia, noted for winter sports. They include the *Snowy mountains* and *Mt Kosciusko*, Australia's highest mountain, 2,229 m/7,316 ft (first noted by Polish-born Paul Strzelecki 1829, and named after a Polish hero).

Alps, Southern range of mountains running the entire length of South Island, New Zealand. They are forested to the W, with scanty scrub to the E. The highest point is Mount Cook 3,764 m/12,349 ft. Scenic features include gorges, glaciers, lakes and waterfalls. Among its most famous lakes are those at the southern end of the range: Manapouri, Te Anau, and the largest, Wakatipu, 83 km/52 mi long, which lies about 300 m/1,000 ft above sea level and has a depth of 378 m/1,242 ft.

Alsace region of France; area 8,300 sq km/3,204 sq mi; population (1986) 1,600,000. It consists of the *départements* of Bas-Rhin and Haut-Rhin, and its capital is Strasbourg.

Alsace-Lorraine area of NE France, lying west of the river Rhine. It forms the modern French regions of ◊Alsace and ◊Lorraine. The former iron and steel industries are being replaced by electronics, chemicals, and precision engineering.

The German dialect spoken does not have equal rights with French, and there is autonomist sentiment. Alsace-Lorraine formed part of Celtic Gaul in Caesar's time, was invaded by the Alemanni and other Germanic tribes in the 4th century, and remained part of the German Empire until the 17th century. In 1648 part of the territory was ceded to France; in 1681 Louis XIV seized Strasbourg. The few remaining districts were seized by France after the Revolution. Conquered by Germany 1870–71 (chiefly for its iron ores), it was regained by France 1919, then again annexed by Germany 1940–44, when it was liberated by the Allies.

Altai territory of the Russian Soviet Federal Socialist Republic in SW Siberia; area 261,700 sq km/101,043 sq mi; population (1985) 2,744,000. The capital is Barnaul.

Altai Mountains mountain system of W Siberia and Mongolia. It is divided into two parts, the Russian Altai, which includes the highest peak, Mount Belukha, 4,506 m/14,783 ft, and the Mongolian or Great Altai.

Altamira caves with Palaeolithic paintings of animals discovered in 1879 in the province of Santander, N Spain.

Altamira an Amazonian town in the state of Pará, NE Brazil, situated at the junction of the Trans-Amazonian Highway with the Xingu river, 700 km SW of Belam. In 1989 a protest against the building of six dams by Brazilian Indians and environmentalists focused world attention on the devastation of the Amazon rainforest.

Altdorf capital of the Swiss canton Uri at the head of Lake Lucerne, Switzerland; population 9,000. It was the scene of the legendary exploits of William Tell.

Altiplano the densely populated upland plateau of the Andes of South America, stretching from Ecuador to NW Argentina. Height 3,000–4,000 m/10,000–13,000 ft.

Alwar city in Rajasthan, India, chief town of the district (formerly princely state) of the same name; population (1981) 146,000. It has fine palaces, temples, and tombs. Flour milling and trade in cotton goods and millet are important.

Amagasaki industrial city on the NW outskirts of Osaka, Honshu island, Japan; population (1987) 500,000.

Amalfi port 39 km/24 mi SE of Naples, Italy, situated at the foot of Monte Cerrato, on the Gulf of Salerno; population 7,000. For 700 years it was an independent republic. It is an ancient archiepiscopal see (seat of an archbishop) and has a Romanesque cathedral.

Amarillo town in the Texan panhandle, USA; population (1980) 149,230. The centre of the world's largest cattle-producing area, it processes the live animal into frozen supermarket packets in a single continuous operation on an assembly

Amazon

line. It is also a centre for assembly of nuclear warheads.

Amazon South American river, the world's second longest, 6,570 km/4,080 mi, and the largest in volume of water. Its main headstreams, the Maraǹn and the Ucayali, rise in central Peru and unite to flow eastwards across Brazil for about 4,000 km/2,500 mi. It has 48,280 km/30,000 mi of navigable waterways, draining 7,000,000 sq km/2,750,000 sq mi, nearly half the South American land mass. It reaches the Atlantic on the Equator, its estuary 80 km/50 mi wide, discharging a volume of water so immense that 64 km/40 mi out to sea fresh water remains at the surface.

The opening up of the Amazon river basin to settlers from the overpopulated E coast has resulted in a massive burning of tropical forest to create both arable and pasture land. Brazil, with one third of the world's remaining tropical rainforest, has 55,000 species of flowering plant – half of which are only found in Brazilian Amazonia. The problems of massive soil erosion, the disappearance of potentially useful plant and animal species, and the possible impact of large-scale forest clearance on global warming of the atmosphere have become environmental issues of international concern.

Ambala or *Umballa* city in N India; population (1981) 121,200. It is a railway junction situated 176 km/110 mi northwest of Delhi. Food processing, flour milling, and cotton ginning are among its most important industries. It is an archaeological site with prehistoric artefacts.

Amboina or *Ambon* small island in the Moluccas, republic of Indonesia; population (1980) 209,000.

The town of Amboina, formerly a historic centre of Dutch influence, has shipyards.

America the western hemisphere of the earth, containing the continents of North America and South America, with Central America in between. This great land mass extends from the Arctic to the Antarctic, from beyond 75° N to past 55° S. The area is about 42,000,000 sq km/16,000,000 sq mi, and the estimated population is over 500,000,000.

The name America is derived from Amerigo Vespucci, the Florentine navigator who was falsely supposed to have been the first European to reach the American mainland 1497. The name is also popularly used to refer to the United States of America, a usage which many Canadians, South Americans, and other non-US Americans dislike.

American Samoa see ◊Samoa, American.

Amersfoort town in the Netherlands, 19 km/12 mi northeast of Utrecht; population (10984) 86,896. Industries include brewing, chemicals, and light engineering.

Amiens ancient city of NE France at the confluence of the rivers Somme and Avre; capital of Somme *département* and centre of a market-gardening region irrigated by canals; population (1982) 154,500. It has a magnificent Gothic cathedral with a spire 113 m/370 ft high, and gave its name to the battles of Aug 1918, when Gen Haig launched his victorious offensive in World War I.

Amman capital and chief industrial centre of Jordan; population (1980) 1,232,600. It is an important communications centre, linking historic trade routes across the Middle East.

Amman is built on on the site of the Old Testament Rabbath-Ammon (Philadelphia), capital of the Ammonites. There is a Roman amphitheatre.

Amoy ancient name for ◊Xiamen, a port in SE China.

Amritsar industrial city in the Punjab, India; population (1981) 595,000. It is the holy city of Sikhism, with the Guru Nanak University (named after the first Sikh guru) and the Golden Temple from which armed demonstrators were evicted by the Indian army under Gen Dayal in 1984, 325 being killed. Subsequently, Indian prime minister Indira Gandhi was assassinated in reprisal. In 1919 it was the scene of the Amritsar Massacre.

Amsterdam capital of the Netherlands; population (1988) 1,031,000. Canals cut through the city link it with the North Sea and the Rhine, and as a port it is second only to Rotterdam. There is shipbuilding, printing, food processing, banking, and insurance.

Art galleries include Rijksmuseum, Stedelijk, Vincent Van Gogh Museum, and Rembrandt house. Notable also are the Royal Palace (1655) and the Anne Frank house.

Amu Darya river formerly called *Oxus* in Soviet central Asia, flowing 2,540 km/1,490 mi from the Pamirs to the ◊Aral Sea.

Amur river in E Asia. Formed by the Argun and the Shilka, the Amur enters the Sea of Okhotsk. At its mouth at Nikolaevsk it is 16 km/10 mi wide. For much of its course of over 4,400 km/2,730 mi it forms, together with its tributary, the Ussuri, the boundary between the USSR and China.

Under the treaties of Aigun (1858) and Peking (1860), 984,200 sq km/380,000 sq mi of territory N and E of the two rivers were ceded by China to the tsarist government. From 1963 China raised the question of its return and there have been border clashes.

Anaconda town in Montana, USA, which has the world's largest copper plant; population (1980) 12,518. The city was founded as Copperopolis 1883 by the Anaconda Copper Mining Company, and was incorporated as Anaconda 1888. The town is 1,615 m/5,300 ft above sea level, and 42 km/26 mi NW of Butte.

Anatolia (Turkish *Anadolu*) alternative name for Turkey-in-Asia.

Anchorage port and largest town of Alaska, USA, at the head of Cook Inlet; population (1984) 244,030.

Established 1918, Anchorage is an important centre of administration, communication, and commerce. Industries include salmon canning, and coal and gold are mined.

Ancona Italian town and naval base on the Adriatic Sea, capital of Marche region; population (1988) 104,000. It has a Romanesque cathedral and a former palace of the popes.

Andalusia (Spanish *Andalucía*) fertile autonomous region of S Spain, including the provinces of Almería, Cádiz, Córdoba, Granada, Huelva, Jaén, Málaga, and Seville; area 87,300 sq km/33,698 sq mi; population (1986) 6,876,000. Málaga, Cádiz, and Algeciras are the chief ports and industrial centres. The *Costa del Sol* on the south coast is famous for its tourist resorts, including Marbella and Torremolinos.

Andalusia has Moorish architecture, having been under Muslim rule 8th–15th centuries.

Andaman and Nicobar Islands two groups of islands in the Bay of Bengal, between India and Burma, forming a Union Territory of the Republic of India; area 8,300 sq km/3,204 sq mi; population (1981) 188,000. The economy is based on fishing, timber, rubber, fruit, and rice.

The *Andamans* consist of five principal islands (forming the Great Andaman), the Little Andaman, and about 204 islets; area 6,340 sq km/2,447 sq mi; population (1981) 158,000. They were used as a penal settlement 1857–1942.

The *Nicobars*, consisting of 19 islands (7 of which are uninhabited), are 120 km/75 mi south of Little Andaman; area 1,953 sq km/754 sq mi;

population (1981) 30,500. The main items of trade are coconut and areca nut. The Nicobars were British 1869–1947.

Andes the great mountain system or *cordillera* that forms the western fringe of South America, extending through some 67° of latitude and the republics of Colombia, Venezuela, Ecuador, Peru, Bolivia, Chile, and Argentina. The mountains exceed 3,600 m/12,000 ft for half their length of 6,500 km/4,000 mi.

Geologically speaking, the Andes are new mountains, having attained their present height by vertical upheaval of the entire strip of the Earth's crust as recently as the latter part of the Tertiary era and the Quaternary. But they have been greatly affected by weathering. Rivers have cut profound gorges, and glaciers have produced characteristic valleys. The majority of the individual mountains are volcanic; some are still active.

The whole system may be divided into two almost parallel ranges. The southernmost extremity is Cape Horn, but the range extends into the sea and forms islands. Among the highest peaks are Cotopaxi and Chimborazo in Ecuador, Cerro de Pasco and Misti in Peru, Illampu and Illimani in Bolivia, Aconcagua in Argentina (the highest mountain in the New World), and Ojos del Salado in Chile.

Andean mineral resources include gold, silver, tin, tungsten, bismuth, vanadium, copper, and lead. Difficult communications make mining expensive. Transport was for a long time chiefly by pack animals, but air transport has greatly reduced difficulties of communications. Three railways cross the Andes from Valparaiso to Buenos Aires, Antofagastato Salta, and Antofagasta via Uyuni to Asunción. New roads are being built, including the ◊Pan-American Highway.

The majority of the sparse population are dependent on agriculture, the nature and products of which vary with the natural environment. Newcomers to the Andean plateau, which includes Lake ◊Titicaca, suffer from *puna*, mountain sickness, but indigenous peoples have hearts and lungs adapted to altitude.

Andhra Pradesh state in E central India
area 276,800 sq km/106,845 sq mi
capital Hyderabad
towns Secunderabad
products rice, sugar cane, tobacco, groundnuts, and cotton
population (1981) 53,404,000
languages Telugu, Urdu, Tamil
history formed 1953 from the Telegu-speaking areas of Madras, and enlarged 1956 from the former Hyderabad state.

Andorra landlocked country in the E Pyrenees, bounded to the N by France and to the S by Spain.

Andhra Pradesh

INDIAN OCEAN

Aneto, Pico highest peak of the Pyrenees mountains, rising to 3,4040 m/11,052 ft in the Spanish province of Huesca.

Angel Falls highest waterfalls in the New World, on the river Caroní in the tropical rainforest of Bolivar Region, Venezuela; total height 978 m/3,210 ft. Named after the aviator and prospector James Angel who flew over the falls and crash-landed nearby 1935.

Angers ancient French town, capital of Maine-et-Loire *département*, on the river Maine; population (1982) 196,000. Products include electrical machinery and Cointreau liquer. It has a 12th–13th-century cathedral and castle, and was formerly the capital of the duchy and province of Anjou.

Angkor site of the ancient capital of the Khmer Empire, in NW Cambodia, N of lake Tonle Sap. The remains date mainly from the 10th–12th centuries AD, and comprise temples originally dedicated to the Hindu gods, shrines associated with Theravāda Buddhism, and royal palaces. Many are grouped within the enclosure called *Angkor Thom*, but the great temple of *Angkor Wat* (early 12th century) lies outside. Angkor was abandoned in the 15th century, and the ruins were overgrown by jungle and not adequately described until 1863. Buildings on the site suffered damage during the civil war 1970–75.

Anglesey (Welsh *Ynys Môn*) island off the NW coast of Wales; area 720 sq km/278 sq mi; population (1981) 67,000. It is separated from the mainland by the Menai Straits, which are crossed by the Britannia tubular railway bridge and Telford's suspension bridge, built 1819–26 but since rebuilt. It is a holiday resort with rich fauna (especially bird life) and flora and many buildings and relics of historic interest. The ancient granary of Wales, Anglesey now has industries such as toy-making, electrical goods, and bromine

Andorra
Principality of
(Principat d'Andorra)

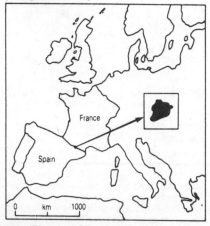

France

Spain

|0   km   1000|

area 470 sq km/181 sq mi
capital Andorra-la-Vella
physical mountainous, with narrow valleys

features the E Pyrenees
head of state Joan Marti y Alanis (bishop of Seo de Urgel, Spain) and François Mitterrand (president of France)
head of government Josep Pintat Solens from 1984
political system feudal
political parties none
exports main industries tourism and smuggling
currency French franc (9.70 = £1 Feb 1990) and Spanish peseta (183.95 = £1 Feb 1990)
population (1988) 51,400 (25% Andorrans, 75% immigrant Spanish workers)
language Catalan (official) 30%; Spanish 59%, French 6%
religion Roman Catholic
literacy 100% (1987)
chronology
1970 Extension of franchise to third-generation women and second-generation men.
1976 First political organization (Democratic Party of Andorra) formed
1977 Franchise extended to first-generation Andorrans.
1981 First prime minister appointed by General Council.

Angola
People's Republic of
(República Popular de Angola)

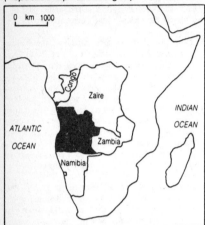

area 1,246,700 sq km/481,226 sq mi
capital and chief port Luanda
towns Lobito and Benguela, also ports
physical elevated plateau, desert in the south
features Kwanza river and Cabinda rainforest
head of state and government José Eduardo dos Santos from 1979
political system one-party socialist republic
political parties People's Movement for the Liberation of Angola-Workers' Party (MPLA-PT), Marxist-Leninist
exports oil, coffee, diamonds, palm oil, sisal, iron ore, fish
currency kwanza (50.97 = £1 Feb 1990)
population (1988 est) 9,387,000 (largest ethnic group Ovimbundu); annual growth rate 2.5%
life expectancy men 40, women 44
language Portuguese (official); Umbundu, Kimbundu
religion Roman Catholic 46%, Protestant 12%, animist 42%
literacy 59% (1985)
GDP $4.5 bn (1982); $478 per head of population

chronology
1951 Angola became an overseas territory of Portugal.
1956 First independence movement formed, the People's Movement for the Liberation of Angola (MPLA).
1961 Unsuccessful independence rebellion.
1962 Second nationalist movement formed, the National Front for the Liberation of Angola (FNLA).
1966 Third nationalist movement formed, the National Union for the Total Independence of Angola (UNITA).
1975 Transitional government of independence formed from representatives of MPLA, FNLA, UNITA, and Portuguese government. MPLA supported by USSR and Cuba, FNLA by 'non-left' power groups of southern Africa, and UNITA by Western powers. Angola declared independent. MPLA proclaimed People's Republic under the presidency of Dr Agostinho Neto. FNLA and UNITA proclaimed People's Democratic Republic of Angola.
1976 MPLA gained control of most of the country. South African troops withdrawn but Cuban units remained.
1977 MPLA restructured to become the People's Movement for the Liberation of Angola - Workers' Party (MPLA-PT).
1979 Death of Neto, succeeded by José Eduardo dos Santos.
1980 Constitution amended to provide for an elected people's assembly. UNITA guerrillas, aided by South Africa, continued to operate South African raids on the South West Africa People's Organization's bases in Angola.
1984 The Lusaka agreement.
1985 South African forces officially withdrawn.
1986 Further South African raids into Angola. UNITA continuing to receive South African support.
1988 Peace treaty, providing for the withdrawal of all foreign troops, signed with South Africa and Cuba.
1989 Ceasefire agreed with UNITA broke down and guerrilla activity restarted.

---

extraction from the sea. Holyhead is the principal town and port; Beaumaris was the county town until the county of Anglesey was merged in Gwynedd 1974.

Angola country in SW Africa, bounded to the west by the Atlantic ocean, to the north and northeast by Zaïre, to the east by Zambia, and to the south by Namibia.

Angostura former name of ◊Ciudad Bolívar.

Angoulême French town, capital of the *département* of Charente, on the Charente; population (1982) 104,000. It has a cathedral, and a castle and papermills dating from the 16th century.

Anguilla island in the E Caribbean
area 160 sq km/62 sq mi
capital the Valley
features white coral sand beaches
exports lobster, salt

currency Eastern Caribbean dollar
population (1988) 7,000
language English and Creole
government from 1982, governor, executive council, and legislative house of assembly (chief minister Emile Gumbs from 1984)
recent history a British colony from 1650, Anguilla was long associated with ◊St Christopher, but revolted against alleged domination by the larger island, and in 1969 declared itself a republic. A small British force restored order, and Anguilla retained a special position at its own request, since 1980 a separate dependency of the UK.

Angus former county and modern district on the E coast of Scotland, merged in 1975 in Tayside region.

Anhui formerly *Anhwei* province of E China, watered by the Chang Jiang (Yangtze river)
area 139,900 sq km/54,000 sq mi
capital Hefei
products cereals in the north, and cotton, rice and tea in the south
population (1986) 52,170,000.

Anhwei former name of ◊Anhui.

Anjou an old countship and former province in northern France; capital Angers. In 1154 the count of Anjou became king of England as Henry II, but the territory was lost by King John 1204. In 1480 the countship was annexed to the French crown. The *département*s of Maine-et-Loire and part of Indre-et-Loire, Mayenne, and Sarthe cover the area, whose people are called Angevins – a name also applied by the English to the Plantagenet kings.

Ankara formerly *Angora* capital of Turkey; population (1985) 2,252,000. Industries include cement, textiles, and leather products. It replaced Istanbul (then in Allied occupation) as capital 1923.

It has the presidential palace and Grand National Assembly buildings; three universities, including a technical university to serve the whole Middle East; the Atatürk mausoleum on a nearby hilltop, and the largest mosque in Turkey at Kocatepe.

Annaba formerly *Bône* seaport in Algeria; population (1983) 348,000. The name means 'city of jujube trees'. There are metallurgical industries, and iron ore and phosphates are exported.

Annam former country of SE Asia, incorporated in Vietnam 1946 as Central Vietnam. A Bronze Age civilization was flourishing in the area when China conquered it about 214 BC. The Chinese named their conquest An-Nam, 'peaceful south'. Independent from 1428, Annam signed a treaty with France 1787, and became a French protectorate, part of Indochina 1884. During World War II Annam was occupied by Japan.

Annapolis seaport and capital of Maryland, USA; population (1984) 31,900. It was named after Princess (later Queen) Anne 1695. It was in session here Nov 1783–June 1784 that Congress received George Washington's resignation as commander in chief 1783, and ratified the peace treaty of the War of American Independence. The US Naval Academy is here, and the naval hero John Paul Jones is buried in the chapel crypt.

Annapurna mountain 8,075 m/26,502 ft in the Himalayas, Nepál. The north face was climbed by a French expedition (Maurice Herzog) 1950 and the south by a British one 1970.

Annecy capital of the *département* of Haute-Savoie, SE France, at the northern end of Lake Annecy; population (1982) 112,600 (conurbation). It has some light industry, including precision instruments, and is a tourist resort.

Annobón former name (1973–79) *Pagalu* island in Equatorial Guinea; area 17 sq km/7 sq mi; its inhabitants are descended from slaves of the Portuguese and still speak a form of that language.

Anshan Chinese city in Liaoning province, 89 km/55 mi SE of Shenyang (Mukden); population (1986) 1,280,000. The iron and steel centre started here 1918 was expanded by the Japanese, dismantled by the Russians, and restored by the Communist government of China. It produces 6 million tonnes of steel annually.

Antakya or *Hatay* city in SE Turkey, site of the ancient Antioch; population (1985) 109,200.

Antalya Mediterranean port on the W coast of Turkey and capital of a province of the same name; population (1985) 258,000. The port trades in agricultural and forest produce.

Antananarivo formerly *Tananarive* capital of Madagascar, on the interior plateau, with a rail link to Tamatave; population (1986) 703,000.

Antarctica the continent covering the South Pole
area 13,727,000 sq km/5,300,000 sq mi
physical the continent, once part of Gondwanaland, is a vast plateau, of which the highest point is the Vinson Massif in the Ellsworth mountains, 5,139 m/16,866 ft high. The Ross Ice Shelf is

Anguilla

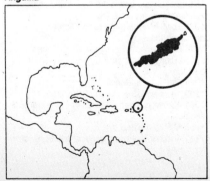

formed by several glaciers coalescing in the Ross Sea, and Mount Erebus on Ross Island is the world's southernmost active volcano. There is less than 50 mm/2 in of rainfall a year (less than in the Sahara). Little more than 1% of the land is ice-free, the temperature falling to –70°C/–100°F and below, and in places the ice is 5,000 m/16,000 ft deep, comprising over two-thirds of the world's fresh water. Each annual layer of snow preserves a record of global conditions, and where no melting at the surface of the bedrock has occurred the ice can be a million years old. It covers extensive mineral resources, including iron, coal, and probably uranium and other strategic metals, as well as oil

features there are only two species of flowering plants, plus a number of mosses, algae, and fungi. Animal life is restricted to visiting whales, seals, penguins, and other seabirds. Fossils of apes resembling humans have been found

population settlement is limited to scientific research stations with changing personnel

history in 1988, nine countries signed the Minerals Convention, laying Antarctica open to commercial exploitation; Australia refused to sign. Guidelines on environmental protection were included but regarded as inadequate by environmental pressure groups.

1773–77 James Cook first sailed in Antarctic seas, but exploration was difficult before the development of iron ships able to withstand ice pressure.

1819–21 Antarctica circumnavigated by Bellinge-hausen.

1823 James Weddell sailed into the sea named after him.

1841–42 James Ross sighted the Great Ice Barrier named after him.

1895 Borchgrevink was one of the first landing party on the continent.

1898 Borchgrevink's British expedition first wintered in Antarctica.

1901–04 Scott first penetrated the interior of the continent.

1907–08 Shackleton came within 182 km/113 mi of the Pole.

1911 Amundsen reached the Pole, 14 Dec, overland with dogs.

1912 Scott reached the Pole, 18 Jan, initially aided by ponies.

1928–29 Byrd made the first flight to the Pole.

1935 Ellsworth first flew across Antarctica.

Antigua and Barbuda
State of

area Antigua 280 sq km/108 sq mi, Barbuda 161 sq km/62 sq mi, plus Redonda 1 sq km/0.4 sq mi

capital and chief port St John's

physical tropical island country

features Antigua is the largest of the Leeward Islands; Redonda is uninhabited

head of state Elizabeth II from 1981 represented by Wilfred Ebenezer Jacobs

head of government Vere C Bird from 1981

political system liberal democracy

political parties Antigua Labour Party (ALP), moderate, left-of-centre; Progressive Labour Movement (PLM), left-of-centre

exports sea-island cotton, rum

currency East Caribbean dollar (4.60 = £1 Feb 1990)

population (1986) 81,500; annual growth rate 1.3%

language English

religion Christian

literacy 90% (1985)

GDP $130 million (1983); $1,850 per head of population

chronology

1967 Antigua and Barbuda became an associated state within the Commonwealth, with full internal independence.

1971 PLM won the general election by defeating the ALP.

1976 PLM called for early independence but ALP urged caution. ALP won the general election.

1981 Full independence.

1983 Assisted US invasion of Grenada.

1984 ALP won a decisive victory in the general election.

1985 ALP re-elected.

1989 Another sweeping general election victory for the ALP.

1957–58 Fuchs made the first overland crossing.
1959 Soviet expedition from the West Ice Shelf to the Pole.
1959 International Antarctic Treaty suspended all territorial claims, reserving an area south of 60° S latitude for peaceful purposes.
1961–62 Bentley Trench discovered, which suggested that there may be an Atlantic–Pacific link beneath the Continent.
1966–67 Specially protected areas established internationally for animals and plants.
1979 Fossils of apes resembling E Africa's *Proconsul* found 500 km/300 mi from the Pole.
1980 International convention on the exploitation of resources – oil, gas, fish, krill.
1982 First circumnavigation of Earth (2 Sept 1979–29 Aug 1982) via the Poles by Sir Ranulph Fiennes and Charles Burton (UK).

Antarctic Ocean popular name for the reaches of the Atlantic, Indian, and Pacific oceans extending south of the Antarctic Circle (66° 32′ S). The term is not used by the International Hydrographic Bureau.

Antarctic Peninsula mountainous peninsula of W Antarctica extending *c.*1,930 km/1,200 mi N toward South America. Originally named *Palmer Land* after a US navigator, Captain Nathaniel Palmer, who was the first to explore the region in 1820. Claimed by Britain (1832), Chile (1942) and Argentina (1940), its name was changed to the Antarctic Peninsula in 1964.

Antibes resort, which includes Juan les Pins, on the French Riviera, in the *département* of Alpes Maritimes; population (1982) 63,248. There is a Picasso collection in the 17th-century castle museum.

Antigua and Barbuda country comprising three islands (Antigua, Barbuda, and uninhabited Redonda) in the eastern Caribbean.

Anti-Lebanon or *Antilibanus* mountain range on the Lebanese-Syrian border, including Mt Hermon, 2,800 m/9,200 ft. It is separated from the Lebanon mountains by the Bekaa valley.

Antilles

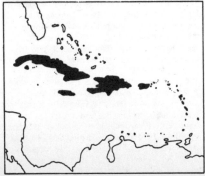

Antilles the whole group of West Indian islands, divided north–south into the *Greater Antilles* (Cuba, Jamaica, Haiti–Dominican Republic, Puerto Rico) and *Lesser Antilles*, subdivided into the Leeward Islands (Virgin Islands, St Kitts–Nevis, Antigua and Barbuda, Anguilla, Montserrat and Guadeloupe) and the Windward Islands (Dominica, Martinique, St Lucia, St Vincent and the Grenadines, Barbados, and Grenada).

Antofagasta port of N Chile, capital of a region of the same name. The area of the region is 125,300 sq km/48,366 sq mi, its population (1982) 341,000. The population of the town of Antofagasta is 175,000. Nitrates from the Atacama desert are exported.

Antrim county of Northern Ireland
area 2,830 sq km/1,092 sq mi
towns Belfast (county town), port of Larne
features Giant's Causeway of natural hexagonal basalt columns which, in legend, was built to enable the giants to cross between Ireland and Scotland; Antrim borders Lough Neagh, and is separated from Scotland by the 32 km/20 mi wide North Channel.
products potatoes, oats, linen, synthetic textiles
population (1981) 642,000.

Antwerp (Flemish *Antwerpen*, French *Anvers*) port in Belgium on the river Scheldt, capital of the province of Antwerp; population (1988) 476,000. One of the world's busiest ports, it has shipbuilding, oil-refining, petrochemical, textile, and diamond-cutting industries. The home of Rubens is preserved, and many of his works are in the Gothic cathedral. The province of Antwerp has an area of 2,900 sq km/1,119 sq mi, and a population (1987) 1,588,000.

It was not until the 15th century that Antwerp rose to prosperity; from 1500 to 1560 it was the richest port in N Europe. After this Antwerp was beset by religious troubles and the Netherlands revolt against Spain. In 1648 the Treaty of Westphalia gave both shores of the Scheldt estuary to the United Provinces, which closed it to Antwerp trade. The Treaty of Paris 1814 opened the estuary to all nations on payment of a small toll to the Dutch, abandoned 1863. During World War I Antwerp was occupied by Germany Oct 1914–Nov 1918; during World War II May 1940–Sept 1944.

Anuradhapura ancient city in Sri Lanka; population (1981) 36,000. It was the capital of the Sinhalese kings of Sri Lanka 5th century BC–8th century AD; rediscovered in the mid-19th century. Sacred in Buhdhism, it claims a bo tree descended from the original one under which Buddha became enlightened.

Anvers French form of ◊Antwerp.

Anyang city in Henan province, E China; population (1980) 430,000. It was the capital of the Shang dynasty (13th–12th centuries BC). Rich archaeological remains have been uncovered since the 1930s.

Anzhero-Sudzhensk town in W Siberia, USSR, 80 km/50 mi N of Kemerovo in the Kuznetsk basin; population (1985) 110,000. Its chief industry is coal mining.

Aomori port at the head of Mutsu Bay, on the N coast of Honshu Island, Japan; 40 km/25 mi NE of Hirosaki; population (1980) 288,000. The port handles a large local trade in fish and timber.

Aosta Italian city, 79 km/49 mi NW of Turin; population (1981) 37,200. It is the capital of Valle d'Aosta (French-speaking) autonomous region, and has extensive Roman remains.

Aouzu Strip disputed territory 100 km/60 mi wide on the Chad–Libya frontier, occupied by Libya 1973. Lying to the N of the Tibesti massif, the area is rich in uranium and other minerals.

Apeldoorn commercial city in Gelderland province, E central Netherlands. Population (1982) 142,400. Het Loo, which is situated nearby, has been the summer residence of the Dutch royal family since the time of William of Orange.

Apennines chain of mountains stretching the length of the Italian peninsula. A continuation of the Maritime Alps, from Genoa it swings across the peninsula to Ancona on the E coast, and then back to the W coast and into the 'toe' of Italy. The system is continued over the Strait of Messina along the N Sicilian coast, then across the Mediterranean sea in a series of islands to the Atlas mountains of North Africa. The highest peak is Gran Sasso d'Italia at 2,914 m/9,560 ft.

Apia capital and port of Western ◊Samoa, on the north coast of Upolu island, in the W Pacific; population (1981) 33,000. It was the home of the writer Robert Louis Stevenson.

Apo, Mount active volcano and highest peak in the Philippines, rising to 2,954 m/9,692 ft on the island of Mindanao.

Appalachians mountain system of E North America, stretching about 2,400 km/1,500 mi from Alabama to Québec, composed of very ancient eroded rocks. The chain includes the Allegheny, Catskill, and Blue Ridge mountains, the last-named having the highest peak, Mount Mitchell, 2,045 m/6,712 ft. The eastern edge has a fall line to the coastal plain where Philadelphia, Baltimore, and Washington stand.

Apulia English form of ◊Puglia, region of Italy.

Aqaba, Gulf of gulf extending for 160 km/100 mi between the Negev and the Red Sea; its coastline is uninhabited except at its head, where the frontiers of Israel, Egypt, Jordan, and Saudi Arabia converge. Here are the two ports Eilat (Israeli Elath) and Aqaba, Jordan's only port.

Aquitaine region of SW France; capital Bordeaux; area 41,300 sq km/15,942 sq mi; population (1986) 2,718,000. It comprises the *département*s of

Dordogne, Gironde, Landes, Lot-et-Garonne, and Pyrénées-Atlantiques. Red wines (Margaux, St Julien) are produced in the Medoc district, bordering the Gironde. Aquitaine was an English possession 1152–1452.

history Early human remains have been found in the Dordogne region. Aquitaine coincides roughly with the Roman province of Aquitania and the ancient French province of Aquitaine. Eleanor of Aquitaine married the future Henry II of England 1152, and brought it to him as her dowry; it remained in English hands until 1452.

AR abbreviation for ◊*Arkansas*.

Arab Emirates see ◊United Arab Emirates.

Arabia the peninsula between the Persian Gulf and the Red Sea, in SW Asia; area 2,590,000 sq km/1,000,000 sq mi. The peninsula contains the world's richest oil and gas reserves. It comprises the states of Bahrain, Kuwait, North Yemen, Oman, Qatar, Saudi Arabia, the United Arab Emirates, and South Yemen.

physical A sandy coastal plain of varying width borders the Red Sea, behind which a mountain chain rises to about 2,000–2,500 m/6,600–8,200 ft. Behind this range is the plateau of the Nejd, averaging 1,000 m/3,300 ft. The interior comprises a vast desert area: part of the Hamad (Syrian) desert in the far north; Nafud in northern Saudi Arabia, and Rub'al Khali in S Saudi Arabia.

history The Arabian civilization was revived by Muhammad during the 7th century AD, but in the new empire created by militant Islam, Arabia became a subordinate state, and its cities were eclipsed by Damascus, Baghdad, and Cairo. Colonialism only touched the fringe of Arabia in the 19th century, and until the 20th century the interior was unknown to Europeans. Nationalism began actively to emerge at the period of World War (1914–18), and the oil discoveries from 1953 gave the peninsula significant economic power.

Arabian Gulf another name for the ◊Persian Gulf.

Arabian sea the NW branch of the ◊Indian Ocean.

Arabistan former name of the Iranian province of Khuzestan, revived in the 1980s by the two million Sunni Arab inhabitants who demand autonomy. Unrest and sabotage 1979–80 led to a pledge of a degree of autonomy by Ayatollah Khomeini.

Arad Romanian town on the river Mures, 160 km/100 mi NE of Belgrade; population (1985) 185,900. It is an important route centre with many industries.

Arafura Sea the area of the Pacific Ocean between N Australia and Indonesia, bounded by the Timor Sea in the west and the Coral Sea in the east. It is 1,290 km/800 mi long and 560 km/350 mi wide.

Aragón autonomous region of NE Spain including the provinces of Huesca, Teruel, and Zaragoza; area 47,700 sq km/18,412 sq mi; population (1986) 1,215,000. Its capital is Zaragoza, and products include almonds, figs, grapes, and olives. Aragón was an independent kingdom 1035–1479.

history A Roman province until taken in the 5th century by the Visigoths, who lost it to the Moors in the 8th century, it became a kingdom 1035. It was united with Castile 1479 under Ferdinand and Isabella.

Aral Sea inland sea in the USSR; the world's fourth largest lake; divided between Kazakhstan and Uzbekistan; former area 62,000 sq km/24,000 sq mi, but decreasing. Water from its tributaries, the Amu Darya and Syr Darya, has been diverted for irrigation and city use, and the sea is disappearing, with long-term consequences for the climate.

Between 1960 and 1990 the water level dropped 13 m/40 ft, reducing the lake to two-thirds of its original area and increasing the area of the surrounding Aralkum salt desert.

Aran Islands three rocky islands (Inishmore, Inishmaan, Inisheer) in the mouth of Galway Bay, Republic of Ireland; population approximately 4,600. The capital is Kilronan. J M Synge used the language of the islands in his plays.

Aranjuez Spanish town on the river Tagus, 40 km/25 mi SE of Madrid; population (1981) 36,000. The palace was a royal residence for centuries.

Ararat double-peaked mountain on the Turkish-Iranian border; the higher, Great Ararat, 5,156 m/17,000 ft, was the reputed resting place of Noah's Ark after the Flood.

Ararat wheat and wool centre in NW Victoria, Australia; population (1986) 8,000. It is a former gold-mining town.

Arbil Kurdish town in a province of the same name in N Iraq. Occupied since Assyrian times, it was the site of a battle in 331 BC at which Alexander the Great defeated the Persians under Darius III. In 1974 Arbil became the capital of a Kurdish autonomous region set up by the Iraqi government. Population (1985) 334,000.

Arctic, the

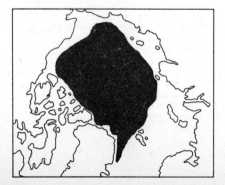

Arbroath fishing town in Tayside, Scotland; population (1981) 24,100. In 1320 the Scottish Parliament asserted Scotland's independence here in a letter to the pope.

Arcadia (Greek *Arkadhia*) central plateau of S Greece; area 4,419 sq km/1,706 sq mi; population (1981) 108,000. Tripolis is the capital town. The English poet Philip Sidney idealized the life of shepherds here in antiquity.

Archangel (Russian *Arkhangelsk*) port in the northern USSR; population (1987) 416,000. It was made an open port by Boris Godunov and was of prime importance until Peter the Great built St Petersburg. It was used 1918–20 by the Allied interventionist armies in collaboration with the White Army in their effort to overthrow the newly established Soviet state. In World War II it was the receiving station for Anglo-American supplies. An open city in a closed area, it can be visited by foreigners only by air, and is a centre for ICBMs (intercontinental ballistic missiles). Although the port is blocked by ice during half the year, it is the chief timber-exporting port of the USSR. Plesetsk, to the south, is a launch site for crewed space flight.

Arctic, the region north of the Arctic Circle. There is no Arctic continent, merely pack ice (which breaks into ice floes in summer) surrounding the Pole and floating on the Arctic Ocean. Pack ice is carried by the south-flowing current into the Atlantic Ocean as icebergs. In winter the sun disappears below the horizon for a time (and in summer, which only lasts up to two months, remains above it), but the cold is less severe than in parts of E Siberia or Antarctica. Land areas in the Arctic have mainly stunted tundra vegetation, with an outburst of summer flowers. Animals include reindeer, caribou, musk ox, fox, hare, lemming, wolf, polar bear, seal, and walrus. There are few birds, except in summer, when insects, especially mosquitoes, are plentiful. The aboriginal people are the Inuit of the Alaskan/Canadian Arctic and Greenland. The most valuable resource is oil. The International Arctic Sciences Committee was established 1987 by the countries with Arctic coastlines to study ozone depletion and climatic change.

Arctic Ocean ocean surrounding the North Pole; area 14,000,000 sq km/5,400,000 sq mi. Because of the Siberian and North American rivers flowing into it, it has comparatively low salinity and freezes readily.

It comprises:

Beaufort Sea off Canada/Alaska coast, named after British admiral Francis Beaufort; oil drilling is allowed only in winter because the sea is the breeding and migration route of the bowhead whales, staple diet of the local Inuit.

Greenland Sea between Greenland and Svalbard, and *Norwegian Sea* between Greenland and

Argentina
Republic of
(República Argentina)

PACIFIC
OCEAN

Brazil

Bolivia

Chile

Paraguay

Uruguay

ATLANTIC
OCEAN

0   1000 km

area 2,780,092 sq km/1,073,116 sq mi
capital Buenos Aires
towns Rosario, Córdoba, Tucumán, Mendoza, Santa Fé; ports are La Plata and Bahïa Blanca
physical mountains in the W, forest in the N and E, pampas (treeless plains) in the central area; rivers Colorado, Paraná, Uruguay, Rio de la Plata estuary
territories Tierra del Fuego; disputed claims to S Atlantic islands; part of Antarctica
features Andes, with Aconcagua the highest peak in the W hemisphere
head of state and government Carlos Menem from 1989
political system emergent democratic federal republic
political parties Radical Union Party (UCR), moderate centrist; Justice Party, right-wing Peronist
exports beef, livestock, cereals, wool, tannin, groundnuts, linseed oil, minerals (coal, copper, molybdenum, gold, silver, lead, zinc, barium, uranium), and the country has huge resources of oil, natural gas, hydroelectric power
currency austral (7,203.85 = £1 Feb 1990)
population (1986) 31,060,000 (mainly of Spanish or Italian origin, only about 30,000 American Indians surviving); annual growth rate 1.6%
life expectancy men 66, women 73
language Spanish

religion Roman Catholic (state-supported)
literacy 96% male/95% female (1985 est)
GDP $58 bn (1983); $2,350 per head of population
chronology
1816 Achieved independence from Spain, followed by civil wars.
1946 Juan Perón elected president, supported by his wife 'Evita'.
1952 'Evita' Perón died.
1955 Perón overthrown and civilian administration restored.
1966 Coup brought back military rule.
1973 The Perónist party won the presidential and congressional elections. Perón returned from exile in Spain as president, with his third wife, 'Isabelita', as vice-president.
1974 Perón died, succeeded by 'Isabelita'.
1976 Coup resulted in rule by a military junta led by Lt-Gen Jorge Videla. Congress dissolved and hundreds of people, including 'Isabelita' Perón, detained.
1976–78 Ferocious campaign against left-wing elements. The start of the 'dirty war'.
1978 Videla retired. Succeeded by Gen Roberto Viola, who promised a return to democracy.
1981 Viola died suddenly. Replaced by Gen Leopoldo Galtieri.
1982 With a deteriorating economy, Galtieri sought popular support by ordering an invasion of the British-held Falkland Islands. After losing the short war, Galtieri was removed and replaced by Gen Reynaldo Bignone.
1983 Amnesty law passed and 1853 democratic constitution revived. General elections won by Dr Raúl Alfonsín and his party. Armed forces under scrutiny.
1984 Commission on the Disappearance of Persons (CONADEP) reported on over 8,000 people who had disappeared during the 'dirty war' of 1976–83.
1985 A deteriorating economy forced Alfonsín to seek help from the IMF and introduce a harsh austerity programme.
1986 Unsuccessful attempt on Alfonsín's life.
1988 Unsuccessful army coup attempt.
1989 Carlos Menem, of the Justice Party, elected president. Pressure put on Alfonsín to hand over power before Dec 1989. 30-day state of emergency declared after rioting following price measures and dramatic inflation, 120% in June; annual rate in 1989 4,923%.
1990 Full diplomatic relations with the UK restored.

Norway. West to east along the north coast of the USSR:

Barents Sea named after Dutch explorer Willem Barents, which has oil and gas reserves and is strategically important as the meeting point of the NATO and Warsaw Pact forces. The ◊White Sea is its southernmost gulf.

Kara Sea renowned for bad weather, and known as the 'great ice cellar'.

Laptev Sea between Taimyr Peninsula and New Siberian Island.

East Siberian Sea and *Chukchi Sea* between the USSR and the USA; the semi-nomadic Chukchi people of NE Siberia accepted Soviet rule only in the 1930s.

Ardebil town in NW Iran, near the Soviet frontier; population (1983) 222,000. Ardebil exports dried fruits, carpets, and rugs.

Ardèche river in SE France, a tributary of the Rhône. Near Vallon it flows under the Pont d'Arc, a natural bridge. It gives its name to a *département*.

Arden, Forest of former forest region of N Warwickshire, England, the setting for Shakespeare's play *As You Like It*.

Ardennes wooded plateau in NE France, SE Belgium, and N Luxembourg, cut through by the river Meuse; also a *département* of ◊Champagne-Ardenne. There was heavy fighting here in World War I and World War II (during the Battle of the Bulge).

Arequipa city in Peru at the base of the volcano El Misti; population (1988) 592,000. Founded by Pizarro 1540, it is the cultural focus of S Peru, and a busy commercial (soap, textiles) centre.

Arezzo town in the Tuscan region of Italy; 80 km/50 mi SE of Florence; population (1981) 92,100. The writers Petrarch and Aretino were born here. It is a mining town and also trades in textiles, olive oil, and antiques.

Argenteuil NW suburb of Paris, France, on the Seine; population (1982) 96,045.

Argentina country in South America, bounded by Chile to the south and west, Bolivia to the northwest, and Paraguay, Brazil, Uruguay, and the Atlantic Ocean to the east.

Arizona

Argyllshire former county on the W coast of Scotland, including many of the Western Isles, which was for the most part merged in Strathclyde region 1975, although a small area to the NW including Ballachulish, Ardgour, and Kingairloch went to the Highland region.

Århus alternative form of ◊Aarhus, Denmark.

Arica port in Chile; population (1987) 170,000. Much of Bolivia's trade passes through it, and there is contention over the use of Arica by Bolivia to allow access to the Pacific Ocean. It is Chile's most northerly city.

It is on a rainless coastline. It was several times devastated by earthquake, and was razed 1880 when captured by Chile from Peru.

Ariège river in southern France, a tributary of the Garonne. It gives its name to a *département*.

Arizona state in SW USA; nickname Grand Canyon State

area 294,100 sq km/113,523 sq mi

capital Phoenix

towns Tucson, Scottsdale, Tempe, Mesa, Glendale, Flagstaff

physical Colorado Plateau in the north and east, desert basins and mountains in the south and west; Colorado River; Grand Canyon

features Grand Canyon National Park (the multicoloured gorge through which the Colorado flows, 6–29 km/4–18 mi wide, up to 1.5 km/1 mi deep and 350 km/217 mi long), the Painted Desert (including the Petrified Forest of fossil trees), Organ Pipe Cactus National Monument Park, Gila Desert, and Sonoran Desert; Roosevelt and Hoover dams; old London Bridge was transported 1971 to the tourist resort of Lake Havasu City

products cotton under irrigation, livestock, copper, molybdenum, silver, electronics, aircraft

population (1987) 3,469,000 including over 150,000 American Indians (Navajo, Hopi, Apache), who still own a quarter of the state

famous people Geronimo, Barry Goldwater, Zane Grey, Percival Lowell, Frank Lloyd Wright

history part of New Spain 1715; part of Mexico 1824; passed to USA after Mexican War 1848; territory 1863; state 1912.

Arizona is believed to derive its name from the Spanish *arida-zona* (dry belt). The first Spaniard to visit Arizona was the Franciscan Marcos de Niza 1539. After 1863, it developed rapidly as a result of the gold rush in neighbouring California. Irrigation has been carried out since the 1920s on a colossal scale. The Roosevelt Dam on the Salt River and the Hoover Dam on the Colorado, between Arizona and Nevada, provide the state with both hydroelectric power and irrigation water. At the end of the 19th century rich copper deposits were found in Arizona and subsequently deposits of many other minerals.

Arkansas state in S central USA; nickname Wonder State/Land of Opportunity

Arkansas

area 137,800 sq km/53,191 sq mi
capital Little Rock
towns Fort Smith, Pine Bluff, Fayetteville
physical Ozark Mountains in the west; lowlands in the east; Arkansas River; many lakes
features Hot Springs National Park
products cotton, soya beans, rice, oil, natural gas, bauxite, timber, processed foods
population (1986) 2,372,000
famous people Douglas MacArthur
history explored by de Soto 1541; European settlers 1648, who traded with local Indians; part of Louisiana Purchase 1803; state 1836.

The first European settlement was Arkansas Post, founded by some of the companions of the French explorer La Salle. After seceding from the Union 1861 to join the Confederacy, Arkansas was readmitted 1886.

Arles town in Bouches-du-Rhône *département*, SE France, on the left bank of the Rhône; population (1982) 50,772. It is a great fruit- and vine-growing district. Roman relics include an amphitheatre for 25,000 spectators. The cathedral of St Trophime is a notable Romanesque structure. The painters Van Gogh and Gauguin lived here 1888.

Arlington town in Virginia, USA, and suburb of Washington DC. It is the site of the National Cemetery for the dead of the United States wars. The grounds were first used as a military cemetery in 1864 during the US Civil War. By 1975, military, naval, and civilian persons buried there numbered 165,142, including the Unknown Soldier of both world wars, President J F Kennedy, and his brother Robert Kennedy.

Armagh county of Northern Ireland
area 1,250 sq km/483 sq mi
towns county town Armagh; Lurgan, Portadown, Keady
physical flat in the north, with many bogs; low hills in the south; Lough Neagh
features smallest county of Northern Ireland. There are crops in the better-drained parts, especially flax. The chief rivers are the Bann and Blackwater, flowing into Lough Neagh, and the Callan tributary of the Blackwater

products chiefly agricultural: apples, potatoes, flax
population (1981) 119,000.
Armagh county town of Armagh, Northern Ireland; population (1981) 13,000. It became the religious centre of Ireland in the 5th century when St Patrick was made archbishop. For 700 years, it was the seat of the kings of Ulster. The Protestant archbishop of Armagh is nominally 'Primate of All Ireland'.
Armenia constituent republic of the Soviet Union from 1936
area 29,800 sq km/11,506 sq mi
capital Yerevan
towns Leninakan
physical mainly mountainous (including Mt Ararat), wooded
products copper, molybdenum, cereals, cotton, silk
population (1987) 3,412,000; 90% Armenian, 5% Azeri, 2% Kurd, 2% Russian
language Armenian
religion traditionally Armenian Christian
history an ancient kingdom formerly occupying what is now the Van region of Turkey, part of NW Iran, and what is now the Armenian republic, it became an independent republic 1918, was occupied by the Red Army 1920, and became a constituent republic of the USSR 1936. An earthquake 1988 caused extensive loss of life and property.
Armentières town in N France on the Lys River; population about 26,000. The song 'Mademoiselle from Armentières' originated during World War I, when the town was held by the British. It was flattened by German bombardment in 1918 and rebuilt.
Armidale town in New South Wales, Australia; population (1985) 21,500. The University of New England is here, and mansions of the squatters survive.
Arnhem city in the Netherlands, on the Rhine SE of Utrecht; population (1988) 297,000. It produces salt, chemicals, and pharmaceuticals. The English poet Sir Philip Sidney died here 1586. The Battle of Arnhem in World War II was an airborne operation by the Allies, 17–26 Sept 1944, to secure a bridgehead over the Rhine, thereby opening the way for a thrust towards the Ruhr and a possible early end to the war. It was only partly successful, with 7,600 casualties.
Arnhem Land plateau of the central peninsula in Northern Territory, Australia. It is named after a Dutch ship which came to port 1618. The chief town is Nhulunbuy. It is the largest of the Aboriginal reserves, and a traditional way of life is maintained, now threatened by mineral exploitation.
Arno Italian river 240 km/150 mi long, rising in the Apennines, and flowing westward to the Mediterranean. Florence and Pisa stand on its banks. A

flood in 1966 damaged virtually every Renaissance landmark in Florence.

Arran large mountainous island in the Firth of Clyde, Scotland, in Strathclyde; area 427 sq km/165 sq mi; population (1981) 4,726. It is popular as a holiday resort. The chief town is Brodick.

Arras French town on the Scarpe river NE of Paris; population (1982) 80,500 (conurbation). It is the capital of Pas-de-Calais *département*, and was formerly known for making tapestry. It was the birthplace of Robespierre.

Arthur's Pass road-rail link across the Southern Alps, New Zealand, at 926 m/3,038 ft, linking Christchurch with Greymouth.

Arthur's Seat hill of volcanic origin, Edinburgh, Scotland; height 251 m/823 ft; only fancifully linked with King Arthur.

Artois former province of N France, bounded by Flanders and Picardie, and almost corresponding with the modern *département* of Pas-de-Calais. Its capital was Arras. Its Latin name *Artesium* lent its name to the Artesian well first sunk at Lillers 1126.

Aruba island in the Caribbean, the westernmost of the Lesser Antilles; an overseas part of the Netherlands
area 193 sq km/75 sq mi
population (1985) 61,000
history Aruba obtained separate status from the other Netherlands Antilles 1986 and has full internal autonomy.

Arunachal Pradesh state of India, in the Himalayas on the borders of Tibet and Burma
area 83,600 sq km/32,270 sq mi
capital Itanagar
products rubber, coffee, spices, fruit, timber
population (1981) 628,000
language 50 different dialects
history formerly nominally part of Assam, and known as the North East Frontier Agency, it became a Union Territory 1972, and was renamed Arunachal Pradesh ('Hills of the Rising Sun'). It became a state 1986.

Arundel town in Sussex, England, on the river Arun; population (1981) 2,200. It has a magnificent castle (much restored and rebuilt), the seat for centuries of the earls of Arundel and dukes of Norfolk.

Arvand River Iranian name for the ◊Shatt al-Arab waterway.

Aryana ancient name of Afghanistan.

Ascension British island of volcanic origin in the S Atlantic, a dependency of ◊St Helena since 1922; population (1982) 1,625. The chief settlement is Georgetown.

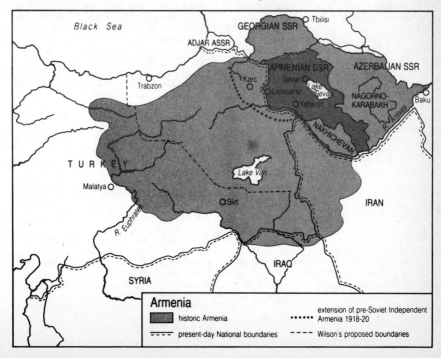

Armenia
▨ historic Armenia
‑ ‑ ‑ present-day National boundaries
•••••• extension of pre-Soviet Independent Armenia 1918-20
‑ ‑ ‑ Wilson's proposed boundaries

A Portuguese navigator landed there on Ascension Day 1501, but it remained uninhabited until occupied by Britain in 1815. There are sea turtles and sooty terns, and it is a staging post to the Falkland Islands.

Ascot village in Berkshire, England, 9.5 km/6 mi SW of Windsor. Queen Anne established the racecourse on Ascot Heath 1711, and the Royal Ascot meeting is a social as well as a sporting event. Horse races include the Gold Cup, Ascot Stakes, Coventry Stakes, and King George VI and Queen Elizabeth Stakes.

Ashanti or *Asante* region of Ghana, W Africa; area 25,100 sq km/9,700 sq mi; population (1984) 2,089,683. Kumasi is the capital. The main crop is cocoa, and the region is noted for its metalwork and textiles.

For more than 200 years Ashanti was an independent kingdom, lost during the 19th century to the British, who sent four expeditions against them and formally annexed their country 1901. Otomfuo Sir Osei Agyeman, nephew of the deposed king, Prempeh I, was made head of the re-established Ashanti confederation 1935 as Prempeh II, and the Golden Stool (actually a chair), symbol of the Ashanti peoples since the 17th century, was returned to Kumasi. (The rest of the Ashanti treasure is in the British Museum.) The Asantahene (King of the Ashanti) still holds ceremonies in which this stool is ceremonially paraded.

Ashby-de-la-Zouch market town in Leicestershire, England; 26 km/16 mi NW of Leicester; population (1985) 11,906. It was named from the La Zouche family who built the castle, which was used to imprison Mary Queen of Scots 1569. The 15th-century castle features in Sir Walter Scott's novel *Ivanhoe.*

Ashdod deep-water port of Israel, on the Mediterranean 32 km/20 mi south of Tel-Aviv, which it superseded in 1965; population (1982) 66,000. It stands on the site of the ancient Philistine stronghold of Askalon.

Asheville textile town in the Blue Ridge Mountains of North Carolina, USA; population (1980) 53,583. Showplaces include the 19th-century Biltmore mansion, home of millionaire George W Vanderbilt, and the home of the writer Thomas Wolfe.

Ashford town in Kent, England, on the river Stour, SW of Canterbury; population (1985) 47,000. It expanded in the 1980s as a new commercial and industrial centre for SE England.

Ashkhabad capital of Republic of Turkmen, USSR; population (1987) 382,000. 'Bukhara' carpets are made here.

It was established 1881 as a military fort on the Persian frontier, occupying an oasis on the edge of the Kara-Kum desert. It is the hottest place in the USSR.

Ashmore and Cartier Islands group of islands comprising Middle, East, and West Islands (the Ashmores), and Cartier Island, in the Indian Ocean about 180 km/120 mi off the NW coast of Australia; area 5 sq km/2 sq mi. They were transferred to the authority of Australia by Britain 1931. Formerly administered as part of the Northern Territory, they became a separate territory 1978. They are uninhabited, and West Ashmore has an automatic weather station. Ashmore reef was declared a national nature reserve 1983.

Ashton under Lyne town in Greater Manchester, England; population (1981) 44,476. There are light industries, coal, and cotton.

Asia largest of the continents, forming the eastern part of Eurasia to the east of the Ural mountains, one third of the total land surface of the world.

area 44,000,000 sq km/17,000,000 sq mi

largest cities (over 5 million) Tokyo, Shanghai, Osaka, Beijing, Seoul, Calcutta, Bombay, Jakarta, Bangkok, Tehran, Hong Kong

physical five main divisions: (1) Central triangular mountain mass, including the Himalayas; to the N the great Tibetan plateau, bounded by the Kunlun mountains, to the N of which lie further ranges, as well as the Gobi Desert. (2) The SW plateaux and ranges, forming Afghanistan, Baluchistan, Iran. (3) The northern lowlands, from the central mountains to the Arctic Ocean, much of which is frozen for several months each year. (4) The eastern margin and islands, where much of the population is concentrated. (5) The southern plateau and river plains, including Arabia, the Deccan, and the alluvial plains of the Euphrates, Tigris, Indus, Ganges, and Irrawaddy. The climate shows great extremes and contrasts, the heart of the continent becoming bitterly cold in winter and very hot in summer. This, with the resulting pressure and wind systems, accounts for the Asiatic monsoons, bringing heavy rain to all SE Asia, China, and Japan, between May and October

features rivers (over 2,000 miles) Ob-Irtysh, Chang Jiang, Huang He, Amur, Lena, Mekong, Yenisei, Euphrates; lakes (over 18,000 sq km/ 7,000 sq mi) Caspian and Aral seas, Baikal, Balkhash

population (1984) 2,778,000,000, the most densely populated of the continents; annual growth rate 1.7%

language predominantly tonal languages (Chinese, Japanese) in the east, Indo-Iranian languages in central India and Pakistan (Hindi/Urdu), and Semitic (Arabic) in the SW

religion Hinduism, Islam, Buddhism, Christianity, Confucianism, Shintoism.

Asia Minor historical name for *Anatolia*, the Asian part of Turkey.

Asia, Soviet Central see ◊Soviet Central Asia.

Asmara or *Asmera* capital of Eritrea, Ethiopia; 64 km/40 mi SW of Massawa on the Red Sea;

Assam

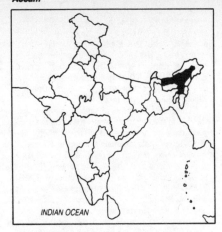

INDIAN OCEAN

population (1984) 275,385. Products include beer, clothes, and textiles.

In 1974, unrest here precipitated the end of the Ethiopian Empire. It has a naval school.

Asnières NW suburb of Paris, France, on the left bank of the Seine; population (1982) 71,220. It is a boating centre and pleasure resort.

Assam state of NE India

area 78,400 sq km/30,262 sq mi

capital Dispur

towns Shilling

products half India's tea is grown here, and half its oil produced; rice, jute, sugar, cotton, coal

population (1981) 19,903,000, including 12,000,000 Assamese (Hindus), 5,000,000 Bengalis (chiefly Muslim immigrants from Bangladesh), and Nepális; and 2,000,000 native people (Christian and traditional religions)

language Assamese

history Assam, a thriving region from 1000 BC, absorbed immigrants from China and Burma. After Burmese invasion 1826, Britain took control, and made it a separate province 1874, which was included in the Dominion of India, except for most of the Muslim district of Silhet, which went to Pakistan 1947. Ethnic unrest started in the 1960s when Assamese was declared the official language. After protests, the Gara, Khasi, and Jaintia tribal hill districts became the state of ◊Meghalaya 1971; the Mizo hill district became the Union Territory of Mizoram 1972. There were massacres of Muslim Bengalis by Hindus 1983. In 1987 members of the Bodo ethnic group began fighting for a separate homeland.

Assisi town in Umbria, Italy, 19 km/12 mi south east of Perugia; population (1981) 25,000. St Francis was born here and is buried in the Franciscan monastery, completed 253. The churches of St Francis are adorned with frescoes by Giotto, Cimabue, and others.

Assiut alternative transliteration of ◊Asyut.

ASSR abbreviation for *Autonomous Soviet Socialist Republic*.

Assuan alternative transliteration of ◊Aswan.

Assy plateau in Haute-Savoie, E France, 1,000 m/3,280 ft above sea level. The area has numerous sanatoriums. The church of Nôtre Dame de Toute Grâce, begun 1937 and consecrated 1950, is adorned with works by Braque, Chagall, Matisse, Derain, Rouault, and other artists.

Asti town in Piedmont, SE of Turin, Italy; population (1983) 76,439. Asti province is famed for its sparkling wine. Other products include chemicals, textiles, and glass.

Astrakhan city in the USSR, on the delta of the Volga, capital of Astrakhan region; population (1987) 509,000. In ancient times a Tatar capital, it becamè Russian 1556. It is the chief port for the Caspian fisheries.

Asturias autonomous region of N Spain; area 10,600 sq km/4,092 sq mi; population (1986) 1,114,000. Half of Spain's coal is produced from the mines of Asturias. Agricultural produce includes maize, fruit, and livestock. Oviedo and Gijon are the main industrial towns.

It was once a separate kingdom and the eldest son of a king of Spain is still called prince of Asturias.

Asunción capital and port of Paraguay, on the Paraguay river; population (1984) 729,000. It produces textiles, footwear, and food products.

Founded 1537, it was the first Spanish settlement in the La Plata region.

Aswan winter resort town in Upper Egypt; population (1985) 183,000. It is near the High Dam built 1960–70, which keeps the level of the Nile constant throughout the year without flooding. It produces steel and textiles.

Asyut commercial centre in Upper Egypt, near the Nile, 322 km/200 mi S of Cairo; population (1985) 274,400. An ancient Graeco-Egyptian city, it has many tombs of 11th- and 12th-dynasty nobles.

Atacama desert in N Chile; area about 80,000 sq km/31,000 sq mi. Inland are mountains, and the coastal area is rainless and barren. There are silver and copper mines and extensive nitrate deposits.

Athabasca lake and river in Alberta and Saskatchewan, Canada, with huge tar sand deposits (source of the hydrocarbon mixture 'heavy oil') to the SW of the lake.

Athens (Greek *Athinai*) capital city of modern Greece and of ancient Attica; population (1981) 885,000, metropolitan area 3,027,000. Situated 8 km/5 mi NE of its port of Piraeus on the Gulf of Aegina, it is built around the rocky hills of the Acropolis 169 m/555 ft and the Areopagus 112 m/368 ft, and is overlooked from the NE by the hill of Lycabettus 277 m/909 ft. It lies in the south of the central plain of Attica, watered by the mountain streams of Cephissus and Ilissus.

features The Acropolis dominates the city. Remains of ancient Greece include the Parthenon, the Erechtheum, and the temple of Athena Nike. Near the site of the ancient Agora (marketplace) stands the Theseum, and south of the Acropolis is the theatre of Dionysus. To the SE stand the gate of Hadrian and the columns of the temple of Olympian Zeus. Nearby is the marble stadium built about 330 BC and restored 1896.

history The site was first inhabited about 3000 BC and Athens became the capital of a united Attica before 700 BC. Captured and sacked by the Persians 480 BC, subsequently under Pericles it was the first city of Greece in power and culture. After the death of Alexander the Great the city fell into comparative decline, but it flourished as an intellectual centre until 529 AD, when the philosophical schools were closed by Justinian. In 1458 it was captured by the Turks who held it until 1833; it was chosen as the capital of modern Greece 1834. Among the modern buildings are the royal palace and several museums.

Athos a mountainous peninsula on the Macedonian coast of Greece. Its peak is 2,033 m/6,672 ft high. The promontory is occupied by a community of 20 Basilian monasteries inhabited by some 3,000 monks and lay brothers.

Atlanta capital and largest city of Georgia, USA; population (1980) 422,000, metropolitan area 2,010,000. There are Ford and Lockheed assembly plants, and it is the headquarters of Coca-Cola.

Originally named *Terminus* 1837, and renamed 1845, the city was burned 1864 by General Sherman during the American Civil War. Nearby Stone Mountain Memorial shows the Confederate heroes Jefferson Davis, Robert E Lee, and Stonewall Jackson on horseback.

Atlantic City seaside resort in New Jersey, USA; population (1980) 40,000. It is noted for its boardwalk (a wooden pavement along the beach). Formerly a family resort, it has become a centre for casino gambling, which was legalized in New Jersey in the 1970s.

Atlantic Ocean ocean lying between Europe and Africa to the east and the Americas to the west, probably named after the legendary Atlantis; area of basin 81,500,000 sq km/31,500,000 sq mi; including Arctic Ocean and Antarctic seas, 106,200,000 sq km/41,000,000 sq mi. The average depth is 3 km/2 mi; greatest depth the Milwaukee Depth in the Puerto Rico Trench 8,650 m/28,389 ft. The Mid-Atlantic Ridge, of which the Azores, Ascension, St Helena, and Tristan da Cunha form part, divides it from north to south. Lava welling up from this central area annually increases the distance between South America and Africa. The North

Atlantic is the saltiest of the main oceans, and it has the largest tidal range. In the 1960s–80s average wave heights have increased by 25%, the largest from 12 m/40 ft to 18 m/60 ft.

Atlas Mountains mountain system of NW Africa, stretching 2,400 km/1,500 mi from the Atlantic coast of Morocco to the Gulf of Gabes, Tunisia, and lying between the Mediterranean on the north and the Sahara on the south. The highest peak is Mount Toubkal 4,165 m/13,670 ft.

Geologically the Atlas Mountains compare with the Alps in age, but their structure is much less complex. They are recognized as the continuation of the great Tertiary fold mountain systems of Europe.

Attica (Greek *Attikí*) region of Greece comprising Athens and the district around it; area 3,381 sq km/1,305 sq mi; population (1981) 342,000. It is noted for its language, art, and philosophical thought in Classical times. It is a prefecture of modern Greece with Athens as its capital.

Aube river of NE France, a tributary of the Seine, length 248 km/155 mi; it gives its name to a *département*.

Aubusson town in the *département* of Creuse, France; population (1982) 6,500. Its carpet and tapestry industry dates from the 15th century.

Auckland largest city in New Zealand, situated in N North Island; population (1987) 889,000. It fills the isthmus that separates its two harbours (Waitemata and Manukau), and its suburbs spread north across the Harbour Bridge. It is the country's chief port and leading industrial centre, having iron and steel plants, engineering, car assembly, textiles, food-processing, sugar-refining, and brewing.

There was a small whaling settlement on the site 1830s, and Auckland was officially founded as New Zealand's capital 1840, remaining so until 1865. The university was founded 1882.

Auckland Islands six uninhabited volcanic islands 480 km/300 mi south of South Island, New Zealand; area 60 sq km/23 sq mi.

Aude river in SE France, 210 km/130 mi long, which gives its name to a *département*. Carcassonne is the main town through which it passes.

Audenarde French form of ◊Oudenaarde, a town in Belgium.

Augrabies Falls waterfalls in the Orange River, NW Cape Province, South Africa. Height 148 m/480 ft.

Augsburg industrial city in Bavaria, West Germany, at the confluence of the Wertach and Lech rivers, 52 km/32 mi NW of Munich; population (1988) 246,000. It is named after the Roman emperor Augustus who founded it 15 BC.

Austin capital of Texas, USA, on the Colorado River; population (1980) 345,500. It is a centre for electronic and scientific research and country-and-western music.

Australasia loosely applied geographical term, usually meaning Australia, New Zealand, and neighbouring islands.

Australia, Commonwealth of

State (Capital)	Area sq km
New South Wales (*Sydney*)	801,396
Victoria (*Melbourne*)	227,620
Queensland (*Brisbane*)	1,736,524
South Australia (*Adelaide*)	984,341
Western Australia (*Perth*)	2,527,632
Tasmania (*Hobart*)	68,331
Territories	
Northern Territory (*Darwin*)	1,356,165
Capital Territory (*Canberra*)	2,432
	7,704,441

Dependencies	
Ashmore and Cartier Islands	1
Australian Antarctic Territory	5,402,480
Cocos (Keeling) Island	14
Christmas Island	135
Heard and McDonald Islands	412
Norfolk Island	34

Australia country occupying the smallest continent and largest island in the world, situated south of Indonesia, between the Pacific and Indian oceans.

Australian Antarctic Territory the islands and territories south of 60° S, between 160° E and 45° E longitude, excluding Adélie Land; area 6,044,000 sq km/2,332,984 sq mi of land, and 75,800 sq km/29,259 sq mi of ice shelf. The population on the Antarctic continent is limited to research personnel.

There are scientific bases at Mawson (1954) in MacRobertson Land, named after the explorer; at Davis (1957) on the coast of Princess Elizabeth Land, named in after Mawson's second-in-command; at Casey (1969) in Wilkes Land, named after Lord Casey, and at Macquarie Island (1948). It came into being 1933, when established by a British Order in Council.

Australian Capital Territory

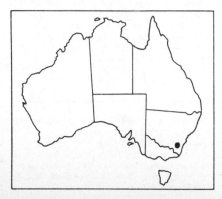

Australian Capital Territory territory ceded to Australia by New South Wales 1911 to provide the site of ◊Canberra, with its port at Jervis Bay, ceded 1915; area 2,400 sq km/926 sq mi; population (1987) 261,000.

Austral Islands alternative name for ◊Tubuai Islands, part of ◊French Polynesia.

Austria landlocked country in central Europe, bounded by Hungary to the E, Yugoslavia to the SE, Italy to the SW, Switzerland to the W, West Germany to the NW, and Czechoslovakia to the NE.

Austria: provinces

province (capital)	Area (sq km)
Burgenland (Eisenstadt)	4,000
Carinthia (Klagenfurt)	9,500
Lower Austria (St Pölten)	19,200
Salzburg (Salzburg)	7,200
Styria (Graz)	16,400
Tirol (Innsbruck)	12,600
Upper Austria (Linz)	12,000
Vienna (Vienna)	420
Vorarlberg (Bregenz)	2,600

Auvergne ancient province of central France and a modern region (*département*s Allier, Cantal, Haute-Loire, and Puy-de-Dôme); area 26,000 sq km/10,036 sq mi; population (1986) 1,334,000. Its capital is Clermont-Ferrand. It lies in the heart of the Central Plateau and is mountainous, composed chiefly of volcanic rocks in several masses.

It is named after the ancient Gallic Avenni tribe whose leader, Vercingetorix, was one of the greatest opponents of the Romans.

Auxerre capital of Yonne *département* France, 170 km/106 mi SE of Paris, on the river Yonne; population about 40,000. The Gothic cathedral, founded 1215, has exceptional sculptures and stained glass.

Avernus circular lake near Naples, Italy. Because it formerly gave off fumes that killed birds, it was thought by the Romans to be the entrance to the lower world.

Aviemore winter sports centre, in the Highlands, Scotland, SE of Inverness among the Cairngorms Mountains.

Avignon city in Provence, France, capital of Vaucluse *département*, on the river Rhône NW of Marseille; population (1982) 174,000. It was an important Gallic and Roman city, and has 14th-century walls, a 12th-century bridge (only half still standing), a 13th-century cathedral, and the palace built 1334–42 during the residence here of the popes. Avignon was papal property 1348–1791.

Avila town in Spain, 90 km/56 mi NW of Madrid; population (1986) 45,000. It is capital of the province of the same name. It has the remains of a Moorish castle, a Gothic cathedral, and the convent and church of St Teresa, who was born here. The town walls are among the

Australia
Commonwealth of

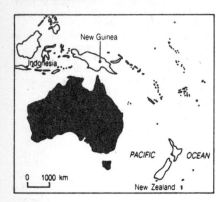

area 7,682,300 sq km/2,966,136 sq mi
capital Canberra
towns Adelaide, Alice Springs, Brisbane,
Darwin, Melbourne, Perth, Sydney
physical the world's driest continent, arid in
north and west Great Dividing Range in the
east; NE peninsula has rainforest; rivers N–S
and Darling River and Murray system E–S; Lake
Eyre basin and fertile Nullarbor Plain in south
territories Norfolk Island, Christmas Island,
Cocos Islands, Ashmore and Cartier Islands,
Coral Sea Islands, Heard Island and McDonald
Islands, Australian Antarctic Territory
features Great Australian Desert, Great
Barrier Reef; unique animals include kangaroo,
koala, numbat, platypus, wombat, Tasmanian
devil and 'tiger'; budgerigar, cassowary,
emu, kookaburra, lyre bird, black swan; and
such deadly insects as the bulldog ant and
funnel-web spider
head of state Elizabeth II from 1952
represented by Bill Hayden
head of government Robert Hawke from 1983
political system federal constitutional
monarchy
political parties Australian Labor Party (ALP),
moderate left-of-centre; Liberal Party of Australia,
moderate, liberal, free-enterprise; National Party
of Australia, centrist non-metropolitan

exports cereals, meat and dairy products,
wool (30% of world production), fruit, wine,
nuts, sugar, honey, bauxite (world's largest
producer), coal, iron, copper, lead, tin, zinc,
opal, mineral sands, uranium, machinery,
transport equipment
currency Australian dollar (2.24 = £1 Feb
1990)
population (1988) 16,250,000; annual growth
rate 1.6%
life expectancy men 72, women 79
language English
religion Anglican 36%, other Protestant 25%,
Roman Catholic 33%
literacy 100% (1984)
GDP $170.2 bn (1984); $9,960 per head of
population
chronology
1901 Creation of Commonwealth of Australia.
1911 Site for capital at Canberra acquired.
1944 Liberal Party founded by Robert Menzies.
1966 Menzies resigned after being Liberal
prime minister for 17 years, and was
succeeded by Harold Holt.
1968 John Gorton became prime minister after
Holt's death.
1971 Gorton succeeded by William McMahon,
heading a Liberal–Country Party coalition.
1972 Gough Whitlam became prime minister,
leading a Labor government.
1975 Senate blocked the government's
financial legislation; Whitlam declined to
resign but was dismissed by the governor
general, who invited Malcom Fraser to form a
Liberal–Country Party caretaker government.
The action of the governor-general, John Kerr,
was widely criticized.
1977 Kerr resigned.
1983 Australian Labor Party, returned to power
under Bob Hawke, sought consensus with
employers and unions on economic policy to
deal with growing unemployment.
1988 Labor foreign minister Bill Hayden
appointed governor-general designate. Free
trade agreement with New Zealand signed.
1989 Andrew Peacock returned as Liberal
Party leader. National Party leader, Ian Sinclair,
replaced by Charles Blunt.
1990 Hawke wins record fourth election victory,
defeating Liberal Party by small majority.

best preserved medieval fortifications of those
in Europe.
Avon county in SW England
area 1,340 sq km/517 sq mi
towns administrative headquarters Bristol; Bath,
Weston-super-Mare
features river Avon

products aircraft and other engineering, tobacco,
chemicals, printing, dairy products
population (1987) 951,000
famous people John Cabot, Thomas Chatterton.
history formed 1974 from the city and county
of Bristol, part of S Gloucestershire, and N
Somerset.

Austria
Republic of
(Republik Österreich)

area 83,920 sq km/32,393 sq mi
capital Vienna
towns Graz, Linz, Salzburg, Innsbruck
physical mountainous, with the Danube river
basin in the east
features Austrian Alps (including Zugspitze
and Brenner and Semmering passes); river
Danube; Hainburg, the largest primeval
rainforest left in Europe, now under threat from
a dam
head of state Kurt Waldheim from 1986
head of government Franz Vranitzky from
1986
political system democratic federal republic
political parties Socialist Party of Austria
(SPÖ), democratic socialist; Austrian People's
Party (ÖVP), progressive centrist; Freedom
Party of Austria (FPÖ), moderate left-of-centre;
United Green Party of Austria (VGÖ),
conservative ecological; Green Alternative
Party (ALV), radical ecological
exports minerals, manufactured goods
currency schilling (20.01 = £1 Feb 1990)
population (1987) 7,576,000; annual growth
rate 0%
life expectancy men 70, women 77
language German
religion Roman Catholic 90%
literacy 98% (1983)
GNP $94.7 bn (1986); $12,521 per head of
population
chronology
1918 Habsburg rule ended, republic
proclaimed.
1938 Incorporated into German Third Reich by
Hitler.
1945 1920 constitution reinstated and coalition
government formed by the SPÖ and the ÖVP.
1955 Allied occupation ended and the
independence of Austria formally recognized.
1966 ÖVP in power with Josef Klaus as
chancellor.
1970 SPÖ formed a minority government, with
Dr Bruno Kreisky as chancellor.
1983 Kreisky resigned and was replaced by Dr
Fred Sinowatz, leading a coalition.
1986 Dr Kurt Waldheim elected president.
Sinowatz resigned and was succeeded by
Franz Vranitzky. In the Nov general election
no party won an overall majority and Vranitzky
formed a coalition of the SPÖ and the ÖVP,
with the ÖVP leader, Dr Alois Mock, as
vice-chancellor. Sinowatz denounced the
coalition as a betrayal of socialist principles
and resigned his SPÖ chair.
1989 Austria sought European Community
membership.

Avon any of several rivers in England and Scotland.
In Warwickshire it is associated with Shakespeare.

The *Upper, or Warwickshire, Avon*, 154 km/
96 mi, rises in the Northampton uplands near
Naseby and joins the Severn at Tewkesbury.

The *Lower, or Bristol, Avon*, 121 km/75 mi,
rises in the Cotswolds and flows into the Bristol
Channel at Avonmouth.

The *East, or Salisbury, Avon*, 104 km/65 mi,
rises S of the Marlborough Downs and flows into
the English Channel at Christchurch.

Awash river that rises to the S of Addis Ababa in
Ethiopia and flows NE to Lake Abba on the frontier with Djibouti. Although deep inside present-
day Ethiopia, the Awash River is considered by
Somalis to mark the eastern limit of Ethiopian
sovereignty prior to the colonial division of
Somaliland in the 19th century.

Awe longest (37 km/23 mi) of the Scottish freshwater lochs, in Strathclyde, SE of Oban. It is
drained by the river Awe into Loch Etive.

Axholme, Isle of area of 2,000 ha/5,000 acres in
Humberside, England, bounded by the Trent,
Don, Idle, and Torne rivers, where medieval-
type open-field strip farming is still practised.
The largest village, Epworth, is the birthplace
of the Methodist John Wesley.

Ayacucho capital of a province of the same name
in the Andean mountains of central Peru; population (1988) 94,200. The last great battle in
the war of independence against Spain was
fought near here in Dec 1824.

Avon

Azerbaijan

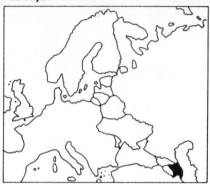

Aycliffe town in Durham, England, on the river Skerne; population (1981) 36,825. It developed from 1947 as a new town.

Ayers Rock vast ovate mass of pinkish rock in Northern Territory, Australia; 335 m/1,100 ft high and 9 km/6 mi round.

It is named after Sir Henry Ayers, a premier of South Australia. For the Aboriginals, whose paintings decorate its caves, it has magical significance.

Ayot St Lawrence village in Hertfordshire, England, where Shaw's Corner (home of the playwright G B Shaw) is preserved.

Ayr town in Strathclyde, Scotland, at the mouth of the river Ayr; population (1981) 49,500. Auld Brig was built in the 15th century, the New Brig 1788 (rebuilt 1879). Ayr has associations with Robert Burns.

Ayrshire former county of SW Scotland, with a 113 km/70 mi coastline on the Firth of Clyde. In 1975 the major part was merged in the region of Strathclyde; the remaining sector, approximately south of the Water of Girvan and including Girvan itself, became part of Dumfries and Galloway.

AZ abbreviation for ◊*Arizona*.

Azerbaijan constituent republic (*Azerbaydzhan* Soviet Socialist Republic) of the USSR from 1936
area 86,600 sq km/33,436 sq mi
capital Baku
towns Kirovabad
physical Caspian Sea; the country ranges from semi-desert to the Caucasus mountains
products oil, iron, copper, fruit, vines, cotton, silk, carpets
population (1987) 6,811,000; 78% Azerbaijani, 8% Russian, 8% Armenian
language Turkic
religion traditionally Shi'ite Muslim

recent history a member of the Transcaucasian Federation 1917, it became an independent republic 1918, but was occupied by the Red Army 1920. Since 1988, claims by the Soviet republic of Armenia over the Nagorno-Karabakh autonomous region have resulted in civil unrest, causing many Armenians to leave.

Azerbaijan, Iranian two provinces of NW Iran: *Eastern Azerbaijan* (capital Tabriz), population (1986) 4,114,000, and *Western Azerbaijan* (capital Orúmiyeh), population 1,972,000. Like the people of Soviet Azerbaijan, the people are Muslim (Shiah) ethnic Turks, descendants of followers of the Khans from the Mongol Empire.

There are about 5 million in Azerbaijan, and 3 million distributed in the rest of the country, where they form a strong middle class. In 1946, with Soviet backing, they briefly established their own republic. Denied autonomy under the Shah, they rose 1979–80 against the supremacy of Ayatollah Khomeini and were forcibly repressed, although a degree of autonomy was promised.

Azincourt French form of ◊Agincourt.

Azores group of nine islands in the N Atlantic, an autonomous region of Portugal; area 2,247 sq km/867 sq mi; population (1987) 254,000. They are outlying peaks of the Mid-Atlantic Ridge, and are volcanic in origin. The capital is Ponta Delgada on the main island, San Miguel.

Portuguese from 1430, the Azores were granted partial autonomy 1976, but remain a Portuguese overseas territory. It has a separatist movement. The Azores command the Western shipping lanes.

Azov (Russian *Azovskoye More*) inland sea of the USSR forming a gulf in the NE of the Black Sea; area 37,555 sq km/14,500 sq mi. Principal ports include Rostov-on-Don, Kerch, and Taganrog. Azov is an important source of freshwater fish.

Baabda capital of the province of Jebel Lubnan in central Lebanon and site of the country's presidential palace. Situated to the SE of Beirut, it is the headquarters of the Christian military leader, Michel Aoun.

Bab-el-Mandeb strait that joins the Red Sea and the Gulf of Aden, and separates Arabia and Africa. The name, meaning 'gate of tears', refers to its currents.

Bacău industrial city in Romania, 250 km/155 mi NNE of Bucharest, on the Bistrita; population (1985) 175,300. It is the capital of Bacău county, and is an important oil-producing region.

Badajoz city in Extremadura, Spain, on the Portuguese frontier; population (1986) 126,000. It has a 13th-century cathedral and ruins of a Moorish castle. Badajoz has often been besieged, and was stormed by Wellington 1812 with the loss of 59,000 British troops.

Baden town in Aargau canton, Switzerland, near Zurich; at an altitude of 388 m/1,273 ft; population (1981) 23,140. Its hot sulphur springs and mineral waters have been visited since Roman times.

Baden-Baden Black Forest spa in Baden-Württemberg, West Germany; population (1984) 49,000. Fashionable in the 19th century, it is now a conference centre.

Baden-Württemberg administrative region (German *Land*) of West Germany
area 35,800 sq km/13,819 sq mi
capital Stuttgart
towns Mannheim, Karlsruhe, Freiburg, Heidelberg, Heilbronn, Pforzheim, Ulm
physical Black Forest; Rhine boundary south and west; source of the Danube; see also ◊Swabia

products wine, jewellery, watches, clocks, musical instruments, textiles, chemicals, iron, steel, electrical equipment, surgical instruments
population (1988) 9,390,000
history formed 1952 (following a plebiscite) by the merger of the *Länder* Baden, Württemberg-Baden, and Württemberg-Hohenzollern.

Bad Godesburg SE suburb of ◊Bonn, West Germany, formerly a spa, and the meeting place of Chamberlain and Hitler before the Munich Agreement 1938.

Baffin Island island in the Northwest Territories, Canada
area 507,450 sq km/195,875 sq mi
features largest island in the Canadian Arctic; mountains rise above 2,000 m/6,000 ft and there are several large lakes. The northernmost part of the strait separating Baffin Island from Greenland forms Baffin Bay, the southern end is Davis Strait.
It is named after William Baffin who carried out research here 1614 during his search for the ◊Northwest Passage.

Baghdad historic city and capital of Iraq, on the Tigris; population (1985) 4,649,000. Industries include oil- refining, distilling, tanning, tobacco processing, and the manufacture of textiles and cement. Founded 762, it became Iraq's capital 1921.
To the SE, on the Tigris, are the ruins of *Ctesiphon*, capital of Parthia about 250 BC–226 AD and of the Sassanian Empire about 226–641; the remains of the Great Palace include the world's largest single-span brick arch 26 m/85 ft wide and 29 m/95 ft high.
A route centre from the earliest times, it was developed by the 8th-century caliph Harun al-Rashid, though little of the Arabian Nights city remains. It was overrun 1258 by the Mongols, who destroyed the irrigation system. In 1639 it was taken by the Turks. During World War I Baghdad was captured by Gen Maude 1917.

Baguio summer resort on Luzon island in the Philippines, 200 km/125 mi N of Manila, 1,370 m/4,500 ft above sea level; population (1980) 119,000. It is the official summer residence of the Philippine president.

Bahamas country comprising a group of islands in the Caribbean, off the SE coast of Florida.

Bahawalpur city in the Punjab, Pakistan; population (1981) 178,000. Once the capital of a former state of Bahawalpur, it is now an industrial town producing textiles and soap. It has a university, established 1975.

Bahia state of E Brazil
area 561,026 sq km/216,556 sq mi
capital Salvador
population (1986) 10,949,000
industry oil, chemicals, agriculture

Bahamas
Commonwealth of the

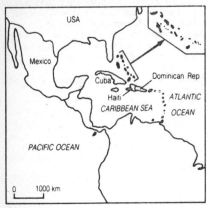

area 13,864 sq km/5,352 sq mi
capital Nassau on New Providence
physical comprises 700 tropical coral islands
and about 1,000 cays
features desert islands: only 30 are inhabited;
Blue Holes of Andros, the world's longest and
deepest submarine caves
head of state Elizabeth II from 1973
represented by Gerald C Cash from 1979
head of government Lynden Oscar Pindling
from 1967

political system constitutional monarchy
political parties Progressive Liberal Party
(PLP), centrist; Free National Movement (FNM),
centre-left
exports cement, pharmaceuticals, petroleum
products, crawfish, rum, pulpwood; over half
the islands' employment comes from tourism
currency Bahamian dollar (1.70 = £1 Feb
1990)
population (1986) 236,171; annual growth
rate 1.8%
language English
religion 26% Roman Catholic, 21% Anglican,
48% other Protestants
literacy 93% (1985)
GDP $780 million (1981); $5,756 per head of
population
chronology
1964 Internal self-government attained.
1967 First national assembly elections.
1972 Constitutional conference to discuss full
independence.
1973 Full independence achieved.
1983 Allegations of drug trafficking by
government ministers.
1984 Deputy prime minister and two cabinet
ministers resigned. Pindling denied any
personal involvement and was endorsed as
party leader.
1987 Pindling re-elected despite claims of
frauds.

Bahía Blanca port in S Argentina, on the Naposta,
5 km/3 mi from its mouth; population (1980)
233,126. It is a major distribution centre for
wool and food processing. The naval base of
Puerto Belgrano is here.

Bahrain country comprising a group of islands in the
Arabian Gulf, between Saudi Arabia and Iran.

Baikal Russian *Baykal Ozero* largest freshwater
lake in Asia 31,500 sq km/12,150 sq mi and deepest in the world (up to 1,740 m/5,710 ft), in S
Siberia, USSR. Fed by more than 300 rivers,
it is drained only by the Lower Angara. It has
sturgeon fisheries and rich fauna.

Baile Atha Cliath official Gaelic name of ◊Dublin,
capital of the Republic of Ireland, from 1922.

Baja California the mountainous peninsula that
forms the twin NW states of Lower (Spanish *baja*)
California, Mexico; area 143,396 sq km/55,351
sq mi; population (1980) 1,440,600. The northern
state, Baja California Norte, includes the busy
towns of Mexicali and Tijuana, but the southern,
Baja California Sur, is sparsely populated.

Bakhtaran formerly (until 1980) *Kermanshah*
capital of Bakhtaran province, NW Iran; population (1986) 561,000. The province (area

23,700 sq km/9,148 sq mi; population 1,463,000)
is on the Iraq border, and is mainly inhabited by
Kurds. Industries include oil refining, carpets, and
textiles.

Baku capital city of the Azerbaijan Republic, USSR,
and industrial port (oil refining) on the Caspian
Sea; population (1987) 1,741,000. Baku is a centre
of the Soviet oil industry, and is linked by pipelines
with Batumi on the Black Sea. In Jan 1990 there
were violent clashes between the Azerbaijani
majority and the Armenian minority, and Soviet
troops were sent to the region. Some 13,000
Armenians subsequently fled from the city.

Bala (Welsh *Llyn Tegid*) lake in Gwynedd, N
Wales, about 6.4 km/4 mi long and 1.6 km/1 mi
wide. Lake Bala has a unique primitive fish, the
gwyniad, protected from 1988.

Balaton lake in W Hungary; area 600 sq km/
230 sq mi.

Bâle French form of Basle or ◊Basel, town in
Switzerland.

Balearic Islands (Spanish *Baleares*) Mediterranean
group of islands forming an autonomous region
of Spain; including ◊Majorca, ◊Minorca, ◊Ibiza,
Cabrera, and Formentera

Bahrain
State of
(Dawlat al Bahrayn)

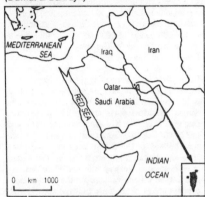

area 688 sq km/266 sq mi
capital Manama on the largest island (also
called Bahrain)
towns oil port Mina Sulman
physical 33 islands, flat and hot
features a causeway 25 km/15 mi long (1985)
links Bahrain to the mainland of Saudi Arabia;
Sitra island is a communications centre for the
lower Persian Gulf, and has a satellite-tracking
station; there is a wildlife park featuring the oryx
on Bahrain, and most of the south of the island
is preserved for the ruling family's falconry

head of state and government Sheikh Isa bin
Sulman al-Khalifa (1933–   ) from 1961
political system absolute emirate
political parties none
exports oil and natural gas
currency Bahrain dinar (0.64 = £1 Feb 1990)
population (1988 est) 421,000 (two thirds are
nationals); annual growth rate 4.4%
life expectancy men 67, women 71
language Arabic, Farsi, English
religion Muslim (Shi'ite 60%, Sunni 40%)
literacy 79% male/64% female (1985 est)
GDP $4.1 bn (1984); $6,315 per head of
population
chronology
1816 Under British protection.
1968 Britain announced its intention to withdraw
its forces. Bahrain formed, with Qatar and the
Trucial States, the Federation of Arab Emirates.
1971 Qatar and the Trucial States left
the federation and Bahrain became an
independent state.
1973 New constitution adopted, with an elected
national assembly.
1975 Prime minister resigned and national
assembly dissolved. Emir and his family
assumed virtually absolute power.
1986 Gulf University established in Bahrain. A
causeway (25 km/15 mi long) linking the island
with Saudi Arabia was opened.

---

area 5,000 sq km/1,930 sq mi
capital Palma de Mallorca
products figs, olives, oranges, wine, brandy,
coal, iron, slate; tourism is important
population (1986) 755,000

Balearic Islands

history a Roman colony from 123 BC, the
Balearic Islands were an independent Moorish
kingdom 1009–1232; the islands were conquered
by Aragon 1343.
Bali island of Indonesia, E of Java, one of the Sunda
Islands
  area 5,800 sq km/2,240 sq mi
  capital Denpasar
  physical volcanic mountains
  features Balinese dancing, music, drama
  products gold and silver work, woodcarving,
  weaving, copra, salt, coffee; tourism
  population (1980) 2,470,000
  history Bali's Hindu culture goes back to the 7th
  century; the Dutch gained control of the island
  by 1908.
Balikesir city in NW Turkey, capital of Aydin province; population (1985) 152,000. There are silver
mines nearby.
Balikpapan port in Indonesia, on the E coast of S
Kalimantan, Borneo; population (1980) 280,900.
It is an oil-refining centre.
Bali Strait a narrow strait between the two islands
of Bali and Java, Indonesia. It was the scene
on 19–20 Feb 1942 of a naval action between

Japanese and Dutch forces which served to delay slightly the Japanese invasion of Java.

Balkans peninsula of SE Europe, stretching into the Mediterranean between the Adriatic and Aegean Seas, comprising Albania, Bulgaria, Greece, Romania, Turkey-in-Europe, and Yugoslavia. It is joined to the rest of Europe by an isthmus 1,200 km/750 mi wide between Rijeka on the W and the mouth of the Danube on the Black Sea to the E.

A byword for political dissension historically, a tendency fostered by the great ethnic diversity resulting from successive waves of invasion, the Balkans' economy developed comparatively slowly until after World War II, largely because of the predominantly mountainous terrain, apart from the plains of the Save-Danube basin in the N. Political differences have remained strong, for example the confrontation of Greece and Turkey over Cyprus, and the differing types of Communism prevailing in the rest, but in the later years of the 20th century, a tendency to regional union emerged. To *Balkanize* is to divide into small warring states.

Balkhash salt lake in Kazakhstan, USSR; area 17,300 sq km/6,678 sq mi. It is 600 km/375 mi long, receives several rivers, but has no outlet. Very shallow, it is frozen throughout the winter.

Balkhash town on the N shore of Lake Balkhash in Kazhakstan, USSR; population (1985) 112,000. It was founded 1928. Chief industries include copper mining and salt extraction.

Ballarat town in Victoria, Australia; population (1986) 75,200. It was founded in the 1851 gold rush, and the mining village and workings have been restored for tourists. The Eureka Stockade miners' revolt took place here 1854.

Ballinasloe town in Galway Bay, Republic of Ireland; population about 6,500. The annual livestock fair every Oct is the largest in Ireland.

Baltic Sea

Baltic Sea large shallow arm of the North Sea, extending NE from the narrow Skagerrak and Kattegat, between Sweden and Denmark, to the Gulf of Bothnia between Sweden and Finland. Its coastline is 8,000 km/5,000 mi long, and its area, including the gulfs of Riga, Finland, and Bothnia, is 422,300 sq km/163,000 sq mi. Its shoreline is shared by Denmark, Germany, Poland, USSR, Finland, and Sweden.

Many large rivers flow into it, including the Oder, Vistula, Niemen, W Dvina, Narva, and Neva. Tides are hardly perceptible, salt content is low; weather is often stormy and navigation dangerous. Most ports are closed by ice from Dec until May. The Kiel canal links the Baltic and the North Sea, the Göta canal connects the two seas by way of the S Swedish lakes, and since 1975 the Baltic has been linked by the Leningrad–Belomorsk seaway with the White Sea.

Baltic States collective name for the former independent states of ◊Estonia, ◊Latvia, and ◊Lithuania, from 1940 republics within the USSR but contemplating secession in 1990.

Baltimore industrial port and largest city in Maryland, USA, on the W shore of Chesapeake Bay, NE of Washington DC; population (1980) 2,300,000. Industries include shipbuilding, oil refining, food processing, and the manufacture of steel, chemicals, and aerospace equipment.

It was named after the founder of Maryland, Lord Baltimore (1606–75). The city of Baltimore dates from 1729 and was incorporated 1797. At Fort McHenry Francis Scott Key wrote 'The Star Spangled Banner'. The writer Edgar Allan Poe and the baseball player Babe Ruth lived here.

Baltistan a region in the Karakoram range of NE Kashmir held by Pakistan since 1949. The home of Balti Muslims of Tibetan origin. The chief town is Skardu, but Ghyari is of greater significance to Muslims as the site of a mosque built by Sayyid Ali Hamadani, a Persian who brought the Shia Muslim religion to Baltistan in the 14th century.

Baluchistan mountainous desert area, comprising a province of Pakistan, part of the Iranian province of Sistán and Balúchestan, and a small area of Afghanistan. The Pakistani province has an area of 347,200 sq km/134,019 sq mi, and a population (1985) 4,908,000; its capital is Quetta. Sistán and Balúchestan has an area of 181,600 sq km/70,098 sq mi, and a population (1986) 1,197,000; its capital is Zahedan. The port of Gwadar in Pakistan is strategically important, on the Indian Ocean and the Strait of Hormuz.

history Originally a loose tribal confederation, Baluchistan was later divided into four principalities that were sometimes under Persian, sometimes under Afghan suzerainty. In the 19th century

British troops tried to subdue the inhabitants until a treaty in 1876 gave them autonomy in exchange for British army outposts along the Afghan border and strategic roads. On the partition of India in 1947 the khan of Khalat declared independence; the insurrection was crushed by the new Pakistani army after eight months. Three rebellions followed, the last 1973–77, when 3,000 Pakistani soldiers and some 6,000 Baloch were killed.

Bamako capital and port of Mali on the River Niger; population (1976) 404,022. It produces pharmaceuticals, chemicals, textiles, tobacco and metal products.

Bamberg town in Bavaria, West Germany, on the river Regnitz; population (1985) 70,400. The economy is based on engineering and the production of textiles, carpets, and electrical goods. It has an early 13th-century Romanesque cathedral.

Banaba formerly *Ocean Island* in the Republic of ◊Kiribati.

Banaras another transliteration of ◊ *Varanasi*, holy Hindu city in Uttar Pradesh, India.

Banbury town in Oxfordshire, England; population (1981) 35,800. The *Banbury Cross* of the nursery rhyme was destroyed by the Puritans 1602, but replaced 1858. *Banbury cakes* are criss-cross pastry cases with a mince-pie-style filling.

Banca alternative form of the Indonesian island ◊Banka.

Bandar Abbas port and winter resort in Iran on the Ormuz strait, Persian Gulf; population (1983) 175,000. Formerly called Gombroon, it was renamed and made prosperous by Shah Abbas I (1571–1629). It is an important naval base.

Bandar Seri Begawan formerly *Brunei Town* capital of Brunei; population (1983) 57,558.

Bandar Shah port in Iran on the Caspian Sea, and northern terminus of the Trans-Iranian railway.

Bandung commercial city and capital of Jawa Barat province on the island of Java, Indonesia; population (1980) 1,463,000. Bandung is the third largest city in Indonesia and was the administrative centre when the country was the Netherlands East Indies.

Banff town and resort in Alberta, Canada; 100 km/62 mi NW of Calgary; population (1984) 4,246. It is a centre for Banff National Park (Canada's first, founded 1885) in the Rocky Mountains. Industries include brewing and ironfounding.

Banffshire former county of NE Scotland, now in Grampian region.

Bangalore capital of Karnataka state, S India; population (1981) 2,914,000. Industries include electronics, aircraft and machine tools construction, and coffee.

Bangkok capital and port of Thailand, on the river Chao Phraya; population (1987) 5,609,000. Products include paper, ceramics, cement, textiles, and aircraft. It is the headquarters of the South-East Asia Treaty Organization.

Bangkok was established as the capital by Phra Chao Tak 1769, after the Burmese had burned down the former capital Avuthia about 65 km/40 mi to the north. Features include the temple of the Emerald Buddha and the vast palace complex.

Bangladesh country in S Asia, surrounded on three sides by India, and bounded to the S by the bay of Bengal.

Bangor cathedral city in Gwynedd, N Wales; population (1981) 46,585. University College, of the University of Wales, is here. The cathedral was begun 1495. Industry includes chemicals and electrical goods.

Bangui capital and port of the Central African Republic on the River Ubangi; population (1988) 597,000. Industries include beer, cigarettes, office machinery, and timber and metal products.

Banjermasin river port in Indonesia, on Borneo; population (1980) 381,300. It is the capital of Kalimantan Selatan province. It exports rubber, timber and precious stones. The university was founded 1960.

Banjul capital and chief port of Gambia, on an island at the mouth of the river Gambia; population (1983) 44,536. Known as Bathurst until 1973. It was established as a settlement for freed slaves in 1816.

Banka or *Bang Ka* island in Indonesia off the E coast of Sumatra
area 12,000 sq km/4,600 sq mi
capital Pangkalpinang
towns port Mintok
products Banka is one of the world's largest producers of tin
population (1970) 300,000.

Bannockburn a town and battlefield to the S of Stirling, central Scotland. The scene of victory by King Robert the Bruce who defeated the English under Edward II in 1314.

Barbados island country in the Caribbean, one of the Lesser Antilles.

Barbican, the arts and residential complex in the City of London. The Barbican Arts Centre 1982 contains theatres, cinemas, exhibition and concert halls.

Barbuda one of the islands which form the state of ◊Antigua and Barbuda.

Barcelona capital, industrial city (textiles, engineering, chemicals), and port of Catalonia, NE Spain; population (1986) 1,694,000. As the chief centre of anarchism and Catalonian nationalism it was prominent in the overthrow of the monarchy 1931, and was the last city of the republic to surrender to Franco 1939.

history It was founded in the 3rd century BC and its importance grew until in the 14th century it had become one of the leading trading cities of the Mediterranean.

features The Ramblas, tree-lined promenades leading from the Plaza de Cataluña, the largest square in Spain; Gaudi's unfinished church of the Holy Family 1883; a replica of Columbus's ship, the *Santa Maria,* in the Maritime Museum; a large collection of art by Picasso.

Bardsey Island former pilgrimage centre in Gwynedd, Wales, with a 6th-century ruined abbey.

Bareilly industrial city in Uttar Pradesh, India; population (1981) 438,000. It was a Mogul capital 1657, and at the centre of the Indian Mutiny 1857.

Barents Sea section of the E ◊Arctic Ocean. It has oil and gas reserves.

Bari capital of Puglia region, S Italy, and industrial port on the Adriatic; population (1988) 359,000. It is the site of Italy's first nuclear power station; the part of the town known as Tecnopolis is the Italian equivalent of ◊Silicon Valley.

Barikot a garrison town in Konar province, E Afghanistan, near the Pakistan frontier. Besieged by mujaheddin rebels in 1985, the relief of Barikot by Soviet and Afghan troops was one of the largest military engagements of the Afghan war during Soviet occupation.

Barisal river port and capital city of Barisal region, S Bangladesh; population (1981) 142,000. It trades in jute, rice, fish, and oilseed.

Barking and Dagenham borough of E Greater London

products Ford motor industry at Dagenham

population (1981) 152,600.

Bangladesh
People's Republic of

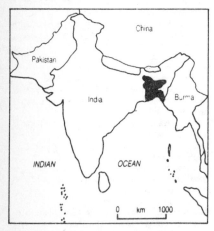

area 144,000 sq km/55,585 sq mi
capital Dhaka (formerly Dacca)
towns ports Chittagong, Khulna
physical flat delta of rivers Ganges and Brahmaputra; annual rainfall of 2,540 mm/100 in; some 75% of the land is less than 3 m/10 ft above sea level and vulnerable to flooding and cyclones
head of state Hussain Mohammad Ershad (president) from 1989
head of government Kazi Zafar Ahmad (prime minister) from 1989
political system restricted democratic republic
political parties Jatiya Dal (National Party), Islamic nationalist; Awami League, secular, moderate socialist; Bangladesh National Party,
Islamic right-of-centre
exports jute (50% of world production), tea
currency taka (54.00 = £1 Feb 1990)
population (1987) 104,100,000; annual growth rate 2.7%
life expectancy men 48, women 47
language Bangla (Bengali)
religion Sunni Muslim 85%, Hindu 14%
literacy 43% male/22% female (1985 est)
GDP $11.2 bn (1983); $119 per head of population
chronology
1947 Formed into E province of Pakistan on partition of British India.
1970 Half a million killed in flood.
1971 Independent Bangladesh emerged under leadership of Sheikh Mujibur Rahman after civil war.
1975 Mujibur Rahman assassinated. Martial law imposed.
1976–77 Maj-Gen Zia ur-Rahman assumed power.
1978–79 Elections held and civilian rule restored.
1981 Assassination of Maj-Gen Zia.
1982 Lt-Gen Ershad assumed power in army coup. Martial law imposed.
1986 Elections held but disputed. Martial law ended.
1987 State of emergency declared in response to opposition demonstrations.
1988 Assembly elections boycotted by main opposition parties. State of emergency lifted. Islam made state religion. Monsoon floods and a cyclone left 35 million homeless and thousands dead.
1989 Power devolved to Chittagong Hill Tracts to end 14-year tribal insurgency.

Barbados

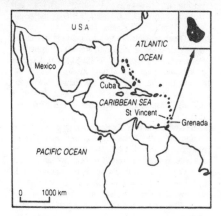

area 430 sq km/166 sq mi
capital Bridgetown
physical most easterly island of the West
Indies; surrounded by coral reefs
features subject to hurricanes
head of state Elizabeth II from 1966
represented by Hugh Springer from 1984
head of government Erskine Lloyd Sandiford
from 1987
political system constitutional monarchy
political parties Barbados Labour Party (BLP),
moderate left-of-centre; Democratic Labour Party
(DLP), moderate left-of-centre

exports sugar, rum, oil
currency Barbados dollar (3.42 = £1 Feb
1990)
population (1985) 253,000; annual growth
rate 0.3%
life expectancy men 70, women 75
language English
religion Christian
literacy 99% (1984)
GDP $1 bn (1984); $3,040 per head of
population
chronology
1951 Universal adult suffrage introduced. BLP
won general election.
1954 Ministerial government established.
1961 Full internal self-government. DLP, led by
Errol Barrow, in power.
1966 Barbados achieved full independence
within the Commonwealth. Barrow became the
new nation's first prime minister.
1972 Diplomatic relations with Cuba
established.
1976 BLP, led by Tom Adams, returned to
power.
1983 Barbados supported US invasion of
Grenada.
1985 Adams died suddenly. Bernard St John
became prime minister.
1986 DLP, led by Barrow, returned to power.
1987 Barrow died, succeeded by Erskine Lloyd
Sandiford.

Barkly Tableland large-scale open-range cattle-raising area in Northern Territory and Queensland, Australia.

Barletta industrial port on the Adriatic, Italy; population (1981) 83,800. It produces chemicals and soap; as an agriculture centre it trades in wine and fruit. There is a Romanesque cathedral and a castle.

Barnaul industrial city in S Siberia, USSR; population (1987) 596,000.

Barnet borough of NW Greater London
features site of the Battle of Barnet 1470 in one of the Wars of the Roses; Hadley Woods; Hampstead Garden Suburb; department for newspapers and periodicals of the British Library at Colindale; residential district of *Hendon*, which includes Metropolitan Police Detective Training and Motor Driving schools and the Royal Air Force Battle of Britain and Bomber Command museums
population (1981) 292,500.

Barnsley town in S Yorkshire, England; population (1981) 128,200. It is an industrial town (iron and

steel, glass, paper, carpet, and clothing) on one of Britain's richest coalfields.

Baroda former name of ◊Vadodara, in Gujarat, India.

Barossa Valley wine-growing area in the Lofty mountain ranges, South Australia.

Barotseland former kingdom in Western Province of ◊Zambia.

Barquisimeto capital of Lara state, NW Venezuela; population (1981) 523,000.

Barra most southerly of the larger Outer Hebrides, Scotland; area 90 sq km/35 sq mi; population (1981) 1,340. It is separated from South Uist by the Sound of Barra. The main town is Castlebay.

Barrancabermeja a port and oil-refining centre on the Magdalena River in the department of Santander, NE Colombia. A major outlet for oil from the De Mares fields which are linked by pipeline to Cartagena on the Caribbean coast.

Barranquilla seaport in N Colombia, on the river Magdalena; population (1985) 1,120,900. Products include chemicals, tobacco, textiles, furniture and footwear.

It is Colombia's chief port on the Caribbean, and is the site of Latin America's first air terminal 1919.

Barren Lands/Grounds the tundra region of Canada, W of Hudson Bay.

Barrow most northerly town in the USA, at Point Barrow, Alaska; the world's largest Inuit settlement. There is oil at nearby Prudhoe Bay.

Barrow-in-Furness port in Cumbria, England; population (1985) 72,600. Industries include shipbuilding and nuclear submarines.

Barry port in S Glamorgan, Wales; population (1981) 44,000. With *Barry Island*, it is a holiday resort.

Basel or *Basle* (French *Bâle*) financial, commercial, and industrial city in Switzerland; population (1987) 363,000. Basel was a strong military station under the Romans. In 1501 it joined the Swiss confederation, and later developed as a centre for the Reformation.

It has the chemical firms Hoffman-La Roche, Sandoz, Ciba-Geigy (dyes, vitamins, agrochemicals, dietary products, genetic products). There are trade fairs, and it is the headquarters of the Bank for International Settlements. There is an 11th-century cathedral (rebuilt after an earthquake 1356), a 16th-century town hall, and a university dating from the 15th century.

Bashkir autonomous republic of the USSR, with the Ural Mountains on the E
area 143,600 sq km/55,430 sq mi
capital Ufa
products minerals, oil
population (1982) 3,876,000
history Bashkir was annexed by Russia 1557, and became the first Soviet autonomous republic 1919.

Basildon industrial new town in Essex, England; population (1981) 152,500. It was designated as a new town in 1949 from several townships. Industries include chemicals, clothing, printing, and engineering.

Basilicata mountainous region of S Italy, comprising the provinces of Potenza and Matera; area 10,000 sq km/3,860 sq mi; population (1988) 622,000. Its capital is Potenza. It was the Roman province of Lucania.

Basingstoke industrial town in Hampshire, England, 72 km/45 mi WSW of London; population (1981) 67,500. It is the headquarters of the UK Civil Service Commission.

Basle alternative form of ◊Basel, city in Switzerland.

Basque Country homeland of the Basque people in the W Pyrenees. The Basque Country includes the Basque Provinces of N Spain and the French *arrondissements* of Bayonne and Maulaon. The Basques are a pre-Indo-European people who largely maintained their independence until the 19th century and speak their own Euskara tongue.

Basque Provinces (Spanish *Vascongadas*, Basque *Euskadi*) autonomous region of NW Spain, comprising the provinces of Vizcaya, Alava, and Guipuzcoa; area 7,300 sq km/2,818 sq mi; population (1986) 2,133,000.

Basra (Arabic *al-Basrah*) principal port in Iraq, in the Shatt-al-Arab delta, 97 km/60 mi from the Persian Gulf; population (1985) 617,000. Exports include wool, oil, cereal, and dates.

Bassein port in Burma, in the Irrawaddy delta, 125 km/78 mi from the sea; population (1983) 355,588. Bassein was founded in the 13th century.

Basse-Normandie or *Lower Normandy* coastal region of NW France lying between Haute-Normandie and Brittany (Bretagne). It includes the *départements* of Calvados, Manche, and Orne; area 17,600 sq km/6,794 sq mi; population (1986) 1,373,000. Its capital is Caen. Apart from stock farming, dairy farming and the production of textiles, the area is noted for its Calvados (apple brandy).

The invasion of Europe by Allied forces began in June 1944 when troops landed on the beaches of Calvados.

Basseterre capital and port of St Kitts-Nevis, in the Leeward Islands; population (1980) 14,000. Industries include data processing, rum, clothes, and electrical components.

Basse-Terre port on the Leeward Island Basse-Terre; population (1982) 13,600. It is capital of the French overseas *département* of Guadeloupe.

Basse-Terre main island of the French West Indian island group of Guadeloupe; area 848 sq km/327 sq mi; population (1982) 141,300. It has an active volcano: Grande Soufrière rising to 1,484 m/4,870 ft.

Bass Rock islet in the Firth of Forth, Scotland, about 107 m/350 ft high, with a lighthouse.

Bass Strait channel between Australia and Tasmania, named after the British explorer George Bass (1760–1912), where oil was discovered in the 1960s.

Bastia port and commercial centre in NE Corsica, France; population (1983) 50,500.

Basutoland former name for ◊Lesotho.

Bataan peninsula in Luzon, the Philippines. Despite Bataan being an earthquake zone, the Marcos government built a nuclear power station here, near a dormant volcano. It has never generated any electricity, but costs the country $350,000 a week in interest payments. In World War II Bataan was held by US and Filipino soldiers under Gen MacArthur until seized by Japanese troops in 1942 after three months of fighting. Some 70,000 Allied prisoners of war died on the Bataan death march to camps in the interior.

Batavia former name until 1949 for ◊Jakarta, capital of Indonesia on Java.

Bath historic city in Avon, England; population (1981) 75,000.

features Bath has hot springs 37°C/93°F, and the ruins of the baths for which it is named, as well as a great temple, are the finest Roman remains in Britain. Excavations in 1979 revealed thousands of coins and 'curses', offered at a place which was thought to be the link between the upper and lower worlds. The Gothic Bath Abbey has an unusually decorated W front and fan vaulting. There is much 18th-century architecture, notably the Royal Crescent by John Wood. The Assembly Rooms 1771 were destroyed in an air raid in 1942 but reconstructed in 1963. The University of Technology was established 1966.

history The Roman city of Aquae Sulis ('waters of Sul' – the British goddess of wisdom) was built in the first 20 years after the Roman invasion. In medieval times the hot springs were crown property, administered by the church, but the city was transformed in the 18th century to a fashionable spa, presided over by 'Beau' Nash. At his home here the astronomer Herschel discovered Uranus 1781. Visitors included the novelists Smollett, Fielding, and Jane Austen.

Bathurst town in New South Wales, on the Macquarie River, Australia; population (1981) 19,600. It dates from the 1851 gold rush.

Bathurst port in New Brunswick, Canada; population (1981) 19,500. Industries include copper and zinc mining. Products include paper and timber.

Bathurst former name (until 1973) of ◊Banjul, capital of the Gambia.

Baton Rouge port on the Mississippi River, USA, the capital of Louisiana; population (1980) 241,500. Industries include oil refining, petrochemicals, and iron. The bronze and marble state capitol was built by Governor Huey Long.

Battersea district of the Inner London borough of Wandsworth on the S bank of the Thames, noted for its park (including a funfair 1951–74), a classically styled power station, now disused, and Battersea Dogs' Home (1860) for strays.

Battle town in Sussex, England, named after the Battle of Hastings, which actually took place here.

Batumi port and capital in the Republic of Adzhar, USSR; population (1984) 111,000. Main industries include oil refining, food canning, and engineering.

Bavaria (German *Bayern*) administrative region (German *Land*) of West Germany

area 70,600 sq km/27,252 sq mi

capital Munich

towns Nuremberg, Augsburg, Würzburg, Regensburg

features largest of the German *Länder*; forms the Danube basin; festivals at Bayreuth and Oberammergau

products beer, electronics, electrical engineering, optics, cars, aerospace, chemicals, plastics, oil-refining, textiles, glass, toys

population (1988) 11,083,000

famous people Lucas Cranach, Hitler, Franz Josef Strauss, Richard Strauss

religion 70% Roman Catholic, 26% Protestant

history the last king, Ludwig III, abdicated 1918, and Bavaria declared itself a republic

The original Bavarians were Teutonic invaders from Bohemia who occupied the country at the end of the 5th century AD. They were later ruled by dukes who recognized the supremacy of the emperor. The house of Wittelsbach ruled parts or all of Bavaria 1181–1918; Napoleon made the ruler a king 1806. In 1871 Bavaria became a state of the German Empire. Prince Albert (1905–), the present claimant to the throne, is also the inheritor of the Stuart claim to the British throne.

Bay City industrial city in Michigan, USA; population (1980) 41,600. Industries include shipbuilding and engineering.

Bayern German name for ◊Bavaria, region of West Germany.

Bayeux town in N France; population (1982) 15,200. Its museum houses the Bayeux Tapestry. There is a 13th-century Gothic cathedral. Bayeux was the first town in W Europe to be liberated by the Allies in World War II, 8 June 1944.

Bay of Pigs inlet on the S coast of Cuba about 145 km/90 mi SW of Havana, the site of an unsuccessful invasion attempt by 1,500 US-sponsored Cuban exiles 17–20 Apr 1961; 1,173 were taken prisoner.

Bayonne river port in SW France; population (1983) 127,000. It trades in timber, steel, fertiliser, and brandy. It is a centre of Basque life. The bayonet was invented here.

Bayreuth town in Bavaria, West Germany; population (1983) 71,000. It was the home of composer Richard Wagner. The Wagner theatre was established 1876, and opera festivals are held every summer.

Beachy Head the loftiest headland 162 m/532 ft on the S coast of England, between Seaford and Eastbourne in Sussex, the E termination of the South Downs. The lighthouse off the shore is 38 m/125 ft high. The French name for the promontory is *Béveziers*.

Beaconsfield town in Buckinghamshire, England; 37 km/23 mi WNW of London; population (1981) 10,900. It has associations with Benjamin Disraeli (whose title was Earl of Beaconsfield), political theorist Edmund Burke, and the poet Edmund Waller.

Beagle Channel channel to the south of Tierra del Fuego, South America, named after the ship of Charles Darwin's voyage. Three islands at its E end, with krill and oil reserves within their 322 km/200 mi territorial waters, and the dependent sector of the Antarctic with its resources, were disputed between Argentina and Chile, and were awarded to Chile 1985.

Beas river in Himachal Pradesh, India, an upper tributary of the Sutlej, which in turn joins the Indus. It is one of the five rivers that give the Punjab its name. The ancient Hyphasis, it marked the limit of the invasion of India by Alexander the Great.

Beaufort Sea section of the Arctic Ocean off Alaska and Canada, named after Francis Beaufort. Oil drilling is allowed only in the winter months because the sea is the breeding and migration route of bowhead whales, the staple diet of local Inuit.

Beaulieu village in Hampshire, England; 9 km/6 mi SW of Southampton; population (1985) 1,200. The former abbey is the home of Lord Montagu of Beaulieu and has the Montagu Museum of vintage cars.

Beauly Firth arm of the North Sea cutting into Scotland N of Inverness, spanned by Kessock Bridge 1982.

Beaune town SW of Dijon, France; population (1982) 21,100. It is the centre of the Burgundian wine trade, and has a wine museum. Other products include agricultural equipment and mustard.

Beauvais town 76 km/47 mi NW of Paris, France; population (1982) 54,150. It is a market town trading in fruit, dairy produce, and agricultural machinery. It has a Gothic cathedral, the tallest in France: 68 m/223 ft, and is famous for tapestries (Gobelin), now made in Paris.

Bebington town on Merseyside, England; population (1981) 64,150. Industries include oil and chemicals. There is a model housing estate originally built 1888 for Unilever workers, Port Sunlight.

Bedfordshire

Bechuanaland former name until 1966 of ◊Botswana.

Bedford administrative headquarters of Bedfordshire, England; population (1983) 89,200. Industries include agricultural machinery and airships. John Bunyan wrote *The Pilgrim's Progress* (1678) while imprisoned here.

Bedfordshire county in central S England
area 1,240 sq km/479 sq mi
towns administrative headquarters Bedford; Luton, Dunstable
features Whipsnade Zoo 1931, near Dunstable, a zoological park belonging to the London Zoological Society (2 sq km/500 acres); Woburn Abbey, seat of the duke of Bedford
products cereals, vegetables, agricultural machinery, electrical goods
population (1987) 526,000
famous people John Bunyan.

Beds abbreviation for ◊*Bedfordshire*.

Beersheba industrial town in Israel; population (1987) 115,000. It is the chief centre of the Negev desert, and has been a settlement from the Stone Age.

Beijing or *Peking* capital of China; part of its NE border is formed by the Great Wall of China; population (1986) 5,860,000. The municipality of Beijing has an area of 17,800 sq km/6,871 sq mi, and a population (1986) of 9,750,000. Industries include textiles, petrochemicals, steel, and engineering.
features Tiananmen Gate (Gate of Heavenly Peace) and Tiananmen Square, where, in 1989, Chinese troops massacred over 1,000 students and civilians demonstrating for greater freedoms and democracy; the Forbidden City, built 1406–20 as Gu Gong (Imperial Palace) of the Ming emperors, where there were 9,000 ladies in waiting and 10,000 eunuchs in service (it is now the seat of the government); the Great Hall of the People 1959 (used for official banquets); museums of Chinese history and of the Chinese revolution; Chairman Mao Memorial Hall 1977 (shared from 1983 with Zhou Enlai, Zhu De, and Liu Shaoqi); the Summer Palace built by the dowager empress Zi Xi (damaged by the European powers 1900, but restored 1903); Temple of Heaven (Tiantan); and Ming tombs 50 km/30 mi to the NW.
history Beijing, founded 3,000 years ago, was the 13th-century capital of the Mongol emperor Kublai Khan. Later replaced by Nanking, it was again capital from 1421, except 1928–49, when it was renamed Peiping. Beijing was held by Japan 1937–45.

Beira port at the mouth of the river Pungwe, Mozambique; population (1986) 270,000. It is a major port, and exports minerals, cotton, and food products. A railway through the *Beira Corridor* links the port with Zimbabwe.

Beirut or *Beyrouth* capital and port of Lebanon, devastated by civil war in the 1970s and 1980s and occupied by armies of neighbouring countries; population (1980) 702,000. The city is divided into a Christian eastern and a Muslim western sector by the Green Line.

history Until the civil war 1975–76, Beirut was an international financial and educational centre, with four universities (Lebanese, Arab, French, and US); it was also a centre of espionage. It was besieged and virtually destroyed by the Israeli army July–Sept 1982 to enforce the withdrawal of the forces of the Palestinian Liberation Organization. After the ceasefire, 500 Palestinians were massacred in the Sabra-Chatila camps 16–18 Sept 1982 by dissident Phalangist and Maronite troops, with alleged Israeli complicity. Civil disturbances continued, characterized by sporadic street fighting and hostage taking. In 1987 Syrian troops were sent in.

Bejaia formerly *Bougie* port in Algeria, 193 km/120 mi E of Algiers; population (1982) 145,000. It is linked by pipeline with oil wells at Hassi Messaoud. It exports wood and hides.

Bekka, the or *El Beqa'a* a governorate of E Lebanon separated from Syria by the Anti-Lebanon mountains. The Bekka Valley has been of strategic importance in the Syrian struggle for control of N Lebanon. In the early 1980s the valley was penetrated by Shia Muslims who established an extremist Hezbollah stronghold with the support of Iranian Revolutionary Guards. Zahlé and the ancient city of Baalbek are the chief towns.

Belau, Republic of formerly *Palau* self-governing island group in Micronesia; area 500 sq km/193 sq mi; population (1988) 14,000. It is part of the US Trust Territory, and became internally self-governing 1980.

There are 26 larger islands (8 inhabited) and about 300 islets. Three referendums have shown that Belau wishes to remain 'non-nuclear', although the USA is exerting strong pressure to secure nuclear facilities for itself.

Spain held the islands from about 1600, and sold them to Germany 1899. Japan seized them in World War I, administered them by League of Nations mandate, and used them as a naval base during World War II. They were captured by the USA 1944, and became part of their Trust Territory 1947.

Belém port and naval base in N Brazil; population (1980) 758,000. The chief trade centre of the Amazon Basin, it is also known as Pará, the name of the state of which it is capital. It was founded about 1615 as Santa Maria de Belém do Grás Pará.

Belfast industrial port (shipbuilding, engineering, electronics, textiles, tobacco) and capital of Northern Ireland since 1920; population (1985) 300,000.

From 1968 it has been heavily damaged by guerrilla activities.

history Belfast grew up around a castle built in 1177 by John de Courcy. With the settlement of English and Scots, Belfast became a centre of Irish Protestantism in the 17th century. An influx of Huguenots after 1685 extended the linen industry and the 1800 Act of Union with England resulted with the promotion of Belfast as an industrial centre. It was created a city in 1888, with a lord mayor from 1892. The former parliament buildings are to the S at Stormont.

Belfort town in NE France; population (1983) 54,500. It is in the strategic *Belfort Gap* between the Vosges and Jura mountains. The capital of the *département* of Territoire de Belfort, industries include chemicals, engineering, plastics and textiles.

Belgaum city in Karnataka, S India; population (1981) 300,000. The main industry is cotton manufacture. It is also known for its Jain temples.

Belgian Congo former name 1908–60 of ◊Zaïre.

Belgium country in N Europe, bounded to the NW by the North Sea, to the SW by France, to the E by Luxembourg and West Germany, and to the NE by the Netherlands.

Belgrade (Serbo-Croat *Beograd*) capital of Yugoslavia and Serbia, and Danube river port linked with the port of Bar on the Adriatic; population (1981) 1,470,000. Industries include light engineering, food processing, textiles, pharmaceuticals and electrical goods.

Belgravia district of London, laid out in squares by Thomas Cubitt (1788–1855) in 1825–30, and bounded to the N by Knightsbridge.

Belitung alternative name for the Indonesian island of ◊Billiton.

Belize country in Central America, bounded to the north by Mexico, to the west and south by Guatemala, and to the east by the Caribbean Sea.

Belize City chief port of Belize, and capital until 1970; population (1980) 40,000. It was destroyed by a hurricane 1961 and it was decided to move the capital inland, to Belmopan.

Bellingshausen Sea the section of the S Pacific off the Antarctic coast. It is named after the Russian explorer Fabian Gottlieb Bellingshausen.

Bellinzona town in Switzerland, on the river Ticino; 16 km/10 m from Lake Maggiore; population (1980) 17,000. It is the capital of Ticino canton and a traffic centre for the St Gotthard Pass. It is a tourist centre.

Belmopan capital of Belize from 1970; population (1980) 3,000. It replaced Belize City as administrative centre of the country.

Belo Horizonte industrial city (steel, engineering, textiles) in SE Brazil, capital of the fast-developing state of Minas Gerais; population (1985) 3,060,000. Built in the 1890s, it was Brazil's first planned modern city.

Belgium
Kingdom of
(French *Royaume de Belgique*, Flemish *Koninkrijk België*)

area 30,600 sq km/11,815 sq mi
capital Brussels
towns Ghent, Liège, Charleroi, Bruges, Mons, Namur, Leuven; ports are Antwerp, Ostend, Zeebrugge
physical mostly flat, with hills and forest in SE
features Ardennes; rivers Scheldt and Meuse
head of state King Baudouin from 1951
head of government Wilfried Martens from 1981
political system liberal democracy
political parties Flemish Social Christian Party (CVP), centre-left; French Social Christian Party (PSC), centre-left; Flemish Socialist Party (SP), left-of-centre; French Socialist Party (PS), left-of-centre; Flemish Liberal Party (PVV), moderate centrist; French Liberal Reform Party (P RL), moderate centrist; Flemish People's Party (VU), federalist
exports iron, steel, textiles, manufactured goods, petrochemicals
currency Belgian franc (59.60 = £1 Feb 1990)
population (1987) 9,880,000 (comprising Flemings and Walloons); annual growth rate 0.1%

life expectancy men 70, women 77
language in the north (Flanders) Flemish (a Dutch dialect, known as *Vlaams*) 55%; in the south (Wallonia) Walloon (a French dialect which is almost a separate language) 44%; 11% bilingual; German (E border) 0.6%; all are official
religion Roman Catholic
literacy 98% (1984)
GDP $111 bn (1986); $9,230 per head of population
chronology
1830 Belgium became an independent kingdom.
1914 Invaded by Germany.
1940 Again invaded by Germany.
1948 Belgium became founder member of Benelux Customs Union.
1949 Belgium became founder member of Council of Europe and North Atlantic Treaty Organization.
1951 Leopold III abdicated in favour of his son Baudouin.
1952 Belgium became founder member of European Coal and Steel Community (ECSC).
1957 Belgium became founder member of the European Community (EEC).
1971 Steps towards regional autonomy taken.
1972 German-speaking members of the cabinet included for the first time.
1973 Linguistic parity achieved in government appointments.
1974 Separate regional councils and ministerial committees established.
1978 Wilfried Martens succeeds Leo Tindemans as prime minister.
1980 Open violence over language divisions. Regional assemblies for Flanders and Wallonia and a three-member executive for Brussels created.
1981 Short-lived coalition led by Mark Eyskens was followed by the return of Martens.
1987 Martens head of caretaker government after breakup of coalition.
1988 Following a general election, Martens formed a new CVP–PS–SP–PSC–VU coalition.

Belorussia alternative spelling for ◊Byelorussia.
Benares transliteration of ◊Varanasi, holy city in India.
Bendigo city in Victoria, Australia, about 120 km/75 mi NNW of Melbourne; population (1986) 62,400. Founded 1851 at the start of a gold rush, the town takes its name from the pugilist William Thompson (1811–89), known as 'Bendigo'.

Benevento historic town in Campania, S Italy; population (1981) 62,500. It is noted for the production of Strega liquer.
Bengal former province of British India, divided 1947 into ◊West Bengal, a state of India, and East Bengal, from 1972 ◊Bangladesh. The famine in 1943, caused by a slump in demand for jute and a bad harvest, resulted in over 3 million deaths.

Belize

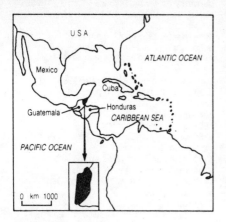

area 22,963 sq km/8,864 sq mi
capital Belmopan
towns port Belize City
physical half the country is forested, much of it high rainforest
head of state Elizabeth II from 1981 represented by Elmira Minita Gordon
head of government Manuel Esquivel from 1984
political system constitutional monarchy
political parties People's United Party (PUP), left-of-centre; United Democratic Party (UDP), moderate conservative
exports sugar, citrus, rice, lobster

currency Belize dollar (3.40 = £1 Feb 1990)
population (1987) 176,000 (including Maya minority in the interior); annual growth rate 2.5%
language English (official), but Spanish is widely spoken
religion Roman Catholic 60%, Protestant 35%, Hindu and Muslim minorities
literacy 80% (1985)
GDP $176 million (1983); $1,000 per head of population
chronology
1862 Belize became a British colony.
1954 Constitution adopted, providing for limited internal self-government. General election won by George Price.
1964 Full internal self-government granted.
1965 Two-chamber national assembly introduced, with Price as prime minister.
1970 Capital moved from Belize City to Belmopan.
1975 British troops sent to defend the frontier with Guatemala.
1977 Negotiations undertaken with Guatemala but no agreemeent reached.
1980 United Nations called for full independence.
1981 Full independence achieved. Price became prime minister.
1984 Price defeated in general election. Manuel Esquivel formed the government. Britain reaffirmed its undertaking to defend the frontier.
1989 Price and the PUP won the general election.

Benghazi or **Banghazi** historic city and industrial port in N Libya on the Gulf of Sirte; population (1982) 650,000. It was controlled by Turkey between the 16th century and 1911, and by Italy 1911–1942; an important naval supply base during World War II.
history Colonized by the Greeks in the 7th century BC (*Euhesperides*), Benghazi was taken by Rome in the 1st century BC (*Berenice*) and by the Vandals in the 5th century AD. It became Arab in the 7th century. With Tripoli, it was co-capital of Libya 1951–72.

Benguela port in Angola, SW Africa; population (1970) 41,000. It was founded 1617. Its railway runs inland to the copper mines of Zaïre and Zambia.

Benin country in W Africa, sandwiched between Nigeria on the E and Togo on the W, with Burkina Faso to the NW, Niger to the NE, and the Atlantic Ocean to the S.

Benin former African kingdom 1200–1897, now part of Nigeria. It reached the height of its power in the 14th– 17th centuries when it ruled the area between the Niger Delta and Lagos. The kingdom traded in spices, ivory, palm oil, and slaves until its decline and eventual incorporation into Nigeria.

Ben Nevis highest mountain in the British Isles (1,342 m/4,406 ft), in the Grampians, Scotland.

Benoni city in the Transvaal, South Africa; 27 km/17 mi E of Johannesburg; population (1980) 207,000. It was founded 1903 as a gold-mining centre.

Bentiu an oil-rich region to the W of the White Nile, in the Upper Nile province of S Sudan.

Benue river in Nigeria, largest affluent of the Niger; it is navigable for most of its length of 1,400 km/870 mi.

Beograd the Serbo-Croatian form of ◊Belgrade, capital of Yugoslavia.

Berbera seaport in Somalia, with the only sheltered harbour on the S side of the Gulf of Aden; population (1982) 55,000. It is in a strategic position on the oil route, and has a new deep sea port completed 1969. Under British control 1884–1960.

Benin
People's Republic of
(République Populaire du Bénin)

area 112,622 sq km/43,472 sq mi
capital Porto Novo
towns Abomey, Natitingou; chief port Cotonou
physical flat, humid, with dense vegetation
features coastal fishing villages on stilts
head of state and government Mathieu Kerekou from 1972
political system one-party socialist republic
political parties Party of the People's Revolution of Benin (PRPB), Marxist-Leninist

exports cocoa, groundnuts, cotton, palm oil
currency CFA franc (485.00 = £1 Feb 1990)
population (1988 est) 4,444,000; annual growth rate 3%
life expectancy men 42, women 46
language French (official); Fan 47%
religion animist 65%, Christian 17%, Muslim 13%
literacy 37% male/16% female (1985 est)
GDP $1.1 bn (1983); $290 per head of population
chronology
1851 Under French control.
1958 Became self-governing dominion within the French Community.
1960–72 Acute political instability, with switches from civilian to military rule.
1972 Military regime established by Gen Mathieu Kerekou.
1974 Kerekou announced that the country would follow a path of 'scientific socialism'.
1975 Name of country changed from Dahomey to Benin.
1977 Return to civilian rule under a new constitution.
1980 Kerekou formally elected president by the National Revolutionary Assembly.
1989 Kerekou re-elected. Marxist-Leninism dropped as official ideology.

Berchtesgaden village in SE Bavaria, West Germany, site of Hitler's country residence, the Berghof, which was captured by US troops 4 May 1945 and destroyed.

Berdichev town in Ukraine, USSR, 48 km/30 mi south of Zhitomir; population (1980) 60,000. Industries include engineering and food processing.

Berdyansk city and port on the Berdyansk Gulf of the Sea of Azov, in SE Ukraine, USSR; population (1985) 130,000.

Berezniki city in the USSR, on the Kama river N of Perm; population (1987) 200,000. It was formed 1932 by the amalgamation of several older towns. Industry includes chemicals and paper.

Bergama modern form of *Pergamum*, ancient city in W Turkey.

Bergamo city in Lombardy, Italy; 48 km/30 mi NE of Milan; population (1988) 119,000. Industries include silk and metal. The Academia Carrara holds a noted collection of paintings.

Bergen industrial port (shipbuilding, engineering, fishing) in SW Norway; population (1988) 210,000. Founded 1070, Bergen was a member of the Hanseatic League.

Bergen-op-Zoom fishing port in SW Netherlands; population (1982) 45,100. It produces chemicals, cigarettes and precision goods.

Bergisch Gladbach industrial city in North Rhine–Westphalia, West Germany; population (1988) 102,000.

Beringia former land bridge 1,600 km/1,000 mi wide between Asia and North America; it existed during the ice ages that occurred before 35000 BC and during the period 2400–9000 BC. It is now covered by Bering Strait and Chukchi Sea.

Bering Sea section of the N Pacific between Alaska and Siberia, from the Aleutian Islands N to Bering Strait.

Bering Strait strait between Alaska and Siberia, linking the N Pacific and Arctic oceans.

Berkeley town on San Francisco Bay in California, USA; population (1980) 103,500. It is the headquarters of the University of California, noted for its nuclear research.

Berks abbreviation for ◊*Berkshire*.

Berkshire or *Royal Berkshire* county in S central England
area 1,260 sq km/486 sq mi
towns administrative headquarters Reading; Eton, Slough, Maidenhead, Ascot, Bracknell, Newbury, Windsor
features rivers Thames and Kennet; Inkpen Beacon 297 m/975 ft; Bagshot Heath; Ridgeway Path, walkers' path (partly prehistoric) running from Wiltshire across the Berkshire Downs into

Berkshire

Hertfordshire; Windsor Forest and Windsor Castle; Eton College; Royal Military Academy at Sandhurst; atomic-weapons research establishment at Aldermaston, and the former main UK base for US cruise missiles at Greenham Common, Newbury
products general agricultural and horticultural, electronics, plastics, pharmaceuticals
population (1987) 741,000
famous people King Alfred, Stanley Spencer.

Berlin industrial city (machine tools, electrical goods, paper and printing) within East Germany, with a Western sector; population (1988) East Berlin 1,223,000; West Berlin 1,879,000. East Berlin is the capital of East Germany, and of the county (*Bezirk*) of East Berlin; area 400 sq km/154 sq mi. West Berlin is an administrative region (*Land*) of West Germany; area 480 sq km/185 sq mi. The ◊Berlin Wall dividing the city was built 1961 and demolished 1989.

Unter den Linden, the tree-lined avenue once the whole city's focal point, has been restored in the East. West Berlin includes the fashionable Kurfürstendamm and the residential Hansa quarter. Prominent buildings include the Reichstag (former parliament building); Schloss Bellevue (Berlin residence of the president); Schloss Charlottenburg (housing several museums); Congress Hall; restored 18th-century State Opera, Dahlem picture gallery. The environs of Berlin include the Grünewald forest and Wannsee lake.

First mentioned about 1230, the city grew out of a fishing village, joined the Hanseatic League in the 15th century, became the permanent seat of the Hohenzollerns, and was capital of the Brandenburg electorate 1486–1701, of the kingdom of Prussia 1701–1871, and of united Germany 1871–1945. From the middle of the 18th century it developed into an important commercial and cultural centre. In World War II air raids and conquest by the Soviet army 23 Apr–2 May 1945 destroyed much of the city. After the war, Berlin was divided into four sectors – British, US, French, and Soviet – and until 1948 was under quadripartite government by the Allies; in that year the USSR withdrew from the combined board, blockaded the city for 327 days (supplies were brought in by air by the Allies), and created a separate municipal government in their sector. The other three sectors (West Berlin) were made a *Land* of the Federal Republic May 1949, and in Oct 1949 East Berlin was proclaimed capital of East Germany.

Bermuda British colony in NW Atlantic
area 54 sq km/21 sq mi
capital and chief port Hamilton
features consists of about 150 small islands, of which 20 are inhabited, linked by bridges and causeways; Britain's oldest colony; the USA has a naval air base and there is a NASA tracking station
products Easter lillies, pharmaceuticals, tourism and banking are important
currency Bermuda dollar
population (1980) 54,900
language English
religion Christian
government under the constitution of 1968, Bermuda is a fully self-governing colony, with a governor, senate, and elected house of assembly

Berlin 1961–89

Berlin
▨ French sector   ▨ US sector
∷ British sector   ▨ Soviet sector

Bermuda

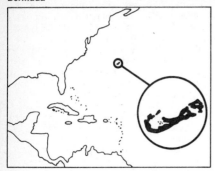

(premier from 1982 John Swan, United Bermuda Party)

history the islands were named after Juan de Bermudez, who visited them in 1515, and were settled by British colonists in 1609. Racial violence in 1977 led to intervention, at the request of the government, by British troops.

Bermuda Triangle the sea area bounded by Bermuda, Florida, and Puerto Rico, which gained the nickname Deadly Bermuda Triangle in 1964 when it was suggested that unexplained disappearances of ships and aircraft were exceptionally frequent there: analysis of the data did not eventually confirm the idea.

Bern (French *Berne*) capital of Switzerland and of Bern canton, in W Switzerland on the Aar; population (1987) 300,000. It joined the Swiss confederation 1353 and became the capital 1848. Industries include textiles, chocolate, pharmaceuticals, light metal, and electrical goods.

It was founded 1191, and made a free imperial city by Frederick II 1218. Its name is derived from the bear in its coat of arms, and there has been a bear pit in the city since the 16th century. The minster was begun 1421, the town hall 1406, and the university 1834. It is the seat of the Universal Postal Union.

Berwickshire former county of SE Scotland, a district of Borders region from 1975.

Berwick-upon-Tweed port in NE England, at the mouth of the Tweed, Northumberland, 5 km/3 mi SE of the Scottish border; population (1981) 26,230. It is a fishing port, other industries include iron foundries and shipbuilding.

features Three bridges cross the Tweed: the Old Bridge 1611–34 with 15 arches, the Royal Border railway bridge 1850 constructed by Robert Stephenson, and the Royal Tweed Bridge 1928.

history Held alternately by England and Scotland for centuries, Berwick was in 1551 made a neutral town; it was attached to Northumberland in 1885.

Besançon town on the river Doubs, France; population (1983) 120,000. It is the capital

of Franche-Comté. The first factory to produce artificial fibres was established here 1890. Industries include textiles and clock-making. It has fortifications by Vauban, Roman remains and a Gothic cathedral. The writer Victor Hugo and the Lumière brothers, inventors of cinematography, were born here.

Bessarabia territory in SE Europe, annexed by Russia 1812, which broke away at the Russian Revolution to join Romania. The cession was confirmed by the Allies, but not by Russia, in a Paris treaty of 1920; Russia reoccupied it 1940 and divided it between the Moldavian and Ukrainian republics. Romania recognized the position in the 1947 peace treaty.

Bethlehem city in E Pennsylvania, USA; population (1980) 70,400. The former steel industry has been replaced by high technology.

Bethlehem (Hebrew *Beit-Lahm*) town on the W bank of the river Jordan, S of Jerusalem. Occupied by Israel in 1967; population (1980) 14,000. In the New Testament it was the birthplace of Jesus and associated with King David.

Béthune city in N France, W of Lille; population (1982) 258,400. Industries include textiles, machinery and tyres.

Betws-y-coed village in Gwynned, Wales; population (1981) 750. It is a tourist centre, noted for its waterfalls.

Beverly Hills residential part of greater Los Angeles, California, USA, known as the home of Hollywood film stars. Population (1980) 32,400.

Bexhill-on-Sea seaside resort in E Sussex, England; population (1981) 35,500.

Béziers city in Languedoc-Roussillon, S France; population (1983) 84,000. It is a centre of the wine trade. It was once a Roman station, and was the site of a massacre 1209 in the Albigensian Crusade.

Bhagalpur town in N India, on the river Ganges; population (1981) 225,000. It manufactures silk and textiles. Several Jain temples are here.

Bhamo town in Burma, near the Chinese frontier, on the Irrawaddy river. It is the inland limit of steam navigation and is mainly a trading centre.

Bharat Hindi name for ◊India.

Bhatgaon *Bhadgaon* or *Bhaktapur* town in Nepál, 11 km/7 mi SE of Katmandu; population (1981) 48,500. A religious centre from the 9th century. It has a palace.

Bhavnagar port in Gujarat, NW India, in the Kathiawar peninsula; population (1981) 308,000. It is a centre for textile industry. It was capital of the former Rajput princely state of Bhavnagar.

Bhopal industrial city (textiles, chemicals, electrical goods, jewellery); capital of Madhya Pradesh, central India; population (1981) 672,000. Nearby Bhimbetka Caves, discovered 1973, have the world's largest collection of prehistoric paintings which are about 10,000 years old. In 1984 some

Bhutan
Kingdom of
(Druk-yul)

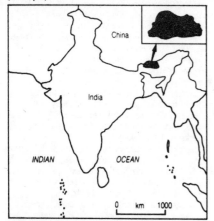

area 46,500 sq km/17,954 sq mi
capital Thimbu
physical occupies S slopes of the Himalayas, and is cut by valleys of tributaries of the Brahmaputra
head of state and government Jigme Singye Wangchuk from 1972
political system absolute monarchy

political parties none
exports timber, minerals
currency ngultrum (28.50 = £1 Feb 1990); also Indian currency
population (1988) 1,400,000; annual growth rate 2%
life expectancy men 47, women 45
language Dzongkha (a Tibetan dialect), Nepáli, and English (all official)
religion Mahayana Buddhist, 35% Hindu
literacy 10%
GDP $150 million (1983); $120 per head of population
chronology
1865 Trade treaty with Britain signed.
1907 First hereditary monarch installed.
1910 Anglo-Bhutanese Treaty signed.
1945 Indo-Bhutan Treaty of Friendship signed.
1952 King Jigme Dorji Wangchuk installed.
1953 National assembly established.
1959 4,000 Tibetan refugees given asylum.
1968 King established first cabinet.
1972 King died and was succeeded by his son Jigme Singye Wangchuk.
1979 Tibetan refugees told to take up Bhutanese citizenship or leave; most stayed.
1983 Bhutan became a founder member of the South Asian Regional Cooperation organization (SARC).

2,000 people died after an escape of poisonous gas from a factory owned by the US company Union Carbide; the long-term effects are yet to be discovered.
history The city was capital of the former princely state of Bhopal, founded 1723, which became allied to Britain in 1817. It was merged with Madhya Pradesh in 1956.

Bhubaneswar city in NE India; population (1981) 219,200. It is the capital of Orissa. Utkal University was founded 1843. A place of pilgrimage and centre of Siva worship, it has temples of the 6th–12th centuries; it was capital of the Kesaris (Lion) dynasty of Orissa 474–950.

Bhutan mountainous, landlocked country in SE Asia, bordered to the north by China and to the south by India.

Biafra, Bight of name until 1975 of the Bight of ◊Bonny, W Africa.

Bialystok city in E Poland; population (1985) 245,000. It is the capital city of Bialystok region. Industries include textiles, chemicals and tools. Founded 1310, the city belonged to Prussia 1795–1807 and to Russia 1807–1919.

Biarritz town on the Bay of Biscay, France; near the Spanish border; population (1982) 28,000. A

seaside resort and spa town, it was popularized by Queen Victoria and Edward VII.

Biel (French *Bienne*) town in NW Switzerland; population (1987) 83,000. Its main industries include engineering, scientific instruments, and watchmaking.

Bielefeld city in North Rhine-Westphalia, West Germany, 55 km/34 mi E of Münster; population (1988) 299,000. Industries include textiles, drinks, chemicals, machinery, and motorcycles.

Bielostok Russian form of ◊Bialystok, city in Poland.

Bienne French form of ◊Biel, town in Switzerland.

Bihar or *Behar* state of NE India
area 173,900 sq km/67,125 sq mi
capital Patna
features river Ganges in the north, Rajmahal Hills in the south
products copper, iron, coal, rice, jute, sugarcane, grain, oilseed
population (1981) 69,823,000
language Hindi, Bihari
famous people Chandragupta, Asoka
history the ancient kingdom of Magadha roughly corresponded to central and S Bihar.

Bikaner city in Rajasthan, N India; population (1981) 280,000. Once capital of the Rajput

Bihar

INDIAN OCEAN

state of Bikaner, it is now noted for carpets.

Bikini atoll in the ◊Marshall Islands, W Pacific, where the USA carried out atom-bomb tests 1946–63. Radioactivity will last there for 100 years. Its name was given to a two-piece swimsuit said to have an explosive effect.

Bilbao industrial port (iron and steel, chemicals, cement, food) in N Spain, capital of Biscay province; population (1986) 378,000.

Billingsgate chief London wholesale fish market, formerly (from the 9th century) near London Bridge. It re-opened in 1982 at the new Billingsgate market, West India Dock, Isle of Dogs.

Billiton Indonesian island in the Java Sea, between Borneo and Sumatra, one of the Sunda Islands; area 4,830 sq km/1,860 sq mi. The chief port is Tanjungpandan. Tin mining is the chief industry.

Biloxi port in Mississippi, USA; population (1980) 49,300. Chief occupations include tourism and seafood canning. Named after a local Indian people.

Bío-Bío longest river in Chile; length 370 km/230 mi from its source in the Andes to its mouth on the Pacific. The name is an Araucanian-language term 'much water'.

Bioko island in the Bight of Bonny, West Africa, part of Equatorial Guinea; area 2,017 sq km/ 786 sq mi; produces coffee, cacao and copra; population (1983) 57,190. Formerly a Spanish possession, as *Fernando Po*, it was known 1973–79 as *Macías Nguema Bijogo*.

Birkenhead seaport in Merseyside, England, on the Mersey estuary opposite Liverpool; population (1981) 123,884. Chief industries include shipbuilding and engineering. The rail Mersey Tunnel 1886 and road Queensway Tunnel 1934 link Birkenhead with Liverpool.

history The first settlement grew up round a Benedictine priory, and Birkenhead was still a small village when William Laird established a small shipbuilding yard, the forerunner of the huge Cammell Laird yards. In 1829 the first iron vessel in Britain was built at Birkenhead. Wallasey dock, first of the series, was opened in 1847.

Birmingham industrial city in the West Midlands, second largest city of the UK; population (1986) 1,006,527, metropolitan area 2,632,000. Industries include motor vehicles, machine tools, aerospace control systems, plastics, chemicals, food.
features It is the site of the National Exhibition Centre. Aston University is linked to a science park; a school of music and symphony orchestra; the art gallery has a Pre-Raphaelite collection; the repertory theatre was founded 1913 by Sir Barry Jackson (1897–1961).
history Lawn tennis was invented here. Sutton Park, in the residential suburb of Sutton Coldfield, has been a public country recreational area since the 16th century. As mayor, Joseph Chamberlain carried out reforms in the 1870s.

Birmingham industrial city (iron, steel, chemicals, building materials, computers, cotton textiles) and commercial centre in Alabama, USA; population (1980) 847,500.

Birobijan town in Kharabovsk Territory, E USSR; near the Chinese border; population (1981) 72,000. Industries include sawmills and clothing. It was capital of the Jewish Autonomous Region 1928–51 (sometimes also called Birobijan).

Biscay, Bay of bay of the Atlantic Ocean between N Spain and W France, known for rough seas and exceptionally high tides.

Biskra oasis town in Algeria on the edge of the Sahara; population (1968) 60,000.

Bismarck Archipelago group of over 200 islands in SW Pacific Ocean, part of ◊Papua New Guinea; area 49,660 sq km/19,200 sq mi. Largest island New Britain.

Bismarck Archipelago

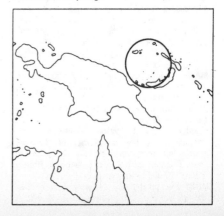

Bissau capital and chief port of Guinea-Bissau, on an island at the mouth of the Geba river; population (1988) 125,000. Originally a fortified slave-trading centre, Bissau became a free port 1869.

Bitolj (or **Bitola**) town in Yugoslavia, 32 km/20 mi north of the Greek border; population (1981) 137,800.

history Held by the Turks (under whom it was known as Monastir) from 1382, it was taken by the Serbs in 1912 during the First Balkan War. Retaken by Bulgaria in 1915, it was again taken by the Allies in November 1916.

Bizerta (or **Bizerte**) port in Tunisia, N Africa; population (1984) 94,500. Chief industries include fishing, oil refining, and metal works.

Björneborg Swedish name of the town of ◊Pori, Finland.

Blackburn industrial town (engineering) in Lancashire, England, 32 km/20 mi NW of Manchester; population (1981) 88,000.

It was pre-eminently a cotton-weaving town until World War II.

Black Country central area of England, around and to the north of Birmingham. Heavily industrialized, it gained its name in the 19th century from its belching chimneys, but pollution laws have given it a changed aspect.

Black Forest (German *Schwarzwald*) mountainous region of coniferous forest in Baden-Württemberg, West Germany. Bounded west and south by the Rhine, which separates it from the Vosges, it has an area of 4,660 sq km/1,800 sq mi and rises to 1,493 m/4,905 ft in the Feldberg. Parts of the forest have recently been affected by acid rain.

Blackheath English common which gives its name to a residential suburb of London partly in Greenwich, partly in Lewisham. Wat Tyler encamped on Blackheath in the 1381 Peasants' Revolt.

Black Hills mountains in the Dakotas and Wyoming, USA.

Black Sea

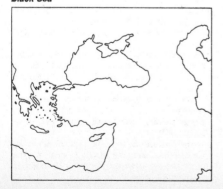

Black Mountains group of hills in S Powys, Wales, overlooking the Wye Valley and honeycombed with caves discovered 1966.

Blackpool seaside resort in Lancashire, England, 45 km/28 mi north of Liverpool; population (1981) 148,000. Amusement facilities include 11 km/7 mi of promenades, known for their 'illuminations' of coloured lights, fun fairs, and a tower 152 m/500 ft high. Political party conferences are often held here.

Black Sea (Russian *Chernoye More*) inland sea in SE Europe, linked with the seas of Azov and Marmara, and via the Dardanelles with the Mediterranean. Uranium deposits beneath it are among the world's largest.

Blantyre-Limbe the chief industrial and commercial centre of Malawi, in the Shiré highlands; population (1985) 355,000. It produces tea, coffee, rubber, tobacco, and textiles.

It was formed by the union of the towns of Blantyre (named after the explorer Livingstone's birthplace) and Limbe in 1959.

Blarney small town in County Cork, Republic of Ireland, possessing, inset in the wall of the 15th-century castle, the *Blarney Stone*, reputed to give persuasive speech to those kissing it.

Blenheim centre of a sheep-grazing area in the NE of South Island, New Zealand; population (1986) 18,300.

Bloemfontein capital of the Orange Free State and judicial capital of the Republic of South Africa; population (1985) 204,000. Founded 1846, the city produces canned fruit, glassware, furniture, and plastics.

Blois town on the river Loire in central France; population (1983) 49,500. It has a château partly dating from the 13th century.

Bloomsbury area in Camden, London, England, between Gower Street and High Holborn. It contains London University headquarters, the British Museum and the Royal Acadamy of Dramatic Arts. Between world wars it was the home of the Bloomsbury Group of writers and artists.

Bluefields one of three major port facilities on the E coast of Nicaragua, situated on an inlet of the Caribbean Sea.

Blue Mountains part of the ◊Great Divide, New South Wales, Australia, ranging 600–1,100 m/2,000–3,600 ft and blocking Sydney from the interior until the crossing 1813 by surveyor William Lawson, Gregory Blaxland, and William Wentworth.

Blue Nile (Arabic *Bahr el Azraq*) river rising in the mountains of Ethiopia. Flowing W then N for 2,000 km/1,250 mi, it eventually meets the White Nile at Khartoum. The river is dammed at Roseires where a hydroelectric scheme produces 70% of Sudan's electricity.

Blue Ridge Mountains range extending from West Virginia to Georgia, USA, and including Mount

Mitchell 2,045 m/6,712 ft; part of the ◊Appalachians.

Bobruisk town in Byelorussia, USSR, on the Beresina river; population (1987) 232,000. Industries include timber, machinery, tyres, and chemicals.

Bochum town in the Ruhr district, West Germany; population (1988) 381,000. Industry includes metallurgy, vehicles, and chemicals.

Bodensee German name for Lake ◊Constance, north of the Alps.

Bodmin administrative headquarters of Cornwall, England, 48 km/30 m from Plymouth; population (1984) 15,000.

Bodmin Moor to the NE is a granite upland, culminating in Brown Willy 419 m/1,375 ft.

Boğazköy village in Turkey 145 km/90 mi E of Ankara. It is on the site of *Hattusas*, the ancient Hittite capital established about 1640 BC. Thousands of tablets discovered by excavations here over a number of years by the German Oriental Society revealed, when their cuneiform writing was deciphered by Bedrich Hrozny (1879–1952), a great deal about the customs, religion, and history of the Hittite people.

Bognor Regis seaside resort in West Sussex, England, 105 km/66 mi SW of London; population (1981) 53,200. It owes the Regis in its name to the convalescent visit by King George V 1929.

Bogotá capital of Colombia, South America; 2,640 m/8,660 ft above sea level on the edge of the plateau of the E Cordillera; population (1985) 4,185,000. It was founded 1538.

Bohemia area of W Czechoslovakia; kingdom of central Europe from the 9th century, under Habsburg rule 1526–1918, when it was included in Czechoslovakia. The name Bohemia derives from the Celtic Boii, its earliest known inhabitants.

It became part of the Holy Roman Empire as the result of Charlemagne's establishment of a protectorate over the Celtic, Germanic, and Slav tribes settled in this area. Christianity was introduced 9th century, the See of Prague being established 975, and feudalism was introduced by King Ottaker I of Bohemia (1197–1230). Mining became increasingly important from the 12th century, and attracted large numbers of German settlers, leading to a strong Germanic influence in culture and society. In 1310, John of Luxemburg (died 1346) founded a German-Czech royal dynasty which lasted until 1437. His son, Charles IV, became Holy Roman Emperor 1355 and, during his reign, the See of Prague was elevated to an archbishopric and a university was founded there. During the 15th century, divisions within the nobility and religious conflicts culminating in the Hussite Wars (1420–36) led to decline.

Bois-le-Duc French form of ◊'s-Hertogenbosch, a town in North Brabant, Netherlands.

Bokhara another form of ◊Bukhara, city in Asian USSR.

Bolivia landlocked country in South America, bordered to the north and east by Brazil, to the southeast by Paraguay, to the south by Argentina, and to the west by Chile and Peru.

Bologna industrial city and capital of Emilia-Romagna, Italy, 80 km/50 mi north of Florence; population (1988) 427,000. It was the site of an Etruscan town, later of a Roman colony, and became a republic in the 12th century. It came under papal rule 1506, and was united with Italy 1860.

The city has a cathedral and medieval towers, and the university, which dates from the 11th century, laid the foundations of the study of anatomy and was attended by the poets Dante, Petrarch, and Tasso, and the astronomer Copernicus.

Bolton city in Greater Manchester, England, 18 km/11 mi NW of Manchester; population (1985) 261,000. Industries include chemicals and textiles.

Bolzano (German *Bozen*) town in Italy, in Trentino-Alto Adige region on the Isarco in the Alps; population (1988) 101,000. Bolzano belonged to Austria until 1919. The people are mostly German-speaking.

Boma port in Zaïre, on the estuary of the river Zaïre 88 km/55 mi from the Atlantic; population (1976) 93,965. The oldest European settlement in Zaïre, it was a centre of the slave trade, and capital of the Belgian Congo until 1927.

Bombay industrial port (textiles, engineering, pharmaceuticals, diamonds), commercial centre, and capital of Maharashtra, W India; population (1981) 8,227,000. It is the centre of the Hindi film industry.

features World Trade Centre 1975, National Centre for the Performing Arts 1969.

history Bombay was founded 13th century, came under Mogul rule, was occupied by Portugal 1530, and passed to Britain 1662 as part of Catherine of Braganza's dowry. It was headquarters of the East India Company 1685–1708. The city expanded rapidly with the development of the cotton trade and the railway in the 1860s.

Bône (or *Bohn*) former name of ◊Annaba, Algerian port.

Bonin and Volcano islands Japanese islands in the Pacific, N of the Marianas and 1,300 km/800 mi E of the Ryukyu islands. They were under US control 1945–68.

The *Bonin Islands* (Japanese *Ogasawara Gunto*) number 27 (in three groups), the largest being Chichijima: area 104 sq km/40 sq mi, population (1970) 300.

The *Volcano Islands* (Japanese *Kazan Retto*) number three, including Iwo Jima, scene of some of the fiercest fighting of World War II; total area 28 sq km/11 sq mi.

Bonn industrial city (chemicals, textiles, plastics, aluminium), capital of West Germany, 18 km/11 mi SSE of Cologne, on the left bank of the Rhine; population (1988) 292,000.

Bonn was an important Roman outpost. It was captured by the French 1794, annexed 1801, and was allotted to Prussia 1815. Beethoven was born here. It became the West German capital 1949.

Bonneville Salt Flats bed of a prehistoric lake in Utah, USA, of which the Great Salt Lake is the surviving remnant. It has been used for motor speed records.

Bolivia
Republic of
(República de Bolivia)

area 1,098,581 sq km/424,052 sq mi
capital La Paz (seat of government), Sucre (legal capital and seat of judiciary)
towns Santa Cruz, Cochabamba
physical high plateau between mountain ridges; forest and lowlands in the E
features Andes, and lakes Titicaca and Poopó
head of state and government Víctor Paz Estenssoro from 1985
political system emergent democratic republic
political parties National Revolutionary Movement (MNR), centre-right; Nationalist Democratic Action Party (ADN), extreme right-wing; Movement of the Revolutionary Left (MIR), left-of-centre
exports tin (second largest world producer), other non-ferrous metals, oil, gas (piped to Argentina), agricultural products
currency boliviano (5.16 = £1 Feb 1990)
population (1988 est) 7,000,000; (Quechua 25%, Aymara 17%, Mestizo 30%, European 14%); annual growth rate 2.7%
language Spanish (official); Aymara, Quechua
religion Roman Catholic (state-recognized)
literacy 84% male/65% female (1985 est)
GDP $3 bn (1983); $570 per head of population

chronology
1825 Independence achieved (formerly known as Upper Peru).
1952 Dr Víctor Paz Estenssoro elected president.
1956 Dr Hernan Siles Zuazo became president.
1960 Estenssoro returned to power.
1964 Army coup led by vice-president.
1966 Gen René Barrientos became president.
1967 Uprising, led by 'Che' Guevara, put down with US help.
1969 Barrientos killed in air crash, replaced by vice-president Siles Salinas. Army coup deposed him.
1970 Army coup put Gen Juan Torres Gonzalez in power.
1971 Torres replaced by Col Hugo Banzer Suarez.
1973 Banzer promised a return to democratic government.
1974 An attempted coup prompted Banzer to postpone elections, and ban political and trade-union activity.
1978 Elections declared invalid after allegations of fraud.
1980 More inconclusive elections followed by another coup, led by Gen Garcia. Allegations of corruption and drug trafficking led to cancellation of US and EEC aid.
1981 Garcia forced to resign. Replaced by Gen Celso Torrelio Villa.
1982 Torrelio resigned. Replaced by military junta led by Gen Vildoso. Because of worsening economy, Vildoso asked congress to install a civilian administration. Dr Siles Zuazo chosen as president.
1983 Economic aid from USA and Europe resumed.
1984 New coalition government formed by Siles. Attempted abduction of president by right-wing officers. The president undertook a five-day hunger strike as an example to the nation.
1985 President Siles resigned. Election result inconclusive. Dr Paz Estenssoro, at the age of 77, chosen by congress.
1989 Jaime Paz Zamora (MIR) elected president.

Bonny, Bight of name since 1975 of the former Bight of Biafra, an area of sea off the coasts of Nigeria and Cameroon.

Bootle port in Merseyside, England, adjoining Liverpool; population (1981) 62,463. The National Girobank headquarters is here.

Bophuthatswana Republic of
area 40,330 sq km/15,571 sq mi
capital Mmbatho or Sun City, a casino resort frequented by many white South Africans
features divided into six 'blocks'
exports platinum, chrome, vanadium, asbestos, manganese
currency South African rand
population (1985) 1,622,000
language Setswana, English
religion Christian
government executive president elected by the Assembly: Chief Lucas Mangope
recent history first 'independent' Black National State from 1977, but not recognized by any country other than South Africa.

Bora-Bora one of the 14 Society Islands of French Polynesia. Situated 225 km/140 mi NW of Tahiti. Area 39 sq km/15 sq mi. Exports include mother-of-pearl, fruit and tobacco.

Borâs town in SW Sweden; population (1982) 211,197. Chief industries include textiles and engineering.

Bordeaux port on the Garonne, capital of Aquitaine, SW France, a centre for the wine trade, oil refining, aeronautics and space industries; population (1982) 640,000. Bordeaux was under the English crown for three centuries until 1453. In 1870, 1914, and 1940 the French government was moved here because of German invasion.

Borders

Borders region of Scotland
area 4,700 sq km/1,815 sq mi
towns administrative headquarters Newtown St Boswells; Hawick, Jedburgh
features river Tweed; Lammermuir, Moorfoot, and Pentland hills; home of the novelist Walter Scott at Abbotsford; Dryburgh Abbey, burial place of Field Marshal Haig and Scott; ruins of 12th-century Melrose Abbey
products knitted goods, tweed, electronics, timber
population (1987) 102,000
famous people Duns Scotus, Mungo Park.

Borneo third largest island in the world, one of the Sunda Islands in the W Pacific; area 754,000 sq km/290,000 sq mi. It comprises the Malaysian territories of ◊*Sabah* and ◊*Sarawak*; ◊*Brunei*; and, occupying by far the largest part, the Indonesian territory of ◊*Kalimantan*. It is mountainous and densely forested. In coastal areas the people of Borneo are mainly of Malaysian origin, with a few Chinese, and the interior is inhabited by the indigenous Dayaks. It was formerly under both Dutch and British colonial influence until Sarawak was formed in 1841.

Bornholm Danish island in the Baltic Sea, 35 km/22 mi SE of the nearest point of the Swedish coast. It constitutes a county of the same name
area 587 sq km/227 sq mi
capital Rönne
population (1985) 47,164.

Borobudur site of Buddhist shrine near ◊Yogyakarta, Indonesia.

Borodino village 110 km/70 mi NW of Moscow. French troops under Napoleon defeated the Russians under Kutusov here 7 Sept 1812.

Bosnia and Herzegovina (Serbo-Croat *Bosna-Hercegovina*) constituent republic of Yugoslavia
area 51,100 sq km/19,725 sq mi
capital Sarajevo
features barren, mountainous country
population (1986) 4,360,000, including 1,630,000 Muslims, 1,320,000 Serbs, and 760,000 Croats
language Serbian variant of Serbo-Croat
religion Sunni Muslim, Serbian Orthodox, and Roman Catholic
history once the Roman province of *Illyria*, it enjoyed brief periods of independence in medieval times, then was ruled by the Ottoman Empire 1463–1878 and Austria 1878–1918, when it was incorporated in the future Yugoslavia.

Bosporus (Turkish *Karadeniz Boğazi*) strait 27 km/17 mi long joining the Black Sea with the Sea of Marmara and forming part of the water division between Europe and Asia. Istanbul stands on its W side. The *Bosporus Bridge* 1973 links Istanbul and Turkey-in-Asia (1,621 m/5,320 ft). In 1988 a second bridge across the straits was opened, linking Asia and Europe.

Boston seaport in Lincolnshire, England, on the Witham river; population (1981) 26,500. St Botolph's is England's largest parish church, and its tower 'Boston stump' is a landmark for sailors.

Boston industrial and commercial centre, capital of Massachusetts, USA; population (1980) 563,000; metropolitan area 2,800,000. It is a publishing centre, and Harvard University and Massachusetts Institute of Technology are nearby. A centre of opposition to British trade restrictions, it was the scene of the Boston Tea Party 1773.

Botany Bay inlet on the E coast of Australia, 8 km/5 mi S of Sydney, New South Wales. Chosen in 1767 as the site for a penal colony, it proved unsuitable. Sydney now stands on the site of the former settlement. The name Botany Bay continued to be popularly used for any convict settlement in Australia.

Botswana landlocked country in central southern Africa, bounded to the south and east by South Africa, to the west and north by Namibia, and to the northeast by Zimbabwe.

Bottrop city in North Rhine-Westphalia, West Germany; population (1988) 112,000.

Bougainville island province of Papua New Guinea; largest of the Solomon Islands archipelago
area 10,620 sq km/4,100 sq mi
capital Kieta
products copper, gold and silver
population (1989) 128,000
history named after the French navigator Bougainville who arrived in 1768. In 1976 Bougainville became a province (with substantial autonomy) of Papua New Guinea. A state of emergency declared 1989 after secessionist violence.

Bougie name until 1962 of ◊Bejaia, port in Algeria.

Bou Kraa the principal phosphate-mining centre of Western Sahara, linked by conveyor belt to the Atlantic coast near La'youn.

Boulogne-sur-Mer town on the English Channel, Pas-de-Calais *département*, France; population

Botswana

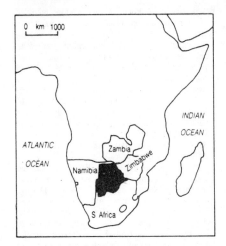

area 582,000 sq km/225,000 sq mi
capital Gaborone
physical desert in SW, plains in E, fertile lands and swamp in N
features larger part of Kalahari Desert, including Okavango Swamp, remarkable for its wildlife; diamonds are mined at Orapa and Jwaneng in partnership with De Beers of South Africa
head of state and government Quett Ketamile Joni Masire from 1980
political system democratic republic
political parties Botswana Democratic Party (BDP), moderate centrist; Botswana National Front (BNF), moderate left-of-centre
exports diamonds, copper-nickel, meat
currency pula (3.14 = £1 Feb 1990)
population (1988) 1,210,000 (80% Bamangwato, 20% Bangwaketse); annual growth rate 3.8%
life expectancy men 53, women 56
language English (official); Setswana (national)
religion Christian (majority)
literacy 73% male/69% female (1985 est)
GDP $810 million (1984); $544 per head of population
chronology
1885 Became a British protectorate.
1960 New constitution created a legislative council.
1963 End of high-commission rule.
1965 Capital transferred from Mafeking to Gaborone. Internal self-government granted. Seretse Khama elected head of government.
1966 Full independence achieved. New constitution came into effect. Name changed from Bechuanaland to Botswana. Seretse Khama elected president.
1980 Seretse Khama died and was succeeded by vice-president Quett Masire.
1984 Masire re-elected.
1985 South African raid on Gaborone.
1987 Joint permanent commission with Mozambique established, to improve relations.
1989 The BDP and Masire re-elected.

(1983) 99,000. Industries include oil refining, food processing, and fishing. It is also a ferry port and seaside resort. Boulogne was a medieval countship, but became part of France 1477.

Boundary Peak highest mountain in Nevada State, USA, rising to 4,006 m/13,143 ft on the Nevada–California frontier.

Bourbon name 1649–1815 of the French island of ◊Réunion in the Indian Ocean.

Bourges city in central France, 200 km/125 mi south of Paris; population (1982) 92,000. Industries include aircraft, engineering, and tyres. It has a 13th-century Gothic cathedral and notable art collections.

Bourgogne region of France, which includes the *département*s of Côte-d'Or, Nièvre, Sâone-et-Loire, and Yonne; area 31,600 sq km/12,198 sq mi; population (1986) 1,607,000. Its capital is Dijon. It is famous for its wines, such as Chablis and Nuits-Saint-Georges, and for its cattle (the Charolais herdbook is maintained at Nevers). A former independent kingdom and duchy (English name **Burgundy**), it was incorporated into France 1477.

Bournemouth seaside resort in Dorset, England; population (1981) 145,000.

Bouvet Island uninhabited island in the S Atlantic Ocean, area 48 sq km/19 sq mi, a dependency of Norway since 1930. Discovered by the Frenchman Jacques Bouvet in 1738, it was made the subject of a claim by Britain in 1825, but this was waived in Norway's favour in 1928.

Boyne a river in the Irish Republic. Rising in the Bog of Allen in County Kildare, it flows 110 km/69 mi NE to the Irish Sea near Drogheda. The Battle of the Boyne was fought at Oldbridge near the mouth of the river in 1690.

Boyoma Falls series of seven cataracts in under 100 km/60 mi in the Lualaba (upper Zaïre river) above Kisangani, central Africa. They have a total drop of over 60 m/200 ft.

Bozen German form of ◊Bolzano, town in Italy.

Brabant (Flemish *Braband*) former duchy of W Europe, comprising the Dutch province of ◊North Brabant, and the Belgian provinces of Brabant and Antwerp. They were divided when Belgium became independent 1830. The present-day Belgian province of Brabant has an area of 3,400 sq km/1,312 sq mi, and a population (1987) of 2,222,000.

During the Middle Ages it was an independent duchy, and after passing to Burgundy, and thence to the Spanish crown, was divided during the Dutch War of Independence. The southern portion was Spanish until 1713, then Austrian until 1815, when the whole area was included in the Netherlands. In 1830 the influential French-speaking part of the population in the S Netherlands rebelled and when Belgium was recognized 1839, S Brabant was included in it.

Bracknell new town in Berkshire, England, founded 1949; population (1981) 49,000. The headquarters of the Meteorological Office is here, and (with Washington DC) is one of the only two global area forecasting centres (of upper-level winds and temperatures) for the world's airlines.

Bradford industrial city (engineering, machine tools, electronics, printing) in West Yorkshire, England, 14 km/9 mi W of Leeds; population (1981) 281,000.

features A 15th-century cathedral; Cartwright Hall art gallery; the National Museum of Photography, Film, and Television 1983 (with Britain's largest cinema screen 14 m × 20 m); and the Alhambra, built as a music hall and restored for ballet, plays, and pantomime.

history From the 13th century, Bradford developed as a great wool- and, later, cloth-manufacturing centre, but the industry declined from the 1970s with Third World and Common Market competition. The city has received a succession of immigrants, Irish in the 1840s, German merchants in the mid-19th century, then Poles and Ukrainians, and more recently West Indians and Asians.

Braga city in N Portugal 48 km/30 mi NNE of Oporto; population (1981) 63,800. Industries include textiles, electrical goods and vehicle manufacture. It has a 12th-century cathedral, and the archbishop is primate of the Iberian peninsula. As *Bracara Augusta* it was capital of the Roman province Lusitania.

Braganua capital of a province of the same name in NE Portugal, 176 km/110 mi NE of Oporto. Population (1981) 13,900. It was the original family seat of the House of Braganua which ruled Portugal 1640–1910.

Brahmaputra river in Asia 2,900 km/1,800 mi long, a tributary of the Ganges.

It rises in the Himalayan glaciers as Zangbo and runs E through Tibet, to the mountain mass of Namcha Barwa. Turning S, as the Dihang, it enters India and flows into the Assam valley near Sadiya. Now known as the Brahmaputra, it flows generally W until, shortly after reaching Bangladesh, it turns S and divides into the Brahmaputra proper, without much water, and the main stream, the Jamuna, which joins the Padma arm of the Ganges. The river is navigable for 1,285 km/800 mi from the sea.

Brăila port in Romania on the river Danube; 170 km/106 mi from its mouth; population (1983) 226,000. It is a naval base. Industries include the manufacture of artificial fibres, iron and steel, machinery, paper. Controlled by the Ottoman Empire 1544–1828.

Brandenburg town in E Germany, on the river Havel; 60 km/36 mi W of Berlin; population (1981) 94,700. Industries include textiles, cars, and aircraft. It has a 12th-century cathedral.

Brasília capital of Brazil from 1960, some 1,000 m/3,000 ft above sea level; population (1980) 411,500. It was designed by Lucio Costa (1902–63), with Oscar Niemeyer as chief architect, as a completely new city to bring life to the interior.

Braşov (Hungarian *Brassó*, German *Krondstadt*) industrial city (machine tools, industrial equipment, chemicals, cement, woollens) in central Romania at the foot of the Transylvanian Alps; population (1985) 347,000. It belonged to Hungary until 1920.

Bratislava (German *Pressburg*) industrial port (engineering, chemicals, oil refining) in Czechoslovakia, on the Danube; population (1986) 417,000. It was the capital of Hungary 1526–1784, and is now capital of the Slovak Socialist Republic and second largest city in Czechoslovakia.

Braunschweig German form of ◊Brunswick.

Brazil country in South America, bounded to the southwest by Uruguay, Argentina, Paraguay and Bolivia, to the west by Peru and Colombia, to the north by Venezuela, Guyana, Suriname, and French Guiana, and to the west by the Atlantic Ocean.

Brazzaville capital of the Congo, industrial port (foundries, railway repairs, shipbuilding, shoes, soap, furniture, bricks) on the river Zaïre, opposite Kinshasa; population (1984) 595,000.

There is a cathedral 1892 and the Pasteur Institute 1908. It stands on Pool Malebo (Stanley Pool).

Brazzaville was founded by the Italian Count Pierre Savorgnan de Brazza (1852–1905), employed in African expeditions by the French government. It was the African headquarters of the Free (later Fighting) French during World War II.

Brecknockshire former county of Wales, merged in ◊Powys in 1974.

Breda town in North Brabant, Netherlands; population (1988) 156,000. It was here that Charles II of England made the declaration that paved the way for his restoration 1660.

Breizh Celtic name for ◊Brittany, region of France.

Bremen industrial port (iron, steel, oil refining, chemicals, aircraft, shipbuilding, cars) in West Germany, on the Weser 69 km/43 mi from the open sea; population (1988) 522,000.

Bremen was a member of the Hanseatic League, and a free imperial city from 1646. It became a member of the North German Confederation 1867, and of the German Empire 1871.

Bremen administrative region (German *Land*) of West Germany, consisting of the cities of Bremen and Bremerhaven; area 400 sq km/154 sq mi; population (1988) 652,000.

Bremerhaven formerly (until 1947) *Wesermünde* port at the mouth of the Weser, Germany; population (1988) 132,000. Industries include fishing

and shipbuilding. It serves as an outport for Bremen.

Brenner Pass lowest of the Alpine passes, 1,370 m/4,495 ft; it leads from Trentino–Alto Adige, Italy, to the Austrian Tirol, and is 19 km/12 mi long.

Brescia ancient *Brixia* historic and industrial city (textiles, engineering, firearms, metal products) in N Italy, 84 km/52 mi E of Milan; population (1988) 199,000. It has medieval walls and two cathedrals (12th and 17th century).

Breslau German name of ◊Wroclaw, town in Poland.

Brest naval base and industrial port (electronics, engineering, chemicals) on *Rade de Brest* (Brest Roads), a great bay at the western extremity of Bretagne, France; population (1983) 201,000. Occupied as a U-boat base by the Germans 1940–44, the town was destroyed by Allied bombing and rebuilt.

Brest town in Byelorussia, USSR, on the river Bug and the Polish frontier; population (1987) 238,000. It was in Poland (*Brześć nad Bugiem*) until 1795 and 1921–39. The *Treaty of ◊Brest-Litovsk* (an older Russian name of the town) was signed here.

Bretagne (English *Brittany*) region of NW France in the Breton peninsula between the Bay of Biscay and the English Channel; area 27,200 sq km/10,499 sq mi; population (1986) 2,764,000. Its capital is Rennes, and includes the *départements* of Côte-du-Nord, Finistère, Ille-et-Vilaine, and Morbihan. It is a farming region.

history Bretagne was established by the Celts in the 5th century and was the Gallo-Roman province of Armorica after being conquered by Julius Caesar 56 BC. It was devastated by Norsemen after the Roman withdrawal. During the Anglo-Saxon invasion of Britain so many Celts migrated across the Channel that it gained the name of Brittany. It became a strong, expansionist state which maintained its cultural and political independence, despite pressure from the Carolingians, Normans, and Capetians. In 1171, the duchy of Brittany was inherited by Geoffrey, son of Henry II of England, and remained in the Angevin dynasty's possession until 1203, when Geoffrey's son Arthur was murdered by King John, and the title passed to the Capetian Peter of Dreux. Under the Angevins, feudalism was introduced, and French influence greatly increased under the Capetians. By 1547 it had been formally annexed by France, and the Breton language was banned in education. A separatist movement developed after World War II, and there has been guerrilla activity.

Bridgeport city in Connecticut, USA, on Long Island Sound; population (1980) 142,500. Industries include metal goods, electrical appliances, and aircraft.

Brazil
Federative Republic of
(República Federativa do Brasil)

area 8,511,965 sq km/3,285,618 sq mi
capital Brasília
towns São Paulo, Belo Horizonte, Curitiba, Fortaleza; ports are Rio de Janeiro, Recife, Porto Alegre, Salvador
physical the densely forested Amazon basin covers the N half of the country with a network of rivers; the S is fertile; enormous energy resources, both hydroelectric (Itaipú dam on the Paraná, and Tucurui on the Tocantins) and nuclear (uranium ores)
features Mount Roraima, Xingu National Park. Brazil is the world's sixth largest arms exporter, and sells training planes to the RAF. In 1988, the annual inflation rate was 600%.
head of state and government Fernando Collor from 1989
political system emergent democratic federal republic
political parties Social Democratic Party (PDS), moderate left-of-centre; Brazilian Democratic Movement Party (PMDB), centre-left; Liberal Front Party (PFL), moderate left-of-centre; Workers' Party, left-of-centre; National Reconstruction Party (PRN), centre-right
exports coffee, sugar, cotton, textiles, motor vehicles, iron, chrome, manganese, tungsten and other ores, as well as quartz crystals, industrial diamonds

currency cruzado (introduced 1986; value = 100 cruzeiros, the former unit) (44.13 = £1 Feb 1990)
population (1988) 144,262,000 (including 200,000 Indians, survivors of 5 million, especially in Rondonia and Mato Grosso, mostly living on reserves); annual growth rate 2.2%
life expectancy men 61, women 66
language Portuguese; 120 Indian languages
religion Roman Catholic 89%, Indian faiths
literacy 79% male/76% female (1985 est)
GDP $218 bn (1984); $1,523 per head of population
chronology
1822 Brazil became an independent empire, ruled by Dom Pedro, son of the refugee King John VI of Portugal.
1889 Monarchy abolished and republic established.
1891 Constitution for a federal state adopted.
1930 Dr Getulio Vargas became president.
1945 Vargas deposed by the military.
1946 New constitution adopted.
1950 Vargas returned to office.
1954 Vargas committed suicide.
1956 Juscelino Kubitschek became president.
1960 Capital moved to Brasília.
1961 Joao Goulart became president.
1964 Bloodless coup made Gen Castelo Branco president. He assumed dictatorial powers, abolishing free political parties.
1967 New constitution adopted. Branco succeeded by Marshal da Costa e Silva.
1969 Da Costa e Silva resigned and a military junta took over.
1974 Gen Ernesto Geisel became president.
1978 Gen Baptista de Figueiredo became president.
1979 Political parties legalized again.
1984 Mass calls for a return to fully democratic government.
1985 Tancredo Neves became first civilian president for 21 years. Neves died and was succeeded by the vice-president, José Sarney.
1988 New constitution approved, transferring power from the president to the congress. Measures announced to halt large-scale burning of Amazonian rainforest for cattle grazing.
1989 Forest Protection Service and Ministry for Land Reform abolished. International concern over how much of the Amazon has been burned. Fernando Color (PRN) elected president.

Bridgetown port and capital of Barbados, founded 1628; population (1987) 8,000. Sugar is exported through the nearby deep-water port.

Bridgwater port in Somerset, England, on the river Parret; population (1981) 26,000. Industries include plastics and electrical goods. 5 km/3 mi SE is the site of the Battle of Sedgemoor.

Brighton resort on the E Sussex coast, England; population (1981) 146,000. It has Regency architecture and Brighton Pavilion 1782 in oriental style. There are two piers and an aquarium. The University of Sussex was founded 1963.

history Originally a fishing village called Brighthelmstone, it became known as Brighton at the beginning of the 19th century, when it was already a fashionable health resort patronized by the Prince Regent, afterwards George IV.

Brindisi (ancient *Brundisium*) port and naval base on the Adriatic, in Puglia, on the heel of Italy; population (1981) 90,000. Industries include food processing and petrochemicals. It is one of the oldest Mediterranean ports, at the end of the Appian Way from Rome. The poet Virgil died here 19 BC.

Brisbane industrial port (brewing, engineering, tanning, tobacco, shoes; oil pipeline from Moonie), capital of Queensland, E Australia, near the mouth of Brisbane river, dredged to carry ocean-going ships; population (1986) 1,171,300

Bristol industrial port (aircraft engines, engineering, microelectronics, tobacco, chemicals, paper, printing), administrative headquarters of Avon, SW England; population (1986) 391,000. The old docks have been redeveloped for housing, industry, yachting facilities, and the National Lifeboat Museum.

features 12th-century cathedral; 14th-century St Mary Redcliffe; 16th-century Acton Court, built by Sir Nicholas Poynz, a courtier of Henry VIII; the Georgian residential area of Clifton; the Clifton Suspension Bridge designed by Brunel and his SS *Great Britain*, which is being restored in dry dock.

history John Cabot sailed from here 1497 to Newfoundland, and there was a great trade with the American colonies and the West Indies in the 17th–18th centuries, including slaves. The poet Chatterton was born here.

Britain or *Great Britain* island off the NW coast of Europe, one of the British Isles. It consists of ◊England, ◊Scotland, and ◊Wales, and is part of the ◊United Kingdom. The name is derived from the Roman name Britannia, which is in its turn derived from the ancient Celtic.

British Antarctic Territory colony created in 1962 and comprising all British territories S of latitude 60°S: the South Orkney Islands, the South Shetland Islands, the Antarctic Peninsula and all adjacent lands, and Coats Land, extending to the South Pole; total land area

British Columbia

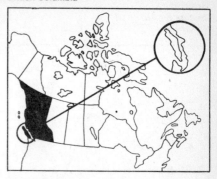

660,000 sq km/170,874 sq mi. Scientific personnel are the only population: about 300.

British Columbia province of Canada on the Pacific

area 947,800 sq km/365,851 sq mi

capital Victoria

towns Vancouver, Prince George, Kamloops, Kelowna

physical Rocky Mountains and Coast Range; the coast is deeply indented; rivers include the Fraser and Columbia; there are more than 80 lakes; more than half the land is forested

products fruit and vegetables; timber and wood products; fish; coal, copper, iron, lead; oil and natural gas, and hydroelectricity

population (1986) 2,889,000

history Captain Cook explored the coast in 1778; a British colony was founded on Vancouver Island in 1849, and the gold rush of 1858 extended settlement to the mainland; it became a province in 1871. In 1885 the Canadian Pacific Railroad linking British Columbia to the E coast was completed.

British Honduras former name of ◊Belize, a country in Central America.

British Indian Ocean Territory British colony in the Indian Ocean directly administered by the Foreign and Commonwealth Office. It consists of the Chagos Archipelago some 1,900 km/1,200 mi NE of Mauritius

area 60 sq km/23 sq mi

features lagoons; US naval and air base on Diego Garcia

products copra, salt fish, tortoiseshell

population (1982) 3,000

history purchased in 1965 for $3 million by Britain from Mauritius to provide a joint US/UK base

The island of Aldabra, Farquhar, and Desroches, some 485 km/300 mi N of Madagascar, originally formed part of the British Indian Ocean Territory, but were returned to the administration of the Seychelles in 1976.

Brunei
(Negara Brunei Darussalam)

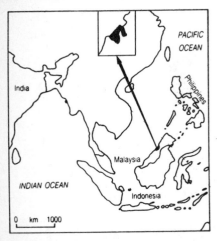

PACIFIC OCEAN

India

Philippines

Malaysia

INDIAN OCEAN

Indonesia

0   km   1000

area 5,765 sq km/2,225 sq mi
capital and chief port Bandar Seri Begawan
physical 75% of the area is forested; the Limbang valley splits Brunei in two, and its cession to Sarawak 1890 is disputed by Brunei
head of state and of government Muda Hassanal Bolkiah Mu'izzaddin Waddaulah from 1968
political system absolute monarchy
political parties Brunei National United Party (BNUP)

exports liquefied natural gas (world's largest producer) and oil, both expected to be exhausted by 2000
currency Brunei dollar (3.17 = £1 Feb 1990)
population (1986) 226,300 (65% Malay, 25% Chinese; few Chinese granted citizenship); annual growth rate 12%
language 50% Malay (official), 26% Chinese (Hokkien), English
religion Muslim
literacy 75% male/50% female (1971)
GDP $3.8 bn (1983); $20,000 per head of population
chronology
1888 Brunei became a British protectorate.
1941–45 Occupied by Japan.
1959 Written constitution made Britain responsible for defence and external affairs.
1962 Sultan began rule by decree.
1963 Proposal to join Malaysia abandoned.
1967 Sultan abdicated in favour of his son Hassanal Bolkiah.
1971 Brunei given internal self-government.
1975 UN resolution called for independence for Brunei.
1984 Full independence achieved, with Britain maintaining a small force to protect the oil and gas fields.
1985 A 'loyal and reliable' political party, the Brunei National Democratic Party (BNDP), legalized.
1986 Death of former sultan, Sir Omar. Formation of multi-ethnic Brunei National United Party (BNUP).
1988 BNDP disbanded.

British Isles group of islands off the NW coast of Europe, consisting of Great Britain (England, Wales, and Scotland), Ireland, the Channel Islands, Orkney and Shetland, the Isle of Man, and many others which are included in various counties, such as the Isle of Wight, Scilly Isles, Lundy Island, and the Inner and Outer Hebrides. The islands are divided from Europe by the North Sea, Strait of Dover, and the English Channel, and face the Atlantic to the west.

British Somaliland a British protectorate over 176,000 sq km/67,980 sq mi of territory on the Somali coast of Africa from 1884 until the independence of Somalia in 1960. British authorities were harassed by a self-proclaimed messiah known as the 'Mad Mullah' from 1901 until 1910.

British Virgin Islands part of the ◊Virgin Islands group in the West Indies.

Brittany English name for ◊Bretagne, region of W France.

Brno industrial city in central Czechoslovakia (chemicals, arms, textiles, machinery), population (1984) 380,800. Now third largest city in Czechoslovakia, Brno was formerly capital of the Austrian crownland of Moravia.

Broads, Norfolk area of some 12 interlinked freshwater lakes in E England, created about 600 years ago by the digging out of peat deposits; they are noted for wildlife and boating facilities.

Brocken highest peak of the Harz Mountains (1,142 m/3,746 ft) in East Germany. On 1 May (Walpurgis night) witches were said to gather here.

The Brocken Spectre is a phenomenon of mountainous areas, so named because first scientifically observed at Brocken in 1780. The greatly enlarged shadow of the observer, accompanied by coloured rings, is cast by a low sun upon a cloud bank.

Broken Hill mining town in New South Wales, Australia; population (1981) 27,000. It is the base of the Royal Flying Doctor Service.

Broken Hill former name until 1967 of ◊Kabwe, town in Zambia.

Bromberg German name of ◊Bydgoszcz, port in Poland.

Bronx, the borough of New York City, USA, NE of Harlem River; area 109 sq km/ 42 sq mi; population (1980) 1,169,000. Largely residential, it is named after an early Dutch settler, James Bronck.

Brooklyn borough of New York City, USA, occupying the SW end of Long Island. It is linked to Manhattan Island by Brooklyn Bridge 1883 and others, and by the Verrazano-Narrows Bridge 1964 to Staten Island. Brooklyn US Navy Yard is here. Of the more than 60 parks, Prospect is the most important. There is also a botanic garden, and a beach and funfair at Coney Island.

Browns Ferry site of a nuclear power station on the Alabama River, central Alabama. A nuclear accident in 1975 resulted in the closure of the plant for 18 months. This incident marked the beginning of widespread disenchantment with nuclear power in the USA.

Bruges (Flemish *Brugge*) historic city in NW Belgium; capital of W Flanders province, 16 km/10 mi from the North Sea, with which it is connected by canal; population (1985) 117,700. Bruges was the capital of medieval Flanders, and was the chief European wool manufacturing town as well as its chief market.

features Among many notable buildings are the 14th-century cathedral, the church of Nôtre Dame with a Michelangelo statue of the Virgin and Child, the Gothic town hall and market hall; there are remarkable art collections. It was named for its many bridges. The College of Europe is the oldest centre of European studies. The modern port handles coal, iron ore, oil and fish. Local manufacturers include lace, textiles, paint, steel, beer, furniture and motors.

Brugge Flemish form of ◊Bruges, town in Belgium.

Brunei country on the N coast of Borneo, surrounded to the landward side by Sarawak, and bounded to the N by the South China Sea.

Brunei Town former name (until 1970) of ◊Bandar Seri Begawan, Brunei.

Brünn German form of ◊Brno, a town in Czechoslovakia.

Brunswick (German *Braunschweig*) former independent duchy, a republic from 1918, which is now part of ◊Lower Saxony, West Germany.

Brunswick (German *Braunschweig*) industrial city (chemical engineering, precision engineering, food processing) in Lower Saxony, West Germany; population (1988) 248,000. It was one of the chief cities of N Germany in the Middle Ages, and a member of the Hanseatic League. It was capital of the duchy of Brunswick from 1671.

Brusa alternative form of ◊Bursa, a town in Turkey.

Brussels (Flemish *Brussel*/French *Bruxelles*) capital of Belgium, industrial city (lace, textiles, machinery, chemicals); population (1987) 974,000

(80% French-speaking, the suburbs Flemish-speaking). It is the headquarters of the European Economic Community and since 1967 of the international secretariat of NATO. First settled in the 6th century AD, and a city from 1321, Brussels became the capital of the Spanish Netherlands 1530 and of Belgium 1830.

features Notable buildings include the 13th-century church of Sainte Gudule; the Hôtel de Ville, Maison du Roi, and others in the Grand Place; and the royal palace; the Musées Royaux des Beaux-Arts de Belgique hold a large art collection. Its most famous statue is the bronze fountain Manneken Pis (1388), of a tiny naked boy urinating.

Bruxelles French form of ◊Brussels, capital of Belgium.

Bryansk city in W central USSR, SW of Moscow on the Desna; population (1987) 445,000. Industries include sawmilling, textiles, and steel.

Brześć nad Bugiem Polish name of ◊Brest, a town in the USSR.

Bubiyan an island of Kuwait claimed by Iraq.

Bucaramanga industrial (coffee, tobacco, cacao, cotton) and commercial city in N central Colombia; population (1985) 493,929. Founded by the Spanish in 1622.

Bucharest (Romanian *Bucureşti*) capital and largest city of Romania; population (1985) 1,976,000, the conurbation of Bucharest district having an area of 1,520 sq km/587 mi and a population of 2,273,000. Originally a citadel built by Vlad the Impaler to stop the advance of the Ottoman invasion in the 14th century. It became the capital of the princes of Wallachia 1698 and of Romania 1861.

Buckingham market town in Buckinghamshire, England; on the river Ouse. University College was established 1974, and was given a royal charter as the University of Buckingham 1983.

Buckinghamshire county in SE central England
area 1,880 sq km/726 sq mi
towns administrative headquarters Aylesbury; Buckingham, High Wycombe, Beaconsfield, Olney
features Chequers (country seat of the prime minister); Burnham Beeches and the church of the poet Gray's 'Elegy' at Stoke Poges; Cliveden, a country house designed by Charles Barry (now a hotel, it was used by the newspaper-owning Astors for house parties); Bletchley Park, home of World War II code-breaking activities, now used as a training post for GCHQ (Britain's electronic surveillance centre); homes of the poets William Cowper at Olney and John Milton at Chalfont St Giles, and of the Tory prime minister Disraeli at Hughenden
products furniture, especially beech; agricultural
population (1987) 621,000.

Bucks abbreviation for ◊*Buckinghamshire*.

Budapest capital of Hungary, industrial city (chemicals, textiles) on the Danube; population (1985) 2,089,000. Buda, on the right bank of the Danube, became the Hungarian capital 1867 and was joined with Pest, on the left bank, 1872.

Budapest saw fighting between German and Soviet troops in World War II 1944–45, and between the Hungarians and Soviet troops in the rising of 1956.

Budějovice see ◊České Budějovice, town in Czechoslovakia.

Bulgaria
People's Republic of
(Narodna Republika Bulgaria)

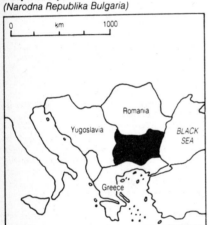

area 110,912 sq km/42,812 sq mi
capital Sofia
towns Plovdiv, Rusé; Burgas and Varna are Black Sea ports
physical Balkan and Rhodope mountains; river Danube in the north
features Black Sea coast
head of state Petar Mladenov from 1989
head of government Andrey Loukanov from 1990
political system socialist pluralist republic
political parties Bulgarian Communist Party (BCP), socialist ; Bulgarian Agrarian People's Union (BZNS), peasants' organization loyal (to 1989) to BCP; Union of Democratic Forces (UDF), pro-democracy opposition movement
exports textiles, chemicals, non-ferrous metals, timber, minerals, machinery

currency lev (1.34 = £1 Feb 1990)
population (1988) 8,970,000 (including 9,000,000–1,500,000 ethnic Turks, concentrated in the S and NE); annual growth rate 0.5%
life expectancy men 69, women 74
language Bulgarian, Turkish
religion Eastern Orthodox Christian 90%, Sunni Muslim 10%
literacy 96% male/93% female (1980 est)
GNP $26 bn (1983); $2,625 per head of population
chronology
1908 Bulgaria became a kingdom independent of Turkish rule.
1944 Soviet invasion of German-occupied Bulgaria.
1946 Monarchy abolished and communist-dominated people's republic proclaimed.
1947 Soviet-style constitution adopted.
1949 Death of Georgi Dimitrov.
1954 Election of Todor Zhivkov as Communist Party general secretary.
1971 Constitution modified. Zhivkov elected president.
1985–88 Large-scale administrative and personnel changes made haphazardly under Soviet stimulus.
1987 New electoral law introduced multi-candidate elections.
1989 310,000 ethnic Turks fled in opposition to the 'Bulgarianization' campaign of forced assimilation. Zhivkov ousted by Petar Mladenov in Nov and expelled from BCP. Sweeping pluralist reforms instituted, and opposition parties allowed to form; Bulgarianization abandoned.
1990 BCP monopoly of power ends (Jan); Alexander Lilov elected new BCP leader and Andrey Loukanov prime minister (Feb).

Budweis German form of České Budějovice, a town in Czechoslovakia.

Buenos Aires capital and industrial city of Argentina, on the south bank of the River Plate; population (1980) 9,927,000. It was founded 1536, and became the capital 1853.

features Palace of Congress; on the Plaza de Mayo, the cathedral and presidential palace (known as the Pink House); university 1821.

Buffalo industrial port in New York State, USA, at the E end of Lake Erie; population (1980) 1,200,000. It is linked with New York City by the New York State Barge Canal.

Bug two rivers in E Europe: the *West Bug* rises in SW Ukraine and flows to the Vistula, and the *South Bug* rises in W Ukraine and flows to the Black Sea.

Buganda two provinces (North and South Buganda) of Uganda, home of the Baganda people, and formerly a kingdom from the 17th century. The *kabaka* or king, Sir Edward Mutesa II (1924–69), was the first president of independent Uganda 1962–66, and his son Ronald Mutebi (1955–) is *sabataka* (head of the Baganda clans).

Bujumbura capital of Burundi; population (1986) 272,600. Formerly called *Usumbura* (until 1962), the town was founded in 1899 by German colonists. The university was established 1960.

Bukavu port in E Zaïre, on Lake Kivu; population (1982) 209,050. Mining is the chief industry. Called *Costermansville* until 1966, it is capital of Itivu region.

Bukhara city in Uzbekistan, USSR; population (1987) 220,000. It is capital of Bukhara region which has given its name to carpets (made in

Burkina Faso
'Land of Upright Men'

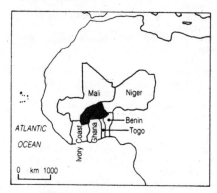

area 274,122 sq km/105,811 sq mi
capital Ouagadougou
towns Bobo-Doiulasso
physical landlocked plateau, savannah country; headwaters of the river Volta
head of state and government Blaise Compaore from 1987
political system one-party military republic
political parties Organization for Popular Democracy – Workers' Movement (ODP-MT), nationalist left-wing
exports cotton, groundnuts, livestock, hides, skins
currency CFA franc (485.00 = £1 Feb 1990)
population (1988) 8,530,000; annual growth rate 2.4%
life expectancy men 44, women 47
language French (official); about 50 native languages
religion animist 53%, Sunni Muslim 36%, Roman Catholic 11%
literacy 21% male/6% female (1985 est)
GDP $1.2 bn (1983); $180 per head of population
chronology
1958 Became a self-governing republic within the French Community.
1960 Full independence achieved, with Maurice Yameogo as the first president.
1966 Military coup led by Col Lamizana. Constitution suspended, political activities banned, and a supreme council of the armed forces established.
1969 Ban on political activities lifted.
1970 Referendum approved a new constitution leading to a return to civilian rule.
1974 After experimenting with a mixture of military and civilian rule, Lamizana reassumed full power.
1977 Ban on political activities removed. Referendum approved a new constitution based on civilian rule.
1978 Lamizana elected president.
1980 Lamizana overthrown in a bloodless coup led by Col Zerbo.
1982 Zerbo ousted in a coup by junior officers. Maj Ouédraogo became president and Thomas Sankara prime minister.
1983 Sankara seized complete power.
1984 Upper Volta renamed Burkina Faso.
1987 Sankara killed in coup led by Blaise Compaore.
1989 New government party ODP-MT formed by merger of other pro-government parties. Coup against Compaore foiled.

Burundi
Republic of
(Republika y'Uburundi)

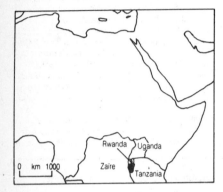

Rwanda Uganda
0 km 1000 Zaïre
Tanzania

area 27,834 sq km/10,744 sq mi
capital Bujumbura
towns Kitega
physical grassy highland
features Lake Tanganyika, Great Rift Valley;
source of the White Nile
head of state and government Pierre Buyoya
from 1987
political system one-party military republic
political parties Union for National Progress
(UPRONA), nationalist socialist
exports coffee, cotton, tea, nickel, hides,
livestock; there are also 500 million tonnes of
peat reserves in the basin of the Akanyaru river
currency Burundi franc (295.25 = £1 Feb 1990)
population (1988) 5,130,000 (of whom 15%

are the Nilotic Tutsi, still holding most of the
land and political power, and the remainder the
Bantu Hutu); annual growth rate 2.8%
life expectancy men 45, women 48
language Kirundi (a Bantu language) and
French (official); Kiswahili
religion Roman Catholic over 50%, with a
Sunni Muslim minority
literacy 43% male/26% female (1985)
GDP $1 bn (1983); $273 per head of population
chronology
1962 Separated from Ruanda-Urundi, as
Burundi, and given independence as a
monarchy under King Mwambutsa IV.
1966 King deposed by his son Charles, who
became Ntare V and was in turn deposed by
his prime minister, Capt Michel Micombero,
who declared Burundi a republic.
1972 Ntare V killed, allegedly by the Hutu ethnic
group. Massacres of 150,000 Hutus by the rival
Tutsi ethnic group, of which Micombero was a
member.
1973 Micombero made president and prime
minister.
1974 UPRONA declared the only legal political
party, with the president as its secretary
general.
1976 Army coup deposed Micombero. Col
Jean-Baptiste Bagaza appointed president by
Supreme Revolutionary Council.
1981 New constitution adopted, providing for a
national assembly.
1984 Bagaza elected president as sole
candidate.
1987 Bagaza deposed in coup in Sept. Maj
Pierre Buyoya headed new Military Council for
National Redemption.
1988 Some 24,000 majority Hutus killed by
Tutsis. First Hutu prime minister appointed.

Ashkhabad). It is an Islamic centre, with a Muslim
theological training centre. An ancient city in central Asia, it was formerly the capital of the independent emirate of Bukhara, annexed to Russia
1868. It was included in Bukhara region 1924.
Bukharest alternative form of ◊Bucharest, capital
of Romania.
Bukovina region in SE Europe, divided between
the USSR and Romania. It covers 10,500 sq km/
4,050 sq mi.
history Part of Moldavia during the Turkish regime,
it was ceded by the Ottoman Empire to Austria
1777, becoming a duchy of the Dual Monarchy
1867–1918; then it was included in Romania.
N Bukovina was ceded to the USSR 1940 and
included in Ukraine as the region of Chernovtzy;
the cession was confirmed by the peace treaty
1947, but the question of its return has been

raised by Romania. The part of Bukovina remaining in Romania became the district of Suceava.
Bulawayo industrial city and railway junction in
Zimbabwe; population (1982) 415,000. It lies
at an altitude of 1,355 m/4,450 ft on the river
Matsheumlope, a tributary of the Zambezi, and
was founded on the site of the kraal (enclosed
village), burned down 1893, of the Matabele chief
Lobenguela. It produces agricultural and electrical
equipment. The former capital of Matabeleland,
Bulawayo developed with the exploitation of
goldmines in the neighbourhood.
Bulgaria country in SE Europe, bounded to the N
by Romania, to the W by Yugoslavia, to the S by
Greece, to the SW by Turkey, and to the E by
the Black Sea.
Burgas Black Sea port and resort in Bulgaria; population (1987) 198,000.

Burgenland federal state of SE Austria, extending from the Danube south along the west border of the Hungarian plain; area 4,000 sq km/1,544 sq mi; population (1987) 267,000. It is a largely agricultural region adjoining the Neusiedler See, and produces timber, fruit, sugar, wine, lignite, antimony, and limestone. Its capital is Eisenstadt.

Burgess Shale Site the site of unique fossil-bearing rock formations in Yoho National Park, British Colombia, Canada. The shales in this corner of the Rocky Mountains contain more than 120 species of marine invertebrate fossils. Although discovered in 1909 by Charles Walcott, the Burgess Shales have only recently been used as evidence in the debate concerning the evolution of life.

Burgos city in Castilla-León, Spain, 217 km/135 mi north of Madrid; population (1986) 164,000. It produces textiles, motor parts, and chemicals. It was capital of the old kingdom of Castile and the national hero El Cid is buried in the Gothic cathedral, built 1221–1567.

Burkina Faso landlocked country in W Africa, bounded to the E by Niger, to the NW and W by Mali, to the S by Ivory Coast, Ghana, Togo and Benin.

Burma former name (to 1989) of ◊Myanmar.

Burnley town in Lancashire, England, 19 km/12 mi NE of Blackburn; population (1983) 92,000. Formerly a cotton-manufacturing town.

Bursa city in NW Turkey, with a port at Mudania; population (1985) 614,000. It was the capital of the Ottoman Empire 1326–1423.

Burton upon Trent town in Staffordshire, England, NE of Birmingham; population (1983) 57,725. Industries include brewing, tyres and engineering.

Burundi country in east central Africa, bounded to the N by Rwanda, to the W by Zaïre, to the S by Lake Tanganyika, and to the SE and E by Tanzania.

Bury town in Greater Manchester, England, on the river Irwell, 16 km/10 mi N of central Manchester; population (1986) 173,650. Industries include cotton, chemicals and engineering.

Buryat republic of the USSR, in Soviet central Asia
area 351,300 sq km/135,600 sq mi
capital Ulan-Udé
physical bounded on the south by Mongolia, on the west by Lake Baikal; mountainous and forested
products coal, timber, building materials, fish, sheep, cattle
population (1986) 1,014,000
history settled by Russians 17th century; annexed from China by treaties 1689 and 1727.

Bury St Edmunds market town in Suffolk, England, on the river Lark; population (1985) 29,500. It was named after St Edmund, and there are remains of a Benedictine abbey founded in 1020.

Byelorussia

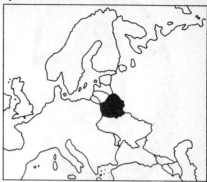

Bute island and resort in the Firth of Clyde, Scotland; area 120 sq km/46 sq mi. The chief town is Rothesay. It is separated from the mainland in the north by a winding channel, the *Kyles of Bute*. With Arran and the adjacent islands it comprised the former county of Bute, merged 1975 in the region of Strathclyde.

Butte mining town in Montana, USA, in the Rocky Mountains; population (1980) 37,200. Butte was founded in 1864 during a rush for gold, soon exhausted; copper was found some 20 years later.

Buxton spa town in Derbyshire, England; population (1981) 21,000. Known from Roman times for its hot springs. It has a restored Edwardian opera house.

Bydgoszcz industrial river port in N Poland, 105 km/65 mi NE of Poznan on the Warta; population (1985) 361,000. As *Bromberg* it was under Prussian control 1772–1919.

Byelorussia or *Belorussia* (Russian *Belaruskaya* or 'White Russia') constituent republic of western USSR since 1919
area 207,600 sq km/80,154 sq mi
capital Minsk
features more than 25% forested; rivers W Dvina, Dnieper and its tributaries, including the Pripet and Beresina; the Pripet Marshes in the east. The climate is mild and damp
products peat, agricultural machinery, fertilizers, glass, textiles, leather, salt, electrical goods, meat, dairy produce
population (1987) 10,078,000; 79% Byelorussian, 12% Russian, 4% Polish, 2% Ukrainian, 1% Jewish
history in a series of mass executions ordered by Stalin in 1937–41, more than 100,000 people were shot. The republic suffered severely under German invasion and occupation during World War II. A Byelorussia Popular Front was established in Feb 1989 and a more extreme nationalist organization, the Toloka group, in Nov 1989.

CA abbreviation for ◊*California*.

Cabinda or *Kabinda* African coastal enclave, a province of Angola; area 7,770 sq km/3,000 sq mi; population (1980) 81,300. The capital is also called Cabinda. There are oil reserves. Cabinda, which was attached to Angola in 1886, has made claims to separate independence.

Cádiz Spanish city and naval base, capital and seaport of the province of Cádiz, standing on Cádiz Bay, an inlet of the Atlantic, 103 km/64 mi south of Seville; population (1986) 154,000. After the discovery of the Americas 1492, Cádiz became one of the most important ports in Europe. Francis Drake burned a Spanish fleet here 1587 to prevent the sailing of the Armada.

Probably founded by the Phoenicians about 1100 BC, it was a centre for the tin trade with Cornwall, England. It was recaptured from the Moors by the king of Castile 1262. Modern development was restricted by its peninsular location until a bridge to the further shore of Cádiz Bay was completed 1969.

Caen capital of Calvados *département*, France, on the river Orne; population (1982) 183,526. It is a business centre, with ironworks, and electric and electronic industries. Caen building stone is famous. The town is linked by canal with the English Channel 14.5 km/9 mi to the north east. The church of St Étienne was founded by William the Conqueror, and the university by Henry VI of England in 1432. Caen was captured by the British in World War II, after five weeks' fighting, on 9 July 1944, during which the town was badly damaged.

Caerleon small town in Gwent, Wales, on the Usk, 5 km/3 mi NE of Newport; population (1981) 6,711. It stands on the site of the Roman fortress of Isca. There is a Legionary Museum and remains of an amphitheatre.

Caernarvon or *Caernarfon* administrative headquarters of Gwynedd, N Wales, situated on the SW shore of the Menai Strait; population (1981) 10,000. Formerly a Roman station, it is now a market town and port. The first Prince of Wales (later Edward II) was born in Caernarvon Castle; Edward VIII was invested here 1911 and Prince Charles 1969. The Earl of Snowdon became Constable of the castle 1963.

Caernarvonshire former county of N Wales, merged in ◊Gwynedd 1974.

Caerphilly market town in Mid Glamorgan, Wales, 11 km/7 mi N of Cardiff; population (1981) 42,736. The castle was built by Edward I. The town is noted for its mild Caerphilly cheese.

Caesarea Mazaca ancient name for the Turkish city of ◊Kayseri.

Cagliari capital and port of Sardinia, Italy, on the Gulf of Cagliari; population (1988) 222,000.

Cagnes-sur-Mer capital of the *département* of Alpes-Maritimes; to the south west of Nice, France; population (1986) 35,214. The château (13th–17th century) contains mementos of Renoir, who lived and died here 1900–19.

Cahora Bassa the largest hydro-electric scheme in Africa, created as a result of the damming of the Zambezi River to form a 230 km/144 mi-long reservoir in W Mozambique.

Cairngorms mountain group in Scotland, north part of the ◊Grampians, the highest peak being Ben Macdhui 1,309 m/4,296 ft. Aviemore (Britain's first complete holiday and sports centre) was opened in 1966, and 11 km/7 mi to the south is the Highland Wildlife Park at Kincraig.

Cairns seaport of Queensland, Australia; population (1984) 38,700. Its chief industry is sugar exporting.

Cairo (Arabic *El Qahira*) capital of Egypt, on the east bank of the Nile 13 km/8 mi above the apex of the Delta and 160 km/100 mi from the Mediterranean; the largest city in Africa and in the Middle East; population (1985) 6,205,000, Greater Cairo (1987) 13,300,000. El Fustat (Old Cairo) was founded by Arabs about AD 64, Cairo itself about 1000 by the Fatimid ruler Gowhar. The Great Pyramids and Sphinx are at nearby Giza.

It is the site of the mosque which houses the El Azhar university AD 972. The city is 32 km/20 mi north of the site of the ancient Egyptian centre of ◊Memphis. The Mosque of Amr dates from AD 643; the Citadel, built by Sultan Saladin in the 12th century, contains the impressive 19th-century Mohammed Ali mosque.

The modern government and business quarters reflect Cairo's importance as an administrative and commercial centre, and the semi-official newspaper *al Ahram* is an influential voice in the Arab world. At Helwan, 24 km/15 mi to the south, an industrial centre is developing, with iron and steel works powered by electricity from the Aswan High Dam. There are two secular universities: Cairo University (1908) and Ein Shams (1950).

Calabar port and capital of Cross River State, SE Nigeria, on the Cross River, 64 km/40 mi from the Atlantic; population (1983) 126,000. Rubber, timber, and vegetable oils are exported. It was a centre of the 18th–19th-century slave trade.

Calabria mountainous earthquake region occupying the 'toe' of Italy, comprising the provinces of Catanzaro, Cosenza, and Reggio; capital Catanzaro; area 15,100 sq km/5,829 sq mi; population (1988) 2,146,000. Reggio is the industrial centre.

Calais port in N France; population (1982) 101,000. Taken by Edward III in 1347, it was saved from destruction by the personal surrender of the Burghers of Calais commemorated in Rodin's sculpture; the French retook it 1558. Following German occupation May 1940–Oct 1944, it surrendered to the Canadians.

Calais, Pas de French name for the Strait of ◊Dover.

Calcutta largest city of India, on the Hooghly, the most westerly mouth of the Ganges, some 130 km/80 mi N of the Bay of Bengal. It is the capital of West Bengal; population (1981) 9,166,000. Chiefly a commercial and industrial centre (engineering, shipbuilding, jute, and other textiles). Calcutta was the seat of government of British India 1773–1912.

features Buildings include a magnificent Jain temple, the palaces of former Indian princes; and the Law Courts and Government House, survivals of the British Raj. Across the river is ◊Howrah, and between Calcutta and the sea there is a new bulk cargo port, Haldia, which is the focus of oil refineries, petrochemical plants, and fertilizer factories.

Educational institutions include the University of Calcutta (1857), oldest of several universities; the Visva Bharati at Santiniketan, founded by Rabindranath Tagore; the Bose Research Institute; and a fine museum.

history Calcutta was founded 1686–90 by Job Charnock, head of Hooghli factory of the East India Company. Captured by Suraj-ud-Dowlah in 1756, during the Anglo-French wars in India, in 1757 it was retaken by Robert Clive.

Caldey Island island off the coast of ◊Dyfed, Wales, near Tenby.

Caledonian Canal a waterway in north west Scotland, 98 km/61 mi long, linking the Atlantic and the North Sea. Of its 98 km/61 mi length only a 37 km/23 mi stretch is artificial, the rest being composed of lochs Lochy, Oich, and Ness. The canal was built by Thomas Telford, 1803–23.

Calgary city in Alberta, Canada, on the Bow River, in the foothills of the Rockies; at 1,048 m/3,440 ft it is one of the highest Canadian towns; population (1986) 671,000. It is the centre of a large agricultural region, and the oil and financial centre of Alberta and W Canada. Founded as Fort Calgary by the North West Mounted Police 1875, it was reached by the Canadian Pacific Railway 1885, and developed rapidly after the discovery of oil 1914.

It has oil-linked and agricultural industries, such as fertilizer factories and flour mills, and is also a tourist centre; the annual Calgary Exhibition and Stampede is held in July. The University of Calgary became independent of the University of Alberta 1966.

Cali city in SW Colombia, in the Cauca Valley 975 m/3,200 ft above sea level, founded in 1536. Cali has textile, sugar and engineering industries. Population (1985) 1,398,276.

California Pacific state of the USA; nickname the Golden State, originally because of its gold mines, but more recently because of its sunshine

area 411,100 sq km/158,685 sq mi

capital Sacramento

towns Los Angeles, San Diego, San Francisco, San José, Fresno

physical Sierra Nevada (including Yosemite and Sequoia National Parks, Lake Tahoe and Mount Whitney, 4,418 m/14,500 ft, the highest mountain in the lower 48 states); and the Coast Range; Death Valley 86 m/282 ft below sea level; Colorado and Mojave deserts (Edwards Air Force base is in the latter); Monterey Peninsula; Salton Sea; offshore in the Pacific there are huge underwater volcanoes with tops 8 km/5 mi across

features California Institute of Technology (Caltech); Lawrence Livermore Laboratory (named after Ernest Lawrence), which shares nuclear weapons research with Los Alamos; Stanford University, which has the Hoover Institute and is the powerhouse of ◊Silicon Valley; Paul Getty art museum at Malibu, built in the style of a Roman villa

products leading agricultural state with fruit (peaches, citrus, grapes in the valley of the San

California

Joaquin and Sacramento rivers), nuts, wheat, vegetables, cotton, rice, all mostly grown by irrigation, the water being carried by immense concrete-lined canals to the Central Valley and Imperial Valley; beef cattle, timber, fish, oil, natural gas, aerospace, electronics (Silicon Valley), food-processing, films and television programmes. There are also great reserves of energy (geothermal) in the hot water which lies beneath much of the state

population (1987) 27,663,000, most populous state of the USA, 66% non-Hispanic white; 20% Hispanic; 7.5% Black; 7% Asian (including many Vietnamese)

famous people Bret Harte, W R Hearst, Jack London, Marilyn Monroe, Richard Nixon, William Saroyan, John Steinbeck

history colonized by Spain 1769, it was ceded to the USA after the Mexican War 1848, and became a state 1850. Gold had been discovered in the Sierra Nevada Jan 1848, and was followed by the gold rush 1849–56.

California, Lower English name for ◊Baja California.

Callao chief commercial and fishing port of Peru, 12 km/7 mi SW of Lima; population (1988) 318,000. Founded 1537, it was destroyed by an earthquake 1746. It is Peru's main naval base, and produces fertilizers.

Calpe former name of ◊Gibraltar.

Caltanissetta town in Sicily, Italy, 96 km/60 mi south east of Palermo; population (1981) 61,146. It is the chief centre of the island's sulphur industry. It has a baroque cathedral.

Calvados *département* in Basse-Normandie region of France, which has given its name to an apple brandy distilled from cider.

Camagüey city in Cuba; population (1986) 260,800. It is capital of Camagüey province in the centre of the island. Founded about 1514, it was capital of the Spanish West Indies during the 19th century. It has a 17th-century cathedral.

Camargue the marshy area of the ◊Rhône delta, S of Arles, France: area about 780 sq km/300 sq mi. Bulls and horses are bred there, and the nature reserve, which is known for its bird life, forms the southern part.

Cambodia country in SE Asia, bordered to the N and NW by Thailand, N by Laos, E and SE by Vietnam, and SW by the South China Sea.

Camborne-Redruth town in Cornwall, 16 km/10 mi south west of Truro, England; population (1985) 18,500. It has tin mines and there is a School of Metalliferous Mining.

Cambrai chief town of Nord *département*, France; on the river Escaut (Scheldt); population (1982) 36,600. Industries include light textiles (cambric is named after the town), and confectionery. The Peace of Cambrai or Ladies' Peace (1529) was concluded on behalf of Francis I of France by his mother Louise of Savoy and on behalf of Charles

V by his aunt Margaret of Austria. Cambrai was severely damaged during World War I.

Cambridge city in England, on the river Cam (a river sometimes called by its earlier name, Granta) 80 km/50 mi north of London; population (1989) 101,000. It is the administrative headquarters of Cambridgeshire. The city is centred on Cambridge University (founded 12th century).

As early as 100 BC, a Roman settlement grew up on a slight rise in the low-lying plain, commanding a ford over the river. Apart from those of Cambridge University, notable buildings include St Benet's church, the oldest building in Cambridge; the round church of the Holy Sepulchre; and the Guildhall 1939. The Cambridge Science Park was started by Trinity College 1973. Industries include the manufacture of scientific instruments, radio, electronics, paper, flour milling, and fertilizers.

Cambridge city in Massachusetts, USA; population (1980) 95,322. Industries include paper and publishing. Harvard University 1636 (the oldest educational institution in the USA, named after John Harvard 1607–38, who bequeathed it his library and half his estate), Massachusetts Institute of Technology 1861, and the John F Kennedy School of Government and Memorial Library are here, as well as a park named after him.

Cambridgeshire county in E England

area 3,410 sq km/1,316 sq mi

towns administrative headquarters Cambridge; Ely, Huntingdon, Peterborough

features rivers Ouse, Cam, and Nene; Isle of Ely; Cambridge University; RAF Molesworth, near Huntingdon, Britain's second cruise missile base was de-activated Jan 1989

Cambridgeshire

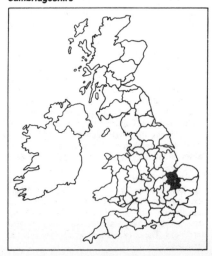

Cambodia
State of
(Former name to 1989 .
Kampuchea)

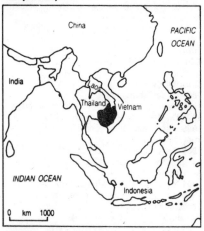

China

PACIFIC
OCEAN

India

Laos

Thailand Vietnam

INDIAN OCEAN

Indonesia

0   km   1000

area 181,035 sq km/69,880
sq mi
capital Phnom Penh
towns Battambang, and the seaport Kompong
Som
physical mostly forested; flat, with mountains in
S; Mekong River runs N–S
features ruins of ancient capital Angkor
head of state Heng Samrin from 1979
head of government Hun Sen from 1985

political system communism
political parties Kampuchean People's
Revolutionary Party (K PRP), Marxist-Leninist;
Party of Democratic Kampuchea (Khmer
Rouge), exiled ultra-nationalist communist;
Khmer People's National Liberation Front
(KPNLF), exiled anti-communist; Sihanoukists,
exiled pro-democracy forces allied to Prince
·Sihanouk
exports rubber, rice
currency Cambodian riel (371.14 = £1 Feb
1990)
population (1985 est) 7,280,000; annual
growth rate 2.6%
life expectancy men 42, women 45
language Khmer (official), French
religion Theravada Buddhist
literacy 78% male/39% female (1980 est)
GDP $100 per head of population (1984)
chronology
1863–1941 French protectorate.
1941–45 Occupied by Japan.
1946 Recaptured by France.
1953 Granted full independence.
1970 Prince Sihanouk overthrown by US-backed
Lon Nol.
1975 Lon Nol overthrown by Khmer Rouge.
1978–79 Vietnamese invasion and installation
of Heng Samrin government.
1987 Partial withdrawal of Vietnamese troops.
1988 Vietnamese troop withdrawal continued.
1989 Name of State of Cambodia re-adopted
and Buddhism declared state religion.
Vietnamese forces fully withdrawn (Sept). Civil
war intensified.

---

products mainly agricultural
population (1987) 642,000.
Cambs abbreviation for ◊*Cambridgeshire*.
Camden industrial city of New Jersey, USA, on the
Delaware River; population (1980) 84,900. The
city is linked with Philadelphia, Pennsylvania, by
the Benjamin Franklin suspension bridge (1926).
The Walt Whitman House, where the poet lived
1884–92, is a museum.
Camden inner borough of NW Greater London
features the Camden Town Group of artists;
includes the districts of
Bloomsbury with London, University, Royal
Academy of Dramatic Art (RADA), and the
British Museum; and home between World War
I and II of writers and artists including Leonard
and Virginia Woolf, and Lytton Strachey;
Fitzrovia W of Tottenham Court Road with
the Telecom Tower and Fitzroy Square as its
focus;
Hampstead, with Primrose Hill, Hampstead
Heath, and nearby Kenwood House; Keats's
home, now a museum; the churchyard where

the painter Constable is buried; and Hampstead
Garden Suburb;
Highgate, with a cemetery which has the
graves of George Eliot, Michael Faraday, and
Karl Marx;
Holborn, with the Inns of Court (Lincoln's Inn
and Gray's Inn); Hatton Garden (diamond deal-
ers), the London Silver Vaults;
Somers Town between Euston and King's Cross
railway stations
population (1981) 171,563.
Camembert village in Normandy, France, where
Camembert cheese originated.
Cameroon country in W Africa, bounded NW by
Nigeria, NE by Chad, E by the Central African
Republic, S by Congo, Gabon, and Equatorial
Guinea, and W by the Atlantic.
Campagna Romana lowland stretch of the Italian
peninsula, including and surrounding the city of
Rome. Lying between the Tyrrhenian Sea and
the Sabine Hills to the NE, and the Alban Hills
to the SE, it is drained by the lower course of
the Tiber and a number of small streams, most

Cameroon
United Republic of
(République du Cameroun)

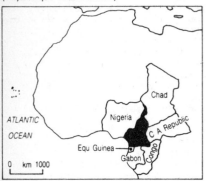

area 465,054 sq km/179,511 sq mi
capital Yaoundé
towns chief port Douala
physical desert in the far N in the Lake Chad basin, dry savanna plateau in the intermediate area, and in the S dense tropical rainforest
features Mount Cameroon 4,070 m/13,358 ft, an active volcano on the coast, W of the Adamawa Mountains
head of state and of government Paul Biya from 1982
political system authoritarian nationalism
political parties Democratic Assembly of the Cameroon People (RDPC), nationalist left-of-centre
exports cocoa, coffee, bananas, cotton, timber, rubber, groundnuts, gold, aluminium
currency CFA franc (485.00 = £1 Feb 1990)
population (1988 est) 11,082,000; annual growth rate 2.7%

life expectancy men 49, women 53
language French and English in pidgin variations (official), but there has been discontent with the emphasis on French; there are 163 indigenous peoples with many African languages
religion Roman Catholic 35%, animist 25%, Muslim 22%, Protestant 18%
literacy 68% male/45% female (1985 est)
GDP $7.3 bn (1984); $802 per head of population
chronology
1884 Under German rule.
1916 Captured by Allied forces in World War I.
1922 Divided between Britain and France.
1946 French and British Cameroons made UN trust territories.
1960 French Cameroon became the independent Republic of Cameroon. Ahmadou Ahidjo elected president.
1961 N part of British Cameroon merged with Nigeria and S part joined the Republic of Cameroon to become the Federal Republic of Cameroon.
1966 A one-party regime introduced.
1972 New constitution made Cameroon a unitary state, the United Republic of Cameroon.
1973 New national assembly elected.
1982 Ahidjo resigned and was succeeded by Paul Biya.
1983 Biya began to remove his predecessor's supporters and was accused by Ahidjo of trying to create a police state. Ahidjo went into exile in France.
1984 Biya re-elected and defeated a plot to overthrow him. Country's name changed to Republic of Cameroon.
1988 Biya re-elected.

---

of which dry up in the summer. Prosperous in Roman times, it later became virtually derelict through over-grazing, lack of water, and the arrival in the area of the malaria-carrying *Anopheles* mosquito. Extensive land reclamation and drainage in the 19th and 20th centuries restored its usefulness.

Campania agricultural region (wheat, citrus, wine, vegetables, tobacco) of S Italy, including the volcano ◊Vesuvius; capital Naples; industrial centres Benevento, Caserta, and Salerno; area 13,600 sq km/5,250 sq mi; population (1988) 5,732,000. There are ancient sites at Pompeii, Herculaneum, and Paestum.

Campeche port on the Bay of ◊Campeche, Mexico; population (1984) 120,000. It is the capital of Campeche state. Timber and fish are exported, and there is a university, established 1756.

Campeche, Bay of area of the southwest Gulf of Mexico, site of a major oil pollution disaster from the field off Yucatan peninsula in 1979.

Campinas city of São Paulo state, Brazil, situated on the central plateau; population (1980) 566,700. It is a coffee-trading centre; there are also metallurgical and food industries.

Campobasso capital of Molise region, Italy, about 190 km/120 mi southeast of Rome; population (1981) 48,300. It is noted for cutlery.

Cam Ranh port in South Vietnam. In the Vietnam War it was a US base, and is now a major staging complex for the Soviet Pacific fleet.

Canada country occupying the N part of the North American continent, bounded to the S by the USA, to the N by the Arctic Ocean, to the NW by Alaska, to the E by the Atlantic Ocean, and to the W by the Pacific Ocean.

Canada
Dominion of

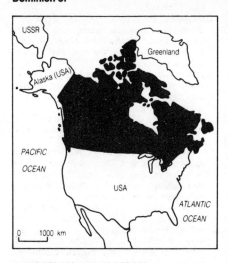

USSR

Greenland

Alaska (USA)

PACIFIC
OCEAN

USA

ATLANTIC
OCEAN

0   1000 km

area 9,971,000 sq km/3,849,803 sq
mi
capital Ottawa
towns Toronto, Montréal, Vancouver,
Edmonton, Calgary, Winnipeg, Québec,
Hamilton
physical St Lawrence Seaway, Mackenzie
river; Great Lakes; Arctic Archipelago; Rocky
Mountains; Great Plains or Prairies; Canadian
Shield
head of state Elizabeth II from 1952
represented by Governor-General Jeanne
Sauvé
head of government Brian Mulroney from 1984
political system federal constitutional
monarchy
political parties Progressive Conservative
Party, free-enterprise centrist; Liberal Party,
nationalist left-of-centre; New Democratic Party,
moderate left-of-centre
exports wheat, timber, pulp, newsprint, fish
(especially salmon), furs (ranched fox and
mink exceed the value of wild furs), oil, natural

gas, aluminium, asbestos, coal, copper, iron,
nickel, motor vehicles and parts, industrial and
agricultural machinery, fertilizers
currency Canadian dollar (2.04 = £1 Feb
1990)
population (1987) 25,600,000 (including
300,000 North American Indians, of whom
75% live on over 2,000 reserves in Ontario
and the four western provinces; some 300,000
Métis (of mixed descent) and 19,000 Inuit (or
Eskimo), of whom 75% live in the Northwest
Terri-tories). Over half Canada's population
lives in Ontario and Québec. Annual growth
rate 1.1%
life expectancy men 72, women 79
language English, French (both official) (about
70% speak English, 20% French, and the rest
are bilingual); there are also North American
Indian languages and the Inuit Inuktitut
religion Roman Catholic 40%, Protestant 35%
literacy 99%
GDP $317 bn (1984); $13,000 per head of
population
chronology
1957 Progressive Conservatives returned to
power after 22 years in opposition.
1961 New Democratic Party (NDP) formed.
1963 Liberals elected under Lester Pearson.
1968 Pearson succeeded by Pierre Trudeau.
1979 Joe Clark, leader of the Progressive
Conservatives, formed a minority government.
1980 Clark defeated on budget proposals.
Liberals under Trudeau returned with a large
majority.
1982 Canada Act removed Britain's last legal
control over Canadian affairs.
1983 Clark replaced as leader of the
Progressive Conservatives by Brian Mulroney.
1984 Trudeau retired and was succeeded
as Liberal leader and prime minister by John
Turner. Progressive Conservatives won the
federal election with a large majority, and
Mulroney became prime minister.
1988 Conservatives re-elected with reduced
majority on platform of free trade with the USA.
1989 Free trade agreement signed. Turner
resigned as Liberal Party leader, and Ed
Broadbent as New Democratic Party leader.

Canary Islands (Spanish *Canarias*) group of volcanic islands 100 km/60 mi off the NW coast
of Africa, forming the Spanish provinces of
Las Palmas and Santa Cruz de Tenerife;
area 7,300 sq km/2,818 sq mi; population (1986)
1,615,000
features the chief centres are Santa Cruz on
Tenerife (which also has the highest peak
in extra-continental Spain, Pico de Teide

3,713 m/12,186 ft), and Las Palmas on Gran
Canaria. The province of Santa Cruz comprises
Tenerife, Palma, Gomera, and Hierro, and the
province of Las Palmas comprises Gran Canaria,
Lanzarote, and Fuerteventura. There are also
six uninhabited islets. The Northern Hemisphere
Observatory (1981) is on the island of Las Palmas,
the first in the world to be remotely controlled.
Observation conditions are among the best in the

world, since there is no moisture, no artificial light pollution, and little natural airglow. The Organization of African Unity (OAU) supports an independent Guanch Republic (so called from the indigenous islanders, a branch of the N African Berbers) and revival of the Guanch language.

Canberra capital of Australia (since 1908), situated in the Australian Capital Territory enclosed within New South Wales, on a tributary of the Murrumbidgee; area (Australian Capital Territory including the port at Jervis Bay) 2,432 sq km/939 sq mi; population (1986) 285,800.

It contains the Parliament House, first used by the Commonwealth Parliament in 1927, the Australian National University (1946), the Canberra School of Music (1965), and the National War Memorial.

Candia Italian name for the Greek island of ◊Crete, also formerly the name of the largest city, ◊Iráklion, founded about AD 824.

Canea (Greek *Khania*) principal port of Crete, roughly midway along the north coast; population (1981) 47,338. It was founded in 1252 by the Venetians, and is still surrounded by a wall. Vegetable oils, soap, and leather are exported. Heavy fighting took place here during World War II, after the landing of German parachutists in May 1941. In 1971 it was replaced by Iraklion as administrative capital of Crete.

Cannes resort in Alpes-Maritimes *département*, S France; population (1982) 73,000, conurbation 296,000. An important film festival is held here annually. Formerly only a small seaport, in 1834 it attracted the patronage of Lord Brougham (who died here) and other distinguished visitors, and became a fashionable and popular holiday resort. A new town (La Bocca) grew up facing the Mediterranean.

Canada: provinces

Province (Capital)	Area sq km
Alberta (*Edmonton*)	661,187
British Columbia (*Victoria*)	948,599
Manitoba (*Winnipeg*)	650,088
New Brunswick (*Fredericton*)	73,437
Newfoundland (*St John's*)	404,517
Nova Scotia (*Halifax*)	54,558
Ontario (*Toronto*)	1,068,587
Prince Edward Island (*Charlottetown*)	5,657
Québec (*Québec*)	1,540,676
Saskatchewan (*Regina*)	651,901
Territories	
Northwest Territories (*Yellowknife*)	3,379,689
Yukon Territory (*Whitehorse*)	536,327
	9,975,223

Cantabria autonomous region of N Spain; area 5,300 sq km/2,046 sq mi; population (1986) 525,000; capital Santander.

Cantabrian Mountains (Spanish *Cordillera Cantabrica*) mountains running along the north coast of Spain, reaching 2,648 m/8,688 ft in the Picos de Europa massif. The mountains have coal and iron deposits.

Cantal volcanic mountain range in central France, which gives its name to Cantal *département*. The highest point is the Plomb du Cantal, 1,858 m/6,096 ft.

Canterbury city in Kent, England, on the Stour, 100 km/62 m SE of London; population (1984) 39,000.

The Roman Durovernum, Canterbury was the Saxon capital of Kent. The modern name derives from *Cantwarabyrig* (Old English 'fortress of the men of Kent'). In 597 King Ethelbert welcomed Augustine's mission to England here, and the city has since been the metropolis of the Anglican Communion and seat of the archbishop of Canterbury. The foundations of the present cathedral were laid by Lanfranc, archbishop 1070–89, but subsequent additions range from Norman to Perpendicular. In the Middle Ages it was a centre of pilgrimage to the tomb of St Thomas à Becket, murdered in the cathedral 1170, but the shrine was destroyed by Henry VIII. The Black Prince and Henry IV are buried there. The city has links with the writers Geoffrey Chaucer, Christopher Marlowe, and Somerset Maugham, who was educated at the King's School (refounded by Henry VIII 1541) on the site of the Benedictine Abbey of St Augustine, of which only fragments remain. The first college of the University of Kent, established 1965, was named after T S Eliot.

Canterbury Plains area of rich grassland between the mountains and the sea on the east coast of South Island, New Zealand, source of Canterbury lamb. Area 10,000 sq km/4,000 sq mi.

canton in France, an administrative district, a subdivision of the *arrondissement*; in Switzerland, one of the 23 subdivisions forming the Confederation.

Canton former name of Kwangchow or ◊Guangzhou in China.

Canton and Enderbury two atolls in the Phoenix group which forms part of the Republic of Kiribati. They were a UK–USA condominium 1939–80, and there are US aviation, radar and tracking stations.

Cape Breton island forming the northern part of the province of Nova Scotia, Canada; area 10,282 sq km/3,970 sq mi; population (1988) 170,000. Bisected by a waterway, it has road and rail links with the mainland across the Strait of Canso. It has coal resources and steelworks, and there has been substantial development in the strait area, with docks, oil refineries, and newsprint production from local timber. In the north the surface rises to 550 m/1,800 ft at North Cape, and the coast has many fine harbours. There are cod fisheries. The climate is mild and very moist. The chief towns are Sydney and Glace Bay.

history The first British colony was established in 1629, but was driven out by the French. In 1763 Cape Breton was ceded to Britain and attached to Nova Scotia 1763–84 and from 1820.

Cape Byron the eastern extremity of Australia, in New South Wales, just south of the border with Queensland.

Cape Coast port of Ghana, West Africa, 130 km/80 mi west of Accra; population (1982) 73,000. It was superseded as the main port since 1962 by Tema. The town, first established by the Portuguese in the 16th century, is built on a natural breakwater, adjoining the castle.

Cape Cod hook-shaped peninsula in SE Massachusetts, USA; 100 km/60 mi long and 1.6–32 km/1–20 mi wide; population (1980) 150,000. Its beaches and woods make it a popular tourist area. It is separated from the rest of the state by the Cape Cod Canal. The islands of Martha's Vineyard and Nantucket are just south of the cape.

Basque and Norse fishermen are believed to have visited Cape Cod many years before the English Pilgrims landed at Provincetown 1620. It was named after the cod which were caught in the dangerous shoals of the cape. The Kennedy family home is at the resort of Hyannis Port.

Cape Horn most southerly point of South America, in the Chilean part of the archipelago of ◊Tierra del Fuego; notorious for gales and heavy seas. It was named in 1616 by its Dutch discoverer Willem Schouten (1580–1625) after his birthplace (Hoorn).

Cape of Good Hope South African headland forming a peninsula between Table Bay and False Bay, Cape Town. The first European to sail round it was Bartholomew Diaz in 1488. Formerly named Cape of Storms, it was given its present name by King John II of Portugal.

Cape Province (Afrikaans *Kaapprovinsie*) largest province of the Republic of South Africa, named after the Cape of Good Hope.

area 641,379 sq km/247,638 sq mi, excluding Walvis Bay

capital Cape Town

towns Port Elizabeth, East London, Kimberley, Grahamstown, Stellenbosch

physical Orange River, Drakensberg, Table Mountain (highest point Maclear's Beacon 1087 m/3567 ft); Great Karoo Plateau, Walvis Bay

products fruit, vegetables, wine; meat, ostrich feathers; diamonds, copper, asbestos, manganese

population (1985) 5,041,000, officially including 2,226,200 Coloured; 1,569,000 Black; 1,264,000 White; 32,120 Asian

history the Dutch occupied the Cape in 1652, but it was taken by the British in 1795 after the French Revolutionary armies had occupied the Netherlands, and was sold to Britain for £6 million in 1814. The Cape achieved self-government in 1872. It was an original province of the Union in 1910.

The Orange River was proclaimed the northern boundary in 1825. Griqualand West (1880) and the southern part of Bechuanaland (1895) were later incorporated; and Walvis Bay, although administered with SW Africa, is legally an integral part of Cape Province.

Cape Town (Afrikaans *Kaapstad*) port and oldest town in South Africa, situated in the SW on Table Bay; population (1985) 776,617. Industries include horticulture and trade in wool, wine, fruit, grain, and oil. It is the legislative capital of the Republic of South Africa, and capital of Cape Province, and was founded in 1652.

It includes the Houses of Parliament, City Hall, Cape Town Castle (1666), and Groote Schuur, 'great barn', the estate of Cecil Rhodes (he designated the house as the home of the premier, and a university and the National Botanical Gardens occupy part of the grounds). The naval base of *Simonstown* is to the SE; in 1975 Britain's use of its facilities was ended by the Labour government in disapproval of South Africa's racial policies.

Cape Verde country comprising a group of islands in the Atlantic, off the coast of Senegal.

Cape Wrath headland at the NW extremity of Scotland.

Cape York peninsula, the most northerly point (10° 41′S) of the Australian mainland, so named by Captain James Cook in 1770. The peninsula is about 800 km/500 mi long and 640 km/400 mi wide at its junction with the mainland. Its barrenness deterred early Dutch explorers, although the south is being developed for cattle (Brahmin type) and in the north there are large bauxite deposits.

Caporetto former name of ◊Kobarid, Yugoslavia.

Capri Italian island at the south entrance of the Bay of Naples; 32 km/20 mi S of Naples; area 13 sq km/5 sq mi. It has two towns, Capri and Anacapri, and is famous for its flowers, beautiful scenery, and ideal climate.

Caprivi Strip NE access strip for Namibia to the Zambezi River.

Capua Italian town in Caserta province on the Volturno, in a fertile plain N of Naples; population (1981) 18,000. There was heavy fighting here in 1943 during World War II, and the Romanesque cathedral was almost destroyed.

Caracas chief city and capital of Venezuela; situated on the Andean slopes, 13 km/8 mi south of its

Cape Verde
Republic of
(República de Cabo Verde)

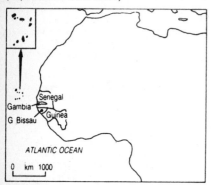

ATLANTIC OCEAN

0   km   1000

area 4,033 sq km/1,557 sq mi
capital Praia
physical archipelago of ten islands
565 km/350 mi W of Senegal
features strategically important because it
dominates the western shipping lanes
head of state and government Aristides

Pereira from 1975
political system one-party socialist state
political parties African Party for the Independence of Cape Verde (PAICV), African-nationalist
exports bananas, coffee
currency Cape Verde escudo (123.10 = £1
Feb 1990)
population (1988) 359,000 (including 100,000
Angolan refugees); annual growth rate 1.9%
life expectancy men 57, women 61
language Creole dialect of Portuguese
religion Roman Catholic 80%
literacy 61% male/39% female (1985)
GDP $110 million (1983); $300 per head of
population
chronology
1974 Moved towards independence through
a transitional Portuguese-Cape Verde
government.
1975 Full independence achieved. National
people's assembly elected. Aristides Pereira
became the first president.
1980 Constitution adopted providing for
eventual union with Guinea-Bissau.
1981 Union with Guinea-Bissau abandoned and
the constitution amended; became one-party
state.

port La Guaira on the Caribbean coast; population
of metropolitan area (1981) 1,817,000. Founded
1567, it is now a major industrial and commercial
centre, notably for oil companies.

It is the birthplace of Simón Bolívar and has
many fine buildings, including Venezuela University, which forms a city within a city, and
has gates guarded by university police. As
in most Latin American countries, the university is independent and self-governing, and no
state police or soldiers are allowed to enter.
The city has suffered several severe earthquakes.

Carcassonne city in SW France, capital of Aude
département, on the river Aude, which divides
it into the ancient and modern town; population (1982) 42,450. Its medieval fortifications
(restored) are the finest in France.

Cardiff capital of Wales (from 1955), and administrative headquarters of South and Mid Glamorgan, at
the mouth of the Taff, Rhymney, and Ely rivers;
population (1983) 279,800. Besides steelworks,
there are automotive component, flour milling,
paper, cigar, and other industries.

The city dates from Roman times, the later
town being built around a Norman castle. The castle was the residence of the earls and marquesses
of Bute from the 18th century and was given to the
city 1947 by the fifth marquess. Coal was exported
until the 1920s. As coal declined, iron and steel
exports continued to grow, and an import trade in

timber, grain and flour, tobacco, meat, and citrus
fruit developed.

The docks on the Bristol Channel were opened
1839 and greatly extended by the second Marquess of Bute (1793–1848). The derelict docks
have now been redeveloped for industry.

In Cathays Park is a group of public buildings
including the Law Courts, City Hall, the National
Museum of Wales, the Welsh Office (established
1964), a major part of the University of Wales
(Institute of Science and Technology, National
School of Medicine, and University College of
South Wales), and the Temple of Peace and
Health. Llandaff, on the right bank of the Taff,
seat of an archbishop from the 6th century, was
included in Cardiff 1922; its cathedral, virtually
rebuilt in the 19th century and restored 1948–57
after air raid damage in World War II, has Jacob
Epstein's sculpture *Christ in Majesty*. At St
Fagan's is the Welsh National Folk Museum,
containing small rebuilt historical buildings from
rural Wales in which crafts are demonstrated.
The city is the headquarters of the Welsh National
Opera.

Cardiganshire former county of Wales, which was
in 1974 merged, together with Pembroke and
Carmarthen, into Dyfed.

Caribbean Sea part of the Atlantic Ocean between
the N coasts of South and Central America and
the West Indies, about 2,740 km/1,700 mi long
and between 650 km/400 mi and 1,500 km/900 mi

wide. It is here that the Gulf Stream turns towards Europe.

Carinthia (German *Kärnten*) alpine federal province of SE Austria, bordering Italy and Yugoslavia in the south; capital Klagenfurt; area 9,500 sq km/3,667 sq mi; population (1987) 542,000. It was an independent duchy from 976, and a possession of the Habsburg dynasty 1276–1918.

Carisbrooke village SW of Newport, Isle of Wight. Charles I was imprisoned in its castle 1647–48.

Carlisle city in Cumbria, England; situated on the river Eden at the W end of Hadrian's Wall; population (1981) 71,000. It is the administrative headquarters of Cumbria, England, the county town of the former county of Cumberland, situated on the Eden at the W end of Hadrian's Wall. It is an important railway centre; textiles, engineering, and biscuit making are the chief industries. There is a Norman cathedral and a castle. The bishopric dates from 1133. Population (1981) 70,706.

Carlow county in the Republic of Ireland, in the province of Leinster; county town Carlow; area 900 sq km/347 sq mi; population (1986) 41,000. Mostly flat except for mountains in the south, the land is fertile, and dairy farming is important.

Carlsbad German name of ◊Karlovy Vary, a spa town in W Bohemia, Czechoslovakia.

Carmarthenshire former county of S Wales, and formerly also the largest Welsh county. It bordered on the Bristol Channel, and was merged in 1974, together with Cardigan and Pembroke, into Dyfed. The county town was Carmarthen, population (1981) 12,302.

Carnac village in Brittany, France; population (1982) 4,000. It has megalithic remains of tombs and stone alignments of the period 2000–1500 BC. The largest of the latter has 1,000 stones up to 4 m/13 ft high arranged in 11 rows, with a circle at the western end.

Carnarvon alternate spelling of ◊Caernarvon.

Carnarvon Range section of the Great Divide, Queensland, Australia, about 900 m/1,000 ft high. There are many Aboriginal paintings in the sandstone caves along its 160 km/100 mi length.

Carnatic region of SE India, in Madras state. It is situated between the Eastern Ghats and the Coromandel Coast, and was formerly an important trading centre.

Carniola a former crownland and duchy of Austria, most of which was included in Slovenia, part of the kingdom of the Serbs, Croats, and Slovenes (later Yugoslavia) in 1919. The westerly districts of Idrija and Postojna, then allocated to Italy, were transferred to Yugoslavia in 1947.

Carolina two separate states of the USA; see ◊North Carolina and ◊South Carolina.

Carolines scattered archipelago in Micronesia, Pacific Ocean, consisting of over 500 coral islets; area 1,200 sq km/463 sq mi. The chief islands are Ponape, Kusai, and Truk in the eastern group, and Yap and Belau in the western.

They are well watered and productive. Occupied by Germany 1899, Japan 1914, and mandated by the League of Nations to that country 1919, they were fortified, contrary to the terms of the mandate. Under Allied air attack in World War II, they were not conquered. In 1947 they became part of the US Trust Territory of the ◊Pacific Islands.

Carpathian Mountains Central European mountain system, forming a semicircle through Czechoslovakia-Poland-USSR-Romania, 1,450 km/900 mi long. The central *Tatra mountains* on the Czechoslovak-Polish frontier include the highest peak, Gerlachovka, 2,663 m/8,737 ft.

Carpentaria, *Gulf of*, a shallow gulf opening out of the Arafura Sea on the N of Australia. It was discovered by Tasman in 1606 and named in 1623 in honour of Pieter Carpentier, Governor-General of the Dutch East Indies.

Carrara town in Tuscany, Italy, 60 km/37 mi NW of Livorno; population (1981) 66,000. It is known for its quarries of fine white marble, which were worked by the Romans, abandoned in the 5th century AD, and came into use again with the revival of sculpture and architecture in the 12th century.

Carrickfergus seaport on Belfast Lough, County Antrim, N Ireland; population (1985) 30,000.

Carse of Gowrie fertile lowland plain bordering the Firth of Tay. It is 24 km/15 mi long, and is one of Scotland's most productive agricultural areas. William III landed here before the Battle of the Boyne, 1690.

Carson City capital of Nevada, USA; population (1980) 30,810. Smallest of the state capitals, named after Kit Carson.

Cartagena city in the province of Murcia, Spain; on the Mediterranean; population (1986) 169,000. It is a seaport and naval base. It was founded as *Carthago Nova* about 225 BC by the Carthaginian Hasdrubal, son-in-law of Hamilcar Barca. It continued to flourish under the Romans and the Moors, and was conquered by the Spanish 1269. It has a 13th-century cathedral and Roman remains.

Cartagena or *Cartagena de los Indes* port, industrial centre, and capital of the department of Bolívar, NW Colombia; population (1985) 531,000. Plastics and chemicals are produced here. A pipeline brings petroleum to the city from the De Manes oilfields. The city was founded 1533, and taken by Drake 1586.

Casablanca (Arabic *Dar el-Beida*) port, commercial and industrial centre on the Atlantic coast of Morocco; population (1981) 2,409,000. It trades in fish, phosphates, and manganese. The Great Hassan II Mosque, completed 1989, is the world's largest; it is built on a platform

(40,000 sq m/430,000 sq ft) jutting out over the Atlantic, with walls 60 m/200 ft high, topped by a hydraulic sliding roof, and a minaret 175 m/574 ft high.

Casablanca was occupied by the French from 1907 until Morocco became independent 1956.

Cascade Range volcanic mountains in western USA and Canada, extending 1,120 km/700 mi from N California through Oregon and Washington to the Fraser River. They include Mount St Helens and Mount Rainier (the highest peak, 4,392 m/14,408 ft), which is noted for its glaciers. The mountains are the most active in the USA, excluding Alaska and Hawaii.

Cascais fishing port and resort town on the Costa do Sol, 25 km/16 mi W of Lisbon, Portugal.

Caserta town in S Italy 33 km/21 mi NE of Naples; population (1981) 66,318. It trades in chemicals, olive oil, wine and grain. The base for Garibaldi's campaigns in the 19th century, it was the Allied headquarters in Italy 1943–45, and the German forces surrendered to Field Marshal Alexander here in 1945.

Caspian Sea world's largest inland sea, divided between Iran and the USSR. Area about 400,000 sq km/155,000 sq mi, with a maximum depth of 1,000 m/3,250 ft. The chief ports are Astrakhan and Baku. It is now approximately 28 m/90 ft below sea level due to drainage in the north, and the damming of the Volga and Ural rivers for hydroelectric power.

An underwater ridge divides it into two halves, of which the shallow north is almost salt-free. There are no tides. The damming has led to shrinkage over the last 50 years, and the growth of industry along its shores has caused pollution and damaged the Russian and Iranian caviar industries.

Cassel alternative spelling of ⟨Kassel, an industrial town in West Germany.

Cassino town in S Italy, 80 km/50 mi NW of Naples; at the foot of Monte Cassino; population (1981) 31,139. It was the scene of heavy fighting during World War II in 1944, when most of the town was destroyed. It was rebuilt 1.5 km/1 mi to the north. The famous abbey on the summit of Monte Cassino, founded by St Benedict in 529, was rebuilt in 1956.

Castel Gandolfo village in Italy 24 km/15 mi SE of Rome. The castle, built by Pope Urban VIII in the 17th century, is still used by the pope as a summer residence.

Castellón de la Plana port in Spain, facing the Mediterranean to the east; population (1981) 124,500. It is the capital of Castellón province, and is the centre of an orange-growing district.

Castilla-La Mancha autonomous region of central Spain; area 79,200 sq km/30,571 sq mi; population (1986) 1,665,000. It includes the provinces of Albacete, Ciudad Real, Cuenca, Guadalajara,

and Toledo. Irrigated land produces grain and chickpeas, and merino sheep graze here.

Castilla-León autonomous region of central Spain; area 94,100 sq km/36,323 sq mi; population (1986) 2,600,000. It includes the provinces of Ávila, Burgos, León, Palencia, Salamanca, Segovia, Soria, Valladolid, and Zamora. Irrigated land produces wheat and rye. Cattle, sheep, and fighting bulls are bred in the uplands.

Castleford town in West Yorkshire, England; population (1981) 36,000.

Castries port and capital of St Lucia, on the NW coast of the island; population (1988) 53,000. It produces textiles, chemicals, wood products, tobacco, and rubber products. The town was rebuilt after destruction by fire 1948.

Catalonia (Spanish *Cataluña*) autonomous region of NE Spain; area 31,900 sq km/12,313 sq mi; population (1986) 5,977,000. It includes Barcelona (the capital), Gerona, Lérida, and Tarragona. Industries include wool and cotton textiles, and hydroelectric power is produced.

The north is mountainous, and the Ebro basin breaks through the Castellón mountains in the south. The soil is fertile, but the climate in the interior is arid. Catalonia leads Spain in industrial development. Tourist resorts have developed along the Costa Brava.

history The region has a long tradition of independence, enjoying autonomy 1932–39, but lost its privileges for supporting the Republican cause in the Spanish Civil War. Autonomy and official use of the Catalan language were restored 1980.

French Catalonia is the adjacent *département* of Pyrénées-Orientales.

Catania industrial port in Sicily; population (1988) 372,000. It exports local sulphur.

Catskills US mountain range, mainly in SE New York state; the highest point is Slide Mt, 1,281 m/4,204 ft.

Cayman Islands

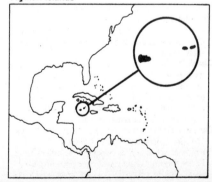

Central African Republic
(République centrafricaine)

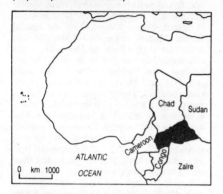

area 622,436 sq km/240,260 sq mi
capital Bangui
physical most of the country is on a plateau, with rivers flowing N and S. The N is dry and there is rainforest in the SW
head of state and government André Kolingba from 1981
political system one-party military republic
political parties Central African Democratic Assembly (RDC), nationalist
exports diamonds, uranium, coffee, cotton, timber
currency CFA franc (485.00 = £1 Feb 1990)
population (1988) 2,860,000; annual growth rate 2.3%

life expectancy men 41, women 45
language Sangho, French (both official)
religion animist over 50%; Christian 35%, both Catholic and Protestant; Muslim 10%
literacy 53% male/29% female (1985 est)
GNP $690 million (1983); $310 per head of population
chronology
1960 Central African Republic achieved independence from France with David Dacko elected president.
1962 The republic made a one-party state.
1965 Dacko ousted in a military coup led by Col Bokassa.
1966 Constitution rescinded and national assembly dissolved.
1972 Bokassa declared himself president for life.
1976 Bokassa made himself emperor of the Central African Empire.
1979 Bokassa deposed by Dacko following violent repressive measures by the self-styled emperor, who went into exile.
1981 Dacko deposed in a bloodless coup, led by Gen André Kolingba, and a military government established.
1983 Clandestine opposition movement formed.
1984 Amnesty for all political party leaders announced.
1985 New constitution introduced, with some civilians in the government.
1986 Formal trial of Bokassa started. Kolingba re-elected.
1988 Bokassa found guilty and received death sentence, later commuted to life imprisonment.

Catterick village near Richmond in N Yorkshire, England, where there is an important military camp.

Caucasus series of mountain ranges between the Caspian and Black Seas, USSR; 1200 km/750 mi long. The highest is Elbruz, 5633 m/18,480 ft. Arabian thoroughbreds are raised at Tersk farm in the northern foothills.

Cauvery or *Kaveri* river of S India, rising in the W Ghats and flowing 765 km/475 mi SE to meet the Bay of Bengal in a wide delta. A major source of hydroelectric power since 1902 when India's first hydropower plant was built on the river.

Cavan agricultural inland county of the Republic of Ireland, in the province of Ulster; area 1,890 sq km/730 sq mi; population (1986) 54,000.

The river Erne divides it into a narrow, mostly low-lying peninsula, 30 km/20 mi long, between Leitrim and Fermanagh, and an eastern section of wild and bare hill country. The soil is generally poor, and the climate moist and cold. The chief towns are Cavan, the capital, population about 3,000; Kilmore, seat of Roman Catholic and Protestant bishoprics; and Virginia.

Cavite town and port of the Philippine Republic; 13 km/8 mi S of Manila; population (1980) 88,000. It is the capital of Cavite province, Luzon. It was in Japanese hands Dec 1941–Feb 1945. After the Philippines achieved independence in 1946, the US Seventh Fleet continued to use the naval base.

Cawnpore former spelling of ◊Kanpur, Indian city.

Cayenne capital and chief port of French Guiana, on Cayenne island at the mouth of the river Cayenne; population (1982) 38,135. It was founded in 1634, and used as a penal settlement from 1854 to 1946.

Cayman Islands British island group in the West Indies
area 260 sq km/100 sq mi
features comprises three low-lying islands, Grand Cayman, Cayman Brac, and Little Cayman
government governor, executive council, and legislative assembly

Central Region

exports seawhip coral, a source of prostaglandins; shrimps; honey; jewellery
currency CI dollar
population (1988) 22,000
language English
GNP $10,900 per head of population
history settled by military deserters in the 17th century, the islands became a pirate lair in the 18th century. Administered with Jamaica until 1962, when they became a separate colony, they are now a tourist resort, international financial centre, and tax haven.

Cebu chief city and port of the island of Cebu in the Philippines; population (1980) 490,000; area 5,086 sq km/1,964 sq mi. The oldest city of the Philippines, founded as San Miguel in 1565, it became the capital of the Spanish Philippines.

Cedar Rapids town in E Iowa, USA; population (1980) 110,243. Communications equipment is manufactured here.

Celebes English name for ◊Sulawesi, an island of Indonesia, one of the Great Sunda Islands.

Celtic Sea name commonly used by workers in the oil industry for the sea area between Wales, Ireland, and SW England, to avoid nationalist significance. It is separated from the Irish Sea by St George's Channel.

Central African Republic landlocked country in Central Africa, bordered NE and E by the Sudan, S by Zaïre and the Congo, W by Cameroon, and NW by Chad.

Central America the part of the Americas that links Mexico with the isthmus of Panama, comprising Belize, Costa Rica, El Salvador, Guatemala, Honduras, Nicaragua, and Panama.

It is also an isthmus, crossed by mountains that form part of the *Cordilleras*. Much of Central America formed part of the Maya civilization. Spanish settlers married indigenous women, and the area remained out of the mainstream of Spanish Empire history. When the Spanish Empire collapsed in the early 1800s, the area formed the Central American Federation, with a constitution based on that of the USA. Demand for cash crops (bananas, coffee, cotton), especially from the USA, created a strong landowning class controlling a serflike peasantry by military means. There has been US military intervention in the area, for example in Nicaragua, where the dynasty of Gen Anastasio Somoza was founded. US president Carter reversed support for such regimes, but in the 1980s, the Reagan and Bush administrations again favoured military and financial aid to right-wing political groups, including the Contras in Nicaragua.

Central Mount Stuart flat-topped mountain 844 m/2,770 ft high, at approximately the central point of Australia. It was originally named in 1860 by explorer J McDouall Stuart after another explorer, Charles Sturt – Central Mount Sturt—but later became known by his own name.

Central Provinces and Berar former British province of India, now part of ◊Madhya Pradesh.

Central Region region of Scotland, formed 1975 from the counties of Stirling, S Perth, and W Lothian
area 2,600 sq km/1,004 sq mi
towns administrative headquarters Stirling; Falkirk, Alloa, Grangemouth
features Stirling Castle; field of Bannockburn; Loch Lomond; the Trossachs
products agriculture; industries including brewing and distilling, engineering, electronics
population (1987) 272,000
famous people Rob Roy Macgregor.

Centre region of N central France; area 39,200 sq km/15,131 sq mi; population (1986) 2,324,000. It includes the *départements* of Cher, Eure-et-Loire, Indre, Indre-et-Loire, Loire-et-Cher, and Loiret. Its capital is Orléans.

Centre, the region of central Australia, including the tourist area between the Musgrave and MacDonnell ranges which contains Ayers Rock and Lake Amadeus.

Cephalonia former name of ◊Kefallinia, largest of the Ionian islands, off the W coast of Greece.

Ceram or *Seram* Indonesian island, in the Moluccas; area 17,142 sq km/6,621 sq mi. Chief town is Ambon.

Cernăuți Romanian form of ◊Chernovtsy.

České Budějovice (German *Budweis*) town in Czechoslovakia, on the river Vltava; population (1984) 92,800. It is a commercial and industrial centre for S Bohemia, producing beer, timber, and metal products.

Cetinje town in Montenegro, Yugoslavia, 19 km/
12 mi SE of Kotor; population (1981) 20,213.
Founded 1484 by Ivan the Black, it was capital
of Montenegro until 1918. It has a palace built by
Nicholas, the last king of Montenegro.

Ceuta Spanish seaport and military base in
Morocco, Spanish N Africa; 27 km/17 mi south
of Gibraltar and overlooking the Mediterranean approaches to the Straits of Gibraltar;
area 18 sq km/7 sq mi; population (1986)
71,000. It trades in tobacco and petrol
products.

Cevennes collective name given to a series of
mountain ranges on the southern, southeastern
and eastern borders of the Central Plateau of
France. The highest peak is Mt Mézenc 1,754 m/
5,755 ft.

Ceylon former name of ◊Sri Lanka.

Chablis town in the Yonne *département* of central
France, famous for white burgundy wine of the
same name.

Chaco province of Argentina; area 99,633 sq km/
38,458 sq mi; population (1980) 701,400. Its capital is Resistencia, in the SE. The chief crop is
cotton, and there is forestry.

It includes many lakes, swamps, and forests,
producing timber and quebracho (a type of wood
used in tanning). Until 1951, it was a territory,
part of Gran Chaco, a great zone, mostly level,
stretching into Paraguay and Bolivia. The north
of Gran Chaco was the scene of the Bolivia-
Paraguay border dispute 1932–35, settled by
arbitration 1938.

Chad landlocked country in central N Africa,
bounded to the north by Libya, to the east
by Sudan, to the south by the Central African

Chad

Republic of *(République du
Tchad)*

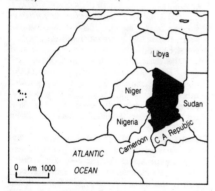

area 1,284,000 sq km/495,624 sq mi
capital N'djamena
physical savanna and part of Sahara Desert in
the N; rivers in the S flow N to Lake Chad in the
marshy E
head of state and government Hissène Habré
from 1982
political system authoritarian nationalism
political parties National Union for
Independence (UNIR), nationalist
exports cotton, meat, livestock, hides, skins,
bauxite, uranium, gold, oil
currency CFA franc (485.00 = £1 Feb 1990)
population (1987) 5,241,000; annual growth
rate 2.3%
life expectancy men 41, women 45
language French (official), Arabic
religion Muslim (north); Christian, animist (south)
literacy 40% male/11% female (1985 est)

GDP $360 million (1984); $88 per head of
population
chronology
1960 Independence from France achieved,
with François Tombalbaye as president.
1963 Violent opposition in the Muslim north,
led by the Chadian National Liberation Front
(Frolinat), backed by Libya.
1968 Revolt quelled with French help.
1975 Tombalbaye killed in military coup led by
Felix Malloum. Frolinat continued its resistance.
1978 Malloum brought former Frolinat leader
Hissène Habré into his government but they
were unable to work together.
1979 Malloum forced to leave the country.
An interim government was set up under Gen
Goukouni. Habré continued his opposition with
his Army of the North (FAN).
1981 Habré now in control of half the country,
forcing Goukouni to flee to Cameroon and then
Algeria, where, with Libyan support, he set up a
government in exile.
1983 Habré's regime recognized by the
Organization for African Unity (OAU) but in the
north Goukouni's supporters, with Libyan help,
fought on. A ceasefire was agreed, dividing the
country into two halves either side of latitude
16° N.
1984 Libya and France agreed a withdrawal of
forces.
1985 Fighting between Libyan-backed and
French-backed forces intensified.
1987 Chad, France, and Libya agree on
ceasefire proposed by OAU.
1988 Full diplomatic relations with Libya
restored.
1989 Libyan troop movements reported on
border. Habré met Col Khaddafi. In Dec
Habré re-elected and a new constitution
announced.

Republic, and to the west by Cameroon, Nigeria, and Niger.

Chad, Lake lake on the NE boundary of Nigeria. It once varied in extent between rainy and dry seasons from 50,000 sq km/20,000 sq mi to 20,000 sq km/7,000 sq mi, but a series of droughts 1979–89 reduced its area by 80%. The Lake Chad basin is being jointly developed for oil and natron by Cameroon, Chad, Niger, and Nigeria. The lake was first seen by European explorers 1823.

Chagos Archipelago island group in the Indian Ocean; area 60 sq km/23 sq mi. Formerly a dependency of Mauritius, it now forms the ◊British Indian Ocean Territory. The chief island is Diego Garcia, now a UK/USA strategic base.

Chalatenango a department on the N frontier of El Salvador; area 2507 sq km/968 sq mi; population (1981) 235,700; capital Chalatenango. It is largely controlled by FMLN guerrilla insurgents.

Châlons-sur-Marne capital of the *département* of Marne, NE France; population (1982) 54,400. It is a market town and trades mainly in champagne. Tradition has it that Attila was defeated in his attempt to invade France, at the *Battle of Châlons* (451), by the Roman general Aëtius and the Visigoth Theodoric.

Chalon-sur-Saône town in the *département* of Saône-et-Loire, France, on the river Saône and the Canal du Centre; population (1982) 58,000. It has mechanical and electrical engineering, and chemical industries.

Chambéry former capital of Savoy, now capital of Savoie *département*, France; population (1982) 96,000. It is the seat of an archbishopric, and has some industry; it is also a holiday and health resort. The town gives its name to a French vermouth.

Chamonix holiday resort at the foot of Mont Blanc, in the French Alps; population (1982) 9,255. Site of the first Winter Olympics in 1924.

Champagne-Ardenne region of NE France; area 25,600 sq km/9,882 sq mi; population (1986) 1,353,000. Its capital is Reims, and it comprises the *département*s of Ardennes, Aube, Marne, and Haute-Marne. It has sheep and dairy farming, and vineyards.

It forms the plains east of the Paris basin. Its chief towns are Epernay, Troyes, and Chaumont. The capital of the ancient province of Champagne was Troyes.

Champlain lake situated in northeast USA, named after Samuel de Champlain, who saw it in 1609. It is linked to the St Lawrence and Hudson rivers.

Chan Chan capital of the pre-Inca ◊Chimu kingdom in Peru.

Chandernagore ('city of sandalwood') city on the river Hooghly, India, in the state of West Bengal; population (1981) 102,000. Formerly a French settlement, it was ceded to India by treaty in 1952.

Chandigarh city of N India, in the foothills of the Himalayas; population (1981) 421,000. It is also a Union Territory; area 114 sq km/44 sq mi; population (1981) 450,000.

Planned by the architect Le Corbusier, it was inaugurated 1953 to replace Lahore (capital of British Punjab), which went to Pakistan under partition 1947. Since 1966, when it became a Union Territory, it has been the capital city of both Haryana and Punjab, until a new capital is built for the former.

Changchiakow former name for ◊Zhangjiakou, trading centre in Hesei province, China.

Changchun industrial city and capital of Jilin province, China; population (1986) 1,860,000. Machinery and motor vehicles are manufactured. It is also the centre of an agricultural district. As Hsingking ('new capital'), it was the capital of Manchukuo 1932–45 during Japanese occupation.

Chang Jiang longest river (formerly Yangtze Kiang) of China, flowing about 6,300 km/3,900 mi from Tibet to the Yellow Sea. It is a major commercial waterway.

It has 204 km/127 mi of gorges, below which is Gezhou Ba, the first dam to harness the river. The entire length of the river was first navigated 1986.

Changsha river port, on the Chang Jiang, capital of Hunan province, China; population (1986) 1,160,000. It trades in rice, tea, timber, and nonferrous metals; works antimony, lead, and silver; and produces chemicals, electronics, porcelain, and embroideries. Mao Zedong was a student here 1912–18.

Channel Country area of SW Queensland, Australia, in which channels such as Cooper's Creek (where explorers Burke and Wills died in 1861) are cut by intermittent rivers. Summer rains supply rich grass for cattle, and there are the 'beef roads', down which herds are taken in linked trucks for slaughter.

Channel Islands a group of islands in the English Channel, off the NW coast of France; they are a possession of the British crown
area 194 sq km/75 sq mi
islands Jersey, Guernsey, Alderney, Great and Little Sark, with the lesser Herm, Brechou, Jethou, and Lihou
features the climate is very mild, and the soil productive. Financially the islands are a 'tax haven'
exports flowers, early potatoes, tomatoes, butterflies
government the main islands have their own parliaments and laws. Unless specially signified, the Channel Islands are not bound by British acts of parliament, though the British government is responsible for defence and external relations
currency English pound, also local coinage
population (1981) 128,878

Channel Islands

language official language French (Norman French) but English more widely used

religion chiefly Anglican

famous people Lillie Langtry

history originally under the duchy of Normandy, they are the only part still held by Britain. The islands came under the same rule as England 1066, and are dependent territories of the English crown. Germany occupied the islands during World War II from June 1940 to May 1945.

Chantilly town in Oise *département*, France, NE of Paris; population (1982) 10,208. It is the centre of French horseracing, and was the headquarters of the French military chief Joffre 1914–17. Formerly renowned for its lace and porcelain.

Chao Phraya chief river (formerly Menam) of Thailand, flowing 1,200 km/750 mi into the Bight of Bangkok, an inlet of the Gulf of Thailand.

Charente French river, rising in Haute-Vienne *département* and flowing past Angoulême and Cognac into the Bay of Biscay below Rochefort. Length 360 km/225 mi. Its wide estuary is much silted up. It gives its name to two *département*s, Charente and Charente-Maritime (formerly Charente-Inférieure).

Charing Cross district in Westminster, London, around Charing Cross mainline railway station, deriving its name from the site of the last of twelve stone crosses erected by Edward I in 1290 at the resting-places of the coffin of his queen, Eleanor. The present cross is modern.

Charleroi town in Belgium on the river Sambre, Hainault province; population (1985) 212,000. Its coal industry declined in the 1970s.

Charleston main port and city of South Carolina, USA; population (1980) 486,000. Industries include textiles, clothing, and paper products. The city dates from 1670. Fort Sumter, in the sheltered harbour of Charleston, was bombarded by Confederate batteries 12–13 April 1861, thus beginning the Civil War. There are many historic houses and fine gardens.

Charleston chief city of West Virginia, USA, on the Kanawha river; population (1980) 64,000. It is the centre of a district producing coal, natural gas, salt, clay, timber and oil. Home of the pioneer Daniel Boone.

Charlotte city in North Carolina, USA, on the border with South Carolina; population (1980) 314,500. Industries include data processing, textiles, chemicals, machinery, and food products. It was the gold-mining centre of the country until 1849. The Mint Museum of Arts has paintings, sculpture, and ceramics. Birthplace of James K Polk, 11th president of the USA.

Charlotte Amalie capital and tourist resort of the US Virgin Islands; population (1980) 11,756.

Charlottetown capital of Prince Edward Island, Canada; population (1986) 16,000. The city trades in textiles, fish, timber, vegetables, and dairy produce. It was founded by the French in the 1720s.

Chartres capital of the *département* of Eure-et-Loir, NW France, 96 km/59 mi SW of Paris, on the river Eure; population (1982) 39,243. The city is an important agricultural centre for the fertile Plaine de la Beauce. Its cathedral of Notre Dame, completed about 1240, is considered a masterpiece of Gothic architecture.

Chatham town in Kent, England; population (1983) 146,000. The Royal Dockyard 1588–1984 was from 1985 converted to a 'new town' including an industrial area, marina, and museum as a focus of revival for the whole Medway area.

Chatham Islands two Pacific islands (Chatham and Pitt), forming a county of South Island, New Zealand; area 960 sq km/371 sq mi; population (1981) 750. The chief settlement is ◊Waitangi.

Chattanooga city in Tennessee, USA on the Tennessee River; population (1986) 426,000. It is the focus of the Tennessee Valley Authority area. Developed as a salt-trading centre after 1835, it now produces chemicals, textiles, and metal products.

Cheapside a street running from St Paul's Cathedral to Poultry, in the City of London, England. The scene of the 13th-century 'Cheap', a permanent fair and general market. Christopher Wren's church of St Mary-le-Bow in Cheapside has the famous Bow Bells.

Checheno-Ingush autonomous republic in the W USSR; area 19,300/7,350 sq mi; population (1986) 1,230,000. It was conquered in the 1850s, and is a major oilfield. The capital is Grozny. The population includes Chechens (53%) and Ingushes (12%).

Cheddar village in Somerset, England; population (1983) 3,994. It is famous for cheese, its limestone gorge, and caves with stalactites and stalagmites. In 1962 excavation revealed the site of a Saxon palace.

Chefoo former name of part of ◊Yantai in China.

Chekiang former name for ◊Zhejiang province of SE China.

Chelmsford town in Essex, England, 48 km/30 mi NE of London; population (1981) 58,000. It is the administrative headquarters of the county, and a market town with radio, electrical, engineering, and agricultural machinery industries.

Chelsea historic area of the Royal Borough of Kensington and Chelsea, London, immediately north of the Thames, where it is crossed by the Albert and Chelsea bridges. The Royal Hospital was founded in 1682 by Charles II for old and disabled soldiers, 'Chelsea Pensioners', and the National Army Museum/1960 covers campaigns 1485–1914. The Physic Garden for botanical research was established in the 17th century; and the home of Thomas Carlyle in Cheyne Row is a museum. The Chelsea Flower Show is held annually by the Royal Horticultural Society in the grounds of Royal Hospital. Ranelagh Gardens 1742–1804 and Cremorne Gardens 1845–77 were celebrated places of entertainment.

Cheltenham spa at the foot of the Cotswolds, Gloucestershire, England; population (1981) 73,000. There are annual literary and music festivals, a racecourse (the Cheltenham Gold Cup is held annually), and Cheltenham College (founded 1854). The home of the composer Gustav Holst is now a museum, and to the SW is Prinknash Abbey, a Benedictine house that produces pottery. Cheltenham is also the centre of the British government's electronic surveillance operations (GCHQ). The Universities' Central Council on Admissions (UCCA) 1963 and the Polytechnics and Colleges Admissions System (PCAS) 1985 are here.

Chelyabinsk industrial town and capital of Chelyabinsk region, W Siberia, USSR; population (1987) 1,119,000. It has iron and engineering works, and makes chemicals, motor vehicles, and aircraft.

It lies east of the Ural Mountains, 240 km/150 mi SE of Sverdlovsk. It was founded 1736 as a Russian frontier post.

Chemnitz former name for ◊Karl-Marx-Stadt, industrial city in East Germany.

Chemulpo former name for ◊Inchond, port and summer resort on the W coast of South Korea.

Chenab a tributary of the river ◊Indus.

Chengchow former name of ◊Zhengzhou, capital of Henan province of China.

Chengde town, formerly *Chengteh* in Hebei province, China, NE of Beijing; population (1984) 325,800. It is a market town for agricultural and forestry products. It was the summer residence of the Manchu rulers and has an 18th-century palace and temples.

Chengdu formerly *Chengtu* ancient city, capital of Sichuan province, China; population (1986) 2,580,000. It is an important rail junction and has

railway workshops, textile, electronics, and engineering industries, and well-preserved temples.

Chengteh former name for ◊Chengde.

Chengtu former name for ◊Chengdu.

Chepstow market town in Gwent, Wales, on the Wye; population (1984) 12,500. The high tides, sometimes 15 m/50 ft above low level, are the highest in Britain. There is a Norman castle, and the ruins of Tintern Abbey are 6.5 km/4 mi to the N.

Cher French river which rises in Creuse *département* and flows into the Loire below Tours. Length 355 km/220 mi. It gives its name to a *département*.

Cherbourg French port and naval station at the northern end of the Cotentin peninsula, in Manche *département*; population (1982) 85,500 (conurbation). There is an institute for studies in nuclear warfare, and Cherbourg has large shipbuilding yards. During World War II, Cherbourg was captured June 1944 by the Allies, who thus gained their first large port of entry into France. Cherbourg was severely damaged; restoration of the harbour was completed 1952. There is a nuclear processing plant at nearby Cap la Hague. There are ferry links to Southampton, Weymouth, and Rosslare.

Cherepovets iron and steel city in W USSR, on the Volga-Baltic waterway; population (1985) 299,000.

Chernigov town and port on the river Desna in N Ukraine; population (1987) 291,000. It has an 11th-century cathedral. Lumbering, textiles, chemicals, distilling, and food-canning are among its industries.

Chernobyl town in Ukraine, USSR. In Apr 1986, a leak, caused by overheating, occurred in a non-pressurized boiling-water nuclear reactor. The resulting clouds of radioactive isotopes were traced as far away as Sweden; over 250 people were killed, and thousands of square kilometres contaminated.

Chernovtsy city in Ukraine, USSR; population (1987) 254,000. Industries include textiles, clothing, and machinery. Former names: Czernowitz (before 1918), Cernăuţi (1918–1940, when it was part of Romania), Chrenovitsy (1940–44).

Ches. abbreviation for ◊*Cheshire.*

Chesapeake Bay largest of the inlets on the Atlantic coast of the USA, bordered by Maryland and Virginia. Its wildlife is threatened by urban and industrial development.

Cheshire county in NW England
area 2,320 sq km/896 sq mi
towns administrative headquarters Chester; Warrington, Crewe, Widnes, Macclesfield, Congleton
physical chiefly a fertile plain; Mersey, Dee, and Weaver rivers
features salt mines and geologically rich former copper workings at Alderley Edge (in use from

Cheshire

Roman times until the 1920s); Little Moreton Hall; discovery of Lindow Man, the first 'bogman', dating from around 500 BC, to be found in mainland Britain; Quarry Bank Mill at Styal is a cotton-industry museum
products textiles, chemicals, dairy products
population (1987) 952,000
famous people the novelist Mrs Gaskell lived at Knutsford (the locale of *Cranford*).

Chesil bank shingle bank extending 19 km/11 mi along the coast of Dorset, England, from Abbotsbury to the Isle of Portland.

Chester city in Cheshire, England; on the river Dee 26 km/16 mi S of Liverpool; population (1984) 117,000. It is the administrative headquarters of Cheshire. Industries include engineering and the manufacture of car components. Its name derives from the Roman *Castra Devana*, 'the camp on the Dee', and there are many Roman and later remains. It is the only English city to retain its city walls (two miles long) intact. The cathedral dates from the 11th century but was restored in 1876. The church of St John the Baptist is a well-known example of early Norman architecture. The 'Rows' are covered arcades dating from the Middle Ages. From 1070 to the reign of Henry III, Chester was the seat of a county palatine (a county whose lord exercised some of the roles usually reserved for the monarch). The town hall dates from 1869. The silting-up of the Dee destroyed Chester's importance as a port during the Middle Ages.

Chesterfield market town of Derbyshire, England; 40 km/25 mi N of Derby, on the Rother river; population (1981) 78,200. Industries include coal-mining, engineering, and glass. It is the burial place of the engineer George Stephenson. All Saints' Church is renowned for its crooked spire.

Cheviots range of hills 56 km/35 mi long, mainly in Northumberland, forming the border between England and Scotland for some 48 km/30 mi. The highest point is the Cheviot 816 m/2,676 ft. For centuries the area was a battleground between the English and the Scots. It gives its name to a breed of sheep.

Chiba industrial city (paper, steel, textiles) in Kanton region, E Honshu island, Japan, 40 km/25 mi west of Tokyo; population (1987) 793,000.

Chicago financial and industrial (iron, steel, chemicals, textiles) city in Illinois, USA, on Lake Michigan; population (1980) 3,005,000, metropolitan area 7,581,000. The famous stockyards are now closed.

It contains the world's first skyscraper (built 1887–88) and some of the world's tallest modern skyscrapers, including the Sears Tower, 443 m/1,454 ft. The Museum of Science and Industry, opened 1893, has 'hands on' exhibits including a coal-mine, a World War II U-boat, an Apollo spacecraft and lunar module; and exhibits by industrial firms. 50 km/30 mi to the west is the Fermilab, the US centre for particle physics. The Chicago River cuts the city into three 'sides'. Chicago is known as the Windy City, possibly from the breezes of Lake Michigan, and its citizens' (and, allegedly, politicians') voluble talk; the lake shore ('the Gold Coast') is occupied by luxury apartment blocks. It has a renowned symphony orchestra, an art institute, the University of Chicago, and five professional sports teams.
history The site of Chicago was visited by Jesuit missionaries 1673, and Fort Dearborn, then a frontier fort, was built here 1803. The original layout of Chicago was a rectangular grid, but many outer boulevards have been constructed on less rigid lines. As late as 1831 Chicago was still an insignificant village, but railways connected it with the east coast by 1852, and by 1871, when it suffered a disastrous fire, it was a city of more than 300,000 inhabitants. Rapid development began again in the 1920s, and during the years of Prohibition 1919–33, the city became notorious for the activities of its gangsters. The opening of the St Lawrence Seaway 1959 brought Atlantic shipping to its docks.

Chichester city and market town in Sussex; 111 km/69 mi SW of London, near Chichester Harbour; population (1981) 24,000 It is the administrative headquarters of West Sussex. It was a Roman township, and the remains of the Roman palace built around AD 80 at nearby Fishbourne are unique outside Italy. There is a cathedral consecrated 1108, later much rebuilt and restored, and the Chichester Festival Theatre (1962).

Chiclayo capital of Lambayeque department, NW Peru; population (1988) 395,000.

Chiengmai or *Chiang Mai* town in N Thailand; population (1982) 104,910. There is a trade in teak and lac (as shellac, a resin used in varnishes and polishes), and many handicraft industries. It is the former capital of the Lan Na Thai kingdom.

Chihuahua capital of Chihuahua state, Mexico, 1,285 km/800 mi NW of Mexico City; population (1984) 375,000. Founded in 1707, it is the centre of a mining district.

Chile South American country, bounded to the north by Peru and Bolivia, to the east by Argentina, and to the south and west by the Pacific Ocean.

Chilterns range of chalk hills extending for some 72 km/45 mi in a curve from a point N of Reading to the Suffolk border. Coombe Hill, near Wendover, 260 m/852 ft high, is the highest point.

Chimbote largest fishing port in Peru; population (1981) 216,000.

China country in SE Asia, bounded N by Mongolia, NW and NE by the USSR, SW by India and Nepál, S by Bhutan, Burma, Laos, and Vietnam, SE by the South China Sea, and E by the East China Sea, North Korea, and the USSR.

China Sea area of the Pacific Ocean bordered by China, Vietnam, Borneo, the Philippines, and Japan. Various groups of small islands and shoals, including the Paracels, 500 km/300 mi east of Vietnam, have been disputed by China and other powers because they lie in oil-rich areas.

Chile
Republic of
(República de Chile)

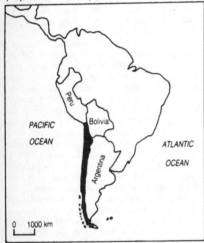

0   1000 km

area 736,905 sq km/284,445 sq mi
capital Santiago
towns Concepción, Viña del Mar, Temuco; ports are Valparaíso, Antofagasta, Arica, Iquique
physical Andes mountains along E border, Atacama Desert in N, arable land and forest in the S
territories Easter Island, Juan Fernández Island, half of Tierra del Fuego, and part of Antarctica
head of state and government Patricio Aylwin Azodar from 1990
political system emergent democratic republic
political parties Christian Democratic Party (PDC), moderate centrist; National Renewal Party (RN), right-wing
exports copper, iron, nitrate (Chile is the chief mining country of South America), pulp and paper
currency peso (491.48 = £1 Feb 1990)
population (1988) 12,680,000 (the majority mestizo, of mixed American Indian and Spanish descent); annual growth rate 1.6%
life expectancy men 67, women 73
language Spanish
religion Roman Catholic
literacy 95.4% (1985)
GNP $21.8 bn (1983); $1,950 per head of population
chronology
1818 Achieved independence from Spain.
1964 PDC formed government under Eduardo Frei.
1970 Dr Salvador Allende became the first democratically elected Marxist president. He embarked on an extensive programme of nationalization and social reform.
1973 Government overthrown by the CIA-backed military, led by Gen Augusto Pinochet. Allende killed. Policy of repression began during which all opposition was put down and political activity banned.
1983 Growing opposition to the regime from all sides, with outbreaks of violence.
1988 Plebiscite asking whether Pinochet should serve a further term resulted in a clear 'No' vote.
1989 President Pinochet agreed to constitutional changes to allow pluralist politics. Patricio Aylwin (PDC) elected president.
1990 (Jan) Aylwin reaches accord on end to military junta government.

China
People's Republic of
(Zhonghua Renmin Gonghe Guo)

area 9,139,300 sq km/3,528,684 sq mi
capital Beijing (Peking)
towns Chongqing (Chungking), Shenyang (Mukden), Wuhan, Nanjing (Nanking), Harbin; ports Tianjin (Tientsin), Shanghai, Qingdao (Tsingtao), Lüda (Lü-ta), Guangzhou (Canton)
physical two-thirds of China is mountains (in the N and SW) or desert; the east is irrigated by rivers Huang He (Yellow River), Chang Jiang (Yangtze-Kiang), Xi Jiang (Si Kiang)
features Great Wall of China; Kongur Shan mountain
head of state Yang Shangkun from 1988
head of government Li Peng from 1987
political system communis republic
political parties Chinese Communist Party (CCP), Marxist-Leninist-Maoist
exports tea, livestock and animal products, silk, cotton, oil, minerals (China is the world's largest producer of tungsten), chemicals, light industrial goods
currency yuan (8.03 = £2 Feb 1990)
population (1989) 1,112,000,000 (of whom the majority are Han or ethnic Chinese; the 67 million of other ethnic groups, including Tibetan, Uigur, and Zhuang, live in border areas). The number of people of Chinese origin outside China, Taiwan, and Hong Kong is estimated at 15–24 million. Annual growth rate 1.2%
life expectancy men 67, women 69
language Chinese
religion officially atheist, but traditionally Taoist, Confucianist, and Buddhist; Muslim 13 million; Catholic 3–6 million (divided between the 'patriotic' church established 1958 and the 'loyal' church subject to Rome); Protestant 3 million
literacy 82% male/66% female (1985 est)
GDP $313 bn (1983); $566 per head of population
chronology
1949 People's Republic of China proclaimed by Mao Zedong.
1954 Soviet-style constitution adopted.
1956–57 Hundred Flowers Movement encouraged criticism of the government.
1958–60 Great Leap Forward commune experiment to achieve 'true communism'.
1960 Withdrawal of Soviet technical advisers.
1962 Sino-Indian border war.
1962–65 Economic recovery programme under Liu Shaoqi; Maoist 'socialist education movement' rectification campaign.
1966–68 Great Proletarian Cultural Revolution and overthrow of Liu Shaoqi.
1969 Ussuri river border clashes with USSR.
1970–76 Reconstruction under Mao and Zhou Enlai; purge of extreme left.
1971 Entry into United Nations.
1972 US president Nixon visited Beijing.
1975 New state constitution. Unveiling of Zhou's Four Modernizations programme.
1976 Death of Zhou Enlai and Mao Zedong; appointment of Hua Guofeng as prime minister and Communist Party chairman. Deng in hiding. Gang of Four arrested.
1977 Rehabilitation of Deng Xiaoping.
1979 Economic reforms introduced. Diplomatic relations opened with USA. Punitive invasion of Vietnam.
1980 Zhao Ziyang appointed prime minister.
1981 Hu Yaobang succeeded Hua as party chairman. Imprisonment of Gang of Four.
1982 New state constitution adopted.
1984 'Enterprise management' reforms for industrial sector.
1986 Student demonstrations for democracy.
1987 Hu was replaced as party leader by Zhao, with Li Peng as prime minister. Deng left the Politburo but remained influential.
1988 Yang Shankun became state president. Economic reforms encountered increasing problems; inflation rocketing.
1989 Following the death of Hu Yaobang pro-democracy student demonstrations in Tiananmen Square, Beijing, were crushed by the army, who killed over 2000 demonstrators. Zhao Ziyang replaced as party leader by Jiang Zemin in a swing towards conservatism.

China: Provinces

Province	Former name	Capital	Area sq km
Anhui	Anhwei	Hefei	139
Fujian	Fukien	Fuzhou	121
Gansu	Kansu	Lanzhou	454
Guangdong	Kwangtung	Guangzhou	212
Guizhou	Kweichow	Guiyang	176
Hebei	Hopei	Shijiazhuang	188
Heilongjiang	Heilungkiang	Harbin	469
Henan	Honan	Zhengzhou	167
Hubei	Hupeh	Wuhan	186
Hunan	Hunan	Changsha	210
Jiangsu	Kiangsu	Nanjing	103
Jiangxi	Kiangsi	Nanchang	169
Jilin	Kirin	Changchun	187
Liaoning	Liaoning	Shenyang	146
Quinghai	Tsinghai	Xining	721
Shaanxi	Shensi	Xian	206
Shanxi	Shansi	Taiyuan	156
Shandong	Shantung	Jinan	153
Sichuan	Szechwan	Chengdu	567
Yunnan	Yunnan	Kunming	394
Zhejiang	Chekiang	Hangzhou	102

Autonomous Regions

Guangxi Zhuang	Kwangsi Chuang	Nanning	236
Nei Monggol	Inner Mongolia	Hohhot	1,183
Ningxia Hui	Ningshia Hui	Yinchuan	66
Xinjiang Uygur	Sinkiang Uighur	Urumqi	1,600
Xizang	Tibet	Lhasa	1,228

Municipalities

Beijing	Peking		17
Shanghai	Shanghai		6
Tianjin	Tientsin		11
		Total	9,571

North of Taiwan it is known as the *East China Sea* and to the south as the *South China Sea*.

Chinghai former name of ◊Qinghai, NW province of China.

Chita town in E Siberia, USSR, on the Chita river; population (1987) 349,000. It is on the Trans-Siberian railway, and has chemical works, engineering works, and coal mines.

Chittagong city and port in Bangladesh, 16 km/10 mi from the mouth of the Karnaphuli river, on the Bay of Bengal; population (1981) 1,388,476. Industries include steel, engineering, chemicals, and textiles.

Chkalov name 1938–57 of ◊Orenburg, town in the USSR.

Chongjin capital of North Hamgyong province on the NE coast of North Korea; population (1984) 754,000.

Chongqing or *Chungking*, also known as *Pahsien* city in Sichuan province, China, which stands at the confluence of the ◊Chang Jiang and the Jialing Jiang; population (1984) 2,733,700. Industries include iron, steel, chemicals, synthetic rubber, and textiles.

For over 4,000 years it has been an important commercial centre in one of the most remote and economically deprived regions of China. It was opened to foreign trade in 1891, and it remains a focal point of road, river, and rail transport. When both Beijing and Nanjing were occupied by the Japanese, it was the capital of China 1938–46.

Christchurch town in Dorset, England, adjoining Bournemouth at the junction of the Stour and Avon rivers, population (1983) 40,300. Light industry includes the manufacture of plastics and electronics. There is a Norman and Early English priory church.

Christchurch city on South Island, New Zealand, 11 km/7 mi from the mouth of the Avon river: population (1986) 299,300. Principal city of the Canterbury plains, it is the seat of the University of Canterbury. Industries include fertilizers and chemicals, canning and meat-processing, rail workshops, and shoes. Christchurch uses as its port a bay in the sheltered Lyttelton Harbour on the N shore of the Banks Peninsula, which forms a denuded volcanic mass. Land has been reclaimed for service facilities, and rail and road tunnels (1867 and 1964 respectively) link Christchurch with Lyttelton.

Christiania former name of Norwegian capital of ◊Oslo (1624–1924), after King Christian IV who replanned it after a fire in 1624.

Christmas Island island in the Indian Ocean, 360 km/224 mi south of Java; area 140 sq km/54 sq mi; population (1986) 2,000. It has phosphate deposits. Found to be uninhabited when reached by Captain W Mynars on Christmas Day 1643, it was annexed by Britain 1888; occupied by Japan 1942–45, and transferred to Australia 1958. After a referendum 1984, it was included in Northern Territory.

Chubu mountainous coastal region of central Honshu island, Japan; population (1986) 20,694,000; area 66,774 sq km/25,791 sq mi. The chief city is Nagoya.

Chufu former name for ◊Qufu, town in Shandong province, China.

Chugoku southwestern region of Honshu island, Japan; area 31,881 sq km/12,314 sq mi; population (1986) 7,764,000. Chief city is Hiroshima.

Chukchi Sea part of the Arctic Ocean, situated to the north of Bering Strait between Asia and North America.

Chungking former name for ◊Chongqing, city in Sichuan province, China.

Churchill town in province of Manitoba, Canada, situated on Hudson Bay.

Chuvash autonomous republic of the USSR, lying W of the Volga, 560 km/350 mi E of Moscow; area 18,300 sq km /7,100 sq mi; population (1986) 1,320,000. The capital is Cheboksary, population (1985) 389,000. Lumbering and grain-growing are important and there are phosphate and limestone deposits, and electrical and engineering industries.

Cienfuegos port and naval base in Cuba; population (1985) 124,600. It trades in sugar, fruit and tobacco.

Cincinnati city and port in Ohio, USA, on the Ohio River; population (1980) 1,400,000. Chief industries include machinery, clothing, furniture making, wine, chemicals, and meat-packing. Founded 1788, it became a city 1819. It attracted large numbers of European immigrants, particularly Germans, during the 19th century. It has two universities, and a major symphony orchestra.

Circassia former name of an area of the N Caucasus, ceded to Russia by Turkey in 1829 and now part of the Karachai-Cherkess region of the USSR.

Cirencester market town in Gloucestershire, England; population (1981) 15,620. It is the 'capital' of the Cotswolds. Light industry is based on engineering and the manufacture of electrical goods. It was the second largest town in Roman Britain, and has an amphitheatre which seated 8,000, and the Corinium Museum. The Royal Agricultural College is based here.

Ciskei, Republic of a Bantu homeland in South Africa, which became independent 1981, although this is not recognized by any other country.
area 7,700 sq km/2,974 sq mi
capital Bisho
features one of the two homelands of the Xhosa people created by South Africa (the other is Transkei).
products pineapples, timber, metal products, leather, textiles
population (1984) 903,681
language Xhosa
government president (Brig Oupa Gqozo from 1990), with legislative and executive councils.

Citlaltépetl (Aztec 'star mountain') a dormant volcano, the highest mountain in Mexico, height 5,700 m/18,700 ft, north of the city of Orizaba (after which it is sometimes named). It last erupted in 1687.

Ciudad Bolívar city in SE Venezuela, on the river Orinoco, 400 km/250 mi from its mouth; population (1981) 183,000. Gold is mined in the vicinity. The city is linked with Soledad across the river by the Angostura bridge (1967), the first to span the Orinoco. Capital of Bolívar state, it was called Angostura 1824–49.

Ciudad Guayana city in Venezuela, on the S bank of the river Orinoco, population (1981) 314,500. Main industries include iron and steel. The city

was formed by the union of Puerto Ordaz and San Felix, and has been opened to ocean-going ships by dredging.

Ciudad Juárez city on the Rio Grande, in Chihuahua state, N Mexico, on the border with the USA; population (1986) 596,000. It is a centre for cotton.

Ciudad Real city of central Spain; 170 km/105 mi S of Madrid; population (1981) 50,150. It is capital of Ciudad Real province. It trades in livestock and produces textiles and pharmaceuticals. Its chief feature is its huge Gothic cathedral.

Ciudad Trujillo name 1936–1961 of ◊Santo Domingo, capital city and seaport of the Dominican Republic.

Civitavecchia ancient port on the W coast of Italy, in Lazio region; 64 km/40 mi NW of Rome; population (1971) 42,300. Industries include fishing, and the manufacture of cement and calcium carbide.

Clackmannanshire former county (the smallest) in Scotland, bordering the Firth of Forth. It was merged with Central Region in 1975. The county town was Alloa.

Clacton-on-Sea seaside resort in Essex, England; 19 km/12 mi SE of Colchester; population (1981) 43,600. The 16th-century St Osyth's priory is nearby.

Clare county on the west coast of the Republic of Ireland, in the province of Munster; area 3,190 sq km/1,231 sq mi; population (1986) 91,000. Shannon airport is here.

The coastline is rocky and dangerous, and inland Clare is an undulating plain, with mountains on the E, W, and NW, the chief range being the Slieve Bernagh mountains in the SE rising to over 518 m/1,700 ft. The principal rivers are the Shannon and its tributary, the Fergus. There are over 100 lakes in the county, Lough Derg is on the E border. The county town is Ennis. At Ardnachusha, 5 km/3 mi north of Limerick, is the main power station of the Shannon hydroelectric installations. The county is said to be named after Thomas de Clare, an Anglo-Norman settler to whom this area was granted 1276.

Cleethorpes seaside resort in Humberside, NE England, on the Humber estuary; population (1981) 35,500.

Clermont-Ferrand city, capital of Puy-de-Dôme *département*, in the Auvergne region of France; population (1983) 256,000. It is a centre for agriculture, and its rubber industry is the largest in France.

Car tyres are manufactured here; other products include chemicals, preserves, foodstuffs, and clothing. The Gothic cathedral is 13th-century. Urban II ordered the First Crusade at a council here 1095. The 17th-century writer Blaise Pascal was born here.

Cleveland county in NE England
area 580 sq km/224 sq mi

Cleveland

towns administrative headquarters Middlesbrough; Stockton on Tees, Billingham, Hartlepool

features river Tees, with Seal Sands wildfowl refuge at its mouth; North Yorkshire Moors National Park. Teesside, the industrial area at the mouth of the Tees, has Europe's largest steel complex (at Redcar) and chemical site (ICI, using gas and local potash), as well as an oil-fuel terminal at Seal Sands and natural-gas terminal at St Fergus, 19 km/12 mi south of Fraserburgh in the Grampians

products steel, chemicals

population (1987) 555,000.

Cleveland largest city of Ohio, USA, on Lake Erie at the mouth of the river Cuyahoga; population (1981) 574,000, metropolitan area 1,899,000. Its chief industries are iron and steel, and petroleum refining. Iron ore from the Lake Superior region and coal from Ohio and Pennsylvania mines are brought here.

Cluj (German *Klausenberg*) city in Transylvania, Romania, located on the river Somes; population (1985) 310,000. It is a communications centre for Romania and the Hungarian plain. Industries include machine tools, furniture, and knitwear.

There is a 14th-century cathedral, and Romanian (1872) and Hungarian (1945) universities.

Cluny town in Saône-et-Loire *département*, France; on the river Grosne; population (1982) 4,500. Its abbey, now in ruins, was the foundation house 910–1790 of the Cluniac order, originally a reformed branch of the Benedictines. Cluny, once a lace-making centre, has an important cattle market.

Clutha longest river in South Island, New Zealand, 322 km/201 mi long. It rises in the Southern Alps,

has hydroelectric installations and flows to meet the sea near Kaitangata.

Clwyd county in N Wales

area 2,420 sq km/934 sq mi

towns administrative headquarters Mold; Flint, Denbigh, Wrexham; seaside resorts Colwyn Bay, Rhyl, Prestatyn

physical rivers Dee and Clwyd; Clwydian Range with Offa's Dyke along the main ridge

features Chirk, Denbigh, Flint, and Rhuddlan castles; Greenfield Valley, NW of Flint, was in the forefront of the industrial revolution before the advent of steam, and now has a museum of industrial archaeology

products dairy and meat products, optical glass, chemicals, limestone, microprocessors, plastics

population (1987) 403,000

language 19% Welsh, English.

Clyde river in Strathclyde, Scotland; 170 km/103 mi long. The Firth of Clyde and Firth of Forth are linked by the Forth and Clyde canal, 56 km/35 mi long. The shipbuilding yards have declined in recent years. The nuclear submarine bases of Faslane (Polaris) and Holy Loch (US Poseidon) are here.

Clydebank town on the Clyde, Strathclyde, Scotland, 10 km/6 mi NW of Glasgow; population (1981) 51,700. At the John Brown yard famous liners such as the *Queen Elizabeth II* were built.

Coatbridge town in Strathclyde, Scotland; 13 km/8 mi E of Glasgow; population (1981) 51,000. Coal and iron are mined nearby. Industries include iron, ore, steel, and engineering.

Cobh seaport and market town on Great Island, Republic of Ireland; in the estuary of the Lee, county Cork; population (1981) 8,400. Formerly

Clwyd

a port of call for transatlantic steamers. The town was known as Cove of Cork until 1849 and Queenstown until 1922.

Coblenz alternative spelling of the German city ◊Koblenz.

Coburg town in Bavaria, West Germany, on the river Itz; 80 km/50 mi SE of Gotha; population (1984) 44,500. Industries include machinery, toys and porcelain. Formerly the capital of the duchy of Coburg, it was part of Saxe-Coburg-Gotha 1826–1918, and a residence of its dukes.

Cochabamba city in central Bolivia, SE of La Paz; population (1985) 317,000. Its altitude is 2,550 m/8,370 ft; it is important for agricultural trading and oil refining.

Its refinery is linked by pipeline with the Camiri oilfields. It is the third largest city in Bolivia.

Cochin former princely state lying west of the Anamalai hills in S India. It was part of Travancore-Cochin from 1949 until merged into Kerala in 1956.

Cochin seaport in Kerala state, India, on the Malabar coast; population (1983) 686,000. It is a fishing port and naval training base. An industrial centre with oil refineries, ropes and clothing are also manufactured here. It exports coir, copra, tea, and spices. Vasco da Gama established a Portuguese factory at Cochin 1502, and St Francis Xavier made it a missionary centre 1530. The Dutch held Cochin from 1663–1795 when it was taken by the English.

Cochin-China region of SE Asia. With Cambodia it formed part of the ancient Khmer empire. In the 17th–18th centuries it was conquered by Annam. Together with Kampuchea it became, 1863–67, the first part of the Indochinese peninsula to be occupied by France. Since 1949 it has been part of Vietnam.

Cocos Islands or *Keeling Islands* group of 27 small coral islands in the Indian Ocean, about 2,770 km/1,720 mi NW of Perth, Australia; area 14 sq km/5.5 sq mi; population (1986) 616. They are owned by Australia.

Discovered by William Keeling 1609, they were uninhabited until 1826, annexed by Britain 1857, and transferred to Australia as the Territory of Cocos (Keeling) Islands 1955. The Australian government purchased them from John Clunies-Ross 1978.

Cognac town in Charente *département*, France, 40 km/25 mi W of Angoulême; population (1982) 21,000. Situated in a vine-growing district, Cognac has given its name to a brandy. Bottles, corks, barrels, and crates are manufactured here.

Coimbatore city in Tamil Nadu, S India, on the Noyil river; population (1981) 917,000. It has textile industries and the Indian Air Force Administrative College.

Coimbra city in Portugal, on the Mondego river, 32 km/19 mi from the sea; population (1981) 71,800. It produces fabrics, paper, pottery and biscuits. There is a 12th-century Romanesque cathedral incorporating part of an older mosque, and a university, founded in Lisbon 1290 and transferred to Coimbra 1537. Coimbra was the capital of Portugal 1139–1385.

Colchester town and river port in England, on the river Colne, Essex; 80 km/50 mi NE of London; population (1981) 82,000. In an agricultural area, it is a market centre with clothing manufacture and engineering and printing works. The University of Essex (1961) is to the SE at Wivenhoe.

history Claiming to be the oldest town in England (Latin *Camulodunum*), Colchester dates from the time of Cymbeline (*c.* AD 10–43). It became a colony of Roman ex-soldiers in AD 50, and one of the most prosperous towns in Roman Britain despite its burning by Boudicca (Boadicea) in 61. Most of the Roman walls remain, as well as ruins of the Norman castle, and St Botolph's priory. Holly Tree Mansion (1718) is a museum of 18th–19th-century social life.

Colmar capital of Haut-Rhin *département*, France, between the river Rhine and the Vosges mountains; population (1983) 82,500. It is the centre of a wine-growing and market-gardening area. Industries include engineering, food processing, and textiles. The church of St Martin is 13th–14th century, and the former Dominican monastery, now the Unterlinden Museum, contains a famed Grünewald altarpiece.

Cologne (German *Köln*) industrial and commercial port in North Rhine-Westphalia, West Germany, on the left bank of the Rhine, 35 km/22 mi from Düsseldorf; population (1988) 914,000. To the north is the Ruhr coalfield, on which many of Cologne's industries are based. They include motor vehicles, railway wagons, chemicals, and machine tools.

Cologne can be reached by ocean-going vessels and has developed into a great transshipment centre, and is also the headquarters of Lufthansa, the state airline.

Founded by the Romans 38 BC and made a colony 50 AD under the name Colonia Claudia Arae Agrippinensis (hence the name Cologne), it became an important Frankish city and during the Middle Ages was ruled by its archbishops. It was a free imperial city from 1288 until the Napoleonic age. In 1815 it passed to Prussia. The great Gothic cathedral was begun in the 13th century but its towers were not built until the 19th century (completed 1880). Its university (1388–1797) was refounded 1919. Cologne suffered severely from aerial bombardment during World War II; 85% of the city and its three Rhine bridges were destroyed.

Colombes suburb of Paris, France; population (1983) 83,260. It is capital of Hauts-de-Seine

Colombia
Republic of
(República de Colombia)

area 1,141,748 sq km/440,715 sq mi
capital Bogotá
towns Medellin, Cali, Bucaramanga; ports
Barranquilla, Cartagena
physical the Andes mountains run N–S;
plains in the E; Magdalena River runs N to the
Caribbean
head of state and government Virgilio Barco
Vargas from 1986
political system emergent democratic republic
political parties Liberal Party, centrist;
Conservative Party, right-of-centre
exports emeralds (world's largest producer),
coffee (second largest world producer),
bananas, cotton, meat, sugar, oil, skins, hides
currency peso (769.83 = £1 Feb 1990)
population (1985) 29,482,000 (68% mestizo,
20% white); annual growth rate 2.2%
life expectancy men 61, women 66

language Spanish
religion Roman Catholic
literacy 89% male/87% female (1985 est)
GNP $42.5 bn (1983); $1,112 per head of
population
chronology
1886 Full independence achieved.
Conservatives in power.
1930 Liberals in power.
1946 Conservatives in power.
1948 Left-wing mayor of Bogotá assassinated.
Widespread outcry.
1949 Start of civil war, La Violencia, during
which 280,000 people died.
1957 Hoping to halt the violence, Conservatives
and Liberals agreed to form a National Front,
sharing the presidency.
1970 National Popular Alliance (ANAPO) formed
as a left-wing opposition to the National Front.
1974 National Front accord temporarily ended.
1975 Civil unrest because of disillusionment
with the government.
1978 Liberals, under Julio Turbay, revived the
accord and began an intensive fight against
drug dealers.
1982 Liberals maintained their control of
Congress but lost the presidency. The
Conservative president, Belisario Betancur,
attempted to end the violence by granting
left-wing guerrillas an amnesty, freeing political
prisoners, and embarking on a public works
programme.
1984 Minister of justice assassinated, allegedly
by drug dealers. Campaign against them
stepped up.
1986 Virgilio Barco Vargas, Liberal, elected
president by a record margin.
1989 Campaign against drug traffickers
intensified.

département. Tyres, electronic equipment, and
chemicals are manufactured.

Colombey-les-Deux-Egllses village (the name
means Colombey with the two churches) in
Haute-Marne, France; population (1981) 700.
General de Gaulle lived and was buried here.

Colombia country in South America, bounded N and
W by the Caribbean and the Pacific, and having
borders with Panama to the NW, Venezuela to
the E and NE, Brazil to the SE, and Peru and
Ecuador to the SW.

Colombo capital and principal seaport of Sri Lanka,
on the west coast near the mouth of the Kelani;
population (1981) 588,000, Greater Colombo
about 1,000,000. It trades in tea, rubber, and
cacao. It has iron and steel works, and an oil
refinery.

Colombo was mentioned as Kalambu about
1340, but the Portuguese renamed it in honour
of the explorer Christopher Columbus. The Dutch
seized it 1656 and surrendered it to Britain 1796.
Since 1983, the chief government offices have
been located at nearby Sri-Jayawardenapura east
of the city.

Colón second largest city in Panama, at the Caribbean end of the Panama Canal; population (1980)
60,000. Founded in 1850, and named Aspinwall
in 1852, it was renamed Colón in 1890 in honour
of the explorer Christopher Columbus.

Colón, Archipiélago de official name of the
◊Galápagos Islands.

Colorado state of the central W USA; nickname
Centennial State
area 269,700 sq km/104,104 sq mi

capital Denver

towns Colorado Springs, Aurora, Lakewood, Fort Collins, Greeley, Pueblo, Boulder

physical Great Plains in the east; the main ranges of the Rocky Mountains; high plateaux of the Colorado Basin in the west

features Rocky Mountain National Park; Pikes Peak; prehistoric cliff dwellings of the Mesa Verde National Park; Garden of the Gods (natural sandstone sculptures); Dinosaur and Great Sand Dunes national monuments; 'ghost' mining towns

products cereals, meat and dairy products, oil, coal, molybdenum, uranium, iron, steel, machinery

population (1986) 3,267,000

famous people Jack Dempsey, Douglas Fairbanks

history it first attracted fur traders, and Denver was founded following the discovery of gold 1858. Colorado became a state 1876.

Colorado River river in North America, rising in the Rocky Mountains and flowing 2,333 km/1,450 mi to the Gulf of California through Colorado, Utah, Arizona, and N Mexico. The many dams along its course, including Hoover and Glen Canyon, provide power and irrigation water, but have destroyed wildlife and scenery, and very little water now reaches the sea. To the west of the river in SE California is the *Colorado Desert*, an arid area of 5,000 sq km/2,000 sq mi.

Colorado Springs health resort in Colorado, USA, 120 km/75 mi SE of Denver; population (1986) 380,000. At an altitude of about 1,800 m/6,000 ft, and surrounded by magnificent scenery, it is also a local trade centre.

Columbia river in W North America, over 1,950 km/1218 mi; it rises in British Columbia, Canada, and flows through Washington state, USA, to the Pacific below Astoria. It is harnessed for irrigation and power by the Grand Coulee and other great dams. It is famous for salmon fishing.

Columbia capital of South Carolina, USA, on the Congaree River; population (1980) 445,000. Manufacturing includes textiles, plastics, electrical goods, fertilizers, and hosiery.

Columbia, District of seat of the federal government of the USA, bordering the capital, Washington; area 178 sq km/69 sq mi. Situated on the Potomac River, it was ceded by Maryland as the national capital site 1790.

Columbus capital city of Ohio, USA, on the rivers Scioto and Olentangy; population (1980) 1,093,000. It has coalfield and natural gas resources nearby; its industries include the manufacture of cars, planes, missiles, electrical goods, mining machinery, refrigerators, and telephones.

Colwyn Bay seaside town in Clwyd, North Wales, known as the 'garden resort of Wales'. Population (1981) 26,300.

Communism Peak (Russian *Pik Kommunizma*) highest mountain in the USSR, in the Pamir range in Tadzhikistan; 7,495 m/24,599 ft.

It was known as Mount Garmo until 1933, and Mount Stalin 1933–62.

Como city in Lombardy, Italy; on Lake Como at the foot of the Alps; population (1981) 95,500. Motor cycles, glass, silk, and furniture are produced here. The river Adda flows N–S through the lake, and the shores are famous for their beauty. Como has a marble cathedral, built 1396–1732, and is a tourist resort.

Comodoro Rivadavia port in Patagonia, SE Argentina; population (1984) 120,000. Argentina's main oilfields and natural gas are nearby.

Comorin the most southerly cape of the Indian sub-continent, in Tamil Nadu, where the Indian Ocean, Bay of Bengal and Arabian Sea meet.

Comoros group of islands in the Indian Ocean between Madagascar and the E coast of Africa. Three of them – Njazidja, Nzwani, and Mwali – form the republic of Comoros. The fourth island in the group, Mayotte, is a French dependency.

Compiègne town in Oise *département*, France, on the river Oise near its confluence with the river Aisne; population (1983) 37,250. It has an enormous chateau, built by Louis XV. The armistices of 1918 and 1940 were signed (the latter by Hitler and Pétain) in a railway coach in the forest of Compiègne.

Conakry capital and chief port of the Republic of Guinea; population (1980) 763,000. It is on the island of Tumbo, linked with the mainland by a causeway and by rail with Kankan, 480 km/300 mi NE. Bauxite and iron ore are mined nearby.

Concepción city in Chile, near the mouth of the river Bió-Bió; population (1987) 294,000. It is capital of the province of Concepción. It is in a rich agricultural district, and is also an industrial centre for coal, steel, paper, and textiles.

Concord town in Massachusetts, USA; population (1980) 16,300. Site of the first battle of the War of American Independence, 19 Apr 1775. The writers Ralph Emerson, Henry

Colorado

Comoros
Federal Islamic Republic of
(République fédérale islamique des Comores)

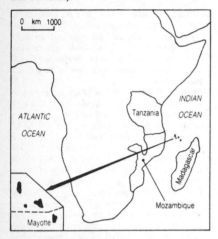

area 1,862 sq km/719 sq mi
capital Moroni
physical comprises the islands of Njazidja, Nzwani, and Mwali (formerly Grand Comoro, Anjouan, Maheli); poor soil
features active volcano on Njazidja
head of state and government vacant; interim military administration
political system authoritarian nationalism
political parties Comoran Union for Progress (Udzima), nationalist Islamic
exports copra, vanilla, cocoa, sisal, coffee, cloves, essential oils
currency CFA franc (485.00 = £1 Feb 1990)
population (1987) 423,000; annual growth rate 3.1%
life expectancy men 48, women 52
language Comorian (Swahili and Arabic dialect), Makua, French, Arabic (official)
religion Muslim (official)
literacy 15%
GNP $154 million (1982); $339 per head of population
chronology
1975 Independence achieved, but Mayotte remained part of France. Ahmed Abdallah elected president. The Comoros joined United Nations.
1976 Abdallah overthrown by Ali Soilih.
1978 Soilih killed by mercenaries working for Abdallah. Islamic republic proclaimed and Abdallah elected president.
1979 The Comoros became a one-party state. Powers of the federal government increased.
1985 Constitution amended to make Abdallah head of government as well as head of state.
1989 Abdallah killed by French mercenaries. Interim military government installed.

Thoreau, Nathaniel Hawthorne and Louisa Alcott lived here.

Coney Island seaside resort on a peninsula in the south west of Long Island, New York, USA. It has been popular for its amusement parks since the 1840s.

Congo former name (1960–71) of ◊Zaïre.

Congo country in W central Africa, bounded to the north by Cameroon and the Central African Republic, to the east and south by Zaïre, to the west by the Atlantic Ocean, and to the northwest by Gabon.

Connacht province of the Republic of Ireland, comprising the counties of Galway, Leitrim, Mayo, Roscommon, and Sligo; area 17,130 sq km/6,612 sq mi; population (1986) 431,000. The chief towns are Galway, Roscommon, Castlebar, Sligo, and Carrick-on-Shannon. Mainly lowland, it is agricultural and stock-raising country, with poor land in the west.

The chief rivers are the Shannon, Moy, and Suck, and there are a number of lakes. The Connacht dialect is the national standard.

Connecticut state in New England, USA; nickname Constitution State/Nutmeg State
area 13,000 sq km/5,018 sq mi
capital Hartford
towns Bridgeport, New Haven, Waterbury
physical highlands in the NW; Connecticut River
features Yale University; Mystic Seaport (reconstruction of 19th-century village, with restored ships)

Connecticut

products dairy, poultry, and market garden products; tobacco, watches, clocks, silverware, helicopters, jet engines, nuclear submarines
population (1983) 3,138,000
famous people Phineas T Barnum, George Bush, Katharine Hepburn, Harriet Beecher Stowe, Mark Twain
history settled by Puritan colonists from Massachusetts 1635, it was one of the Thirteen Colonies, and became a state 1788.

Connemara the western part of county Galway, Republic of Ireland, noted for its rocky coastline and mountainous scenery.

Constance (German *Konstanz*) town in Baden-Württemberg, Germany, on the section of the Rhine joining Lake Constance and the Untersee; population (1983) 69,100. Suburbs stretch across the frontier into Switzerland. Constance has clothing, machinery, and chemical factories and printing works.

Constance, Lake (German *Bodensee*) lake between Germany, Austria, and Switzerland, through which the river Rhine flows; area 540 sq km/200 sq mi.

Constanţa chief Romanian port on the Black Sea, capital of Constanţa region, and third largest city of Romania; population (1985) 323,000. It is the exporting centre for the Romanian oilfields, to which it is connected by pipeline. It has refineries, shipbuilding yards, and food factories.

It was founded as a Greek colony in the 7th century BC, and later named after the Roman emperor Constantine I (4th century AD). Ovid, the Roman poet, lived in exile here.

Constantine city in Algeria; population (1983) 449,000. It produces carpets and leather goods. It was one of the important towns in the Roman province of Numidia, but declined and was ruined, then restored 313 by Constantine the Great, whose name it bears. It was subsequently ruled by Arabs, Turks, and Salah Bey 1770–92, who built many of the Muslim buildings. It was captured by the French 1837.

Contadora Panamanian island of the Pearl Island group in the Gulf of Panama. It was the first meeting place 1983 of the foreign ministers of Colombia, Mexico, Panama, and Venezuela (now known as the *Contadora Group*) who came together to discuss the problems of Central America.

Conwy port in Wales on the river Conwy, Gwynedd; population (1981) 12,950. Known until 1972 by the anglicized form *Conway*. Still surrounded by walls,

---

Congo
People's Republic of the
(République Populaire du Congo)

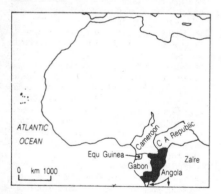

area 342,000 sq km/132,012 sq mi
capital Brazzaville
towns chief port Pointe Noire
physical Zaïre (Congo) river on the border; half the country is rainforest
head of state and government Denis Sassau-Nguesso from 1979
political system one-party socialist republic

political parties Congolese Labour Party (PCT), Marxist-Leninist
exports timber, potash, petroleum
currency CFA franc (485.00 = £1 Feb 1990)
population (1987) 2,270,000 (chiefly Bantu); annual growth rate 2.6%
life expectancy men 45, women 48
language French (official)
religion animist 50%, Christian 48%
literacy 79% male/55% female (1985 est)
GDP $2.1 bn (1983); $500 per head of population
chronology
1960 Achieved full independence from France, with Abbe Youlou as the first president.
1963 Youlou forced to resign. New constitution approved, with Alphonse Massamba-Débat as president.
1964 The Congo became a one-party state.
1968 Military coup, led by Capt Marien Ngouabi, ousted Massamba-Débat.
1970 A Marxist state, the People's Republic of the Congo, was announced, with the PCT as the only legal party.
1977 Ngouabi assassinated. Col Yhombi-Opango became president.
1979 Yhombi-Opango handed over the presidency to PCT, who chose Col Denis Sassau-Ngessou as his successor.
1984 Sassou-Ngessou elected for another five-year term.

Conwy has the ruins of a castle rebuilt by Edward I in 1284.

Coober Pedy (native Australian 'white man in a hole') town in the Great Central Desert, Australia; 700 km/437 mi NW of Adelaide, S Australia; population (1976) 1,900. Opals were discovered in 1915, and are mined amid a moonscape of diggings in temperatures up to 60°C/140°F.

Cooch Behar former princely state in India, it was merged in West Bengal in 1950.

Cook, Mount highest point, 3,764 m/12,353 ft, of Southern Alps, range of mountains running through New Zealand.

Cookham-on-Thames village in Berkshire, England. The artist Stanley Spencer lived here for many years and a memorial gallery of his work was opened in 1962.

Cook Islands group of six large and a number of smaller Polynesian islands 2,600 km/1,600 mi NE of Auckland, New Zealand; area 290 sq km/112 sq mi; population (1986) 17,000. Their main products include fruit, copra, and crafts. They became a self-governing overseas territory of New Zealand 1965.

The chief island, Rarotonga, is the site of Avarua, the seat of government. Niue, geographically part of the group, is separately administered. The Cook Islands were visited by Capt Cook 1773, annexed by Britain 1888, and transferred to New Zealand 1901. They have common citizenship with New Zealand.

Cook Strait strait dividing North and South Island, New Zealand. A submarine cable carries electricity from South to North Island.

Cooper's Creek river, often dry, in ◊Channel Country, SW Queensland, Australia.

Coorg or *Kurg* mountainous district of the state of Karnataka, in the Western Ghats of India. Formerly the princely state of Coorg, it was merged in Karnataka in 1956.

Copán town in W Honduras; population (1983) 19,000. The nearby site of a Maya city, including a temple and pyramids, was bought by John Stephens of the USA in the 1830s for $50.

Copenhagen (Danish *København*) capital of Denmark, on the islands of Zealand and Amager; population (1988) 1,344,000 (including suburbs).

To the NE is the royal palace at Amalienborg; the 17th-century Charlottenburg Palace houses the Academy of Arts, and parliament meets in the Christiansborg Palace. The statue of Hans Andersen's 'Little Mermaid' (by Edvard Eriksen) is at the harbour entrance. The Tivoli amusement park is on the shore of the Øresund.

Copenhagen was a fishing village until 1167, when the bishop of Roskilde built the castle on the site of the present Christiansborg palace. A settlement grew up, and it became the Danish capital 1443. The university was founded

1479. The city was under German occupation Apr 1940–May 1945.

Coral Sea or *Solomon Sea* part of the Pacific Ocean lying between NE Australia, New Guinea, the Solomon Islands, Vanuatu, and New Caledonia. It contains numerous coral islands and reefs. The Coral Sea Islands are a Territory of Australia; they comprise scattered reefs and islands over an area of about 1,000,000 sq km. They are uninhabited except for a meteorological station on Willis Island. The ◊Great Barrier Reef lies along its western edge.

Corby town in Northamptonshire, England; population (1981) 52,500. Formerly a major steel centre, it is now an enterprise zone producing plastics.

Cordilleras, the the mountainous western section of North America, with the Rocky Mountains and the coastal ranges parallel to the contact between the North American and the Pacific plates.

Córdoba city in central Argentina, on the Rio Primero; population (1980) 982,000. It is capital of Córdoba province. Main industries include cement, glass, textiles and vehicles. Founded in 1573, it has a university founded 1613, a military aviation college, an observatory, and a cathedral.

Córdoba capital of Córdoba province, Spain, on the river Guadalquivir; population (1986) 305,000. Paper, textiles, and copper products are manufactured here. It has many Moorish remains, including the mosque, now a cathedral, founded by 'Abd-ar-Rahman I in 785; it is one of the largest Christian churches in the world. Córdoba was probably founded by the Carthaginians, and held by the Moors 711–1236.

Corfe Castle village in the Isle of Purbeck, Dorset, England, built around the ruins of a Norman castle destroyed in the Civil War.

Corfu (Greek *Kérkira*) most northerly, and second largest of the Ionian islands, off the coast of Epirus in the Ionian Sea; area 1,072 sq km/414 sq mi; population (1981) 96,500. Its businesses include tourism, fruit, olive oil, and textiles. Its largest town is the port of Corfu (Kérkira), population (1981) 33,560. Corfu was colonized by Corinthians about 700 BC, Venice held it 1386–1797, Britain from 1815–64.

Corinth (Greek *Kórinthos*) port in Greece, on the isthmus connecting the Peloponnesos with the mainland; population (1981) 22,650. The rocky isthmus is bisected by the 6.5 km/4 mi Corinth canal, opened 1893. The site of the ancient city-state of Corinth lies 7 km/4.5 mi SW.

Corinth was already a place of some commercial importance in the 9th century BC. At the end of the 6th century BC it joined the Peloponnesian League, and took a prominent part in the Persian and the Peloponnesian wars. In 146 BC it was conquered by the Romans. The emperor Augustus (63 BC–AD 14) made it capital of the Roman province of Achaea. St Paul visited

Corinth AD 51 and addressed two epistles to its churches. After many changes of ownership it became part of independent Greece in 1822. Corinth's ancient monuments include the ruined temple of Apollo (6th century BC).

Cork largest county of the Republic of Ireland, in the province of Munster; county town Cork; area 7,460 sq km/2,880 sq mi; population (1986) 413,000. It is agricultural but there is also some copper and manganese mining, marble quarrying, and river and sea fishing. Natural gas and oil fields are found off the S coast at Kinsale.

It includes Bantry Bay and the village of Blarney. There is a series of ridges and vales running NE-SW across the county. The Nagles and Boggeraph mountains run across the centre, separating the two main rivers, the Blackwater and the Lee. Towns are Cobh, Bantry, Youghal, Fermoy, and Mallow. Natural gas, found off the S coast at Kinsale, is supplied to Northern Ireland.

Cork city and seaport of county Cork, on the river Lee, at the head of the long inlet of Cork Harbour; population (1986) 174,000. Cork is the second port of the Republic of Ireland. The lower section of the harbour can berth liners, and the town has distilleries, shipyards, and iron foundries. St Finbarr's seventh-century monastery was the original foundation of Cork. It was eventually settled by Danes who were dispossessed by the English 1172. University College (1845) became the University of Cork 1968. The city hall was opened 1937. There is a Protestant cathedral dedicated to the city's patron saint, St Finbarr, and a Roman Catholic cathedral of St Mary and St Finbarr.

Corniche (French 'mountain ledge') *la Grande* (Great) *Corniche*, a road with superb alpine and coastal scenery, built between Nice and Menton, S France, by Napoleon; it rises to 520 m/1,700 ft. *La Moyenne* (Middle) and *la Petite* (Little) *Corniche* are supplementary parallel roads, the latter being nearest the coast.

Cornwall county in SW England including ◊Scilly Islands (Scillies)

area (excluding Scillies) 3,550 sq km/1,370 sq mi

towns administrative headquarters Truro; Camborne, Launceston; resorts of Bude, Falmouth, Newquay, Penzance, St Ives

physical Bodmin Moor (including Brown Willy 419 m/1,375 ft), Land's End peninsula, St Michael's Mount, rivers Tamar, Fowey, Fal, and Camel

features Poldhu, site of first transatlantic radio signal 1901. The Stannary has six members from each of the four Stannary towns: Losthwithiel, Launceston, Helston, and Truro. The flag of St Piran, a white St George's cross on a black ground, is used by separatists

products electronics; spring flowers; tin (mined since Bronze Age, some workings renewed in

Cornwall

1960s, though the industry has all but disappeared), kaolin (St Austell); fish

population (1987) 453,000

famous people John Betjeman, Humphry Davy, Daphne Du Maurier, William Golding

history the Stannary or Tinners' Parliament, established in the 11th century, ceased to meet 1752 but its powers were never rescinded at Westminster, and it was revived 1974 as a separatist movement.

Coromandel the east coast of Tamil Nadu, India.

Coromandel Peninsula peninsula on North Island, New Zealand, east of Auckland.

Corrèze river of central France flowing 89 km/55 mi from the Plateau des Millevaches, past Tulle, capital of Corrèze *département* (to which it gives its name), to join the Vézère. It is used for generating electricity at Bar, 9.5 km/6 mi NW of Tulle.

Corrientes city of Argentina, on the Paraná river; population (1980) 180,000. Capital of Corrientes province, it is an important river port in a stock-raising district. Industries include tanning, sawmilling and textiles.

Corse French name for ◊Corsica.

Corsica (French *Corse*) island region of France, in the Mediterranean off the W coast of Italy, north of Sardinia; it comprises the *départements* of Haute Corse and Corse du Sud

area 8,700 sq km/3,358 sq mi

capital and port Ajaccio

features maquis vegetation; its mountain bandits were eradicated 1931, but the tradition of the vendetta or blood feud lingers; it is the main base of the Foreign Legion

government its special status involves a 61-member regional parliament with the power to

Corsica

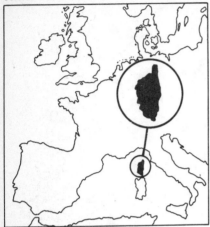

scrutinize French National Assembly bills applicable to the island and propose amendments

exports wine, olive oil

population (1986) 249,000, of whom just under 50% are native Corsicans; there are about 400,000 *émigrés*, mostly in Mexico and Central America, who return to retire

language French (official); the majority speak Corsican, an Italian dialect

famous people Napoleon

history the Phocaeans of Ionia founded Alalia about 570 BC, and were succeeded in turn by the Etruscans, the Carthaginians, the Romans, the Vandals, and the Arabs. In the 14th century, Corsica fell to the Genoese, and in the second half of the 18th century a Corsican nationalist, Pasquale Paoli (1725–1807), led an independence movement. Genoa sold Corsica to France 1768. In World War II Corsica was occupied by Italy 1942–43. From 1962, French *pieds noir* (refugees from Algeria), especially vine growers, were settled in Corsica, and their prosperity helped to fan nationalist feeling, which demands an independent Corsica. This fuelled a 'national liberation front' (FNLC), banned 1983.

Cortona town in Tuscany, N Italy, 22 km/13 mi SE of Arezzo; population (1981) 22,000. One of Europe's oldest cities. It is encircled by walls built by the Etruscans, and has a medieval castle and an 11th-century cathedral.

Corunna (Spanish *La Coruña*) city in the extreme NW of Spain; population (1986) 242,000. It is the capital of Corunna province. Industry is centred upon the fisheries; tobacco, sugar refining, and textiles are also important. The Armada sailed from Corunna 1588, and the town was sacked by Francis Drake 1589.

Cos alternative spelling of ◊Kos, a Greek island.

Cosenza town in Calabria, S Italy; at the junction of the river crati and the river Busento; population (1988) 106,000. It is the capital of Cosenza province and is an archiepiscopal see. Alaric, king of the Visigoths, is buried here.

Cossyra ancient name for ◊Pantelleria, Italian island in the Mediterranean.

Costa Rica country in Central America, bounded to the N by Nicaragua, to the S by Panama, to the E by the Caribbean, and to the W by the Pacific Ocean.

Côte d'Azur the Mediterranean coast from Menton to St Tropez, France, renowned for its beaches; part of ◊Provence-Côte d'Azur.

Cotonou chief port and largest city of Benin, on the Bight of Benin; population (1982) 487,000. Palm products and timber are exported. Although not the official capital, it is the seat of the president, and the main centre of commerce and politics.

Cotopaxi an active volcano, situated to the south of Quito in Ecuador. It is 5,897 m/19,347 ft high, and was first climbed 1872. Its name is Quechua for 'shining peak'.

Cotswolds range of hills in Avon-Gloucestershire, England, some 80 km/50 mi long, between Bristol and Chipping Camden. They rise to 333 m/1,086 ft at Cleeve Cloud, but average about 200 m/600 ft.

Cottbus capital of Cottbus county, East Germany, on the Spree river SE of Berlin; population (1986) 126,000. Industries include textiles and carpets. Cottbus county has an area of 8,260 sq km/3,188 sq mi, and a population of 883,000.

Courtrai (Flemish *Kortrijk*) town in Belgium on the river Lys, in West Flanders; population (1985) 76,110. It is connected by canal with the coast, and by river and canal with Antwerp and Brussels. It has a large textile industry, especially damask, linens, and lace.

Covent Garden London square (named from the convent garden once on the site) laid out by Inigo Jones in 1631. The buildings which formerly housed London's fruit and vegetable market (moved to Nine Elms, Wandsworth, in 1973) were adapted for shops and leisure. The Royal Opera House, also housing the Royal Ballet, is here, also the London Transport Museum. The Theatre Museum, opened 1987, is in the Old Flower Market.

Coventry industrial city in West Midlands, England; population (1981) 313,800. Manufacturing includes cars, electronic equipment, machine tools, and agricultural machinery.

history it originated when Leofric, Earl of Mercia and husband of Lady Godiva, founded a priory in 1043. Its modern industry began with bicycle manufacture in 1870. Features include the cathedral, designed by Basil Spence, and incorporating the steeple of the church built 1373–95 and destroyed in an air raid Nov 1940; St Mary's

Costa Rica
Republic of
(República de Costa Rica)

area 51,100 sq km/19,725 sq mi
capital San José
towns ports Limón, Puntarenas
physical high central plateau and tropical coast
head of state and government Oscar Arias Sánchez from 1986
political system liberal democracy
political parties National Liberation Party (PLN), left-of-centre; Christian Socialist Unity Party (PUSC), centrist
exports coffee, bananas, cocoa, sugar
currency colón (144.88 = £1 Feb 1990)
population (1988) 2,810,000 (including 1,200 Guaymí Indians); annual growth rate 2.6%
life expectancy men 71, women 76
language Spanish
religion Roman Catholic
literacy 94% male/93% female (1985 est)
GDP $2 bn (1982); $2,238 per head of population
chronology
1821 Independence achieved.
1949 New constitution adopted. National army abolished. José Figueres, co-founder of the PLN, elected president. He embarked on an ambitious socialist programme.
1958–73 Mainly Conservative administrations returned.
1974 PLN regained the presidency and returned to socialist policies.
1978 Rodrigo Carazo, Conservative, elected president. Sharp deterioration in the state of the economy.
1982 Luis Alberto Monge of the PLN elected president. Harsh austerity programme introduced to rebuild the economy. Pressure from the USA to abandon neutral stance and condemn the Sandinista regime in Nicaragua.
1983 Policy of neutrality reaffirmed.
1985 Following border clashes with Sandinista forces, a US-trained anti-guerrilla guard was formed.
1986 Oscar Arias Sánchez won the presidency on a neutralist platform.
1987 Oscar Arias Sánchez awarded Nobel Peace Prize.
1990 Rafael Calderón (PUSC) elected president.

Hall, built 1394–1414 as a guild centre; two gates of the old city walls 1356; Belgrade Theatre 1958; Art Gallery and Museum; Museum of British Road Transport, and Lanchester Polytechnic.

Cowes seaport and resort on the north coast of the Isle of Wight, England, on the Medina estuary, opposite Southampton Water; population (1981) 19,500. It is the headquarters of the Royal Yacht Squadron which holds the annual Cowes Regatta, and has maritime industries. In East Cowes is Osborne House, a favoured residence of Queen Victoria, now used as a museum.

Cracow alternative form of ◊Kraków, Polish city.

Craigavon town in Armagh, Northern Ireland; population (1981) 73,000. It was created from 1965 by the merging of Lurgan and Portadown, and named after the first prime minister of Northern Ireland.

Craiova town in S Romania, near the river Jiu; population (1985) 275,000. Industries include electrical engineering, food processing, textiles, fertilisers, and farm machinery.

Crater Lake lake in the centre of Chubb Crater, Oregon, USA.

Crawley town in West Sussex, England, NE of Horsham; population (1981) 73,000. It was chartered by King John 1202, and developed as a 'new town' from 1946. Industries include plastics, engineering, and printing.

Cremona city in Italy, Lombardy, on the river Po, 72 km/45 mi SE of Milan; population (1981) 81,000. It is the capital of Cremona province. Once a famous violin-making centre, it now produces food products and textiles. It has a 12th-century cathedral.

Crete (Greek *Kríti*) the largest Greek island, in the E Mediterranean Sea, 100 km/62 mi SE of Greece
area 8,378 sq km/3,234 sq mi
capital Iráklion
towns Khaniá (Canea), Rethymnon, Aghios Nikolaos

Crete

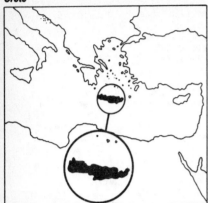

products citrus fruit, olives, wine
population (1981) 502,000
language Cretan dialect of Greek
history it has remains of the Minoan civilization 3000–1400 BC, including the palace of Knossos, and was successively under Roman, Byzantine, Venetian, and Turkish rule. The island was annexed by Greece 1913. In 1941, it was captured by German forces from Allied troops who had retreated from the mainland, and was retaken by the Allies 1944.

Creuse river in central France flowing 255 km/158 mi generally N from the Plateau des Millevaches to the Vienne river. It traverses Creuse *département*, to which it gives its name.

Creusot, Le town in Saône-et-Loire *département*, France; population (1982) 32,100. It is a coal mining centre and has foundries, locomotive shops, and armaments factories.

Crewe town in Cheshire, England; population (1981) 59,300. It owed its growth to its position as a railway junction. At Crewe are the chief construction workshops of British Rail. Other occupations include chemical works, clothing factories and vehicles.

Crimea N peninsula on the Black Sea, a region of ◊Ukraine Republic, USSR, from 1954.
area 27,000 sq km/10,425 sq mi
capital Simferopol
towns Sevastopol, Yalta
features mainly steppe, but the southern coast is a holiday resort
products iron, oil
recent history under Turkish rule 1475–1774, a subsequent brief independence was ended by Russian annexation 1783. It was the republic of Taurida 1917–20, and the Crimean Autonomous Soviet Republic from 1920 until occupied by Germany July 1942–May 1944. It was then reduced to a region, its Tatar people being deported

to Uzbekistan for collaboration. Although they were exonerated 1967, and some were allowed to return, others were forcibly re-exiled 1979.

Croatia (Serbo-Croat *Hrvatska*) constituent republic of Yugoslavia
area 56,500 sq km/21,809 sq mi
capital Zagreb
physical Adriatic coastline with large islands; very mountainous, with part of the Karst region and the Julian and Styrian Alps; some marshland
population (1985) 4,660,000 including 3,500,000 Croats, 530,000 Serbs, and 25,000 Hungarians
language the Croatian variant of Serbo-Croat
history part of Pannonia in Roman times; settled by Carpathian Croats 7th century; for 800 years from 1102 an autonomous kingdom under the Hungarian crown; Austrian crownland 1849; Hungarian crownland 1868; included in the kingdom of the Serbs, Croats, and Slovenes (called Yugoslavia from 1931) 1918; Nazi puppet state during World War II; it has remained a centre for nationalist and separatist demands from the 1970s.

Croydon borough of S London, England; it includes the suburbs of Croydon, Purley, and Coulsdon
features 11th-century Lanfranc's palace, former residence of archbishops of Canterbury; Ashcroft Theatre, founded 1962; overspill office development from central London
industries engineering, electronics, foodstuffs, pharmaceuticals
population (1981) 316,557.

CT abbreviation for ◊*Connecticut*.

Cuba island in the Caribbean, the largest of the West Indies, off the south coast of Florida.

Cubango Portuguese name for the ◊Okavango river in Africa.

Cúcuta capital of Norte de Santander department, NE Colombia; population (1985) 379,000. It is situated in a tax-free zone close to the Venezuelan border, and trades in coffee, tobacco, and cattle. It was a focal point of the independence movement, and meeting place of the first Constituent Congress 1821.

Cuenca city in S Ecuador; population (1980) 140,000. It is capital of Azuay province. Industries include chemicals, food processing, agricultural machinery and textiles. It was founded by the Spanish in 1557.

Cuenca city in Spain, at the confluence of the rivers Júcar and Huécar; 135 km/84 mi SE of Madrid; population (1981) 42,000. It is the capital of Cuenca province. It has a 13th-century cathedral.

Cuiaba town in Brazil, on the Cuiaba river; population (1980) 168,000. It is the capital of Mato Grosso state. Gold and diamonds are worked nearby.

Culham village near Oxford, England, site of a British nuclear research establishment.

Cuba
Republic of
(República de Cuba)

area 114,524 sq km/44,206 sq mi
capital Havana
physical comprises Cuba, the largest and westernmost of the West Indian islands, and smaller islands including Isle of Youth; low hills; Sierra Maestra mountains in E
features US base (on perpetual lease since 1934) at Guantánamo Bay (Gitmo), and Soviet base at Cienfuegos
head of state and government Fidel Castro Ruz from 1959
political system communist republic
political parties Communist Party of Cuba (PCC); Marxist-Leninist
exports sugar (largest producer after USSR), tobacco, coffee, iron, copper, nickel
currency Cuban peso (1.36 = £1 Feb 1990, official rate)
population (1987) 10,240,000 (plus 125,000 refugees from the Cuban port of Mariel – *marielitos* – in US); 66% are of Spanish descent, and a large number are of African origin; annual growth rate 0.6%
life expectancy men 72, women 75
language Spanish
religion Roman Catholic 45%
literacy 96% male/95% female (1979)
disposable national income $15.8 bn (1983);

$1,590 per head of population
chronology
1901 Cuba achieved independence.
1933 Fulgencia Batista seized power.
1944 Batista retired.
1952 Batista seized power again to begin an oppressive regime.
1953 Fidel Castro led an unsuccessful coup against Batista.
1956 Castro led a second unsuccessful coup.
1959 Batista overthrown by Castro. Constitution of 1940 replaced by a 'Fundamental Law', making Castro prime minister, his brother Raul Castro his deputy, and Ché Guevara his number three.
1960 All US businesses in Cuba appropriated without compensation. US broke off diplomatic relations.
1961 US sponsored an unsuccessful invasion, the Bay of Pigs episode. Castro announced that Cuba had become a communist state, with a Marxist-Leninist programme of economic development.
1962 Cuba expelled from the Organization of American States (OAS). Soviet nuclear missiles removed from Cuba at US insistence.
1965 Cuba's sole political party renamed Cuban Communist Party (PCC). With Soviet help, Cuba began to make considerable economic and social progress.
1972 Cuba became a full member of the Moscow-based Council for Mutual Economic Assistance (CMEA).
1976 New socialist constitution approved and Castro elected president.
1976–81 Castro became involved in extensive international commitments, assisting Third World countries, particularly in Africa.
1982 Cuba joined other Latin American countries in giving moral support to Argentina in its dispute with Britain.
1984 Castro tried to improve US-Cuban relations by discussing the exchange of US prisoners in Cuba with Cuban 'undesirables' in the US.
1988 Peace accord with South Africa signed, agreeing to withdrawal of Cuban troops from Angola.
1989 Reduction in Cuba's overseas military activities.

Culiacán Rosales capital of Sinaloa state, NW Mexico; population (1980) 560,000. It trades in vegetables and textiles.

Cumberland former county of NW England, merged in 1974 with ◊Cumbria.

After the Roman withdrawal, Cumberland became part of Strathclyde, a British kingdom.

In 945 it passed to Scotland, in 1157 to England, and until the union of the English and Scottish crowns in 1603 Cumberland was the scene of frequent battles between the two countries.

Cumbernauld new town in Strathclyde, Scotland; 18 km/11 mi from Glasgow; population (1981) 48,000. It was founded 1955 to take in city

Cyprus

divided between the southern
Republic of Cyprus (Greek
Kypriaki Dimokratia), and the Turkish
**Republic of Northern
Cyprus** (Turkish *Kibris Cumhuriyeti)*

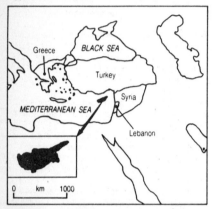

area 9,251 sq km/3,571 sq mi, 37% in Turkish
hands
capital Nicosia (divided between the Greeks
and Turks)
towns ports Paphos, Limassol, and Larnaca
(Greek); and Morphou, and ports Kyrenia and
Famagusta (Turkish)
physical central plain between two E–W
mountain ranges
features Attila Line; two British military
enclaves on the S coast at Episkopi (includes
Royal Air Force Akrotiri) and Dhekelia; there is
also an outpost of British Government Communications Headquarters in the mountains
heads of state and government Georgios
Vassilou (Greek) from 1988, Rauf Denktaş
(Turkish) from 1976
political system democratic divided republic
political parties Democratic Front (DIKO),
centre-left; Progressive Party of the Working
People (AKEL), socialist; Democratic Rally
(DISY) , centrist; Socialist Party (EDEK),
socialist
exports citrus, grapes, Cyprus sherry,

potatoes, copper, pyrites
currency Cyprus pound (0.79 = £1 Feb 1990)
population (1987) 680,400 (Greek Cypriot
81%, Turkish Cypriot 19%); annual growth
rate 1.2%
life expectancy men 72, women 76
language Greek and Turkish (official); English
religion Greek Orthodox, Sunni Muslim
literacy 99% (1984)
GNP $2.11 bn (1983); $3,986 per head of
population
chronology
1955 Guerrilla campaign for *enosis*, or union
with Greece, started by Archbishop Makarios
and Gen Grivas.
1956 Makarios and *enosis* leaders deported.
1959 Compromise agreed and Makarios
returned to be elected president of an
independent Greek-Turkish Cyprus.
1960 Full independence achieved, with Britain
retaining its military bases.
1963 Turks set up their own government in N
Cyprus. Fighting broke out between the two
communities.
1964 UN peacekeeping force installed.
1971 Grivas returned to start a guerrilla war
against the Makarios government.
1974 Grivas died. A military coup deposed
Makarios, who fled to Britain. Nicos Sampson
appointed president. Turkish army sent to N
Cyprus to confirm the Turkish Cypriots' control.
The military regime in S Cyprus collapsed and
Makarios returned. N Cyprus declared itself the
Turkish Federated State of Cyprus (TFSC), with
Rauf Denktaş as president.
1977 Makarios died and was succeeded by
Spyros Kyprianou.
1983 An independent Turkish Republic of
Northern Cyprus (TRNC) was proclaimed but
was recognized only by Turkey.
1984 UN peace proposals rejected.
1985 Summit meeting between Kyprianou and
Denktaş failed to reach agreement.
1988 Georgios Vassilou elected president.
Talks with Denktaş, under UN auspices, began.
1989 Vassilou and Denktaş agreed to draft an
agreement for the future reunification of the
island, but peace talks abandoned in Sept.

overspill. In 1966 it won a prize as the world's
best-designed community.
Cumbria county in NW England
area 6,810 sq km/2,629 sq mi
towns administrative headquarters Carlisle; Barrow, Kendal, Whitehaven, Workington, Pennith
physical Lake District National Park, including
Scafell Pike 978 m/3,210 ft, highest mountain in

England; Helvellyn 950 m/3,118 ft; Lake Windermere, the largest lake in England, 17 km/10.5 mi
long, 1.6 km/1 mi wide
features the Grizedale Forest sculpture project is
nearby; other lakes including Derwentwater, Ullswater; Furness peninsula; atomic stations at Calder
Hall and Sellafield (reprocessing plant), formerly
Windscale (site of a nuclear accident Oct 1957)

Cumbria

products the traditional coal, iron, and steel of the coast towns has been replaced by newer industries including chemicals, plastics, and electronics; in the N and E there is dairying, and West Cumberland Farmers is the country's largest agricultural cooperative
population (1987) 487,000
famous people birthplace of Wordsworth at Cockermouth, and home at Grasmere; homes of Coleridge and Southey at Keswick; Ruskin's home, Brantwood, on Coniston Water; de Quincey.

Cunene or **Kunene** river rising near Nova Lisboa in W central Angola. It flows S to the frontier with Namibia then W to the Atlantic. Length 250 km/156 mi.

Curaçao island in the West Indies, one of the ◊Netherlands Antilles; area 444 sq km/171 sq mi; population (1981) 147,000. The principal industry, dating from 1918, is the refining of Venezuelan petroleum. Curaçao was colonized by Spain 1527, annexed by the Dutch West India Company 1634, and gave its name from 1924 to the group of islands renamed Netherlands Antilles in 1948. Its capital is the port of Willemstad.

Curitiba city in Brazil, on the Curitiba river; population (1980) 844,000. The capital of Paraná state, it dates from 1654. It has a university (1912) and makes paper, furniture, textiles, and chemicals. Coffee, timber and maté are exported.

Curragh, the plain in County Kildare, Republic of Ireland. It is the headquarters of Irish racing and site of the national stud.

Cuttack city and river port in E India; on the Mahanadi river delta; population (1981) 327,500. It was the capital of Orissa state until 1950. The old fort (Kataka) from which the town takes its name is in ruins.

Cuxhaven seaport in Germany on the S side of the Elbe estuary, at its entrance into the North Sea; population (1983) 57,800. It acts as an outport for Hamburg.

Cuzco city in S Peru, capital of Cuzco department, in the Andes, over 3,350 m/11,000 ft above sea

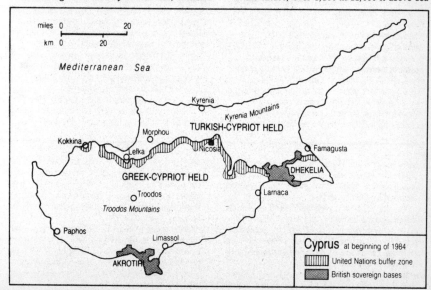

Czechoslovakia
Socialist Republic of
*(Československá Socialistická
Republika)*

area 127,903 sq km/49,371 sq mi
capital Prague
towns Brno, Bratislava, Ostrava
physical Carpathian Mountains, rivers Morava,
Labe (Elbe), Vltava (Moldau); hills and plateau;
Danube plain in S
features divided by valley of the Morava
into the W, densely populated area with
good communications, and the E, sparsely
populated, comparatively little-developed
Slovak area
head of state Vaclav Havel from 1989
head of government Marion Calfa from 1989
political system socialist pluralist republic
political parties Communist Party of Czechoslovakia (CCP), Marxist-Leninist; Civic Forum,
Czech pluralist reform coalition; Public Against
Violence, Slovak pluralist reform coalition;
Agrarian Party, farmers' party supporting
collectivization; Czechoslovak Socialist Party

and Czechoslovak Freedom Party, pre-1989
allies of CCP; Green Party
exports machinery, timber, ceramics, glass,
textiles
currency koruna (61.11 commercial rate, 27.96
tourist rate = £1 Feb 1990)
population (1986) 15,521,000 (63% Czech,
31% Slovak, with Hungarian, Polish, German,
Russian, and other minorities); annual growth
rate 0.4%
life expectancy men 68, women 75
language Czech and Slovak (official)
religion 75% Roman Catholic, 15% Protestant
literacy 99% (1981)
GNP $85.8 bn (1982); $5,800 per head of
population
chronology
1945 Liberation of Czechoslovakia.
1948 Communists assumed power in coup and
new constitution framed.
1968 Prague Spring experiment with
liberalization ended by Soviet invasion.
1969 Czechoslovakia became a federal state.
Husák elected Communist Party leader.
1977 Emergence and suppression of Charter
77 human-rights movement.
1985–86 Criticism of Husák rule by new Soviet
leadership.
1987 Husák resigned as Communist leader;
replaced by Miloš Jakeš.
1988 Personnel overhaul of party and state
bodies, including replacement of Prime Minister
Štrougal by the technocrat Adamec.
1989 Communist regime of Jakeš, Husák, and
Adamec overthrown in Nov-Dec bloodless 'gen-
tle revolution' following mass pro-democracy
protests in Prague and throughout the country,
directed by the newly formed Civic Forum.
Communist monopoly of power ended, with
'Grand Coalition' government formed. Václav
Havel appointed president and Alexander
Dubček chair of national parliament.
1990 22,000 prisoners released (Jan). Havel
announced agreement with USSR for complete
withdrawal of Soviet troops by May 1991 (Feb).

---

level and 560 km/350 mi SE of Lima; population
(1988) 255,000. It was founded in the 11th century
as the ancient capital of the Inca empire, and was
captured by Pizarro 1533.

The university was founded 1598. The city has
a Renaissance cathedral and other relics of the
early Spanish conquerors. There are many Inca
remains and in the 1970s and 1980s the Inca
irrigation canals and terracing nearby were being
restored to increase cultivation.

Cwmbran (Welsh 'Vale of the Crow') town in Wales,
NW of Newport, on the Afon Lywel, a tributary

of river Usk; population (1981) 45,000. It is the
administrative headquarters of Gwent. It was
established in 1949 to provide a focus for new
industrial growth in a depressed area, producing
scientific instruments, car components, nylon, and
biscuits.

Cyclades group of about 200 Greek islands (Greek
Kikládhes) in the Aegean Sea, lying between
Greece and Turkey; area 2,579 sq km/996 sq mi;
population (1981) 88,500. They include Andros,
Melos, Paros, Naxos, and Siros, on which is the
capital Hermoupolis.

Cymru Celtic name for ◊Wales.

Cyprus island in the Mediterranean, off the S coast of Turkey.

Czechoslovakia landlocked country in E central Europe, bounded to the NE by Poland, E by the USSR, S by Hungary and Austria, W by West Germany, and NW by East Germany.

Częstochowa town in Poland, on the river Vistula; 193 km/120 mi SW of Warsaw; population (1985) 247,000. It produces iron goods, chemicals, paper, and cement. The basilica of Jasna Góra is a centre for Catholic pilgrims (it contains the painting known as the Black Madonna).

Dacca former spelling (until 1984) of ◊Dhaka, capital of Bangladesh.

Dacia ancient region forming much of modern Romania. The various Dacian tribes were united around 60 BC, and for many years posed a threat to the Roman empire; they were finally conquered by the Roman emperor Trajan AD 101–106, and the region became a province of the same name. It was abandoned to the invading Goths in about 275.

Dadra and Nagar Haveli since 1961 a Union Territory of W India; capital Silvassa; area 490 sq km/189 sq mi; population (1981) 104,000. Formerly part of Portuguese Daman. It produces rice, wheat, millet, and timber.

Dagestan autonomous republic of western USSR, situated E of the Caucasus, bordering the Caspian Sea. Capital Makhachkala; area 50,300 sq km/14,700 sq mi; population (1982) 1,700,000. It is mountainous, with deep valleys, and its numerous ethnic groups speak a variety of distinct languages. Annexed from Iran in 1723, which strongly resisted Russian conquest, it became an autonomous republic in 1921.

Dairen former name for the Chinese port of Dalian, part of ◊Lüda.

Dakar capital and chief port (with artificial harbour) of Senegal; population (1984) 1,000,000.

It is an industrial centre, and there is a university 1957. Founded 1862, it was formerly the seat of government of French West Africa. In July 1940 an unsuccessful naval action was undertaken by British and Free French forces to seize Dakar as an Allied base.

Dakota see ◊North Dakota and ◊South Dakota.

Dalian one of the two cities comprising the Chinese port of ◊Lüda.

Dallas commercial city in Texas, USA; population (1980) 904,000, metropolitan area (with Fort Worth) 2,964,000. Industries include banking, insurance, oil, aviation, aerospace and electronics. Dallas-Fort Worth Regional Airport (opened 1973) is one of the world's largest. John F Kennedy was assassinated in Dallas 1963.

It is a cultural centre, with a symphony orchestra, opera, ballet, and theatre; there is an annual Texas State Fair. Founded as a trading post 1844, it developed as the focus of a cotton area, and then as a mineral and oil-producing centre, with banking and insurance operations. After World War II growth increased rapidly.

Dalmatia region of Croatia, Bosnia and Herzegovina, and Montenegro in Yugoslavia. The capital is Split. It lies along the eastern shore of the Adriatic and includes a number of islands. The interior is mountainous. Important products are wine, olives, and fish. Notable towns in addition to the capital are Zadar, Sibenik, and Dubrovnik.

history Dalmatia became Austrian 1815, and by the treaty of Rapallo 1920 became part of the kingdom of the Serbs, Croats, and Slovenes (Yugoslavia from 1931), except for the town of Zadar (Zara), and the island of Lastovo (Lagosta), which, with neighbouring islets, were given to Italy until transferred to Yugoslavia 1947. Dalmatia was made a region of Croatia 1949.

Daman or *Dama*part of the Union Territory of Daman and ◊Diu; area 110 sq km/42 sq mi; capital Panaji; population (1981) 79,000. Daman has an area of 72 sq km/28 sq mi and a population (1981) 49,000. The town of Daman is a port on the W coast of India, 160 km/100 mi north of Bombay; population (1981) 21,000. Daman was seized by Portugal 1531 and ceded to Portugal by the Shar of Gujarat 1539. It was annexed by India 1961 and was part of the Union Territory of ◊Goa, Daman, and Diu until Goa became a separate state 1987. The economy is based on tourism and fishing.

Damaraland central region of Namibia, home of the nomadic Bantu-speaking Hereros.

Damascus (Arabic *Dimashq*) capital of Syria, on the river Barada, SE of Beirut; population (1981) 1,251,000. It produces silk, wood products, and brass and copper ware. Said to be the oldest continuously inhabited city in the world, Damascus was an ancient city even in Old Testament times; most notable of the old buildings is the Great Mosque, completed as a Christian church in the 5th century.

The Assyrians destroyed it about 733 BC. In 332 BC it fell to one of the generals of Alexander the Great; in 63 BC it came under Roman rule. In AD 635 it was taken by the Arabs, and has since been captured many times, by Egyptians, Mongolians, and Turks. In 1918, during World War I, it was taken from the Turks by the British with Arab aid, and in

Danube

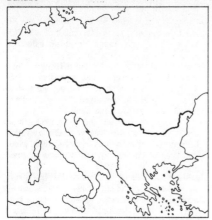

Dardanelles

1920 became the capital of French-mandated Syria.

The 'street which is called straight' is associated with St Paul, who was converted while on the road to Damascus. The tomb of Saladin is here. The fortress dates from 1219.

Damietta English name for the Egyptian port of ◊Dumyat.

Damodar Indian river flowing 560 km/350 mi from Chota Nagpur plateau in Bihar, through Bihar and West Bengal states to join the ◊Hooghly River 40 km/25 mi SW of Calcutta. The Damodar Valley is an industrial centre with a hydroelectric project, combined with irrigation works.

Da Nang formerly *Tourane* port and second city of S Vietnam, 80 km/50 mi SE of Hué; population (1975) 500,000. Following the reunion of North and South Vietnam, the major part of the population was dispersed 1976 to rural areas. A US base in the Vietnam War, it is now used by the USSR.

Danube (German *Donau*) second longest of European rivers, rising on the east slopes of the Black Forest, and flowing 2,858 km/1,776 mi across Europe to enter the Black Sea in Romania by a swampy delta.

The head of river navigation is Ulm, in Baden-Württemberg; Braila, Romania, is the limit for ocean-going ships. Cities on the Danube include Linz, Vienna, Bratislava, Budapest, Belgrade, Ruse, Braila, and Galati. A canal connects the Danube with the ◊Main, and thus with the Rhine system. Plans to dam the river for hydroelectric power at Nagymaros in Hungary, with participation by Austria and Czechoslovakia, were abandoned on environmental grounds 1989.

Danzig German name for the Polish port of ◊Gdańsk.

Dardanelles (ancient name *Hellespont*; Turkish name *Canakkale Boğazi*) Turkish strait connecting the Sea of Marmara with the Aegean Sea; its shores are formed by the ◊Gallipoli peninsula on the NW and the mainland of Turkey-in-Asia on the SE. It is 75 km/47 mi long and 5–6 km/3–4 mi wide.

Dar el-Beida Arabic name for the port of ◊Casablanca, Morocco.

Dar es Salaam (Arabic 'haven of peace') chief seaport in Tanzania, on the Indian Ocean, and capital of Tanzania until its replacement by ◊Dodoma in 1974; population (1985) 1,394,000.

It is the Indian Ocean terminus of the TanZam Railway, and a line also runs to the lake port of Kigoma; a road links it with Ndola in the Zambian copperbelt, and oil is carried to Zambia by pipeline from Dar es Salaam's refineries. University College (1963) became the University of Dar es Salaam in 1970.

Darfur province in the west of the Republic of Sudan; area 196,555 sq km/75,920 sq mi; population (1983) 3,093,699. The capital is El Fasher (population 30,000). The area is a vast rolling plain producing gum arabic, and there is also some stock raising. Darfur was an independent sultanate until conquered by Egypt in 1874.

Darien former name for the Panama isthmus as a whole, and still the name of an eastern province of Panama; area 16,803 sq km/6,490 sq mi; population (1980) 26,500. The *Gulf of Darien*, part of the Caribbean, lies between Panama and Colombia. The *Darien Gap* is the complex of swamp, jungle and ravines, which long prevented the linking of the North and South American sections of the Pan-American Highway, stretching about 300 km/200 mi between Canitas, Panama, and Chigorodo, Colombia. At the Colombian end is the Great Atrato Swamp, 60 km/35 mi across and over 300 m/1,000 ft deep.

Darjeeling town and health resort in West Bengal, India; situated 2,150 m/7,000 ft above sea level, on the southern slopes of the Himalayas; population (1981) 57,600. It is connected by rail with Calcutta, 595 km/370 mi to the south. It is the centre of a tea-producing district.

Darkhan or *Darhan* industrial town in Outer Mongolia, near the border with the USSR; population (1988) 80,000. Cement and bricks are made, and to the south is Erdenet, where copper and molybdenum are mined.

Darling river in SE Australia, a tributary of the Murray, which it joins at Wentworth. It is 3,075 km/1,910 mi long and its waters are conserved in Menindee Lake 155 sq km/60 sq mi, and others nearby. The name comes from Sir Ralph Darling (1775–1858), governor of New South Wales 1825–31. The *Darling Range*, a ridge in W Australia, has a highest point of about 582 m/1,669. The *Darling Downs* in SE Queensland is an agricultural and stockraising area.

Darlington town in Durham, England, on the river Skerne, near its junction with the Tees; population (1981) 85,400. It has coal and ironstone mines, and produces iron and steel goods, and knitting wool. The world's first passenger railway was opened between Darlington and Stockton on 27 Sept 1825.

Darmstadt town in the *Land* of Hessen, West Germany, 29 km/18 mi south of Frankfurt-am-Main; population (1988) 134,000. Industries include iron founding, and the manufacture of chemicals, plastics, and electronics. It is a centre of the European space industry. It has a ducal palace and a technical university.

Dartford industrial town in Kent, England, 27 km/17 mi SE of London; population (1981) 42,000. Cement, chemicals, and paper are manufactured. The *Dartford Tunnel* (1963) runs under the Thames to Purfleet, Essex.

Dartmoor plateau of SW Devon, England, over 1,000 sq km/400 sq mi in extent, of which half is some 300 m/1,000 ft above sea level. Most of Dartmoor is a National Park. The moor is noted for its wild aspect, and rugged blocks of granite, or 'tors', crown its higher points, the highest being *Yes Tor* 618 m/2,028 ft and *High Willhays* 621 m/2,039 ft. Devon's chief rivers have their sources on Dartmoor. There are numerous prehistoric remains. Near Hemerdon there are tungsten reserves.

Dartmoor Prison, opened in 1809 originally to house French prisoners-of-war, is at Princetown in the centre of the moor, 11 km/7 mi east of Tavistock.

Dartmouth English seaport at the mouth of the river Dart; 43 km/27 mi east of Plymouth, on the Devon coast; population (1981) 62,298. It is a centre for yachting, and has an excellent harbour. The Britannia Royal Naval College dates from 1905.

Dartmouth port in Nova Scotia, Canada, on the NE of Halifax harbour; population (1986) 65,300. It is virtually part of the capital city itself. Industries include oil refining and shipbuilding.

Darwin capital and port in Northern Territory, Australia, in NW Arnhem Land; population (1986) 69,000. It serves the uranium mining site at Rum Jungle to the south. Destroyed 1974 by a cyclone, the city was rebuilt on the same site.

Darwin is the north terminus of the rail line from Birdum; commercial fruit and vegetable growing is being developed in the area. Founded 1869, under the name of Palmerston, the city was renamed after Charles Darwin 1911.

Dasht-e-Kavir Desert or *Dasht-i-Davir Desert* salt desert SE of Tehran, Iran; US forces landed here in 1980 in an abortive mission to rescue hostages held at the American Embassy in Tehran.

Daugavpils (Russian *Dvinsk*) town in Latvia, USSR, on the river Daugava (west Dvina); population 1985 est.) 124,000. A fortress of the Livonian Knights 1278, it became the capital of Polish ◊Livonia. Industries include timber, textiles, engineering and food products.

Daulaghiri a mountain in the ◊Himalayas, NW of Pokhara, Nepál; it rises to 8,172 m/2,681 ft.

Davao town in the Philippine Republic, at the mouth of the Davao river on the island of Mindanao; population (1980) 611,310. It is the capital of Davao province. It is the centre of a fertile district and trades in pearls, copra, rice and corn.

Daventry town in Northamptonshire, England, 19 km/12 mi west of Northampton; population (1981) 16,200. Because of its central position, it became in 1925 the site of the BBC high-power radio transmitter. Originally specializing in footwear manufacture, it received London and Birmingham overspill from the 1950s, and developed varied light industries.

Davos town in an Alpine valley in Grisons canton, Switzerland; at 1,559 m/5,115 ft above sea level; population (1980) 10,500. It is recognised as a health resort and as a winter sports centre.

Dawson City town in Canada, capital until 1953 of ◊Yukon Territory, at the junction of the Yukon and Klondike rivers; population (1986) 1,700. It was founded 1896, at the time of the Klondike gold rush, when its population was 25,000.

Dawson Creek town in British Columbia, Canada; population (1981) 11,500. It is the south east terminus of the Alaska Highway.

Dayton city in Ohio, USA; population (1980) 830,000. It produces precision machinery, household appliances, and electrical equipment. It has an aeronautical research centre and a Roman Catholic university, and was the home of aviators Wilbur and Orville Wright.

Delaware

Dayton small town in Tennessee, USA, notorious as the scene of the Scopes monkey trial 1925.

Daytona Beach US resort on the Atlantic coast of Florida; population (1980) 54,176. It is a motor-racing centre.

DE abbreviation for ◊*Delaware*.

Dead Sea large lake, partly in Israel and partly in Jordan; area 1,020 sq km/394 sq mi; lying 394 m/1,293 ft below sea-level. The chief river entering it is the Jordan; it has no outlet to the sea, and the water is very salty.

Since both Israel and Jordan are using the waters of the Jordan river, the Dead Sea is now dried up in the centre and divided into two halves, but in 1980 Israel announced a plan to link it by canal with the Mediterranean. The Dead Sea Rift is part of the fault between the African and Arab plates.

Deal port and resort on the east coast of Kent, England; population (1981) 26,000. It was one of the Cinque ports. Julius Caesar is said to have landed here in 55 BC. The castle was built by Henry VIII and houses the town museum.

Dearborn city in Michigan, USA; on the Rouge River; 16 km/10 mi SW of Detroit; population (1980) 158,366. Settled in 1795, it was the birthplace and home of Henry Ford, who built his first car factory here. Car manufacture is still the main industry. Dearborn also makes aircraft parts, steel, and bricks.

Death Valley depression 225 km/140 mi long and 6–26 km/4–16 mi wide, in SE California, USA. At 85 mi/280 ft below sea level, it is the lowest point in North America. Bordering mountains rise to 3,000 mi/10,000 ft. It is one of the world's hottest places, with an average annual rainfall of 35 mm/1.4 in.

Deauville holiday resort of Normandy in Calvados *département*, France, on the English Channel and at the mouth of the Touques, opposite Trouville; population (1982) 4,800.

Debrecen third largest city in Hungary, 193 km/120 mi E of Budapest, in the Great Plain (*Alföld*) region; population (1988) 217,000. It produces tobacco, agricultural machinery and pharmaceuticals. Kossuth declared Hungary independent of the Habsburgs here 1849.

Decatur city in central Illinois, USA, on Lake Decatur, population (1980) 94,000. It has engineering, food processing, and plastics industries. It was founded in 1829 and named after Stephen Decatur, a naval hero.

Deccan triangular tableland in eastern India, stretching between the Vindhya Hills in the north, and the Western and Eastern Ghats in the south.

Dee river in Grampian region, Scotland; length 139 km/87 mi. From its source in the Cairngorms, it flows E into the North Sea at Aberdeen (by an artificial channel). It is noted for salmon fishing. Also a river in Wales and England; length 112 km/70 mi. Rising in Lake Bala, Gwynnedd, it flows into the Irish Sea W of Chester. There is another Scottish river Dee (61 km/38 mi) in Kirkcudbright.

Dehra Dun town in Uttar Pradesh, India; population (1981) 220,530. It is the capital of Dehra Dun district. It has a military academy, a forest research institute, and a Sikh temple built in 1699.

Delaware state of NE USA; nickname the First State or Diamond State
area 5,300 sq km/2,046 sq mi
capital Dover
towns Wilmington, Newark
physical divided into two physical areas, one hilly and wooded, and the other gently undulating
features one of the most industrialized states; headquarters of the Dupont chemical firm (nylon)
population (1987) 644,000
products dairy, poultry, and market-garden produce; chemicals, motor vehicles, textiles
famous people J P Marquand
history the first settlers were Dutch and Swedes about 1638, but in 1664 the area was captured by the British. Delaware was made a separate colony 1702, and organized as a state 1776. It was one of the original 13 states of the USA.

Delft town in the Netherlands in the province of S Holland, 14 km/9 mi NW of Rotterdam; population (1984) 87,000. It produces pottery and porcelain. The Dutch nationalist leader William the Silent was murdered here in 1584. It is the birthplace of the artist Vermeer.

Delhi Union Territory of the Republic of India from 1956; capital New Delhi; area 1,500 sq km/579 sq mi; population (1981) 6,196,000. It produces grains, sugar cane, fruits, and vegetables.

Delos Greek island, smallest in the ◊Cyclades group, in the SW Aegean; area about 5 sq km/2 sq mi.

Denmark
Kingdom of
(Kongeriget Danmark)

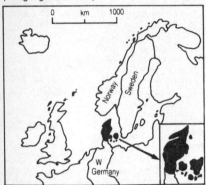

area 43,075 sq km/16,627 sq mi
capital Copenhagen
towns Aarhus, Odense, Aalborg, Esbjerg, all ports
physical the land is flat and cultivated; sand dunes and lagoons on the W coast and long inlets on the E
territories Faeroe Islands and Greenland
features comprises the peninsula of Jylland/Jutland, plus the main island Sjælland (Zealand), Fünen, Lolland, Bornholm, and smaller islands
head of state Margrethe II from 1972
head of government Poul Schlüter from 1982
political system liberal democracy
political parties Social Democrats (SD), left-of-centre; Conservative People's Party (KF), moderate centre-right; Liberal Party

(V), centre-left; Socialist People's Party (SF), moderate left-wing; Radical Liberals (RV), radical internationalist left-of-centre; Centre Democrats (CD), moderate centrist; Progress Party (FP), radical anti-bureaucratic; Christian People's Party (KrF), interdenominational, family values
exports bacon, dairy produce, eggs, fish, mink pelts, car and aircraft parts, electrical equipment, textiles
currency krone (11.00 = £1 Feb 1990)
population (1988) 5,129,000; annual growth rate 0%
life expectancy men 72, women 78
language Danish (official)
religion Lutheran
literacy 99% (1983)
GNP $50.4 bn (1983); $12,956 per head of population
chronology
1940–45 Occupied by Germany.
1945 Iceland's independence recognized.
1947 Frederik IX succeeded Christian X.
1948 Home rule granted for Faeroe Islands.
1949 Became a founder member of NATO.
1960 Joined European Free Trade Association (EFTA).
1972 Margrethe II became Denmark's first queen for nearly 600 years.
1973 Left EFTA and joined European Community.
1979 Home rule granted for Greenland.
1985 Strong non-nuclear movement in evidence.
1987 Inconclusive general election, minority government formed.
1989 Another inconclusive election; new centre-right coalition government formed.

The great temple of Apollo (4th century BC) is still standing.

Demerara river in Guyana, 174 km/180 mi long, which gives its name to the country's chief sugar cane growing area, after which Demerara sugar is named.

Denbighshire former county of Wales, largely merged in 1974, together with Flint and part of Merioneth, in Clwyd; a small area along the W border was included in Gwynedd. Denbigh, in the Clwyd valley (population about 9,000), was the county town.

Den Haag Dutch form of The ◊Hague.

Den Helder port in North Holland province, Netherlands, 65 km/40 mi N of Amsterdam, on the entrance to the North Holland Canal from the North Sea; population (1985) 63,538. It is a fishing port and naval base.

Denmark peninsula and islands in N Europe, bounded to the N by the Skagerrak, to the

E by the Kattegat, to the S by West Germany, and to the W by the North Sea.

Denpasar capital town of Bali in the Lesser Sunda Islands of Indonesia. Population (1980) 88,100.

Denver city in Colorado, USA, on the South Platte river, near the foothills of the Rocky Mountains; population (1980) 492,365, Denver-Boulder metropolitan area 1,850,000. It is a processing and distribution centre for a large agricultural area, and for natural resources (minerals, oil, gas).

Denver was founded 1858 with the discovery of gold, becoming a mining camp supply centre during the gold and silver boom in the 1870s and 1880s, and for oil in the 1970s; coal is also mined nearby. There is a university, a mining school, and many medical institutions, and the US mint is sited here.

Deptford district in SE London, in the borough of Lewisham, mainly residential, with industries including engineering and chemicals. It was an

Derbyshire

important Royal naval dockyard from 1513 to 1869, on the south bank of the the river Thames.

Derby industrial city in Derbyshire, England; population (1981) 216,000. Rail locomotives, Rolls-Royce cars and aero-engines, chemicals, paper, electrical, mining and engineering equipment are manufactured here.
features the museum collections of Crown Derby china; the Rolls-Royce collection of aero engines; and the Derby Playhouse.

Derbyshire county in N central England
area 2,630 sq km/1,015 sq mi
towns administrative headquarters Matlock; Derby, Chesterfield, Ilkeston
features Peak District National Park (including Kinder Scout 636 m/2,088 ft); rivers Derwent, Dove, Rother, Trent; Chatsworth House, Bakewell (seat of the duke of Devonshire), Haddon Hall
products cereals; dairy and sheep farming. There have been pit and factory closures, but the area is being redeveloped, and there are large reserves of fluorspar
population (1987) 919,000.

Derry county of Northern Ireland
area 2,070 sq km/799 sq mi
towns Derry (county town, formerly Londonderry), Coleraine, Portstewart
features rivers Foyle, Bann, and Roe; borders Lough Neagh
products mainly agricultural, but farming is hindered by the very heavy rainfall; flax, cattle, sheep, food processing, textiles, light engineering
population (1981) 187,000
famous people Joyce Cary.

Derry (Gaelic *doire*, 'a place of oaks') historic city and port on the river Foyle, County Derry, Northern Ireland; population (1981) 89,100. Known as Londonderry until 1984, Derry dates from the foundation of a monastery by St Columba in AD 546. James I of England granted the borough and surrounding land to the citizens of London and a large colony of imported Protestants founded the present city which they named Londonderry. Textiles and chemicals are produced.

Derwent river in N Yorkshire, NE England; length 112 km/70 mi. Rising in the N Yorkshire moors it joins the river Ouse SE of Selby. Other rivers of the same name in the UK are found in Derbyshire (96 km/60 mi), Cumbria (56 km/35 mi), and Northumberland (26 km/16 mi).

Des Moines capital and largest town in Iowa, USA, on the Des Moines River, a tributary of the Mississippi; population (1980) 371,800. It is an important road, railway, and air centre with many manufactures.

Dessau town of Halle county, East Germany, on the River Mulde, 115 km/70 mi SW of Berlin; population (1986) 104,000. It is the former capital of Anhalt duchy and state. It manufactures chemicals, machinery, and chocolate, and was the site of the Junkers aeroplane works.

Detroit city of Michigan, USA, situated on Detroit River; population (1980) 1,203,339, metropolitan area 4,353,000. It is an industrial centre with the headquarters of Ford, Chrysler, and General Motors, hence its nickname, Motown from 'motor town'.

It was founded 1701 and is the oldest city of any size west of the original colonies of the east coast. In 1805 it was completely destroyed by fire, but soon rebuilt. A recent major development is the waterfront Renaissance Center complex. In the 1960s and 1970s, Detroit was the home of Motown Records.

Detsko Selo former name of ◊Pushkin, near Lenigrad, which was renamed after the Russian poet in 1937.

Deventer town in Overijssel province, the Netherlands, on the Ijssel, 45 km/28 mi S of the Ijssel Meer; population (1984) 64,800. It is an agricultural and transport centre, and produces carpets, precision equipment and packaging machinery.

Devil's Island (French *Ile du Diable*) smallest of the Iles du Salut, off French Guiana, 43 km/27 mi NW of Cayenne. The group of islands was collectively and popularly known by the name Devil's Island, and formed a penal colony notorious for its terrible conditions.

Alfred Dreyfus was imprisoned there 1895–99. Political prisoners were held on Devil's Island, and dangerous criminals on St Joseph, where they were subdued by solitary confinement in tiny cells or subterranean cages. The largest island, Royale,

Devon

now has a tracking station for the French rocket site at Kourou.

Devil's Marbles area of granite boulders, S of Tennant Creek, off the Stuart Highway in Northern Territory, Australia.

Devizes historic market town in Wiltshire, England; population (1982) 13,000. Formerly noted for its trade in cloth, but now a centre for brewing, engineering and food processing. Special features include ancient earthworks and the shattered remains of a Norman castle stormed by Cromwell in 1645.

Devon or *Devonshire* county in SW England
area 6,720 sq km/2,594 sq mi
towns administrative headquarters Exeter; Plymouth, and the resorts Paignton, Torquay, Teignmouth, and Ilfracombe
features rivers Dart, Exe, Tamar; Dartmoor and Exmoor National Parks
products mainly agricultural, with sheep and dairy farming; cider and clotted cream; kaolin in the south; Honiton lace; Dartington glass
population (1987) 1,010,000
famous people Francis Drake, John Hawkins, Charles Kingsley, Robert F Scott.

Dhaka (formerly *Dacca* until 1982) capital of Bangladesh from 1971, in Dhaka region, W of the river Meghna; population (1984) 3,600,000. It trades in jute, oilseed, sugar, and tea, and produces textiles, chemicals, glass, and metal products.
history a former French, Dutch, and English trading post, Dhaka became capital of East Pakistan 1947; it was handed over to Indian troops Dec 1971 to become capital of the new country of Bangladesh.

Dhaulagiri mountain in the Himalayas of W central Nepál rising to 8,172 m/26,811 ft.

Dhofar mountainous western province of Oman, on the border with South Yemen; population (1982) 40,000. South Yemen supported guerrilla activity here in the 1970s, while Britain and Iran supported the government's military operations. The capital is Salalah, which has a port at Rasut.

Diego Garcia island in the ◊Chagos Archipelago, named after its Portuguese discoverer in 1532. See ◊British Indian Ocean Territory.

Dieppe channel port at the mouth of the river Arques, Seine-Maritime *département*, N France; population (1983) 39,500. There are ferry services from its harbour to Newhaven and elsewhere, and fishing, shipbuilding and pharmaceutical industries.

Dijon city and capital of Bourgogne (Burgundy), France; population (1983) 216,000. As well as metallurgical, chemical, and other industries, it has a wine trade and is famed for its mustard.

Dinan town in Côtes-du-Nord *département*, N France, on the river Rance; population (1982) 14,150. The river is harnessed for tidal hydro-electric power.

Dinant ancient town in Namur province, Belgium, on the river Meuse; population (1982) 12,000. It is a tourist centre for the Ardennes.

Dinaric Alps extension of the European Alps in Western Yugoslavia and NW Albania. The highest peak is Durmitor at 2,522 m/8,274 ft.

Diomede two islands off the tip of the Seward peninsula, Alaska. *Little Diomede* 6.2 sq km/2.4 sq mi, belongs to the USA, and is only 3.9 km/2.4 mi from *Big Diomede* 29.3 sq km/11,3 sq mi, owned by the USSR. They were first sighted by Vitus Bering 1728.

District of Columbia federal district of the USA, see ◊Washington.

Diu island off the Kathiawar peninsular, NW India, part of the Union Territory of ◊Daman and Diu; area 38 sq km/15 sq mi; population (1981) 30,000. The main town is also called Diu, and has a population of 8,020. The economy is based on tourism, coconuts, pearl millet, and salt. Diu was captured by the Portuguese 1534.

Diyarbakir town in Asiatic Turkey, on the river Tigris; population (1985) 305,000. It has a trade in gold and silver filigree work, copper, wool, and mohair, and manufactures textiles and leather goods.

Djakarta variant spelling of ◊Jakarta, capital of Indonesia.

Djibouti chief port and capital of the Republic of Djibouti, on a peninsula 240 km/149 mi SW of Aden and 565 km/351 mi NE of Addis Ababa; population (1988) 290,000. The city succeeded Obock as capital of French Somaliland 1896, and was the official port of Ethiopia from 1897.

Djibouti
Republic of
(Jumhouriyya Djibouti)

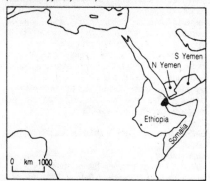

area 23,200 sq km/8,955 sq mi
capital and chief port Djibouti
physical mountains divide an inland plateau
from a coastal plain; hot and arid
head of state and government Hassan
Gouled Aptidon from 1977

political system authoritarian nationalism
political parties People's Progress Assembly
(RPP), nationalist
exports acts mainly as a transit port for
Ethiopia
currency Djibouti franc (299 = £1 Feb 1990)
population (1988) 484,000 (Issa 47%, Afar
37%, European 8%, Arab 6%); annual growth
rate 3.4%
language Somali, Afar, French, Arabic
religion Sunni Muslim
literacy 17% (1985)
GNP $307 (1984); $400 per head of population
chronology
1977 Full independence achieved. Hassan
Gouled elected president.
1979 All political parties combined to form the
People's Progress Assembly (RPP).
1981 New constitution made RPP the only legal
party. Gouled re-elected. Treaties of friendship
signed with Ethiopia, Somalia, Kenya, and
Sudan.
1984 Policy of neutrality reaffirmed.
1987 Gouled re-elected for a final term.

Djibouti country on the E coast of Africa, at
the S end of the Red Sea, bounded to the
E by the Gulf of Aden, to the SE by the
Somali Republic, and to the S, W, and N by
Ethiopia.

Dneprodzerzhinsk port in Ukraine, USSR, on the
river Dnieper, 48 km/30 mi NW of Dnepropetrovsk; population (1987) 279,000. It produces
chemicals, iron, and steel.

Dnepropetrovsk city in Ukraine, USSR, on the
right bank of the Dnieper; population (1987)
1,182,000. It is the centre of an important
industrial region, with iron, steel, chemical,

and engineering industries. It is linked with the
Dnieper Dam, 60 km/37 mi downstream.

Dnieper or *Dnepr* Russian river rising in the
Smolensk region and flowing S past Kiev,
Dnepropetrovsk, and Zaporozhe, to enter the
Black Sea E of Odessa. Total length 2,250
km/1,400 mi.

Dobruja district in the Balkans, bounded to the N
and W by the Danube, and to the E by the Black
Sea. It is low-lying, partly marshland, partly fertile
steppe land. Constanta is the chief town. Dobruja
was divided between Romania and Bulgaria in

Dnieper

Dodecanese

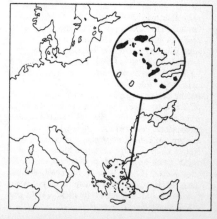

Dominica
Commonwealth of

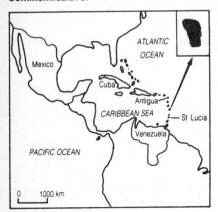

area 751 sq km/290 sq mi
capital Roseau, with a deepwater port
physical largest of the Windward Islands,
mountainous, tropical
features of great beauty, it has mountains
of volcanic origin rising to 1,620 m/5,317 ft;
Boiling Lake, an effect produced by escaping
subterranean gas
head of state Clarence Seignoret from 1983
head of government Mary Eugenia Charles
from 1980

political system liberal democracy
political parties Dominica Freedom Party
(DFP), centrist; Labour Party of Dominica (LPD),
left-of-centre
exports bananas, coconuts, citrus, lime, bay oil
currency E Caribbean dollar (4.60 = £1 Feb
1990), pound sterling, French franc
population (1987) 94,200 (mainly black African
in origin, but with a small Carib reserve of some
500); annual growth rate 1.3%
language English (official), but the Dominican
patois reflects earlier periods of French rule
religion Roman Catholic 80%
literacy 80%
GNP $79 million (1983); $460 per head of
population
chronology
1978 Dominica achieved full independence
within the Commonwealth. Patrick John, leader
of the Dominica Labour Party (DLP), elected
prime minister.
1980 DFP, led by Eugenia Charles, won a
convincing victory in the general election.
1981 Patrick John was implicated in a plot to
overthrow the government.
1982 John tried and acquitted.
1985 John retried and found guilty. Regrouping
of left-of-centre parties resulted in the new
Labour Party of Dominica (LPD). DFP, led by
Eugenia Charles, re-elected.

1878. In 1913, after the second Balkan War,
Bulgaria ceded its part to Romania, but received
it back in 1940, a cession confirmed by the peace
treaty of 1947.
Dodecanese (Greek *Dhodhekánisos*, 'twelve islands')
group of islands in the Aegean sea; area 1,028
sq m/2,663 sq km. Once Turkish, the islands
were Italian 1912–47, when they were ceded to
Greece. They include ◊Rhodes, and ◊Kos. Chief
products include fruit, olives and sponges.
Dodge City city in SW Kansas, USA, on the river
Arkansas; population (1980) 18,000. On the Santa
Fé Trail, it was a noted frontier cattle town in the
days of the Wild West.
Dodoma capital (replacing Dar-es-Salaam in 1974)
of Tanzania; 1,132 m/3,713 ft above sea level;
population (1984) 180,000. It is a centre of communications, linked by rail with Dar-es-Salaam and
Kigoma on Lake Tanganyika, and by road with
Kenya to the N, and Zambia and Malawi to the S.
Dogger Bank submerged sandbank in the North
Sea, about 115 km/70 mi off the coast of Yorkshire. In places the water is only 11 m/36 ft deep,
but the general depth is 18–36 m/60–120 ft; it is
a well-known fishing ground.

Dogs, Isle of district of E London, England, part of
the Greater London borough of Tower Hamlets.
Doha (Arabic *Ad Dawḥah*) capital and chief port
of Qatar; population (1986) 217,000. Industries
include oil refining, refrigeration plants, engineering, and food processing. It is the centre of voca-
tional training for all the Gulf states.
Doi Inthanon highest mountain in Thailand, rising
to 2,595 m/8,513 ft SW of Chiang Mai in NW
Thailand.
Dolgellau (formerly *Dolgelly*) market town at the
foot of Cader Idris in Gwynedd, Wales; on the
river Wnion; population (1981) 2,400. The town is
also a tourist centre. Nearby are the Gwynfynydd
('White mountain') and Clogau goldmines; a nug-
get from the latter has supplied gold for the wed-
ding rings of royal brides since 1923.
Dominica island in the West Indies, between
Guadeloupe and Martinique, the largest of the
Windward Islands, with the Atlantic to the E and
the Caribbean to the W.
Dominican Republic country in the West Indies,
occupying the E of the island of Hispaniola, with
Haiti to the W. The island is surrounded by the
Caribbean Sea.

Dominican Republic
(República Dominicana)

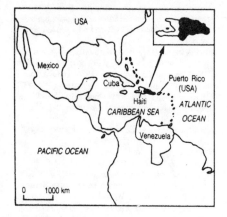

area 48,446 sq km/18,700 sq mi
capital Santo Domingo
physical comprises E part of island of
Hispaniola; central mountain range; fertile
valley in N
features Pico Duarte 3,174 m/10,417 ft, highest
point in the Caribbean islands
head of state and government Joaquín
Balaguer from 1986
political system democratic republic
political parties Dominican Revolutionary Party

(PRD), moderate left-of-centre; Christian Social
Reform Party (PRSC), independent socialist;
Dominican Liberation Party (PLD), nationalist
exports sugar, gold, coffee, ferro-nickel
currency peso (14.35 = £1 Feb 1990)
population (1987) 6,708,000; annual growth
rate 2.3%
life expectancy men 61, women 65
language Spanish (official)
religion Roman Catholic
literacy 78% male/77% female (1985 est)
GNP $8.7 bn (1983); $1,221 per head of
population
chronology
1930 Military coup established the dictatorship
of Rafael Trujillo.
1961 Trujillo assassinated.
1962 First democratic elections resulted in
Juan Bosch, founder of the PRD, becoming
president.
1963 Bosch overthrown in military coup.
1966 New constitution adopted. Joaquín
Balaguer, leader of the PRSC, became
president.
1978 PRD returned to power, with Silvestre
Antonio Guzmán as president.
1982 PRD re-elected, with Jorge Blanco as
president.
1985 Blanco forced by International Monetary
Fund to adopt austerity measures to save the
economy.
1986 PRSC returned to power, with Balaguer
re-elected president.

Don river in Soviet Union, rising to the south of
Moscow and entering the NE extremity of the
Sea of Azov; length 1,900 km/1,180 mi. In its
lower reaches the Don is 1.5 km/1 mi wide, and
for about four months of the year it is closed by
ice. Its upper course is linked with the Volga by
a canal.
Donau German name for the ◊Danube.
Donbas abbreviation of ◊Donets Basin, a coal-rich
area in the USSR.
Doncaster town in South Yorkshire, England, on
the river Don; population (1981) 81,600. It has a
racecourse; famous races here are the St Leger
(1776) in Sept and the Lincolnshire Handicap
in Mar.
history Doncaster was originally a Roman station. Conisbrough, a ruined Norman castle to the
SW, features in Scott's *Ivanhoe* as Athelstan's
stronghold. Coal, iron, and steel have been the
dominant industries in this area for hundreds of
years, though they have recently declined and
are being replaced by other manufactures, such
as synthetic textiles.

Donegal mountainous county in Ulster province
in the NW of the Republic of Ireland, surrounded on three sides by the Atlantic;
area 4,830 sq km/1,864 sq mi; population (1986)
130,000. The county town is Lifford; the market
town and port of Donegal is at the head of Donegal
Bay in the SW. Commercial activities include sheep
and cattle raising, tweed and linen manufacture,
and some deep-sea fishing. The river Erne hydroelectric project (1952) involved the building of large
power stations at Ballyshannon.
Donets river of the USSR rising in Kursk region
and flowing 1,080 km/670 mi through Ukraine to
join the river Don 100 km/60 mi east of Rostov;
see also ◊Donets Basin.
Donets Basin area in the bend formed by the rivers Don and Donets, which holds one of Europe's
richest coalfields, together with salt, mercury, and
lead, so that the *Donbas*, as the name is abbreviated, is one of the greatest industrial regions of
the USSR.
Donetsk city in Ukraine, capital of Donetsk region,
situated in the Donets Basin, 600 km/372 mi SE

Dorset

of Kiev, USSR; population (1987) 1,090,000. It has blast furnaces, rolling mills, and other heavy industries.

It developed from 1871 when a Welshman, John Hughes, established a metallurgical factory, and the town was first called *Yuzovka* after him; renamed *Stalino* 1924, and Donetsk 1961.

Dongola town in the Northern Province of the Sudan, above the third cataract on the river Nile. It was founded about 1812 to replace *Old Dongola*, 120 km/75 mi up river, which was destroyed by the Mamelukes. The latter, a trading centre on a caravan route, was the capital of the Christian kingdom of Nubia during the 6th–14th centuries.

Dongting lake in Hunan province, China; area 10,000 sq km/4,000 sq mi.

Donnybrook former village, now part of Dublin, Republic of Ireland, notorious until 1855 for riotous fairs.

Dorchester market town in Dorset, England, on the river Frome, north of Weymouth; population (1985) 14,000. It is administrative centre for the county. *Maiden Castle* to the SW was occupied as a settlement from about 2000 BC. The novelist Thomas Hardy was born nearby.

Dordogne river in SW France, rising in Puy-de-Dôme *département* and flowing 490 km/300 mi to join the Garonne, 23 km/14 mi N of Bordeaux. It gives its name to a *département* and is an important source of hydroelectric power.

The valley of the Dordogne is a popular tourist area and the caves of the wooded valleys of its tributary, the Vézère, have signs of early human occupation. Famous sites include Cromagnon, Moustier, and the Lascaux caves, discovered in

1940, which have the earliest known examples of cave art. Images of bulls, bison and deer were painted by the Cromagnon people (named from skeletons found 1868 in Cromagnon Cave, near Les Eyzies). The opening of the caves to tourists led to deterioration of the paintings; the caves were closed in 1963 and a facsimile opened in 1983.

Dordrecht or *Dort* river port on an island in the Maas, South Holland, Netherlands, 19 km/12 mi SE of Rotterdam; population (1988) 108,000, metropolitan area of Dordrecht-Zwijndrecht 203,000. It is an inland port with shipbuilding yards and makes heavy machinery, plastics, and chemicals.

Dorpat German name for the Estonian city of ◊Tartu.

Dorset county in SW England

   area 2,650 sq km/1,023 sq mi

   towns administrative headquarters Dorchester; Poole, Shaftesbury, Sherborne; resorts Bournemouth, Lyme Regis, Weymouth

   features Chesil Bank (shingle bank along the coast 19 km/11 mi long); Isle of Purbeck, a peninsula where china clay and Purbeck 'marble' are quarried, and which includes Corfe Castle and the holiday resort of Swanage; Dorset Downs; Cranborne Chase; rivers Frome and Stour; Maiden Castle; Tank Museum at Royal Armoured Corps Centre, Bovington, where the cottage of T E Lawrence is a museum.

   products Wytch Farm is the largest onshore oilfield in the UK

   population (1987) 649,000

   famous people Thomas Hardy, the novelist, born at Higher Bockhampton (Dorchester is 'Casterbridge', the heart of Hardy's Wessex).

Dort another name for ◊Dordrecht, a port in the Netherlands.

Dortmund industrial centre in the Ruhr, West Germany, 58 km/36 mi NE of Düsseldorf; population (1988) 568,000. It is the largest mining town of the Westphalian coalfield and the southern terminus of the Dortmund-Ems canal. Industries include iron, steel, construction machinery, engineering, and brewing.

Douai town in the Nord *département*, France, on the river Scarpe; population (1982) 44,515, conurbation 202,000. It has coal-mines, iron foundries, and breweries. An English Roman Catholic college was founded there 1568 by English Catholics in exile. The Douai-Reims Bible, published 1582–1610, influenced the translators of the King James Version.

Douala or *Duala* chief port and industrial centre (aluminium, chemicals, textiles, pulp) of Cameroon, on the Wouri river estuary; population (1981) 637,000. Known as Kamerunstadt until 1907, it was capital of German Cameroon 1885–1901.

Doubs river in France and Switzerland, rising in the Jura mountains and flowing 430 km/265 mi to join the river Saône. It gives its name to a *département*.

Douglas capital of the Isle of Man in the Irish Sea; population (1981) 20,000. It is a holiday resort and terminus of shipping routes to and from Fleetwood and Liverpool.

Dounreay an experimental nuclear reactor site on the north coast of Scotland, 12 km/7 mi W of Thurso. Development started here in 1974 and continued until a decision was made in 1988 to decommission the site by 1994.

Douro (Spanish *Duero*) river rising in N central Spain and flowing through N Portugal to the Atlantic at Porto; length 800 km/500 mi. Navigation at the river mouth is hindered by sand bars. There are hydro-electric installations.

Dover market town and seaport on the SE coast of Kent, England; population (1981) 33,000. It is Britain's nearest point to mainland Europe, being only 34 km/21 mi from Calais. Dover's modern development has been chiefly due to the cross-Channel traffic, which includes train, ferry, hovercraft, and other services. It was one of the Cinque Ports.

history Under Roman rule, Dover (Portus Dubris) was the terminus of Watling Street, and the beacon or 'lighthouse' in the grounds of the Norman castle dates from about AD 50, making it one of the oldest buildings in Britain. The Lord Warden of the Cinque Ports is Constable of Dover Castle.

Dover, Strait of (French *Pas-de-Calais*) stretch of water separating England from France, and connecting the English Channel with the North Sea. It is about 35 km/22 mi long and 34 km/21 mi wide at its narrowest part. It is one of the world's busiest sea lanes, and by 1972 increasing traffic, collisions, and shipwrecks had become so frequent that traffic-routeing schemes were enforced.

Down county in SE Northern Ireland, facing the Irish Sea on the east; area 2,470 sq km/953 sq mi; population (1981) 53,000. In the south are the Mourne mountains, in the east Strangford sea lough. The county town is Downpatrick; the main industry is dairying.

Downs, North and South two lines of chalk hills in SE England. They form two scarps which face each other across the Weald of Kent and Sussex, and are much used for sheep pasture. The *North Downs* run from Salisbury Plain across Hampshire, Surrey, and Kent to the cliffs of S Foreland. The *South Downs* run across Sussex to Beachy Head.

Downs, the roadstead (partly sheltered anchorage) off E Kent, England, between Deal and the Goodwin Sands. Several 17th-century naval battles took place here, including a defeat of Spain by the Dutch in 1639.

Drakensberg ('dragon's mountain'; Sesuto name *Quathlamba*) mountain range in South Africa, on the boundary of Lesotho and the Orange Free State with Natal; highest point is Thaban Ntlenyana, 3,482 m/10,822 ft, near which is Natal National Park.

Drenthe low-lying northern province of the Netherlands; area 2,660 sq km/1,027 sq mi; population (1988) 437,000. Chief town is Assen. Although it is a thinly populated province of woods, fenlands and moors, stock rearing and mixed arable farming predominate on the well-drained clay and peat soils.

Dresden city in East Germany, capital of Dresden county, formerly capital of Saxony; population (1986) 520,000. Industries include chemicals, machinery, glassware, and musical instruments. It was one of the most beautiful German cities prior to its devastation by Allied fire-bombing 1945. Dresden county has an area of 6,740 sq km/2,602 sq mi, and a population of 1,772,000.

history Under the elector Augustus II the Strong (1694–1733), it became a centre of art and culture. The manufacture of Dresden china, started at Dresden 1709, was transferred to Meissen 1710. The city was bombed by the Allies on the night 13–14 Feb 1945, 15.5 sq km/6 sq mi of the inner town being destroyed, and deaths being estimated at 35,000–135,000.

Drogheda seaport near the mouth of the Boyne, County Louth, Republic of Ireland. The port trades in cattle and textiles; chemicals and foodstuffs are produced. In 1649 the town was stormed by Oliver Cromwell, who massacred most of the garrison, and in 1690 it surrendered to William III after the battle of the Boyne.

Drôme river in France, rising in Dauphiné Pre-Alps and flowing NW for 101 km/63 mi to join the river Rhône below Livron. It gives its name to Drôme *département*.

Dubai one of the ◊United Arab Emirates.

Dublin county in Leinster province, Republic of Ireland, facing the Irish Sea; area 920 sq km/355 sq mi; population (1986) 1,021,000. It is mostly level and low-lying, but rises in the south to 753 m/2,471 ft in Kippure, part of the Wicklow mountains. The river Liffey enters Dublin Bay; Dún Laoghaire is the only other large town.

Dublin (Gaelic *Baile Atha Cliath*) capital and port on the E coast of the Republic of Ireland, at the mouth of the Liffey, facing the Irish Sea; population (1981) 526,000, Greater Dublin (including Dún Laoghaire) 921,000. It is the site of one of the world's largest breweries (Guinness); other industries include textiles, pharmaceuticals, electrical goods, and machine tools. It was the centre of English rule from 1171 (exercised from Dublin Castle 1220) until 1922.

history The city was founded 840 by the invading Danes, who were finally defeated 1014

Dumfries and Galloway

at Clontarf, now a N suburb of the city. In the Georgian period many fine squares were laid out, and the Custom House was damaged in the 1921 rising but later restored.

features There is a Roman Catholic procathedral, St Mary's (1816), two Protestant cathedrals, and two universities: the University of Dublin and the National University of Ireland. Trinity College library contains the Book of Kells, a splendidly illuminated 8th-century gospel book produced at the monastery of Kells in county Meath, founded by St Columba. Other buildings are the City Hall (1779), the Four Courts (1796), the National Gallery, Dublin Municipal Gallery, National Museum, Leinster House (where the *Dáil Eireann* sits), and the Abbey and Gate theatres.

Dubna town in USSR, 40 km/25 mi W of Tula; population (1985) 61,000. It is a metal-working centre, and has the Volga Nuclear Physics Centre.

Dubrovnik (Italian *Ragusa*) port in Yugoslavia on the Adriatic sea; population (1985) 35,000. It manufactures cheese, liqueurs, silk and leather. Once a Roman station, it was for a long time an independent republic, but passed to Austrian rule 1814–1919.

Dudley town NW of Birmingham, West Midlands, England; population (1981) 187,000. Industries include light engineering and clothing manufacture.

Dufourspitze second highest of the alpine peaks, 4,634 m/15,203 ft high. It is the highest peak in the Monte Rosa group of the Pennine alps on the Swiss–Italian frontier.

Duisburg city in North Rhine-Westphalia, West Germany; population (1988) 515,000.

Duisburg river port and industrial city in North Rhine-Westphalia, West Germany, at the confluence of the Rhine and Ruhr rivers; population (1987) 515,000. It is the largest inland river port in Europe. Heavy industries include oil refining and the production of steel, copper, zinc, plastics, and machinery.

Dukeries an area of estates in Nottinghamshire, England, with magnificent noblemen's mansions, few now surviving. Thoresby Hall, said to be the largest house in England (about 365 rooms), was sold as a hotel 1989 and the contents dispersed.

Duluth port in the USA on Lake Superior; by the mouth of the St Louis River, Minnesota; population (1980) 92,000. It manufactures steel, flour, timber, and dairy produce; it trades in iron ore and grain.

Dulwich suburb, part of the inner London borough of Southwark, England. It contains Dulwich College (founded in 1619 by Edward Alleyn, an Elizabethan actor), the Horniman Museum (1901), with a fine ethnological collection, Dulwich Picture Gallery (1814), rebuilt in 1953 after being bombed during World War II, Dulwich Park, and Dulwich Village.

Dumbarton town in Strathclyde, Scotland; population (1981) 23,204. Industries include marine engineering, whisky distilling and electronics.

Dumfries administrative headquarters of Dumfries and Galloway region, Scotland; population (1981) 32,000. It has knitwear, plastics and other industries.

Dumfries and Galloway region of Scotland
area 6,500 sq km/2,510 sq mi
towns administrative headquarters Dumfries
features Solway Firth; Galloway Hills, setting of John Buchan's *The Thirty-Nine Steps*; Glen Trool National Park; Ruthwell Cross, a runic cross of about AD 800 at the village of Ruthwell; Stranraer provides the shortest sea route to Ireland
products horses and cattle (for which the Galloway area was especially famous), sheep, timber
population (1987) 147,000
famous people Robert Burns, Thomas Carlyle.

Dumfriesshire former county of S Scotland, merged in 1975 in the region of Dumfries and Galloway.

Dumyat (English *Damietta*) town in Egypt at the mouth of the Nile; population (1986) 121,200.

Duna Hungarian name for the ◊Danube.

Dunarea Romanian name for the ◊Danube.

Dunav Bulgarian name for the ◊Danube.

Dunbar port and resort in Lothian region, Scotland; population (1981) 6,000. Torness nuclear power station is nearby. Oliver Cromwell defeated the Scots here in 1650.

Dunbartonshire former county of Scotland, bordering the N bank of the Clyde estuary, on which stand Dunbarton (the former county town),

Clydebank, and Helensburgh. It was merged 1975 in the region of Strathclyde.

Dundee city and fishing port, administrative headquarters of Tayside, Scotland, on the north side of the Firth of Tay; population (1981) 175,000. Important shipping and rail centre with marine engineering, watch and clock, and textile industries.

The city developed around the jute industry in the 19th century, and has benefited from the North Sea oil discoveries of the 1970s. There is a university (1967) derived from Queen's College (founded 1881), and other notable buildings include the Albert Institute (1867) and Caird Hall.

Dunedin port on Otago harbour, South Island, New Zealand; population (1986) 106,864. Also a road, rail and air centre, with engineering and textile industries. The city was founded in 1848 by members of the Free Church of Scotland and the university established 1869.

Dunfermline industrial town near the Firth of Forth in Fife region, Scotland; population (1981) 52,000. Site of the naval base of Rosyth; industries include engineering, shipbuilding, electronics, and textiles. Many Scottish kings, including Robert the Bruce, are buried in Dunfermline Abbey. Birthplace of the industrialist Andrew Carnegie.

Dungeness shingle headland on the south coast of Kent, England. It has nuclear power stations, a lighthouse, and a bird sanctuary.

Dunkirk (French **Dunkerque**) seaport on the N coast of France, in Nord *département*, on the Strait of Dover; population (1983) 83,760, conurbation 196,000. Its harbour is one of the most important in France, and it has widespread canal links with the rest of France and Belgium; ferry service to Ramsgate. Industries include oil refining and fishing; textiles, machinery, and soap are manufactured.

It was close to the front line during much of World War I, and in World War II, 337,131 Allied troops (including about 110,000 French) were evacuated from the beaches.

Dún Laoghaire (former name **Kingstown** 1821–1921) port and suburb of Dublin, Republic of Ireland. It is a terminal for ferries to Britain, and there are fishing industries. Before 1821 it was called *Dunleary*.

Dunmow, Little village in Essex, England, scene every four years of the Dunmow Flitch trial (dating from 1111), in which a side of bacon is presented to any couple who 'will swear that they have not quarrelled nor repented of their marriage within a year and a day after its celebration'; they are judged by a jury whose members are all unmarried.

Dunstable town in SW Bedfordshire, England; at the N end of the Chiltern Hills; 48 km/30 mi NW of London; population (1981) 31,000. Whipsnade

Durham

Zoo is nearby. Industries include printing and engineering.

Durazzo Italian form of ◊Dürres, Albanian port.

Durban principal port of Natal, South Africa, and second port of the republic; population (1985) 634,000, urban area 982,000. It exports coal, maize, and wool, imports heavy machinery and mining equipment, and is also an important holiday resort.

Founded 1824 as Port Natal, it was renamed 1835 after Gen Benjamin d'Urban (1777–1849), lieutenant-governor of the east district of Cape Colony 1834–37. Natal university 1949 is divided between Durban and Pietermaritzburg.

Durham county in NE England
area 2,440 sq km/942 sq mi
towns administrative headquarters Durham; Darlington, and the new towns of Peterlee and Newton Aycliffe
features Beamish open-air industrial museum
products sheep and dairy produce; the county lies on one of Britain's richest coalfields.
population (1987) 599,000.

Durham city in the county of Durham, England; population (1983) 88,600. It is administrative headquarters of the county. Founded in 995, it has a Norman cathedral dating from 1093, where the remains of the historian Bede were transferred in 1370; the castle was built by William I in 1072, and the university founded in 1832. Textiles, engineering and coal mining are the chief industries.

Durrës chief port of Albania; population (1983) 72,000. It is an important commercial and communications centre, with flour mills, soap and cigarette factories, distilleries, and an electronics plant. It was the capital of Albania 1912–21.

Dyfed

Dushanbe formerly (1929–69) *Stalinabad* capital of Tadzhik Republic, USSR, 160 km/100 mi north of the Afghan frontier; population (1987) 582,000. It is an important road, rail, and air centre. Industries include cotton mills, tanneries, meat-packing factories, and printing works. It is the seat of Tadzhik state university.

Düsseldorf industrial city of West Germany, on the right bank of the Rhine, 26 km/16 mi NW of Cologne, capital of North Rhine-Westphalia; population (1988) 561,000. It is a river port and the commercial and financial centre of the Ruhr area, with food processing, brewing, agricultural machinery, textile, and chemical industries.

Dutch East Indies former Dutch colony which in 1945 became independent as ◊Indonesia.

Dutch Guiana former Dutch colony which in 1948 became independent as ◊Suriname.

Dyfed county in SW Wales
area 5,770 sq km/2,227 sq mi
towns administrative headquarters Carmarthen; Aberystwyth, Cardigan, Lampeter
features Pembrokeshire Coast National Park, part of the Brecon Beacons National Park, including the Black Mountain, and part of the Cambrian Mountains, including Plynlimon Fawr 752 m/2,468 ft; the village of Laugharne, at the mouth of the Towey, was the home of Dylan Thomas, and features in his work as 'Milk Wood'; Museum of the Woollen Industry at Dre-fach Felindre, and of Welsh religious life at Tre'rddôl. Anthracite mines produce about 50,000 tonnes a year
population (1987) 343,000
language 46% Welsh, English
famous people Taliesin.

Dzerzhinsk city in central USSR, on the Oka river, 32 km/20 mi west of Gorky; population (1987) 281,000. There are engineering, chemical, and timber industries.

Dzhambul city in S Kazakhstan, USSR, in a fruit-growing area NE of Tashkent. Industries include fruit canning, sugar refining, and the manufacture of phosphate fertilizers. Population (1985) 303,000.

Dzo a river in central Portugal that flows 80 km/50 mi through a region noted for its wine.

Ealing borough of Greater London, England. Population (1981) 280,000. The first British sound-film studio was built here in 1931, and 'Ealing comedies' became a noted genre in British film-making. There are many engineering and chemical industries.

East Anglia region of E England, formerly a Saxon kingdom, including Norfolk, Suffolk, and parts of Essex and Cambridgeshire. The University of East Anglia was founded at Norwich 1962, and the Sainsbury Centre for the Visual Arts, opened 1978, has a collection of ethnographic art and sculpture.

Eastbourne English seaside resort in East Sussex, 103 km/64 mi SE´ of London; population (1981) 77,500. The old town was developed in the early 19th century as a model of town planning, largely due to the 7th duke of Devonshire. The modern town extends along the coast for 5 km/3 mi. To the E the South Downs terminate in ◊Beachy Head.

Easter Island or *Rapa Nui* Chilean island in the S Pacific Ocean, part of the Polynesian group, about 3,500 km/2,200 mi W of Chile; area about 166 sq km/64 sq mi; population (1985) 2,000. It was first reached by Europeans on Easter Sunday 1722. It is famous for its huge carved statues and stone houses, the work of neolithic peoples of unknown origin. The chief centre is Hanga-Roa.

East Germany see ◊Germany, East.

East Kilbride town in Strathclyde, Scotland; population (1985) 72,000. It was an old village developed as a 'new town' from 1947 to take overspill from Glasgow, 11 km/6 mi to the NE. It is the site of the National Engineering Laboratory. There are various light industries and some engineering, including jet engines.

East London port and resort on the SE coast of Cape Province, South Africa. Population (1980) 160,582. Founded 1846 as Port Rex, its name was changed to East London 1848. It has a good harbour, is the terminus of a railway from the interior, and is a leading wool-exporting port.

East Lothian former county of SE Scotland, merged with West Lothian and Midlothian in 1975 in the new region of ◊Lothian. Haddington was the county town.

East River tidal strait 26 km/16 mi long, between Manhattan and the Bronx, and Long Island, in New York, USA. It links Long Island Sound with New York Bay, and is also connected, via the Harlem River, with the Hudson. There are both commercial and naval docks, and most famous of its many bridges is the Brooklyn.

East Siberian Sea part of the ◊Arctic Ocean, off the N coast of USSR, between the New Siberian Islands and Chukchi Sea. The world's widest continental shelf, with an average width of nearly 650 km/404 mi, lies in the East Siberian Sea.

East Sussex county in SE England
area 1,800 sq km/695 sq mi
towns administrative headquarters Lewes; cross-channel port of Newhaven; Brighton, Eastbourne, Hastings, Bexhill, Winchelsea, Rye
features Beachy Head, highest headland on the S coast at 180 m/590 ft, the E end of the South ◊Downs; the Weald (including Ashdown Forest); the modern Friston Forest; rivers Ouse, Cuckmere, East Rother; Romney Marsh; the 'Long Man' chalk hill figure at Wilmington, near Eastbourne; Herstmonceux, with a 15th-century castle (conference and exhibition centre) and adjacent modern buildings housing 1958–1990 the

East Sussex

Greenwich Royal Observatory; other castles at Hastings, Lewes, Pevensey, and Bodiam; Battle Abbey and the site of the Battle of Hastings; Michelham Priory; Sheffield Park garden; University of Sussex at Falmer, near Brighton, founded in 1961.

products electronics, gypsum, timber

population (1987) 698,000

famous people former homes of Henry James at Rye, Rudyard Kipling at Burwash, Virginia Woolf at Rodmell.

East Timor disputed territory on the island of ◊Timor in the Malay Archipelago; prior to 1975, a Portuguese colony for almost 460 years

area 14,874 sq km/5,706 sq mi

capital Dili

products coffee

population (1980) 555,000

history Following Portugal's withdrawal 1975, the left-wing Revolutionary Front of Independent East Timor (Fretilin) occupied the capital, Dili, calling for independence. In opposition, troops from neighbouring Indonesia invaded the territory, declaring East Timor (*Loro Sae*) the 17th province of Indonesia July 1976. This claim is not recognized by the United Nations.

The Portuguese colonizers left behind a literacy rate of under 10% and no infrastructure. A brief civil war followed their departure and, after the nationalist guerrillas' calls for independence, the invading Indonesian troops bombed villages and carried out mass executions of suspected Fretilin sympathizers. The war and its attendant famine are thought to have caused more than 100,000 deaths, but starvation had been alleviated by the mid-1980s, and the Indonesian government has built schools, roads, and hospitals. Fretilin guerrillas were still active 1988, claiming to have the support of the population; the number of Indonesian troops in East Timor was estimated at 20,000.

Ebbw Vale town in Gwent, Wales; population (1981) 21,100. The iron and steel industries ended in the 1970s, but tin-plate manufacture and engineering continues. To the east is Blaenavon, where the Big Pit (no longer working) is a tourist attraction.

Ebro river in NE Spain, which rises in the Cantabrian Mountains and flows some 800 km/500 mi SE to meet the Mediterranean SW of Barcelona. Zaragoza is on its course, and ocean-going ships can sail as far as Tortosa, 35 km/22 mi from its mouth. It is a major source of hydro-electric power.

Eccles town near Manchester, England, 8 km/5 mi W of Manchester, on the river Irwell and Manchester Ship Canal. Population (1981) 37,166. Industries include cotton textiles, machinery, and pharmaceuticals. Eccles cakes, rounded pastries with a dried fruit filling, originated here.

Ecuador country in South America, bounded to the N by Colombia, to the E and S by Peru, and to the W by the Pacific Ocean.

Edam town in the Netherlands on the river Ij, North Holland province, Population (1987) 24,200. It is famous for its round cheeses covered in red wax.

Eddystone Rocks rocks in the English Channel, 23 km/14 mi S of Plymouth. The lighthouse, built in 1882, is the fourth on this exposed site.

Eden river in Cumbria, NW England; length 104 km/65 mi. From its source in the Pennines, it flows NW to enter the Solway Firth NW of Carlisle.

Edinburgh capital of Scotland and administrative centre of the region of Lothian, near the S shores of the Firth of Forth; population (1985) 440,000. A cultural centre, it is known for its annual festival of music and the arts; the university was established 1583. Industries include printing, publishing, banking, insurance, chemical manufactures, distilling, brewing, and some shipbuilding.

features the university has a famous medical school and the Koestler chair of parapsychology (instituted 1985), the only such professorship in the UK. The Heriot-Watt University (established 1885; university status 1966) is mainly a technical institution.

Edinburgh Castle contains the 12th-century St Margaret's chapel, the oldest building in Edinburgh. The palace of Holyrood House was built in the 15th and 16th centuries on the site of a 12th-century abbey; it is the British sovereign's official Scottish residence. Rizzio was murdered here 1566, in the apartments of Mary Queen of Scots. The *Parliament House*, begun 1632, is now the seat of the supreme courts. The Royal Scottish Academy and the National Gallery of Scotland (renovated 1989) in Classical style are by William Henry Playfair (1789–1857). The episcopal cathedral of St Mary, opened 1879, and St Giles parish church (mostly 15th-century) are the principal churches. The Royal Observatory has been at Blackford Hill since 1896. The two best known thoroughfares are Princes Street and the Royal Mile.

history In Roman times the site was occupied by Celtic peoples, and about 617 was captured by Edwin of Northumbria, from whom the town took its name. The early settlement grew up round a castle on Castle Rock, while about a mile to the east another burgh, Canongate, developed round the abbey of Holyrood, founded 1128 by David I. It remained separate from Edinburgh until 1856. Robert Bruce made Edinburgh a burgh 1329, and established its port at Leith. In 1544 the town was destroyed by the English. After the union with England 1707, Edinburgh lost its political importance, but remained culturally pre-eminent. Development of the area known as New Town was started 1767.

Ecuador
Republic of
(República del Ecuador)

ATLANTIC
OCEAN

Colombia

Peru

Brazil

PACIFIC

OCEAN

0   1000 km

area 270,670 sq km/104,479 sq mi
capital Quito
towns Cuenca; chief port Guayaquil
physical Andes mountains, divided by a
central plateau, or Valley of the Volcanoes,
including Chimborazo and Cotopaxi, which has
a large share of the cultivable land and is the
site of the capital
features the untouched rainforest of the
Amazon basin has a wealth of wildlife; Ecuador
is crossed by the equator, from which it derives
its name; Galapagos Islands
head of state and government Rodrigo Borja
Cevallos from 1988
political system emergent democracy
political parties Progressive Democratic
Front coalition, left-of-centre (composed of six
individual parties); Concentration of Popular

Forces (CFP), right-of-centre; Social Christian
Party (PSC), right-wing; Conservative Party (PC),
right-wing; and others
exports bananas, cocoa, coffee, sugar, rice,
balsa wood, fish
currency sucre (1,186.06 = £1 Feb 1990,
official rate)
population (1986) 9,640,000; annual growth
rate 2.9%
life expectancy men 62, women 66
language Spanish (official); Quechuan,
Jivaroan
religion Roman Catholic
literacy 85% male/80% female (1985 est)
GNP $11.6 bn (1983); $1,428 per head of
population
chronology
1830 Ecuador became an independent
republic.
1930–48 Great political instability.
1948–55 Liberals in power.
1956 First Conservative president for 60 years.
1960 Liberals returned, with José Velasco as
president.
1961 Velasco deposed and replaced by the
vice-president.
1963 Military junta installed.
1968 Velasco returned as president.
1972 A coup put the military back in power.
1978 New democratic constitution adopted.
1979 Liberals in power but opposed by
right- and left-wing parties.
1982 Deteriorating economy provoked strikes,
demonstrations, and a state of emergency.
1983 Austerity measures introduced.
1985 No party with a clear majority in the
national congress. Febres Cordero narrowly
won the presidency for the Conservatives.
1988 Roderigo Borja elected president for
moderate left-wing coalition.
1989 Guerrilla left-wing group, *Alfaro Vive,
Carajo* ('Alfaro lives, Dammit'), numbering
about 1,000, lays down arms after 9 years.

Edirne town in European Turkey, on the Maritza,
about 225 km/140 mi NW of Istanbul. Population
(1985) 86,700. Founded on the site of ancient
Uscadama, it was formerly known as Adrianople,
named after the Emperor Hadrian *c.* AD 125.
Edmonton locality, once a town, part of the London
borough of Enfield. John Keats lived at Edmonton,
and Charles Lamb lived and died here. The Bell
Inn is referred to in William Cowper's poem *John
Gilpin.*
Edmonton capital of Alberta, Canada, on the North
Saskatchewan River; population (1986) 785,000.
It is the centre of an oil and mining area to
the north, and also an agricultural and dairying

region. Petroleum pipelines link Edmonton with
Superior, Wisconsin, USA, and Vancouver, British
Columbia.
Edward, Lake lake in Uganda, area 2,150 sq km/
830 sq mi, at about 900 m/3,000 ft above sea
level in the Albertine rift valley. In 1973–79 it
was known as Lake Idi Amin Dada, after President
Amin of Uganda.
Egmont, Mount (Maori *Taranaki*) symmetrical
extinct volcano in North Island, New Zealand;
situated S of New Plymouth; 2,517 m/8,260 ft
high.
Egypt country in NE Africa, bounded to the N by
the Mediterranean, to the E by the Suez Canal

Egypt
Arab Republic of
(Jumhuriyat Misr al-Arabiya)

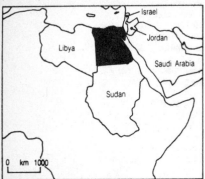

area 1,002,000 sq km/386,772 sq mi
capital Cairo
towns Gîza; ports Alexandria, Port Said
physical mostly desert; hills in E; fertile land
along river Nile; the cultivated and settled area
is about 35,500 sq km/13,700 sq mi
features Aswan High Dam and Lake Nasser;
Sinai; remains of Ancient Egypt (Pyramids,
Sphinx, Luxor, Karnak, Abu Simbel, El Faiyum)
head of state and government Hosni Mubarak
from 1981
political system democratic republic
political parties National Democratic Party
(NDP), moderate left-of-centre; Socialist Labour
Party, right-of-centre; Socialist Liberal Party,
free-enterprise; New Wafd Party, nationalist
exports cotton and textiles
currency Egyptian pound (4.45 = £1 Feb
1990)
population (1987) 49,280,000; annual growth
rate 2.4%
life expectancy men 57, women 60
language Arabic (ancient Egyptian survives to
some extent in Coptic)
religion Sunni Muslim 95%, Coptic Christian
5%
literacy 59% male/30% female (1985 est)
GDP $32 bn (1983); $686 per head of

population
chronology
1914 Egypt became a British protectorate.
1936 Independence recognized. King Fuad
succeeded by his son Farouk.
1946 Withdrawal of British troops except from
Suez Canal Zone.
1952 Farouk overthrown by the army in a
bloodless coup.
1953 Egypt declared a republic, with Gen
Neguib as president.
1956 Neguib replaced by Col Gamal Nasser.
Nasser announced nationalization of Suez
Canal; Egypt attacked by Britain, France
and Israel. Ceasefire agreed because of US
intervention.
1958 Short-lived merger of Egypt and Syria
as United Arab Republic (UAR). Subsequent
attempts to federate Egypt, Syria, and Iraq
failed.
1967 Six-Day War with Israel ended in Egypt's
defeat and Israeli occupation of Sinai and the
Gaza strip.
1970 Nasser died suddenly and was
succeeded by Anwar Sadat.
1973 Attempt to regain territory lost to Israel led
to fighting. Ceasefire arranged by US secretary
of state Henry Kissinger.
1977 Visit by Sadat to Israel to address the
Israeli parliament was criticized by Egypt's
Arab neighbours.
1978–79 Camp David talks in the USA resulted
in a treaty between Egypt and Israel. Egypt
expelled from the Arab League.
1981 Sadat assassinated and succeeded by
Hosni Mubarak.
1983 Improved relations between Egypt and
the Arab world; only Libya and Syria maintained
a trade boycott.
1984 Mubarak's party victorious in the people's
assembly elections.
1987 Mubarak re-elected. Egypt readmitted to
Arab League.
1988 Full diplomatic relations with Algeria
restored.
1989 Improved relations with Libya; diplomatic
relations with Syria restored.

---

and Red Sea, to the S by Sudan, and to the W
by Libya.
Eiger mountain peak in the Swiss ◊Alps.
Eilat alternative spelling of ◊Elat, a port in Israel.
Eindhoven town in North Brabant province, Netherlands, on the river Dommel; population (1988)
381,000. Industries include electrical and electronic equipment.
Eire Gaelic name for the Republic of ◊Ireland.

Eisenhower, Mount Rocky Mountain peak in
Alberta, Canada, included in Banff National Park,
2,862 m/9,390 ft.
Ekaterinburg pre-revolutionary name of ◊Sverd-
lovsk, a town in the western USSR, the site of
the assassination of Tsar Nikolai II and his family
in 1918.
Ekaterinodar pre-revolutionary name of ◊Krasno-
dar, an important industrial town in the USSR.

Ekaterinoslav pre-revolutionary name of ◊Dnepropetrovsk, centre of an industrial region in Ukraine, USSR.

El Aaiún Arabic name of ◊La'Youn.

Elat port at the head of the Gulf of Aqaba, Israel's only outlet to the Red Sea; population (1982) 19,500. Founded in 1948, on the site of the Biblical Elath, it is linked by road with Beersheba. There are copper mines and granite quarries nearby, and a major geophysical observatory opened in 1968 is 16 km/10 mi to the N.

Elba island in the Mediterranean, 10 km/6 mi off the W coast of Italy; population (1981) 35,000; area 223 sq km/86 sq mi. Iron ore is exported from the capital, Portoferraio, to the Italian mainland, and there is a fishing industry. The small uninhabited island of *Monte Cristo* 40 km/25 mi to the S, supplied the title of Alexandre Dumas' hero in *The Count of Monte Cristo*. Elba was Napoleon's place of exile 1814–15.

Elbe one of the principal rivers of Germany, 1,166 km/725 mi long, rising on the S slopes of the Riesengebirge, Czechoslovakia, and flowing NW across the German plain to the North Sea.

Elberfeld West German industrial town, merged with ◊Wuppertal in 1929.

Elbing German name for ◊Elbląg, a Polish port.

Elbląg Polish port 11 km/7 mi from the mouth of the river Elbląg which flows into the Vistula Lagoon, an inlet of the Baltic; population (1983) 115,900. It has shipyards, engineering works, and car and tractor factories.

Elbruz or *Elbrus* highest mountain, 5,642 m/18,517 ft, on the continent of Europe, in the Caucasus, Georgian Republic, USSR.

Elburz volcanic mountain range in NW Iran, close to the S shore of the Caspian Sea, rising in Mount Damavand to 5,670 m/18,602 ft.

Elephanta island in Bombay harbour, Maharashtra, India, some 8 km/5 mi from Bombay. The Temple Caves (6th century), cut out of solid rock, have sculptures of many Hindu deities executed 450–740. There was formerly a large stone elephant near the island's landing place.

El Faiyûm city in N Egypt, 90 km/56 mi SW of Cairo; population (1985) 218,500. A centre of prehistoric culture; the crocodile god Sobek used to be worshipped nearby, and famous realistic mummy portraits of 1st–4th centuries AD were found in the area.

El Ferrol full name *El Ferrol del Caudillo* city and port in La Coruña province, on the NW coast of Spain; population (1986) 88,000. It is a naval base, and has a deep, sheltered harbour and shipbuilding industries. It is the birthplace of Francisco Franco.

Elgin chief town of Moray District, Grampian region, NE Scotland, on the river Lossie 8 km/5 mi S of its port of Lossiemouth on the S shore of the Moray Firth; population (1983) 20,065. There are sawmills and whisky distilleries. Gordonstoun public school is nearby. Elgin Cathedral, founded 1224, was destroyed 1390.

Elisabethville former name of ◊Lubumbashi, a town in Zaïre.

Elizabeth city in NE New Jersey, USA; population (1980) 106,000. It was the first English settlement in New Jersey, established 1664. It has automobile, sewing machine, and tool factories, oil refineries, and chemical works.

Elizavetpol former name of ◊Kirovabad, industrial town in Azerbaijan Republic, USSR.

Ellesmere second largest island of the Canadian Arctic archipelago, Northwest Territories; area 212,687 sq km/82,097 sq mi. It is for the most part barren or glacier-covered.

Ellesmere Port oil port and industrial town in Cheshire, England, on the river Mersey and the Manchester Ship Canal. Population (1983) 81,900. Formerly the biggest transshipment canal port in NW England, it now has the National Waterways Museum, 1976, with old narrow boats and a blacksmith's forge.

Ellice Islands former name of ◊Tuvalu, a group of islands in the W Pacific Ocean.

El Obeid capital of Kordofan province, Sudan; population (1984) 140,025. Linked by rail with Khartoum, it is a market for cattle, gum arabic, and durra (Indian millet).

El Paso city in Texas, USA, situated at the base of the Franklin Mountains, on the Rio Grande, opposite the Mexican city of Ciudad Juárez; population (1980) 425,200. It is the centre of an agricultural and cattle-raising area, and there are electronics, food processing and packing, and leather industries, as well as oil refineries and industries based on local iron and copper mines.

El Salvador country in Central America, bounded N and E by Honduras, S and SW by the Pacific Ocean, and NW by Guatemala.

Elsinore another form of ◊Helsingør, a port on the NE coast of Denmark.

Ely city in Cambridgeshire, England, on the Great Ouse river 24 km/15 mi NE of Cambridge; population (1983) 11,030. It has sugar beet, paper, and engineering factories.

history It was the chief town of the former administrative district of the *Isle of Ely*, so called because the area was once cut off from the surrounding countryside by the fens. Hereward the Wake had his stronghold here. The 11th-century cathedral is one of the largest in England. At the annual feast of St Ethelreda (Audrey), founder of a religious community at Ely in the 7th century, cheap, low-quality souvenirs were sold; the word 'tawdry', a corruption of St Audrey, derives from this practice.

El Salvador
Republic of
(República de El Salvador)

area 21,393 sq km/8,258 sq mi
capital San Salvador
physical flat in S, rising to mountains in N
features smallest and most thickly populated
Central American country
head of state and government Alfredo
Cristiani from 1989
political system emergent democracy
political parties Christian Democrats (PDC),
anti-imperialist; National Republican Alliance
(ARENA), right-wing; National Conciliation Party
(PCN), right-wing
exports coffee, cotton
currency colón (10.91 = £1 Feb 1990)

population (1985) 5,480,000 (mainly of
Spanish-Indian extraction, including some
500,000 illegally in the US); annual growth
rate 2.9%
life expectancy men 63, women 67
language Spanish
religion Roman Catholic
literacy 75% male/69% female (1985 est)
GDP $4.3 bn (1984); $854 per head of
population
chronology
1829 Achieved independence.
1961 Right-wing coup.
1972 Allegations of human-rights violations
and growth of left-wing guerrilla activities. Gen
Carlos Romero elected president.
1979 A coup replaced Romero with a
military-civilian junta.
1980 Archbishop Oscar Romero assassinated.
Country on verge of civil war. José Duarte
became president.
1981 The Mexican and French governments
recognized the guerrillas as a legitimate
political force but the USA actively assisted the
government in its battle against them.
1982 Assembly elections boycotted by left-wing
parties and held amid considerable violence.
1985 Right-wing majority in the national
assembly elections.
1986 Duarte sought a negotiated settlement
with the guerrillas.
1988 Duarte resigned following diagnosis of
terminal cancer.
1989 Alfredo Cristiani (ARENA) elected
president, amid allegations of rigging; guerrillas
agreed to hold peace talks.

Emba river 612 km/380 mi long in the Kazakh
Republic, USSR, draining into the N part of the
Caspian Sea.

Emden port in Lower Saxony, West Germany, at
the mouth of the river Ems; population (1984)
51,000. It is an important fishing port and export
outlet for the ◊Ruhr, with which it is connected
by the Dortmund–Ems canal. There are oil refineries here.

Emi Koussi highest point of the Tibesti massif in
N Chad, rising to 3,425 m/11,204 ft.

Emilia-Romagna region of N central Italy including much of the Po valley; area 22,100 sq km/
8,531 sq mi; population (1988) 3,924,000. The
capital is Bologna; other towns include Reggio,
Rimini, Parma, Ferrara, and Ravenna. Agricultural produce includes fruit, wine, sugar beet,
beef, and dairy products; oil and natural gas
resources have been developed in the Po valley.

Emmental district in the valley of the Emme river,
Berne, Switzerland, where a hard cheese of the

same name has been made since the mid-15th
century.

Enfield borough of NE Greater London; population (1981) 259,000. Industries include engineering – the Royal Small Arms factory was
famous for its production of the Enfield rifle –
textiles, furniture, and cement. Little remains
of Edward VI's palace, but the royal hunting
ground of Enfield Chase partly survives in the
'green belt'. The borough includes the district
of Edmonton, where John Keats and Charles and
Mary Lamb once lived (the Lambs are buried
there); and the Bell Inn, referred to in William
Cowper's poem 'John Gilpin'. From the 1970s
the Lea Valley has been developed as London's
first regional park.

Engadine the upper valley of the river Inn in Switzerland, famous as a winter sports resort.

England largest division of the ◊United Kingdom
area 130,357 sq km/50,318 sq mi
capital London

towns Birmingham, Cambridge, Coventry, Leeds, Leicester, Manchester, Newcastle-upon-Tyne, Nottingham, Oxford, Sheffield, York; ports Bristol, Dover, Felixstowe, Harwich, Liverpool, Portsmouth, Southampton

England: counties

County	Administrative headquarters	Area sq km
Avon	Bristol	1,340
Bedfordshire	Bedford	1,240
Berkshire	Reading	1,260
Buckinghamshire	Aylesbury	1,880
Cambridgeshire	Cambridge	3,410
Cheshire	Chester	2,320
Cleveland	Middlesbrough	580
Cornwall	Truro	3,550
Cumbria	Carlisle	6,810
Derbyshire	Matlock	2,630
Devon	Exeter	6,720
Durham	Durham	2,440
East Sussex	Lewes	1,800
Essex	Chelmsford	3,670
Gloucestershire	Gloucester	2,640
Hampshire	Winchester	3,770
Hereford & Worcs	Worcester	3,930
Hertfordshire	Hertford	1,630
Humberside	Kingston upon Hull	3,510
Isle of Wight	Newport	380
Kent	Maidstone	3,730
Lancashire	Preston	3,040
Leicestershire	Leicester	2,550
Lincolnshire	Lincoln	5,890
London, Greater		1,580
Manchester, Greater		1,290
Merseyside	Liverpool	650
Norfolk	Norwich	5,360
Northamptonshire	Northampton	2,370
Northumberland	Newcastle-upon-Tyne	5,030
North Yorkshire	Northallerton	8,320
Nottinghamshire	Nottingham	2,160
Oxfordshire	Oxford	2,610
Shropshire	Shrewsbury	3,490
Somerset	Taunton	3,460
South Yorkshire	Barnsley	1,560
Staffordshire	Stafford	2,720
Suffolk	Ipswich	3,800
Surrey	Kingston upon Thames	1,660
Tyne & Wear	Newcastle-upon-Tyne	540
Warwickshire	Warwick	1,980
West Midlands	Birmingham	900
West Sussex	Chichester	2,020
West Yorkshire	Wakefield	2,040
Wiltshire	Trowbridge	3,480

features variability of climate and diversity of scenery; among European countries, only the Netherlands is more densely populated
exports agricultural (cereals, rape, sugar beet, potatoes); meat and meat products; electronic (especially software), and telecommunications equipment (main centres Berkshire and Cambridge); scientific instruments; textiles and fashion goods; North Sea oil and gas, petrochemicals, pharmaceuticals, fertilizers; beer; china clay, pottery, porcelain, and glass; film and television programmes, and sound recordings. Tourism is important. There are worldwide banking and insurance interests
currency pound sterling
population (1986) 47,255,000
language English, with more than 100 minority languages
religion Christian, with the Anglican Communion as the established church, 1,600,000; and various Protestant groups, of which the largest is the Methodist 1,400,000; Roman Catholic about 5,000,000; Jewish 410,000; Muslim 900,000; Sikh 175,000; Hindu 140,000.

Eniwetok atoll in the ◊Marshall Islands, in the central Pacific Ocean; population (1980) 453. It was taken from Japan by the USA 1944, which made the island a naval base and conducted 43 atomic tests there from 1947. The inhabitants were re-settled at Ujelang, but insisted on returning home in 1980. Despite the clearance of nuclear debris and radioactive soil to the islet of Runit, high radiation levels persisted.

Ennis county town of County Clare, Republic of Ireland, on the river Fergus, 32 km/20 mi NW of Limerick; population (1981) 14,600. There are distilleries, flour mills, and furniture manufacturing.

Enniskillen county town of Fermanagh, Northern Ireland, between Upper and Lower Lough Erne; population (1981) 10,500. There is some light industry (engineering, food processing) and it has been designated for further industrial growth. A bomb exploded there at a Remembrance Day service in Nov 1987, causing many casualties.

Enschede textile manufacturing centre in Overijssel province, the Netherlands; population (1988) 145,000, urban area of Enschede-Hengelo 250,000.

Entebbe town in Uganda, on the NW shore of Lake Victoria, 20 km/12 mi SW of Kampala, the capital; 1,136 m/3,728 ft above sea level; population (1983) 21,000. Founded 1893, it was the administrative centre of Uganda 1894–1962.

In 1976, a French aircraft was hijacked by a Palestinian liberation group. It was flown to Entebbe airport, where the hostages on board were rescued six days later by Israeli troops.

Enugu town in Nigeria, capital of Anambra state; population (1983) 228,400. It is a coal-mining centre, with steel and cement works, and is linked by rail with Port Harcourt.

Epernay town in Marne *département*, Champagne-Ardenne region, France; population (1986) 29,000. It is the centre of the champagne industry.

Equatorial Guinea
Republic of
(República de Guinea Ecuatorial)

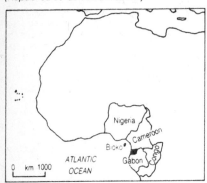

Nigeria

Bioko · Cameroon

ATLANTIC
OCEAN
Gabon

Congo

0   km 1000

area 28,051 sq km/10,828 sq mi
capital Malabo
physical comprises mainland Rio Muni, plus
the small islands of Corisco, Elobey Grande
and Elobey Chico, and Bioko (formerly
Fernando Po) and Annobón (formerly Pagalu)
features volcanic mountains on Bioko
head of state and government Teodoro
Obiang Nguema Mbasogo from 1979
political system one-party military republic

political parties Democratic Party of Equatorial
Guinea (PDGE), militarily controlled
exports cocoa, coffee, bananas, timber
currency ekuele; CFA franc (485.00 = £1 Feb
1990)
population (1988 est) 336,000 (plus 110,000
estimated to live in exile abroad); annual growth
rate 2.2%
life expectancy men 42, women 46
language Spanish (official); pidgin English is
widely spoken, and on Pagalu (whose people
were formerly slaves of the Portuguese) a
Portuguese dialect
religion nominally Christian, mainly Catholic,
but in 1978 Roman Catholicism was banned
literacy 55% (1984)
GDP $60 million (1983); $250 per head of
population
chronology
1968 Achieved full independence from Spain.
Francisco Macias Nguema became first
president, soon assuming dictatorial powers.
1979 Macias overthrown and replaced by his
nephew, Teodoro Obiang Nguema Mbasogo,
who established a military regime. Macias tried
and executed.
1982 Obiang elected president for another
seven years. New constitution, promising a
return to civilian government, adopted.
1989 Obiang re-elected president.

Epinal capital of Vosges *département*, on the
Moselle, France. Population (1982) 40,954. A
cotton textile centre, it dates from the 10th
century.

Epirus (Greek *Ipiros*) region of NW Greece;
area 9,200 sq km/3,551 sq mi; population (1981)
325,000. Its capital is Yannina, and it consists
of the nomes (provinces) of Arta, Thesprotia,
Yannina, and Preveza. There is livestock farming.

Epping Forest a forest in ◊Essex, SE England.

Epsom town in Surrey, England; population (1981)
68,535. In the 17th century it was a spa producing
Epsom salts. There is a racecourse, where the
Derby and the Oaks are held. The site of Henry
VIII's palace of Nonsuch was excavated in 1959.

Equatorial Guinea country in W central Africa,
bounded N by Cameroon, E and S by Gabon,
and W by the Atlantic Ocean; also several small
islands off the coast and the larger island of Bioko
off the coast of Cameroon.

Erebus, Mount the world's southernmost active
volcano, 3,794 m/12,452 ft high, on Ross Island,
Antarctica. It contains a lake of molten lava which
scientists are investigating in the belief that it can
provide a 'window' onto the magma beneath the
Earth's crust.

Erfurt city in East Germany on the river Gera, capital of Erfurt county; population (1986) 217,000.
It is a rich horticultural area, and its industries
include textiles, typewriters, and electrical goods.
Erfurt county has an area of 7,350 sq km/2,837 sq
mi, and a population of 1,235,000.

Erie city and port on the Pennsylvania bank of
Lake Erie, USA, population (1981) 120,000. It
has heavy industries and a trade in iron, grain,
and freshwater fish.

Erie, Lake fourth largest of the Great Lakes of
North America, connected to Lake Ontario by
the Niagara River, and bypassed by the Welland
Canal; area 25,720 sq km/9,930 sq mi.

Eritrea province of N Ethiopia
area 117,600 sq km/45,394 sq mi
capital Asmara
towns ports Assab and Massawa are Ethiopia's
outlets to the sea
physical coastline on the Red Sea 1,000 km/620
mi; narrow coastal plain which rises to an inland
plateau
products coffee, salt, citrus fruits, grains, cotton
currency birr
population (1984) 2,615,000
language Amharic (official)
religion Islam

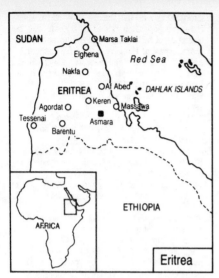

Eritrea

Essex

history part of an ancient Ethiopian kingdom until the 7th century; under Ethiopian influence until it fell to the Turks mid-16th century; Italian colony 1889–1941, where it was the base for Italian invasion of Ethiopia; under British administration 1941–52, when it became an autonomous part of Ethiopia; since 1962, when it became a region, various secessionist movements have risen; civil war from the 1970s, during which guerrillas held most of Eritrea; Ethiopian government, backed by Soviet and Cuban forces, recaptured most towns 1978; resistance continued in the 1980s, aided by conservative Gulf states, and some cooperation with guerrillas in Tigré province.

Erivan alternative transliteration of ◊Yerevan, capital of Armenian Republic, USSR.

Erlangen industrial town in Bavaria, West Germany; population (1988) 100,000.

Erzgebirge mountain range (German 'ore mountains') on the German-Czech frontier, where the rare metals uranium, cobalt, bismuth, arsenic, and antimony are mined. Some 145 km/90 mi long, its highest summit is Mount Klinovec (Keilberg) 1,244 m/4,080 ft, in Czechoslovakia.

Erzurum capital of Erzurum province, NE Turkey; population (1985) 253,000. It is a centre of agricultural trade and mining, and has a military base.

Esbjerg port of Ribe county, Denmark, on the west coast of Jutland; population (1988) 81,000. It is the terminus of links with Sweden and the UK, and is a base for Danish North Sea oil exploration.

Eskilstuna town W of Stockholm, Sweden; population (1986) 88,400. It has iron foundries, steel and armament works.

Eskişehir city in Turkey, 200 km/125 mi west of Ankara; population (1985) 367,000. Products include meerschaum, chromium, magnesite, cotton goods, tiles, and aircraft.

Esquipulas a pilgrimage town in Chiquimula department, SE Guatemala; seat of the 'Black Christ' which is a symbol of peace throughout Central America. In May 1986 five Central American presidents met here to discuss a plan for peace in the region.

Essen city in North Rhine-Westphalia, West Germany; population (1988) 615,000. It is the administrative centre of the Ruhr, with textile, chemical, and electrical industries.

Essequibo the longest river in Guyana, South America, rising in the Guiana Highlands of S Guyana; length 1014 km/630 mi. Part of the district of Essequibo, which lies to the west of the river, is claimed by Venezuela.

Essex county in SE England
area 3,670 sq km/1,417 sq mi
towns administrative headquarters Chelmsford; Colchester; ports Harwich, Tilbury; resorts Southend, Clacton
features former royal hunting ground of Epping Forest (controlled from 1882 by the City of London); the marshy coastal headland of the Naze; birdlife at Maplin Sands; Stansted, site of London's third airport
products dairying, cereals, fruit
population (1987) 1,522,000
famous people William Harvey.

Estonia constituent republic of the USSR from 1940
area 45,100 sq km/17,413 sq mi
capital Tallinn

Estonia

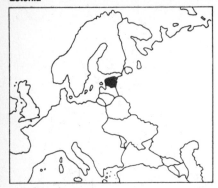

features mild climate, lakes and marshes in a partly forested plain

products oil from shale, wood products, flax, dairy and pig products

population (1987) 1,556,000; 61% Estonian, 28% Russian, 3% Ukrainian, 2% Byelorussian

language Estonian, allied to Finnish

religion traditionally Lutheran

history the workers' and soldiers' soviets took control Nov 1917, were overthrown by German troops Mar 1918, and were restored Nov 1918. The soviets were overthrown with the help of the British navy May 1919, and Estonia was a democratic republic until overthrown by a fascist coup 1934. It was incorporated into the USSR 1940. Nationalist dissent grew from 1980. In 1988 Estonia adopted its own constitution, with a power of veto on all Soviet legislation. The new constitution allowed private property and placed land and natural resources under Estonian control. An Estonian popular front (Rahvarinne) was established in Oct 1988 to campaign for democratization, increased autonomy, and eventual independence, and held mass rallies. In Nov 1988 Estonia's Supreme Soviet (state assembly) voted to declare the republic 'sovereign' and thus autonomous in all matters except military and foreign affairs, although the Presidium of the USSR's Supreme Soviet rejected this as unconstitutional. In Nov 1989 Estonia's assembly also denounced the 1940 incorporation of the republic into the USSR as 'forced annexation'. A multi-party system is effectively in place in the republic, embracing the Popular Front, Christian Democrats, Independence League, and republican Communist Party, and coalition governments seemed set to be formed following the elections of Dec 1989. In 1989 parliament passed a law replacing Russian with Estonian as the main language.

Estoril fashionable resort on the coast 20 km/13 mi W of Lisbon, Portugal. There is a Grand Prix motor racing circuit. Population (1981) 16,000.

Esztergom city on the Danube, NW of Budapest, Hungary; population (1986) 31,000. It was the birthplace of St Stephen, and the former ecclesiastical capital of Hungary, with a fine cathedral.

Etaples fishing port and seaside resort on the Canche estuary, Pas de Calais *département*, France; population (1985) 11,500. During World War I it was an important British base and hospital centre.

Ethiopia country in E Africa, bounded NE by the Red Sea, E and SE by Somalia, S by Kenya, and W and NW by Sudan.

Etna volcano on the E coast of Sicily, 3,323 m/10,906 ft, the highest in Europe; its most recent eruptions were Dec 1985.

Eton town in Berkshire, England, on the N bank of the Thames, opposite Windsor; population (1981) 3,500.

Euboea (Greek *Evvoia*) mountainous island off the E coast of Greece, in the Aegean Sea; area 3,755 sq km/1,450 sq mi; about 177 km/110 mi long; population (1981) 188,410. Mount Delphi reaches 1,743 m/5,721 ft. The chief town, Chalcis, is connected by a bridge to the mainland.

Eupen-et-Malmédy region of Belgium around the towns of Eupen and Malmédy. It was Prussian from 1814 until it became Belgian 1920 after a plebiscite; there was fierce fighting here in the German Ardennes offensive Dec 1944.

Euphrates (Arabic *Furat*) river rising in E Turkey, flowing through Syria and Iraq and joining the Tigris above Basra to form the Shatt-al-Arab, at the head of the Persian/Arabian Gulf; 3,600 km/2,240 mi in length. The ancient cities of Babylon, Eridu, and Ur were situated along its course.

Eure river rising in Orne *département*, France, and flowing SE, then N, to the Seine; length 115 km/70 mi. Chartres is on its banks. It gives its name to two *départements*, Eure and Eure-et-Loire.

Europe second smallest continent, comprising the land west of the Ural mountains; it has 8% of the Earth's surface, with 14.5% of world population

area 10,400,000 sq km/4,000,000 sq mi

largest cities (over 1.5 million inhabitants) Athens, Barcelona, Berlin, Birmingham, Budapest, Hamburg, Istanbul, Kiev, Leningrad, London, Madrid, Manchester, Milan, Moscow, Paris, Rome, Vienna, Warsaw

features North European Plain on which stand London, Paris, Berlin, and Moscow; Central European Highlands (Sierra Nevada, Pyrenees, Alps, Apennines, Carpathians, Balkans); and Scandinavian highland, which takes in the Scottish Highlands; highest point Mount Elbruz in Caucasus mountains. Rivers (over 1,600 km/1,000 mi) Volga, Don, Dnieper, Danube; lakes

Ethiopia
People's Democratic Republic of
(Hebretesebawit Ityopia, formerly also known as **Abyssinia***)*

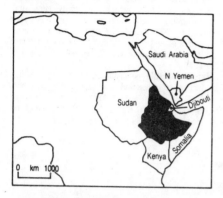

area 1,221,900 sq km/471,653 sq mi
capital Addis Ababa
towns Asmara (capital of Eritrea), Dire Dawa; ports are Massawa, Assab
physical a high plateau with mountains; plains in east; Blue Nile river
features Danakil and Ogaden deserts; ancient remains at Aksum, Gondar, Lalibela among other places; only African country to retain its independence during the colonial period
head of state and government Mengistu Haile Mariam from 1977
political system one-party socialist republic
political parties Workers' Party of Ethiopia (WPE), Marxist-Leninist; Eritrean People's Liberation Front (EPLE) a guerrilla army fighting for an independent Eritrea.
exports coffee, pulses, oilseeds, hides, skins
currency birr (3.50 = £1 Feb 1990)
population (1986) 46,000,000 (Oromo 40%, Amhara 25%, Tigré 12%, Sidama 9%); annual growth rate 2.5%
language Amharic (official); Tigré, Galla, Arabic
religion Christian (Ethiopian Orthodox church, which has had its own patriarch since 1976) 50%, Sunni Muslim 50%
literacy 18% (1985)
GNP $4.7 bn (1984); $141 per head of population
chronology
1974 Haile Selassie deposed and replaced by a military government led by Gen Teferi Benti. Ethiopia declared a socialist state.
1977 Teferi Benti killed and replaced by Col Mengistu Haile Mariam.
1984 WPE declared the only political party.
1985 Worst famine for more than a decade. Western aid sent and internal resettlement programmes undertaken.
1987 New constitution adopted, Mengistu Mariam elected president. Provisional Military Administrative Council dissolved and elected National Assembly introduced. New famine; food aid hindered by guerrillas.
1988 Mengistu agreed to adjust his economic policies in order to secure IMF assistance. Influx of refugees from Sudan.
1989 Government forces routed from Eritrea and Tigré, rebels claimed. Coup attempt against Mengistu foiled. Another famine in north feared.
1990 Rebels capture part of Massawa.

(over 5,000 sq km/2,000 sq mi) Ladoga, Onega, Vänern. The climate ranges from the variable NW, modified by the Gulf Stream, through the central zone with warm summers and cold winters, becoming bitterly cold in E Europe, to the Mediterranean zone with comparatively mild winters and hot summers. The last is the richest zone for plant life, but animal species have long been reduced everywhere by the predominance of humans.
population (1985) 492,000,000 (excluding Turkey and USSR)
languages mostly of Indo-European origin, with a few exceptions, including Finno-Ugrian (Finnish and Hungarian) and Basque
religion Christianity (Protestantism, Roman Catholicism, Greek Orthodox), Islam, Judaism.
Euskadi the Basque name for the ◊Basque Country.

Evansville industrial city (pharmaceuticals, plastics) in SW Indiana, USA, on the Ohio River; population (1980) 130,500. Abraham Lincoln spent his boyhood in nearby Spencer County.
Everest, Mount the world's highest mountain, in the Himalayas, on the China-Nepál frontier; height 8,872 m/29,118 ft. It was first climbed by Edmund Hillary and Norgay Tenzing 1953.

The English name comes from George Everest (1790–1866), surveyor-general of India. In 1987 a US expedition obtained measurements of ◊K2 which disputed Everest's claim to be the highest mountain.
Everglades area of swamps and lakes in S ◊Florida, USA; area 12,950 sq km/6,000 sq mi.
Evesham town in Hereford and Worcester, England, on the Avon SE of Worcester; population (1981) 15,250. Fruit and vegetables from the

fertile *Vale of Evesham* are canned. In the Battle of Evesham, 4 Aug 1265, Edward, Prince of Wales, defeated Simon de Montfort, who was killed.

Evreux capital of Eure *département* in NW France; population (1983) 46,250. It produces pharmaceuticals and rubber.

Evvola Greek name for the island of ◊Euboea.

Exeter city, administrative headquarters of Devon, England, on the river Exe; population (1981) 96,000. It has medieval, Georgian, and Regency architecture, including a cathedral 1280–1369, a modern market centre, and a university 1955. It manufactures agricultural machinery, pharmaceuticals, and textiles.

Exmoor moorland in Devon and Somerset, England, forming (with the coast from Minehead to Combe Martin) a National Park since 1954. It includes Dunkery Beacon 520 m/1,707 ft, and the Doone Valley.

Extremadura autonomous region of W Spain including the provinces of Badajoz and Cáceres; area 41,600 sq km/16,058 sq mi; population (1986) 1,089,000. Irrigated land is used for growing wheat; the remainder is either oak forest or used for pig or sheep grazing.

Eyre, Lake Australia's largest lake, in central South Australia, which frequently runs dry, becoming a salt marsh in dry seasons; area up to 9,000 sq km/3,500 sq mi. It is the continent's lowest point, 12 m/39 ft below sea level. It is named after E J Eyre, who reached it 1840.

Eyre Peninsula peninsula in S Australia, which includes the iron and steel city of Whyalla. Over 50% of the iron used in Australia's steel industry is mined at Iron Knob; the only seal colony on mainland Australis is at Point Labatt.

Faenza city on the river Lamone in Ravenna province, Emilia-Romagna, Italy; population (1985) 54,900. It has many medieval remains, including the 15th-century walls. It gave its name to 'faience' pottery, a type of tin-glazed earthenware first produced there.

Faeroe Islands or *Faeroes* alternative spelling of the ◊Faroe Islands, a group of islands in the N Atlantic.

Fagatogo capital of American Samoa. Situated on Pago Pago Harbour, Tutuila Island.

Fairbanks town in central Alaska, USA, situated on the Chena Slough, a tributary of the river Tanana; population (1983) 65,000. Founded 1902, it is a goldmining and fur-trading centre, and the terminus of the Alaska Railroad and of the Pan-American Highway.

Faisalabad city in Punjab province, Pakistan; population (1981) 1,092,000. It trades in grain, cotton, and textiles.

Faizabad town in Uttar Pradesh, N India; population (1981) 143,167. It lies at the head of navigation of the river Ghaghara, and has sugar refineries and an agricultural trade.

Falaise town 32 km/20 mi SE of Caen, in Calvados *département*, Normandy, France; population (1982) 8,820. It is a market centre, and manufactures cotton and leather goods. The castle was that of the first dukes of Normandy, and William the Conqueror was born here.

Falkirk town in Central Region, Scotland, 37 km/23 mi W of Edinburgh; population (1981) 37,734. An iron-founding centre, Falkirk has brewing, distilling, tanning and chemical industries.

Falkland Islands British Crown Colony in the S Atlantic

area 12,173 sq km/4,700 sq mi, made up of two main islands: East Falkland 6,760 sq km/2,610 sq mi, and West Falkland 5,413 sq km/2,090 sq mi

capital Stanley; new port facilities were opened 1984, and Mount Pleasant airport 1985

features in addition to the two main islands, there are about 200 small islands, all with wild scenery and rich bird life

exports wool, alginates (used as dyes and as a food additive) from seaweed beds

population (1986) 1,916

government there is a governor (Gordon Jewkes from Oct 1985) advised by an executive council, and a mainly elected legislative council. Administered with the Falklands, but separate dependencies of the UK, are South Georgia and the South ◊Sandwich Islands; see also ◊British Antarctic Territory.

history the first European to visit the islands was Englishman John Davis 1592, and at the end of the 17th century they were named after Lord Falkland, treasurer of the British navy. The first British settlers arrived 1765; Spain bought out a French settlement 1766, and the British were ejected 1770–71, but British sovereignty was never ceded, and from 1833, when a few Argentines were expelled, British settlement was continuous.

history Argentina asserts its succession to the Spanish claim to the 'Islas Malvinas', but the inhabitants oppose cession. Occupied by Argentina Apr 1982, the islands were recaptured by British military forces in May–June of the same year. The cost of the British military presence was officially £257 million for 1987.

Fall River city and port in Massachusetts, USA; population (1980) 95,900. It stands at the mouth

Falkland Islands

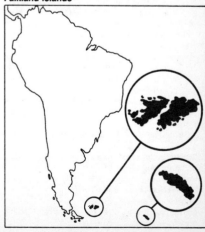

of the Taunton River, over the Little Fall River which gave it its name. Cotton, rubber and paper are the chief industries.

Falmouth port on the S coast of Cornwall, England, on the estuary of the Fal; population (1981) 18,525. There are ship-repairing and marine engineering industries.

Famagusta seaport on the E coast of Cyprus, in the Turkish Republic of Northern Cyprus; population (1985) 19,500. It was the chief port of the island prior to the Turkish invasion 1974.

Fao or *Faw* an oil port on a peninsula at the mouth of the Shatt al-Arab in Iraq. Iran launched a major offensive against Iraq in 1986, capturing Fao for two years.

Far East geographical term for all Asia east of the Indian subcontinent.

Fareham town in Hampshire, England, 10 km/6 mi NW of Portsmouth; population (1981) 88,250. Bricks, ceramics, and rope are made and there is engineering and boat-building as well as varied light industries.

Farnborough town in Hampshire, England, N of Aldershot; population (1981) 45,500. The mansion of Farnborough Hill was occupied by Napoleon III and the Empress Eugénie, and she, her husband and her son, are buried in a mausoleum at the Roman Catholic church she built. Experimental work is carried out at the Royal Aircraft Establishment.

Farne rocky island group in the North Sea, off Northumberland, England. A chapel stands on the site of the hermitage at St Cuthbert on Inner Farne; there are two lighthouses, the Longstone lighthouse being the scene of the rescue of shipwrecked sailors by Grace Darling. The islands are a sanctuary for birds and grey seals.

Farnham town in Surrey, England, on the river Wey; population (1981) 35,250. The parish church was once part of Waverley Abbey (1128), the first Cistercian house in England: Walter Scott named his first novel after the abbey. At Moor Park, the writer Jonathan Swift met Stella.

Faroe Islands or *Faroes* or *Faeroe Islands* or *Faeroes* (Danish *Færøerne*) island group (18 out of 22 inhabited) in the N Atlantic, between the Shetland Islands and Iceland, forming an outlying part of Denmark
area 1,399 sq km/540 sq mi; largest islands are Strømø, Østerø, Vagø, Suderø, Sandø, and Bordø.
capital Thorshavn on Strømø, population (1986) 15,287
features the name means 'Sheep Islands'; they do not belong to the EC
exports fish, crafted goods
population (1986) 46,000
language Færøese, Danish
government since 1948 the islands have had full self-government

history first settled by Norsemen in the 9th century, they were a Norwegian province 1380–1709. Their parliament was restored 1852. They withdrew from EFTA 1972
currency Danish krone.

Fars province of SW Iran, comprising fertile valleys among mountain ranges running NW–SE. Population (1982) 2,035,600; area 133,300 sq km/51,487 sq mi. The capital is Shiraz, and there are imposing ruins of Cyrus the Great's city of Parargardae and of Persepolis.

Fashoda former name (until 1905) of the town of Kodok, situated on the White Nile in SE Sudan. The capture of this town by French troops caused an international incident in 1898.

Fécamp a seaport and resort of France, NE of Le Havre in the *département* of Seine Maritime; population (1982) 21,696. The main industries are shipbuilding and fishing. Benedictine liqueur was first produced here in the early 16th century.

Felixstowe port and resort opposite Harwich in Suffolk, England, between the Orwell and Deben estuaries; population (1981) 21,000. It is Britain's busiest container port, and also has ferry services to Gothenburg, Rotterdam, and Zeebrugge.

Fens level, low-lying tracts of land in E England, west and south of the Wash, about 115 km/70 mi N–S and about 55 km/34 mi E–W. They fall within the counties of Lincolnshire, Cambridgeshire, and Norfolk, consisting of a huge area, formerly a bay of the North Sea, but now crossed by numerous drainage canals and forming some of the most productive agricultural land in Britain. The peat portion of the Fens is known as the *Bedford Level*.

The first drainage attempts were made by the Romans. In 1634 the 4th earl of Bedford brought over the Dutch water-engineer Vermuyden, who introduced Dutch methods. Burwell Fen and Wicken Fen, NE of Cambridge, have been preserved undrained as nature reserves.

Ferghana town in Uzbekistan, USSR, in the fertile Ferghana valley; population (1987) 203,000. It is the capital of the important cotton and fruit-growing Ferghana region; nearby are petroleum fields.

Fermanagh county in the southern part of Northern Ireland
area 1,680 sq km/648 sq mi
towns Enniskillen (county town), Lisnaskea, Irvinestown
physical in the centre is a broad trough of low-lying land, in which lie Upper and Lower Lough Erne
products mainly agricultural; livestock, tweeds, clothing
population (1981) 52,000.

Fernando Po former name (until 1973) of ◊Bioko, Equatorial Guinea.

Ferrara industrial city and archbishopric in Emilia-Romagna region, N Italy, on a branch of the Po delta 52 km/32 mi west of the Adriatic Sea; population (1988) 143,000. There are chemical industries and textile manufacturers.

It has the Gothic castle of its medieval rulers, the House of Este, palaces, museums, and a cathedral, consecrated 1135. The university was founded 1391. Savonarola was born here, and the poet Tasso was confined in the asylum 1579–86.

Ferrol alternative name for ◊El Ferrol, a city and port in NW Spain.

Fertő tó Hungarian name for the ◊*Neusiedler Sea*.

Fès or *Fez* former capital of Morocco 808–1062, 1296–1548, and 1662–1912, in a valley north of the Great Atlas mountains, 160 km/100 mi E of Rabat; population (1982) 563,000. Textiles, carpets, and leather are manufactured, and the *fez*, a brimless hat worn in S and E Mediterranean countries, is traditionally said to have originated here.

Kairwan Islamic University dates from 859; the second university was founded 1961.

Fez alternative spelling of ◊Fès, a city in Morocco.

Fezzan former province of Libya, a desert region, with many oases, and with rock paintings from about 3000 BC. It was captured from Italy 1942, and placed under French control until 1951 when it became a province of the newly independent United Kingdom of Libya. It was split into smaller divisions 1963.

Fichtelgebirge chain of mountains in Bavaria, West Germany, on the Czechoslovak border. The highest peak is the *Schneeberg* 1,051 m/3,448 ft. There are granite quarries, uranium mining, china and glass industries, and forestry.

Fiesole resort town 6 km/4 mi NE of Florence, Italy, with many Etruscan and Roman relics; population (1971) 14,400. The Romanesque cathedral was completed 1028.

Fife region of E Scotland (formerly the county of Fife) facing the North Sea and Firth of Forth
area 1,300 sq km/502 sq mi
towns administrative headquarters Glenrothes; Dunfermline, St Andrews, Kirkcaldy, Cupar
physical the only high land is the Lomond Hills, in the NW chief rivers Eden and Leven
features Rosyth naval base and dockyard (used for nuclear submarine refits) on N shore of the Firth of Forth; Tentsmuir, possibly the earliest settled site in Scotland. The ancient palace of the Stuarts was at Falkland, and eight Scottish kings are buried at Dunfermline
products potatoes, cereals, electronics, petrochemicals (Mossmorran), light engineering
population (1987) 345,000.

Fiji group of 332 islands in the SW Pacific, about 100 of which are inhabited.

Fingal's Cave cave on the island of Staffa, Inner Hebrides, Scotland. It is lined with natural basalt columns, and is 60 m/200 ft long and 20 m/

Fife

65 ft high. Fingal, based on the Irish hero Finn mac Cumhaill, was the leading character in Macpherson's Ossianic forgeries. Visited by Mendelssohn in 1829, the cave was the inspiration of his *Hebrides* overture, otherwise known as Fingal's Cave.

Finistère *département* of Brittany, NW France; area 7,030 sq km/2,740 mi; population (1982) 828,500. The administrative centre is Quimper.

Finisterre, Cape promontory in the extreme NW of Spain.

Finland country in Scandinavia, bounded N by Norway, E by the USSR, S and W by the Baltic Sea, and NW by Sweden.

Finland, Gulf of eastern arm of the ◊Baltic Sea, separating Finland from Estonia.

Finsteraarhorn the highest mountain, 4,274 m/14,020 ft, in the Bernese Alps, Switzerland.

Firenze Italian form of ◊Florence.

Fishguard seaport on an inlet on the S side of Fishguard Bay, Dyfed, SW Wales; population about 5,000. There is a ferry service to Rosslare in the Republic of Ireland.

FL abbreviation for ◊*Florida*.

Flanders a region of the Low Countries which in the 8th and 9th centuries extended from Calais to the Scheldt, and is now covered by the Belgian provinces of Oost Vlaanderen and West Vlaanderen (East and West Flanders), the French *département* of Nord, and part of the Dutch province of Zeeland. The language is Flemish. East Flanders, capital Ghent, has an area of 3,000 sq km/1,158 sq mi, and a population (1987) of 1,329,000. West Flanders, capital Bruges, has an area of 3,100 sq km/1,197 sq mi, and a population (1987) of 1,035,000.

Fiji

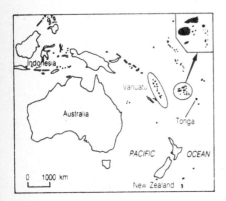

area 18,337 sq km/7,078 sq mi
capital Suva on Viti Levu
physical comprises some 800 Melanesian islands (about 100 inhabited), the largest being Viti Levu (10,386 sq km/400 sq mi) and Vanua Levu (5,535 sq km/2,137 sq mi); mountainous, with tropical forest
features Nadi airport is an international Pacific staging post
head of state Ratu Sir Penaia Ganilau from 1987
head of government Ratu Sir Kamisese Mara from 1987

political system democratic republic
political parties Alliance Party (AP), moderate centrist; National Federation Party (NFP), moderate left-of-centre; Fijian Labour Party (FLP), left-of-centre Indian
exports sugar, coconut oil, ginger, timber, canned fish; tourism is important
currency Fiji dollar (2.57 = £1 Feb 1990)
population (1986) 714,000 (46% Fijian, holding 80% of the land communally, and 49% Indian, introduced in the 19th century to work the sugar crop); annual growth rate 1.9%
life expectancy men 67, women 71
language English (official); Fijian, Hindi
religion Hindu 50%, Methodist 44%
literacy 88% male/77% female (1980 est)
GDP $1.2 bn (1984); $1,086
chronology
1970 Full independence achieved. Ratu Sir Kamisese Mara elected as first prime minister.
1987 General election in Apr brought to power an Indian-dominated coalition led by Dr Timoci Bavadra. Military coup May by Col Sitiveni Rabuka removed new government at gunpoint. Governor General Ratu Sir Penaia Ganilau regained control within weeks. A second military coup Sept by Rabuka proclaimed Fiji a republic and suspended the constitution. In Oct Fiji ceased to be a member of the Commonwealth. In Dec a civilian government was restored with Rambuka retaining control of security as minister for home affairs.
1989 New constitution proposed.

Fleet Street street in London, England (named after the subterranean river Fleet), traditionally the centre of British journalism. It runs from Temple Bar eastwards to Ludgate Circus. With adjoining streets it contained the offices and printing works of many leading British newspapers until the mid-1980s, when most moved to sites farther from the centre of London.

Fleetwood port and seaside resort in Lancashire, England, at the mouth of the river Wyre; population (1981) 28,530. The fishing industry has declined, but the port still handles timber, petroleum, and chemicals. Ferry services operate to the Isle of Man and Belfast.

Flensburg port on the E coast of Schleswig-Holstein, West Germany, with shipyards and breweries; population (1984) 86,700.

Flevoland formerly *IJsselmeerpolders* a low-lying province of the Netherlands established 1986; area 1,410 sq km/544 sq mi; population (1988) 194,000. The chief town is Dronten. The polder land of the IJsselmeer was reclaimed during 1950–57.

Flint city in Michigan, USA, on the Flint River, 90 km/56 mi NW of Detroit. The manufacture of cars is the chief industry; population (1980) 522,000.

Flintshire former county of Wales, and smallest of the Welsh counties. It was merged in 1974, with Denbigh and part of Merioneth, into the new county of Clwyd; the county town of Mold became the administrative headquarters of the new region.

Florence (Italian *Firenze*) capital of Tuscany, N Italy, 88 km/55 mi from the mouth of the river Arno; population (1988) 421,000. It has printing, engineering, and optical industries, many crafts, including leather, gold and silver work, and embroidery, and its art and architecture attract large numbers of tourists.

history The Roman town of Florentia was founded in the 1st century BC on the site of the Etruscan town of Faesulae. It was besieged by the Goths AD 405, and visited by Charlemagne 786.

In 1052, Florence passed to Countess Matilda of Tuscany (1046–1115), and from the 11th century onwards gained increasing autonomy. In

Finland
Republic of
(Suomen Tasavalta)

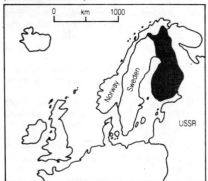

area 352,752 sq km/136,162 sq mi
capital Helsinki
towns Tampere, the port of Turku, Espoo, Vantaa
physical archipelago in south; most of the country is forest, with about 60,000 lakes; one third is within the Arctic Circle; mountains in the north
head of state Mauno Koivisto from 1982
head of government Harri Holkeri from 1987
political system democratic republic
political parties Social Democratic Party (SDP), moderate left-of-centre; National Coalition Party (KOK), moderate right-of-centre; Centre Party (KP), radical centrist, rural-orientated; Finnish People's Democratic League (SKDL), left-wing; Swedish People's Party, independent Swedish-orientated; Finnish Rural Party (SMP), farmers and small businesses
exports metal, chemical and engineering products (icebreakers and oil rigs), paper, timber, textiles, fine ceramics, glass, furniture
currency markka (6.73 = £1 Feb 1990)
population (1987) 4,938,600; annual growth rate 0.5%
life expectancy men 70, women 78
language Finnish 94%, Swedish (official), Lapp
religion Lutheran 90%, Eastern Orthodox
literacy 99%
GNP $50.6 bn (1984); $10,477 per head of population
chronology
1917 Independence declared.
1939 Defeated by USSR in Winter War.
1941 Joined Hitler in invasion of USSR.
1944 Concluded separate armistice with Allies.
1948 Finno-Soviet Pact of Friendship, Co-operation, and Mutual Assistance signed.
1973 Trade treaty with EEC signed.
1977 Trade agreement with USSR signed.
1987 KOK–SDP coalition formed.
1988 Koivisto re-elected president.
1989 Finland joined Council of Europe.

1198, it became an independent republic, with new city walls, and governed by a body of 12 citizens. In the 13th–14th centuries, the city was the centre of the struggle between the Guelphs (papal supporters) and Ghibellines (supporters of the Holy Roman emperor). Despite this, Florence became immensely prosperous, and went on to reach its cultural peak during the 14th–16th centuries.

From the 15th to the 18th century, the Medici family, originally bankers, were the predominant power, in spite of their having been twice expelled by revolutions. In the first of these, in 1493, a year after Lorenzo de' Medici's death, a republic was proclaimed (with Machiavelli as secretary) which lasted until 1512. From 1494–98, the city was under the control of Savonarola. In 1527, the Medicis again proclaimed a republic. Notable Medieval and Renaissance citizens included the writers Dante and Boccaccio, and the artists Giotto, Leonardo da Vinci, and Michelangelo.

The republic lasted through many years of gradual decline until 1737 when the city passed to Maria Theresa of Austria. From 1737, the city was ruled by the Habsburg imperial dynasty. The city was badly damaged in World War II, and by floods 1966
features Firenze's architectural treasures include the Ponte Vecchio 1345; the Pitti and Vecchio palaces; the churches of Santa Croce and Santa Maria Novella; the cathedral of Santa Maria del Fiore 1314; and the Uffizi Gallery, which has one of Europe's finest art collections, based on that of the Medici.

Florianópolis seaport and resort on Santa Caterina Island, Brazil; population (1980) 153,500. It is linked to the mainland by two bridges, one of which is the largest expansion bridge in Brazil.

Florida most southeasterly state of the USA; mainly a peninsula jutting into the Atlantic, which it separates from the Gulf of Mexico; nickname Sunshine State
area 152,000 sq km/58,672 sq mi
capital Tallahassee
towns Miami, Tampa, Jacksonville
physical 50% forested; lakes (including Okeechobee 1,800 sq km/695 sq mi); Everglades National Park (5,000 sq km/1,930 sq mi, with birdlife, cypresses, alligators)

Florida

features Palm Beach, an island resort between the lagoon of Lake Worth and the Atlantic; Florida Keys; John F Kennedy Space Center at Cape Canaveral; Disney World theme park
products citrus fruit, melons, vegetables, fish, shellfish, phosphates (one third of world supply), chemicals, uranium (largest US producer), space research
population (1989) 13,000,000; the fastest growing state
history under Spanish rule from 1513 until its cession to England 1763, Florida was returned to Spain 1783, and purchased by the USA 1819, becoming a state 1845. It is a centre for drug trade with Latin America.

Florida Keys series of small coral islands which curve over 240 km/150 mi SW from the southern tip of Florida. The most important are Key Largo and Key West (with a US naval and air station); they depend on fishing and tourism.

Flushing port (Dutch *Vlissingen*) on Walcheren Island, Zeeland, Netherlands; population (1987) 44,900. It stands at the entrance to the Scheldt estuary, one of the principal sea routes into Europe. Industries include fishing, shipbuilding, and petrochemicals, and there is a ferry service to Harwich. Admiral de Ruyter was born at Flushing and is commemorated in the Jacobskerk.

Foggia city of Puglia region, S Italy; population (1988) 159,000. The cathedral, dating from about 1170, was rebuilt after an earthquake 1731. Natural gas is found nearby.

Folkestone port and holiday resort on the SE coast of Kent, England, 10 km/6 mi SW of Dover; population (1983) 44,200. There are ferry and hovercraft services to and from Boulogne. It is the birthplace of the physician William Henry.

Fontainebleau town to the SE of Paris, in Seine-et-Marne *département*; population (1982) 18,753. The palace was built by François I in the 16th century. Mme de Montespan lived there in the reign of Louis XIV, and Mme du Barry in that of Louis XV. Napoleon signed his abdication there in 1814. Nearby is the village

of Barbizon, the haunt of several 19th-century painters.

Foochow former name of ◊Fuzhou, port and capital of Fujian province, SE China.

Foreland *North* and *South* headlands on the Kent coast, England. *North Foreland*, with one lighthouse, lies 4 km/2.5 mi E of Margate; *South Foreland*, with two, lies 4.8 km/3 mi NE of Dover.

Forfarshire former name (16th century–1928) of Angus, which was absorbed in Tayside, Scotland, in 1975.

Forlì city and market centre in Emilia-Romagna region, NE Italy, south of Ravenna; population (1988) 110,000. Felt, maiolica, and paper are manufactured.

Formentor, Cape northern extremity of ◊Majorca, in the Balearic Islands of the West Mediterranean.

Formosa former name of ◊Taiwan.

Fortaleza Ceará industrial port in NE Brazil; population (1980) 648,815. It has textile, flour-milling, and sugar-refining industries.

Fort-de-France capital, chief commercial centre, and port of ◊Martinique, West Indies; population (1982) 99,844.

Forth river in SE Scotland, with its headstreams rising on the NE slopes of Ben Lomond. It flows approximately 72 km/45 mi to Kincardine where the *Firth of Forth* begins. The Firth is approximately 80 km/50 mi long, and is 26 km/16 mi wide where it joins the North Sea.

At Queensferry near Edinburgh are the Forth rail (1890) and road (1964) bridges. The *Forth and Clyde Canal* (1768–90) across the lowlands of Scotland links the Firth with the river Clyde, Grangemouth to Bowling (53 km/33 mi). A coalfield was located beneath the Firth of Forth in 1976.

Fort Lamy former name of ◊N'djaména, capital of Chad.

Fort Wayne town in NE Indiana, USA; population (1980) 172,000. Industries include electrical goods, electronics, and farm machinery. A fort was built here against the North American Indians in 1794 by Gen Anthony Wayne (1745–96), hero of a surprise attack on a British force at Stony Point, New York, in 1779, which earned him the nickname 'Mad Anthony'.

Fort Worth city in NE Texas, USA; population (1980) 385,164, metropolitan area (with ◊Dallas) 2,964,000. Formerly an important cow town, it is now a grain, petroleum, aerospace, and railway centre serving the S USA.

Fos-sur-Mer harbour and medieval township near Marseille, France, forming the southern focus of a direct Rhône-Rhine route to the North Sea.

Fou-Liang former name of ◊Jingdezhen, a town in China.

Foveaux Strait stretch of water between the extreme south of South Island, New Zealand, and Stewart Island. It is a fishing area, and produces a considerable oyster catch.

Fowey port and resort in Cornwall, England, near the mouth of the Fowey estuary; population, with ◊St Austell (1981) 36,500. It is an outlet for the Cornish clay mining industry.

Foyle sea-lough on the N coast of Ireland, traversed by the frontier of Northern Ireland and the Irish Republic.

France: regions and départements

Region and Département	Capital	Area sq km
Alsace		*8,300*
Bas-Rhin	Strasbourg	
Haut-Rhin	Colmar	
Aquitaine		*41,300*
Dordogne	Périgueux	
Gironde	Bordeaux	
Landes	Mont-de-Marsan	
Lot-et-Garonne	Agen	
Pyrénées-Atlantiques	Pau	
Auvergne		*26,000*
Allier	Moulins	
Cantal	Aurillac	
Haute-Loire	Le Puy	
Puy-de-Dôme	Clermont-Ferrand	
Basse-Normandie		*17,600*
Calvados	Caen	
Manche	St-Lô	
Orne	Alençon	
Bourgogne		*31,600*
Côte-d'Or	Dijon	
Nièvre	Nevers	
Saône-et-Loire	Mâcon	
Yonne	Auxerre	
Bretagne		*27,200*
Côtes-du-Nord	St Brieuc	
Finistère	Quimper	
Ille-et-Vilaine	Rennes	
Morbihan	Vannes	
Centre		*39,200*
Cher	Bourges	
Eure-et-Loire	Chartres	
Indre	Châteauroux	
Indre-et-Loire	Tours	
Loire-et-Cher	Blois	
Loiret	Orléans	
Champagne-Ardenne		*25,600*
Ardenne	Charleville-Mézières	
Aube	Troyes	
Marne	Châlons-sur-Marne	
Haute-Marne	Chaumont	
Corsica		*8,700*
Haute Corse	Bastia	
Corse du Sud	Ajaccio	
Franche-Comté		*16,200*
Doubs	Besançon	
Jura	Lons-le-Saunier	
Haute Saône	Vesoul	
Terre de Belfort	Belfort	
Haute-Normandie		*12,300*
Eure	Evreux	
Seine-Maritime	Rouen	
Ile de France		*12,000*
Essonne	Évry	
Val-de-Marne	Créteil	
Val d'Oise	Cergy-Pontoise	
Ville de Paris		
Seine-et-Marne	Melun	
Hauts-de-Seine	Nanterre	
Seine-St-Denis	Bobigny	
Yvelines	Versailles	
Languedoc-Roussillon		*27,400*
Aude	Carcassonne	
Gard	Nimes	
Hérault	Montpellier	
Lozère	Mende	
Pyrènées-Orientales	Perpignan	
Limousin		*16,900*
Corrèze	Tulle	
Creuse	Guéret	
Haute-Vienne	Limoges	
Lorraine		*23,600*
Meurthe-et-Moselle	Nancy	
Meuse	Bar-le-Duc	
Moselle	Metz	
Vosges	Épinal	
Midi-Pyrénées		*45,300*
Ariège	Foix	
Aveyron	Rodez	
Haute-Garonne	Toulouse	
Gers	Auch	
Lot	Cahors	
Hautes-Pyrénées	Tarbes	
Tarn	Albi	
Tarn-et-Garonne	Montauban	
Nord-Pas-de-Calais		*12,400*
Nord	Lille	
Pas-de-Calais	Arras	
Pays de la Loire		*32,100*
Loire Atlantique	Nantes	
Maine-et-Loire	Angers	
Mayenne	Laval	
Sarthe	Le Mans	
Vendée	La Roche-sur-Yon	
Picardie		*19,400*
Aisne	Laon	
Oise	Beauvais	
Somme	Amiens	
Provence-Alpes-Côte d'Azur		*31,400*
Alpes-de-Haute Provence	Digne	
Hautes-Alpes	Gap	
Alpes Maritimes	Nice	
Bouches-du-Rhône	Marseille	
Var	Toulon	
Vaucluse	Avignon	

France
French Republic
(République Française)

area (including Corsica) 543,965 sq
km/209,970 sq mi
capital Paris
towns Lyon, Lille, Bordeaux, Toulouse, Nantes,
Strasbourg; ports Marseille, Le Havre
physical rivers Seine, Loire, Garonne,
Rhône; mountain ranges Alps, Massif Central,
Pyrenees, Jura, Vosges, Cévennes
territories Guadeloupe, French Guiana,
Martinique, Réunion, St Pierre and Miquelon,
Southern and Antarctic Territories, New
Caledonia, French Polynesia, Wallis and Futuna
features Ardennes forest, Auvergne mountain
region, caves of Dordogne with relics of early
humans, Riviera
head of state François Mitterrand from 1981
head of government Michel Rocard from 1988
political system liberal democracy
political parties Socialist Party (PS), left-of-centre; Rally for the Republic (RPR), neo-Gaullist
conservative; Union for French Democracy
(UDF), centre-right; Republican Party (RP),
centre-right; French Communist Party (PCF),
Marxist-Leninist; National Front, far-right; Greens,
environmentalist
exports fruit (especially apples), wine, cheese,
cars, aircraft, chemicals, jewellery, silk, lace;
tourism is important
currency franc (9.70 = £1 Feb 1990)
population (1988 est) 55,854,000 (including
4,500,000 immigrants, chiefly from Portugal,
Algeria, Morocco, and Tunisia); annual growth
rate 0.3%
life expectancy men 71, women 79
language French (regional languages include
Breton)
religion mainly Roman Catholic; Muslim 3
million, Protestant 750,000
literacy 99% (1984)
GNP $568 bn (1983); $7,179 per head of
population
chronology
1944–46 De Gaulle provisional government.
Commencement of Fourth Republic.
1954 Independence of Indochina.
1956 Moroccan and Tunisian independence.
1957 Entry into EEC.
1958 Recall of de Gaulle following Algerian
crisis. Commencement of Fifth Republic.
1959 De Gaulle became president.
1962 Algerian independence.
1966 France withdrew from NATO.
1968 'May events' crisis.
1969 De Gaulle resigned following referendum
defeat. Pompidou became president.
1974 Giscard d'Estaing elected president.
1981 Mitterrand elected Fifth Republic's first
socialist president.
1986 'Cohabitation' experiment, with the
conservative Jacques Chirac as prime minister
1988 Mitterrand re-elected. The moderate
socialist Michel Rocard became prime minister
and continued in this post despite the Socialist
Party failing to obtain a secure majority in the
National Assembly elections. Matignon Accord
on future of New Caledonia approved by
referendum.
1989 Greens gained 11% of vote in elections to
European Parliament.

France country in W Europe, bounded NE by
Belgium and West Germany, E by Switzerland
and Italy, S by the Mediterranean, SW by
Spain and Andorra, and W by the Atlantic
Ocean.

Franche-Comté region of E France; area 16,200
sq km/6,253 sq mi; population (1987) 1,086,000.
Its capital is Besançon, and it includes the
départements of Doubs, Jura, Haute Saône, and
Territoire de Belfort. In the mountainous Jura,
there is farming and forestry, and elsewhere there
are engineering and plastics industries.

Once independent and ruled by its own count,
it was disputed by France, Burgundy, Austria, and Spain from the 9th century until it
became a French province under the Treaty of
Nijmegen 1678.

Frankfurt-am-Main city in Hessen, West Germany,
72 km/45 mi NE of Mannheim; population (1988)
592,000. It is a commercial and banking centre,

with electrical and machine industries, and an inland port on the river Main. An international book fair is held annually.

history Frankfurt was a free imperial city 1372–1806, when it was incorporated into ◊Prussia. It is the birthplace of the poet Goethe. It was the headquarters of the US zone of occupation in World War II and of the Anglo-US zone 1947–49.

Frankfurt-an-der-Oder city in East Germany 80 km/ 50 mi SE of Berlin, capital of Frankfurt county; population (1981) 81,000. It is linked by the river Oder and its canals to the Vistula and Elbe. Industries include chemicals, engineering, paper, and leather. Frankfurt county has an area of 7,190 sq km/2,775 sq mi, and a population (1986) of 708,000.

Franklin a district of ◊Northwest Territories, Canada; area 1,422,550 sq km/549,104 sq mi.

Franz Josef Land (Russian *Zemlya Frantsa Iosifa*) archipelago of some 85 islands in the Arctic Ocean, E of Spitsbergen and NW of Novaya Zemlya, USSR. Area 20,720 sq km/8,000 sq mi. There are scientific stations.

Fraser river in British Columbia, Canada. It rises in the Yellowhead Pass of the Rockies and flows NW, then S, then W to the Strait of Georgia. It is 1,370 km/850 mi long, and famous for salmon.

Fray Bentos river port in Uruguay; population (1985) 20,000. Linked by a bridge over the Uruguay with Puerto Unzué in Argentina (1976), it is famous for its meat-packing industry, particularly corned beef.

Fredericton capital of New Brunswick, Canada, on the St John River; population (1986) 44,000. It was formerly known as St Anne's Point, and in 1785 was named after Prince Frederick, second son of George III.

Fredrikstad Norwegian port at the mouth of the river Glomma, dating from 1570; population (1987) 26,650. It is a centre of the timber trade, and has shipyards.

Freetown capital of Sierra Leone, W Africa; population (1988) 470,000. It has a naval station and a harbour. Industries include cement, plastics, footwear, and oil refining. Platinum, chromite, diamonds, and gold are traded.

It was founded as a settlement for freed slaves in the 1790s.

Freiburg-im-Breisgau industrial city (pharmaceuticals, precision instruments) in Baden-Württemberg, West Germany; population (1988) 186,000. It is the seat of a university, and has a 12th-century cathedral.

Fremantle chief port of Western Australia, at the mouth of the Swan river, SW of Perth; population (1981) 23,780. It has shipbuilding yards, sawmills, and iron foundries, and exports wheat, fruit, wool, and timber. It was founded as a penal settlement 1829.

French Guiana

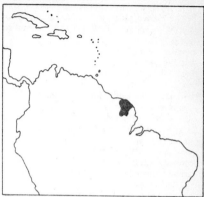

French Antarctica territory, in full *French Southern and Antarctic Territories*, created 1955; area 10,100 sq km/3,900 sq mi; population about 200 research scientists. It includes Adélie Land, on the Antarctic continent, the Kerguelen and Crozet archipelagos, and Saint Paul and Nouvelle Amsterdam islands in the southern seas. It is administered from Paris, but Port-aux-Français on Kerguelen is the chief centre, with several research stations. There are also research stations on Nouvelle Amsterdam and in Adélie Land; and a meteorological station on Possession Island in the Crozet archipelago. Saint Paul is uninhabited. In 1988, French workers, who were illegally building an airstrip, thus violating a United Nations treaty on Antarctica, attacked Greenpeace workers.

French Community former association consisting of France and those overseas territories joined with it by the constitution of the Fifth Republic, following the 1958 referendum. Many of the constituent states withdrew during the 1960s, and it no longer formally exists, but in practice all former French colonies have close economic and cultural as well as linguistic links with France.

French Guiana (French *Guyane Française*) French overseas *département* from 1946, and administrative region from 1974, on the N coast of South America, bounded to the W by Suriname and to the E and S by Brazil

area 83,500 sq km/32,230 sq mi

capital Cayenne

towns St Laurent

features Eurospace rocket launch pad at Kourou; Îles du Salut, which include ◊Devil's Island

exports timber, shrimps, gold

population (1987) 89,000

language 90% Creole, French, Amerindian

history first settled by France 1604, the territory became a French possession 1817; penal colonies,

including Devil's Island, were established from 1852; by 1945, the shipments of convicts from France ceased, and the status changed to an overseas department 1946, and an administrative region 1974.
currency franc
famous people Capt Dreyfus.

French Polynesia French Overseas Territory in the S Pacific, consisting of five archipelagoes: Windward Islands, Leeward Islands (the two island groups comprising the ◊Society Islands), ◊Tuamotu Archipelago (including ◊Gambier Islands), ◊Tubuai Islands, and ◊Marquesas Islands
total area 3,940 sq km/1,521 sq mi
capital Papeete on Tahiti
exports cultivated pearls, coconut oil, vanilla; tourism is important
population (1987) 185,000
languages Tahitian (official), French
government a high commissioner (Alain Ohrel) and Council of Government; two deputies are returned to the National Assembly in France
history first visited by Europeans 1595; French Protectorate 1843; annexed to France 1880–82; became an Overseas Territory, changing its name from French Oceania 1958; self-governing 1977; following demands for independence in ◊New Caledonia 1984–85, agitation increased also in Polynesia.

French Somaliland former name, until 1967, of ◊Djibouti, in E Africa.

French Sudan former name (1898–1959) of ◊Mali, NW Africa.

French West Africa group of French colonies administered from Dakar 1895–1958. They have become the modern Senegal, Mauritania, Sudan, Burkina Faso, Guinea, Niger, Ivory Coast, and Benin.

Fribourg city in W Switzerland, on the river Sarine, capital of the canton of Fribourg; population (1980) 37,400. It is noted for its food products, particularly the cheese of the Gruyère district.

Friendly Islands another name for ◊Tonga.

Friesland maritime province of the N Netherlands, which includes the Frisian Islands and land which is still being reclaimed from the former Zuyder Zee; area 3,400 sq km/1,312 sq mi; population (1988) 599,000. Its capital is Leeuwarden. Friesian cattle originated here.

Frisian Islands chain of low-lying islands 5–32 km/3–20 mi off the NW coasts of the Netherlands and Germany, with a northerly extension off the W coast of Denmark. They were formed by the sinking of the intervening land. *Texel* is the largest and most westerly.

Friuli-Venezia Giulia autonomous agricultural and wine-growing region of NE Italy, bordered on the east by Yugoslavia; area 7,800 sq km/3,011 sq mi; population (1988) 1,210,000. It

includes the capital Udine, Gorizia, Pordenone, and Trieste.
Formed 1947 from the province of Venetian Fruli and part of Eastern Friuli, to which Trieste was added after its cession to Italy 1954, it was granted autonomy 1963. The Slav minority numbers about 100,000, and in Friuli there is a movement for complete independence.

Frunze capital (formerly Pishpek) of Kirghiz Republic, USSR; population (1987) 632,000. It produces textiles, farm machinery, metal goods, and tobacco.

Fujairah or *Fujayrah* one of the seven constituent member states of the ◊United Arab Emirates; area 1,150 sq km/450 sq mi; population (1985) 54,000.

Fujian formerly *Fukien* province of SE China, bordering Taiwan Strait, opposite Taiwan
area 123,100 sq km/47,517 sq mi
capital Fuzhou
physical dramatic mountainous coastline
features it is being developed for tourists; designated as pace-setting province for modernization 1980
products sugar, rice, special aromatic teas, tobacco, timber, fruit
population (1986) 27,490,000.

Fujiyama or *Mount Fuji* Japanese volcano and highest peak, on Honshu Island; height 3,778 m/12,400 ft. Extinct since 1707, it has a Shinto shrine and a weather station on its summit.

Fukien former name of ◊Fujian, a province of SE China.

Fukuoka formerly *Najime* Japanese industrial port on the NW coast of Kyushu island; population (1987) 1,142,000. It produces chemicals, textiles, paper, and metal goods.

Fukuyama port in SW Honshu, Japan, at the mouth of the Ashida river; population (1985) 360,000. It has cotton, rubber and other industries.

Funabashi city in Kanto region, Honshu island, east of Tokyo; population (1987) 508,000.

Funafuti atoll consisting of 30 islets in the West Pacific and capital of the state of Tuvalu; area 2.8 sq km/1.1 sq mi; population 900.

Funchal capital and chief port of the Portuguese island of Madeira, on the S coast; population (1980) 100,000. Tourism and wine are the main industries.

Fundy, Bay of Canadian Atlantic inlet between New Brunswick and Nova Scotia, with a rapid tidal rise and fall of 18 m/60 ft (harnessed for electricity since 1984). In summer, fog increases the dangers to shipping.

Fünen German form of ◊Fyn, an island forming part of Denmark.

Fünfkirchen (German 'five churches') German name for ◊Pécs, a town in SW Hungary.

Furness peninsula in England, formerly a detached northern portion of Lancashire, separated from the main part by Morecambe Bay. In 1974 it was included in the new county of Cumbria. Barrow is its ship-building and industrial centre.

Fürth town in Bavaria, West Germany, adjoining Nuremberg; population (1984) 98,500. It has electrical, chemical, textile, and toy industries.

Fushun coal-mining and oil-refining centre in Liaoning province, China, 40 km/25 mi E of Shenyang; population (1984) 636,000. It has aluminium, steel, and chemical works.

Fuzhou formerly *Foochow* industrial port and capital of Fujian province, SE China; population (1986) 1,190,000. It is a centre for shipbuilding and steel production, and rice, sugar, tea, and fruit pass through the port. There are joint foreign and Chinese factories.

The Mazu (Matsu) island group, occupied by the Nationalist Chinese, is offshore.

Fyn (German *Fünen*) island forming part of Denmark and lying between the mainland and Zealand: area 2,976 sq km/1,149 sq mi; capital Odense; population (1984) 454,000.

GA abbreviation for ◊*Georgia* (USA).

Gabès port in E Tunisia; population (1984) 92,300. Fertilizers and dates are exported. The town stands on the site of the Roman town of Tacapae.

Gabon country in central Africa, bounded N by Cameroon, E and S by the Congo, W by the Atlantic Ocean, and NW by Equatorial Guinea.

Gaborone capital of Botswana from 1965, mainly an administrative centre; population (1988) 111,000. Light industry includes textiles.

Gafsa oasis town in central Tunisia, centre of a phosphate-mining area; population (1984) 60,900.

Gainsborough market town in Lincolnshire, England; population (1985) 18,715. It is an agricultural marketing centre with flour mills and the manufacture of agricultural machinery. It stands on the river Trent, which periodically rises in a tidal wave, the 'eagre'.

Galápagos Islands (official name *Archipeliégo de Colón*) group of 15 islands in the Pacific, belonging to Ecuador; area 7,800 sq km/3,000 sq mi; population (1982) 6,120. The capital is San Cristóbal on the island of the same name. The islands are a nature reserve. Their unique fauna (including giant tortoises, iguanas, penguins, flightless cormorants, and Darwin's finches) is under threat from introduced species.

Galaţi (German *Galatz*) port on the river Danube in Romania; population (1985) 293,000. Industries include ship-building, iron, steel, textiles, food processing, and cosmetics.

Galicia mountainous but fertile autonomous region of NW Spain, formerly an independent kingdom; area 29,400 sq km/11,348 sq mi; population (1986) 2,785,000. It includes La Coruña,

Gabon
Gabonese Republic
(*République Gabonaise*)

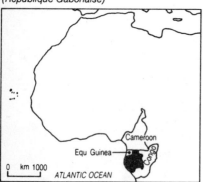

area 267,667 sq km/103,319 sq mi
capital Libreville
physical virtually the whole country is tropical rainforest; mountains alternate with lowlands; Ogooué River flows S–W
features Schweitzer hospital at Lambaréné
head of state and government Omar Bongo from 1967

political system authoritarian nationalism
political parties Gabonese Democratic Party (PDG), nationalist
exports petroleum, manganese, iron, uranium, timber
currency CFA franc (485.00 = £1 Feb 1990)
population (1988) 1,226,000; annual growth rate 1.6%
life expectancy men 47, women 51
language French (official), Bantu
religion animist 60%, Roman Catholic 35%, small Muslim minority
literacy 70% male/53% female (1985 est)
GNP $3 bn (1983); $2,613 per head of population
chronology
1960 Independence from France achieved. Léon M'ba became the first president.
1967 Attempted coup by rival party foiled with French help. M'ba died and was succeeded by his protégé, Albert-Bernard Bongo.
1968 One-party state established.
1973 Bongo re-elected; converted to Islam, he changed his first name to Omar.
1986 Bongo re-elected.
1989 Coup attempt against Bongo defeated.

Gambia
Republic of The

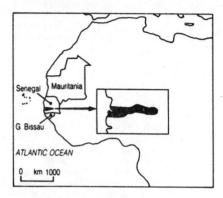

Senegal | Mauritania

G Bissau

ATLANTIC OCEAN

0   km 1000

area 10,689 sq km/4,126 sq mi
capital Banjul
physical banks of the river Gambia
features the smallest state in black Africa
head of state and government Dawda
Kairaba Jawara from 1970
political system liberal democracy

political parties Progressive People's Party
(PPP), moderate centrist; National Convention
Party (NCP), left-of-centre
exports groundnuts, palm oil, fish
currency dalasi (14.17 = £1 Feb 1990)
population 788,200 (1988); annual growth
rate 1.9%
life expectancy men 34, women 37
language English (official)
religion Muslim 70%, with animist and
Christian minorities
literacy 36% male/15% female (1985 est)
GNP $200 million (1983); $330 per head of
population
chronology
1965 Achieved independence as a constitutional monarchy within the Commonwealth, with
Dawda K Jawara as prime minister.
1970 Declared itself a republic, with Jawara as
president.
1972 Jawara re-elected.
1981 Attempted coup foiled with the help of
Senegal.
1982 Formed with Senegal the Confederation of
Senegambia. Jawara re-elected.
1987 Jawara re-elected.
1989 Confederation of Senegambia dissolved.

Lugo, Orense, and Pontevedra. Industries include
fishing and the mining of tungsten and tin. The
language is similar to Portuguese.

Galicia former province of central Europe, extend-
ing from the N slopes of the Carpathians to the
Czech-Romanian border. Once part of the Aus-
trian Empire, it was included in Poland after World
War I, and divided in 1945 between Poland and the
USSR.

Gallipoli port in European Turkey, giving its name
to the peninsula (ancient name *Chersonesus*) on
which it stands. In World War I an unsuccessful
Allied landing Feb 1915–Jan 1916 cost the lives
of many British, French, Australian, and New
Zealand troops.

Gällivare iron-mining town above the Arctic Circle in Norrbotten county, N Sweden; population
(1976) 25,279.

Galloway ancient area of SW Scotland, now part of
the region of ◊Dumfries and Galloway.

Galveston port in Texas, USA; population (1980)
61,902. It exports cotton, petroleum, wheat, and
timber; and has chemical works and petroleum
refineries. In 1900, 8,000 people died in one of
the hurricanes which periodically hit the region.

Galway county on the W coast of the Republic of Ireland, in the province of Connacht;
area 5,940 sq km/2,293 sq mi; population (1986)
178,000. Towns include Galway (county town),

Ballinasloe, Tuam, Clifden, and Loughrea (near
which deposits of lead, zinc, and copper were
found 1959). The east is low-lying. In the south
are the Slieve Aughty mountains and Galway Bay,
with the Aran islands. West of Lough Corrib is
Connemara, a wild area of moors, hills, lakes, and
bogs. The Shannon is the principal river.

Galway fishing port and county town of county
Galway, Republic of Ireland; population (1986)
47,000. It produces textiles and chemicals. University College is part of the national university,
and Galway Theatre stages Irish Gaelic plays.

Gambia river in W Africa, which gives its name to
◊Gambia; 1,000 km/620 mi long.

Gambia, The country in W Africa, surrounded to
the N, E, and S by Senegal, and bordered to the
W by the Atlantic Ocean.

Gambier Islands island group, part of ◊French
Polynesia, administered with the ◊Tuamotu Archipelago; area 36 sq km/14 sq mi; population (1983)
582. It includes four coral islands and many small
islets. The main island is Mangareva, with its town
Rikitea.

Ganges (Hindi *Ganga*) major river of India and
Bangladesh; length 2,510 km/1,560 mi. It is the
most sacred river for Hindus.

Its chief tributary is the **Yamuna** (Jumna);
length 1,385 km/860 mi, which joins the Ganges
near Allahabad, where there is a sacred bathing

place. The Ganges is joined in its delta in Bangladesh by the ◊Brahmaputra, and its most commercially important and westernmost channel to the Bay of Bengal is the *Hooghly*.

The area regularly flooded in the wet season has almost doubled and the annual cost of flood damage has risen to $1 billion as a consequence of deforestation of the Ganges watershed, which has also decreased the river's flow in the dry season by 20%.

Gannet Peak the highest peak in Wyoming State, USA, rising to 4,207 m/13,804 ft.

Gansu formerly *Kansu* province of NW China
area 530,000 sq km/204,580 sq mi
capital Lanzhou
features subject to earthquakes; the 'Silk Road' (now a motor road) passed through it in the Middle Ages, carrying trade to central Asia
products coal, oil, hydroelectric power from the Huang He (Yellow) River
population (1986) 20,710,000, including many Muslims.

Gaoxiong mainland Chinese form of ◊Kaohsiung, a port in W Taiwan.

Garching town N of Munich, West Germany, site of a nuclear research centre.

Gard French river, 133 km/83 mi long, a tributary of the Rhône, which it joins above Beaucaire. It gives its name to Gard *département* in Languedoc-Roussillon region.

Garda, Lake largest lake in Italy; situated on the border between the regions of Lombardia and Veneto; 370 sq km/143 sq mi.

Garonne river in SW France, rising on the Spanish side of the Pyrenees and flowing to the ◊Gironde estuary; length 580 km/350 mi.

Gary city in NW Indiana, USA; population (1980) 151,953. It contains the steel and cement works of the United States Steel Corporation, and was named after E H Gary (1846–1927), its chair.

Gaspé Peninsula mountainous peninsula in SE Québec, Canada; area 29,500 sq km/11,390 sq mi. It has fishing and lumbering industries.

Gateshead port in Tyne and Wear, England; population (1981) 81,000. Industries include engineering, chemicals, and glass.

Gatwick site of Gatwick Airport, West Sussex, England, constructed 1956–58.

Gaya ancient city in Bihar state, NE India; population (1986) 200,000. It is a centre of pilgrimage for Buddhists and Hindus with many temples and shrines. A bo tree at ◊Buddh Gaya is said to be a direct descendant of the original tree under which Buddha sat.

Gaza capital of the ◊Gaza Strip, once a Philistine city, and scene of three World War I battles; population (1979) 120,000.

Gazankulu Black National State in Transvaal province, South Africa, with self-governing status from 1971; population (1985) 497,200.

Gaza Strip strip of Palestine under Israeli administration; capital Gaza; area 363 sq km/140 sq mi; population (1988) 564,000. It was invaded by Israel 1956, reoccupied 1967, and regained 1973. Clashes between the Israeli authorities and the Palestinian people escalated to *intifada* (uprising) 1988.

Gaziantep Turkish city 185 km/115 mi NE of Adana; population (1985) 466,000. It has textile and tanning industries. Until 1922 it was known as Antep or Aintab.

Gdańsk (German *Danzig*) Polish port; population (1985) 467,000. Oil is refined, and textiles, televisions, and fertilizers are produced. Up to 1989 there were repeated strikes at the Lenin shipyards against the communist government.

Formerly a member of the Hanseatic League, it was in almost continuous Prussian possession 1793–1919, when it again became a free city under the protection of the League of Nations. Annexed by Germany 1939, it reverted to Poland 1945, when the churches and old merchant houses were restored. Possession was disputed by Germany until 1990.

GDR abbreviation for *German Democratic Republic* (East ◊Germany).

Gdynia port in N Poland; population (1985) 243,000. It was established in 1920 to give newly constituted Poland a sea outlet to replace lost ◊Gdańsk. It has a naval base and shipyards and is now part of the 'Tri-city' which includes Sopot and Gdańsk.

Geelong industrial port in S Victoria, Australia; population (1986) 148,300. In addition to oil refining and trade in grain, it produces aluminium, motor vehicles, textiles, glass, and fertilizers.

Gelderland or *Guelders* province of the E Netherlands; area 5,020 sq km/1,938 sq mi; population (1988) 1,784,000. Its capital is Arnhem. In the NW is the Veluwe, a favourite holiday resort.

Gelsenkirchen industrial city in the Ruhr, West Germany, 25 km/15 mi west of Dortmund; population (1988) 284,000. It has iron, steel, chemical, and glass industries.

Geneva (French *Genève*) Swiss city, capital of Geneva canton, on the shore of Lake Geneva; population (1987) 385,000. It is a point of convergence of natural routes, and is a cultural and commercial centre. Industries include the manufacture of watches, scientific and optical instruments, foodstuffs, jewellery, and musical boxes.

The site on which Geneva now stands was the chief settlement of the Allobroges, a central European tribe who were annexed to Rome 121 BC; Caesar built an entrenched camp here. In the Middle Ages, Geneva was controlled by the prince-bishops of Geneva and the rulers of Savoy. Under Calvin, it became a centre of the

Reformation 1536–64; the Academy, which he founded 1559, became a university 1892. Geneva was annexed by France 1798; it was freed 1814 and entered the Swiss Confederation 1815. In 1864 the International Red Cross Society was established in Geneva. It was the headquarters of the League of Nations, whose properties in Geneva passed 1946 into the possession of the United Nations.

Geneva, Lake (French *Lac Léman*) largest of the central European lakes, between Switzerland and France; area 580 sq km/225 sq mi.

Genf German form of ◊Geneva, Switzerland.

Gennesaret, Lake of another name for Lake ◊Tiberias (Sea of Galilee) in N Israel.

Genoa historic city in NW Italy, capital of Liguria; population (1988) 722,000. It is Italy's largest port; industries include oil-refining, chemicals, engineering, and textiles.

Decline followed its conquest by the Lombards 640, but from the 10th century, it established a commercial empire in the W Mediterranean, pushing back the Muslims, and founding trading posts in Corsica, Sardinia, and N Africa; during the period of the Crusades, further colonies were founded in the kingdom of Jerusalem and on the Black Sea, where Genovese merchants enjoyed the protection of the Byzantine empire. At its peak about 1300, the city had a virtual monopoly of European trade with the East. Strife between lower-class Genovese and the ruling mercantile-aristocratic oligarchy led to weakness and domination by a succession of foreign powers, including Pope John XXII (1249–1334), Robert of Anjou, king of Naples (1318–35), and Charles VI of France (1368–1422). During the 15th century, most of its trade and colonies were taken over by Venice or the Ottomans. Rebuilt after World War II, it became the busiest port on the Mediterranean, and the first to build modern container facilities. The nationalist Giuseppe Mazzini and the explorer Columbus were born here.

Genova Italian form of ◊Genoa, Italy.

Georgetown capital and port of Guyana; population (1983) 188,000. Founded 1781 by the British, it was held 1784–1812 by the Dutch, who renamed it *Stabroek*, and ceded to Britain 1814.

Georgetown or *Penang* chief port of the Federation of Malaysia, and capital of Penang, on the Island of Penang; population (1980) 250,600. It produces textiles and toys. It is named after King George III.

Georgia state of the S USA; nickname Empire State of the South/Peach State

area 152,600 sq km/58,904 sq mi

capital Atlanta

towns Columbus, Savannah, Macon

features Okefenokee National Wildlife Refuge (1,700 sq km/656 sq mi)

Georgia (USA)

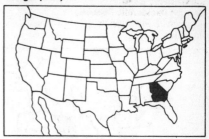

products poultry, livestock, tobacco, maize, peanuts, cotton, china clay, crushed granite, textiles, carpets, aircraft

population (1987) 6,222,000

famous people Jim Bowie, Erskine Caldwell, Jimmy Carter, Martin Luther King, Margaret Mitchell

history named after George II of England, it was founded 1733 and was one of the original Thirteen States of the USA.

Georgia (Georgian *Sakartvelo*, Russian *Gruzia*) constituent republic of the SW USSR from 1936

area 69,700 sq km/26,911 sq mi

capital Tbilisi

features holiday resorts and spas on the Black Sea; good climate

products tea, citrus, orchard fruits, tung oil, tobacco, vines, silk, hydroelectricity

population (1987) 5,266,000; 69% Georgian, 9% Armenian, 7% Russian, 5% Azerbaijani, 3% Ossetian, 2% Abkhazian

language Georgian

religion Georgian Church, independent of the Russian Orthodox Church since 1917

famous people Stalin

recent history independent republic 1918–21; uprising 1921 quelled by Soviet troops, who

Georgia (USSR)

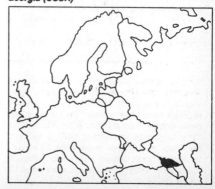

Germany, East
German Democratic Republic
*(Deutsche Demokratische
Republik)*

area 108,350 sq km/41,823 sq mi
capital East Berlin
towns Leipzig, Dresden, Karl-Marx-Stadt, Magdeburg; chief port Rostock
physical flat in north, mountains in south; rivers Elbe, Oder, and Neisse; many lakes, including Müritz
features Harz Mountains, Erzgebirge, Fichtelgebirge, Thüringer Wald
head of state Manfred Gerlach from 1989
head of government
political system socialist pluralist republic
political parties Socialist Unity Party (SED), Marxist-Leninist; New Forum, opposition umbrella pressure group; Social Democratic Party (SPD), left-of-centre; Liberal Democratic Party, Christan Democratic Union (CDU), National Democratic Party and Democratic Farmers Party, until 1989 allies of the SED; Free Democratic Party (FDP), liberal; Green Party, environmentalist
exports lignite, uranium, cobalt, coal, iron, steel, fertilizers, plastics
currency GDR Mark, or Ostmark (2.86 = £1 Feb 1990, not free rate)
population (1986) 16,640,000; annual growth rate –0.1%
life expectancy men 70, women 75
language German
religion Protestant 80%, Roman Catholic 11%
literacy 99% (1985)
GNP $86 bn (1983); $8,000 per head of population
chronology
1949 The German Democratic Republic established as an independent state.
1953 Riots in East Berlin suppressed by Soviet troops.
1961 The Berlin Wall erected to stem flow of refugees.
1964 Treaty of Friendship and Mutual Assistance signed with USSR.
1971 Erich Honecker elected Socialist Unity Party (SED) leader.
1973 Basic Treaty ratified, normalizing relations with Federal Republic.
1975 Friendship Treaty with USSR renewed for 25 years.
1987 Official visit of Honecker to the Federal Republic.
1989 East German visitors to Hungary permitted to enter Austria and the west; mass exodus to West Germany began (344,000 left during 1989). Oct: Honecker replaced by Egon Krenz following mass demonstrations calling for reform after Gorbachev's visit to East Berlin. Nov: New Forum opposition movement legalized; national borders, including Berlin Wall, opened. Reformist Hans Modrow appointed prime minister. Dec: Krenz replaced as party leader by Gysi and as president by Gerlach. Honecker placed under house arrest.
1990 Jan: Secret-police *(Stasi)* headquarters in East Berlin stormed by demonstrators. Feb: 'Grand Coalition' government formed; Modrow called for a neutral united Germany; Mar: multi-party electrons won by the right-wing Christian Democratic Union (CDU).

occupied Georgia; proclaimed republic 1921; linked with Armenia and Azerbaijan as the Transcaucasian Republic within the SW USSR 1922–36; increasing demands for autonomy from 1981, spearheaded by a Georgian Popular Front. Within the republic there have been inter-ethnic conflicts between the Osset and Abkhaz communities. Nationalist demonstrators clashed with Soviet troops in Tbilisi 1989, leaving 19 demonstrators killed by poison gas.

Gera capital of Gera county and industrial city (engineering, textiles) in S East Germany; population (1986) 132,000. Gera county has an area of 4,000 sq km/1,544 sq mi, and a population of 741,000.
Germany nation of central Europe, divided after World War II into East Germany and West Germany, with land to the east of the Oder and western Neisse rivers being divided between the USSR and Poland. Restoration of these

Germany, West
Federal Republic of Germany
(Bundesrepublik Deutschland)

area 248,706 sq km/96,001 sq mi
capital Bonn
towns West Berlin, Cologne, Munich, Essen, Frankfurt-am-Main, Dortmund, Düsseldorf; ports Hamburg, Kiel, Cuxhaven, Bremerhaven
physical flat in N, mountainous in S with Alps; rivers Rhine, Weser, Elbe flow N, Danube flows SE
features Black Forest
head of state Richard von Weizsäcker from 1984
head of government Helmut Kohl from 1982
political system democratic republic
political parties Christian Democratic Union (CDU), right-of-centre; Social Democratic Party (SPD), left-of-centre; Free Democratic Party (FDP), liberal; Christian Social Union (CSU), Bavarian-based conservative; Greens,

environmentalist; Republicans, far-right
exports machine tools (world's leading exporter), cars, commercial vehicles, electronics, industrial goods, textiles, chemicals, iron, steel, wine
currency Deutschmark (2.89 = £1 Sept 1987)
population (1986) 61,170,000 (including 4,400,000 'guest workers', *Gastarbeiter*, of whom 1,600,000 are Turks; the rest are Yugoslavs, Italians, Greeks, Spanish, and Portuguese); annual growth rate –0.2%
life expectancy men 70, women 77
language German
religion Protestant 49%, Roman Catholic 47%
literacy 99% (1985)
GNP $655 bn (1983); $9,450 per head of population
chronology
1945 German surrender and division into four (US, French, British, Soviet) occupation zones.
1948 Berlin crisis.
1949 Establishment of Federal Republic under the 'Basic Law' Constitution with Adenauer as chancellor.
1954 Grant of full sovereignty.
1957 Entry into EEC. Recovery of Saarland.
1961 Construction of Berlin Wall.
1963 Retirement of Chancellor Adenauer.
1969 Willy Brandt became chancellor.
1972 Basic Treaty with East Germany.
1974 Resignation of Brandt. Helmut Schmidt became chancellor.
1982 Kohl became chancellor.
1988 Death of Bavarian CSU leader Franz-Josef Strauss.
1989 Rising support for far-right in local and European elections, and declining support for Kohl. Cabinet reshuffle announced. Mass influx of refugees from East Germany (May onwards). In Dec Kohl unveiled ten-point plan for reunification with East Germany.

'lost territories' (Silesia, Pomerania, Sudetenland, and East Prussia), a third of the former area, remains a political issue. After the opening of the Berlin Wall 1989, the two Germanys moved rapidly towards reunification. A treaty committing East and West to economic, monetary, and social union under the West German system from July 1990 was signed in May, and joint elections were scheduled for Dec 1990.

Germany, East country in E Europe, bounded to the N by the Baltic Sea, E by Poland, S by Czechoslovakia, and SW and W by West Germany.

Germany, West country in W Europe, bounded to the N by the North Sea and Denmark, E by East Germany and Czechoslovakia, S by Austria and

Switzerland, and W by France, Belgium, Luxembourg, and the Netherlands.

Germiston town in the Transvaal, South Africa; population (1980) 155,435. Industries include gold refining, chemicals, steel, textiles.

Gerona town in Catalonia, NE Spain, capital of Gerona province; population (1986) 68,000. Industries include textiles and chemicals. There are ferry links with Ibiza, Barcelona, and Málaga.

Gers river in France, 178 km/110 mi in length; it rises in the Lannemezan Plateau and flows north to join the Garonne 8 km/5 mi above Agen. It gives its name to a *département* in Midi-Pyrénées region.

Gethsemane site of the garden where Judas Iscariot, according to the New Testament, betrayed Jesus.

It is on the Mount of Olives, east of Jerusalem. When Jerusalem was divided between Israel and Jordan 1948, Gethsemane fell within Jordanian territory.

Germany: regions

Republic	Capital	Area sq km
WEST GERMANY Land (Region)	BONN	248,710
Baden-Württemberg	Stuttgart	35,800
Bavaria	Munich	70,600
Bremen	Bremen	400
Hamburg	Hamburg	760
Hessen	Wiesbaden	21,100
Lower Saxony	Hanover	47,400
North Rhine-Westphalia	Düsseldorf	34,100
Rhineland-Palatinate	Mainz	19,800
Saarland	Saarbrücken	2,570
Schleswig-Holstein	Kiel	15,700
West Berlin	West Berlin	480
EAST GERMANY Bezirk (County)	EAST BERLIN	108,350
East Berlin		400
Cottbus	Cottbus	8,260
Dresden	Dresden	6,740
Erfurt	Erfurt	7,350
Frankfurt	Frankfurt	7,190
Gera	Gera	4,000
Halle	Halle	8,770
Karl-Marx-Stadt	Karl-Marx-Stadt	6,010
Leipzig	Leipzig	4,970
Magdeburg	Magdeburg	11,530
Neubrandenburg	Neubrandenburg	10,950
Potsdam	Potsdam	12,570
Rostock	Rostock	7,080
Schwerin	Schwerin	8,670
Suhl	Suhl	3,860

Gezira, El plain in the Republic of Sudan, between the Blue and White Niles. The cultivation of cotton, sorghum, wheat, and groundnuts is made possible by irrigation.

Ghaghara or *Gogra* river in N India, a tributary of the ◊Ganges, which rises in Tibet and flows through Nepál and the state of Uttar Pradesh; length 1,000 km/600 mi.

Ghana country in W Africa, bounded to the N by Burkina Faso, E by Togo, S by the Gulf of Guinea, and W by the Ivory Coast.

Ghats, Eastern and Western twin mountain ranges in S India, to the E and W of the central plateau; a few peaks reach about 3,000 m/9,800 ft. They are connected by the Nilgiri Hills. The name is a European misnomer, the Indian word *ghat* meaning pass, not mountain.

Ghent (Flemish *Gent*, French *Gand*) city and port in East Flanders, NW Belgium; population (1982) 237,500. Industries include textiles, chemicals, electronics, and metallurgy. The cathedral of St Bavon (12th–14th centuries) has paintings by van Eyck and Rubens, and the university was established 1816.

Gibraltar British dependency, situated on a narrow rocky promontory in S Spain

area 6.5 sq km/2.5 sq mi

features strategic naval and air base, with NATO underground headquarters and communications centre; colony of Barbary apes; the frontier zone is adjoined by the Spanish port of La Línea

exports mainly a trading centre for the import and re-export of goods

population (1988) 30,000

recent history captured from Spain 1704 by English admiral George Rooke (1650–1709), it was ceded to Britain under the Treaty of Utrecht 1713. A referendum 1967 confirmed the wish of the people to remain in association with the UK, but Spain continues to claim sovereignty, and closed the border 1969–85. In 1989, the UK government announced it would reduce the military garrison by half

currency Gibraltar government notes and UK coinage

language English

religion mainly Roman Catholic

government the governor has executive authority, with the advice of the Gibraltar council, and there is an elected house of assembly (chief minister Joshua Hassan 1964–69 and from 1972).

Gibson Desert desert in central Western Australia; area 220,000 sq km/85,000 sq mi.

Giessen manufacturing town on the Lahn, Hessen, West Germany; population (1984) 71,800. Its university was established 1605.

Gijón port on the Bay of Biscay, Oviedo province, N Spain; population (1986) 259,000. It produces iron, steel, chemicals, and oil, is an outlet for the coalmines of Asturias, and is an important fishing and shipbuilding centre.

Gilbert and Ellice Islands former British colony in the Pacific, known since independence 1978 as ◊Tuvalu and ◊Kiribati.

Gilgit town and region on the NW frontier of Kashmir, under the rule of Pakistan.

Gippsland Lakes series of shallow lagoons on the coast of Victoria, Australia. The main ones are Wellington, Victoria and King (broadly interconnected), and Reeve.

Girgenti former name (until 1927) of ◊Agrigento, a town in Sicily, Italy.

Gironde navigable estuary 80 km/50 mi long, formed by the mouths of the ◊Garonne, length 580 km/360 mi, and ◊Dordogne rivers, in SW France. The Lot, length 480 km/300 mi, is a tributary of the Garonne.

Ghana
Republic of

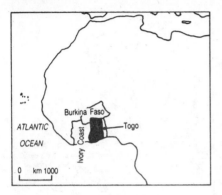

area 238,305 sq km/91,986 sq mi
capital Accra
towns Kumasi, and ports Sekondi-Takoradi,
Tema
physical mostly plains; bisected by river Volta
features artificial Lake Volta; relics of traditional
kingdom of Ashanti
head of state and government Jerry Rawlings
from 1981
political system military republic
political parties all political parties were
banned 1981

exports cocoa, coffee, timber, gold, diamonds,
manganese, bauxite
currency cedi (524.37 = £1 Feb 1990)
population (1988) 13,812,000; annual growth
rate 3.2%
life expectancy men 50, women 54
language English (official)
religion Christian 43%, animist 38%, Muslim
12%
literacy 64% male/43% female (1985 est)
GNP $3.9 bn (1983); $420 per head of
population
chronology
1957 Independence achieved, within the
Commonwealth, with Kwame Nkrumah as
president.
1960 Ghana became a republic and a one-party
state.
1966 Nkrumah deposed and replaced by Gen
Joseph Ankrah.
1969 Ankrah replaced by Gen Akwasi Afrifa,
who initiated a return to civilian government.
1970 Edward Akufo-Addo elected president.
1972 Another coup placed Col Acheampong at
the head of a military government.
1978 Acheampong deposed in a bloodless
coup led by Frederick Akuffo. Another coup put
Flight Lt Jerry Rawlings in power.
1979 Return to civilian rule under Hilla Limann.
1982 Rawlings seized power again, citing the
incompetence of previous governments.
1989 Coup attempt against Rawlings foiled.

Gisborne port on the E coast of North Island, New
Zealand, exporting dairy products, wool and meat;
population (1986) 32,200.
Giza, El or **al-Jizah** site of the Great Pyramids
and Sphinx, a suburb of ◊Cairo, Egypt; popu-
lation (1983) 1,500,000. It has textile and film
industries.
Glace Bay port on Cape Breton Island, Nova Scotia,
Canada, centre of a coal-mining area; population
(1986) 20,500.
Glamorgan three counties of S Wales – ◊Mid,
◊South, and ◊West Glamorgan – created in 1974
from the former county of Glamorganshire. Mid
Glamorgan also takes in a small area of the former
county of Monmouthshire to the east. All are on
the Bristol Channel.
Glasgow city and administrative headquarters of
Strathclyde, Scotland; population (1985) 734,000.
Industries include engineering, chemicals, print-
ing, and distilling.
    Buildings include the 12th-century cathedral
of St Mungo, and the Cross Steeple (part
of the historic Tolbooth); the universities of
Glasgow, established 1451 (19th-century buildings

by Sir Gilbert Scott) and Strathclyde, established
1964; the Royal Exchange, the Stock Exchange,
Kelvingrove Art Gallery (Impressionist collection); the Glasgow School of Art, designed by
C R Mackintosh; the Burrell Collection at Pollock
Park, bequeathed by shipping magnate Sir William
Burrell (1861–1958); Mitchell Library.
Glastonbury market town in Somerset, England;
population (1981) 6,773. Nearby are two excavated lake villages thought to have been occupied
for about 150 years before the Romans came to
Britain.
    The first church on the site was traditionally
founded in the 1st century by Joseph of Arima-
thea. The ruins of the Benedictine abbey built in
the 10th–11th centuries by Dunstan and his followers were excavated in 1963 and the site of the
grave of King Arthur and Queen Guinevere was
thought to have been identified. One of Europe's
largest pop festivals is held annually in June to
benefit CND.
Glencoe glen in Strathclyde region, Scotland,
where members of the Macdonald clan were
massacred in 1692. John Campbell, Earl of

Gibraltar

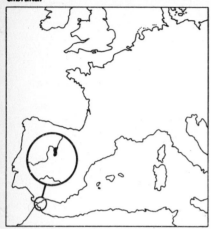

Gloucestershire

Breadalbane, was the chief instigator. It is now a winter sports area.

Gleneagles glen in Tayside, Scotland, famous for its golf course and for the *Gleneagles Agreement*, formulated in 1977 at the Gleneagles Hotel by Commonwealth heads of government, that 'every practical step (should be taken) to discourage contact or competition by their nationals' with South Africa, in opposition to apartheid.

Glenrothes town and administrative headquarters of Fife, Scotland, 10 km/6 mi N of Kirkcaldy, developed as a 'new town' from 1948; population (1981) 32,700. Industries include electronics, plastics, and paper.

Glittertind the highest mountain in Norway, rising to 2,470 m/8,110 ft in the Jotunheim range.

Gliwice city in Katowice region, S Poland, formerly in German Silesia; population (1985) 213,000. It has coal-mining, iron, steel, and electrical industries. It is connected to the river Oder by the Gliwice Canal.

Glomma river in Norway, 570 km/350 mi long. The largest river in Scandinavia, it flows into the Skagerrak at Frederikstad.

Glos abbreviation for ◊*Gloucestershire*.

Gloucester city, port, and administrative headquarters of Gloucestershire, England; population (1983) 92,200. Industries include the manufacture of aircraft and agricultural machinery. Its 11th–14th-century cathedral has a Norman nucleus and additions in every style of Gothic.

Gloucestershire county in SW England
area 2,640 sq km/1,019 sq mi
towns administrative headquarters Gloucester; Stroud, Cheltenham, Tewkesbury, Cirencester
features Cotswold Hills; river Severn and tributaries; Berkeley Castle, where Edward II was murdered; Prinknash Abbey, famous for pottery; Cotswold Farm Park, near Stow-on-the Wold, for rare and ancient breeds of farm animals
products cereals, fruit, dairy products; engineering, coal in the Forest of Dean
population (1987) 522,000.
famous people Edward Jenner.

Goa state of India
area 3,700 sq km/1,428 sq mi
capital Panaji
population (1981) 1,003,000
history Goa was captured by the Portuguese 1510, and the inland area was added in the 18th century. Goa was incorporated into India as a Union Territory with ◊Daman and ◊Diu 1961, and became a state 1987.

Gobi Asian desert divided between the Mongolian People's Republic and Inner Mongolia, China; 800 km/500 mi N–S, and 1,600 km/1,000 mi E–W. It is rich in fossil remains of extinct species.

Godalming town in Surrey, England; population (1981) 18,200. Industries include engineering and textiles.

Godavari river in central India, flowing from the Western Ghats to the Bay of Bengal; length 1,450 km/900 mi. It is sacred to Hindus.

Godthaab (Greenlandic *Nuuk*) capital and largest town of Greenland; population (1982) 9,700. It is a storage centre for oil and gas, and the chief industry is fish processing.

Gogra alternative transcription of river ◊Ghaghara in India.

Golan Heights (Arabic *Jawlan*) plateau on the Syrian border with Israel, bitterly contested in the Arab-Israeli Wars, and annexed by Israel on 14 Dec 1981.

Gold Coast the former name for ◊Ghana, but historically, the W coast of Africa from Cape Three Points to the Volta river, where alluvial gold is washed down. Portuguese and French navigators visited this coast in the 14th century, and a British trading settlement developed into the colony of the Gold Coast 1618. With its dependencies of Ashanti and Northern Territories plus the trusteeship territory of Togoland, it became Ghana 1957. The name is also used for many coastal resort areas; for example, in Queensland, Australia, and Florida, USA.

Gold Coast resort region on the east coast of Australia, stretching 32 km/20 mi along the coast of Queensland and New South Wales south of Brisbane; population (1986) 219,000.

Golden Gate strait in California, USA, linking ◊San Francisco Bay with the Pacific, spanned by a bridge which was completed 1937. The longest span is 1,280 m/4,200 ft.

Gondar town in Ethiopia about 2,300 m/7,500 ft above sea level and 40 km/25 mi N of Lake Tana; population (1984) 69,000.

Goodwin Sands sandbanks off the coast of Kent, England, exposed at low tide, and famous for wrecks. According to legend, they are the remains of the island of Lomea, owned by Earl Godwin in the 11th century.

Goose Bay a settlement at the head of Lake Melville on the Labrador coast of Newfoundland, Canada. In World War II it was used as a staging post by US and Canadian troops on their way to Europe. Until 1975 it was used by the US Air Force as a low-level-flying base.

Gorakhpur city in Uttar Pradesh, N India, situated on the Rapti river, at the centre of an agricultural region producing cotton, rice, and grain; population (1981) 306,000.

Gorgonzola small town NE of Milan, Italy, famous for cheese.

Gorizia town in Friuli-Venezia-Giulia region, N Italy, on the Isonzo, SE of Udine; population (1981) 41,500. Industries include textiles, furniture, and paper. It has a 16th-century castle, and was a cultural centre during Habsburg rule.

Gorky (Russian *Gor'kiy*) (former name Nizhny-Novgorod until 1932) city in central USSR; population (1987) 1,425,000. Cars, locomotives, and aircraft are manufactured here.

Görlitz manufacturing town in Dresden county, East Germany; population (1981) 81,000.

Gorlovka industrial town (coalmining, chemicals, engineering) on the ◊Donbas coalfield, Ukraine, USSR; population (1987) 345,000.

Gosport naval port opposite ◊Portsmouth, Hampshire, England; population (1981) 77,250.

Göteborg (German *Gothenburg*) port and industrial (ships, vehicles, chemicals) city on the west

Grampian

coast of Sweden, on the Göta Canal (built 1832), which links it with Stockholm; population (1988) 432,000. It is Sweden's second largest city.

Gotha town in Erfurt county, SW East Germany, former capital of the duchy of Saxe-Coburg-Gotha; population (1981) 57,600. It has a castle and two observatories; pottery, soap, textiles, precision instruments, and aircraft are manufactured here.

Gothenburg German form of ◊Göteborg, city in Sweden.

Gotland Swedish island in the Baltic Sea; area 3,140 sq km/1,212 sq mi; population (1986) 56,200. The capital is Visby. Its products are mainly agricultural (sheep and cattle), and there is tourism. It was an area of dispute between Sweden and Denmark, but became part of Sweden 1645.

Göttingen town in Lower Saxony, West Germany; population (1988) 134,000. Industries include printing, publishing, precision instruments, and chemicals. Its university was founded by George II of England 1734.

Gouda town in Zuid Holland, W Netherlands; population (1987) 61,500. It produces round flat cheeses.

Goulburn town in New South Wales, Australia, SW of Sydney; population (1983) 22,500. It is an agricultural centre, and manufactures bricks, tiles, and pottery.

Gower Peninsula peninsula in West ◊Glamorgan, S Wales.

Grafton town in New South Wales, Australia, S of Brisbane; population (1985) 17,600. Industries include sugar, timber, and dairy products.

Graham Land mountainous peninsula in Antarctica, formerly a dependency of the Falkland Islands, and from 1962 part of the ◊British Antarctic Territory.

It was discovered by John Biscoe in 1832, and until 1934 was thought to be an archipelago.

Grahamstown town in SE Cape Province, South Africa; population (1985) 75,000. It is the seat of Rhodes University, established 1951, founded in 1904 as Rhodes University College.

Grampian region of Scotland
area 8,600 sq km/3,320 sq mi
towns administrative headquarters Aberdeen
features part of the Grampian Mountains (the Cairngorms); valley of the river Spey, with its whisky distilleries; Balmoral Castle (royal residence on the river Dee near Braemar, bought by Prince Albert 1852, and rebuilt in Scottish baronial style); Braemar Highland Games in Aug
products beef cattle (Aberdeen Angus and Beef Shorthorn), fishing, North Sea oil service industries, tourism (winter skiing)
population (1987) 503,000.

Grampian Mountains a range that separates the Highlands from the Lowlands of Scotland, running NE from Strathclyde. It takes in the S Highland region (which includes **Ben Nevis**, the highest mountain in the British Isles at 1,340 m/4,406 ft), northern Tayside, and the S border of Grampian region itself (the Cairngorms, which include **Ben Macdhui** 1,309 m/4,296 ft). The region includes Aviemore, a winter holiday and sports centre.

Grampians western end of Australia's eastern highlands, in Victoria; the highest peak is Mount William 1,167 m/3,829 ft.

Granada city in the Sierra Nevada in Andalucia, S Spain; population (1986) 281,000. It produces textiles, soap, and paper.
history Founded by the Moors in the 8th century, it became the capital of an independent kingdom 1236–1492, when it was the last Moorish stronghold to surrender to the Spaniards. Ferdinand and Isabella, the first sovereigns of a united Spain, are buried in the cathedral (built 1529–1703). The *Alhambra*, a fortified hilltop palace, was built in the 13th–14th centuries by the Moorish kings.

Granada Nicaraguan city on the NW shore of Lake Nicaragua; population (1985) 89,000. It has shipyards, and manufactures sugar, soap, clothing, and furniture. Founded 1523, it is the oldest city in Nicaragua.

Gran Chaco large lowland plain in N Argentina, W Paraguay, and SE Bolivia; area 650,000 sq km/251,000 sq mi. It consists of swamps, forests (a source of quebracho timber), and grasslands, and there is cattle-raising.

Grand Canal (Chinese *Da Yune*) the world's longest canal. It is 1,600 km/1,000 mi long, and runs north from Hangzhou to Tianjin, China. It is 30–61 m/100–200 ft wide, and 0.6–4.6 m/2–15 ft deep. The earliest section was completed 486 BC, and the northern section was built 1282–92 AD, during the reign of Kublai Khan.

Grand Canyon vast gorge containing the Colorado River, Arizona, USA. It is 350 km/217 mi long, 6–29 km/4–18 mi wide, and reaches depths of over 1.5 km/1 mi. It was made a national park in 1919.

Grand Falls town in Newfoundland, Canada; population (1986) 9,100. It is the site of large paper and pulp mills.

Grand Rapids city in W Michigan, USA, on the river Grand; population (1980) 602,000. It produces furniture, motor bodies, plumbing fixtures, and electrical goods.

Grand Teton highest point of the spectacular Teton range, NW Wyoming, USA, rising to 4,197 m/13,770 ft. Grand Teton National Park was established 1929.

Grantham market town in SE Lincolnshire, England; population (1981) 30,084. It is an agricultural centre, dating from Saxon times. Margaret Thatcher was born here.

Grasmere English lake and village in the Lake District, Cumbria. William Wordsworth and his sister Dorothy lived at Dove Cottage (now a museum) 1799–1808, Thomas de Quincey later made his home in the same house, and both Samuel Coleridge and Wordsworth are buried in the churchyard of St Oswald's.

Grasse town near Cannes, SE France; population (1982) 38,360. It is the centre of a perfume-manufacturing region, and flowers are grown on a large scale for this purpose.

Graubünden Swiss canton, the largest in Switzerland; area 7,106 sq km/2,743 sq mi; population (1986) 167,000. The inner valleys are the highest in Europe, and the main sources of the river Rhine rise here. It also includes the resort of Davos, and, in the Upper Engadine, St Moritz. The capital is Chur. Romansch is still widely spoken. Graubünden entered the Swiss Confederation 1803.

Gravesend town on the Thames, Kent, SE England, linked by ferry with Tilbury opposite; population (1981) 52,963.

Graz capital of Styria province, and second largest city in Austria; population (1981) 243,400. Industries include engineering, chemicals, iron, and steel. It has a 15th-century cathedral and a university founded in 1573. The famous Lippizaner horses are bred near here.

Great Barrier Reef chain of coral reefs and islands about 2,000 km/1,250 mi long, off the E coast of Queensland, Australia at a distance of 15–45 km/10–30 mi. It forms an immense natural breakwater, and the coral rock forms a structure larger than all human-made structures on Earth combined.

The reef is in danger from a swarm of starfish, which are reported to have infested 35% of the reef. Some scientists fear the entire reef will disappear within 50 years.

Greece
Hellenic Republic
(Elliniki Dimokratia)

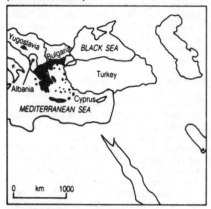

area 131,957 sq km/50,935 sq mi
capital Athens
towns ports Thessaloniki, Patras, Larisa,
Iráklion
physical mountainous; a large number of
islands, notably Crete, Corfu, and Rhodes
features Corinth canal; Mount Olympus;
archaeological sites; US military bases at
Hellenikon, Nea Makri (both near Athens), and
(on Crete) at Souda Bay near Iráklion
head of state Christos Sartzetakis from 1985
head of government Xenophon Zolotas
from 1989
political system democratic republic
political parties Panhellenic Socialist
Movement (PASOK), democratic socialist; New
Democracy Party (ND), centre-right
exports tobacco, fruit (including currants),
vegetables, olives, olive oil, textiles
currency drachma (268.50 = £1 Feb 1990)
population (1987) 9,990,000; annual growth
rate 0.5%
life expectancy men 72, women 76

language Greek
religion Greek Orthodox, Christian 97%
literacy 96% male/89% female (1985)
GNP $32.4 bn (1984); $3,260 per head of
population
chronology
1946 Civil war between royalists and
communists. Communists defeated.
1949 Monarchy re-established with Paul as king.
1964 King Paul succeeded by his son
Constantine.
1967 Army coup removed the king and Col
George Papadopoulos became prime minister.
Martial law imposed and all political activity
banned.
1973 Republic proclaimed, with Papadopoulos
as president.
1974 Former premier Constantine Karamanlis
recalled from exile to lead government.
Martial law and ban on political parties lifted.
Restoration of the monarchy rejected by a
referendum.
1975 New constitution adopted, making Greece
a republic.
1980 Karamanlis resigned as prime minister
and was elected president.
1981 Greece became a full member of the EC
Andreas Papandreou elected Greece's first
socialist prime minister.
1983 Five-year defence and economic
cooperation agreement signed with the US.
Ten-year economic cooperation agreement
signed with USSR.
1985 Papandreou re-elected.
1988 Relations with Turkey improved. Major
cabinet reshuffle following mounting criticism of
Papandreou.
1989 Papandreou defeated in elections.
Tzannis Tzannetakis, Conservative
backbencher, became prime minister, heading
first all-party government, including communists,
for 15 years. This broke up and Xenophon
Zolotas formed new unity government.

Great Bear Lake lake on the Arctic Circle,
in the Northwest Territories, Canada; area
31,800 sq km/12,275 sq mi.

Great Britain official name for ◊England, ◊Scotland,
and ◊Wales, and the adjacent islands, from 1603
when the English and Scottish crowns were
united under James I of England (James VI of
Scotland). With Northern ◊Ireland it forms the
◊United Kingdom.

Great Divide or *Great Dividing Range* E Australian mountain range, extending 3,700 km/2,300 mi
N–S from Cape York Peninsula, Queensland,
to Victoria. It includes the Carnarvon Range,

Queensland, which has many Aboriginal cave
paintings, the Blue Mountains in New South
Wales, and the Australian Alps.

Great Lake Australia's largest freshwater lake,
1,025 m/3,380 ft above sea level, in Tasmania;
area 114 sq km/44 sq mi. It is used for hydroelectric power and is a tourist attraction.

Great Lakes series of five freshwater lakes
along the USA–Canada border: Lakes Superior,
Michigan, Huron, Erie, and Ontario; total
area 245,000 sq km/94,600 sq mi. Interconnect-
ing canals make them navigable by large ships,
and they are drained by the ◊St Lawrence River.

They are said to contain 20% of the world's fresh water.

Great Plains a semiarid region to the E of the Rocky Mountains, USA, stretching as far as the 100th meridian of longitude through Oklahoma, Kansas, Nebraska and the Dakotas. The plains, which cover one-fifth of the USA, extend from Texas in the S over 2,400 km/ 1,500 mi N to Canada. Ranching and wheat farming have resulted in overexploitation of the water resources to such an extent that available farmland has been reduced by erosion.

Great Rift Valley longest 'split' in the Earth's surface, 8,000 km/5,000 mi long, running south from the Dead Sea (Israel/Jordan) to Mozambique; see ◊Rift Valley, Great.

Great Sandy Desert desert in N Western Australia; area 415,000 sq km/160,000 sq mi. It is also the name of an arid region in S Oregon, USA.

Great Slave Lake lake in the Northwest Territories, Canada; area 28,450 sq km/10,980 sq mi. It is the deepest lake (615 m/2,020 ft) in North America.

Great Wall of China continuous wall stretching 2,250 km/1,450 mi from W Gansu to the Gulf of Liaodong; it was once even longer. A brick-faced wall of earth and stone, some 8 m/25 ft high, with a series of square watch towers, it was built under the Qin dynasty from 214 BC to prevent incursions by Turks and Mongols, and has been carefully restored.

Great Yarmouth alternative name for the resort and port of ◊Yarmouth in Norfolk, England.

Greece country in SE Europe, comprising the S Balkan peninsula, bounded N by Yugoslavia and Bulgaria, NE by Turkey, E by the Aegean Sea, S by the Mediterranean Sea, W by the Ionian Sea, NW by Albania, and numerous islands to the S and E.

Greenland (Greenlandic *Kalaalit Nunaat*) world's largest island. It lies between the North Atlantic and Arctic Oceans.
area 2,175,600 sq km/840,000 sq mi
capital Godthaab (Greenlandic *Nuuk*) on the W coast
features the whole of the interior is covered by a vast ice-sheet; the island has importance in civil aviation and strategically, and military activities are shared with the USA; there are lead and cryolite deposits, and offshore oil is being explored
economy fishing and fish processing
population (1983) 51,903; Inuit, Danish, and other European
language Greenlandic
history Greenland was discovered about 982 by Eric the Red, who founded colonies on the W coast. Christianity was introduced about 1000.

In 1261 the colonies accepted Norwegian sovereignty, but early in the 15th century all communication with Europe ceased, and by the 16th century the colonies had died out. It became a Danish colony in the 18th century, and following a referendum 1979 was granted full internal self-government 1981.

Greenland Sea area of the ◊Arctic Ocean between Spitsbergen and Greenland, and north of the Norwegian Sea.

Greenock port on the S shore of the Firth of Clyde, Strathclyde, Scotland; population (1981) 59,000. Industries include shipbuilding, engineering, and electronics. It is the birthplace of James Watt.

Greenwich inner borough of Greater London, England; population (1981) 212,001.
features the *Queen's House* 1637, designed by Inigo Jones, the first Palladian-style building in England, since 1937 housing part of the *National Maritime Museum*; the *Royal Naval College*, designed by Christopher Wren in 1694 as a naval hospital to replace a palace previously on this site (the birthplace of Henry VIII, Mary and Elizabeth I), and used as a college since 1873; the *Royal Greenwich Observatory* (founded here in 1675). The source of Greenwich Mean Time has been moved to ◊Herstmonceux, but the Greenwich meridian (0°) remains unchanged. Part of the buildings have been taken over by the National Maritime Museum, and named Flamsteed House after the first Astronomer Royal. The *Cutty Sark*, most celebrated of the great tea clippers, is preserved as a museum of sail, and Francis Chichester's *Gipsy Moth IV* is also here. The borough also includes *Woolwich* with the Royal Arsenal; and Eltham Palace 1300.

Grenada island in the Caribbean, the southernmost of the Windward Islands.

Grenadines chain of about 600 small islands in the Caribbean, part of the group known as the Windward Islands. They are divided between ◊St Vincent and ◊Grenada.

Grenoble alpine town in Rhône-Alpes region, SE France; population (1982) 159,500, conurbation 392,000. Industries include engineering, nuclear research, hydroelectric power, computers, technology, chemicals, plastics, and gloves. It was the birthplace of the novelist Stendhal, commemorated by a museum, and the Beaux Arts gallery has a modern collection. There is a 12th–13th-century cathedral, a university 1339, and the Institut Laue-Langevin for nuclear research. The 1968 Winter Olympics were held here.

Grimsby fishing port in Humberside, England; population (1985) 95,000. It declined in the 1970s when Icelandic waters were closed to British fishermen.

Grisons French name for the Swiss canton of ◊Graubünden.

Grenada

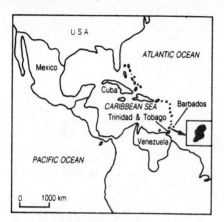

area (including the Grenadines, notably Carriacou) 310 sq km/120 sq mi
capital St George's
physical southernmost of the Windward Islands; mountainous
features smallest independent nation in the western hemisphere
head of state Elizabeth II from 1974 represented by Paul Scoon
head of government Ben Jones from 1989
political system emergent democracy
political parties New National Party (NNP), centrist; Grenada United Labour Party (GULP), nationalist left-of-centre

exports cocoa, nutmeg, bananas, mace
currency Eastern Caribbean dollar (4.56 = £1 Feb 1990)
population (1987) 92,000; annual growth rate 1.2%
language English
religion Roman Catholic
literacy 85% (1985)
GDP $116 million (1983); $500 per head of population
chronology
1974 Full independence achieved, with Eric Gairy elected prime minister.
1979 Gairy was removed in a bloodless coup led by Maurice Bishop. Constitution suspended and a people's revolutionary government established.
1982 Relations with the US and Britain deteriorated as ties with Cuba and USSR strengthened. Bishop feared impending US invasion.
1983 After Bishop's attempt to improve relations with the US, he was overthrown by left-wing opponents. A coup established the Revolutionary Military Council (RMC) and Bishop and some of his colleagues were executed. The US, accompanied by troops from some other E Caribbean countries, invaded Grenada, overthrowing the RMC. The 1974 constitution was reinstated.
1984 The newly formed NNP won 14 of the 15 seats in the house of representatives, and its leader, Herbert Blaize, became prime minister.
1989 Herbert Blaize died and was succeeded by Ben Jones.

Grodno industrial town in Byelorussia, USSR, on the Sozh river; population (1987) 263,000. Part of Lithuania from 1376, it passed to Poland 1596, Russia 1795, Poland 1920, and Russia 1939.

Groningen most northerly province of the Netherlands; area 2,350 sq km/907 sq mi; population (1988) 557,000. Capital is Groningen; population (1988) 207,000. Industries include textiles, tobacco, and sugar refining.

Grossglockner highest mountain in Austria, rising to 3,797 m/12,457 ft in the Hohe Tauern range of the Tirol alps.

Grozny capital of the Checheno-Ingush republic, USSR; population (1987) 404,000. It is an oil-producing centre.

Gruyère district in W Switzerland, famous for pale yellow cheese with large holes.

Guadalajara industrial (textiles, glass, soap, pottery) capital of Jalisco state, W Mexico; population (1986) 2,587,000. It is a key communications centre. It has a 16th–17th-century cathedral, the Governor's Palace, and an orphanage with murals by the Mexican painter José Orozco.

Guadalcanal largest of the ◊Solomon Islands; area 6,500 sq km/2,510 sq mi; population (1987) 71,000. Gold, copra, and rubber are produced. During World War II it was the scene of a battle which was won by US forces after six months of fighting.

Guadeloupe an island group in the Leeward Islands, West Indies, an overseas department of France; area 1,705 sq km/658 sq mi; population (1982) 328,400. The main islands are Basse-Terre, on which is the chief town of the same name, and Grande-Terre. Sugar refining and rum distilling are the main industries.

Guam largest of the ◊Mariana Islands in the W Pacific, an unincorporated territory of the USA
area 540 sq km/208 sq mi
capital Agaña

Guatemala
Republic of
(República de Guatemala)

area 108,889 sq km/42,031 sq mi
capital Guatemala City
towns Quezaltenango, Puerto Barrios (naval base)
physical mountainous, tropical
features earthquakes are frequent
head of state and government Mario Vinicio Cerezo Arevalo from 1986
political system democratic republic
political parties Guatemalan Christian Democratic Party (PDCG), Christian centre-left; Centre Party (UCN), centrist; National Democratic Co-operation Party (PDNC), centre-right; Revolutionary Party (PR), radical; Movement of National Liberation (MLN), extreme right-wing; Democratic Institutional Party (PID),

moderate conservative
exports coffee, bananas, cotton
currency quetzal (6.42 = £1 Feb 1990)
population (1988) 8,990,000 (Mayaquiche Indians 54%, mestizos 42%); annual growth rate 2.8%
life expectancy men 57, women 61
language Spanish
religion Roman Catholic
literacy 63% male/47% female (1985 est)
GDP $9.9 bn (1984); $1,085 per head of population
chronology
1839 Independent republic.
1954 Col Carlos Castillo became president in a US-backed coup, halting land reform.
1963 Military coup made Col Enrique Peralta president.
1966 Cesar Méndez elected president.
1970 Carlos Araña elected president.
1974 Gen Kjell Laugerud became president. Widespread political violence.
1978 Gen Fernando Romeo became president.
1981 Growth of anti-government guerrilla movement.
1982 Gen Angel Anibal became president. An army coup installed Gen Ríos Montt as head of a junta and then as president. Political violence continued.
1983 Montt removed in a coup led by Gen Mejía Victores, who declared amnesty for the guerrillas.
1985 New constitution adopted; PDCG won congressional elections; Vincio Cerezo elected president.
1989 Coup attempt against Cerezo foiled. Over 100,000 people killed and 40,000 reported missing since 1979.

towns port Apra
features major US air and naval base, much used in the Vietnam War; tropical, with much rain
products sweet potatoes, fish; tourism is important
currency US dollar
population (1984) 116,000
language English, Chamorro (basically Malay-Polynesian)
religion Roman Catholic 96%
government popularly elected governor (Ricardo Bordallo from 1985) and single-chamber legislature
recent history Guam was ceded by Spain to the USA 1898, and occupied by Japan 1941–44. It was granted full US citizenship and self-government from 1950. A referendum 1982 favoured Commonwealth status.

Guanch Republic proposed name for an independent state in the ◊Canary Islands.
Guangdong formerly *Kwantung* province of S China
area 231,400 sq km/89,320 sq mi
capital Guangzhou
features tropical climate; Hainan, Leizhou peninsula, and the foreign enclaves of Hong Kong and Macao in the Pearl River delta
products rice, sugar, tobacco, minerals, fish
population (1986) 63,640,000.
Guangxi formerly *Kwangsi Chuang* autonomous region in S China
area 220,400 sq km/85,074 sq mi
capital Nanning
products rice, sugar, fruit
population (1986) 39,460,000, including the Zhuang people, allied to the Thai, who form China's largest ethnic minority.

Guinea
Republic of
(République de Guinée)

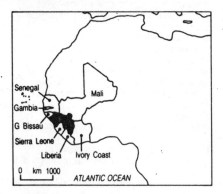

Senegal
Mali
Gambia
G Bissau
Sierra Leone
Liberia   Ivory Coast
0   km 1000
ATLANTIC OCEAN

area 245,857 sq km/94,901 sq mi
capital Conakry
towns Labe, N'Zerekore, KanKan
physical mainly mountainous; sources of rivers
Niger, Gambia, and Senegal; forest in SE
features Fouta Djallon, area of sandstone
plateaus, cut by deep valleys
head of state and government Lansana Conté
from 1984

political system military republic
political parties none since 1984
exports coffee, rice, palm kernels, alumina,
bauxite, diamonds
currency syli or franc (510.75 = £1 Feb 1990)
population (1988) 6,533,000 (chief peoples are
Fulani 40%, Mandingo 25%); annual growth
rate 2.3%
life expectancy men 39, women 42
language French (official)
religion Muslim 62%, Christian 15%, local 35%
literacy 40% male/17% female (1985 est)
GNP $1.6 bn (1983); $305 per head of
population
chronology
1958 Full independence from France achieved.
Sékou Touré elected president.
1977 Strong opposition to Touré's policies of
rigid Marxism forced him to accept the return of
a mixed economy.
1980 Touré returned unopposed for a fourth
seven-year term of office.
1984 Touré died. A bloodless coup established
a military committee for national recovery, with
Col Lansana Conté at its head.
1985 Attempted coup against Conté while
he was out of the country was foiled by loyal
troops.

Guangzhou formerly *Kwangchow/Canton* capital of Guangdong province, S China; population
(1986) 3,290,000. Its industries include shipbuilding, engineering, chemicals, and textiles. Sun
Yat-sen Memorial Hall, a theatre, commemorates
the politician, who was born nearby and founded
the university. There is a rail link with Beijing and
one is planned with Liuzhai.
history It was the first Chinese port opened to
foreign trade, the Portuguese visiting it 1516, and
was a treaty port from 1842 until its occupation
by Japan 1938.
Guantanamo capital of a province of the same name
in SE Cuba; population (1986) 174,400; a trading
centre in a fertile agricultural region producing
sugar. Iron, copper, chromium and manganese
are mined nearby. There is a US naval base.
Guatemala country in Central America, bounded N
and NW by Mexico, E by Belize and the Caribbean
Sea, SE by Honduras and El Salvador, and SW by
the Pacific Ocean.
Guatemala City capital of Guatemala; population
(1983) 1,300,000. It produces textiles, tyres,
footwear, and cement. It was founded in 1776
when its predecessor (Antigua) was destroyed
in an earthquake. It was severely damaged by
another earthquake 1976.

Guayaquil city and chief Pacific port of Ecuador, at
the mouth of the Guayas River; population (1982)
1,300,868.
Guelders another name for ◊Gelderland, a region
of the Netherlands.
Guelph industrial town and agricultural centre in SE
Ontario, Canada, on the Speed River; population
(1981) 71,250. Industries include food processing,
electricals, and pharmaceuticals.
Guernica town in the ◊Basque provinces of Vizcaya,
N Spain; population (1981) 18,000. It was where
the Castilian kings formerly swore to respect
the rights of the Basques. It was almost completely destroyed in 1937 by German bombers
aiding Franco in the Spanish Civil War, and
rebuilt in 1946. The bombing inspired a painting by Picasso, and a play by Fernando Arrabal
(1932–   ).
Guernsey second largest of the ◊Channel Islands;
area   63 sq km/24.5 sq mi;   population   (1986)
55,500. The capital is St Peter Port. From
1975 it has been a major financial centre. Guernsey
cattle originated here.
   Products include electronics, tomatoes, flowers, and more recently butterflies. Guernsey
cattle are a pale fawn colour, and give rich
creamy milk. Guernsey has belonged to the

Guinea-Bissau
(Republica da Guiné-Bissau)

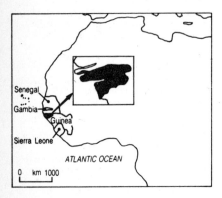

Senegal
Gambia
Guinea
Sierra Leone
ATLANTIC OCEAN
0   km 1000

area 36,125 sq km/13,944 sq mi
capital and chief port Bissau
physical flat lowlands
features the archipelago of Bijagos
head of state and government João Bernardo
Vieira from 1980
political system one-party socialist republic
political parties African Party for the

Independence of Portuguese Guinea and Cape
Verde (PAIGC), nationalist socialist
exports rice, coconuts, peanuts, fish, salt
currency peso (1,106.62 = £1 Feb 1990)
population (1988 est) 932,000; annual growth
rate 1.9%
life expectancy men 41, women 45
language Crioulo, Cape Verdean dialect of
Portuguese
religion Muslim 40%, Christian 4%
literacy 46% male/17% female (1985 est)
GDP $177 million (1982); $165 per head of
population
chronology
1956 PAIGC formed to secure independence
from Portugal.
1973 Two-thirds of the country declared
independent, with Luiz Cabral as president of a
state council.
1974 Portugal recognized independence of
Guinea-Bissau.
1980 Cape Verde decided not to join a unified
state. Cabral deposed and João Vieira became
chair of a council of revolution.
1981 PAIGC confirmed as the only legal party,
with Vieira as its secretary general.
1982 Normal relations with Cape Verde
restored.
1984 New constitution adopted, making Vieira
head of government as well as head of state.
1989 Vieira re-elected.

English Crown since 1066, but was occupied
by German forces 1940–45. Guernsey has no
jury system; instead, it has a Royal Court with
12 jurats (full-time unpaid jurors appointed by
an electoral college) with no legal training. This
system dates from Norman times. Jurats cannot
be challenged or replaced.

Guiana the NE part of South America, which includes
◊French Guiana, ◊Guyana, and ◊Suriname.

Guildford city in Surrey, England, on the river
Wey; population (1981) 56,500. It has a ruined
Norman castle; a cathedral designed by Edward
Maufe 1936–61; the University of Surrey 1966,
and a theatre (1964) named after the comedy
actress Yvonne Arnaud (1895–1958). There is a
cattle market, and industries include flour-milling,
plastics, and engineering.

Guilin formerly *Kweilin* principal tourist city of
S China, on the Li river, Guangxi province.
The dramatic limestone mountains are a major
attraction.

Guinea country in W Africa, bounded to the N by
Senegal, NE by Mali, SE by the Ivory Coast, SW
by Liberia and Sierra Leone, W by the Atlantic,
and NW by Guinea-Bissau.

Guinea-Bissau country in W Africa, bounded to the
N by Senegal, E and SE by Guinea, and SW by
the Atlantic.

Guinea Coast the coast of W Africa between
Gambia and Cape Lopez.

Guiyang formerly *Kweiyang* capital and industrial
city of Guizhou province, S China; population
(1986) 1,380,000. Industries include metals and
machinery.

Guizhou formerly *Kweichow* province of S China
area 174,000 sq km/67,164 sq mi
capital Guiyang
features includes many minority groups which
have often been in revolt
products rice, maize, nonferrous minerals
population (1986) 30,080,000.

Gujarat state of W India
area 196,000 sq km/75,656 sq mi
capital Ahmedabad
features heavily industrialized; includes most of
the Rann of Kutch; the Gir Forest is the last home
of the wild Asian lion
products cotton, petrochemicals, oil, gas, rice,
textiles
population (1984) 33,961,000

Guyana
Cooperative Republic of

area 214,969 sq km/82,978 sq mi
capital and port Georgetown
physical mostly tropical rainforest
features Mount Roraima; Kaietur National Park including Kaietur Fall on the Potaro (tributary of Essequibo) 250 m/821 ft
head of state and government Desmond Hoyte from 1985
political system democratic republic

political parties People's National Congress (PNC), Indian nationalist socialist; People's Progressive Party (PPP), Afro-Indian Marxist-Leninist
exports sugar, rice, rum, timber, diamonds
currency Guyana dollar (50.96 = £1 Feb 1990)
population (1987) 812,000 (51% E Indians, introduced to work the sugar plantations after the abolition of slavery, 30% black, 5% Amerindian); annual growth rate 2%
life expectancy men 66, women 71
language English (official), Hindi
religion Christian 57%, Hindu 33%, Sunni Muslim 9%
literacy 97% male/95% female (1985 est)
GNP $419 million (1983); $457 per head of population
chronology
1953 Assembly elections won by left-wing party. Britain installed interim administration, claiming fear of communist takeover.
1961 Internal self-government granted.
1966 Full independence achieved.
1970 Guyana became a republic within the Commonwealth.
1980 Forbes Burnham became the first executive president under new constitution.
1985 Burnham died and was succeeded by Desmond Hoyte.

languages Gujarati, Hindi.
Gujranwala city in Punjab province, Pakistan; population (1981) 597,000. It is a centre of grain trading. It is a former Sikh capital, and the birthplace of Sikh leader Ranjit Singh (1780–1839).

Gujarat

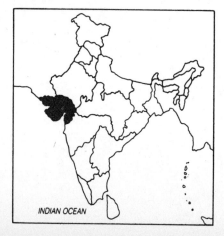

Gulf States oil-rich countries sharing the coastline of the ◊Persian Gulf (Bahrain, Iran, Iraq, Kuwait, Oman, Qatar, Saudi Arabia, and the United Arab Emirates). In the USA, the term refers to those states bordering the Gulf of Mexico (Alabama, Florida, Louisiana, Mississippi, and Texas).
Except for Iran and Iraq, the Persian Gulf States formed a Gulf Co-operation Council (GCC) 1981.
Guyana country in South America, bounded to the N by the Atlantic Ocean, E by Suriname, S and SW by Brazil, and NW by Venezuela.
Gwalior city in Madhya Pradesh, India; population (1981) 543,862. It was formerly a small princely state, and has Jain and Hindu monuments.
Gwent county in S Wales
area 1,380 sq km/533 sq mi
towns administrative headquarters Cwmbran; Abergavenny, Newport, Tredegar
features Wye Valley; Tintern Abbey; Legionary Museum of Caerleon, and Roman amphitheatre; Chepstow and Raglan castles
products salmon and trout on the Wye and Usk; iron and steel at Llanwern
population (1987) 443,000
language 2.5% Welsh, English
famous people Aneurin Bevan and Neil Kinnock, both born in Tredegar; Alfred Russel Wallace.

Gwent

Gwynedd

Gwynedd county in NW Wales
area 3,870 sq km/1,494 sq mi
towns administrative headquarters Caernarvon; Bangor, resorts Pwllheli, Barmouth
features Snowdonia National Park, including Snowdon (Welsh *Yr Wyddfa*; the highest mountain in Wales, with a rack railway to the top from Llanberis) 1,085 m/3,561 ft, Cader Idris 892 m/2,928 ft, and the largest Welsh lake, Llyn Tegid (Bala) 6 km/4 mi long, 1.6 km/1 mi wide; Caernarvon Castle; ◊Anglesey is across the Menai Straits; Lleyn Peninsula and to the SW Bardsey Island, with a 6th-century ruined abbey, once a centre for pilgrimage; Welsh Slate Museum at Llanberis; Segontium Roman Fort Museum, Caernarvon; Criccieth and Harlech castles; Bodnant Garden; and the fantasy resort of Portmeirion by the architect Williams-Ellis
products cattle, sheep, gold (at Dolgellau), textiles, electronics, slate
population (1987) 236,000
language 61% Welsh, English.

Györ industrial city (steel, vehicles, textiles, foodstuffs) in NW Hungary, near the frontier with Czechoslovakia; population (1988) 131,000.

Haarlem industrial town in the W Netherlands, 20 km/12 mi west of Amsterdam; population (1988) 214,000. At Velsea to the north a road-rail tunnel runs under the North Sea Canal, linking North and South Holland. Industries include chemicals, pharmaceuticals, textiles, and printing. Haarlem is famous for bulbs, and has a 15th–16th-century cathedral and a Frans Hals Museum.

Hackney inner borough of N central Greater London; population (1984) 187,900.

features Hackney Downs and Hackney Marsh, formerly the haunt of highwaymen, now a leisure area; includes *Shoreditch*, site of England's first theatre (The Theatre) in 1576; *Hoxton*, with the Geffrye Museum of the domestic arts; *Stoke Newington*, where the writer Daniel Defoe once lived. The horse-drawn hackney carriage is so named because horses were bred in Hackney in the 14th century.

Haddington agricultural market town in Lothian, Scotland, on the river Tyne, 16 km/10 mi SW of Dunbar; population (1981) 8,117. The Protestant reformer John Knox was born here.

Hadhramaut district of the People's Democratic Republic of Yemen (South Yemen), which was formerly ruled by Arab chiefs in protective relations with Britain. A remote plateau region at 1,400 m/4,500 ft, it was for a long time unknown to westerners and later attracted such travellers as Harry St John Philby and Freya Stark. Cereals, tobacco, and dates are grown by settled farmers and there are nomadic Bedouin. The chief town is Mukalla.

Hagen industrial city in the Ruhr, North Rhine-Westphalia, West Germany; population (1988) 206,000. It produces iron, steel, and textiles.

Hague, The (Dutch *Gravenhage* or *Den Haag*) seat of the Netherlands government, linked by canal with Rotterdam and Amsterdam; population (1988) 680,000. It is also the seat of the United Nations International Court of Justice.

The seaside resort of *Scheveningen* (patronized by Wilhelm II and Churchill), with its Kurhaus, is virtually incorporated.

Haifa port in NE Israel; population (1987) 223,000. Industries include oil refining and chemicals.

Hainan island in the South China Sea; area 34,000 sq km/13,124 sq mi; population (1986) 6,000,000. The capital is Haikou. In 1987 Hainan was designated a Special Economic Zone; in 1988 it was separated from Guangdong and made a new province. It is China's second largest island.

Hainaut industrial province of SW Belgium; capital Mons; area 3,800 sq km/1,467 sq mi; population (1987) 1,272,000. It produces coal, iron, and steel.

Haiphong industrial port in N Vietnam; population (1980) 1,305,000. It has shipyards, and industries include cement, plastics, phosphates, and textiles.

Haiti country in the Caribbean, occupying the W part of the island of Hispaniola; to the E is the Dominican Republic.

Hakodate port in Hokkaido, Japan; population (1985) 319,000. It was the earliest port opened to the West, in 1854.

Halab Arabic name of ◊Aleppo, a city in Syria.

Halabja Kurdish town near the Iran border in Sulaymaniyah province, NE Iraq. In Aug 1988 international attention was focused on the town when Iraqi planes dropped poison gas, killing 5,000 of its inhabitants.

Halifax capital of Nova Scotia, E Canada's main port; population (1986) 296,000. Its industries include lumber, steel, and sugar refining. It was founded 1749. It is the terminus of North America's two transcontinental railways.

Halifax woollen textile town in W Yorkshire, England; population (1981) 87,500.

St John's parish church is Perpendicular Gothic; All Souls' is by Gilbert Scott (built for a mill owner named Ackroyd, whose home, Bankfield, is now a museum); the Town Hall is by Charles Barry; and the Piece Hall of 1779 (former cloth market) has been adapted to modern use; the surviving gibbet (predecessor of the guillotine) was used to behead cloth stealers 1541–1650.

Halle capital of Halle county and industrial city in East Germany, on the river Saale, NW of Leipzig; population (1986) 235,000. Industries include mechanical engineering, the production of salt from brine springs, and lignite mining. Halle county has an area of 8,770 sq km/3,385 sq mi, and a population of 1,786,000.

Hamadán city in NW Iran on the site of the ancient Ecbatana, capital of the Medes; population (1986) 274,300.

Haiti
Republic of
(République d'Haiti)

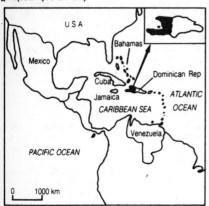

area 27,750 sq km/10,712 sq mi
capital Port-au-Prince
physical mainly mountainous
features only French-speaking republic in the Americas; the island of La Tortuga off the N coast was formerly a pirate lair; US military base at Le Môle St Nicolas, the nearest point to Cuba
head of state and government Prosper Avril from 1988
political system military republic
political parties National Progressive Party (PNP), right-wing military
exports coffee, sugar, sisal, cotton, cocoa, rice

currency gourde (8.51 = £1 Feb 1990)
population (1985) 5,272,000; annual growth rate 2.5%
life expectancy men 51, women 54
language French (official, spoken by bourgeoisie), creole (spoken by 90% black majority)
religion Roman Catholic (official, but opposed to the regime)
literacy 40% male/35% female (1985 est)
GNP $1.6 bn (1983); $300 per head of population
chronology
1804 Independence from France achieved.
1915 Haiti invaded by USA, and remained under US control to 1934.
1957 Dr François Duvalier (Papa Doc) elected president.
1964 Duvalier pronounced himself president for life.
1971 Constitution amended to allow the president to nominate his successor. Duvalier died and was succeeded by his son, Jean-Claude (Baby Doc). Thousands murdered during Duvalier era.
1986 Duvalier deposed and replaced by Lt-Gen Henri Namphy, as head of a governing council.
1988 Leslie Manigat became president in Feb despite allegations of fraudulent elections. Namphy staged a military coup in June, but another coup in Sept led by Prosper Avril replaced him with a civilian government under military control.
1989 Coup attempt against Avril foiled.
1990 Opposition elements expelled.

Hamamatsu industrial city (textiles, chemicals, motorcycles) in Chubu region, central Honshu island, Japan; population (1987) 518,000.

Hambledon village in SE Hampshire, England. The first cricket club was founded here in 1750.

Hamburg largest port of Europe, in West Germany, on the Elbe; population (1988) 1,571,000. Industries include oil, chemicals, electronics, and cosmetics. It is the capital of the *Land* of Hamburg, and an archbishopric from 834. In alliance with Lübeck, it founded the Hanseatic League.

Hamburg administrative region (German *Land*) of West Germany
area 760 sq km/293 sq mi
capital Hamburg
features comprises the city and surrounding districts; the hamburger, a fried and seasoned patty of chopped beef, said to have been invented by medieval Tatar invaders of this Baltic area, was taken to the USA in the 19th century, from where it was reintroduced to Europe in the 1960s

products refined oil, chemicals, electrical goods, ships, processed food
population (1988) 1,570,000
religion Protestant 74%, Roman Catholic 8%
history in 1510 the emperor Maximilian I made Hamburg a free imperial city, and in 1871 it became a state of the German Empire. There is a university, established 1919, and the Hamburg Schauspielhaus is one of the republic's leading theatres.

Hameln (English *Hamelin*) town in Lower Saxony, West Germany; population (1984) 56,300. Old buildings include the Rattenhaus, rat-catcher's house, and the town is the setting of the Pied Piper legend.

Hamersley Range range of hills above the Hamersley Plateau, Western Australia, with coloured rocks and river gorges, as well as iron reserves.

Hamilton capital (since 1815) of Bermuda, on Bermuda Island; population (1980) 1,617. It was founded in 1612.

Hampshire

Hamilton town in Strathclyde, Scotland; population (1981) 52,000. Industries include textiles, electronics, and engineering.

Hamilton port in Ontario, Canada; population (1986) 557,000. Linked with Lake Ontario by the Burlington Canal, it has a hydroelectric plant, and steel, heavy machinery, electrical, chemical, and textile industries.

Hamilton industrial and university town on North Island, New Zealand, on the Waikato river; population (1986) 101,800. It trades in forest, horticulture, and dairy-farming products. Waikato University was established here in 1964.

Hamm industrial town in North Rhine-Westphalia, West Germany; population (1988) 166,000. There are coal mines and chemical and engineering industries.

Hammerfest fishing port in NW Norway, northernmost town of Europe; population (1985) 7,500.

Hampshire county of S England

area 3,770 sq km/1,455 sq mi

towns administrative headquarters Winchester; Southampton, Portsmouth, Gosport

features New Forest, area 373 sq km/144 sq mi, a Saxon royal hunting ground; Hampshire Basin, where Britain has onshore and offshore oil; Danebury, 2,500-year-old Celtic hillfort; Beaulieu (including National Motor Museum); Broadlands (home of Lord Mountbatten); Highclere (home of the Earl of Carnarvon, with gardens by Capability Brown); Hambledon, where the first cricket club was founded in 1750; site of the Roman town of Silchester, the only one in Britain known in such detail

products agricultural; oil from refineries at Fawley; chemicals, pharmaceuticals, electronics

population (1987) 1,537,000

famous people Jane Austen, Charles Dickens, Gilbert White.

Hampstead district of N London, part of the borough of ◊Camden.

Hangchow former name for ◊Hangzhou, port in Zhejiang province, China.

Hangzhou formerly *Hangchow* port and capital of Zhejiang province, China; population (1986) 1,250,000. It has jute, steel, chemical, tea, and silk industries. It has fine landscaped gardens, and was the capital of China 1127–1278 under the Sung dynasty.

Hanley one of the old Staffordshire pottery towns in England, now part of ◊Stoke-on-Trent.

Hannibal town in Missouri, USA, population (1980) 18,811. Mark Twain lived here as a boy, and made it the setting of the events of his novel *The Adventures of Huckleberry Finn.*

Hanoi capital of Vietnam, on the Red River; population (1979) 2,571,000. Industries include textiles, paper, and engineering.

Captured by the French in 1873, it was the capital of French Indochina 1887–1946 and the capital of North Vietnam 1954–76. Hanoi University was founded 1918.

Hanover industrial city, capital of Lower Saxony, West Germany; population (1988) 506,000. Industries include machinery, vehicles, electrical goods, rubber, textiles, and oil refining.

From 1386, it was a member of the Hanseatic League, and from 1692 capital of the electorate of Hanover (created a kingdom 1815). George I of England was also Elector of Hanover, and the two countries shared the same monarch until the accession of Victoria 1837. Since Salic Law meant a woman could not rule in Hanover, the throne passed to her uncle, Ernest, Duke of Cumberland. His son was forced by Bismarck to abdicate 1866, and Hanover became a Prussian province. In 1946, Hanover was merged with Brunswick and Oldenburg to form the *Land* of Lower Saxony.

Hants abbreviation for ◊*Hampshire.*

Hanyang former Chinese city, now merged in ◊Wuhan, in Hubei province.

Harare capital of Zimbabwe, on the Mashonaland plateau about 1,525 m/5,000 ft above sea level; population (1982) 656,000. It is the centre of a rich farming area (tobacco and maize), with metallurgical and food-processing industries.

The British occupied the site in 1890, and named it Fort Salisbury in honour of Lord Salisbury, then prime minister of the UK. It was capital of the Federation of Rhodesia and Nyasaland 1953–63.

Harbin formerly *Haerhpin* and *Pinkiang* port on the Songhua river, NE China; capital of Heilongjiang province; population (1986) 2,630,000. Industries include metallurgy, machinery, paper, food processing, and sugar refining, and

Haryana

INDIAN OCEAN

it is a major rail junction. Harbin was developed by Russian settlers after Russia was granted trading rights there 1896, and more Russians arrived as refugees after the October Revolution 1917.

Hardwar town in Uttar Pradesh, India, on the right bank of the Ganges; population (1981) 115,513. The name means 'door of Hari' (or Vishnu). It is one of the holy places of the Hindu religion and a pilgrimage centre. The *Kumbhmela* festival, held every 12th year in honour of the god Siva, is the most important and attracts about 1 million pilgrims.

Harfleur port in NW France; population (1985) 9,700. Important in medieval times, it was superseded by ◊Le Havre.

Hargeisa trading centre in NW Somalia; population (1988) 400,000.

Haringey borough of N Greater London; population (1984) 200,100. It includes the suburbs of Wood Green, Tottenham, and Hornsey.

features Alexandra Palace, with a park; Finsbury Park (once part of Hornsey Wood); includes *Tottenham* with Bruce Castle, originally built in the 16th century on a site belonging to Robert Bruce's father (Rowland Hill, inventor of the postage stamp, once ran a school here).

Harlech town in Gwynedd, N Wales; population (1980) 1,250. The song 'March of the Men of Harlech' originated in the siege when the town was captured in 1468 by the Yorkists in the Wars of the Roses.

Harlem commercial and residential district of Manhattan, New York City, USA. It is a centre for music, particularly jazz.

Harper's Ferry village in W Virginia, USA, where the Potomac meets the Shenandoah. It is famous for the incident in 1859 when anti-slavery leader

John Brown seized the government's arsenal here.

Harris southern part of ◊Lewis with Harris, in the Outer ◊Hebrides; area 500 sq km/193 sq mi; population (1971) 2,900. It is joined to Lewis by a narrow isthmus. Harris tweeds are produced here.

Harrogate resort and spa in N Yorkshire, England; population (1981) 66,500. There is a US communications station at Menwith Hill.

Hartz Mountains range running north to south in Tasmania, Australia, with two remarkable peaks: Hartz Mountain 1,254 m/4,113 ft and Adamsons Peak 1,224 m/4,017 ft.

Harwich seaport in Essex, England, with ferry services to Scandinavia and NW Europe; population (1981) 15,076. Reclamation of Bathside Bay mudflats is making it a rival, as a port, to Felixstowe.

Haryana state of NW India
area 44,200 sq km/17,061 sq mi
capital Chandigarh
features part of the Ganges plain, and a centre of Hinduism
products sugar, cotton, oilseed, textiles, cement, iron ore
population (1981) 12,851,000
language Hindi.

Hastings resort in East Sussex, England; population (1981) 74,803. The chief of the Cinque Ports, it has ruins of a Norman castle, and the wreck of the Dutch East Indiaman *Amsterdam* 1749 is under excavation. It is adjoined by St Leonard's, developed in the 19th century.

Hatteras cape on the coast of N Carolina, USA, noted for shipwrecks.

Haute-Normandie or *Upper Normandy* coastal region of NW France lying between Basse-Normandie and Picardy and bisected by the Seine; area 12,300 sq km/4,757 sq mi; population (1986) 1,693,000. It consists of the *départements* of Eure and Seine-Maritime; its capital is Rouen. Major ports include Dieppe and Fécamp. The area is noted for its beech forests.

Havana capital and port of Cuba; population (1986) 2,015,000. Products include cigars and tobacco. The palace of the Spanish governors and the stronghold of La Fuerza (1583), survive. In 1898 the blowing up of the US battleship *Maine* in the harbour began the Spanish-American War.

Havre, Le see ◊Le Havre, port in France.

Hawaii Pacific state of the USA; nickname Aloha State
area 16,800 sq km/6,485 sq mi
capital Honolulu on Oahu
towns Hilo
physical features Hawaii consists of a chain of some 20 volcanic islands, of which the chief are: *Hawaii* itself, noted for *Mauna Kea* 4,201 m/13,788 ft, the world's highest island mountain

Hawaii

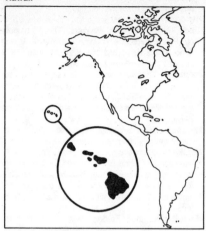

(site of a UK infrared telescope) and Mauna Loa, 4,170 m/13,686 ft, the world's largest active volcanic crater; *Maui*, second largest island; *Oahu*, third largest, with the greatest concentration of population and tourist attractions, for example, Waikiki beach, and site of Pearl Harbor; *Kauai*; and *Molokai*
products sugar, coffee, pineapples, bananas, flowers; offshore cobalt, nickel, and manganese deposits
population (1987) 1,083,000, of whom about 34% are European, 25% Japanese, 14% Filipino, 12% Hawaiian, and 6% Chinese
language English
religion Christian; minority Buddhist
famous people Father Joseph Damien
history Capt Cook, who called them the Sandwich Islands, was the first known European visitor 1778. A kingdom until 1893, Hawaii became a republic 1894, ceded itself to the USA 1898, and became a state 1959.

Hawarden town in Clwyd, N Wales; population 8,500. Prime Minister W E Gladstone lived at Hawarden Castle for many years, and founded St Deiniol's theological library in Hawarden.

Hawkesbury river in New South Wales, Australia; length 480 km/300 mi. It is a major source of Sydney's water.

Haworth village in W Yorkshire, home of the Brontë family of writers. It is now part of ◊Keighley.

Hay-on-Wye town in Powys, Wales, known as the 'town of books' because of the huge secondhand bookshop started in 1961 by Richard Booth, which was followed by others.

Heard Island and McDonald Islands group of islands forming an Australian external territory in the S Indian Ocean, about 4,000 km/2,500 mi SW of Fremantle; area 410 sq km/158 sq mi. They

were discovered 1833, annexed by Britain 1910, and transferred to Australia 1947. *Heard Island* 42 km/26 mi by 19 km/12 mi is glacier-covered, although the volcanic mountain *Big Ben* 2,742 m/ 9,000 ft is still active. A weather station was built 1947. Shag Island is 8 km/5 mi to the north and the craggy McDonalds are 42 km/26 mi to the west.

Heathrow site of Heathrow Airport, W of ◊London, England.

Hebei formerly *Hopei* or *Hupei* province of N China
area 202,700 sq km/78,242 sq mi
capital Shijiazhuang
features include special municipalities of Beijing and Tianjin
products cereals, textiles, iron, steel
population (1986) 56,170,000.

Hebrides group of over 500 islands (fewer than 100 inhabited) off W Scotland; total area 2,900 sq km/ 1,120 sq mi. The Hebrides were settled by Scandinavians in the 6th–9th centuries, and passed under Norwegian rule about 890–1266.

The *Inner Hebrides* are divided between Highland and Strathclyde regions, and include ◊Skye, ◊Mull, ◊Jura, ◊Islay, ◊Iona, ◊Rum, Raasay, Coll, Tiree, Raasay, Colonsay, Muck, and uninhabited ◊Staffa. The *Outer Hebrides* form the islands area of the ◊Western Isles administrative area, separated from the Inner Hebrides by the Little Minch. They include ◊Lewis with Harris, ◊North Uist, ◊South Uist, ◊Barra, and ◊St Kilda.

Hebron (Arabic *El Khalil*) town on the West Bank of the Jordan, occupied by Israel from 1967; population (1967) 43,000, including 4,000 Jews. It is a frontline position in the confrontation between Israelis and Arabs in the *Intifada* (uprising). Within the mosque is the traditional site of the tombs of Abraham, Isaac, and Jacob.

Hefei formerly *Hofei* capital of Anhui province, China; population (1984) 853,000. Products include textiles, chemicals, and steel.

Heidelberg town on the S bank of the Neckar, 19 km/ 12 mi SE of Mannheim, in Baden-Württemberg, West Germany; population (1988) 136,000. Heidelberg University, the oldest in Germany, was established 1386. The town is overlooked by the ruins of its 13th–17th-century castle, 100 m/ 330 ft above the river.

Heidelberg village near Melbourne, Australia, which gave its name to the Heidelberg School – a group of Impressionist artists (including Roberts, Streeton, and Conder) working in teaching camps in the neighbourhood. Flourishing 1888–90, the school had its most famous exhibition 1889, the '9 by 5', from the size of the cigar-box lids used.

Heilbronn river port in Baden-Württemberg, West Germany, on the Neckor, north of Stuttgart; population (1988) 112,000. It trades extensively in wine.

Heilongjiang formerly *Heilungkiang* province of NE China, in ◊Manchuria
area 463,600 sq km/178,950 sq mi
capital Harbin
features China's largest oilfield, near Anda
products cereals, gold, coal, copper, zinc, lead, cobalt
population (1986) 33,320,000.

Heilungkiang former name of ◊Heilongjiang, a province of NE China.

Hejaz former independent kingdom, merged in 1932 with Nejd to form ◊Saudi Arabia; population (1970) 2,000,000; the capital is Mecca.

Heligoland island in the North Sea, one of the North Frisian Islands; area 0.6 sq km/150 acres. It is administered by the state of Schleswig-Holstein, West Germany, having been ceded to Germany by Britain 1890 in exchange for Zanzibar. It was used as a naval base in both world wars.

Hellespont former name of the ◊Dardanelles, the strait which separates Europe from Asia.

Helmand the longest river in Afghanistan. Rising in the Hindu Kush, W of Kabul, it flows SW for 1,125 km/703 mi before entering the marshland surrounding Lake Saberi on the Iranian frontier.

Helsingborg (Swedish *Hälsingborg*) port in SW Sweden, linked by ferry with Helsingør across the Sound; population (1986) 106,300. Industries include copper-smelting, rubber and chemical manufacture, and sugar refining.

Helsingfors Swedish name for ◊Helsinki.

Helsingør port in NE Denmark; population (1987) 57,000. It is linked by ferry with Helsingborg across the Sound; Shakespeare made it the scene of *Hamlet*.

Helsinki (Swedish *Helsingfors*) capital and port of Finland; population (1988) 490,000, metropolitan area 978,000. Industries include shipbuilding, engineering, and textiles. The homes of the architect Eliel Saarinen and the composer Jean Sibelius outside the town are museums.

Helvellyn peak of the English Lake District in ◊Cumbria, 950 m/3,118 ft high.

Helvetia region, corresponding to W Switzerland, occupied by the Celtic Helvetii 1st century BC–5th century AD. In 58 BC Caesar repulsed their invasion of southern Gaul at Bibracte (near Autun) and Helvetia became subject to Rome.

Hemel Hempstead 'new town' in Hertfordshire, England; population (1981) 80,000. Industries include the manufacture of paper, electrical goods, and office equipment.

Henan formerly *Honan* province of E central China
area 167,000 sq km/64,462 sq mi
capital Zhengzhou
features comprises river plains of the Huang He (Yellow River); in the 1980s the ruins of Xibo, the 16th-century BC capital of the Shang dynasty, were discovered here

products cereals, cotton
population (1986) 78,080,000.

Hendon residential district in the borough of ◊Barnet, Greater London, England. The Metropolitan Police Detective Training and Motor Driving Schools are here, and the RAF Museum 1972 includes the Battle of Britain Museum 1980.

Henley-on-Thames town in Oxfordshire, England; population (1984) 10,976. The regatta, held here annually since 1839, is in July; Henley Management College, established in 1946, was the first in Europe.

Henzada city in S central Myanmar (Burma), on the Irrawaddy river; population 284,000.

Heraklion alternative name for ◊Iráklion.

Herat capital of Herat province, and the largest city in W Afghanistan, on the N banks of the Hari Rud; population (1980) 160,000. A principal road junction, it was a great city in ancient and medieval times.

Herault river in S France, 160 km/100 mi long, rising in the Cévennes and flowing into the Gulf of Lyons near Agde. It gives its name to a *département*.

Herculaneum ancient city of Italy between Naples and Pompeii. Along with Pompeii, it was buried when Vesuvius erupted AD 79. It was excavated from the 18th century onwards.

Hercules, Pillars of rocks (at Gibraltar and Ceuta) which guard the entrance to the Mediterranean.

Hereford town in the county of Hereford and Worcester, on the river Wye, England; population (1981) 630,000. The cathedral, which was begun 1079, contains the *Mappa Mundi*, a medieval map of the world. Products include cider, beer, and metal goods.

Hereford and Worcester county in W central England
area 3,930 sq km/1,517 sq mi
towns administrative headquarters Worcester; Hereford, Kidderminster, Evesham, Ross-on-Wye, Ledbury
features rivers Wye and Severn; Malvern Hills (high point Worcester Beacon 425 m/1,395 ft) and Black Mountains; Droitwich, once a Victorian spa, reopened its baths in 1985 (the town lies over a subterranean brine reservoir with waters buoyant enough to take a laden tea tray); fertile Vale of Evesham
products mainly agricultural, apples, pears, and cider; hops and vegetables; Hereford cattle; carpets, porcelain, some chemicals and engineering
population (1987) 665,000
famous people Edward Elgar, A E Housman, William Langland, John Masefield

Hermon (Arabic *Jebel esh-Sheikh*) snow-topped mountain, 2,814 m/9,232 ft high, on the Syria-Lebanon border. According to tradition, Jesus was transfigured here.

Hereford and Worcester

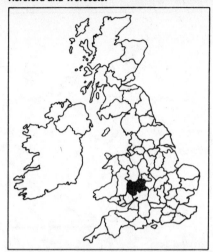

Hertfordshire

Herne industrial city in North Rhine-Westphalia, West Germany; population (1988) 171,000.

Herne Bay seaside resort in Kent, SE England; population (1981) 27,528.

Herstmonceux village 11 km/7 mi N of Eastbourne, East Sussex, England. Since 1958 the buildings of the Royal Greenwich Observatory have been here, alongside the 15th-century castle. The Observatory is, however, to move from Herstmonceux to Cambridge, a process which is expected to take until at least 1991.

Hertford administrative headquarters of Hertfordshire, SE England, on the Lea; population (1981) 21,412. There are brewing, engineering, and brick industries.

Hertfordshire county in SE England
area 1,630 sq km/629 sq mi
towns administrative headquarters Hertford; St Albans, Watford, Hatfield, Hemel Hempstead, Bishop's Stortford, Letchworth (the first garden city, followed by Welwyn 1919, and Stevenage 1947)
features rivers Lea, Stort, Colne; part of the Chiltern Hills; Hatfield House; Knebworth House (home of Lord Lytton); Brocket Hall (home of Palmerston and Melbourne); home of G B Shaw at Ayot St Lawrence; Berkhamsted Castle (Norman); Rothamsted agricultural experimental station
products engineering, aircraft, electrical goods, paper and printing; general agricultural
population (1987) 987,000
famous people Graham Greene was born at Berkhamsted.

Hertogenbosch see ◊'s-Hertogenbosch, capital of North Brabant, Netherlands.

Herts abbreviation for ◊*Hertfordshire*.

Herzegovina or *Hercegovina* part of Yugoslavia, see ◊Bosnia and Herzegovina.

Hessen administrative region (German *Land*) of West Germany
area 21,100 sq km/8,145 sq mi
capital Wiesbaden
towns Frankfurt-am-Main, Kassel, Darmstadt, Offenbach am Main
physical features valleys of the Rhine and Main; Taunus mountains, rich in mineral springs, as at Homburg and Wiesbaden; see also ◊Swabia
products wine, timber, chemicals, cars, electrical engineering, optical instruments
population (1988) 5,550,000
religion Protestant 61%, Roman Catholic 33%
history until 1945, Hessen was divided in two by a strip of Prussian territory, the southern portion consisting of the valleys of the Rhine and the Main, the northern being dominated by the Vogelsberg (744 m/2,442 ft). Its capital was Darmstadt.

HI abbreviation for ◊*Hawaii*.

Higashi-Osaka industrial city (textiles, chemicals, engineering), an eastern suburb of Osaka, Kinki region, Honshu island, Japan; population (1987) 503,000.

High Country in New Zealand, the generally mountainous land above the 750–51,000 m/2,500–30,000 ft level, most of which is in South Island. The lakes, fed by melting snow, are used for hydro-electric power, and it is a skiing, mountaineering, and tourist area.

Highland Region administrative region of Scotland
area 26,100 sq km/10,077 sq mi
towns administrative headquarters Inverness; Thurso, Wick

Highland Region

Himachal Pradesh

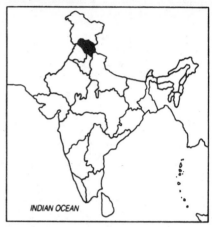

INDIAN OCEAN

features comprises almost half the country; Grampian Mountains; Ben Nevis (highest peak in the UK); Loch Ness, Caledonian Canal; Inner Hebrides; the Queen Mother's castle of Mey at Caithness; John O'Groats' House; Dounreay (with Atomic Energy Authority's prototype fast reactor, and a nuclear processing plant)
products oil services, winter sports, timber, livestock, grouse and deer hunting, salmon fishing
population (1987) 201,000.

Highlands general name for the plateau of broken rock which covers almost all of Scotland, and extends S of the Highland region itself.

High Wycombe market town in Buckinghamshire, on the river Wye, England; population (1981) 60,500. Products include furniture.

Hildesheim industrial town in Lower Saxony, West Germany, linked to the Mittelland Canal; population (1988) 101,000. Products include electronics and hardware. A bishopric from the 9th century, Hildesheim became a free city of the Holy Roman Empire in the 13th century. It was under Prussia 1866–1945.

Hillingdon borough of W London; population (1984) 232,200.
features London Airport at Heathrow (built on the site of a Neolithic settlement); Jacobean mansion (Swakeleys) at Ickenham; Brunel University 1966; Grand Union Canal; includes Uxbridge.

Hilversum town in North Holland province of the Netherlands, 27 km/17 mi SE of Amsterdam; population (1988) 103,000. Besides being a summer resort, Hilversum is the chief centre of Dutch broadcasting.

Himachal Pradesh state of NW India
area 55,700 sq km/21,500 sq mi

capital Simla
features mainly agricultural state, one third forested, with softwood timber industry
products timber, grain, rice, fruit
population (1981) 4,238,000, mainly Hindu
language Pahari
history created as a Union Territory 1948, it became a full state 1971. Certain hill areas were transferred to Himachal Pradesh from the Punjab 1966.

Himalayas vast mountain system of central Asia, extending from the Indian states of Kashmir in the W to Assam in the E, covering the S part of Tibet, Nepál, Sikkim, and Bhutan. It is the highest mountain range in the world. The two highest peaks are *Mount ◊Everest* and ◊*Kangchenjunga*. Other major peaks include Makalu, Annapurna, and Nanga Parbat, all over 8,000 m/26,000 ft.

Hinckley market town in Leicestershire, England; population (1981) 55,250. Industries include engineering and the manufacture of footwear and hosiery.

Hindenburg German name 1915–45 of the Polish city of ◊Zabrze, in honour of General Hindenburg.

Hindu Kush mountain range in central Asia; length 800 km/500 mi; greatest height Tirich Mir 7,690 m/25,239 ft, Pakistan. The *Khyber Pass*, a narrow defile (53 km/33 mi long), separates Pakistan from Afghanistan, and was used by Zahir and other invaders of India. The present road was built by the British in the Afghan Wars.

Hindustan ('land of the Hindus') a term loosely applied to the whole of India, but more specifically to the plain of the Ganges and Jumna rivers, or that part of India N of the Deccan.

Hiroshima industrial city (cars) and port on the S coast of Honshu, Japan, destroyed by the first wartime use of an atomic bomb 6 Aug 1945.

The city has largely been rebuilt since the war; population (1987) 1,034,000.

Towards the end of World War II the city was utterly devastated by the US atom bomb. More than 10 sq km/4 sq mi was obliterated, with very heavy damage outside that area. Casualties totalled at least 137,000 out of a population of 343,000: 78,150 were found dead, others died later.

Hispaniola (Spanish 'little Spain') West Indian island, first landing place of Columbus in the New World, 6 Dec 1492; now divided into ◊Haiti and the ◊Dominican Republic.

Hitachi city on Honshu, Japan; population 204,000. The chief industry is the manufacture of electrical goods.

Hitchin market town in Hertfordshire, England, 48 km/30 mi NW of London; population (1985) 30,000. The cultivation and distillation of lavender, introduced from Naples in the 16th century, still continues.

Hobart capital and port of Tasmania, Australia; population (1986) 180,000. Products include zinc, textiles, and paper. Founded 1804 as a pearl colony, it was named after Lord Hobart, then secretary of state for the colonies. The University of Tasmania, established 1890, is at Hobart.

Hoboken city and port in NE New Jersey, USA, on the Hudson river; population (1980) 42,460.

Ho Chi Minh City formerly (until 1976) *Saigon* chief port and industrial city of S Vietnam; population (1985) 3,500,000. Industries include shipbuilding, textiles, rubber, and food products. Saigon was the capital of the Republic of Vietnam (South Vietnam) 1954–76, when it was renamed.

Hodeida or *Al Hudaydah* Red Sea port of North Yemen; population (1986) 155,000. It trades in coffee and spices.

Hofei former name of ◊Hefei, a city in China.

Hoggar another form of ◊Ahaggar, a plateau in the Sahara.

Hohhot formerly *Huhehot* city and capital of Inner Mongolia (*Nei Mongol*) autonomous region, China; population (1984) 778,000. Industries include textiles, electronics, and dairy products. There are Lamaist monasteries and temples here.

Hokkaido most northerly of the four main islands of Japan, separated from Honshu to the S by Tsugaru Strait and from Sakhalin to the N by Soya Strait; area 83,500 sq km/32,231 sq mi, population (1986) 5,678,000 including 16,000 Ainus. The capital is Sapporo. Natural resources include coal, mercury, manganese, oil and natural gas, timber, and fisheries. Coal mining and agriculture are the main industries.

Snow-covered for half the year, Hokkaido was little developed until the Meiji Restoration 1868 when disbanded samurai were settled here. Intensive exploitation followed World War II, including heavy and chemical industrial plants, development of electric power, and dairy farming. An artificial harbour has been constructed at Tomakomai, and an undersea rail tunnel links Hakodate with Aomori (Honshu), but remains as yet closed to public transport.

Holland two provinces of the Netherlands; see ◊North Holland and ◊South Holland.

Holland, Parts of former separate administrative county of SE Lincolnshire, England.

Holyhead seaport on the N coast of Holyhead Island, off Anglesey, Gwynedd, N Wales; population (1981) 10,467. Holyhead Island is linked by road and railway bridges with Anglesey, and there are regular sailings between Holyhead and Dublin.

Holy Island or *Lindisfarne* island in the North Sea, area 10 sq km/4 sq mi; 3 km/2 mi off Northumberland, England, with which it is connected by a causeway. St Aidan founded a monastery here in 635.

Holy Loch western inlet of the Firth of Clyde, W Scotland, with a US nuclear submarine base.

Homburg or *Bad Homburg* town and spa at the foot of the Taunus mountains, West Germany; population (1984) 41,800. It has given its name to a soft felt hat for men, made fashionable in Homburg by Edward VII of England.

Home Counties the counties in close proximity to London, England: Hertfordshire, Essex, Kent, Surrey, and formerly Middlesex.

Homs or *Hums* city, capital of Homs district, W Syria, near the Orontes River; population (1981) 355,000. Silk, cereals and fruit are produced in the area, and industries include silk textiles, oil refining, and jewellery. Zenobia, Queen of Palmyra, was defeated at Homs by the Roman emperor Aurelian 272.

Honan former name of ◊Henan, a province of China.

Hondo another name for ◊Honshu, an island of Japan.

Honduras country in Central America, bounded to the N by the Caribbean, to the SE by Nicaragua, to the S by the Pacific, to the SW by El Salvador, and to the W and NW by Guatemala.

Hong Kong British crown colony in SE Asia, comprising Hong Kong Island, the Kowloon peninsula, and the mainland New Territories
area 1,070 sq km/413 sq mi
capital Victoria (popularly Hong Kong City)
towns Kowloon, Tsuen Wan (in the New Territories)
features an enclave of Kwantung province, China, it has one of the world's finest natural harbours; Hong Kong Island is connected with Kowloon by undersea railway; a world financial centre, its stock market has four exchanges; across the border of the New Territories in China itself is the Shenzhen special economic zone

Honduras
Republic of
(República de Honduras)

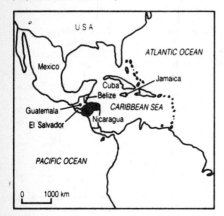

area 112,100 sq km/43,282 sq mi
capital Tegucigalpa
towns San Pedro Sula; ports Henecan (on Pacific), La Ceiba
physical mountainous; 45% forest
features areas still unexplored
head of state and government Rafael Leonardo Callejas from 1990
political system democratic republic
political parties Liberal Party of Honduras (PLH), centre-left; National Party (PN), right-wing

exports coffee, bananas, timber (including mahogany, rosewood)
currency lempira (3.41 = £1 Feb 1990)
population (1985) 4,370,000 (90% mestizo, 10% Indians and Europeans); annual growth rate 3.4%
life expectancy men 58, women 62
language Spanish
religion Roman Catholic
literacy 61% male/58% female (1985 est)
GNP $2.8 bn (1983); $590 per head of population
chronology
1838 Honduras achieved independence.
1980 After more than a century of mostly military rule, a civilian government was elected, with Dr Roberto Suazo as president. The army chief, Gen Gustavo Alvárez, retained considerable power.
1983 Close involvement with the US in providing naval and air bases and allowing Nicaraguan counter-revolutionaries to operate from Honduras.
1984 Alvárez ousted in a coup led by junior officers, resulting in a review of policy towards the US and Nicaragua.
1985 José Azeona elected president after the electoral law changed, making Suazo ineligible for presidency.
1989 Government and opposition declare support for Central American peace plan to demobilize Nicaraguan Contras based in Honduras.
1990 Rafael Callejas (PN) elected president.

exports textiles, clothing, electronic goods, clocks, watches, cameras, plastic products; a large proportion of the exports and imports of S China are transshipped here; tourism is important
currency Hong Kong dollar
population (1986) 5,431,000; 57% Hong Kong Chinese, most of the remainder refugees from the mainland
languages English and Chinese
religion Confucianist, Buddhist, Taoist, with Muslim and Christian minorities
government Hong Kong is a British dependency administered by a crown-appointed governor who presides over an unelected executive council, composed of four ex officio and 11 nominated members, and a legislative council composed of three ex officio members, 29 appointees and 24 indirectly elected members
history formerly part of China, Hong Kong Island was occupied by Britain 1841, during the first of the Opium Wars, and ceded by the Chinese government under the 1842 Treaty of Nanking. The Kowloon Peninsula was acquired under the 1860 Peking (Beijing) Convention and the

New Territories secured on a 99-year lease from 1898.

The colony, which developed into a major *entrepôt* for Sino-British trade during the late 19th and early 20th centuries, was occupied by Japan 1941–45. The restored British administration promised, after 1946, to increase self-government. These plans were shelved, however, after the 1949 Communist revolution in China. During the 1950s almost 1,000,000 Chinese (predominantly Cantonese) refugees fled to Hong Kong. Immigration continued during the 1960s and 1970s, raising the colony's population from 1,000,000 in 1946 to 5,000,000 in 1980, and forcing the imposition of strict border controls during the 1980s. Since 1975, 160,000 Vietnamese 'boat people' have fled to Hong Kong; in 1989 50,000 remained, and the UK government began forced repatriation (51 forced, 630 voluntary, by Dec 1989).

Hong Kong's economy expanded rapidly during the corresponding period, and the colony became one of Asia's major commercial, financial, and industrial centres. As the date (1997)

Hong Kong

for the termination of the New Territories' lease approached, negotiations on Hong Kong's future were opened between Britain and China 1982. These culminated in a unique agreement, signed in Beijing 1984, in which Britain agreed to transfer full sovereignty of the Islands and New Territories to China 1997 in return for Chinese assurance that Hong Kong's social and economic freedom and capitalist lifestyle would be preserved for at least 50 years.

Under this 'one country, two systems' agreement, in 1997 Hong Kong would become a special administrative region within China, with its own laws, currency, budget, and tax system, and would retain its free-port status and authority to negotiate separate international trade agreements. In preparation for its withdrawal from the colony, the British government introduced indirect elections to select a portion of the new legislative council 1984, and direct elections for seats on lower tier local councils 1985. A Sino-British joint liaison group was established to monitor the functioning of the new agreement and a 59-member committee (including 25 representatives from Hong Kong) formed in Beijing 1985 to draft a new constitution. In Dec 1989 the UK government granted British citizenship to 225,000 Hong Kong residents from 1997.

Honiara port and capital of the Solomon Islands, on the NW coast of Guadalcanal island; population (1985) 26,000.

Honiton market town in Devon, SW England, on the river Otter; population (1981) 6,627. Its hand-made pillow-lace industry is undergoing a revival.

Honolulu (Hawaiian 'sheltered bay') capital city and port of Hawaii, USA, on the S coast of Oahu; population (1980) 365,000. It is a holiday resort, noted for its beauty and tropical vegetation, with some industry. 11 km/7 mi SW

is Pearl Harbor with naval and military installations.

Honshu principal island of Japan. It lies between Hokkaido to the NE and Kyushu to the SW; area 231,100 sq km/89,205 sq mi, including 382 smaller islands; population (1986) 97,283,000. A chain of volcanic mountains runs along the island, which is subject to frequent earthquakes. The main cities are Tokyo, Yokohama, Osaka, Kobe, Nagoya, and Hiroshima.

Hooghly or *Hugli* river and town in West Bengal, India; population (1981) 125,193. The river is the western stream of the Ganges delta. The town is on the site of a factory set up by the East India Company 1640, which was moved to Calcutta, 40 km/25 mi downstream, 1686–90.

Hook of Holland (Dutch *Hoek van Holland*, meaning 'corner of Holland') a small peninsula and village in South Holland, the Netherlands, important as the terminus for ferry services with Harwich and Parkeston Quay, England.

Hopei former name of ◊Hebei, a province of China.

Hormuz or *Ormuz* small island, 41 sq km/16 sq mi, in the **Strait of Hormuz**, belonging to Iran. It is strategically important because oil tankers leaving the Persian Gulf for Japan and the West have to pass through the strait to reach the Arabian Sea.

Horsham town and market centre on the river Arun, in West Sussex, England, 26 km/16 mi SE of Guildford; population (1985) 30,000. The public school Christ's Hospital is about 3 km/2 mi to the SW. The poet Shelley was born here.

Hounslow borough of W Greater London; population (1981) 199,782.
features London Airport (established 1946 at Heathrow); Hounslow Heath, formerly the haunt of highwaymen; *Chiswick*, with the Palladian villa by Burlington, and the artist Hogarth's home (now a museum); *Heston*, site of London's first civil airport established in 1919; *Brentford*, reputed site of Caesar's crossing of the Thames in 54 BC, and the duke of Northumberland's seat at Syon House; and *Isleworth*, Osterley, home of the economist Thomas Gresham (both with work by Robert Adam).

Houston port in Texas, USA; population (1981) 2,891,000; linked by canal to the Gulf of Mexico. It is an agricultural centre, and industries include petrochemicals, chemicals, plastics, synthetic rubber, and electronics.

Hove seaside resort in East Sussex, England, adjoining Brighton; population (1981) 66,612.

Howrah or *Haora* city of West Bengal, India, on the right bank of the Hooghly, opposite Calcutta; population (1981) 742,298. The capital of Howrah district, it has jute and cotton factories, rice, flour, and saw mills, chemical factories, and engineering works. Howrah suspension bridge, opened 1943, spans the river.

Humberside

Huallaga River a tributary of the Marayon in NE Peru. The upper reaches of the river valley are used for the growing of coca, a major source of the drug cocaine.

Huambo town in central Angola; population (1970) 61,885. It was founded 1912, and known as *Nova Lisboa* 1928–78, when it was designated by the Portuguese as the future capital. It is an agricultural centre.

Huang He formerly *Hwang-ho* river in China; length 5,464 km/3,395 mi. It gains its name (meaning 'yellow river') from its muddy waters. Formerly known as 'China's sorrow' because of disastrous floods, it is now largely controlled through hydroelectric works and flood barriers. However, the flood barriers are ceasing to work because the silt that gives the river its name 'yellow' is continually raising the river bed.

Huangshan Mountains mountain range in S Anhui province, China; the highest peak is Lotus Flower 1,873 m/5,106 ft.

Huáscaran extinct volcano in the Andes, the highest mountain in Peru, 6,768 m/22,205 ft.

Hubei formerly *Hupei* province of central China, through which flow the Chang Jiang and its tributary the Han Shui
area 187,500 sq km/72,375 sq mi
capital Wuhan
features in the west the land is high, the Chang breaking through from Sichuan in gorges, but elsewhere the land is low-lying and fertile; many lakes
products beans, cereals, cotton, rice, vegetables, copper, gypsum, iron ore, phosphorus, salt
population (1986) 49,890,000.

Huddersfield industrial town in West Yorkshire, on the river Colne, linked by canal with Manchester

and other north of England centres; population (1981) 123,888. A village in Anglo-Saxon times, it was a thriving centre of woollen manufacture by the end of the 18th century, and more recently has diversified to dyestuffs, chemicals, and electrical and mechanical engineering.

Hudson river of the NE USA; length 485 km/ 300 mi. First reached by European settlers 1524, it was explored 1609 by Henry Hudson, and named after him. New York stands at its mouth.

Hudson Bay inland sea of NE Canada, linked with the Atlantic by *Hudson Strait*, and with the Arctic by Foxe Channel; area 1,233,000 sq km/ 476,000 sq mi. It is named after Henry Hudson.

Hue town in central Vietnam, formerly capital of Annam, 13 km/8 mi from the China Sea; population (1973) 209,043. The Citadel, within which is the Imperial City enclosing the palace of the former emperor, lies to the W of the Old City on the N bank of the Huong (Perfume) River; the New City is on the S bank. Hue was once an architecturally beautiful cultural and religious centre, but large areas were devastated, with many casualties, during the Battle of Hue 31 Jan–24 Feb 1968, when US and South Vietnamese forces retook the city after Vietcong occupation by infiltration.

Huelva port and capital of Huelva province, Andalusia, SW Spain, near the mouth of the Odiel; population (1986) 135,000. Industries include ship building, oil refining, fisheries, and trade in ores from Rio Tinto. Columbus began and ended his voyage to America at nearby Palos de la Frontera.

Huesca capital of Huesca province in Aragon, northern Spain; population (1981) 41,455. Industries include engineering and food processing. Among its buldings are a fine 13th-century cathedral and the former palace of the kings of Aragon.

Huhehot former name of ◊Hohhot, a city in Inner Mongolia.

Hull officially *Kingston upon Hull* city and port, through which the river Humber flows, administrative headquarters of Humberside, England; population (1986) 258,000. It is linked with the south bank of the estuary by the Humber Bridge. Industries include fish processing, vegetable oils, flour milling, electricals, textiles, paint, pharmaceuticals, chemicals, caravans, and aircraft. There are ferries to Rotterdam and Zeebrugge. Buildings include the 13th-century Holy Trinity Church, Guildhall, Ferens Art Gallery 1927, and the university 1954.

Humberside county of NE England
area 3,510 sq km/1,355 sq mi
towns administrative headquarters Kingston upon Hull; Grimsby, Scunthorpe, Goole, Cleethorpes
features Humber Bridge; fertile Holderness peninsula; Isle of Axholme, bounded by rivers Trent, Don, Idle, and Torne, where medieval open-field strip farming is still practised

Hungary
Hungarian Republic
(Magyar Köztársaság)

area 93,032 sq km/35,910 sq mi
capital Budapest
towns Miskolc, Debrecen, Szeged, Pécs
physical Great Hungarian Plain covers eastern
half of country; Bakony Forest; rivers Danube,
Tisza; Lake Balaton
head of state Matyas Szuros (acting) from
1989
head of government Károly Grosz from 1988
political system socialist pluralist republic
political parties over 50, including Hungarian
Socialist Party (HSP), left-of-centre; Hungarian
Democratic Forum (MDF), umbrella
pro-democracy grouping; Alliance of Free
Democrats (SzDSz), radical free-market opposition group heading coalition with Alliance
of Young Democrats, Social Democrats, and

Smallholders Party, right-wing
exports machinery, vehicles, chemicals,
textiles
currency forint (108.06 = £1 Feb 1990)
population (1988) 10,604,000 (Magyar
92%, Romany 3%, German 2.5%; there is a
Hungarian minority in Romania; annual growth
rate 0%
life expectancy men 67, women 74
language Hungarian (or Magyar), one
of the few languages of Europe with
non-Indo-European origins. It is grouped with
Finnish and Estonian in the Finno-Ugrian family
religion Roman Catholic 50%, other Christian
denominations 25%
literacy 99.3% male/98.5% female (1980)
GNP $18.6 bn (1983); $4,180 per head of
population
chronology
1946 Republic proclaimed.
1949 Soviet-style constitution adopted.
1956 Hungarian national rising. Workers'
demonstrations in Budapest, democratization
reforms by Imre Nagy overturned by Soviet
tanks, Kádár installed as party leader.
1968 Economic decentralization reforms.
1983 Competition introduced into elections.
1987 VAT and income tax introduced.
1988 Kádár replaced by Károly Grosz. First free
trade union recognized. Rival political parties
legalized.
1989 May: border with Austria opened. July:
new four-man collective leadership of Hungarian
Socialist Workers' Party (HSWP). Oct: new
'transitional constitution' adopted, founded on
multi-party democracy and new presidentialist
executive. HSWP changed name to Hungarian
Socialist Party, with Nyers as new leader.
1990 HSP standing damaged by 'Danubegate'
bugging scandal. March; firts round of
multi-party elections.

---

products petrochemicals, refined oil, processed
fish, cereals, root crops, cattle
population (1987) 847,000
famous people Amy Johnson, Andrew Marvell,
John Wesley.
Hunan province of S central China
area 210,500 sq km/81,253 sq mi
capital Changsha
features Dongting Lake; farmhouse in Shaoshan
village, where Mao Zedong was born
products rice, tea, tobacco, cotton; nonferrous
minerals
population (1986) 56,960,000.
Hungary country in central Europe, bordered to
the N by Czechoslovakia, NE by the USSR, E
by Romania, S by Yugoslavia, and W by Austria.

Hunter river in New South Wales, Australia, which
rises in the Mount Royal Range and flows into the
Pacific near Newcastle, after a course of about
465 km/290 mi. Although the river is liable to
flooding, the Hunter Valley has dairying and market gardening, and produces wines.
Huntingdon town in Cambridgeshire, E England,
on the river Ouse, 26 km/16 mi NW of Cambridge; population (1981) 17,467. It is a market town with a number of light industries.
A bridge built in 1332 connects Huntingdon
with Godmanchester on the S bank of the
river, and the two towns were united in 1961.
Samuel Pepys and Oliver Cromwell attended
the grammar school founded 1565 in a 12th-
century building, formerly part of the medieval

hospital; it was opened in 1962 as a Cromwell museum.

Huntingdonshire former English county, merged 1974 in a much enlarged Cambridgeshire.

Huntsville town in NE Alabama, USA; population (1981) 309,000. It is an aerospace research centre.

Hunza small state on the NW frontier of Kashmir, under the rule of Pakistan.

Hupei former name of ◊Hebei, province of China.

Huron second largest of the Great Lakes of North America, on the US-Canadian border; area 60,000 sq km/23,160 sq mi. It includes Georgian Bay, Saginaw Bay, and Manitoulin Island.

It receives Lake Superior's waters through the St Marys River, and Lake Michigan's through the Straits of Mackinac. It drains south into Lake Erie through the St Clair River–Lake St Clair–Detroit River system.

Hurstmonceux alternative spelling of ◊Herstmonceux, a village in East Sussex.

Hvannadalshnjukur highest peak in Iceland, rising to 2,119 m/6,952 ft in SE Iceland.

Hwange formerly (to 1982) *Wankie* coalmining town in Zimbabwe; population (1982) 39,200. Hwange National Park is nearby.

Hwang-Ho former name of the ◊Huang He, a river in China.

Hydaspes classical name of river ◊Jhelum, a river in Pakistan and Kashmir.

Hyde Park one of the largest open spaces in London, England. It occupies about 146 ha/350 acres in Westminster. It adjoins Kensington Gardens, and includes the Serpentine, a boating lake with a 'lido' for swimming. Rotten Row (a corruption of French *route du roi* 'the king's road') is a riding track. In 1851 the Great Exhibition was held here.

Hyderabad capital city of the S central Indian state of Andhra Pradesh, on the Musi, population (1981) 2,528,000. Products include carpets, silks, and metal inlay work. It was formerly the capital of the state of Hyderabad. Buildings include the Jama Masjid mosque and Golconda fort.

Hyderabad city in Sind province, SE Pakistan; population (1981) 795,000. It produces, gold, pottery, glass, and furniture. The third largest city of Pakistan, it was founded 1768.

Hyères town on the Côte d'Azur in the *département* of Var, S France; population (1982) 41,739. It has a mild climate, and is a winter health resort. Industries include olive-oil pressing and the export of violets, strawberries, and vegetables.

Hyphasis classical name of the river ◊Beas, in India.

Hythe seaside resort (former Cinque Port) in the Romney Marsh area of Kent, SE England; population (1981) 12,723.

population (1984) 1,001,000
religion Christian, predominantly Mormon
history first permanently settled 1860 after the discovery of gold, Idaho became a state 1890.

Idi Amin Dada, Lake former name 1973–79 of Lake ◊Edward in Uganda/Zaïre.

If small French island in the Mediterranean about 3 km/2 mi off Marseille, with a castle, Château d'If, built about 1529. This was used as a state prison, and is the scene of the imprisonment of Dante in Dumas' *Count of Monte Cristo*.

Ifni a former Spanish overseas province in SW Morocco 1860–1969; area 1,920 km/740 sq mi. The chief town is Sidi Ifni.

Igls winter sports resort in the Austrian Tyrol, near Innsbruck; venue for the 1964 Winter Olympics.

Iguaçu Falls or *Iguassú Falls* waterfall in South America, on the border between Brazil and Argentina. The falls lie 19 km/12 mi above the junction of the Iguaç with the Paraná. They are divided by forested rocky islands and form a spectacular tourist attraction. The water plunges in 275 falls, many of which have separate names. They have a height of 82 m/269 ft, and a width about 4 km/2.5 mi.

IJsselmeer lake in the Netherlands, formed 1932 after the Zuider Zee was cut off by a dyke from the North Sea; freshwater since 1944. Area 1,217 sq km/470 sq mi.

IL abbreviation for ◊*Illinois*.

Ile-de-France region of N France; area 12,000 sq km/4,632 sq mi; population (1986) 10,251,000. It includes the French capital, Paris, and the towns of Versailles, Sèvres, and St-Cloud, and is composed of the *départements* of Essonne, Val-de-Marne, Val d'Oise, Ville de Paris, Seine-et-Marne, Hauts-de-Seine, Seine-Saint-Denis, and Yvelines. From here the early French kings extended their authority over the whole country.

Ilfracombe resort on the N coast of Devon, England; population (1981) 10,479.

Ilkeston town in SE Derbyshire, England; population (1981) 33,031. Products include clothing and plastics.

Ilkley town in W Yorkshire, England, noted for nearby *Ilkley Moor*; population (1981) 24,082.

Ille French river 45 km/28 mi long, which rises in

IA abbreviation for ◊*Iowa*.

Iaşi (German *Jassy*) city in NE Romania, capital of Moldavia; population (1985) 314,000. It has chemical, machinery, electronic, and textile industries.

Ibadan city in SW Nigeria and capital of Oyo state; population (1981) 2,100,000. Industries include chemicals, electronics, plastics, and vehicles.

Ibague capital of Tolima department, W central Colombia; population (1985) 293,000.

Iberia name given by ancient Greek navigators to the Spanish peninsula, derived from the river Iberus (Ebro). Anthropologists have given the name *Iberian* to a Neolithic people, traces of whom are found in the Spanish peninsula, southern France, the Canary Isles, Corsica, and part of North Africa.

Ibiza one of the ◊Balearic Islands, a popular tourist resort; area 596 sq km/230 sq mi; population (1986) 45,000. The capital and port, also called Ibiza, has a cathedral.

Içel another name for ◊Mersin, a city in Turkey.

Iceland island in the N Atlantic, situated S of the Arctic Circle, between Greenland and Norway.

Ichang alternative form of ◊Yichang, a port in China.

Iconium city of ancient Turkey; see ◊Konya.

ID abbreviation for ◊*Idaho*.

Idaho state of NW USA; nickname Gem State
area 216,500 sq km/ 83,569 sq mi
capital Boise
towns Pocatello, Idaho Falls
features Rocky Mountains; Snake River, which runs through Hell's Canyon, at 2,330 m/7,647 ft the deepest in North America, and has the National Reactor Testing Station on the plains of its upper reaches; Sun Valley ski and summer resort
products potatoes, wheat, livestock, timber, silver, lead, zinc, antimony

Iceland
Republic of
(Lýdd-veldidd- Ísland)

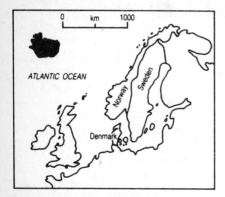

area 103,000 sq km/39,758 sq mi
capital Reykjavik
physical warmed by the Gulf Stream; glaciers and lava fields cover 75% of the country
features active volcanoes (Hekla was once thought the gateway to Hell), geysers, hot springs, and new islands being created offshore (Surtsey in 1963); subterranean hot water heats Iceland's homes
head of state Vigdís Finnbogadóttir from 1980
head of government Thorsteinn Palsson from 1987

political system democratic republic
political parties Independence Party (IP), right-of-centre; Progressive Party (PP), radical socialist; People's Alliance (PA), socialist; Social Democratic Party (SDP), moderate, left-of-centre; Citizen's Party, centrist; Women's Alliance, women and family orientated
exports cod and other fish products
currency krona (102.25 = £1 Feb 1990)
population (1987) 247,400; annual growth rate 1.2%
life expectancy men 74, women 80
language Icelandic, the most archaic Scandinavian language, in which some of the finest sagas were written
religion Evangelical Lutheran
literacy 99.9% (1984)
GDP $2.1 bn (1983); $9,000 per head of population
chronology
1944 Independence from Denmark achieved.
1949 Joined NATO and the Council of Europe.
1953 Joined the Nordic Council.
1976 'Cod War' with the UK.
1979 Iceland announced a 200-mile exclusive fishing zone.
1983 Steingrímur Hermannsson appointed to lead a coalition government.
1985 Iceland declared a nuclear-free zone.
1987 New coalition government formed by Thorsteinn Palsson after general election.
1988 Vigdís Finnbogadóttir re-elected president for a third term.

Lake Boulet and enters the Vilaine at Rennes. It gives its name to the *département* of Ille-et-Vilaine in Brittany.

Illimani highest peak in the Bolivian Andes, rising to 6,402 m/21,004 ft E of La Paz.

Illinois midwest state of the USA; nickname Inland Empire/Prairie State
area 146,100 sq km/56,395 sq mi
capital Springfield

Illinois

towns Chicago, Rockford, Peoria, Decatur
features Lake Michigan, the Mississippi, Illinois, Ohio, and Rock rivers; Cahokia Mounds, the largest group of prehistoric earthworks in the USA; in Des Plaines, the restaurant where the first McDonald's hamburger was served 1955 became a museum 1985
products soybeans, cereals, meat and dairy products, machinery, electric and electronic equipment
population (1987) 11,582,000
famous people Walt Disney, James T Farrell, Ernest Hemingway, Edgar Lee Masters, Ronald Reagan, Frank Lloyd Wright
history originally explored by the French in the 17th century, ceded to Britain by the French 1763, Illinois passed to American control 1783, and became a state 1818.

Ilorin capital of Kwara state, Nigeria; population (1983) 344,000. It trades in tobacco and wood products.

Imbros (Turkish *Imroz*) island in the Aegean; area 280 sq km/108 sq mi. Occupied by Greece in World War I, it became Turkish under the Treaty of Lausanne 1923. Population (1970) 6,786.

Immingham town on the river Humber, Humberside, NE England; population (1981) 11,500. It is a bulk cargo handling port, with petrochemical works and oil refineries.

Imphal capital of Manipur state on the Manipur river, India; population (1981) 156,622, a communications and trade centre (tobacco, sugar, fruit). It was besieged Mar–June 1944, when Japan invaded Assam, but held out with the help of supplies dropped by air.

Imroz Turkish form of ◊Imbros, an island in the Aegean.

IN abbreviation for ◊*Indiana*.

Inchon formerly **Chemulpo** chief port of Seoul, South Korea; population (1985) 1,387,000. It produces steel and textiles.

India

(Hindi *Bharat*)

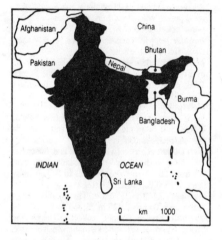

area 3,166,829 sq km/1,222,396 sq mi
capital New Delhi
towns Bangalore, Hyderabad, Ahmedabad; ports Calcutta, Bombay, Madras, Kanpur, Pune, Nagpur
physical Himalaya mountains on the N border; plains around rivers Ganges, Indus, Brahmaputra; Deccan peninsula S of the Narmada River, a plateau between the W and E Ghats mountain ranges
territories Andaman and Nicobar Islands, Lakshadweep
features the Taj Mahal monument; cave paintings (Ajanta); world's fourth-largest military: 1,362,000, behind only the USSR, China, and the US
head of state Ramaswami Iyer Venkataraman from 1987
head of government Vishwanath Pratap Singh from 1989
political system federal democratic republic
political parties Janata Dal, left-of-centre; Congress Party–Indira (Congress (I)), cross-caste and religion left-of-centre; Bharatiya Janata Party (BJP), conservative Hindu-chauvinist; Communist Party of India (CPI), pro-Moscow Marxist-Leninist; Communist Party of India–Marxist (CPI-M), West Bengal-based moderate socialist
exports tea, coffee, fish, iron ore, leather, textiles, polished diamonds
currency rupee (28.50 = £1 Feb 1990)
population (1985) 750,900,000; annual growth rate 1.9%
life expectancy men 56, women 55
language Hindi (official), English, and 14 other recognized languages: Assamese, Bengali, Gujarati, Kannada, Kashmiri, Malayalam, Marathi, Oriya, Punjabi, Sanskrit, Sindhi, Tamil, Telugu, Urdu
religion Hindu 80%, Sunni Muslim 10%, Christian 2.5%, Sikh 2%
literacy 57% male/29% female (1985 est)
GNP $190 bn (1983); $150 per head of population
chronology
1947 Independence achieved from Britain.
1950 Federal republic proclaimed.
1962 Border skirmishes with China.
1964 Death of Prime Minister Nehru. Border war with Pakistan over Kashmir.
1966 Indira Gandhi became prime minister.
1971 War with Pakistan leading to creation of Bangladesh.
1975–77 State of emergency proclaimed.
1977–79 Janata party government in power.
1980 Indira Gandhi returned in landslide victory.
1984 Assassination of Indira Gandhi. Rajiv Gandhi elected with record majority.
1987 Signing of 'Tamil' Colombo peace accord with Sri Lanka; Indian Peacekeeping Force (IPKF) sent there. Public revelation of Bofors scandal.
1988 New opposition party, Janata Dal, established by former finance minister V P Singh. Indian paratroopers foiled attempted coup in Maldives. Voting age lowered from 21 to 18.
1989 Congress (I) lost majority in general election and Janata Dal minority government formed, with V P Singh prime minister.
1990 Central rule imposed in Jammu and Kashmir following Muslim separatist violence.

Indiana

Independence city in W Missouri, USA; population (1980) 111,806. Industries include steel, Portland cement, petroleum refining, and flour milling. President Harry S Truman was raised here, and later made it his home.

India: states and union territories

State	Capital	Area sq km
Andhra Pradesh	Hyderabad	276,800
Arunachal Pradesh	Itanagar	83,600
Assam	Dispur	78,400
Bihar	Patna	173,900
Goa	Panaji	3,700
Gujarat	Gandhinagar	196,000
Haryana	Chandigarh	44,200
Himachal Pradesh	Simla	55,700
Jammu and Kashmir	Srinagar	101,300
Karnataka	Bangalore	191,800
Kerala	Trivandrum	38,900
Madhya Pradesh	Bhopal	442,800
Maharashtra	Bombay	307,800
Manipur	Imphal	22,400
Meghalaya	Shillong	22,500
Mizoram	Aizawl	21,100
Nagaland	Kohima	16,500
Orissa	Bhubaneswar	155,800
Punjab	Chandigarh	50,400
Rajasthan	Jaipur	342,200
Sikkim	Gangtok	7,300
Tamil Nadu	Madras	130,100
Tripura	Agartala	10,500
Uttar Pradesh	Lucknow	294,400
West Bengal	Calcutta	87,900
Union territory		
Andaman and Nicobar Islands	Port Blair	8,300
Chandigarh	Chandigarh	114
Dadra and Nagar Haveli	Silvassa	490
Daman and Diu		110
Delhi	Delhi	1,500
Lakshadweep	Kavaratti Island	32
Pondicherry	Pondicherry	480

India country in S Asia, having borders to the N with Afghanistan, China, Nepál, and Bhutan, to the E with Burma, and to the NW with Pakistan. Situated within the NE corner of India, N of the Bay of Bengal, is Bangladesh, and India is surrounded to the SE, S, and SW by the Indian Ocean.

Indiana state of the midwest USA; nickname Hoosier State
area 93,700 sq km/36,168 sq mi
capital Indianapolis
towns Fort Wayne, Gary, Evansville, South Bend
features Wabash River; Wyandotte Cave; undulating prairies
products cereals, building stone, machinery, electrical goods, coal, steel, iron, chemicals
population (1988) 5,575,000
famous people Theodore Dreiser, Cole Porter, David Letterman, Michael Jackson
history first white settlements established 1731–35 by French traders; ceded to Britain by the French 1763; passed to American control 1783; became a state 1816.

Indianapolis capital and largest city of Indiana, USA, on the White River; population (1986) 720,000. It is an industrial centre and venue of the 'Indianapolis 500' car race.

Indian Ocean ocean between Africa and Australia, with India to the N, and the S boundary being an arbitrary line from Cape Agulhas to S Tasmania; area 73,500,000 sq km/28,371,000 sq mi; average depth 3,872 m/12,708 ft. The greatest depth is the Java Trench 7,725 m/25,353 ft.

Indochina French former collective name for ◊Kampuchea, ◊Laos, and ◊Vietnam, which became independent after World War II.

Indonesia country in SE Asia, made up of over 13,000 islands situated on the equator, between the Indian and Pacific oceans.

Indore city in Madhya Pradesh, India; population (1981) 829,327. A former capital of the princely state of Indore, it now produces cotton, chemicals, and furniture.

Indre river rising in the Auvergne mountains, France, and flowing NW for 170 km/115 mi to join the Loire below Tours. It gives its name to the *départements* of Indre and Indre-et-Loire.

Indus river in Asia, rising in Tibet and flowing 3,180 km/1,975 mi to the Arabian Sea. In 1960 the use of its waters, including those of its five tributaries, was divided between India (rivers Ravi, Beas, Sutlej) and Pakistan (rivers Indus, Jhelum, Chenab).

Inhambane seaport on the SE coast of Mozambique, 370 km/231 mi NE of Maputo. Population (1980) 56,000.

Inland Sea (Japanese *Seto Naikai*) an arm of the Pacific Ocean, 390 km/240 mi long, almost enclosed by the Japanese islands of Honshu, Kyushu and Shikoku. It has about 300 small islands.

Inn river in S central Europe, tributary of the Danube. Rising in the Swiss Alps, it flows 507 km/

317 mi NE through Austria and into Bavaria, West Germany, where it meets the Danube at Passau.

Innsbruck capital of Tirol state, W Austria, population (1981) 117,000. It is a tourist and winter sports centre, and a route junction for the Brenner Pass. The 1964 and 1976 Winter Olympics were held here.

Interlaken chief town of the Bernese Oberland, on the river Aar between lakes Brienz and Thun, Switzerland; population (1985) 13,000. The site was first occupied in 1130 by a monastery, suppressed in 1528.

Invercargill city on the S coast of South Island, New Zealand; population (1986) 52,800. It has saw-mills, and meatpacking and aluminium-smelting plants.

Inverness town in Highland region, Scotland, lying in a sheltered site at the mouth of the Ness; population (1985) 58,000. A tourist centre, it has tweed, tanning, engineering, and distilling industries.

Inverness-shire largest of the former Scottish counties, it was merged in Highland region 1975.

Inyangani highest peak in Zimbabwe, rising to 2,593 m/8,507 ft near the Mozambique frontier in NE Zimbabwe.

Inyökern village in the Mojave desert, California, USA, 72 km/45 mi NW of Mojave. It is the site

Indonesia
Republic of
(Republik Indonesia)

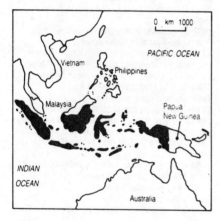

area 1,919,443 sq km/740,905 sq mi
capital Jakarta
towns ports Surabaya, Semarang
physical comprises 13,677 tropical islands, including Islands both the Greater Sunda Islands (including Java and Madura, part of Kalimantan/Borneo, Sumatra, Sulawesi and Belitung) and the Lesser Sundas/Nusa Tenggara (including Bali, Lombok, Sumba, Timor), as well as Malaku/Moluccas and part of New Guinea (Irian Jaya)
features world's largest Islamic state; Java is one of the world's most densely populated areas
head of state and government T N J Suharto from 1967
political system authoritarian nationalist republic

political parties Golkar, military-bureaucrat-farmers ruling party; United Development Party (PPP), moderate Islamic; Indonesian Democratic Party (PDI), nationalist Christian
exports coffee, rubber, palm oil, coconuts, tin, tea, tobacco, oil, liquid natural gas
currency rupiah (3,080.43 £1 Feb 1990)
population (1987) 172,250,000 (including 300 ethnic groups); annual growth rate 2%
life expectancy men 52, women 55
language Indonesian, closely allied to Malay
religion Muslim 90%, Buddhist, Hindu, and Pancasila (a secular official ideology)
literacy 83% male/65% female (1985 est)
GNP $87 bn (1983); $560 per head of population
chronology
17th century Dutch rule established.
1942 Occupied by Japan. Nationalist government established.
1945 Japanese surrender. Nationalists declare independence under Sukarno.
1949 Formal transfer of Dutch sovereignty.
1950 Unitary constitution established.
1963 Western New Guinea (Irian Jaya) ceded by Holland.
1965–66 Attempted communist coup; Gen Suharto emergency administration.
1967 Sukarno replaced as president by Suharto.
1976 Annexation by force of the former Portuguese colony of East Timor.
1986 Institution of 'transmigration programme' to settle large numbers of Javanese on the sparsely populated outer islands, particularly Irian Jaya.
1988 Partial easing of travel restrictions to East Timor. Suharto re-elected for fifth term.
1989 Foreign debt reaches $50 billion; Western creditors offer aid on the condition that concessions are made to foreign companies, and that austerity measures are introduced.

Iran
Islamic Republic of
(Jomhori-e-Islami-e-Irân;
until 1935 **Persia)**

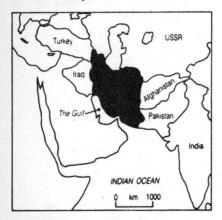

area 1,648,000 sq km/636,128 sq mi
capital Tehran
towns Isfahan, Mashhad, Tabriz, Shiraz, Ahwaz; chief port Abadan
physical plateau surrounded by mountains, including Elburz and Zagros; Lake Rezayeh; Dasht-Ekavir Desert
features ruins of Persepolis
Leader of the Revolution Ali Khamenei from 1989
head of government Ali Akbar Rafsanjani from 1989
political system authoritarian Islamic republic
political parties Islamic Republican Party (IRP), fundamentalist Islamic

exports carpets, cotton textiles, metalwork, leather goods, oil, petrochemicals
currency rial (117.00 = £1 Feb 1990)
population (1988) 53,920,000 (including minorities in Azerbaijan, Baluchistan, Khuzestan/Arabistan, and Kurdistan); annual growth rate 2.9%
life expectancy men 57, women 57
language Farsi, Kurdish, Turk, Arabic, English, French
religion Shi'ite Muslim (official)
literacy 62% male/39% female (1985 est)
GDP $76.37 bn (1977); $2,160 per head of population
chronology
1946 British, US, and Soviet forces left Iran.
1951 Oilfields nationalized by Prime Minister Mohammed Mossadeq.
1953 Mossadeq deposed and the shah took full control of the government.
1975 The shah introduced a single-party system.
1978 Opposition to the shah organized from France by Ayatollah Khomeini.
1979 Shah left the country and Khomeini returned to create an Islamic state. Students seized US hostages at embassy in Tehran.
1980 Start of Gulf War against Iraq.
1981 US hostages released.
1984 Egyptian peace proposals rejected.
1985 Gulf War fighting intensified. UN secretary-general's peace moves were unsuccessful.
1988 Ceasefire in Gulf War, talks with Iraq began.
1989 Khomeini called for the murder of British writer Salman Rushdie. Khomeini died June. Ali Khamenei elected interim Leader of the Revolution. Speaker of the Iranian parliament Ali Akbar Rafsanjani elected president.

---

of a US Naval Ordnance test station, founded in 1944, carrying out research in rocket flight and propulsion.
IOM abbreviation for ◊*Isle of Man.*
Iona an island in the Inner Hebrides; area 850 hectares. It is the site of a monastery founded 563 by St Columba, and a centre of early Christianity. It later became a burial ground for Irish, Scottish, and Norwegian kings. It has a 13th-century abbey.
Ionian Islands island group off the W coast of Greece; area 860 sq km/332 sq mi. A British protectorate from 1815 until their cession to Greece 1864, they include:
Cephalonia (Kefallínia);
Corfu (Kérkyra) a Venetian possession 1386–1797;
Cythera (Kíthira);
Ithaca (Itháki), the traditional home of Odysseus;
Leukas (Levkás);

Paxos (Paxoí);
Zante (Zákynthos).
Ionian Sea the part of the Mediterranean lies between Italy and Greece, to the S of the Adriatic, and containing the Ionian islands.
IOW abbreviation for ◊*Isle of Wight.*
Iowa state of the midwest USA; nickname Hawkeye State
area 145,800 sq km/56,279 sq mi
capital Des Moines
towns Cedar Rapids, Davenport, Sioux City
features Grant Wood Gallery in Davenport and Herbert Hoover birthplace and library in West Branch
products cereals, soya beans, meat, wool, chemicals, machinery, electrical goods
population (1984) 2,837,000
famous people Buffalo Bill Cody

Iraq
Republic of
(al Jumhouriya al 'Iraqia)

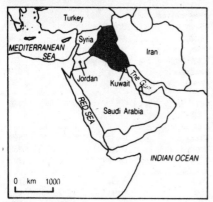

area 434,924 sq km/167,881 sq mi
capital Baghdad
towns Mosul and port of Basra
physical mountains in N, desert in W; wide valley of rivers Tigris and Euphrates NW–SE
features reed architecture of the marsh Arabs; sites of Eridu, Babylon, Nineveh, Ur, Ctesiphon
head of state and government Saddam Hussein At-Takriti from 1979
political system effective one-party socialist republic
political parties Arab Baath Socialist Party, nationalist socialist
exports dates (80% of world supply), wool, oil
currency Iraqi dinar (0.53 = £1 Feb 1990)
population (1987) 17,093,000; annual growth rate 3.6%
life expectancy men 62, women 63
language Arabic (official)
religion Shi'ite Muslim 60%, Sunni Muslim 30%, Christian 3%
literacy 68% male/32% female (1980 est)
GNP $31 bn (1981); $2,410 per head of population
chronology
1920 Iraq became a British League of Nations protectorate.
1921 Hashemite dynasty established, with Faisal I as king.
1932 Achieved full independence.
1958 Monarchy overthrown and Iraq became a republic.
1968 Military coup puts Gen al-Bakr in power.
1979 Al-Bakr replaced by Saddam Hussein.
1980 Gulf War between Iraq and Iran broke out.
1985 Gulf War fighting intensified. UN secretary-general's peace moves were unsuccessful.
1988 Ceasefire in Gulf War, talks began with Iran. Iraq accused of using chemical weapons. Harsh repression of Kurdish rebels seeking greater autonomy.
1989 Unsuccessful coup against President Hussein.

---

history part of the Louisiana Purchase 1803, it remains an area of small farms; it became a state 1846.

Ipoh capital of Perak state, Peninsular Malaysia; population (1980) 301,000. The economy is based on tin mining.

Ipswich river port on the Orwell estuary, administrative headquarters of Suffolk, England; population (1981) 120,500. Industries include engineering and the manufacture of textiles,

Iowa

plastics, and electrical goods. Home of the painter Thomas Gainsborough.

Iquique city and seaport in N Chile, capital of the province of Tarapaca; population (1985) 120,700. It exports nitrate of soda from its desert region.

Iquitos river port on the Amazon, Peru, also a tourist centre for the rainforest; population (1988) 248,000.

Iráklion or *Heraklion* largest city and capital (since 1971) of Crete, Greece; population (1981) 102,000.

Iran country in SW Asia, bounded to the N by the USSR and the Caspian Sea, to the E by Afghanistan and Pakistan, to the S and SW by the Gulf of Oman, to the W by Iraq, and to the NW by Turkey.

Iraq country in SW Asia, bounded to the N by Turkey, to the E by Iran, to the S by the Persian Gulf, Kuwait, and Saudi Arabia, to the SW by Jordan, and to the W by Syria.

Ireland one of the British Isles, lying to the west of Great Britain, from which it is separated by the Irish Sea. It comprises the provinces of Ulster, Leinster, Munster, and Connacht, and is divided between

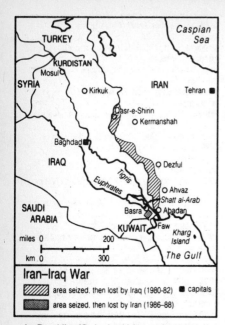

Iran–Iraq War

- ▨ area seized, then lost by Iraq (1980–82)   ■ capitals
- ▨ area seized, then lost by Iran (1986–88)

the Republic of Ireland, which occupies the south, centre, and northwest of the island, and Northern Ireland, which occupies the northeast corner and forms part of the United Kingdom.

The centre of Ireland is a lowland, about 60–120 m/200–400 ft above sea level; hills are mainly around the coasts, though there are a few peaks over 1,000 m/3,000 ft high, the highest being Carrantuohill ('the inverted reaping hook'), 1,040 m/3,415 ft, in Macgillicuddy's Reeks, County Kerry. The entire western coastline is an intricate alternation of bays and estuaries. Several of the rivers flow in sluggish courses through the central lowland, and then cut through fjord-like valleys to the sea. The ◊Shannon in particular falls 30 m/100 ft in its last 26 km/16 mi above Limerick, and is used to produce hydroelectric power.

The lowland bogs which cover parts of central Ireland are intermingled with fertile limestone country where dairy farming is the chief occupation. The bogs are an important source of fuel, in the form of peat.

The climate is mild, moist, and changeable. The annual rainfall on the lowlands varies from 76 cm/30 in in the east to 203 cm/80 in in some western districts, but much higher falls are recorded in the mountains.

Ireland, Northern constituent part of the UK
area 13,460 sq km/5,196 sq mi
capital Belfast
towns Londonderry, Enniskillen, Omagh, Newry, Armagh, Coleraine

Ireland: provinces and counties

County	Administrative headquarters	Area sq km
Ulster province		
Antrim	Belfast	2,830
Armagh	Armagh	1,250
Down	Downpatrick	2,470
Fermanagh	Enniskillen	1,680
Londonderry	Derry	2,070
Tyrone	Omagh	3,160
NORTHERN IRELAND		*13,460*
Ulster province		
Cavan	Cavan	1,890
Donegal	Lifford	4,830
Monaghan	Monaghan	1,290
Munster province		
Clare	Ennis	3,190
Cork	Cork	7,460
Kerry	Tralee	4,700
Limerick	Limerick	2,690
Tipperary (N)	Nenagh	2,000
Tipperary (S)	Clonmel	2,260
Waterford	Waterford	1,840
Leinster province		
Carlow	Carlow	900
Dublin	Dublin	920
Kildare	Naas	1,690
Kilkenny	Kilkenny	2,060
Laois	Portlaoise	1,720
Longford	Longford	1,040
Louth	Dundalk	820
Meath	Trim	2,340
Offaly	Tullamore	2,000
Westmeath	Mullingar	1,760
Wexford	Wexford	2,350
Wicklow	Wicklow	2,030
Connacht province		
Galway	Galway	5,940
Leitrim	Carrick-on-Shannon	1,530
Mayo	Castlebar	5,400
Roscommon	Roscommon	2,460
Sligo	Sligo	1,800
REPUBLIC OF IRELAND		*68,910*

features Mourne mountains, Belfast Lough and Lough Neagh; Giant's Causeway; comprises the six counties (Antrim, Armagh, Down, Fermanagh, Londonderry, and Tyrone) that form part of Ireland's northernmost province of Ulster
exports engineering, especially shipbuilding, textile machinery, aircraft components; linen and synthetic textiles; processed foods, especially dairy and poultry products – all affected by the 1980s depression and political unrest
currency as for the rest of the UK
population (1986) 1,567,000

Atlantic Ocean

KINTYRE

Londonderry   ANTRIM
LONDONDERRY

Ballymena

TYRONE   Belfast

Omagh   Neagh

Enniskillen   Armagh   DOWN
FERMANAGH   ARMAGH   Downpatrick

IRELAND   Irish
                                  Sea

Northern Ireland

☐ Protestant majority
☐ R. Catholic majority

Employment Act 1975 but in 1987 Catholics were two and a half times more likely to be unemployed than their Protestant counterparts – a differential that had not improved since 1971.

Ireland, Republic of country in N W Europe, occupying almost all of the island of Ireland, to the W of England, Scotland, and Wales.

Irian Jaya the western portion of the island of New Guinea, part of Indonesia
area 420,000 sq km/162,000 sq mi
capital Jayapura
population (1980) 1,174,000
history part of the Dutch East Indies 1828 as Western New Guinea; retained by Netherlands after Indonesian independence 1949, but ceded to Indonesia 1963 by the United Nations and remained part of Indonesia by an 'Act of Free Choice' 1969; in the 1980s 283,500 hectares/700,000 acres were given over to Indonesia's controversial transmigration programme for the resettlement of farming families from overcrowded Java, causing destruction of rainforests and displacing indigenous people.

Irkutsk city in S USSR; population (1987) 609,000. It produces coal, iron, steel, and machine tools. Founded 1652, it began to grow after the Trans-Siberian railway reached it 1898.

Ironbridge Gorge site, near Telford New Town, Shropshire, England, of the Iron Bridge (1779), one of the first and most striking products of the Industrial Revolution in Britain: it is now part of an open-air museum of industrial archaeology.

Iron Gate (Romanian *Portile de Fier*) narrow gorge, interrupted by rapids, in Romania. A hydro-electric scheme undertaken 1964–70 by Romania and Yugoslavia transformed this section of the river Danube into a 145 km/90 mi long lake and eliminated the rapids as a navigation hazard. Before flooding, in 1965, an archaeological survey revealed Europe's oldest urban settlement, Lepenski Vir.

Irrawaddy (Burmese *Ayeryarwady*) chief river of Myanmar (Burma), flowing roughly N to S for 2,090 km/1,300 mi across the centre of the country into the Bay of Bengal. Its sources are the Mali and N'mai rivers; its chief tributaries are the Chindwin and Shweli.

Irvine new town in Strathclyde, W Scotland; population (1984) 57,000. It overlooks the Isle of Arran, and is a holiday resort.

Ischia volcanic island about 26 km/16 mi SW of Naples, Italy, in the Tyrrhenian Sea; population (1985) 26,000. It has mineral springs known to the Romans, beautiful scenery, and is a holiday resort.

Ise city SE of Kyoto, on Honshu, Japan. It is the site of the most sacred Shinto shrine, dedicated to sun-goddess Amaterasu. It has been rebuilt every 20 years in the form of a perfect thatched house of the 7th century BC, and contains the octagonal mirror of the goddess.

language English
religion Protestant 54%, Roman Catholic 31%
famous people Montgomery, Alanbrooke
government because of the outbreak of violence, there has been direct rule from the UK since 1972. Northern Ireland is entitled to send 12 members to the Westminster Parliament.

Under the Anglo-Irish Agreement 1985, the Republic of Ireland was given a consultative role (via an Anglo-Irish conference) in the government of Northern Ireland, but agreed that there should be no change in its status except by majority consent, and that there should be greater cooperation against terrorism. The agreement was approved by Parliament, but all 12 Ulster members gave up their seats, so that by-elections could be fought as a form of 'referendum' on the views of the province itself. A similar boycotting of the Northern Ireland Assembly since the Anglo-Irish Agreement led to its dissolution 1986 by the UK government
history the creation of Northern Ireland dates from 1921 when the mainly Protestant counties of Ulster withdrew from the newly established Irish Free State. Spasmodic outbreaks of violence by the IRA continued, but only in 1968–69 were there serious disturbances arising from Protestant political dominance and discrimination against the Roman Catholic minority in employment and housing. British troops were sent to restore peace and protect Catholics, but disturbances continued and in 1972 the parliament at Stormont was prorogued, and superseded by direct rule from Westminster. Job discrimination was outlawed under the Fair

Ireland, Republic of
(Irish *Éire*)

area 68,900 sq km/26,595 sq mi
capital Dublin
towns ports Cork, Dún Laoghaire, Limerick, Waterford
physical central plateau with hills; rivers Shannon, Liffey, Boyne
features Bog of Allen, source of domestic and national power; Magillicuddy's Reeks, Wicklow Mountains; Lough Corrib, lakes of Killarney; Galway Bay and Aran Islands; heavy rainfall
head of state Patrick J Hillery from 1976
head of government Charles Haughey from 1987
political system democratic republic
political parties Fianna Fáil (Soldiers of Destiny), moderate centre-right; Fine Gael (Irish Tribe), moderate centre-left; Labour Party, moderate left-of-centre; Progressive Democrats, radical free-enterprise
exports livestock, dairy products, Irish whiskey, microelectronic components and assemblies, mining and engineering products, chemicals, tobacco, clothing; tourism is important
currency punt (1.08 = £1 Feb 1990)
population (1988) 3,540,000; annual growth rate 1.2%
life expectancy men 70, women 76
language Irish and English (both official)
religion Roman Catholic
literacy 99% (1984)
GNP $16.5 (1983); $4,750 per head of population
chronology
1916 Easter Rising: nationalists seized the Dublin general post office and proclaimed a republic. The revolt was suppressed by the British army and most of the leaders were executed.
1918–21 Guerrilla warfare against British army led to split in rebel forces.
1921 Anglo-Irish Treaty resulted in creation of the Irish Free State (Southern Ireland).
1937 Eire established as an independent state.
1949 Eire left the Commonwealth and became the Republic of Ireland.
1973 Fianna Fáil defeated after 40 years in office. Liam Cosgrave formed a coalition government.
1977 Fianna Fáil returned to power, with Jack Lynch as prime minister.
1979 Lynch resigned and was succeeded by Charles Haughey.
1981 Garret FitzGerald formed a coalition.
1983 New Ireland Forum formed, but rejected by the British government.
1985 Anglo-Irish Agreement signed.
1986 Protests by Ulster Unionists against the agreement.
1987 General election won by Charles Haughey.
1988 Relations with UK at low ebb because of disagreement over extradition decisions.
1989 Haughey failed to win a majority in the general election. Progressive Democrats (a breakaway party of Fianna Fáil) given cabinet positions in a coalition government.

Isère river in SE France, 290 km/180 mi long, a tributary of the Rhône. It gives its name to the *département* of Isère.

Isfahan or *Esfahan* industrial (steel, textiles, carpets) city in central Iran; population (1986) 1,001,000. It was the ancient capital (1598–1722) of Abbas the Great, and its features include the Great Square, Grand Mosque, and Hall of Forty Pillars.

Isis the upper stretches of the river Thames, England, above Oxford.

Iskandarlya Arabic name for ◊Alexandria, Egypt.

Iskenderun port, naval base and steel town in Turkey; population (1980) 125,000. It was founded by Alexander the Great in 333 BC and called Alexandretta until 1939.

Islamabad capital of Pakistan from 1967, in the Potwar district, at the foot of the Margala Hills and immediately NW of Rawalpindi; population (1981) 201,000. The city was designed by Constantinos Doxiadis in the 1960s. The Federal Capital Territory of Islamabad has an area of 907 sq km/ 350 sq mi, and a population (1985) of 379,000.

Islay most southerly island of the Inner Hebrides,

Israel
State of
(Medinat Israel)

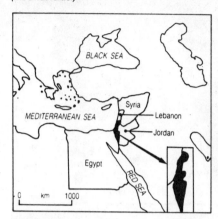

area 20,800 sq km/8,029 sq mi (as at 1949 armistice)
capital Jerusalem (not recognized by the United Nations)
towns ports Tel Aviv/Jaffa, Haifa, Eilat; Bat-Yam, Holon, Ramat Gan, Petach Tikva, Beersheba
physical coastal plain of Sharon between Haifa and Tel Aviv noted since ancient times for fertility; high arid region in south and centre; river Jordan Rift Valley along the east is below sea level
features Dead Sea, Lake Tiberias, Negev Desert, Golan Heights; historic sites: Jerusalem, Bethlehem, Nazareth; Masada, Megiddo, Jericho; caves of the Dead Sea scrolls
head of state Chaim Herzog from 1983
head of government Itzhak Shamir from 1986
political system democratic republic
political parties Israel Labour Party, moderate left-of-cent re; Consolidation Party (Likud), right-of-centre
exports citrus and other fruit, avocados, chinese leaves, fertilizers, plastics, petrochemicals, textiles, electro-optics, precision instruments, aircraft and missiles
currency shekel (3.30 = £1 Feb 1990)
population (1988) 4,442,000 (including 750,000 Arab Israeli citizens and over 1 million

Arabs in the occupied territories); under the Law of Return 1950, 'every Jew shall be entitled to come to Israel as an immigrant', those from the East and E Europe are *Ashkenazim*, and from Spain, Portugal, and Arab N Africa are *Sephardim* (over 50% of the population is now of Sephardic descent). An Israeli-born Jew is a *Sabra*; about 500,000 Israeli Jews are resident in the US. Annual growth rate 1.8%
life expectancy men 73, women 76
language Hebrew and Arabic (official); Yiddish, European and W Asian languages
religion Israel is a secular state, but the predominant faith is Judaism; also Sunni Muslim, Christian, and Druse
literacy 97% male/93% female (1985 est)
GNP $23 bn (1983); $5,609 per head of population
chronology
1948 Independent state of Israel proclaimed with Ben Gurion as prime minister.
1963 Ben Gurion resigned and was succeeded by Levi Eshkol.
1964 Palestine Liberation Organization (PLO) founded with the aim of overthrowing the state of Israel.
1967 Israel victorious in the Six-Day War.
1968 Israel Labour Party formed, led by Golda Meir.
1969 Golda Meir became prime minister.
1974 Yom Kippur War. Golda Meir succeeded by Itzhak Rabin.
1977 Menachem Begin elected prime minister. Egyptian president addressed the Knesset.
1978 Camp David talks.
1979 Egyptian-Israeli agreement signed.
1982 Israel pursued PLO fighters into Lebanon.
1983 Agreement reached for withdrawal from Lebanon.
1985 Israeli prime minister Shimon Peres had secret talks with King Hussein of Jordan.
1986 Itzhak Shamir took over from Peres under power-sharing agreement.
1988 Criticism of Israel's handling of Palestinian uprising in occupied territories. PLO acknowledges Israel's right to exist.
1989 New Likud–Labour coalition government formed under Shamir.
1990 Coalition collapses following disagreement over peace process.

Scotland, in Strathclyde region, separated from Jura by the Sound of Islay; area 610 sq km/235 sq mi; population (1981) 3,800. The principal towns are Bowmore and Port Ellen. It produces malt whisky, and its wildlife includes eagles and rare wintering geese.

Isle of Ely former county of England, in East Anglia. It was merged with Cambridgeshire in 1965.
Isle of Man see ◊Man, Isle of.
Isle of Wight see ◊Wight, Isle of.
Islington borough of N Greater London including

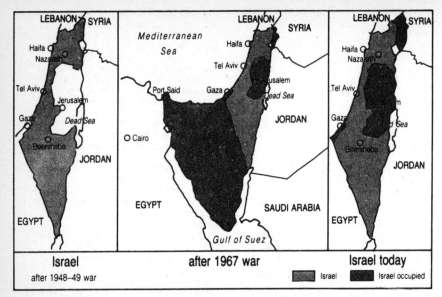

Israel after 1948–49 war | after 1967 war | Israel today

Israel | Israel occupied

the suburbs of Islington and Finsbury; population (1985) 167,900.

features 19th-century squares and terraces at Highbury, Barnsbury, Canonbury; Wesley Museum in City Road. Mineral springs (Sadler's Wells) in Clerkenwell were exploited in conjunction with a music-hall in the 17th century, and Lilian Baylis developed a later theatre as an 'Old Vic' annexe.

Ismailia city in NE Egypt; population (1985) 191,700. It was founded in 1863 as the head-quarters for construction of the Suez Canal, and was named after the Khedive Ismail.

Israel ancient kingdom of N ◊Palestine, formed after the death of Solomon by Jewish peoples seceding from the rule of his son Rehoboam, and electing Jeroboam in his place.

Israel country in SW Asia, bounded to the N by Lebanon, to the E by Syria and Jordan, to the S by the Gulf of Aqaba, and to the W by Egypt and the Mediterranean.

Istanbul city and chief seaport of Turkey; population (1985) 5,495,000. It produces textiles, tobacco, cement, glass, and leather. Founded as *Byzantium* about 660 BC, it was renamed *Constantinople* 330, and was the capital of the Byzantine Empire until captured by the Turks 1453. As *Istamboul* it was capital of the Otto-man Empire until 1922.

features the harbour of the Golden Horn; Hagia Sophia (Emperor Justinian's church of the Holy Wisdom, 537, now a mosque); Sultan Ahmet Mosque, known as the Blue Mosque, from its tiles; Topkapi Palace of the Sultans (with a harem of 400 rooms), now a museum. The Selimye Barracks in the suburb of *Usküdar* (Scutari) was used as a hospital in the Crimean War. The rooms used by Florence Nightingale, with her personal possessions, are preserved as a museum.

Italy: regions

Region	Capital	Area sq km
Abruzzi	Aquila	10,800
Basilicata	Potenza	10,000
Calabria	Catanzaro	15,100
Campania	Naples	13,600
Emilia-Romagna	Bologna	22,100
Friuli-Venezia Giulia*	Udine	7,800
Lazio	Rome	17,200
Liguria	Genoa	5,400
Lombardy	Milan	23,900
Marche	Ancona	9,700
Molise	Campobasso	4,400
Piedmont	Turin	25,400
Puglia	Bari	19,300
Sardinia*	Cagliari	24,100
Sicily*	Palermo	25,700
Trentino-Alto Adige*	Trento**	13,600
Tuscany	Florence	23,000
Umbria	Perugia	8,500
Valle d'Aosta*	Aosta	3,300
Veneto	Venice	18,400
		301,300

*special autonomous regions
**also Bolzano-Bozen

Italy
Republic of
(Repubblica Italiana)

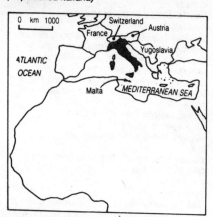

area 301,300 sq km/116,332 sq mi
capital Rome
towns Milan, Turin; ports Naples, Genoa, Palermo, Bari, Catania
physical mountainous (Maritime Alps, Dolomites, Apennines); rivers Po, Adige, Arno, Tiber; islands of Sicily, Sardinia, Elba, Capri, Ischia
features lakes Como, Maggiore, Garda; Europe's only active volcanoes: Vesuvius, Etna, Stromboli; historic towns include Venice, Florence, Siena
political parties Christian Democratic Party (DC), Catholic centrist; Italian Communist Party (PCI), pro-European socialist; Italian Socialist Party (PSI), moderate socialist; Italian Social Movement–National Right (MSI-DN), neo-fascist; Italian Republican Party (PRI), social democratic, left-of-centre; Italian Social Democratic Party (PSDI), moderate left-of-centre;

Liberals (PLI), right-of-centre
exports wine, fruit, vegetables, textiles (Europe's largest silk producer), leather goods, motor vehicles, electrical goods, chemicals, marble (Carrara), sulphur, mercury, iron, steel
head of state Francesco Cossiga from 1985
head of government Giulio Andreotti from 1989
political system democratic republic
currency lira (2116.25 = £1 Feb 1990)
population (1988) 57,397,000; annual growth rate 0.1%
life expectancy men 71, women 78
language Italian, derived from Latin
religion Roman Catholic 90%
literacy 98% male/96% female (1985)
GNP $350 bn (1983); $6,914 per head of population
chronology
1946 Monarchy replaced by a republic.
1948 New constitution adopted.
1954 Trieste returned to Italy.
1976 Communists proposed the establishment of a broad-based, left–right government, the 'historic compromise'. Idea ultimately rejected by the Christian Democrats.
1978 Christian Democrat Aldo Moro, architect of the historic compromise, kidnapped and murdered by Red Brigade guerrillas.
1983 Bettino Craxi, a socialist, became leader of a broad coalition government.
1987 Craxi resigned, and the succeeding coalition fell within months.
1988 After several unsuccessful attempts to form a stable government, the leader of the Christian Democrats, Ciriaco de Mita, established a five-party coalition that included the Socialists.
1989 De Mita resigned after disagreements within his coalition government; eventually succeeded by Giulio Andreotti.

Italian Somaliland former Italian Trust Territory on the Somali coast of Africa extending to 502,300 sq km/194,999 sq mi. Established in 1892, it was extended in 1925 with the acquisition of Jubaland from Kenya; administered from Mogadishu; under British rule 1941–50. Thereafter it reverted to Italian authority before uniting with British Somaliland in 1960 to form the independent state of Somalia.

Italy country in S Europe, bounded N by Switzerland and Austria, E by Yugoslavia and the Adriatic Sea, S by the Ionian and Mediterranean Seas, and W by the Tyrrhenian Sea and France. It includes the Mediterranean islands of Sardinia and Sicily.

Itaipu the world's largest dam, situated on the Paraná River, SW Brazil.

Ithaca (modern Greek *Ithaki*) Greek island in the Ionian Sea, area 93 sq km/36 sq mi. Important in pre-classical Greece, Ithaca was (in Homer's poem) the birthplace of Odysseus.

Ivanovo capital of Ivanovo region, USSR, 240 km/150 mi NE of Moscow; population (1987) 479,000. Industries include textiles, chemicals and engineering.

Iviza alternative spelling of ◊Ibiza, one of the ◊Balearic Islands.

Ivory Coast (French *Côte d'Ivoire*) country in W Africa, bounded to the N by Mali and Burkina

Ivory Coast
Republic of
(République de la Côte d'Ivoire)

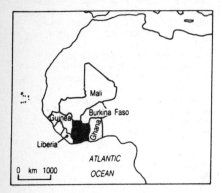

Mali

Burkina Faso

Guinea

Ghana

Liberia

ATLANTIC

0   km   1000   OCEAN

area 322,463 sq km/124,471 sq mi
capital Abidjan; capital designate
Yamoussouko
towns Bouaké

physical tropical rainforest (diminishing as it is
exploited) in the S: savanna and low mountains
in the N
head of state and government Félix
Houphouët-Boigny from 1960
political system effectively one-party republic
political parties Democratic Party of the Ivory
Coast (PDCI), nationalist, free-enterprise
exports coffee, cocoa, timber, petroleum
currency CFA franc (485.00 = £1 Feb 1990)
population (1988) 11,630,000; annual growth
rate 3.7%
life expectancy men 49, women 52
language French (official)
religion animist 65%, Muslim 24%, Christian
11%
literacy 53% male/31% female (1985 est)
GNP $6.7 bn (1983); $1,100 per head of
population
chronology
1958 Achieved internal self-government.
1960 Achieved full independence, with Félix
Houphouët-Boigny as president of a one-party
state.

Faso, E by Ghana, S by the Gulf of Guinea, and
W by Liberia and Guinea.

Iwo Jima largest of the Japanese Volcano Islands
in the W Pacific Ocean, 1,222 km/764 mi S of
Tokyo; area 21 sq km/8 sq mi. Annexed by Japan
1891, it was captured by the US 1945 after heavy
fighting. It was returned to Japan 1968.

Izhevsk industrial city in the E USSR, capital of
Udmurt Autonomous Republic; population (1987)
631,000. Industries include steel, agricultural
machinery, machine tools, and armaments. It
was founded 1760.

Izmir formerly *Smyrna* port and naval base in Turkey; population (1985) 1,490,000. Products include

steel, electronics, and plastics. The largest annual
trade fair in the Middle East is held here. Headquarters of North Atlantic Treaty Organization SE
Command.
history Originally Greek (founded about 1000
BC), it was of considerable importance in ancient
times, vying with Ephesus and Pergamum as the
first city of Asia. It was destroyed by Tamerlane
in 1402, and became Turkish in 1424. It was
occupied by the Greeks in 1919 but retaken by
the Turks in 1922; in the same year it was largely
destroyed by fire.

Iznik modern name of ancient ◊Nicaea, a town in
Turkey.

Jabalpur industrial city on the Narbarda river in Madhya Pradesh, India; population (1981) 758,000. Products include textiles, oil, bauxite, and armaments.

Jablonec town in Czechoslovakia, on the river Neisse, NE of Prague; population (1984) 45,000. It has had a glass industry since the 14th century.

Jackson largest city and capital of Mississippi, USA, on the Pearl River; population (1980) 203,000. It produces furniture, cotton-seed oil, iron and steel castings, and owes its prosperity to the discovery of gasfields to the south. Named after President Andrew Jackson, it dates from 1821 and was almost destroyed in the Civil War by Gen W Sherman 1863.

Jacksonville port, resort, and commercial centre in Florida, USA; population (1980) 541,000. The port has naval installations and ship repair yards. To the N the Cross-Florida Barge Canal links the Atlantic with the Gulf of Mexico.

Jacobabad city in Sind province, SE Pakistan, 400 km/250 mi NE of Karachi; population (1981) 80,000. Founded by General John Jacob as a frontier post, the city now trades in wheat, rice, and millet. It has a very low annual rainfall (about 5 cm/2 in) and temperatures are among the highest in the Indian subcontinent – up to 53°C/127°F.

Jaén capital of Jaén province, S Spain, on the Guadalbullon river; population (1986) 103,000. It has remains of its Moorish walls and citadel.

Jaffa Biblical name *Joppa* port in W Israel, part of ◊Tel Aviv from 1950.

It was captured by the Crusaders in the 12th century, by the French emperor Napoleon in 1799, and by British field marshal Allenby 1917.

Jaffna capital of Jaffna district, Northern Province, Sri Lanka. The focal point of Hindu Tamil nationalism and the scene of recurring riots during the 1980s.

Jaipur capital of Rajasthan, India; population (1981) 1,005,000. Formerly the capital of the state of Jaipur, it was merged with Rajasthan in 1949. Products include textiles and metal products.

Jakarta or *Djakarta* capital of Indonesia on the NW coast of Java; population (1980) 6,504,000. Industries include textiles, chemicals, and plastics; a canal links it with its port of Tanjung Priok where rubber, oil, tin, coffee, tea, and palm oil are among its exports; also a tourist centre. Founded by the Dutch in 1619, and known as Batavia until 1949, it has the president's palace and government offices.

Jalalabad capital of Nangarhar province, E Afghanistan, on the road from Kabul to Peshawar in Pakistan. The city was beseiged by mujaheddin rebels in 1989 after the withdrawal of Soviet troops from Afghanistan.

Jalgava formerly (to 1917) *Mitau* town in Latvian republic, USSR, 48 km/30 mi S of Riga; population about 57,000. Industries include textile and sugar-refining. The town was founded in 1265 by Teutonic knights.

Jamaica island in the Caribbean, to the S of Cuba, and to the W of Haiti.

Jammu winter capital of the state of Jammu and Kashmir, India; population (1981) 206,100. It stands on the river Tavi and was linked to India's rail system in 1972.

Jammu and Kashmir state of N India
area 101,300 sq km/39,102 sq mi; another 78,900 sq km/30,455 is occupied by Pakistan, and 42,700 sq km/16,482 by China
capital Srinagar (winter); Jammu (summer)

Jammu and Kashmir

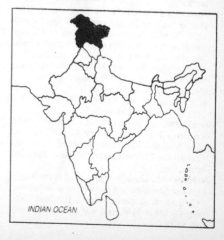

INDIAN OCEAN

Jamaica

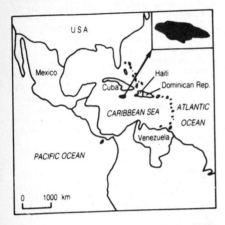

USA

Mexico

Haiti

Cuba

Dominican Rep.

CARIBBEAN SEA

ATLANTIC

OCEAN

Venezuela

PACIFIC OCEAN

0   1000 km

area 11,425 sq km/4,410 sq mi
capital Kingston
towns Montego Bay, Spanish Town, St Andrew
physical mountainous
features Blue Mountains (so called because
of the haze over them, and renowned for
their coffee); partly undersea remains of
the pirate city of Port Royal, destroyed by
earthquake 1692
head of state Elizabeth II from 1962
represented by Florizel Glasspole from 1973

head of government Michael Manley from
1989
political system constitutional monarchy
political parties Jamaica Labour Party (JLP),
moderate, centrist; People's National Party
(PNP), left-of-centre
exports sugar, bananas, bauxite, rum, coffee,
coconuts, liqueurs, cigars
currency Jamaican dollar (11.65 = £1 Feb
1990)
population (1987) 2,300,000 (a mixture
of several ethnic groups); annual growth
rate 1.5%
life expectancy men 70, women 76
language English, Jamaican creole
religion Protestant 70%, Rastafarian
literacy 90% male/93% female (1980 est)
GNP $2.9 bn (1983); $1,340 per head of
population
chronology
1959 Granted internal self-government.
1962 Achieved full independence, with
Alexander Bustamente of the JLP as prime
minister.
1967 JLP re-elected under Hugh Shearer.
1972 Michael Manley of the PNP became prime
minister.
1980 JLP elected, with Edward Seaga as prime
minister.
1983 JLP re-elected, winning all 60 seats.
1988 Island badly damaged by hurricane.
1989 PNP won a decisive victory with Michael
Manley returning as prime minister.

towns Leh
products timber, grain, rice, fruit, silk, carpets
population (1981) 5,982,000 (Indian-occupied
territory)
history part of the Mogul Empire from 1586,
Jammu came under the control of Gulab Singh
1820. In 1947 Jammu was attacked by Pakistan
and chose to become part of the new state of India.
Dispute over the area caused further hostilities
1971 between India and Pakistan (ended by the
Simla agreement 1972). See also ◊Kashmir.

Jamnagar city in Gujarat, India, on the Gulf of
Kutch, SW of Ahmedabad; population (1981)
317,000. Its port is at Bedi.

Jamshedpur city in Bihar, India; population (1981)
439,000. It was built in 1909, and takes its
name from the industrialist Jamsheedji Tata, who
founded the Tata iron and steel works here and
in Bombay.

Jan Mayen Norwegian volcanic island in the Arctic,
between Greenland and Norway; area 380 sq km/
147 sq mi. It is named after a Dutchman who
visited it about 1610, and was annexed by Norway 1929.

Japan country in E Asia, occupying a group of
islands of which the four main ones are Hokkaido,
Honshu, Kyushu, and Shikoku. Japan is situated
in the N Pacific, to the E of North and South
Korea.

Japan, Sea of sea separating Japan from the mainland of Asia.

Jarrow town in Tyne and Wear, NE England, on the
S bank of the Tyne, 10 km/6 mi E of Newcastle
and connected with the N bank by the Tyne Tunnel
(1967); population (1981) 27,075. The closure of
Palmer's shipyard in Jarrow in 1933 prompted
the unemployed to march to London, a landmark
event of the Depression.

Jassy German name for the Romanian city of
◊Iaşi.

Java or *Jawa* the most important island of
Indonesia, situated between Sumatra and Bali
area (with the island of Madura) 132,000 sq km/
51,000 sq mi
capital Jakarta (also capital of Indonesia)
towns ports include Surabaja and Semarang
physical about half the island is under cultivation, the rest being thickly forested. Mountains

Japan
(Nippon)

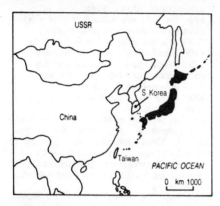

area 377,815 sq km/
145,837 sq mi
capital Tokyo
towns Fukuoka, Kitakyushu, Kyoto, Sapporo;
ports Osaka, Nagoya, Yokohama, Kobe,
Kawasaki
physical mountainous, volcanic; comprises
over 1,000 islands, of which the chief are
Hokkaido, Honshu, Shikoku, Kyushu, Ryukyu
features Mount Fuji
head of state (figurehead) Emperor Akihito
from 1989
head of government Toshiki Kaifu from 1989.
political system constitutional monarchy
political parties Liberal Democratic Party
(LDP), right-of-centre; Japan Socialist Party
(JSP), left-of-centre; Komeito (Clean Government
Party), Buddhist-centrist; Democratic Socialist
Party, centrist; Japanese Communist Party
(JCP), socialist
exports televisions, cassette and video

recorders, radios, cameras, computers, robots,
other electronic and electrical equipment,
cars and other vehicles, ships, iron, steel,
chemicals, textiles
currency yen (246.25 = £1 Feb 1990)
population (1987) 122,264,000; annual growth
rate 0.7%
life expectancy men 74, women 80
language Japanese
religion Shinto and Buddhist (often combined),
Christian (minority). 30% of the population
claim to have a personal religious faith
literacy 99% (1985)
GNP $1,200 bn (1984); $10,266 per head of
population
chronology
1945 Japanese surrender. Allied control
commission in power.
1946 Framing of 'Peace Constitution'.
1952 Full sovereignty regained.
1958 Joined United Nations.
1972 Ryukyu Islands regained.
1974 Resignation of Prime Minister Tanaka over
Lockheed bribes scandal.
1982 Election of Yasuhiro Nakasone as prime
minister.
1987 Noboru Takeshita chosen to succeed
Nakasone.
1988 Recruit corporation insider-trading scandal
cast shadow over government and opposition
parties.
1989 Emperor Hirohito died and was
succeeded by his son Akihito. Two cabinet
ministers forced to resign over Recruit, and
many more implicated. Takeshita eventually
resigned because of the Recruit scandal, and
was succeeded by Sosuke Uno in June. Uno
resigned Aug over revelations that he had had
affairs with geishas, and was succeeded by
Toshiki Kaifu.
1990 New house of councillors' elections (Feb)
won by LDP.

---

and sea breezes keep temperatures down, but
humidity is high, with heavy rainfall from Dec
to Mar
features a chain of mountains, some of which are
volcanic, runs along the centre, rising to 2,750 m/
9,000 ft. The highest mountain, Semeru 3,676 m/
12,060 ft, is in the east.
exports rice, coffee, cocoa, tea, sugar, rubber,
quinine, teak, and petroleum
population (with Madura) (1980) 91,270,000;
including people of Javanese, Sundanese, and
Madurese origin, with differing languages
religion predominantly Muslim
history Fossilized early human remains (*Homo
erectus*) were discovered 1891–92. In central Java

there are ruins of magnificent Buddhist monuments and of the Sivaite temple in Prambanan.
The island's last Hindu kingdom, Majapahit, was
destroyed about 1520 and followed by a number
of short-lived Javanese kingdoms. The Dutch East
India company founded a factory in 1610. Britain
took over during the Napoleonic period, 1811–16,
and Java then reverted to Dutch control. Occupied
by Japan 1942–45 while under Dutch control, Java
then became part of the republic of Indonesia.
Jedburgh small town in the Borders region, SE
Scotland, on Jed Water; population (1981) 4,000.
It has the remains of a 12th-century abbey.
Jedda alternative spelling for the Saudi Arabian port
◊Jiddah.

Jena town SE of Weimar, Gera county, East Germany; population (1985) 107,240. Industries include the Zeiss firm of optical-instrument makers, founded 1846. Here in 1806 Napoleon defeated the Prussians, and Schiller and Hegel taught at the university, which dates from 1558.

Jerez de la Frontera city in Andalusia, SW Spain; population (1986) 180,000. It is famed for sherry, the fortified wine to which it gave its name.

Jersey largest of the ◊Channel Islands; capital St Helier; area 117 sq km/45 sq mi; population (1986) 80,000. It is governed by a lieutenant-governor representing the English Crown and an assembly. Like Guernsey, it is famous for its cattle.

Jersey City city of NE New Jersey, USA; population (1980) 223,500. It faces Manhattan Island, to which it is connected by tunnels. A former port, it is now an industrial centre.

Jerusalem ancient city of Palestine, divided 1948 between Jordan and the new republic of Israel; area (pre-1967) 37.5 sq km/14.5 sq mi, (post-1967) 108 sq km/42 sq mi, including areas of the West Bank; population (1989) 500,000, about 350,000 Israelis and 150,000 Palestinians. In 1950 the western New City was proclaimed as the Israeli capital, and, having captured from Jordan the eastern Old City 1967, Israel affirmed 1980 that the united city was the country's capital; the United Nations does not recognize the claim.

features There are seven gates into the Old City through the walls built by Selim I (1467–1520). Notable buildings include the Church of the Holy Sepulchre (built by Emperor Constantine 335) and the mosque of the Dome of the Rock. The latter stands on the site of the Temple built by King Solomon in the 10th century BC, and the Western ('wailing') Wall, held sacred by Jews, is part of the walled platform on which the Temple once stood. The Hebrew University of Jerusalem opened 1925. Religions are Christian, Hebrew, and Muslim, with Roman Catholic, Anglican, Eastern Orthodox, and a Coptic bishop. In 1967 Israel guaranteed freedom of access for all faiths to their holy places.

history
1400 BC Jerusalem was ruled by a king subject to Egypt.
c.1000 David made it the capital of a united Jewish kingdom.
586 The city was destroyed by Nebuchadnezzar, king of Babylonia, who deported its inhabitants.
539–529 Under Cyrus the Great of Persia the exiled Jews were allowed to return to Jerusalem and a new settlement was made.
c.445 The city walls were rebuilt.
333 Conquered by Alexander the Great.
63 Conquered by the Roman general Pompey.
AD 29 or 30 Under the Roman governor Pontius Pilate, Jesus was executed here.

70 A Jewish revolt led to the complete destruction of the city by the Roman emperor Titus.
135 On its site the emperor Hadrian founded the Roman city of Aelia Capitolina.
615 The city was pillaged by the Persian Chosroës II while under Byzantine rule.
637 It was first conquered by Islam.
1099 Jerusalem captured by the Crusaders.
1187 Recaptured by Saladin, sultan of Egypt.
1516 Became part of the Ottoman Empire.
1917 Britain occupied Palestine.
1922–1948 Jerusalem was the capital of the British mandate.

Jervis Bay deep bay on the coast of New South Wales, Australia, 145 km/90 mi SW of Sydney. The federal government in 1915 acquired 73 sq km/28 sq mi here to create a port for ◊Canberra. It forms part of the Australian Capital Territory and is the site of the Royal Australian Naval College.

Jewish Autonomous Region part of the Khabarovsk Territory, USSR, on the river Amur; capital Birobidzhan; area 36,000 sq km/13,900 sq mi; population (1986) 211,000. Industries include textiles, leather, metallurgy, light engineering, agriculture, and timber. It was established as a Jewish National District 1928, and became an autonomous region 1934, but became only nominally Jewish after the Stalinist purges 1936–47 and 1948–49.

Jhansi city in Uttar Pradesh, NE India, 286 km/178 mi SW of Lucknow; population (1981) 281,000. It is a railway and road junction and a market centre. It was founded 1613, and was the scene of a massacre of British civilians 1857.

Jhelum river rising in Kashmir and flowing into Pakistan; length about 720 km/450 mi. The Mangla Dam 1967, one of the world's largest earth-filled dams, stores flood waters for irrigation and hydroelectricity. The Jhelum is one of the five rivers which give Punjab its name, and was known in the ancient world as the Hydaspes, on whose banks Alexander the Great won a battle in 326 BC.

Jiangsu formerly *Kiangsu* province on the coast of E China
area 102,200 sq km/39,449 sq mi
capital Nanjing
features includes the swampy mouth of the Chang Jiang, and the special municipality of Shanghai
products cereals, rice, tea, cotton, soya, fish, silk, ceramics, textiles, coal, iron, copper, cement
population (1986) 62,130,000

Jiangxi formerly *Kiangsi* province of SE China
area 164,800 sq km/63,613 sq mi
capital Nanchang
products rice, tea, cotton, tobacco, porcelain, coal, tungsten, uranium

Jordan
Hashemite Kingdom of
(Al Mamlaka al Urduniya al Hashemiyah)

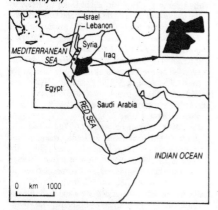

area 89,206 sq km/34,434 sq mi (West Bank, incorporated into Jordan 1950 but occupied by Israel since 1967, area 5,879 sq km/2,269 sq mi)
capital Amman
towns Zarqa, Irbid, Aqaba (the only port)
physical mostly desert
features Dead Sea, river Jordan, archaeological sites including Jerash, Roman forum
head of state and government King Hussein ibn Talai from 1952
political system absolute monarchy
political parties party activity banned 1976, and has not been fully restored
exports potash, phosphates, citrus
currency Jordanian dinar (1.13 = £1 Feb 1990)

population (1988) 2,970,000 (including Palestinian refugees); West Bank (1988) 866,000; annual growth rate 3.7%
life expectancy men 62, women 66
language Arabic
religion Sunni Muslim
literacy 87% male/63% female (1985 est)
GDP $4.2 bn (1984); $552 per head of population
chronology
1946 Achieved full independence as Transjordan.
1949 New state of Jordan declared.
1953 Hussein ibn Talai became king of Jordan.
1958 Jordan and Iraq formed Arab Federation which ended when the Iraqi monarchy was deposed.
1976 Lower house dissolved, and elections postponed until further notice.
1982 Hussein tried to mediate in Arab-Israeli conflict.
1984 Women voted for the first time.
1985 Hussein put forward a framework for a Middle East peace settlement. Secret meeting between Hussein and Israeli prime minister.
1988 Hussein announced a decision to cease administering the West Bank as part of Jordan, passing responsibility to Palestine Liberation Organization, and suspending parliament.
1989 Prime minister Zaid al-Rifai resigned and Hussein promised new parliamentary elections following criticism of economic policies. Riots over price increases up to 50% following fall in oil revenues. 80-member parliament elected and Mudar Badran appointed prime minister. Hussein abolishes martial law after 22 years.

---

population (1986) 35,090,000.
history the province was Mao Zedong's original base in the first phase of the Communist struggle against the Nationalists.
Jibuti variant spelling of ◊Djibouti, republic of NE Africa.
Jiddah or *Jedda* port in Hejaz, Saudi Arabia, on the E shore of the Red Sea; population (1986) 1,000,000. Industries include cement, steel, and oil refining. Pilgrims pass through here on their way to Mecca.
Jilin formerly *Kirin* province of NE China in central ◊Manchuria
area 187,000 sq km/72,182 sq mi
capital Changchun
population (1986) 23,150,000.
Jinan formerly *Tsinan* city and capital of Shandong province, China; population (1986) 1,430,000. It has food processing and textile industries.

Jingdezhen formerly *Chingtechen* or *Fou-liang* town in Jiangxi, China. Ming blue-and-white china was produced here, the name of the clay kaolin coming from Kaoling, a hill east of Jingdezhen; some of the best Chinese porcelain is still made here.
Jinja town in Busoga Province, Uganda, on the Victoria Nile E of Kampala; population (1983) 45,000. Nearby is the Owen Falls Dam 1954.
Jinsha Jiang river of China, which rises in SW China, and forms the Chang Jiang (Yangtze) at Yibin.
Jodhpur city in Rajasthan, India, formerly capital of Jodhpur princely state, founded in 1459 by Rao Jodha; population (1981) 493,600. It is a market centre and has the training college of the Indian air force, an 18th-century Mogul palace, and a red sandstone fort. A style of riding breeches is named after it.

Jogjakarta alternative spelling of ◊Yogyakarta, a city in Indonesia.

Johannesburg largest city of South Africa, situated on the Witwatersrand in Transvaal; population (1985) 1,609,000. It is the centre of a large gold-mining industry; other industries include engineering works, meat-chilling plants, and clothing factories.

Notable buildings include the law courts, Escom House (Electricity Supply Commission), the South African Railways Administration Building, the City Hall, Chamber of Mines and Stock Exchange, the Witwatersrand 1921 and Rand Afrikaans 1966 universities, and the Union Observatory. Johannesburg was founded after the discovery of gold 1886, and was probably named after Jan (Johannes) Meyer, the first mining commissioner.

John o' Groats village in NE Highland region, Scotland, about 3 km/2 mi W of Duncansby Head, proverbially Britain's most northerly point. It is named after the Dutchman John de Groot who built a house there in the 16th century.

Johor state in S Peninsular Malaysia; capital Johor Baharu; area 19,000 sq km/7,334 sq mi; population (1980) 1,638,000. The southernmost point of mainland Asia, it is joined to Singapore by a causeway. It is mainly forested, with swamps. There is bauxite and iron.

Jönköping town at the S end of Lake Vättern, Sweden; population (1985) 107,362. It is an industrial centre in an agricultural and forestry region.

Joppa ancient name of ◊Jaffa, a port in W Israel.

Jordan river rising on Mount Hermon, Syria, at 550 m/1,800 ft above sea level and flowing S for about 320 km/200 mi via the Sea of Galilee to the Dead Sea, 390 m/1,290 ft below sea level. It occupies the northern part of the Great Rift Valley; its upper course forms the boundary of Israel with Syria and the kingdom of Jordan; its lower course runs through Jordan; the West Bank has been occupied by Israel since 1967.

Jordan country in SW Asia, bordered to the N by Syria, NE by Iraq, E and SE by Saudi Arabia, S by the Gulf of Aqaba, and W by Israel.

Jotunheim mountainous region of S Norway, containing the highest mountains in Scandinavia, Glittertind 2,453 m/8,048 ft and Galdhöpiggen 2,468 m/8,097 ft. In Norse myth it is the home of the giants.

Jounieh a port on the Mediterranean coast of Lebanon, 15 km/9 mi N of Beirut. The centre of an anti-Syrian Christian enclave.

Juan Fernández Islands three small volcanic Pacific islands belonging to Chile; almost uninhabited. The largest is Más-a-Tierra (also sometimes called Juan Fernández Island) where Alexander Selkirk was marooned 1704–09. The islands were named after the Spanish navigator who reached them in 1563.

Juba river in E Africa, formed at Dolo, Ethiopia, by the junction of the Ganale Dorya and Dawa rivers. It flows S for about 885 km/550 mi through the Somali Republic (of which its valley is the most productive area) into the Indian Ocean.

Juba capital of Equatoria province, Sudan Republic; situated on the left bank of the White Nile, at the head of navigation above Khartoum, 1,200 km/750 mi to the N; population (1973) 56,700.

Jubbulpore alternative name for the city of ◊Jabalpur in India.

Jugoslavia alternative spelling of ◊Yugoslavia.

Jumna or Yamuna river in India, rising in the Himalayas, in Uttar Pradesh, and joining the Ganges near Allahabad, where it forms a sacred bathing place. Agra and Delhi are also on its course. Length 1,385 km/860 mi.

Juneau ice-free port and state capital of Alaska, USA, on Gastineau Channel in the remote Alaska panhandle; population (1980) 26,000. There is salmon fishing, and gold and furs are exported.

Jungfrau mountain in the Bernese Oberland, Switzerland; 4,166 m/13,669 ft high. A railway ascends to the plateau of the Jungfraujoch, 3,456 m/11,340 ft, where there is a winter sports centre.

Jura island of the Inner Hebrides; area 380 sq km/147 sq mi; population (with Colonsay, 1971) 343. It is separated from Scotland by the Sound of Jura. The whirlpool Corryvreckan (Gaelic 'Brecan's cauldron') is off the north coast.

Jura mountains series of parallel mountain ranges running SW–NE along the French-Swiss frontier between the Rhône and the Rhine, a distance of 250 km/156 mi. The highest peak is *Crête de la Neige*, 1,723 m/5,650 ft. The mountains give their name to a *département* of France; and in 1979 a Jura canton was established in Switzerland, formed from the French-speaking areas of Berne.

Jutland (Danish *Jylland*) a peninsula of N Europe; area 29,500 sq km/11,400 sq mi. It is separated from Norway by the Skagerrak, from Sweden by the Kattegat, with the North Sea to the west. The larger northern part belongs to Denmark, and the southern part to West Germany.

Jylland Danish name for the mainland of Denmark, the N section of the Jutland peninsula. The chief towns are Aalborg, Aarhus, Esbjerg, Fredericia, Horsens, Kolding, Randers, and Vejle.

K2 second highest mountain in the world, about 8,900 m/29,210 ft, in the Karakoram range, Kashmir, N India; it is also known as *Dapsang* (Hidden Peak) and formerly as *Mount Godwin-Austen* (after the son of a British geologist). It was first climbed 1954 by an Italian expedition.

Kabardino-Balkar autonomous republic of the USSR, capital Nalchik; area 12,500 sq km/4,825 sq mi; population (1986) 724,000. Under Russian control from 1557, it was annexed 1827, and became an autonomous republic 1936.

Kabinda part of Angola. See ◊Cabinda.

Kabul capital of Afghanistan, 2,100 m/6,900 ft above sea level, on the river Kabul; population (1984) 1,179,300. Products include textiles, plastics, leather, and glass. It commands the strategic routes to Pakistan via the ◊Khyber Pass.

Kabwe town in central Zambia (formerly *Broken Hill*); mining industry (copper, cadmium, lead, and zinc); population (1980) 143,635.

Kaduna town in N Nigeria, on the Kaduna river; population (1983) 247,000. A market centre for grain and cotton; industries include textiles, cars, timber, pottery, and oil refining.

Kafue river in central Zambia, a tributary of the Zambezi: 965 km/600 mi long. The upper reaches of the river form part of the Kafue national park 1951. *Kafue* town 44 km/27 mi S of Lusaka, population (1980) 35,000, is the centre of Zambia's heavy industry.

Kagoshima industrial city (Satsumayaki porcelain) and port on Kyushu Island, SW Japan; population (1987) 525,000.

Kaieteur waterfall on the river Potaro, a tributary of the Essequibo, Guyana. At 250 m/822 ft it is five times as high as Niagara.

Kaifeng former capital of China, 907–1127, and of Honan province; population (1984) 619,200. It has lost its importance because of the silting-up of the nearby Huang He river.

Kaikouras double range of mountains in the NE of South Island, New Zealand, separated by the Clarence river, and reaching 2,885 m/9,465 ft.

Kaingaroa forest NE of Lake Taupo in North Island, New Zealand, one of the world's largest planted forests.

Kairouan Muslim holy city in Tunisia, N Africa, S of Tunis; population (1984) 72,200. It is a noted centre of carpet production. The city, said to have been founded AD 617, ranks after Mecca and Medina as a place of pilgrimage.

Kaiserslautern industrial town (textiles, cars) in West Germany, in the Rhineland-Palatinate, 48 km/30 mi west of Mannheim; population (1978) 98,700. It dates from 882; the castle from which it gets its name was built by Frederick Barbarossa 1152, and destroyed by the French 1703.

Kakadu a national park E of Darwin in the Alligator Rivers Region of Arnhem Land, Northern Territory, Australia. Established in 1979, it overlies one of the richest uranium deposits in the world. As a result of this, it has become the focal point of controversy between conservationists and mining interests.

Kalahari Desert semi-desert area forming most of Botswana, and extending into Namibia, Zimbabwe, and South Africa; area about 900,000 sq km/347,400 sq mi. The only permanent river, the Okavango, flows into a delta in the NW forming marshes rich in wildlife. Its inhabitants are the nomadic Bushmen.

Kalgan city in NE China, now known as ◊Zhangjiakou.

Kalgoorlie town in Western Australia, 545 km/340 mi NE of Perth, amalgamated with Boulder in 1966; population (1986) 25,000. Gold has been mined here since 1893.

Kalimantan provinces of the republic of Indonesia occupying part of the island of Borneo
area 543,900 sq km/210,000 sq mi
towns Banjermasin and Balikpapan
physical features mostly low-lying, with mountains in the N
products petroleum, rubber, coffee, copra, pepper, timber
population (1980) 6,723,086

Kalinin formerly (until 1933) *Tver* city of the USSR, capital of Kalinin region, a transport centre on the Volga, 160 km/100 mi NW of Moscow; population (1987) 447,000. It was renamed in honour of President Kalinin.

Kaliningrad formerly *Königsberg* Baltic naval base in the USSR; population (1987) 394,000. Industries include engineering and paper. It was the capital of East Prussia until the latter was divided between the USSR and Poland 1945 under the Potsdam Agreement, when it was renamed in honour of President Kalinin.

Kalmar port on the SE coast of Sweden; population (1986) 55,000. Industries include paper, matches, and the Orrefors glassworks.

Kalmyk or **Kalmuck** Autonomous Republic within the Russian SFSR, USSR, on the Caspian Sea; area 75,900 sq km/29,300 sq mi; population (1986) 325,000; capital Elista. Industry is mainly agricultural. It was settled by migrants from China in the 17th century, and abolished 1943–57 because of alleged collaboration of the people with the Germans during the siege of Stalingrad.

Kaluga town in the USSR, on the river Oka, 160 km/100 mi SW of Moscow, capital of Kaluga region; population (1987) 307,000. Industries include hydroelectric installations and engineering works, telephone equipment, chemicals, and measuring devices.

Kamakura city on Honshu island, Japan; population 175,000. It was the seat of the first shogunate 1192–1333, which established the rule of the samurai class, and the Hachimangu Shrine is dedicated to the gods of war; the 13th-century statue of Buddha (Daibutsu) is 13 m/43 ft high. From the 19th century artists and writers, for example the novelist Kawabata, settled here.

Kamara'n island in the Red Sea, formerly belonging to South Yemen, but occupied by North Yemen 1972; area 180 sq km/70 sq mi. The former RAF station is controlled by the USSR.

Kamchatka mountainous peninsula separating the Bering Sea and Sea of Okhotsk, forming (together with the Chukchi and Koryak national districts) a region of the USSR. Its capital Petropavlovsk is the only town; agriculture is possible only in the south. Most of the inhabitants are fishers and hunters.

Kamet Himalayan mountain 7,756 m/25,447 ft high on the Tibet–India border. The British climbers F S Smythe and Eric Shipton were in the group that made the first ascent in 1931.

Kampala capital of Uganda; population (1983) 455,000. It is linked by rail with Mombasa. Products include tea, coffee, textiles, fruit, and vegetables.

Kamperduin Dutch spelling of ◊Camperdown, village in the Netherlands.

Kampuchea former name (1975–89) of ◊Cambodia.

Kananga chief city of Kasai Occidental region, W central Zaïre, on the Lulua river; population (1984) 291,000. It was known as **Luluabourg** until 1966.

Kanazawa industrial city (textiles and porcelain) on Honshu island, in Chubu region, Japan, 160 km/100 mi NNW of Nagoya; population (1985) 430,000.

Kanchenjunga a variant spelling of ◊Kangchenjunga, a Himalayan mountain.

Kandahar city in Afghanistan, 450 km/280 mi SW of Kabul, capital of Kandahar province and a trading centre, with wool and cotton factories; population (1984) 203,200. It is surrounded by a 8 m/25 ft high mud wall. It was the first capital of Afghanistan when it became independent in 1747.

Kandy city in central Sri Lanka, former capital of the kingdom of Kandy 1480–1815; population (1985) 140,000. Products include tea. One of the most sacred Buddhist shrines is situated at Kandy, and the chief campus of the University of Sri Lanka (1942) is at Peradenia, 5 km/3 mi away.

Kangchenjunga Himalayan mountain on the Nepál–Sikkim border, 8,598 m/20,208 ft high, 120 km/75 mi SE of Everest. The name means 'five treasure houses of the great snows'. Kangchenjunga was first climbed by a British expedition 1955.

Ka Ngwane black homeland in Natal province, South Africa; achieved self-governing status 1971; population (1985) 392,800.

Kano capital of Kano state in N Nigeria, trade centre of an irrigated area; population (1983) 487,100. Products include bicycles, glass, furniture, textiles, and chemicals. Founded about 1000 BC, Kano is a walled city, with New Kano extending beyond the walls. Goods still arrive by camel train to a market place holding 20,000 people.

Kanpur (formerly **Cawnpore**) capital of Kanpur district, Uttar Pradesh, India, SW of Lucknow, on the river Ganges; a commercial and industrial centre (cotton, wool, jute, chemicals, plastics, iron, steel); population (1981) 1,688,000.

Kansas state of central USA; nickname Sunflower State
area 213,200 sq km/82,295 sq mi
capital Topeka
towns Kansas City, Wichita, Overland Park
physical features undulating prairie; rivers Missouri, Kansas, and Arkansas
products wheat, cattle, coal, petroleum, natural gas, aircraft
population (1985) 2,450,000.

Kansas City twin city in the USA at the confluence of the Missouri and Kansas rivers, partly in Kansas and partly in Missouri; a market

Kansas

and agricultural distribution centre and, next to Chicago, the chief livestock centre of the USA. Kansas City, Missouri, has car assembly plants and Kansas City, Kansas, has the majority of offices; population (1980) of Kansas City (Kansas) 161,087, Kansas City (Missouri) 448,159, metropolitan area 1,327,000.

history The city was founded as a trading post by French fur trappers about 1826. In the 1920s and 1930s Kansas City was run by boss Tom Pendergast, of the Ready-Mix Concrete Company, and in the nightclubs on Twelfth Street under his 'protection' jazz musicians such as Lester Young, Count Basie, and Charlie Parker performed.

Kansu alternative spelling for Chinese province ◊Gansu.

Kanto flat, densely populated region of E Honshu island, Japan; population (1986) 37,156,000; area 32,377 sq km/12,505 sq mi. The chief city is Tokyo.

Kaohsiung city and port on the west coast of Taiwan; population (1988) 1,300,000. Industries include aluminium ware, fertilizers, cement, oil refineries, iron and steel works, shipyards, and food-processing. Kaohsiung began to develop as a commercial port after 1858; its industrial development came about while it was occupied by Japan, 1895–1945.

Kara Bogaz Gol shallow gulf of the Caspian Sea, USSR; area 20,000 sq km/8,000 sq mi. Rich deposits of sodium chloride, sulphates, and other salts have formed by evaporation.

Karachi largest city and chief seaport of Pakistan, and capital of Sind province, NW of the Indus delta; industry (engineering, chemicals, plastics, textiles); population (1981) 5,208,000. It was the capital of Pakistan 1947–59.

Karafuto Japanese name for ◊Sakhalin island.

Karaganda industrial town (coal, copper, tungsten, manganese) in Kazakh republic of the USSR, linked by canal with the Irtysh River; capital of Karaganda region; population (1987) 633,000.

Kara-Kalpak Autonomous Republic within Uzbekistan, USSR

area 158,000 sq km/61,000 sq mi

capital Nukus

towns Munyak

products cotton, rice, wheat, fish

population (1986) 1,108,000

history called after the Kara-Kalpak people whose name means black bonnet. They live south of the Sea of Aral and were conquered by Russia 1867. An autonomous Kara-Kalpak region was formed 1926 within Kazakhstan, transferred to the Soviet republic 1930, made a republic 1932, and attached to Uzbekistan 1936.

Karakoram mountain range in central Asia, divided among China, Pakistan, and India. Peaks include

K2, Masharbrum, Gasharbrum, and Mustagh Tower. *Ladakh* subsidiary range is in NE Kashmir on the Tibetan border.

Karakoram highway road constructed by China and Pakistan and completed 1978; runs 800 km/500 mi from Havelian (NW of Rawalpindi), via ◊Gilgit in Kashmir and the Khunjerab Pass 4,800 m/16,000 ft, to ◊Kashi in China.

Karakorum ruined capital of Genghis Khan, SW of Ulaanbaatar in Mongolia.

Kara-Kum sandy desert occupying most of ◊Turkmenistan, USSR; area about 310,800 sq km/120,000 sq mi. It is crossed by the Caspian railway.

Kara Sea part of the Arctic Ocean off the N coast of the USSR, bounded to the NW by the island of Novaya Zemlya and to the NE by Severnaya Zemlya. Novy Port on the Gulf of Ob is the chief port, and the Yenisei also flows into it.

Karbala alternative spelling for ◊Kerbela, holy city in Iraq.

Karelia Autonomous Republic of the Russian Soviet Republic (RSFSR), in NW USSR

area 172,400 sq km/66,550 sq mi

capital Petrozavodsk

towns Vyborg

physical features mainly forested; Lake Ladoga

products fishing, timber, chemicals, coal

population (1986) 787,000

history Karelia was annexed to Russia by Peter the Great in 1721 as part of the grand duchy of Finland. In 1917 part of Karelia was retained by Finland when it gained its independence from Russia. The remainder became an autonomous region 1920 and an autonomous republic 1923 of the USSR. Following the wars of 1939–40 and 1941–44, Finland ceded 46,000 sq km/18,000 sq mi to the USSR. Part of this territory was incorporated in the Russian Soviet Republic and part in the Karelian autonomous republic. In 1946 the Karelo-Finnish Soviet Socialist Republic was set up but in 1956 the greater part of the republic returned to its former status as an autonomous Soviet socialist republic.

Karelia, North (Finnish *Pohjois-Karjala*) province of E Finland, area 21,585 sq km/8,337 sq mi, capital Joensuu, population (1989) 208,500. North Karelia was created in 1944 when the rest of Karelia was ceded to the USSR.

Karelian Isthmus strip of land between Lake Ladoga and the Gulf of Finland, USSR, with Leningrad at the S extremity and Vyborg at the N. Finland ceded it to the USSR 1940–41 and after 1944.

Kariba dam concrete dam on the Zambia–Zimbabwe border, about 386 km/240 mi downstream from the Victoria Falls, constructed 1955–60 to supply power to both countries. The dam crosses Kariba Gorge, and the reservoir, Lake Kariba, has important fisheries.

Karikal small port in India, 250 km/155 mi S of Madras, at the mouth of the right branch of the Cauvery delta. On a tract of land acquired by the French in 1739, it was transferred to India in 1954, confirmed by treaty in 1956, together with ◊Pondicherry.

Karl-Marx-Stadt formerly (until 1954) *Chemnitz* town in East Germany, capital of Karl-Marx-Stadt county, on the river Chemnitz, 65 km/40 mi SSE of Leipzig. It is an industrial centre (engineering, textiles, chemicals); population (1986) 314,000. It came within the Soviet zone of occupation after World War II. Karl-Marx-Stadt county has an area of 6,010 sq km/2,320 sq mi and a population of 1,870,000.

Karlovy Vary spa in the Bohemian Forest, W Czechoslovakia, famous from the 14th century for its alkaline thermal springs; population (1983) 59,696.

Karlsbad German name of ◊Karlovy Vary.

Karlsruhe industrial town (nuclear research, oil refining) in Baden-Württemberg, West Germany; population (1988) 268,000.

Karnak village of modern Egypt, on the E bank of the Nile, which gives its name to the temple of Ammon (constructed by Seti I and Ramses I) around which the major part of the city of ◊Thebes was built. An avenue of rams leads to ◊Luxor.

Karnataka formerly (until 1973) *Mysore* state in SW India

area 191,800 sq km/74,035 sq mi

capital Bangalore

products mainly agricultural, but its minerals include manganese, chromite, and India's only sources of gold and silver

population (1981) 37,043,000

language Kannada

famous people Hyder Ali, Tipu Sahib.

Karnataka

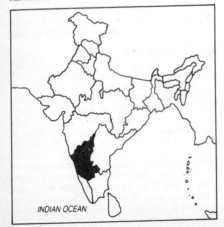

INDIAN OCEAN

Kärnten German name for ◊Carinthia, province of Austria.

Karroo two areas of semi-desert in Cape Province, South Africa, divided into the Great Karroo and Little Karroo by the Swartberg mountains. The two Karroos together have an area of about 260,000 sq km/100,000 sq mi.

Kasai river that rises in Angola and forms the frontier with Zaïre before entering Zaïre and joining the Zaïre river, of which it is the chief tributary. It is rich in alluvial diamonds. Length 2,100 km/1,300 mi.

Kashgar former name of ◊Kashi in China.

Kashi oasis town (formerly Kashgar) in Xinjiang Uyghur autonomous region, China, on the Kaxgar He, capital of Kashi district which adjoins the Kirghiz and Tadzic republics, Afganistan and Kashmir; population (1973) 180,000. It is a trading centre, the Chinese terminus of the ◊Karakoram Highway, and a focus of Muslim culture.

Kashmir former Muslim state of North British India, now an area of contention between India and Pakistan.

history Although Kashmir came under the sway of India for many centuries, Muslim rule was established by the 14th century. The Mogul dynasty held power in Kashmir from the 16th century until the Afghan invasion of 1753. This was followed by a period of Sikh control. The state was then ruled by Hindu maharajahs, the last of whom ceded to the Republic of India in 1947. There was fighting between pro-India and pro-Pakistan factions, and open war between the two countries 1965–66 and 1971. Tension between India and Pakistan increased in 1984 when troops from both countries occupied strategic positions at high altitudes on either side of the loosely defined ceasefire line in the Karakoram Mountains. Attempts by both governments to resolve the conflict in Kashmir were further frustrated during 1989–90 when Kashmiri separatists stepped up their violent protests. A plebiscite decreed by the United Nations for the state has never been held, and it remains divided: the northwest is occupied by Pakistan and the rest by India.

Kashmir Pakistan-occupied area in the NW of the former state of Kashmir, now ◊Jammu and Kashmir. Azad ('free') Kashmir in the west has its own legislative assembly based in Muzaffarabad while Gilgit and Baltistan regions to the north and east are governed directly by Pakistan. The ◊Northern Areas are claimed by India and Pakistan.

population 1,500,000

towns Gilgit, Skardu

features W Himalayan peak Nanga Parbat 8,126 m/26,660 ft, Karakoram Pass, Indus River, Baltoro Glacier.

Kassel industrial town (engineering, chemicals, electronics) in Hessen, West Germany, on the river Fulda; population (1988) 185,000. There is the spectacular Wilhelmshöhe mountain park, and the Grimm Museum commemorates the compilers of fairy tales who lived here.

Katanga former name of the ◊Shaba region in Zaïre.

Kathiawar peninsula on the W coast of India. Formerly occupied by a number of princely states, all Kathiawar (60,723 sq km/23,445 sq mi) had been included in Bombay state by 1956, but was transferred to Gujarat in 1960. Mahatma Gandhi was born in Kathiawar at Porbandar.

Katmai active volcano in Alaska, USA, 2,046 m/6,715 ft. Its major eruption in 1912 created the Valley of Ten Thousand Smokes.

Katmandu or **Kathmandu** capital of Nepál; population (1981) 235,000. Founded in the 8th century on an ancient pilgrim and trade route from India to Tibet and China, it has a royal palace, Buddhist shrines, and monasteries.

Katowice industrial city (anthracite, iron and coal mining, iron foundries, smelting works, machine shops) in Upper Silesia, S Poland; population (1985) 363,000.

Kattegat sea passage between Denmark and Sweden. It is about 240 km/150 mi long and 135 km/85 mi wide at its broadest point.

Katyn Forest forest near Smolensk, W USSR, where during World War II 4,500 Polish officer prisoners of war (captured in the German-Soviet partition of Poland 1940) were shot; 10,000 others were killed elsewhere. The mass murder was instigated by the Soviet secret police.

Kaunas Russian *Kovno* industrial river port (textiles, chemicals, agricultural machinery) in the Lithuanian republic of the USSR, on the Niemen river; population (1987) 417,000. It was the capital of independent Lithuania 1910–40.

Kawasaki industrial city (iron, steel, shipbuilding, chemicals, textiles) on Honshu island, Japan; population (1987) 1,096,000.

Kayah State division of Myanmar (Burma), area 11,900 sq km/4,600 sq mi, formed 1954 from the Karenni states (Kantarawaddy, Bawlake, and Kayebogyi) and inhabited by the Karen people. Kayah State has a measure of autonomy.

Kayseri (ancient name *Caesarea Mazaca*) capital of Kayseri province, central Turkey; population (1985) 378,000. It produces textiles, carpets, and tiles. In Roman times it was capital of the province of Cappadocia.

Kazakhstan constituent republic of the USSR from 1936, part of Soviet Central Asia
area 2,717,300 sq km/1,049,150 sq mi
capital Alma-Ata
towns Karaganda, Semipalatinsk, Petropavlovsk
physical second largest republic in the USSR; Caspian and Aral seas, Lake Balkhash; Steppe region

Kazakhstan

features the Baikonur Cosmodrome (official name for the Soviet space launch site at Tyuratam, near the coalmining town of Baikonur), and a weapons-testing area near the Chinese border
products second only to Ukraine as a grain producer; copper, lead, zinc, manganese, coal, oil
population (1987) 16,244,000; Russian 41%, Kazakh 36%, Ukrainian 6%
language Russian; Kazakh, related to Turkish
history ruled by the Mongols from the 13th century, the region came under Russian control in the 18th century. It became part of the USSR 1922 as an autonomous republic (administrative unit) and became a full union republic 1936. It was the site of Khrushchev's ambitious 'Virgin Lands' agricultural programme during the 1950s, which led to overcropping and harvest failures during the early 1960s, but also to a large influx of Russian settlers, turning the Kazakhs into a minority in their own republic. Today, Kazakhstan produces one-third of Soviet grain output. In Dec 1986 violent nationalist riots erupted in the capital, Alma-Ata, and in June 1989 four died in inter-ethnic violence in the oil town of Novy Uzen.

Kazan capital of the Tatar Autonomous Republic in Russian SFSR, USSR, on the river Volga; population (1987) 1,068,000. It a transport, commercial, and industrial centre (engineering, oil refining, petrochemical, textiles, large fur trade). Formerly capital of a Tatar khanate, Kazan was captured by Ivan IV 'the Terrible' 1552.

The 'Black Virgin of Kazan', an icon so called because blackened with age, was removed to Moscow (1612–1917), where the great Kazan Cathedral was built to house it 1631; it is now in the USA. Among miracles attributed to its presence were the defeat of Poland 1612 and of Napoleon at Moscow 1812.

Kebnekaise highest peak in Sweden, rising to 2,111 m/6,926 ft in the Kolen range, W of Kiruna.

Kecskemét town in Hungary, situated on the Hungarian plain SE of Budapest; population (1988) 105,000. It is a trading centre of an agricultural region.

Kedah state in NW Peninsular Malaysia; capital Alor Setar; area 9,400 sq km/3,628 sq mi; population (1980) 1,116,000. Products include rice, rubber, tapioca, tin, and tungsten. Kedah was transferred by Thailand to Britain 1909, and was one of the Unfederated Malay States until 1948.

Keeling Islands another name for the ◊Cocos Islands, an Australian territory.

Keelung or **Chi-lung** industrial port (shipbuilding, chemicals, fertilizer) on the N coast of Taiwan, 24 km/15 mi NE of Taipei; population (1985) 351,904.

Keewatin eastern district of Northwest Territories, Canada, including the islands in Hudson and James Bays
area 590,935 sq km/228,101 sq mi
towns (trading posts) Chesterfield Inlet, Eskimo Point, and Coral Harbour, the last with an air base set up during World War II
physical the north is an upland plateau, the south low and level, covering the greater part of the Arctic prairies of Canada; there are a number of lakes
products trapping for furs is the main occupation
history Keewatin District was formed 1876, under the administration of Manitoba; it was transferred to Northwest Territories in 1905, and in 1912 lost land south of 60 degrees N to Manitoba and Ontario.

Kefallinia English **Cephalonia** largest of the Ionian Islands off the W coast of Greece; area 935 sq km/360 sq mi; population (1981) 31,300. It was devastated by an earthquake in 1953 which destroyed the capital Argostolion.

Keflavik fishing port in Iceland, 35 km/22 mi SW of Reykjavik; population (1986) 7,500. Its international airport was built during World War II by US forces (who called it Meeks Field). Keflavik became a NATO base in 1951.

Keighley industrial (wool, engineering) town on the river Aire, NW of Bradford in W Yorkshire, England; population (1981) 57,800. Haworth, home of the Brontë family of writers, is now part of Keighley.

Kelantan state in NE Peninsular Malaysia; capital Kota Baharu; area 14,900 sq km/5,751 sq mi; population (1980) 894,000. It produces rice, rubber, copra, tin, manganese, and gold. Kelantan was transferred by Siam to Britain 1909, and until 1948 was one of the Unfederated Malay States.

Kemerovo coalmining town in W Siberia, USSR, centre of Kuznetz coal basin; population (1987) 520,000. It has chemical and metallurgical industries. The town, which was formed out of the villages of Kemerovo and Shcheglovisk, was known as Shcheglovisk 1918–32.

Kendal town in Cumbria, England, on the river Kent; population (1981) 23,411. An industrial centre (light industry; agricultural machinery and, since the 14th century, wool) and tourist centre for visitors to the ◊Lake District.

Kenilworth castle and small town in Warwickshire, England. The Norman castle became a royal residence and was enlarged by John of Gaunt and later by the Earl of Leicester, who entertained Elizabeth I here in 1575. It was dismantled after the Civil War; the ruins were given to the British nation by the 1st Lord Kenilworth in 1937.

Kensington and Chelsea borough of Greater London, England, N of the river Thames
features Kensington Gardens; museums include Victoria and Albert, Natural History, Science; Imperial College of Science and Technology 1907; Commonwealth Institute; Kensington Palace; Holland House (damaged in World War II, and partly rebuilt as a youth hostel); Leighton House
population (1986) 137,600.

Kent county in SE England, nicknamed the 'garden of England'
area 3,730 sq km/1,440 sq mi
towns administrative headquarters Maidstone; Canterbury, Chatham, Rochester, Tunbridge Wells; resorts Folkestone, Margate, Ramsgate
features traditionally, a 'man of Kent' comes from east of the Medway and a 'Kentish man' from W Kent; New Ash Green, a new town; Romney Marsh; the Isles of Grain, Sheppey (on which is

Kent

Kentucky

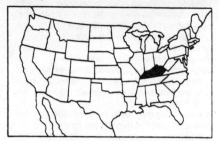

Kerala

INDIAN OCEAN

the resort of Sheerness, formerly a royal dockyard) and Thanet; Weald (agricultural area); rivers Darent, Medway, Stour; Leeds Castle (converted to a palace by Henry VIII), Hever Castle (where Henry VIII courted Anne Boleyn), Chartwell (Churchill's country home), Knole, Sissinghurst Castle and gardens
products hops, apples, soft fruit (on the Weald), coal, cement, paper
population (1987) 1,511,000
famous people Charles Dickens, Christopher Marlowe
Kentucky state of S central USA; nickname Bluegrass State
area 104,700 sq km/40,414 sq mi
capital Frankfort
towns Louisville, Lexington-Fayette, Owensboro, Covington, Bowling Green
features horse racing at Louisville (Kentucky Derby); Mammoth Cave National Park (main cave 6.5 km/4 mi long, up to 38 m/125 ft high, where Indian councils were once held); President Lincoln's birthplace at Hodgenville; Fort Knox, US Gold Bullion Depository
products tobacco, cereals, steel goods, textiles, transport vehicles
population (1987) 3,727,000
famous people Kit Carson, Henry Clay, Jefferson Davis
history Kentucky was first permanently settled after Daniel Boone had blazed his Wilderness Trail. Originally part of Virginia, it became a state 1792.
Kenya country in E Africa, bordered to the N by the Sudan and Ethiopia, E by Somalia, SE by the Indian Ocean, SW by Tanzania, and W by Uganda.
Kenya, Mount or *Kirinyaga* extinct volcano from which Kenya takes its name, 5,200 m/17,058 ft; the first European to climb it was Halford Mackinder in 1899.
Kerala state of SW India, formed 1956 from the former princely states of Travancore and Cochin
area 38,900 sq km/15,015 sq mi
capital Trivandrum
features most densely populated, and most literate (60%) state of India; strong religious

and caste divisions make it politically unstable
products tea, coffee, rice, oilseed, rubber, textiles, chemicals, electrical goods
population (1981) 25,403,000
language Kannada, Malayalam, Tamil
Kerbela or *Karbala* holy city of the Shi'ite Muslims, 96 km/60 m SW of Baghdad, Iraq; population (1985) 184,600. Kerbela is built on the site of the battlefield where Husein, son of Ali and Fatima, was killed in 680 while defending his succession to the Khalifate; his tomb in the city is visited every year by many pilgrims.
Kerch port in the Crimea, Ukraine, USSR, at the eastern end of Kerch peninsula, an important iron-producing area; population (1987) 173,000. Kerch was built on the site of an ancient Greek settlement, and became Russian 1783.
Kerguelen Islands or *Desolation Islands* volcanic archipelago in the Indian Ocean, part of the French Southern and Antarctic Territories; area 7,215 km/2,787 sq mi. It was discovered in 1772 by the Breton navigator Yves de Kerguelen, and annexed by France in 1949. Uninhabited except for scientists (centre for joint study of geomagnetism with the USSR), the islands support a unique wild cabbage containing a pungent oil.
Kerkira Greek form of ◊Corfu, an island in the Ionian Sea.
Kermadec Islands volcanic group, a dependency of New Zealand since 1887; area 30 sq km/12 sq mi. They are uninhabited except for a meteorological station on the largest island, Raoul.
Kerman town in Kerman province SE Iran; population (1986) 254,800. It is a centre for the mining of copper and precious metals.
Kermanshah former name (until 1980) of the town of ◊Bakhtaran in NW Iran.

Kenya
Republic of
(Jamhuri ya Kenya)

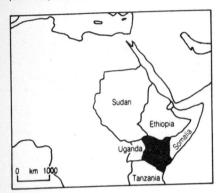

Sudan

Ethiopia

Uganda

Somalia

Tanzania

0 km 1000

area 582,600 sq km/224,884 sq mi
capital Nairobi
towns Kisumu, port Mombasa
physical mountains and highlands in the W and centre; coastal plain in S; the N is arid
features Great Rift Valley, Mount Kenya, Lake Nakuru (flamingos), Lake Turkana (Rudolf), national parks with wildlife, Malindini Marine Reserve, Olduvai Gorge
head of state and government Daniel arap Moi from 1978
political system authoritarian nationalism
political parties Kenya African National Union (KANU), nationalist, centrist

exports coffee, tea, sisal, pineapples
currency Kenya shilling (36.70 = £1 Feb 1990)
population (1988 est) 22,800,000 (the dominant ethnic group is the Kikuyu); annual growth rate 4.1%
life expectancy men 51, women 55
language Kiswahili (official), 21% Kikuyu, 14% Luhya, English is spoken in commercial centres
religion indigenous religions with Christian and Muslim minorities
literacy 70% male/49% female (1985 est)
GDP $5.6 bn (1983); $309 per head of population
chronology
1950 Mau Mau campaign began.
1953 Nationalist leader Jomo Kenyatta imprisoned.
1956 Mau Mau campaign defeated, Kenyatta released.
1963 Granted internal self-government, with Kenyatta as prime minister.
1964 Achieved full independence as a republic, within the Commonwealth, with Kenyatta as president.
1978 Death of Kenyatta. Succeeded by Daniel arap Moi.
1982 Attempted coup against Moi foiled.
1983 Moi re-elected.
1989 Moi announced the release of all political prisoners. Confiscated ivory burned in attempt to stop elephant poaching.
1990 Foreign minister Robert Ouko found murdered (Feb).

Kernow Celtic name for ◊Cornwall, England.
Kerry county of Munster province, Republic of Ireland, E of Cork
area 4,700 sq km/1,814 sq mi
county town Tralee
physical W coastline deeply indented, N part low-lying, but in the S are the highest mountains in Ireland including Carrantuohill 1,041 m/3,417 ft, the highest peak in Ireland; many rivers and lakes
features Macgillicuddy's Reeks; Lakes of Killarney
products engineering, woollens, shoes, cutlery; tourism
population (1986) 124,000.
Kesteven, Parts of SW area of Lincolnshire, England, formerly an administrative unit with county offices at Sleaford 1888–1974.
Key West town at the tip of the Florida peninsula, USA; population (1980) 24,382. As a tourist resort, it was popularized by the novelist Ernest Hemingway. In 1967 it became the first town in the USA to take all its fresh water from the sea.
Khabarovsk industrial city (oil refining, saw milling, meat packing) in SE Siberia, USSR; population (1987) 591,000.
Khabarovsk territory of the Russian Soviet Federal Socialist Republic, USSR, bordering the Sea of Okhotsk and drained by the Amur; area 824,600 km2/318,501; population(1985) 1,728,000. The capital is Khabarovsk. Mineral resources include gold, coal and iron ore.
Khardungla Pass road linking the Indian town of Leh with the high-altitude military outpost on the Siachen Glacier at an altitude of 5,662 m/1,744 ft in the Karakoram range, Kashmir. It is possibly the highest road in the world.
Kharga or *Kharijah* oasis in the Western Desert of Egypt, known to the Romans, and from 1960 headquarters of the New Valley irrigation scheme. An area twice the size of Italy is watered from natural underground reservoirs.

Kharg Island a small island in the Persian Gulf used by Iran as a deepwater oil terminal. Between 1982 and 1988 Kharg Island came under frequent attack during the Gulf War.

Kharkov capital of the Kharkov region, Ukraine, USSR, 400 km/250 mi E of Kiev; population (1987) 1,587,000. It is an important railway junction and industrial city (engineering, tractors), close to the Donets Basin coalfield and Krivoy Rog iron mines. Kharkov was founded 1654 as a fortress town. Its university dates from 1805.

Khartoum capital and trading centre of Sudan, at the junction of the Blue and White Nile; population (1983) 476,000, and of Khartoum North, across the Blue Nile, 341,000. ◊Omdurman is a suburb of Khartoum, giving the urban area a population of over 1.3 million.

It was founded 1830 by Mehemet Ali. General Gordon was killed at Khartoum by the Mahdist rebels 1885. A new city was built after the site was recaptured by British troops under Kitchener 1898.

Kherson port in Ukraine, USSR, on the Dnieper river, capital of Kherson region; population (1987) 358,000. Industries include shipbuilding, soap, and tobacco manufacture. It was founded 1778 by army commander Potemkin as the first Russian naval base on the Black Sea.

Khmer Republic former name of ◊Cambodia, country in SE Asia.

Khorramshahr former port and oil-refining centre in Iran, on the Shatt-al-Arab river and linked by bridge to the islands of Abadan. It was completely destroyed in the 1980s by enemy action in the Iran-Iraq war.

Khulna capital of Khulna region, SW Bangladesh, situated close to the Ganges delta; population (1981) 646,000. Industry includes shipbuilding and textiles; it trades in jute, rice, salt, sugar, and oilseed.

Khuzestan SW province of Iran, which includes the chief Iranian oil resources; population (1986) 2,702,533. Towns include Ahvaz (capital) and the ports of Abadan and Khuninshahr. There have been calls for Sunni Muslim autonomy, under the name Arabistan.

Khyber Pass pass 53 km/33 mi long through the mountain range that separates Pakistan from Afghanistan. The Khyber Pass was used by invaders of India. The present road was constructed by the British during the Afghan Wars.

Kiangsi former spelling of ◊Jiangxi, province of China.

Kiangsu former spelling of ◊Jiangsu, province of China.

Kidderminster market town in the West Midlands of England, on the river Stour; population (1981) 51,300. It has had a carpet industry from about 1735.

Kiel Baltic port (fishing, shipbuilding, electronics engineering), in West Germany, capital of Schleswig-Holstein; population (1988) 244,000. *Kiel Week* in June is a yachting meeting.

Kiel Canal waterway 98.7 km/51 mi long that connects the Baltic with the North Sea. Built by Germany in the years before World War I, the canal allowed the German navy to move from Baltic bases to the open sea without travelling through international waters.

Kielce city in central Poland, NE of Krakow; population (1985) 201,000; industrial rail junction (chemicals, metals).

Kiev capital of Ukraine, industrial centre (chemicals, clothing, leatherwork) and third largest city of the USSR, on the confluence of the Desna and Dnieper rivers; population (1987) 2,554,000.

Founded in the 5th century by Vikings, Kiev replaced Novgorod as the capital of Slav-dominated Russia 882, and was the original centre of the Orthodox Christian faith 988. It was occupied by Germany 1941. St Sophia cathedral (11th century) and Kiev-Pechersky Monastery (both now museums) survive, and also remains of the Golden Gate. The Kiev ballet and opera are renowned.

Kigali capital of Rwanda, central Africa; population (1981) 157,000. Products include coffee and minerals.

Kigoma town and port on the E shore of Lake Tanganyika, Tanzania, at the W terminal of the railway from Dar es Salaam; population (1978) 50,044.

Kildare county of Leinster province, Republic of Ireland, S of Meath
area 1,690 sq km/652 sq mi
county town Naas
physical wet and boggy in the north
features includes part of the Bog of Allen; the village of Maynooth, with a training college for Roman Catholic priests; and the Curragh, a plain which is the site of the national stud and headquarters of Irish horse racing
products oats, barley, potatoes, cattle
population (1986) 116,000.

Kilimanjaro volcano in Tanzania, the highest mountain in Africa, 5,900 m/19,364 ft.

Kilkenny county of Leinster province, Republic of Ireland, E of Tipperary
area 2,060 sq km/795 sq mi
county town Kilkenny
features river Nore
products agricultural, coal
population (1986) 73,000.

Killarney market town in County Kerry, Republic of Ireland; population (1981) 7,693. A famous beauty spot in Ireland, it has ◊Macgillycuddy's Reeks (a range of mountains) and the Lakes of Killarney to the SW.

Kilmarnock town in Strathclyde region, Scotland, 32 km/20 mi SW of Glasgow; population (1981)

52,083. Products include carpets, agricultural machinery, and whisky; Robert Burns's first book of poems was published here 1786.

Kimberley diamond-mining town in Cape Province, South Africa, 153 km/95 mi NW of Bloemfontein; population (1980) 144,923. Its mines have been controlled by De Beers Consolidated Mines since 1887.

Kimberley diamond site in Western Australia, found in 1978–79, estimated to have 5 per cent of the world's known gem-quality stones and 50 per cent of its industrial diamonds.

Kincardineshire former county of E Scotland, merged in 1975 in Grampian region. The county town was Stonehaven.

King's County older name of ◊Offaly, an Irish county.

King's Lynn port and market town at the mouth of the Great Ouse river, Norfolk, E England; population (1981) 38,000. An important port in medieval times, its name was changed by Henry VIII from Lynn to King's Lynn.

Kingston capital and principal port of Jamaica, West Indies; the cultural and commercial centre of the island; population (1983) 101,000, metropolitan area 525,000. Founded 1693, Kingston became the capital of Jamaica 1872.

Kingston town in E Ontario, Canada, on Lake Ontario; population (1981) 60,313. Industries include shipbuilding yards, engineering works, and grain elevators. It grew from 1782 around the French Fort Frontenac, was captured by the English 1748, and renamed in honour of George III.

Kingston-upon-Hull official name of ◊Hull, city in Humberside in NE England.

Kingston upon Thames borough of Greater London, England, on the S bank of the Thames, 16 km/10 mi SW of London; administrative headquarters of Surrey; population (1983) 133,600. Industries include metalworking, plastic and paint. The coronation stone of the Saxon kings is still preserved here.

Kingstown former name for ◊Dún Laoghaire, port near Dublin, Ireland.

Kingstown capital and principal port of St Vincent and the Grenadines, West Indies, in the SW of the island of St Vincent; population (1987) 29,000.

King-Te-Chen former spelling of ◊Jingdezhen, town in China.

Kinki region of S Honshu island, Japan; population (1986) 21,932,000; area 33,070 sq km/12,773 sq mi. Chief city is Osaka.

Kinshasa formerly *Léopoldville* capital of Zaïre on the river Zaïre, 400 km/250 mi inland from Matadi; population (1984) 2,654,000. Industries include chemicals, textiles, engineering, food processing, and furniture. It was founded by the explorer Henry Stanley 1887.

Kirghizia

Kirghizia constituent republic of the USSR from 1936, part of Soviet Central Asia
area 198,500 sq km/76,641 sq mi
capital Frunze
physical mountainous, an extension of the Tian Shan range
products cereals, sugar, cotton, coal, oil, sheep, yaks, horses
population (1987) 4,143,000; Kirghiz 48% (related to the Kazakhs, they are of Mongol-Tatar origin), Russian 26%, Uzbek 12%, Ukrainian 3%, Tatar 2%
language Kirghiz
religion Sunni Islam
history annexed by Russia 1864, it was part of an independent Turkestan republic 1917–24, when it was reincorporated in the USSR.

Kiribati republic in the central Pacific, comprising three groups of coral atolls: the 16 Gilbert Islands, eight uninhabited Phoenix Islands, eight of the 11 Line Islands, and the volcanic island of Banaba.

Kirin former name for ◊Jilin, Chinese province.

Kirkcaldy seaport on the Firth of Forth, Fife region, Scotland; population (1981) 46,300. Manufactures include floor coverings and paper. Birthplace of the economist Adam Smith and the architect Robert Adam.

Kirkcudbright former county of S Scotland, merged 1975 in Dumfries and Galloway region. The county town was Kirkcudbright.

Kirkuk town in NE Iraq; population (1985) 208,000. It is the centre of a major oilfield. Formerly it was served by several pipelines providing outlets to Lebanon, Syria, and other countries, but closures caused by the Iran-Iraq war left only the pipeline to Turkey operational.

Kirkwall administrative headquarters and port of the Orkneys, Scotland, on the N coast of the largest island, Mainland; population (1985)

Kiribati
Republic of

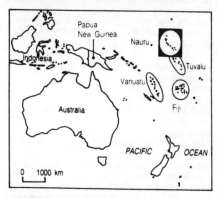

area 717 sq km/277 sq mi
capital and port Bairiki (on Tarawa Atoll)
physical comprises 33 Pacific islands: the Gilbert, Phoenix, and Line Islands, and Banaba (Ocean Island)
head of state and government Ieremia T Tabai from 1979

political system liberal democracy
political parties Christian Democratic Party, opposition faction within assembly; National Party, governing faction
exports copra
currency Australian dollar (2.24 = £1 Feb 1990)
population (1987) 66,250; annual growth rate 1.7%
language English and Gilbertese (official)
religion Christian, both Roman Catholic and Protestant
literacy 90% (1982)
GNP $30 million (1983) per capita.
chronology
1977 Gilbert Islands granted internal self-government.
1979 Achieved full independence, within the Commonwealth, as the Republic of Kiribati, with Ieremia Tabai as president.
1983 Tabai re-elected.
1985 Fishing agreement with Soviet state-owned company negotiated, prompting formation of Kiribati's first political party, the opposition Christian Democrats.
1987 Tabai re-elected.

6,000. The Norse cathedral of St Magnus dates from 1137.

Kirov formerly (until 1934) *Vyatka* town NE of Gorky, on the Vyatka river, USSR; population (1987) 421,000. It is a rail and industrial centre for rolling stock, tyres, clothing, toys, and machine tools.

Kirovabad city in Azerbaijan Republic, USSR; population (1987) 270,000. Industries include cottons, woollens, and processed foods. It was known as *Elizavetpol* 1804–1918 and *Gandzha* prior to 1804 and again 1918–35.

Kirovograd city in Ukrainian Republic, USSR; population (1987) 269,000. Manufacturing includes agricultural machinery and food processing. The city is on a lignite field. It was known as *Yelizavetgrad* until 1924 and *Zinovyevsk* 1924–36.

Kisangani formerly (until 1966) *Stanleyville* town in NE Zaïre, on the upper Zaïre river, below Stanley Falls; population (1984) 283,000. It is a communications centre.

Kishinev capital of the Moldavian Republic, USSR; population (1987) 663,000. Industries include cement, food processing, tobacco, and textiles. Founded 1436, it became Russian 1812. It was taken by Romania 1918, by the USSR 1940, and by Germany 1941, when it was totally destroyed. The USSR recaptured the site 1944, and rebuilding soon began. A series of large nationalist demonstrations were held in the city during 1989.

Kitakyushu industrial (coal, steel, chemicals, cotton thread, plate glass, alcohol) city and port in Japan, on the Hibiki Sea, N Kyushu, formed 1963 by the amalgamation of Moji, Kokura, Tobata, Yawata, and Wakamatsu; population (1987) 1,042,000. A tunnel 1942 links it with Honshu.

Kitchener city in SW Ontario, Canada; population (1986) 151,000, metropolitan area (with Waterloo) 311,000. Manufacturing includes agricultural machinery and tyres. Settled by Germans from Pennsylvania in the 1800s, it was known as Berlin until 1916.

Kitimat port near Prince Rupert, British Columbia, Canada; population (1981) 4,300. Founded 1955, it has one of the world's largest aluminium smelters, powered by the Kemano hydro-electric scheme.

Kitwe commercial centre for the Zambian copperbelt; population (1987) 450,000. To the south are Zambia's emerald mines.

Kitzbühel winter-sports resort in the Austrian Tirol, NE of Innsbruck; population (1985) 9,000.

Kivu lake in the Great Rift Valley between Zaïre and Rwanda, about 105 km/65 mi long. The chief port is Bukavu.

Klaipeda formerly *Memel* port in the Lithuanian Republic of the USSR, on the Baltic coast at the mouth of the Dange river; population (1987) 201,000. Industries include shipbuilding and iron foundries. It was founded 1252 as the castle of

Korea, North
Democratic People's Republic of *(Chosun Minchu-chui Inmin Konghwa-guk)*

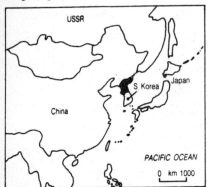

area 120,538 sq km/46,528 sq mi
capital Pyongyang
physical mountainous
features the richest of the two Koreas in mineral resources
head of state Kim Il Sung from 1972 (also head of Communist Party)
head of government Yon Hyong Muk from 1988

political system communism
political parties Korean Workers' Party (KWP), Marxist-Leninist-Kim Il Sungist
exports coal, iron, copper, textiles, chemicals
currency won (1.65 = £1 Feb 1990)
population (1988) 21,890,000; annual growth rate 2.5%
life expectancy men 65, women 71
language Korean
religion traditionally Buddhist and Confucian
literacy 99% (1984)
GNP $18.1 bn (1982 est); $570 per head of population
chronology
1948 Democratic People's Republic of Korea declared.
1950 North Korea invaded South Korea to begin Korean War.
1953 Armistice agreed to end Korean War.
1961 Friendship and mutual assistance treaty signed with China.
1972 New constitution, with executive president, was adopted. Talks took place with South Korea about possible reunification.
1980 Reunification talks broke down.
1983 Four South Korean cabinet ministers assassinated in Rangoon, Burma, by North Korean army officers.
1985 Increased relations with the USSR.

Memelburg by the Teutonic Knights, joined the Hanseatic League soon after, and has changed hands between Sweden, Russia, and Germany. Lithuania annexed Klaipeda 1923, and after German occupation 1939–45, it was restored to Lithuania.

Klondike former gold-mining area in ◊Yukon, Canada, and named after the river valley where gold was found 1896. About 30,000 people moved there during the following 15 years. Silver is still mined there.

Klosters alpine skiing resort NE of Davos in E Switzerland.

Knaresborough market town in N Yorkshire, England; 6 km/4 mi NE of Harrogate; population (1981) 13,000. It has a castle dating from about 1070.

Knoxville city in E Tennessee, USA; population (1986) 591,000. It is the centre of a mining and agricultural region, and the administrative headquarters of the Tennessee Valley Authority. The university was founded 1794.

Knutsford town in Cheshire, England; the novelist Elizabeth Gaskell, who lived in Knutsford for 22 years and is buried there, wrote of it under the name Cranford; it is now a suburb of Manchester.

Kobarid formerly *Caporetto* village on the Isonzo river, in Slovenia, NW Yugoslavia. Originally in Hungary, it was in Italy from 1918, and in 1947 became Kobarid. During World War I German-Austrian troops defeated Italian forces there 1917.

Kobe deep-water port in S Honshu, Japan; population (1987) 1,413,000. *Port Island*, created 1960–68 from the rock of nearby mountains, area 5 sq km/2 sq mi, is one of the world's largest construction projects.

København Danish name for ◊Copenhagen, capital of Denmark.

Koblenz city in the Rhineland-Palatinate, West Germany, at the junction of the rivers Rhine and Mosel; population (1988) 110,000. The city dates back to Roman times. It is a centre of communications and the wine trade, with industries (shoes, cigars, paper).

Kodiak island off the S coast of Alaska, site of a US naval base; area 9,505 sq km/3,670 sq mi. It is the home of the world's largest bear. The town of Kodiak is the largest US fishing port (mainly salmon).

Kokand oasis town in Uzbek Republic of USSR; population (1981) 156,000. It was the capital of

Korea, South
Republic of
(Daehan Minguk)

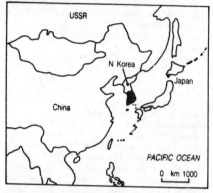

area 99,022 sq km/38,222 sq mi
capital Seoul
towns Taegu, ports Pusan, Inchon
physical mountainous
head of state Roh Tae-Woo from 1988
head of government Kang Young Hoon from 1988
political system emergent democracy
political parties Democratic Liberal Party (DLP), right-of-centre; Party for Peace and Democracy (PPD), left-of-centre
exports steel, ships, chemicals, electronics, textiles, plastics
currency won (1,172 = £1 Feb 1990)
population (1987) 42,082,000; annual growth rate 1.6%
life expectancy men 65, women 71
language Korean
religion traditionally Buddhist and Confucian
literacy 96% male/87% female (1980 est)
GNP $78.9 bn (1984); $1,187 per head of population
chronology
1948 Republic proclaimed.
1950–53 War with North Korea.
1960 President Syngman Rhee resigned amid unrest.
1961 Military coup by Gen Park Chung-Hee. Industrial growth programme.
1979 Assassination of President Park.
1980 Military coup by Gen Chun Doo-Hwan.
1987 Adoption of more democratic constitution following student unrest. Roh Tae-Woo elected president.
1988 Former president Chun, accused of corruption, publicly apologized for the misdeeds of his administration and agreed to hand over his financial assets to the state.
1990 Two minor opposition parties united with Democratic Justice Party to form ruling Democratic Liberal Party.

Kokand khanate when annexed by Russia 1876. Industries include fertilizers, cotton, and silk.

Koko Nor Mongolian form of ◊Qinghai, province of China.

Kola (Russian *Kol'skiy Poluostrov*) peninsula in N USSR, bounded by the White Sea on the S and E, and by the Barents Sea on the N; area 129,500 sq km/50,000 sq mi; coterminous with Murmansk region. Apatite and other minerals are exported. To the NW the low-lying granite plateau adjoins Norway's thinly populated county of Finnmark, and Soviet troops are heavily concentrated here.

Kolchugino former name (to 1925) of ◊Leninsk-Kuznetsky, town in USSR.

Kolhapur industrial city in Maharashtra, India, noted as a film production centre; population (1981) 346,000.

Köln German form of ◊Cologne, city in West Germany.

Kolwezi mining town in Shaba province, SE Zaïre; population (1985) 82,000. It is important for copper and cobalt. In 1978 former police of the province invaded from Angola and massacred some 650 of the inhabitants.

Komi autonomous republic in N central USSR; area 415,900 sq km/160,540 sq mi; population (1986) 1,200,000. Its capital is Syktyvkar.

Königsberg German name of ◊Kaliningrad, port in USSR.

Konstanz German form of the town of ◊Constance.

Konya (Roman *Iconium*) city in SW central Turkey; population (1985) 439,000. Carpets and silks are made here, and the city contains the monastery of the dancing dervishes.

Kordofan province of central Sudan, known as the 'White Land'; area 146,932/ 56,752 sq mi; population (1983) 3,093,300. Although never an independent state, it has a character of its own. It is mainly undulating plain, with acacia scrub producing gum arabic, marketed in the chief town ◊El Obeid. Formerly a rich agricultural region, it has been overtaken by desertification.

Korea, North country in E Asia, bounded N by China, E by the Sea of Japan, S by South Korea, and W by the Yellow Sea.

Korea, South country in E Asia, bordered to the N by North Korea, E by the Sea of Japan, S by the E China Sea, and W by the Yellow Sea.

Korinthos Greek form of ◊Corinth.

Kortrijk Flemish form of ◊Courtrai, town in Belgium.

Kos or *Cos* fertile Greek island, one of the Dodecanese, in the Aegean Sea; area 287 sq km/111 sq mi. It gives its name to the Cos lettuce.

Kosciusko highest mountain in Australia (2,229 m/7,316 ft), in New South Wales. Paul Strzelecki, who was born in Prussian Poland, discovered the mountain 1839 and named it after a Polish revolutionary hero.

Košice town in SE Czechoslovakia; population (1986) 222,000. It has a textile industry and is a road centre; a large part of the population (1980) 204,700 is Magyar-speaking, and Košiče was in Hungary until 1920 and 1938–45.

Kosovo autonomous region (since 1974) in S Serbia, Yugoslavia; capital Priština; area 10,900 sq km/4,207 sq mi; population (1986) 1,800,000. Products include wine, nickel, lead, and zinc. Since it is largely inhabited by Albanians and bordering on Albania, there are demands for unification with that country, while in the late 1980s Serbians were agitating for Kosovo to be merged with the rest of Serbia.

Kota Bharu capital of Kelantan, Malaysia; population (1980) 170,600.

Kota Kinabalu formerly (until 1968) *Jesselton* capital and port in Sabah, Malaysia; population (1980) 59,500. Exports include rubber and timber.

Kottbus alternative spelling of ◊Cottbus, town in East Germany.

Kovno Russian form of ◊Kaunas, port in Lithuania, USSR.

Kowloon peninsula on the Chinese coast forming part of the British crown colony of Hong Kong; the town of Kowloon is a residential area.

Kragujevac garrison town and former capital (1818–39) of Serbia, Yugoslavia; population (1981) 165,000.

Krakatoa (Indonesian *Krakatau*) volcanic island in Sunda strait, Indonesia, which erupted in 1883, causing 36,000 deaths on Java and Sumatra by the tidal waves which followed. The island is now uninhabited.

Kraków or *Cracow* city in Poland, on the Vistula; population (1985) 716,000. It is an industrial centre producing railway wagons, paper, chemicals, and tobacco. It was capital of Poland about 1300–1595.

Founded 1400, its university, at which the astronomer Copernicus was a student, is one of the oldest in central Europe. There is a 14th-century Gothic cathedral.

Kramatorsk industrial town in Ukraine, USSR, in the Donbas, north of Donetsk; population (1987) 198,000. Industries include coalmining machinery, steel, ceramics, and railway repairs.

Krasnodar industrial town at the head of navigation of the Kuban river, in SW USSR; population (1987) 623,000. It is linked by pipeline with the Caspian oilfields. The town was known as Ekaterinodar until 1920.

Krasnodar territory of the USSR in the N Caucasus, adjacent to the Black Sea; area 83,600 sq km/32,290 sq mi; population (1985) 4,992,000. The capital is Krasnodar. In addition to stock rearing and the production of grain, rice, fruit and tobacco, oil is refined.

Krasnoyarsk industrial city in central USSR; population (1987) 899,000. Industries include locomotives, paper, timber, cement, gold refining, and a large hydroelectric works. There is a large early-warning and space-tracking radar phased array device at nearby Abalakova.

Krasnoyarsk territory of the USSR in central Siberia stretching N to the Arctic Ocean; area 2,401,600 sq km/927,617 sq mi; population (1985) 3,430,000. The capital is Krasnoyarsk. It is drained by the Yenisei river. Mineral resources include gold, graphite, coal, iron ore and uranium.

Krefeld industrial town near the river Rhine; 52 km/32 mi NW of Cologne; West Germany; population (1988) 217,000. Industries include chemicals, textiles, and machinery. The town is on the Westphalian coalfield.

Kremenchug industrial town on the river Dnieper, in Ukraine Republic, USSR; population (1987) 230,000. Manufacturing includes road-building machinery, rail wagons, and processed food.

Krivoi Rog town in Ukraine, USSR, 130 km/80 mi SW of Dnepropetrovsk; population (1987) 698,000. The surrounding district is rich in iron ore, and there is a metallurgical industry. The name means 'crooked horn'.

Kruger National Park game reserve in NE Transvaal, South Africa, between the Limpopo and Crocodile rivers; it is the largest in the world (about 20,720 sq km/8,000 sq mi). The Sabie Game Reserve was established 1898 by President Kruger, and the park declared in 1926.

Krugersdorp mining town in the Witwatersrand district, Transvaal, South Africa; population (1980) 103,000. Manganese, uranium, and gold are mined.

KS abbreviation for ◊*Kansas*.

Kuala Lumpur capital of the Federation of Malaysia; population (1980) 938,000. The city developed after 1873 with the expansion of tin and rubber trading; these are now its major industries. Formerly within the state of Selangor, of which it was also the capital, it was created a federal territory 1974; area 240 sq km/93 sq mi; population (1980) 977,000.

Kuban river in the USSR, rising in Georgia (see ◊Krasnodar); length 906 km/563 mi to the Sea of Azov.

Kuching capital and port of Sarawak state, E Malaysia, on the Sarawak river; population (1980) 74,200.

Kuwait
State of
(Dowlat al Kuwait)

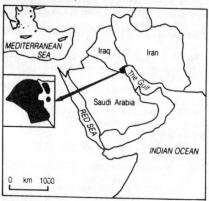

MEDITERRANEAN SEA

Iraq

Iran

The Gulf

Saudi Arabia

RED SEA

INDIAN OCEAN

0   km   1000

area 17,819 sq km/6,878 sq mi
capital Kuwait (also chief port)
physical hot desert
features oil revenues make it one of the world's

best-equipped states in public works, and medical and educational services
head of state and government Jabir al-Ahmad al-Jabir al-Sabah from 1977
political system absolute monarchy
political parties none permitted
exports oil
currency Kuwaiti dinar (0.49 = £1 Feb 1990)
population (1988) 1,960,000 (40% Kuwaitis, 30% Palestinians); annual growth rate 5 5%
life expectancy men 70, women 74
language 78% Arabic, 10% Kurdish, 4% Farsi
religion Sunni Muslim, with Shi'ite minority
literacy 76% male/63% female (1985 est)
GNP $22 bn (1984); $11,431 per head of population
chronology
1961 Achieved full independence, with Sheikh Abdullah al-Salem al-Sabah as emir.
1965 Sheikh Abdullah died and was succeeded by his brother, Sheikh Sabah.
1977 Sheikh Sabah died and was succeeded by Crown Prince Jabir.
1990 Pro-democracy demonstrations suppressed.

Kufra group of oases in the Libyan Desert, N Africa, SE of Tripoli. By the 1970s the vast underground reservoirs were being used for irrigation.

Kuibyshev or *Kuybyshev* capital of Kuibyshev region, USSR, and port at the junction of the rivers Samara and Volga, situated in the centre of the fertile middle Volga plain; population (1987) 1,280,000. Its industries include aircraft, locomotives, cables, synthetic rubber, textiles, fertilizers, petroleum refining, and quarrying. It was provisional capital of the USSR 1941–43.

Founded as Samara, the town was renamed Kuibyshev 1935. *Kuibyshev Sea* is an artificial lake about 480 km/300 mi long, created in the 1950s by damming the Volga river.

Kumamoto city on Kyushu island, Japan, 80 km/50 mi east of Nagasaki; population (1987) 550,000. A military stronghold until the last century, the city is now a centre for fishing, food processing, and textile industries.

Kumasi town in Ghana, W Africa, capital of Ashanti region, with trade in cocoa, rubber, and cattle; population (1984) 350,000.
history In the Fourth Ashanti War, in 1900, Sir Frederic Hodgson, governor of the Gold Coast Colony, his wife, staff, and a small garrison were besieged in the fort at Kumasi Mar–June, when they fought their way out. Soon afterwards the kingdom of Ashanti, of which Kumasi had been the capital since the 17th century, was annexed by the British.

Kunlunshan mountain range on the edge of the great Tibetan plateau, China; 4,000 km/2,500 mi E–W; highest peak Muztag (7,282 m/23,900 ft).

Kunming formerly *Yunnan* capital of Yunnan province, China, on Lake Dian Chi, about 2,000 m/6,300 ft above sea level; population (1986) 1,490,000. Industries include chemicals, textiles, and copper smelted with nearby hydroelectric power.

Kurdistan or *Kordestan* hilly region in SW Asia in the neighbourhood of Mount Ararat, where the borders of Iran, Iraq, Syria, Turkey, and the USSR meet; area 192,000 sq km/74,600 sq mi; total population around 18 million.

Kure naval base and port 32 km/20 mi SE of Hiroshima, on the S coast of Honshu, Japan; population (1980) 234,500. Industries include shipyards and engineering works.

Kuria Muria group of five islands in the Arabian Sea, off the S coast of Oman; area 72 sq km/28 sq mi.

Kuril Islands chain of about 50 small islands stretching from the NE of Hokkaido, Japan, to the S of Kamchatka, USSR; area 14,765 sq km/5,700 sq mi; population (1970) 15,000. Some of them are of volcanic origin. Two of the Kurils are claimed by both Japan and the USSR.

The Kurils were discovered 1634 by a Russian navigator and were settled by Russians. Japan seized them 1875–1945, when under the Yalta agreement they were returned to the USSR. Japan still claims the southernmost (Etorofu and Kunashiri), and also the nearby small islands of

Habomai and Shikotan (not part of the Kurils). The USSR agreed to the latter 1972, but the question of Etorofu and Kunashiri prevents signature of a Japan-Soviet peace treaty.

Kursk town and capital of Kursk region of the USSR; population (1987) 434,000. It dates from the 9th century. Industries include chemicals, machinery, alcohol, and tobacco.

Kūt-al-Imāra or *al Kūt* town in Iraq, on the river Tigris; population (1985) 58,600. It is a grain market and carpet-manufacturing centre. In World War I it was under siege by Turkish forces Dec 1915–Apr 1916, when the British garrison surrendered.

Kutch, Rann of salt, marshy area in Gujarat state, India, which forms two shallow lakes, the *Great Rann* and the *Little Rann*, in the wet season, and is a salt-covered desert in the dry. It takes its name from the former princely state of Kutch, which it adjoined. An international tribunal 1968 awarded 90% of the Rann of Kutch to India and 10% (about 800 sq km/300 sq mi) to Pakistan, the latter comprising almost all the elevated area above water the year round.

Kuwait country in SW Asia, bordered N and NW by Iraq, E by the Persian Gulf, and S and SW by Saudi Arabia.

Kuwait City (Arabic *Al Kuwayt*) formerly *Qurein* chief port and capital of the State of Kuwait, on the S shore of Kuwait Bay; population (1985) 44,300, plus the suburbs of Hawalli, population (1985) 145,100, Jahra, population (1985) 111,200, and as-Salimiya, population (1985) 153,400. Kuwait is a banking and investment centre.

Kuzbas (in full *Kuznetsk Basin*) industrial area in Kemerovo region, S USSR, lying to the Tom river to the N of the Altai mountains. Development began in the 1930s. It takes its name from the old town of Kuznetsk.

Kuznetsk Basin industrial area in Kemorovo region, S USSR, usually abbreviated to ◊Kuzbas.

Kwa Ndebele black homeland in Transvaal province, South Africa; achieved self-governing status 1981; population (1985) 235,800.

Kwangchow former name of ◊Guangzhou, city in China.

Kwangchu or *Kwangju* capital of South Cholla province, SW South Korea; population (1985)

906,000. It is at the centre of a rice-growing region. A museum in the city houses a huge collection of Chinese porcelain dredged up 1976 after lying for over 600 years on the ocean floor.

Kwangsi-Chuang former name of ◊Guanxi Zhuang, region of China.

Kwangtung former name of ◊Guangdong, province of China.

KwaZulu black homeland in Natal province, South Africa; achieved self-governing status 1971; population (1985) 3,747,000.

Kweichow former name of ◊Guizhou, province of China.

Kweilin former name of ◊Guilin in China.

KY abbreviation for ◊*Kentucky*.

Kyoga lake in central Uganda; area 4,425 sq km/1,709 sq mi. The Victoria Nile river passes through the lake.

Kyoto former capital of Japan 794–1868 on Honshu island, linked by canal with Biwa Lake; population (1987) 1,469,000. Industries include silk weaving and manufacture, porcelain, bronze, and lacquer ware.

Kyrenia port in Turkish-occupied Cyprus, about 20 km/12 mi N of Nicosia. Population (1985) 7,000.

Kyushu most southerly of the main islands of Japan, separated from Shikoku and Honshu by Bungo Channel and Suo Bay, but connected to Honshu by bridge and rail tunnel
area 42,150 sq km/16,270 sq mi including about 370 small islands
capital Nagasaki
towns Fukuoka, Kumamoto, Kagoshima
physical mountainous, volcanic, with sub-tropical climate
features the active volcano Aso-take (1,592 m/5,225 ft) has the world's largest crater
products coal, gold, silver, iron, tin, rice, tea, timber
population (1986) 13,295,000.

Kyustendil town in SW Bulgaria, SW of Sofia, noted for its hot springs; population about 25,000.

Kyzyl-Kum desert in Kazakhstan and Uzbekistan, USSR, between the Sur-Darya and Amu-Darya rivers; area about 300,000 sq km/116,000 sq mi. It is being reclaimed for cultivation by irrigation and protective tree-planting.

LA abbreviation for ◊*Louisiana*; *Los Angeles*.

Labrador area of NE Canada, part of the province of Newfoundland, lying between Ungava Bay on the NW, the Atlantic on the E, and the Strait of Belle Isle on the SE; area 266,060 sq km/102,699 sq mi; population (1976) 33,052. It consists primarily of a gently sloping plateau with an irregular coastline of numerous bays, fjords, and inlets, and cliffs 60 m/200 ft to 120 m/400 ft high. Industries include fisheries, timber and pulp, and many minerals. Hydroelectric resources include Churchill Falls on Churchill River, where one of the world's largest underground power houses is situated. The Canadian Air Force base in Goose Bay is on land claimed by the Innu (or Montagnais-Naskapi) Indian people, who call themselves a sovereign nation (in 1989 numbering 9,500).

Labuan a flat, wooded island off NW Borneo, a Federal Territory of East Malaysia; area 100 sq km/39 sq mi; population (1980) 12,000. Its chief town and port is Victoria, population 3,200. Labuan was ceded to Great Britain 1846, and from 1963 included in Sabah, Federation of Malaysia.

Laccadive, Minicoy, and Amindivi Islands former name of Indian island group ◊Lakshadweep.

La Ceiba chief Atlantic port of Honduras; population (1985) 61,900.

Lachlan river in Australia which rises in the Blue Mountains, a tributary of the Murrumbidgee; length 1,485 km/920 mi.

La Condamine a commune of Monaco.

Ladakh subsidiary range of the ◊Karakoram and district of NE Kashmir, India, on the border of Tibet; chief town Leh. After China occupied Tibet in 1951, it made claims on the area.

Ladoga (Russian *Ladozhskoye*) largest lake on the continent of Europe, in the USSR, just NE of Leningrad; area 18,400 sq km/7,100 sq mi. It receives the waters of the Svir, which drains Lake Onega, and other rivers, and runs to the Gulf of Finland by the river Neva.

Ladrones Spanish name (meaning 'thieves') of the ◊Marianas archipelago.

Ladysmith town in Natal, South Africa, 185 km/115 mi NW of Durban, near the Klip. It was besieged by the Boers, 2 Nov 1899–28 Feb 1900, during the South African War. Ladysmith was named in honour of the wife of Sir Henry Smith, a colonial administrator.

Lagos chief port and former capital of Nigeria, located at the western end of an island in a lagoon and linked by bridges with the mainland via Iddo Island; population (1983) 1,097,000. Industries include chemicals, metal products, and fish.
Abuja was established as the new capital 1982.

Lahore capital of the province of Punjab and second city of Pakistan; population (1981) 2,920,000. Industries include engineering, textiles, carpets, and chemicals. It is associated with Mogul rulers Akbar, Jahangir, and Aurangzeb, whose capital it was in the 16th–17th centuries.

Laibach German name of ◊Ljubljana, city in Yugoslavia.

Lake District region in Cumbria, England; area 1,800 sq km/700 sq mi. It embraces the the principal English lakes separated by wild uplands rising to many peaks, including Scafell Pike 978 m/3,210 ft.
Windermere, in the SE, is connected with Rydal Water and Grasmere. The westerly Scafell range extends south to the Old Man of Coniston overlooking Coniston Water, and north to Wastwater. Ullswater lies in the NE of the district, with Hawes Water and Thirlmere nearby. The river Derwent flows north through Borrowdale forming Derwentwater Bassenthwaite. West of Borrowdale lie Buttermere, Crummock Water, and, beyond, Ennerdale Water.
The Lake District has associations with the writers Wordsworth, Coleridge, Southey, De Quincey, Ruskin, and Beatrix Potter, and was made a national park 1951.

Lake Havasu City small town in Arizona, USA, which has been developed as a tourist resort. Old London Bridge was transported and reconstructed there in 1971.

Lakshadweep group of 36 coral islands, 10 inhabited, in the Indian Ocean, 320 km/200 mi off the Malabar coast; area 32 sq km/12 sq mi; population (1981) 40,000. The administrative headquarters is on Kavaratti Island. Products include coir, copra, and fish. The religion is Muslim. The first Western visitor was Vasco da Gama 1499. It was British from 1877 until Indian independence, and created a Union Territory of the Republic of India 1956. Formerly known as the Laccadive,

Minicoy, and Amindivi Islands, they were renamed Lakshadweep 1973.

La Línea town and port on the isthmus of Algeciras Bay, S Spain, adjoining the frontier zone with Gibraltar; population (1981) 56,300.

La Mancha (Arabic *al mansha*, the dry land), former province of Spain now part of the autonomous region of ◊Castilla-La Mancha. Cervantes' *Don Quijote de la Mancha* 1605 begins there.

Lambeth borough of S central Greater London
features Lambeth Palace (chief residence of the archbishop of Canterbury since 1197); Tradescant museum of gardening history; the South Bank (including Royal Festival Hall, National theatre); the Oval (headquarters of Surrey County Cricket Club from 1846) at Kennington, where the first England–Australia test match was played in 1880; Brixton Prison; Brixton had serious riots in 1981 and 1985
population (1981) 245,500.

Lammermuir Hills a range of hills dividing Lothian and Borders regions, Scotland, from Gala Water to St Abb's Head.

Lamu island off the E coast of Kenya.

Lanark former county town of Lanarkshire, Scotland; now capital of Clydesdale district, Strathclyde region; population (1981) 9,800. William Wallace once lived here, and later returned to burn the town and kill the English sheriff. *New Lanark* to the S, founded in 1785 by Robert Owen, was a socialist 'ideal village' experiment.

Lanarkshire former inland county of Scotland, merged 1975 in the region of Strathclyde. The county town was Lanark.

Lancashire county in NW England
area 3,040 sq km/1,173 sq mi

Lancashire

towns administrative headquarters Preston, which forms part of Central Lancashire New Town (together with Fulwood, Bamber Bridge, Leyland, and Chorley), Lancaster, Accrington, Blackburn, Burnley; ports Fleetwood and Heysham; seaside resorts Blackpool, Morecambe, and Southport
features river Ribble; Pennines; Forest of Bowland (moors and farming valleys); Pendle Hill, traditional centre of witchcraft
products formerly a world centre of cotton manufacture, this has been replaced with newer varied industries
population (1987) 1,381,000
famous people Kathleen Ferrier, Gracie Fields, George Formby, Rex Harrison.

Lancaster city in Lancashire, England, on the river Lune; population (1983) 126,400. It was the former county town of Lancashire (now Preston). The university was founded 1964. Industries include textiles, floor coverings, furniture, plastics. There is a castle, which incorporates Roman work, and during the Civil War was captured by Cromwell.

Lancaster city in Pennsylvania, USA, 115 km/70 mi W of Philadelphia; population (1980) 54,700. It produces textiles and electrical goods. It was capital of the USA briefly in 1777.

Lanchow former name of ◊Lanzhou, city in China.

Lancs abbreviation for ◊*Lancashire*.

Landes sandy, low-lying area in SW France, along the Bay of Biscay, about 12,950 sq km/5,000 sq mi in extent. Formerly covered with furze and heath, it has in many parts been planted with pine and oak forests. It gives its name to a *département*, and extends into the *département*s of Gironde and Lot-et-Garonne. There is a testing range for rockets and missiles at Biscarosse, 72 km/45 mi SW of Bordeaux. There is an oilfield in Parentis-en-Born.

Land's End promontory of W Cornwall, 15 km/9 mi WSW of Penzance, the most westerly point of England. It was bought by entrepreneur Peter de Savary in the 1980s.

An extension of Land's End is a group of dangerous rocks, the *Longships*, a mile out, marked by a lighthouse.

Landskrona town and port in Sweden, on the Sound, 32 km/20 mi N of Malmö; population (1983) 36,500. Industries include shipyards, machinery, chemicals and sugar refining. Carl XI defeated the Danes off Landskrona in 1677.

Languedoc former province of S France, lying between the Rhône, the Mediterranean, Guienne, and Gascony.

Languedoc-Roussillon region of S France, comprising the *département*s of Aude, Gard, Hérault, Lozère, and Pyrénées-Orientales; area 27,400 sq km/10,576 sq mi; population (1986) 2,012,000. Its capital is Montpellier, and products include fruit, vegetables, wine, and cheese.

Laos

People's Democratic Republic of
(Saathiaranagroat Prachhathippatay Prachhachhon Lao)

area 236,790 sq km/91,400 sq mi
capital Vientiane
towns Luang Prabang, the former royal capital
physical high mountains in the E; Mekong River in the W; jungle
features hydroelectric power from the Mekong is exported to Thailand; Plain of Jars, where a prehistoric people carved stone jars large enough to hold a person; once known as the Land of a Million Elephants

head of state Prince Souphanouvong from 1975; Phoumi Vongvichit acting president from 1986
head of government Kaysone Phomvihane from 1975
political system communism
exports tin, teak
currency new kip (1213.88 = £1 Feb 1990)
population (1989) 3,923,000; annual growth rate 2.6%
life expectancy men 48, women 51
language Lao
religion traditionally Theravada Buddhist
literacy 76% male/63% female (1985 est)
GNP $601 million (1983); $85 per head of population
chronology
1893–1945 Laos became a French protectorate.
1945 Temporarily occupied by Japan.
1946 Re-taken by France.
1950 Granted semi-autonomy in French Union.
1954 Full independence achieved.
1960 Right-wing government seized power.
1962 Coalition government established; civil war continued.
1973 Vientiane ceasefire agreement.
1975 Communist-dominated republic proclaimed with Prince Souphanouvong as head of state.
1987 Phoumi Vongvichit became acting president.
1988 Plans announced to withdraw 40% of the Vietnamese forces stationed in the country.
1989 First assembly elections since communist takeover.

Lansing capital of Michigan, USA, at the confluence of the Grand and Red Cedar rivers; population (1980) 472,000. Manufacturing includes motor vehicles, diesel engines, pumps, and furniture.

Lanzhou formerly *Lanchow* capital of Gansu province, China, on the Yellow River, 190 km/120 mi south of the Great Wall; population (1986) 1,350,000. Industries include oil refining, chemicals, fertilizers, and synthetic rubber.

Laois or *Laoighis* county in Leinster province, Republic of Ireland
area 1,720 sq km/664 sq mi
county town Portlaoise
physical flat except for the Slieve Bloom mountains in the NW
products sugarbeets, dairy products, woollens, agricultural machinery
population (1986) 53,000.

Laon capital of Aisne *département*, Picardie, N France; 120 km/75 mi NE of Paris; population (1982) 29,000. It was the capital of France and a royal residence until the 10th century. It has a 12th-century cathedral.

Laos landlocked country in SE Asia, bordered to the N by China, E by Vietnam, S by Cambodia, and W by Thailand.

La Palma see under La ◊Palma, one of the Spanish Canary Islands.

La Pampa province in Argentina, see under ◊Pampas.

La Paz city in Bolivia, 3,800 m/12,400 ft above sea level; population (1985) 992,600. Products include textiles and copper. Founded by the Spanish 1548, it has been the seat of government since about 1900.

Lapland region of Europe within the Arctic Circle in Norway, Sweden, Finland, and the USSR, without political definition. Its chief resources are chromium, copper, iron, timber, hydroelectric power, and tourism. There are about 20,000 Lapps, who live by hunting, fishing, reindeer herding, and handicrafts.

La Plata capital of Buenos Aires province, Argentina; population (1980) 560,300. Industries include meat packing and petroleum refining. It was founded 1882.

la Plata, Río de or *River Plate* estuary in South America into which the rivers Paraná and Uruguay flow; length 320 km/200 mi and width up to 240 km/150 mi. The basin drains much of Argentina, Bolivia, Brazil, Uruguay, and Paraguay, who all cooperate in its development.

Laptev Sea part of the Arctic Ocean off the N coast of the USSR between Taimyr Peninsula and New Siberian Island.

Laramie town in Wyoming, USA, on the Laramie Plains, a plateau 2,300 m/7,500 ft above sea level, bounded to the N and E by the Laramie Mountains; population (1980) 24,400. The Laramie River, on which it stands, is linked with the Missouri via the Platte. On the overland trail and Pony Express route, Laramie features in Western legend.

Larderello site in the Tuscan hills, NE Italy, where the sulphur springs were used by the Romans for baths, and exploited for boric acid in the 18th–19th centuries. Since 1904 they have been used to generate electricity: the water reaches 220°C.

Laredo city on the Rio Grande river, Texas, USA; population (1980) 91,450. Indstries include oil refining and meat processing. *Nuevo Laredo*, Mexico, on the opposite bank, is a textile centre; population (1980) 203,300. There is much cross-border trade.

La Rioja region of N Spain; area 5,000 sq km/1,930 sq mi; population (1986) 263,000.

Larisa town in Thessaly, Greece, S of Mount Olympus; population (1981) 102,000. Products include textiles and agriculture.

Larne seaport of County Antrim, N Ireland, on Lough Larne, terminus of sea routes to Stranraer, Liverpool, Dublin, and other places; population (1981) 18,200.

La Rochelle fishing port in W France; population (1982) 102,000. It is the capital of Charente-Maritime *département*. Industries include shipbuilding, chemicals, and motor vehicles. A Huguenot stronghold, it was taken by Cardinal Richelieu in the siege of 1627–28.

Lashio town in Shan state, Myanmar, about 200 km/125 mi NE of Mandalay; beginning of the Burma Road, constructed in 1938, to Kunming in China.

Las Palmas or *Las Palmas de Gran Canaria* tourist resort on the NE coast of Gran Canaria, Canary Islands; population (1986) 372,000. Products include sugar and bananas.

La Spezia port in NW Italy, chief Italian naval base; population (1988) 107,000. Industries include shipbuilding, engineering, electrical goods, and

Latvia

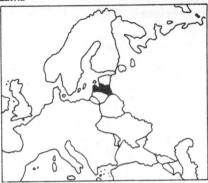

textiles. The poet Shelley drowned in the Gulf of Spezia.

Las Vegas city in Nevada, USA, known for its nightclubs and gambling casinos; population (1986) 202,000.

Latakia port with tobacco industries in NW Syria; population (1981) 197,000.

Latin America countries of South and Central America (also including Mexico) in which Spanish, Portuguese, and French are spoken.

Lattakia alternative form of ◊Latakia in Syria.

Latvia constituent republic of W USSR from 1940
area 63,700 sq km/24,595 sq mi
capital Riga
towns Daugavpils, Liepaja, Jelgava, Ventspils
physical lakes, marshes, wooded lowland
products meat and dairy products, communications equipment, consumer durables, motorcycles, locomotives
population (1987) 2,647,000; Lett 54%, Russian 33%
language Latvian
religion mostly Lutheran Protestant with a Roman Catholic minority
recent history as in the other Baltic republics, there has been nationalist dissent since 1980, influenced by the Polish example and prompted by an influx of Russian workers and officials. A Latvian popular front was established in Oct 1988 to campaign for independence, and a multiparty system is effectively in place, with, following the republic's elections of Dec 1989, a coalition government set to be formed. In Oct 1988 the prewar flag was readopted and official status given to the Latvian language.

In Jan 1990 the Latvian Communist Party broke its links with Moscow and in May of the same year Latvia followed the lead taken by Lithuania when it unilaterally declared its independence from the Soviet Union.

Laugharne village at the mouth of the river Towey, Dyfed, Wales. The home of the poet

Dylan Thomas, it features in his work as 'Milk Wood'.

Launceston port in NE Tasmania, Australia, on the Tamar river; population (1986) 88,500. Founded in 1805, its industries include woollen blankets, saw milling, engineering, furniture and pottery making, and railway workshops.

Lausanne resort and capital of Vaud canton, W Switzerland, above the N shore of Lake Geneva; population (1987) 262,000. Industries include chocolate, scientific instruments, and publishing.

La Vendée see ◊Vendée, La.

Lawrence town in Massachusetts, USA; population (1980) 63,175. Industries include textiles, clothing, paper, and radio equipment. The town was established in 1845 to utilize power from the Merrimack Rapids on a site first settled in 1655.

La'Youn (Arabic ***El Aaiún***) capital of Western Sahara; population (1982) 97,000. The city has expanded from a population of 25,000 in 1970 as a result of Moroccan investment (Morocco lays claim to Western Sahara).

Lazio (Roman ***Latium***) region of W central Italy; area 17,200 sq km/6,639 sq mi; capital Rome; population (1988) 5,137,000. Products include olives, wine, chemicals, pharmaceuticals, and textiles. Home of the Latins from the 10th century BC, it was dominated by the Romans from the 4th century BC.

Lea river rising in Bedfordshire, England, which joins the river Thames at Blackwall.

Leamington officially ***Royal Leamington Spa*** town and health resort in the West Midlands, England, on the river Leam, adjoining Warwick; population (1985) 56,500. The Royal Pump Room offers modern spa treatment.

Leatherhead town in Surrey, England, SW of London, on the river Mole at the foot of the N Downs; population (1985) 40,300. It has industrial research stations, the Thorndike Theatre (1968), and the Royal School for the Blind (1799).

Lebanon country in W Asia, bordered N and E by Syria, S by Israel, and W by the Mediterranean.

Lebda former name of ◊Homs, a city in Syria near the river Orontes.

Lebowa black homeland in Transvaal province, South Africa; achieved self-governing status 1972; population (1985) 1,836,000.

Leeds city in W Yorkshire, England, on the river Aire; population (1984) 712,200. Industries include engineering, printing, chemicals, glass, and woollens.

Noted buildings include the Town Hall designed by Cuthbert Brodrick, Leeds University 1904, the Art Gallery 1844, Temple Newsam (birthplace of Henry Darnley in 1545, now a museum), and the Cistercian Abbey of Kirkstall 1147. It is a centre

Lebanon

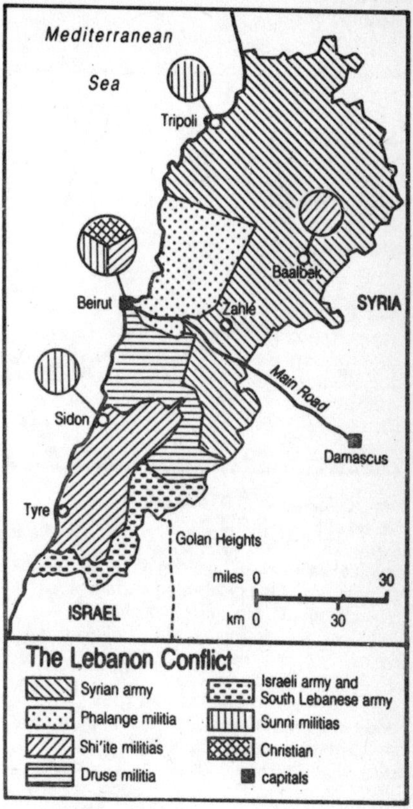
Mediterranean
Sea
Tripoli
Beirut
Baalbek
Zahlé
SYRIA
Main Road
Sidon
Damascus
Tyre
Golan Heights
miles 0
30
km 0
30
ISRAEL
The Lebanon Conflict
Syrian army
Phalange militia
Shi'ite militias
Druse militia
Israeli army and South Lebanese army
Sunni militias
Christian
capitals

of communications where road, rail and canal (to Liverpool and Goole) meet.

Leeuwarden city in the Netherlands, on the Ee river; population (1987) 85,200. It is the capital of Friesland province. A marketing centre, it also makes gold and silver ware. After the draining of the Middelzee fenlands, the town changed from being a port to an agricultural market town. Notable buildings include the palace of the stadholders of Friesland, and the church of St Jacob.

Leeward Islands (1) group of islands, part of the ◊Society Islands, in ◊French Polynesia, S Pacific; (2) general term for the northern half of the Lesser ◊Antilles in the West Indies; (3) former British colony in the West Indies (1871–1956) comprising Antigua, Montserrat, St Christopher/St Kitts-Nevis, Anguilla, and the Virgin Islands.

Lebanon
Republic of
(al-Jumhouria al-Lubnaniya)

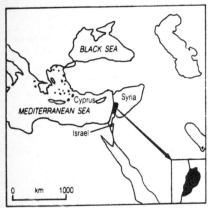

area 10,452 sq km/4,034 sq mi
capital and port Beirut
towns ports Tripoli, Tyre, Sidon
physical valley N—S between mountain ranges
features few of the celebrated cedars of
Lebanon remain; Mount Hermon; Chouf
Mountains; archaeological sites at Baalbeck,
Byblos, Tyre; until the civil war, the financial
centre of the Middle East
head of state Elias Hwrawi from 1989.
heads of government Selim El-Hoss from 1989.
government emergent democratic republic
political parties Phalangist Party, Christian,
radical, right-wing; Progressive Socialist Party
(PSP), Druze, moderate, socialist; National
Liberal Party (NLP), Maronite, centre-left;
Parliamentary Democratic Front, Sunni Muslim,
centrist; Lebanese Communist Party (PCL),
nationalist, communist.
exports citrus and other fruit; industrial
products to Arab neighbours
currency Lebanese pound (937.53 = £1
Feb 90)
population (1985 est) 3,500,000 (including

350,000 Palestinian refugees, many driven
out, killed in fighting or massacred 1982–85);
annual growth rate –0.1%
life expectancy men 63, women 67
language Arabic (official); French and English
religion Muslim 57% (Shi'ite 33%, Sunni
24%), Christian (Maronite and Orthodox) 40%,
Druse 3%
literacy 86% male/69% female (1985 est)
GNP $3 bn (1983); $1,150 per head of
population
chronology
1944 Full independence achieved.
1964 Palestine Liberation Organization (PLO)
founded in Beirut.
1975 Outbreak of civil war between Christians
and Muslims.
1976 Ceasefire agreed,
1978 Israel invaded S Lebanon in search of
PLO fighters. International peacekeeping force
established. Fighting broke out again.
1979 Part of S Lebanon declared an
'independent free Lebanon'.
1982 Bachir Gemayel became president, but
was assassinated before he could assume
office. His brother Amin Gemayel became
president.
1983 Agreement reached for the withdrawal of
Syrian and Israeli troops, but not honoured.
1984 Most of international peacekeeping force
withdrawn.
1985 Lebanon nearing chaos, with many
foreigners being taken hostage.
1987 Syrian troops sent into Beirut.
1988 Attempts to agree a Christian successor
to Gemayel failed. His last act in office was to
establish a military government; Selim El-Hoss
set up a rival government, and the threat of
partition hung over the country.
1989 Arab Peace Plan accepted by Muslims
but rejected by Maronite Christians led by
General Michel Aoun; National Assembly
appointed Rene Muawad as president, in
place of Aoun; Muawad killed by a car bomb,
succeeded by Elias Hwrawi; Hwrawi formally
made Selim El-Hoss prime minister; Aoun
continued his defiance.

Leghorn former English name for the Italian port
ΦLivorno.

Leh capital of Ladakh region, E Kashmir, India,
situated E of the Indus, 240 km/150 mi E of
Srinagar. Leh is the nearest supply base to the
Indian army outpost on the Siachen Glacier.

Le Havre industrial port (engineering, chemicals,
oil refining) in Normandy, NW France, on the
Seine; population (1982) 255,000. It is the third

largest port in Europe, and has a ferry link to
Portsmouth, UK.

Leicester industrial city (food processing, hosiery,
footwear, engineering, electronics, printing, plastics) and administrative headquarters of Leicestershire, England, on the river Soar; population
(1983) 282,300.

Leicestershire county in central England
area 2,550 sq km/984 sq mi

towns administrative headquarters Leicester; Loughborough, Melton Mowbray, Market Harborough

features Rutland district (formerly England's smallest county, with Oakham as its county town); Rutland Water, one of Europe's largest reservoirs; Charnwood Forest; Vale of Belvoir (under which are large coal deposits); the site of Snibston mine (closed 1986) at Coalville is being developed as a science museum to be opened 1992

products horses, cattle, sheep, dairy products, coal

population (1987) 879,000

famous people C P Snow.

Leics abbreviation for ◊*Leicestershire*.

Leiden or *Leyden* city in South Holland province, Netherlands; population (1988) 183,000. Industries include textiles and cigars. It has been a printing centre since 1580, with a university established 1575. It is linked by canal to Haarlem, Amsterdam, and Rotterdam. The painters Rembrandt and Jan Steen were born here.

Leinster SE province of the Republic of Ireland, comprising the counties of Carlow, Dublin, Kildare, Kilkenny, Laois, Longford, Louth, Meath, Offaly, Westmeath, Wexford, and Wicklow; area 19,630 sq km/7,577 sq mi; capital Dublin; population (1986) 1,850,000.

Leipzig capital of Leipzig county, East Germany, 145 km/90 mi SW of Berlin; population (1986) 552,000. Products include furs, leather goods, cloth, glass, cars, and musical instruments. The county of Leipzig has an area of 4,970 sq km/1,918 sq mi, and a population of 1,374,000.

Leith port in Scotland S of the Firth of Forth, incorporated in Edinburgh 1920. Leith was granted to Edinburgh as its port by Robert Bruce in 1329.

Leitrim county in Connacht province, Republic of Ireland, bounded on the NW by Donegal Bay

area 1,530 sq km/591 sq mi

county town Carrick-on-Shannon

features rivers Shannon, Bonet, Drowes and Duff

products potatoes, cattle, linen, woollens, pottery, coal, iron, lead

population (1986) 27,000.

Leix spelling used 1922–35 of ◊Laois, county of Ireland.

Léman, Lac French name for Lake ◊Geneva.

Le Mans industrial town in Sarthe *département*, France; population (1982) 150,000, conurbation 191,000. It has a motor-racing circuit where the annual endurance 24-hour race (established 1923) for sports cars and their prototypes is held.

Lemberg German name of ◊Lvov, city in USSR.

Lemnos (Greek *Límnos*) Greek island in the N of the Aegean Sea

area 476 sq km/184 sq mi

towns Kastron, Mudros

physical of volcanic origin, rising to 430 m/1,411 ft

products mulberries and other fruit, tobacco, sheep

population (1981) 15,700.

Lena longest river in Asiatic Russia, 4,400 km/2,730 mi, with numerous tributaries. Its source is near Lake Baikal and it empties into the Arctic Ocean through a delta 400 km/240 mi wide. It is ice-covered for half the year.

Leninakan town in the Armenian Republic, USSR, 40 km/25 mi NW of Yerevan; population (1987) 228,000. Industries include textiles and engineering. It was founded 1837 as a fortress called Alexandropol, and virtually destroyed by an earthquake 1926 and again 1988.

Leningrad capital of the Leningrad region, at the head of the Gulf of Finland; population (1987) 4,948,000. Industries include shipbuilding, machinery, chemicals, and textiles. Originally called *St Petersburg*, it was renamed *Petrograd* 1914, and *Leningrad* 1924.

features Leningrad is split up by the mouths of the river Neva, which connects it with Lake Ladoga. The site is low and swampy, and the climate severe. The city has wide boulevards and many Baroque and Classical buildings. The oldest building is the fortress of St Peter and St Paul on an island in the Neva, now a prison. Museums include the Winter Palace, used by the tsars until 1917, the Hermitage, the Russian Museum (formerly Michael Palace), and St Isaac's Cathedral.

history Capital of the Russian Empire 1709–1918, it was founded 1703 by Peter the Great, who took up residence there in 1712. Leningrad was the centre of all the main revolutionary movements from the Decembrist revolt of 1825 to the 1917 revolution. During the German invasion in World War II the city withstood siege and bombardment from Sept 1941 to Jan 1944, with great loss of life.

Leningrad became a seaport when it was linked with the Baltic by a ship canal built 1875–93. It is also linked by canal and river with the Caspian and Black seas, and in 1975 a seaway connection was completed via lakes Onega and Ladoga with the White Sea near Belomorsk, so that naval forces can reach the Barents Sea free of NATO surveillance.

Leninsk-Kuznetsky town in Kemerovo region, S USSR, on the Inya river, 320 km/200 mi SSE of Tomsk; population (1985) 110,000. It is a mining centre in the Kuzbas, with a large iron and steel works; coal, iron, manganese, and other metals, and precious stones occur in the neighbourhood. Formerly *Kolchugino*, the town was renamed *Leninsk-Kuznetsky* in 1925.

Lens coalmining town in Pas-de-Calais *département*, France; population (1982) 38,300, conurbation 327,000. During World War I it was in German occupation and close to the front line Oct 1914–Oct 1918, when the town and its mines

Lesotho
Kingdom of

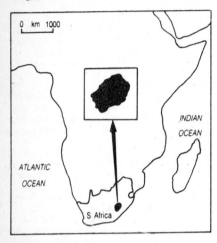

0 km 1000

INDIAN
OCEAN

ATLANTIC
OCEAN

S Africa

area 30,355 sq km/11,717 sq mi
capital Maseru
physical mountainous
features Lesotho is an enclave within South

Africa
government military-controlled monarchy
head of state Moshoeshoe II from 1966
head of government Justin Lekhanya from 1986
political parties Basotho National Party (BNP), traditionalist, nationalist
exports wool, mohair, diamonds
currency maluti (4.33= £1 Feb 1990)
population (1987) 1,627,000; annual growth rate 2.5%
life expectancy men 46, women 52
language Sesotho and English (official)
religion Christian 70% (Roman Catholic 40%)
literacy 62% male/84% female (1985 est)
GNP $678.2 million (1981); $355 per head of population
chronology
1966 Basutoland achieved full independence within the Commonwealth as the Kingdom of Lesotho, with Chief Leabua Jonathan as prime minister.
1975 Members of the ruling party attacked by guerrillas backed by South Africa.
1986 South Africa imposed a border blockade, forcing the deportation of 60 African National Congress members.
1987 Gen Lekhanya ousted Chief Jonathan in a coup.

---

were severely damaged. In World War II it was occupied by Germany May 1940–Sept 1944, but suffered less physical damage.

León city in W Nicaragua, population (1985) 101,000. Industries include textiles and food processing. Founded 1524, it was capital of Nicaragua until 1855.

León city in Castilla-León, Spain; population (1986) 137,000. It was the capital of the kingdom of León 10th century–1230, when it was merged with Castile.

León de los Aldamas industrial city (leather goods, footwear) in central Mexico; population (1986) 947,000.

Léopoldville former name (until 1966) of ◊Kinshasa, city in Zaïre.

Le Puy capital of Haute-Loire *département*, Auvergne, SE France; population (1982) 26,000. It is dramatically situated on a rocky plateau; it has a 12th-century cathedral.

Lérida (Catalan *Lleida*) capital of Lérida province, N Spain, on the river Segre; 132 km/82 mi west of Barcelona; population (1986) 112,000. Industries include leather, paper, glass, and cloth. Lérida was captured by Caesar 49 BC. It has a palace of the kings of Aragon.

Lerwick port in Shetland, Scotland; population (1985) 8,000. It is the administrative headquarters of Shetland. Main occupations include fishing and oil. Hand-knitted shawls are a speciality. A Viking tradition survives in the Jan festival of Up-Helly-Aa when a copy of a longship is burned.

Lesbos ancient name of ◊Lesvos, an island in the Aegean Sea.

Lesotho landlocked country in southern Africa, an enclave within South Africa.

Lesvos Greek island in the Aegean Sea, near the coast of Turkey
area 2,154 sq km/831 sq mi
capital Mytilene
products olives, wine, grain
population (1981) 104,620
history ancient name **Lesbos**; an Aeolian settlement, the home of the poets Alcaeus and Sappho; conquered by the Turks from Genoa 1462; annexed to Greece 1913.

Letchworth town in Hertfordshire, England, 56 km/35 mi NNW of London; population (1981) 31,835. Industries include clothing, furniture, scientific instruments, light metal goods and printing. It was founded in 1903 as the first English garden city.

Le Touquet resort in N France, at the mouth of the river Canche; fashionable in the 1920s–30s.

Levant the E Mediterranean region, or more specifically, the coastal regions of Turkey-in-Asia, Syria, Lebanon, and Israel.

Liberia
Republic of

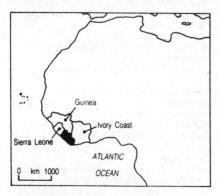

area 111,370 sq km/42,989 sq mi
capital Monrovia
physical forested highlands; swampy coast where six rivers end
features nominally the world's largest merchant navy because minimal controls make Liberia's a flag of convenience
head of state and government Samuel Kanyon Doe from 1980
political parties National Democratic party of Liberia (NDLP), nationalist
government emergent democratic republic
exports iron ore, rubber, diamonds, coffee, cocoa, palm oil
currency Liberian dollar (1.70 = £1 Feb 1990)
population (1988) 2,436,000 (95% belonging to the indigenous peoples); annual growth rate 3.2%
life expectancy men 47, women 51
language English (official)
religion Muslim 20%, Christian 15%, traditional 65%
literacy 47% male/23% female (1985 est)
GNP $900 million (1983); $400 per head of population
chronology
1847 Founded as an independent republic.
1944 William Tubman elected president.
1971 Tubman died and was succeeded by William Tolbert.
1980 Tolbert assassinated in a coup led by Samuel Doe, who suspended the constitution and ruled through a People's Redemption Council (PRC).
1984 New constitution approved. National Democratic Party of Liberia (NDPL) founded by Doe.
1985 NDPL won decisive victory in general election. Unsuccessful coup against Doe.
1990 Gradual movement to more pluralist politics and economic problems threaten President Doe.

Leven town in Fife region, Scotland; at the mouth of the river Leven, where it meets the Firth of Forth; population (1981) 8,600. It has timber, paper, and engineering industries.

Leven, Loch loch in Tayside region, Scotland; area 16 sq km/6 sq mi. It is drained by the river Leven, and has seven islands; Mary Queen of Scots was imprisoned 1567–68 on Castle Island. A national nature reserve since 1964. Leven is also the name of a sea loch in Strathclyde, Scotland.

Leverkusen river port in North Rhine-Westphalia, West Germany, 8 km/5 mi north of Cologne; population (1988) 155,000. It has iron, steel, and chemical industries.

Lewes market town (administrative headquarters) in E Sussex, England, on the river Ouse; population (1981) 13,800. The Glyndebourne music festival is held nearby. Simon de Montfort defeated Henry III here in 1264; there is a house once belonging to Anne of Cleves, and a castle. The town is known for its 5th Nov celebrations.

Lewisham borough of SE Greater London
features at Deptford shipbuilding yard (1512–1869), Drake was knighted and Peter the Great worked here; Crystal Palace (re-erected at Sydenham in 1854) site now partly occupied by the National Sports Centre; the poet James Elroy Flecker was born here
population (1981) 233,225.

Lewis with Harris largest island in the Outer Hebrides; area 2,220 sq km/857 sq mi; population (1981) 23,400. Its main town is Stornoway. It is separated from NW Scotland by the Minch. There are many lakes and peat moors. Harris is famous for its tweeds.

Lexington town in Massachusetts, USA; population (1981) 29,500. Industries include printing and publishing. The Battle of Lexington and Concord 1775 opened the War of American Independence.

Lexington-Fayette town in Kentucky, USA, centre of the bluegrass country; population (1981) 204,160. Race horses are bred in the area, and races and shows are held. There is a tobacco market and the University of Kentucky (1865).

Leyden alternative form of ◊Leiden, city in the Netherlands.

Leyland industrial town in Lancashire, England; population (1981) 37,100. Industries include motor vehicles, paint and rubber. The Rover Group (previously British Leyland), largest of British firms

Libya
Socialist People's Libyan Arab State of the Masses
(al-Jamahiriya al-Arabiya al-Libya al-Shabiya al-Ishtirakiya al-Uzma)

area 1,759,540 sq km/679,182 sq mi
capital Tripoli
towns ports Benghazi, Misurata
physical desert; mountains in N and S
features Gulf of Sirte; rock paintings of about 3000 BC in the Fezzan; Roman city sites of Leptis Magna, Sabratha among others; the plan to pump water from below the Sahara to the coast risks exhaustion of a largely non-renewable supply

government one-party, socialist state
head of state and government Moamar Khaddhafi from 1969
political parties Arab Socialist Union (ASU), radical, left-wing
exports oil, natural gas
currency Libyan dinar (0.49 = £1 Feb 1990)
population (1986) 3,955,000 (including 500,000 foreign workers); annual growth rate 3.9%
life expectancy men 57, women 60
language Arabic
religion Sunni Muslim
literacy 60% (1985)
GDP $25 bn (1984); $7,000 per head of population
chronology
1951 Achieved independence as the United Kingdom of Libya, under King Idris.
1969 King deposed in a coup led by Col Moamar Khaddhafi. Revolution Command Council set up and the Arab Socialist Union (ASU) proclaimed the only legal party.
1972 Proposed federation of Libya, Syria, and Egypt abandoned.
1980 Proposed merger with Syria abandoned. Libyan troops began fighting in Chad.
1981 Proposed merger with Chad abandoned.
1986 US bombing of Khaddhafi's headquarters, following allegations of his complicity in guerrilla activities.
1988 Diplomatic relations with Chad restored.
1989 US accused Libya of building a chemical-weapons factory and shot down two Libyan planes; reconciliation with Egypt.

---

producing cars, buses, and lorries, has its headquarters here.
Lhasa (the 'Forbidden City') capital of the autonomous region of Tibet, China, at 5,000 m/16,400 ft; population (1982) 105,000. Products include handicrafts and light industry. The holy city of Lamaism, Lhasa was closed to Westerners until the early 20th century. It was annexed with the rest of Tibet 1950–51 by China, and the Dalai Lama fled 1959 after a popular uprising against Chinese rule. Monasteries have been destroyed and monks killed, and an influx of Chinese settlers has generated resentment. In 1988 and 1989 nationalist demonstrators were shot by Chinese soldiers.
Liao river in NE China, frozen Dec–Mar; the main headstream rises in the mountains of Inner Mongolia and flows E, then S to the Gulf of Liaodong; length 1,450 km/900 mi.
Liaoning province of NE China
area 151,000 sq km/58,300 sq mi
capital Shenyang

towns Anshan, Fushun, Liaoyang
features it was developed by Japan 1905–45, including the **Liaodong Peninsula** whose ports had been conquered from the Russians, and the province is one of China's most heavily industrialized areas
products cereals, coal, iron, salt, oil
population (1986) 37,260,000.
Liaoyang industrial city (engineering, textiles) in Liaoning province; population (1970) 250,000. In 1904 Russia was defeated by Japan here.
Libau German name of Latvian port ◊Liepāja.
Liberia country in W Africa, bounded to the N and NE by Guinea, E by the Ivory Coast, S and SW by the Atlantic, and NW by Sierra Leone.
Libreville capital of Gabon, on the estuary of the river Gabon; population (1985) 350,000. Products include timber, oil, and minerals. It was founded 1849 as a refuge for slaves freed by the French.
Libya country in N Africa, bordered to the N by the Mediterranean, E by Egypt, SE by the Sudan, S by Chad and Niger, and W by Algeria and Tunisia.

Liechtenstein
Principality of

area 160 sq km/62 sq mi
capital Vaduz

physical Alpine; includes part of Rhine Valley
features only country in the world to take
its name from its reigning family; most highly
industrialized country
head of state Prince Hans Adam II from 1989
head of government Hans Brunhart from 1978
government constitutional monarchy
exports microchips, precision engineering,
processed foods, postage stamps; easy tax
laws make it a haven for foreign companies and
banks
currency Swiss franc (2.53 = £1 Feb 1990)
population (1987) 27,700 (33% foreign);
annual growth rate 1.4%
life expectancy men 65, women 73
language German
religion Roman Catholic
literacy 100% (1986)
GDP 1 bn Swiss francs (1984); $16,440 per
head of population
chronology
1938 Prince Franz Josef II came to power.
1984 Vote extended to women in national
elections.
1989 Prince Franz Joseph II died; Hans Adam
II succeeded him as prince.

Lichfield town in the Trent Valley, Staffordshire, England; population (1985) 26,310. The cathedral, 13th–14th century, has three spires. Samuel Johnson was born here.

Liechtenstein landlocked country in W central Europe, situated between Austria to the E, and Switzerland to the W.

Liège industrial city (weapons, textiles, paper, chemicals), capital of Liège province in Belgium, SE of Brussels, on the Meuse; population (1988) 200,000. The province of Liège has an area of 3,900 sq km/1,505 sq mi, and a population (1987) of 992,000.

Liepāja (German Libau) naval and industrial port in the Republic of Latvia, USSR; population (1985) 112,000. The Knights of Livonia founded Liepāja in the 13th century. Industries include steel, engineering, textiles and chemicals.

Liffey river in E Ireland, flowing from the Wicklow mountains to Dublin Bay; length 80 km/50 mi.

Liguria coastal region of NW Italy, which includes the resorts of the Italian Riviera, lying between the western Alps and the Mediterranean Gulf of Genoa. The region comprises the provinces of Genova, La Spezia, Imperia, and Savona, with a population (1988) of 1,750,000 and an area of 5,418 sq km/2,093 sq mi. Genoa is the chief town and port.

Lille (Flemish Ryssel) industrial city (textiles, chemicals, engineering, distilling), capital of Nord-Pas-de-Calais, France; population (1982) 174,000, metropolitan area 936,000. The world's first entirely automatic underground system was opened here 1982.

Lilongwe capital of Malawi since 1975; population (1985) 187,000. Products include tobacco and textiles.

Lima capital of Peru, an industrial city (textiles, chemicals, glass, cement) with its port at Callao; population (1988) 418,000, metropolitan area 4,605,000. Founded by the conquistador Pizarro 1535, it was rebuilt after destruction by an earthquake 1746.

Survivals of the colonial period are the university 1551, cathedral 1746, government palace (the rebuilt palace of the viceroys), and the senate house (once the headquarters of the Inquisition).

Limassol port in S Cyprus in Akrotiri Bay; population (1985) 120,000. Products include cigarettes and wine. Richard I married Berengaria of Navarre here 1191. The town's population increased rapidly with the influx of Greek Cypriot refugees after the Turkish invasion 1974.

Limburg province of Belgium; capital Hasselt; area 2,400 sq km/926 sq mi; population (1987) 737,000.

Limburg southernmost province of the Netherlands in the plain of the Maas (Meuse); area 2,170 sq km/838 sq mi; population (1988) 1,095,000. Its capital is Maastricht, the oldest city in the Netherlands. Manufacture of chemicals has now replaced coal mining but the coal industry is still remembered at Kerkrade, alleged site of the first European coal mine. The marl soils of S Limburg are used in the manufacture of cement and fertilizer. Mixed arable farming and horticulture are also important.

Limehouse district in E London; part of ◊Tower Hamlets.

Limerick county town of Limerick, Republic of Ireland, the main port of W Ireland, on the Shannon estuary; population (1986) 77,000. It was founded in the 12th century.

Limerick county in SW Republic of Ireland, in Munster province
area 2,690 sq km/1,038 sq mi
county town Limerick
physical fertile, with hills in the south
products dairy products
population (1986) 164,000.

Limoges city and capital of Limousin, France; population (1982) 172,000. Fine enamels were made here in the medieval period, and it is the centre of the modern French porcelain industry. Other industries include textiles, electrical equipment, and metal goods. The city was sacked by the Black Prince 1370.

Limousin former province and modern region of central France; area 16,900 sq km/6,544 sq mi; population (1986) 736,000. It consists of the *départements* of Corréze, Creuse, and Haute-Vienne. Chief town is Limoges. A thinly populated and largely unfertile region, it is crossed by the mountains of the Massif Central. Fruit and vegetables are produced in the more fertile lowlands. Kaolin is mined.

Lincolnshire

Limpopo river in SE Africa, rising in the Transvaal and reaching the Indian Ocean in Mozambique; length 1,600 km/1,000 mi.

Lincoln industrial city in Lincolnshire, England; population (1981) 76,200. Manufacturing includes excavators, cranes, gas turbines, power units for oil platforms and cosmetics. It was the flourishing Roman colony of Lindum, and had a big medieval wool trade. Paulinus built a church here in the 7th century, and the 11th–15th-century cathedral has the earliest Gothic work in Britain. The 12th-century High Bridge is the oldest in Britain still to have buildings on it.

Lincoln industrial city and capital of Nebraska, USA; population (1981) 172,000. Industries include engineering, oil refining, and food processing. Known as *Lancaster* until 1867 when it was renamed after President Lincoln.

Lincolnshire county in E England
area 5,890 sq km/2,274 sq mi
towns administrative headquarters Lincoln; resort Skegness
physical Lincoln Wolds, marshy coastline, the Fens in the SE, rivers Witham and Welland
features 16th-century Burghley House; Belton House, a Restoration mansion
products cattle, sheep, horses, cereals, flower bulbs, oil
population (1987) 575,000
famous people Isaac Newton, Alfred Tennyson, Margaret Thatcher.

Lincs abbreviation for *Lincolnshire*.

Lindisfarne site of monastery off the coast of Northumberland, England; see under ◊Holy Island.

Line Islands coral-island group in the Pacific ocean; population (1985) 2,500. Products include coconut and guano. Eight of the islands belong to Kiribati and two (Palmyra and Jarvis) are administered by the USA.

Linköping industrial town in SE Sweden; 172 km/107 mi SW of Stockholm; population (1986) 117,800. Industries include hosiery, aircraft and engines, and tobacco. It has a 12th-century cathedral.

Linlithgow tourist centre in Lothian region, Scotland; population (1981) 9,600. Linlithgow Palace, now in ruins, was once a royal residence, and Mary Queen of Scots was born there.

Linlithgowshire former name of West Lothian, now included in Lothian region, Scotland.

Linz industrial port (iron, steel, metalworking) on the river Danube in N Austria; population (1981) 199,900.

Lipari or *Aeolian Islands* volcanic group of seven islands off NE Sicily, including Lipari (on which is the capital of the same name), Stromboli (active volcano 926 m/3,038 ft high), and Vulcano (also with an active volcano); area 114 sq km/44 sq mi. In Greek mythology, the god Aeolus kept the winds imprisoned in a cave on the Lipari Islands.

Lippe river of N West Germany flowing into the Rhine; length 230 km/147 mi; also a former German state, now part of North Rhine-Westphalia.

Lisboa Portuguese form of ◊Lisbon, capital of Portugal.

Lisbon (Portuguese *Lisboa*) city and capital of Portugal, in the SW on the tidal lake and estuary formed by the Tagus; population (1984) 808,000. Industries include steel, textiles, chemicals, pottery, shipbuilding, and fishing. It has been capital since 1260, and reached its peak of prosperity in the period of Portugal's empire during the 16th century.

Lisburn cathedral city and market town in Antrim, N Ireland, on the river Lagan; population (1985) 87,900. It is noted for linen and furniture.

Lisieux town in Calvados *département*, France, to the SE of Caen; population (1982) 25,823. St Thérèse of Lisieux spent her religious life in the Carmelite convent here, and her tomb attracts pilgrims.

Litani river rising near Baalbek in the Anti-Lebanon mountains of E Lebanon. It flows NE-SW through the Beqa'a Valley then E to the Mediterranean 8 km/5 mi N of Tyre. The Israelis invaded Lebanon as far as the Litani River in 1978.

Lithuania constituent republic of the W USSR from 1940

area 65,200 sq km/25,174 sq mi

capital Vilnius

towns Kaunas, Klaipeda

physical river Niemen; 25% forested; lakes, marshes, and complex sandy coastline

products bacon, dairy products, cereals, potatoes, heavy engineering, electrical goods, cement

population (1987) 3,641,000; 80% Lithuanian, 9% Russian, 8% Polish

language Lithuanian, an Indo-European tongue which has retained many ancient features and is related to Latvian; it is written in a Latin alphabet

religion only Soviet republic that is predominantly Roman Catholic

Lithuania

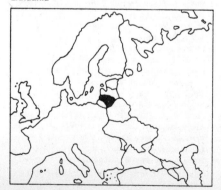

famous people Jacques Lipchitz

history formerly part of the Russian empire, Lithuania became an independent Soviet republic 1918; this was overthrown by Germans, Poles, and nationalist Lithuanians 1919, and a democratic republic was established. It was overthrown by a fascist coup 1926. In 1939 the USSR demanded military bases and in 1940 incorporated Lithuania as a constituent republic. As in the other Baltic republics, there has been nationalist dissent since 1980, influenced by the Polish example and prompted by the influx of Russian workers and officials. A popular front, the Lithuanian Restructuring Movement (Sajudis), was formed in Oct 1988 to campaign for increased autonomy, and in Nov 1989 the republic's Supreme Soviet (state assembly), to the chagrin of Russian immigrants, decreed Lithuanian as the state language and readopted the flag of the independent interwar republic. A month later, the republic's Communist Party split into two, with the majority wing formally breaking away from the Communist Party of the Soviet Union and establishing itself as a social-democratic, Lithiuanian-nationalist body. A multi-party system is effectively in place in the republic. In Mar 1990 Lithuania unilaterally declared its independence.

Littlehampton seaside resort in W Sussex, England, at the mouth of the river Arun, 16 km/10 mi SE of Chichester; population (1981) 22,000.

Little Rock industrial city and capital of Arkansas, USA; population (1980) 394,000. Black/white integration of the schools caused riots here 1957 and was enforced by federal troops. In 1981–82 in the Scopes monkey trial a federal judge ruled that a law requiring schools to teach creationism as well as evolution was a violation of the constitutional separation of church and state.

Liverpool city, seaport, and administrative headquarters of Merseyside, NW England; population (1984) 497,300. In the 19th and early 20th century, it exported the textiles of Lancashire and Yorkshire, and is the UK's chief Atlantic port with miles of specialized, mechanized quays on the river Mersey.

Livingston industrial new town (electronics, engineering) in W Lothian, Scotland, established 1962; population (1985) 40,000.

Livingstone formerly *Maramba* town in Zambia; population (1987) 95,000. Founded 1905, it was named after the explorer, and was capital of Northern Rhodesia 1907–35. Victoria Falls is nearby.

Livorno (English *Leghorn*) industrial port in W Italy; population (1988) 173,000. Industries include shipbuilding, distilling, and motor vehicles. A fortress town since the 12th century, it was developed by the Medici family; it has a naval academy, and is also a resort.

Lizard Point most southerly point of England in Cornwall. The coast is broken into small bays overlooked by two cliff lighthouses.

Ljubljana (German **Laibach**) capital and industrial city (textiles, chemicals, paper, leather goods) of Slovenia, Yugoslavia; population (1981) 305,200. It has a nuclear research centre and is linked with S Austria by the Karawanken road tunnel under the Alps (1979–83).

Llanberis village in Gwynedd, Wales, point of departure for ascents of Mount Snowdon.

Llandaff town in S Glamorgan, Wales, 5 km/3 mi NW of Cardiff, of which it forms part. The 12th-century cathedral, heavily restored, contains Epstein's sculpture 'Christ in Majesty'.

Llandrindod Wells spa in Powys, E Wales, administrative headquarters of the county; population (1981) 4,186.

Llandudno resort and touring centre for N Wales, in Gwynedd. Great Orme's Head is a spectacular limestone headland.

Llanelli (formerly Llanelly) industrial port in Dyfed, Wales; population (1981) 41,391. Industries include tinplate and copper smelting.

Llanfair P G village in Anglesey, Wales; full name **Llanfairpwllgwyngyllgogerychwyrndrobwllllantysiliogogogoch** (St Mary's church in the hollow of the white hazel near the rapid whirlpool of St Tysillio's church, by the red cave).

Lleyn peninsula in Gwynedd, N Wales, between Cardigan Bay and Caernarvon Bay. It included the resort Pwllheli, and Bardsey Island at the tip of Peninsula Lleyn is the traditional burial place of 20,000 saints.

Lobito port in Angola; population (1970) 60,000. It is linked by rail with Beira in Mozambique, via the Zaïre and Zambia copperbelt.

Locarno health resort in the Ticino canton of Switzerland on the north of Lago Maggiore, west of Bellinzona; population (1983) 15,300. Formerly in the duchy of Milan, it was captured by the Swiss in 1803.

Lochaber wild mountainous district of Highland region, Scotland, including Ben Nevis. Fort William is the chief town of the area. It is the site of large hydroelectric installations.

Loch Ness lake in Highland region, Scotland, forming part of the Caledonian Canal; 36 km/22.5 mi long, 229 m/754 ft deep. There have been unconfirmed reports of a **Loch Ness monster** since the 15th century.

Lodi town in Italy, 30 km/18 mi SE of Milan; population (1980) 46,000. It is a market centre for agricultural produce; fertilizers, agricultural machinery and textiles are produced. Napoleon's defeat of Austria at the battle of Lodi in 1796 gave him control of Lombardy. Napoleon was first called Le Petit Caporal at Lodi.

Łódź industrial town (textiles, machinery, dyes) in central Poland, 120 km/75 mi SW of Warsaw; population (1984) 849,000.

Lofoten and Vesterålen island group off NW Norway; area 4,530 sq km/1,750 sq mi. Hinnoy, in the Vesterålens, is the largest island of Norway. The surrounding waters are rich in cod and herring. The **Maelström**, a large whirlpool hazardous to ships which gives its name to similar features elsewhere, occurs in one of the island channels.

Logroño market town in La Rioja, N Spain, on the Ebro river; population (1986) 119,000. It is the centre of a wine region.

Loir French river, rising N of Illiers in the **département** of Eure-et-Loir and flowing SE, then SW to join the Sarthe near Angers; 311 km/500 mi. It gives its name to the **département**s of Loir-et-Cher and Eure-et-Loir.

Loire the longest river in France, rising in the Cévennes at 1,350 m/4,430 ft and flowing for 1,050 km/650 mi first north then west until it reaches the Bay of Biscay at St Nazaire, passing Nevers, Orléans, Tours, and Nantes. It gives its name to the **département**s of Loire, Haute-Loire, Loire-Atlantique, Indre-et-Loire, Maine-et-Loire, and Saône-et-Loire. There are many chateaux and vineyards along its banks.

Loiret French river, 11 km/7 mi long. It rises near Olivet and joins the Loire 8 km/5 mi below Orléans. It gives its name to Loiret **département**.

Lombardy (Italian **Lombardia**) region of N Italy, including Lake Como; capital Milan; area 23,900 sq km/9,225 sq mi; population (1988) 8,886,000. It is the country's chief industrial area (chemical, pharmaceuticals, engineering, textiles).

Lombok (Javanese 'chilli pepper') island of Indonesia, E of Java, one of the Sunda Islands; area 4,730 sq km/1,826 sq mi; population (1980) 1,957,000. Chief town is Mataram. It comprises a fertile plain between N and S mountain ranges.

Lomé capital and port of Togo; population (1983) 366,000. It is a centre for gold, silver, and marble crafts; major industries include steel production and oil refining.

Lomond, Loch largest freshwater Scottish lake, 37 km/21 mi long, area 70 sq km/27 sq mi, divided between Strathclyde and Central regions. It is overlooked by the mountain **Ben Lomond** 296.5 m/973 ft and linked to the Clyde estuary.

London the capital of England and the United Kingdom, on the river Thames; area 1,580 sq km/610 sq mi; population (1987) 6,770,000, larger metropolitan area about 9 million. The **City of London**, known as the 'square mile', area 677 acres, is the financial and commercial centre of the UK. **Greater ◊London** from 1965 comprises the City of London and 32 boroughs. Popular tourist attractions include the Tower of London, St Paul's

London, Greater

Cathedral, Buckingham Palace, and Westminster Abbey.

Roman *Londinium* was established soon after the Roman invasion AD 43; in the 2nd century London became a walled city; by the 11th century, it was the main city of England and gradually extended beyond the walls to link with the originally separate Westminster. The Monument (a column designed by Wren) marks the site in Pudding Lane where the Great Fire of 1666 began.

features The Tower of London, built by William the Conqueror on a Roman site, houses the crown jewels and the royal armouries; 15th-century Guildhall; Mansion House (residence of the lord mayor); Barbican arts and conference centre; Central Criminal Court (Old Bailey) and the Inner and Middle Temples; markets including Covent Garden, Smithfield (meat), and Spitalfields (fruit and vegetables).

government There has since 1986 been no central authority for Greater London; responsibility is divided between individual boroughs and central government.

The City of London has been governed by a corporation from the 12th century. Its structure and the electoral procedures for its common councillors and aldermen are medievally complex and it is headed by the lord mayor (who is, broadly speaking, nominated by the former and elected annually by the latter). After being sworn in at the Guildhall, he or she is presented the next day to the lord chief justice at the Royal Courts of Justice in Westminster, and the *Lord Mayor's Show* is a ceremonial procession there in Nov.

architecture London contains examples of all styles of English architecture since the 11th century. Examples include *Norman*: the White Tower, Tower of London; St Bartholomew's, Smithfield; the Temple Church. *Gothic*: Westminster Abbey; Westminster Hall; Lambeth Palace; Southwark Cathedral. *Tudor*: St James's Palace; Staple Inn, Holborn. *17th century*: Banqueting Hall, Whitehall (Inigo Jones); St Paul's, Kensington Palace, and many City churches (Wren). *18th century*: Somerset House (Chambers); St Martin-in-the-Fields; Buckingham Palace. *19th century*: British Museum (Neo-Classical); Houses of Parliament; Law Courts (Gothic); Westminster Cathedral (Byzantine). *20th century*: Lloyd's of London.

commerce and industry Important from Saxon times, the Port of London once dominated the Thames from Tower Bridge to Tilbury; its activity is now centred outside the metropolitan area, and downstream Tilbury has been extended to cope with container traffic. The prime economic importance of London is as a financial centre. There are various industries, mainly on the outskirts. There are also recording, broadcasting, television, and film studios; publishing companies, and the works and offices of the national press. Tourism is important. Some of the docks in the East End of London, once the busiest in the world, have been sold to the Docklands Development Corporation, which has built new houses, factories, and a railway.

education and entertainment Among its museums are the British, Victoria and Albert, Natural History, and Science museums, the National and Tate galleries. London University is the largest in Britain, while the Inns of Court have been the training school for lawyers since the 13th century. London has been the main centre of English drama ever since its first theatre was built by Burbage 1576.

London city in SW Ontario, Canada, on the river Thames, 160 km/100 mi SW of Toronto; population (1986) 342,000. The centre of a farming district, it has tanneries, breweries, and factories making hosiery, radio and electrical equipment, leather and shoes. It dates from 1826 and is the seat of the University of Western Ontario. A Shakespeare festival is held in Stratford, about 30 km/18 mi to the northwest.

Londonderry former name (until 1984) of the county and city of ◊Derry in Northern Ireland.

London, Greater the metropolitan area of ◊London, England, comprising the City of London, which forms a self-governing enclave, and 32 surrounding boroughs; area 1,580 sq km/610 sq mi; population (1987) 6,770,000. Certain powers were exercised over this whole area by the Greater London Council (GLC) from 1965 until its abolition 1986.

The London boroughs are: Barking and Dagenham, Barnet, Bexley, Brent, Bromley, Camden, Croydon, Ealing, Enfield, Greenwich, Hackney, Hammersmith and Fulham, Haringey, Harrow, Havering, Hillingdon, Hounslow, Islington, Kensington and Chelsea, Kingston upon Thames, Lambeth, Lewisham, Merton, Newham, Redbridge, Richmond upon Thames, Southwark, Sutton, Tower Hamlets, Waltham Forest, and Wandsworth.

Long Beach city in SW California, USA; population (1980) 361,334. It is a naval base and pleasure resort. Industries include oil refineries and aircraft. It forms part of the ◊Los Angeles conurbation.

Longchamp pleasure resort and racecourse in Paris, France, in the Bois de Boulogne. It is on the site of a former nunnery founded in 1260, suppressed 1790.

Longford county of Leinster province, Republic of Ireland
area 1,040 sq km/401 sq mi
county town Longford
features rivers Camlin and Inny; the Shannon marks the W boundary; several lakes
population (1986) 31,000.

Long Island island off the coast of Connecticut and New York, USA, separated from the mainland by Long Island Sound; area 3,627 sq km/1,400 sq mi. It includes two boroughs of New York City (Queens and Brooklyn), John F Kennedy airport, suburbs, and resorts.

It also has Brookhaven National Laboratory for atomic research, the world's largest automotive museum, the New York Aquarium, and a whaling museum. The popular pleasure resort of Coney Island is actually a peninsula in the SW, with a boardwalk 3 km/2 mi long.

Lop Nor series of shallow salt lakes with shifting boundaries in the Taklimakan Shamo (desert) in Xinjiang Uyghur, NW China. Marco Polo visited Lop Nor, then a single lake of considerable extent, about 1273. The area is used for atomic tests.

Lord Howe Island volcanic island and dependency of New South Wales, Australia, 700 km/435 mi NE of Sydney; area 15 sq km/6 sq mi; population (1984) 300. It is a resort and 'world heritage area' because of its scenery and wildlife. The woodhen is a bird found only here.

Lorestan alternative form of ◊Luristan, Iran.

Loreto town in the Marche region of central Italy; population (1981) 10,600. The town allegedly holds the Virgin Mary's house, carried there by angels from Nazareth; hence Our Lady of Loreto is the patron saint of aviators.

Lorient commercial and naval port in Brittany, NW France; population (1983) 104,000. Industries include fishing and shipbuilding.

Lorraine former province and modern region of NE France in the upper reaches of the Meuse

Lothian

and Moselle rivers; bounded to the N by Belgium, Luxembourg, and West Germany and to the E by Alsace; area 23,600 sq km/9,095 sq mi; population (1986) 2,313,000. It consists of the *départements* of Meurthe-et-Moselle, Meuse, Moselle, and Vosges, and its capital is Nancy. There are deposits of coal, iron ore, and salt; grain, fruit, and livestock are important. In 1871 the region was ceded to Germany as part of Alsace-Lorraine.

Los Angeles city and port in SW California, USA; population of urban area (1980) 2,967,000, the metropolitan area of Los Angeles-Long Beach 9,478,000. Industries include aerospace, electronics, chemicals, clothing, printing, and food-processing. Features include the suburb of Hollywood, centre of the film industry since 1911; the Hollywood Bowl concert arena; observatories at Mt Wilson and Mt Palomar; Disneyland; the Huntingdon Art Gallery and Library; and the Getty Museum.

Greater Los Angeles comprises 86 towns, including Long Beach, Redondo Beach, Venice, Santa Monica, Burbank, Compton, Beverly Hills, Glendale, Pasadena, and Pomona. It covers 10,000 sq km/4,000 sq mi. There are 6.3 million cars to 5.5 million drivers.

Lossiemouth fishing port and resort in Grampian, Scotland; population (1981) 6,800. Ramsay MacDonald was born and buried here.

Lot French river; see under ◊Gironde.

Lothian region of Scotland
area 1,800 sq km/695 sq mi
towns administrative headquarters Edinburgh; Livingston

features Lammermuir, Moorfoot, and Pentland Hills; Bass Rock in the Firth of Forth, noted for seabirds
products bacon, vegetables, coal, whisky, engineering, electronics
population (1987) 744,000
famous people birthplace of R L Stevenson in Howard Place, Edinburgh.
Loughborough industrial town in Leicestershire, England; population (1981) 47,647. Occupations include engineering, bell-founding, electrical goods, and knitwear. The university of technology was established 1966.
Louisiana state of the S USA; nickname Pelican State
area 135,900 sq km/52,457 sq mi
capital Baton Rouge
towns New Orleans, Shreveport, Lafayette, Lake Charles
features Mississippi delta
products rice, cotton, sugar, maize, oil, natural gas, sulphur, salt, processed foods, petroleum products, lumber, paper
population (1987) 4,461,000, which includes the Cajuns, descendants of 18th-century religious exiles from Canada, who speak a French dialect
famous people Louis Armstrong, Pierre Beauregard, Huey Long
history explored by La Salle; named after Louis XIV and claimed for France 1682; became Spanish 1762-1800; passed to the USA under the Louisiana Purchase 1803; admitted to the Union as a state 1812.
Louisville industrial city and river port on the Ohio, Kentucky, USA; population (1980) 655,000. Products include electrical goods, agricultural machinery, motor vehicles, tobacco, and baseball bats. It is noted for its Kentucky Fair and Exposition Center, and the Kentucky Derby horse race.
Lourdes town in SW France with a Christian shrine to St Bernadette which has a reputation for miraculous cures; population (1982) 18,000.
Lourenço Marques former name of ◊Maputo, capital of Mozambique.

Louisiana

Louth smallest county of the Republic of Ireland, in Leinster province; county town Dundalk; area 820 sq km/317 sq mi; population (1986) 92,000.
Louvain (Flemish *Leuven*) industrial town in Brabant province, central Belgium; population (1985) 85,000. Manufacturing includes fertilizers and food processing. Its university dates from 1425, and there is a Science City.
Low Countries the region of Europe which consists of ◊Belgium and the ◊Netherlands, and usually includes ◊Luxembourg.
Lowell city in Massachusetts, USA; population (1980) 92,500. Industries include electronics, plastics, and chemicals. Once a textile centre, it was designated a national park in 1978 as a birthplace of the US industrial revolution.
Lower Austria (German *Niederösterreich*) largest federal state of Austria; drained by the Danube; area 19,200 sq km/7,411 sq mi; population (1987) 1,426,000. Its capital is St Pölten. In addition to wine, sugar beet, and grain, there are reserves of oil. Manufactured products include textiles, chemicals, and metal goods.
Lower California English name for ◊Baja California, Mexico.
Lower Saxony (German *Niedersachsen*) administrative region (German *Land*) of N West Germany
area 47,400 sq km/18,296 sq mi
capital Hanover
towns Brunswick, Osnabrück, Oldenburg, Göttingen, Wolfsburg, Salzgitter, Hildesheim
features Lüneburg Heath; Harz mountains
products cereals, cars, machinery, electrical engineering
population (1988) 7,190,000
religion 75% Protestant, 20% Roman Catholic
history formed 1946 from Hanover, Oldenburg, Brunswick, and Schaumburg-Lippe.
Lowestoft most easterly port in Britain, in Suffolk; population (1981) 55,000. The composer Benjamin Britten was born here.
Lozère section of the Cévennes Mountains, S France. It rises in Finiels to 1,702 m/5,584 ft, and gives its name to a *département* in Languedoc-Roussillon region.
Lualaba another name for the upper reaches of the river ◊Zaïre in Africa, as it flows N through Zaïre from near the Zambia border.
Luanda formerly *Loanda* capital and industrial port (cotton, sugar, tobacco, timber, paper, oil) of Angola; population (1988) 1,200,000. It was founded 1575 and became a Portuguese colonial administrative centre as well as an outlet for slaves transported to Brazil.
Luang Prabang or *Louangphrabang* Buddhist religious centre in Laos, on the Mekong at the head of river navigation; population (1984) 44,244. It was the capital of the kingdom of

Luang Prabang, incorporated in Laos in 1946, and the royal capital of Laos 1946–75.

Lübeck seaport of Schleswig-Holstein, West Germany, on the Baltic Sea, 60 km/37 mi NE of Hamburg; population (1988) 209,000. Founded 1143, it has five Gothic churches and a cathedral from 1173. Once head of the powerful Hanseatic League, it later lost much of its trade to Hamburg and Bremen, but improved canal and port facilities helped it to retain its position as a centre of Baltic trade. Lübeck was a free state of both the empire and the Weimar Republic. The name Lübeck is of Wendish origin and means 'lovely one'.

Lublin city in Poland, on the Bystrzyca river, 150 km/95 mi SE of Warsaw; population (1985) 324,000. Industries include textiles, engineering, aircraft, and electrical goods. A trading centre from the 10th century, it has an ancient citadel, 16th-century cathedral, and a university (1918). A council of workers and peasants proclaimed Poland's independence at Lublin in 1918; and a Russian-sponsored committee of national liberation, which proclaimed itself the provincial government of Poland at Lublin on 31 Dec 1944, was recognized by Russia five days later.

Lubumbashi formerly (until 1986) *Elisabethville* town in Zaïre, on the Lualaba river; population (1984) 543,000. It is chief commercial centre of the Shaba copper-mining region.

Lucca city in NW Italy; population (1981) 91,246. It was an independent republic from 1160 until its absorption into Tuscany in 1847. The composer Puccini was born here.

Lucerne (German *Luzern*) capital and tourist centre of Lucerne canton, Switzerland, on the Reuss where it flows out of Lake Lucerne; population (1987) 161,000. It developed around the Benedictine monastery, established about 750, and owes its prosperity to its position on the St Gotthard road and railway.

Lucerne, Lake (German *Luzern*) scenic lake in central Switzerland; area 114 sq km/44 sq mi.

Lucknow capital and industrial city (engineering, chemicals, textiles, many handicrafts) of the state of Uttar Pradesh, India; population (1981) 1,007,000. During the Indian Mutiny against British rule, it was besieged 2 Jul–16 Nov 1857.

Lüda formerly *Hüta* industrial port (engineering, chemicals, textiles, oil refining, shipbuilding, food processing) in Liaoning, China, on Liaodong Peninsula, facing the Yellow Sea; population (1986) 4,500,000. It comprises the naval base of Lüshun (known under 19th-century Russian occupation as Port Arthur) and the commercial port of Dalien (formerly Talien/Dairen).

Both were leased to Russia (who needed an ice-free naval base) 1898, but were ceded to Japan after the Russo-Japanese War; Lüshun was under Japanese siege Jun 1904–Jan 1905. After World War II Lüshun was occupied by Russian airborne troops (returned to China 1955) and Russia was granted shared facilities at Dalien (ended on the deterioration of Sino-Russian relations 1955).

Lüderitz port on Lüderitz Bay, SW Africa; population (1970) 6,500. It is a centre for diamond-mining. The town, formerly a German possession, was named after a German merchant who acquired land here in 1883.

Ludlow market town in Shropshire, England, on the river Teme, 42 km/26 mi S of Shrewsbury; population (1983) 8,130. Milton's masque *Comus* was presented at Ludlow Castle in 1634.

Ludwigshafen city and Rhine river port, Rhineland-Palatinate, West Germany; population (1988) 152,000. Industries include chemicals, dyes, fertilizers, plastics, and textiles.

Lugano resort town on Lake Lugano, Switzerland; population (1980) 28,600.

Lugano, Lake lake partly in Italy, between lakes Maggiore and Como, and partly in Switzerland; area 49 sq km/19 sq mi.

Lugansk formerly (1935–58 and 1970–89) *Voroshilovgrad* industrial city (locomotives, textiles, mining machinery) in the Ukraine, USSR; population (1987) 509,000.

Luik Flemish name of ◊Liège, town in Belgium.

Luleå port in N Sweden, on the Gulf of Bothnia at the mouth of the river Luleå; population (1986) 66,500. It is the capital of Norrbotten county. Exports include iron ore and timber in ice-free months.

Lund city in Malmöhus county, SW Sweden; 16 km/10 mi NE of Malmö; population (1986) 83,400. It has an 11th-century Romanesque cathedral and a university established 1666. The treaty of Lund was signed in 1676 after Carl XI had defeated the Danes.

Lundy rocky island at the entrance to the Bristol Channel; 19 km/12 mi NW of Hartland Point, Devon, England; area 9.6 sq km/3.7 sq mi; population (1975) 40. Formerly used by pirates and privateers for a lair, it is now a National Trust bird sanctuary and the first British marine reserve (1987).

Lüneburg town in Lower Saxony, West Germany; on the river Ilmenau; population (1985) 61,000. Industries include chemicals, paper, and iron works. It is a health resort.

Lüneburg Heath German *Lüneburger Heide* area in Lower Saxony, West Germany, between the Elbe and Aller rivers. It was here that more than a million German soldiers surrendered to Montgomery on 4 May 1945.

Luoyang (formerly *Loyang*) industrial city in Henan province; south of the Yellow River; population 1,114,000. Formerly the capital of China, industries include machinery and tractors.

Lurgan see ◊Craigavon, town in Northern Ireland.

Luristan or *Lorestan* mountainous province in W Iran; area 28,800 sq km/11,117 sq mi; population

Luxembourg
Grand Duchy of
(Grand-Duché de Luxembourg)

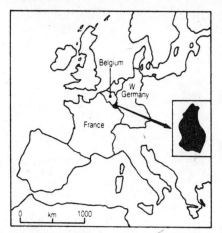

area 2,586 sq km/998 sq mi
capital Luxembourg
physical on the river Moselle; part of the Ardennes (Oesling) forest in the north
features Rupert Murdoch's television satellite Astra is based here

head of state Grand Duke Jean from 1964
head of government Jacques Santer from 1984
political system liberal democracy
political parties Christian Social Party (PCS), moderate, left-of-centre; Luxembourg Socialist Workers' Party (POSL), moderate, socialist; Democratic Party (PD), centre-left; Communist Party of Luxembourg, pro-European left-wing
exports pharmaceuticals, synthetic textiles; international banking is important; Luxembourg is economically linked with Belgium
currency Luxembourg franc (59.60 = £1 Feb 1990)
population (1989) 380,000; annual growth rate 0%
life expectancy men 68, women 74
language French (official); local Letzeburgesch; German
religion Roman Catholic
literacy 100% (1983)
GDP $3.8 bn (1981); $10,444 per head of population
chronology
1948 With Belgium and the Netherlands formed the Benelux customs union.
1958 Benelux became economic union.
1961 Prince Jean became acting head of state on behalf of his mother, Grand Duchess Charlotte.
1964 Grand Duchess Charlotte abdicated and Prince Jean became grand duke.

(1986) 1,367,000. The capital is Khorramabad. The province is inhabited by Lur tribes who live by their sheep and cattle. Excavation in the area has revealed a culture of the 8th–7th centuries BC with bronzes decorated with animal forms; its origins are uncertain.

Lusaka capital of Zambia from 1964 (of Northern Rhodesia 1935–64), 370 km/230 mi NE of Livingstone; commercial and agricultural centre (flour mills, tobacco factories, vehicle assembly, plastics, printing); population (1987) 819,000.

Lüshun-Dalien see ◊Lüda, port in China.

Lusitania an area of the Iberian peninsula, roughly equivalent to modern Portugal. Conquered by Rome in 139 BC, the province of Lusitania rebelled periodically until final conquest by Pompey 73–72 BC.

Lü-ta former name of ◊Lüda, port in China.

Luton industrial town in Bedfordshire, England, 53 km/33 mi SW of Cambridge; population (1985) 165,000. Luton airport is a secondary one for London. Manufacturing includes cars, chemicals, electrical goods, ballbearings, and, traditionally, hats. Luton Hoo, a Robert Adam mansion, was built in 1762.

Lützen town in Halle county, East Germany, SW of Leipzig, where in 1632 Gustavus Adolphus, king of Sweden, defeated the German commander Wallenstein in the Thirty Years' War; Gustavus was killed in the battle. Napoleon overcame the Russians and Prussians here in 1813.

Luxembourg capital of Luxembourg; population (1985) 76,000. The 16th-century Grand Ducal Palace, European Court of Justice, and European Parliament secretariat are situated here, but plenary sessions of the parliament are now held only in ◊Strasbourg. Products include steel, chemicals, textiles, and processed food.

Luxembourg landlocked country in W Europe, bordered to the N and W by Belgium, E by West Germany, and S by France.

Luxembourg province of Belgium; capital Arlon; area 4,400 sq km/1,698 sq mi; population (1987) 227,000.

Luxor (Arabic *al-Uqsur*) village in Egypt on the E bank of the Nile near the ruins of ◊Thebes.

Luzern German name of ◊Lucerne, town and lake in Switzerland.

Luzon largest island of the ◊Philippines; area 108,130 sq km/41,750 sq mi; capital Quezon

City; population (1970) 18,001,270. The chief city is Manila, capital of the Philippines. Products include rice, timber, and minerals. It has US military bases.

Lvov (Ukrainian *Lviv*) capital and industrial city of Lvov region in the Ukrainian Republic, USSR; population (1987) 767,000. Industries include textiles, metals, and engineering. The university was founded 1661. It was formerly an important centre on the Black Sea-Baltic trade route.

Lvov, founded in the 13th century by a Galician prince (the name means city of Leo or Lev), was Polish 1340–1772, Austrian 1772–1919, Polish 1919–39, and annexed by the USSR 1945. It was the site of violent nationalist demonstrations in Oct 1989.

Lwów Polish form of ◊Lvov, city in Ukraine, USSR.

Lyme Regis seaport and resort in Dorset, S England; population (1981) 3,500. The rebel duke of Monmouth landed here in 1685. The Cobb (a massive stone pier) features in Jane Austen's *Persuasion* 1818 and John Fowles's *The French Lieutenant's Woman* 1969.

Lymington port and yachting centre in Hampshire, S England; 8 km/5 mi SW of Southampton; population (1981) 39,698. It has a ferry link with the Isle of Wight.

Lynn industrial city in Massachusetts, USA, on Massachusetts Bay; population (1980) 78,471. Founded as *Saugus* in 1629, it was renamed 1637 after King's Lynn, England.

Lyon (English *Lyons*) industrial city (textiles, chemicals, machinery, printing) and capital of Rhône *département*, Rhône-Alpes region, and third largest city of France, at the confluence of the Rhône and Saône, 275 km/170 mi NNW of Marseille; population (1982) 418,476, conurbation 1,221,000. Formerly a chief fortress of France, it was the ancient *Lugdunum*, taken by the Romans 43 BC.

Lyons English form of ◊Lyon, city in France.

Lytham St Annes resort in Lancashire, England, on the river Ribble; 10 km/6 mi SE of Blackpool; population (1982) 39,641. It has a championship golf course.

Maas Dutch or Flemish name for the river ◊Meuse.

Maastricht industrial city (metallurgy, textiles, pottery) and capital of the province of Limburg, Netherlands, on the river Maas, near the Dutch-Belgian frontier; population (1988) 160,000. Maastricht dates from Roman times.

Macao Portuguese possession on the south coast of China, about 65 km/40 mi west of Hong Kong, from which it is separated by the estuary of the Canton River; it consists of a peninsula and the islands of Taipa and Colôane

area 17 sq km/7 sq mi

capital Macao, on the peninsula

features the peninsula is linked to Taipa by a bridge and to Colôane by a causeway, both 2 km long

government internal self-government with a consultative council and a legislative council

Macao

under a Portuguese governor. Under the constitution (organic statute) of 1976, Macao enjoys considerable political autonomy. The Portuguese president controls the colony's external affairs but appoints, in consultation with the local legislative assembly, a governor to exercise control over domestic matters. The governor works with a cabinet of five appointed secretaries and confers with a ten-member consultative council and a 17-member legislative council, both composed of a mixture of elected and nominated members. The legislative council frames internal legislation, but any bills passed by less than a two-thirds majority can be vetoed by the governor. A number of 'civic associations' and interest groups function, sending representatives to the legislative council

currency pataca

population (1986) 426,000

language Cantonese; Portuguese (official)

religion Buddhist, with 6% Catholic minority

history Macao was first established as a Portuguese trading and missionary post in the Far East 1537, and was leased from China 1557. It was annexed 1849 and recognized as a Portuguese colony by the Chinese government in a treaty 1887. The port declined in prosperity during the late 19th and early 20th centuries, as its harbour silted up and international trade was diverted to Hong Kong and the new treaty ports. The colony thus concentrated instead on local 'country trade' and became a centre for gambling and, later, tourism.

In 1951 Macao became an overseas province of Portugal, sending an elected representative to the Lisbon parliament. After the Portuguese revolution 1974, it became a 'special territory' and was granted considerable autonomy.

In 1986 negotiations opened between the Portuguese and the Chinese government over the question of the return of Macao's sovereignty under similar 'one country, two systems' terms to those agreed by China and the UK for ◊Hong Kong. These negotiations proved successful and were concluded Apr 1987 by the signing of the Macao Pact, under which Portugal agreed to hand over sovereignty to the People's Republic Dec 1999, and China agreed in return to guarantee to maintain the port's capitalist economic and social system for at least 50 years.

Macassar another name for ◊Ujung Pandang, port in Sulawesi, Indonesia.

Macclesfield industrial town (textiles, light engineering, paper, plastics) in Cheshire, NW England; population (1986) 151,800.

Macdonnell Ranges mountain range in central Australia, Northern Territory, with the town of Alice Springs; highest peak Mount Zeil 1,510 m/4,955 ft.

Madagascar
Democratic Republic of
*(Repoblika Demokratika n'i
Madagaskar)*

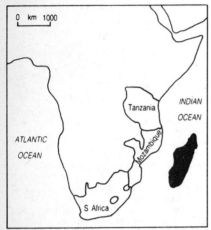

area 587,041 sq km/226,598 sq mi
capital Antananarivo
towns chief port Toamasina
physical central highlands; humid valleys and
coastal plains
features one of the last places in the world to
be inhabited, it evolved in isolation with unique
animals, for example the lemur, now under
threat from destruction of the forests
head of state and government Didier
Ratsiraka from 1975

government one-party socialist republic
political parties National Front for the Defence
of the Malagasy Socialist Revolution (FNDR)
exports coffee, sugar, spice, textiles
currency Malagasy franc (2,500 = £1 Mar
1989)
population (1988) 10,919,000; annual growth
rate 2.8%
life expectancy men 49, women 50
language Malagasy (of the Malayo-Polynesian
family, official); French and English
religion animist 50%, Christian 40%, Muslim
10%
literacy 74% male/62% female (1985 est)
GNP $2.7 bn (1983); $279 per head of
population
chronology
1960 Achieved full independence, with Philibert
Tsiranana as president.
1972 Army took control of the government.
1975 Martial law imposed under a national
military directorate. New constitution proclaimed
the Democratic Republic of Madagascar, with
Didier Ratsiraka as president.
1976 Front-Line Revolutionary Organisation
(AREMA) formed.
1977 National Front for the Defence of the
Malagasy Socialist Revolution (FNDR) became
the sole legal political organization.
1983 Ratsiraka re-elected, despite strong
opposition from radical socialist National Movement for the Independence of Madagascar
(MONIMA) under Monja Jaona.
1989 Ratsiraka re-elected for third term.

Macedonia ancient region of Greece, forming parts of modern Greece, Bulgaria, and Yugoslavia. Macedonia gained control of Greece after Philip II's victory at Chaeronea in 338 BC. His son, Alexander the Great, conquered a vast empire. Macedonia became a Roman province in 146 BC.

Macedonia (Greek *Makedhonia*) mountainous region of N Greece, bounded to the W and N by Albania and Yugoslavia; population(1981) 2,122,000; area 34,177 sq km/13,200 sq mi. Chief city is Thessaloniki. Fertile valleys produce grain, olives, grapes, tobacco and livestock. Mt Olympus rises to 2,918 m/9,570 ft on the border with Thessaly.

Macedonia (Serbo-Croat *Makedonija*) a federal republic of Yugoslavia
area 25,700 sq km/9,920 sq mi
capital Skopje
physical mountainous; chief rivers Struma and Vardar
population (1981) 2,040,000, including 1,280,000 Macedonians, 380,000 Albanians, and 90,000 Turks
language Macedonian, closely allied to Bulgarian and written in Cyrillic
religion Macedonian Orthodox Christian
history Macedonia was an ancient country of SE Europe between Illyria, Thrace, and the Aegean Sea; settled by Slavs in the 6th century; conquered by Bulgars in the 7th century, by Byzantium 1014, by Serbia in the 14th century, and by the Ottoman Empire 1355; divided between Serbia, Bulgaria, and Greece after the Balkan Wars of 1912–13.

Maceió industrial town (sugar, tobacco, textile, timber industries) in NE Brazil, capital of Alagaos state with its port at Jaraguá; population (1980) 375,800.

Macgillycuddy's Reeks a range of mountains in SW Ireland lying W of Killarney, in County Kerry; includes Carrantuohill 1,041 m/3,414 ft, the highest peak in Ireland.

Machu Picchu a ruined Inca city in Peru, built *c.*AD 1500, NW of Cuzco, discovered in 1911 by Hiram Bingham. It stands at the top of 300 m/1,000 ft high cliffs, and contains the well-preserved remains of houses and temples.

Macias Nguema former name (until 1979) of ◊Bioko, an island of Equatorial Guinea in the Bight of Bonny, West Africa.

Mackenzie River river in the Northwest Territories, Canada, flowing from Great Slave Lake NW to the Arctic Ocean; about 1,800 km/1,120 mi long. It is the main channel of the Finlay-Peace-Mackenzie system, 4,241 km/2,635 mi long. It was named after the British explorer Alexander Mackenzie, who saw it 1789.

McKinley, Mount peak in Alaska, USA, the highest in North America, 6,194 m/20,320 ft; named after US president William McKinley. It is part of the ◊Rocky Mountains.

Mâcon capital of the French *département* of Saône-et-Loire, on the Saône, 72 km/45 mi N of Lyons; population (1983) 39,000. It produces wine. Mâcon dates from ancient Gaul, when it was known as Matisco. The French writer Lamartine was born here.

Madagascar island country in the Indian Ocean, off the coast of E Africa, about 400 km/280 mi from Mozambique.

Madeira group of islands forming an autonomous region of Portugal off the NW coast of Africa, about 420 km/260 mi N of the Canary Islands. Madeira, the largest, and Porto Santo are the only inhabited islands. The Desertas and Selvagens are uninhabited islets. Their mild climate makes them an all-year-round resort.
area 796 sq km/308 sq mi
capital Funchal, on Madeira

Madeira

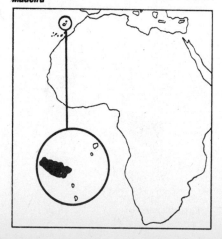

Madhya Pradesh

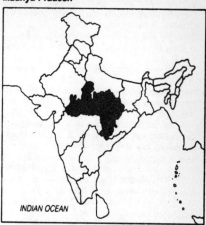

INDIAN OCEAN

physical Pico Ruivo, on Madeira, is the highest mountain at 1,861 m/6,056 ft
products madeira (a fortified wine), sugar cane, fruit, fish, handicrafts
population (1986) 269,500
history Portuguese from the 15th century; occupied by Britain in 1801 and 1807–14. In 1980 Madeira gained partial autonomy but remains a Portuguese overseas territory.

Madeira River river of W Brazil; length 3,250 km/2,020 mi. It is formed by the rivers Beni and Mamoré, and flows NE to join the Amazon.

Madhya Bharat state of India 1950–56. It was a union of 24 states of which Gwalior and ◊Indore were the most important. In 1956 Madhya Bharat was absorbed in ◊Madhya Pradesh.

Madhya Pradesh state of central India
area 442,800 sq km/170,921 sq mi
capital Bhopal
towns Indore, Jabalpur, Gwalior, Durg-Bhilainagar, Raipur, Ujjain
features it is the largest of the states
products cotton, oilseed, sugar, textiles, engineering, paper, aluminium
population (1981) 52,132,000
language Hindi
history formed 1950 from the former British province of Central Provinces and Berar and the princely states of Makrai and Chattisgarh. In 1956 it lost some SW districts, including ◊Nagpur, and absorbed Bhopal, Madhya Bharat, and Vindhya Pradesh.

Madison capital of Wisconsin, USA, 193 km/120 mi NW of Chicago, between lakes Mendota and Monona; population (1980) 323,545; products include agricultural machinery and medical equipment.

Madras industrial port (cotton, cement, chemicals, iron and steel) and capital of Tamil Nadu, India, on the Bay of Bengal; population (1981) 4,277,000. Fort St George 1639 remains from the East India Company when Madras was the chief port on the E coast. Madras was occupied by the French 1746–48, and shelled by the German ship *Emden* in 1914, the only place in India attacked in World War I.

Madras former name of ◊Tamil Nadu, state of India.

Madrid industrial city (leather, chemicals, furniture, tobacco, paper) and capital of Spain and Madrid province; population (1986) 3,124,000. Built on an elevated plateau in the centre of the country, at 655 m/2,183 ft it is the highest capital city in Europe and has excesses of heat and cold. Madrid province has an area of 8,000 sq km/3,088 sq mi, and a population of 4,855,000. Madrid began as a Moorish citadel captured by Castile 1083, became important in the times of Charles V and Philip II and was designated capital 1561.

Features include the Real Academia de Bellas Artes 1752, the Prado Museum 1785, and the royal palace 1764. During the civil war Madrid was besieged by the Nationalists 7 Nov 1936–28 Mar 1939.

Madura an island in Indonesia, off Surabaya, Java; one of the Sunda Islands
area 4,564 sq km/1,762 sq mi; with offshore islands, more than 5,000 sq km/2,000 sq mi
capital Pamekasan
features central hills rising to 4,800 m/1,545 ft; forested
products rice, tobacco, salt, cattle, fish
population (1970) 2,447,000
history See ◊Java.

Madurai city in Tamil Nadu, India; site of the 16th–17th century Hindu temple of Sundareswara, and of Madurai University 1966; cotton industry; population (1981) 904,000.

Maeander anglicized form of the ancient Greek name of the river ◊Menderes in Turkey.

Maestricht alternative form of ◊Maastricht, city in the Netherlands.

Mafeking former name of ◊Mafikeng, town in South Africa, incorporated into Bophuthatswana in 1980.

Mafikeng town (until 1980 Mafeking) in Bophuthatswana, South Africa; it was the capital of Bechuanaland, and the British officer Baden-Powell held it under Boer siege 12 Oct 1899–17 May 1900.

Magadan port for the gold mines in East Siberia, USSR, off the N shore of the Sea of Okhotsk; population (1985) 142,000.

Magdeburg industrial city (vehicles, paper, chemicals, iron, steel, textiles, machinery) and port on the river Elbe, in East Germany, capital of Magdeburg county; population (1986) 289,000. Magdeburg was a member of the Hanseatic League, and

has a 13th-century Gothic cathedral. Magdeburg county has an area of 11,530 sq km/4,451 sq mi, and a population of 1,250,000.

Magellan, Strait of channel between South America and Tierra del Fuego, named after the navigator. It is 595 km/370 mi long, and joins the Atlantic and Pacific Oceans.

Magenta town in Lombardy, Italy, 24 km/15 mi W of Milan, where France and Sardinia defeated Austria in 1859 during the struggle for Italian independence. Magenta dye was named in honour of the victory.

Maggiore, Lago lake partly in Italy, partly in Swiss canton of Ticino, with Locarno on its N shore; 63 km/39 mi long and up to 9 km/5.5 mi wide (area 212 sq km/ 82 sq mi), with fine scenery.

Maghreb name for NW Africa (Arabic 'far west', 'sunset'). The Maghreb powers – Algeria, Libya, Morocco, Tunisia, and Western Sahara – agreed on economic coordination 1964–65, with Mauritania cooperating from 1970. Chad and Mali are sometimes included. The NE African countries form part of ◊Mashraq.

Magnitogorsk industrial town (steel, motor vehicles, tractors, railway rolling stock) in Chelyabinsk region, USSR, on the E slopes of the Ural Mountains; population (1987) 430,000. It was developed in the 1930s to work iron, manganese, bauxite, and other metals in the district.

Mahabad Kurdish town in Azerbaijan, W Iran, population (1983) 63,000. Occupied by Russian troops in 1941, it formed the centre of a short-lived Kurdish republic (1945–46) before being reoccupied by the Iranians. In the 1980s Mahabad was the focal point of resistance by Iranian Kurds against the Islamic republic.

Maharashtra state in W central India
area 307,800 sq km/118,811 sq mi
capital Bombay

Maharashtra

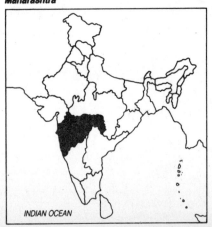

INDIAN OCEAN

towns Pune, Nagpur, Ulhasnagar, Sholapur, Nasik, Thana, Kolhapur, Aurangabad, Sangli, Amravati

features cave temples of Ajanta, containing 200 BC–7th century AD Buddhist murals and sculptures; Ellora cave temples 6th–9th century with Buddhist, Hindu, and Jain sculptures

products cotton, rice, groundnuts, sugar, minerals

population (1981) 62,694,000

language Marathi 50%

religion Hindu 80%, Parsee, Jain, and Sikh minorities

history formed 1960 from the southern part of the former Bombay state.

Mahón or *Port Mahon* capital and port of the Spanish island of Minorca; population (1981) 21,900. Probably founded by the Carthaginians, it was in British occupation 1708–56 and 1762–82.

Maidenhead town in Berkshire, S England, 40 km/ 25 mi W of London, on the river Thames; boating centre; it manufactures computer software, plastics, pharmaceuticals, and has a printing industry. Population (1983) 48,473.

Maidstone town in Kent, SE England, on the river Medway, administrative headquarters of the county; prison, law courts; population (1986) 133,700. Industries include agricultural machinery and paper. Maidstone has the ruins of All Saints' College 1260. The Elizabethan Chillington Manor is an art gallery and museum.

Maiduguri capital of Borno state, NE Nigeria; population (1983) 230,900.

Maikop capital of Adyge autonomous region of the USSR on the river Bielaia, with timber mills, distilleries, tanneries, and tobacco and furniture factories; population (1985) 140,000. Oilfields, discovered in 1900, are linked by pipeline with Tapse on the Black Sea.

Main river in central West Germany, flowing through Frankfurt to join the river Rhine at Mainz. A canal links it with the Danube. Length 515 km/320 mi.

Maine old French province bounded on the N by Normandy, on the W by Brittany, and on the S by Anjou. The modern *département*s of Sarthe and Mayenne approximately correspond with it.

Maine French river, 11 km/7 mi long, formed by the junction of the Mayenne and Sarthe; it enters the Loire below Angers, and gives its name to Maine-et-Loire *département*.

Maine northeasternmost state of the USA, largest of the New England states; nickname Pine Tree State

area 86,200 sq km/33,273 sq mi

capital Augusta

towns Portland, Lewiston, Bangor

physical Appalachian Mountains; Acadia National Park; 80% of the state is forested

products dairy and market garden produce, paper, pulp, timber, textiles; tourism and fishing are also important

Maine

population (1986) 1,174,000

famous people Longfellow, Edna St Vincent Millay, Kate Douglas Wiggin

history settled from 1623, it became a state 1820.

Mainz (French *Mayence*) capital of Rhineland-Palatinate, West Germany, on the Rhine, 37 km/ 23 mi WSW of Frankfurt-am-Main; population (1988) 189,000. In Roman times it was a fortified camp and became the capital of Germania Superior. Printing was possibly invented here about 1448 by Gutenberg.

Majorca (Spanish *Mallorca*) largest of the ◊Balearic Islands, belonging to Spain, in the W Mediterranean

area 3,640 sq km/1,405 sq mi

capital Palma

features the highest mountain is Puig Mayor 1,445 m/4,741 ft

products olives, figs, oranges, wine, brandy, timber, sheep; tourism is the mainstay of the economy

population (1981) 561,215

history captured 797 by the Moors, it became the kingdom of Majorca 1276, and was united with Aragon in 1343.

Makeyevka formerly (until 1931) *Dmitrievsk* city in the Donets Basin, SE Ukraine, USSR; population (1987) 455,000. Industries include coal, iron, steel, and chemicals.

Makhachkala formerly (until 1922) *Port Petrovsk* capital of Dagestan, USSR, on the Caspian Sea, ESE of Grozny, from which pipelines bring petroleum to Makhachkala's refineries; population (1987) 320,000. Other industries include shipbuilding, meat packing, chemicals, matches, and cotton textiles.

Malabar Coast the coastal area of Karnataka and Kerala states, India, lying between the Arabian Sea and the Western Ghats; about 65 km/40 mi W to E, 725 km/450 mi N to S. A fertile area with heavy rains, it produces food grains, coconuts, rubber, spices; teak, ebony, and other woods. Lagoons fringe the shore. It includes a district transferred in 1956 to Kerala from Tamil Nadu.

Malawi
Republic of
(Malawi) former name
Nyasaland

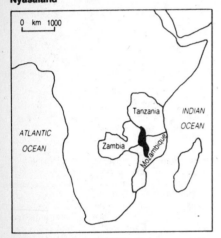

0 km 1000

ATLANTIC
OCEAN

Tanzania INDIAN
OCEAN

Zambia

Mozambique

area 118,000 sq km/45,560 sq mi
capital Lilongwe
towns Blantyre-Limbe
physical occupies the mountainous west side of Lake Malawi
features Livingstonia National Park on the Nyika Plateau in the north, rich in orchids, arthropods, elephants; Shiré Highlands, noted for tea and tobacco, and rising to 1,750 m/5,750 ft.
head of state and government Hastings Kamusu Banda from 1966 for life
government one-party republic
political parties Malawi Congress Party (MCP), multi-racial, right-wing
exports tea, tobacco, cotton, groundnuts, sugar
currency kwacha (4.42 = £1 Feb 1990)
population (1985) 7,059,000; annual growth rate 3.1%; Malawi contains a refugee population of about 500,000 in camps and possibly as many settled among local people. About 70,000 refugees crossed the border Sept 1986.
life expectancy men 44, women 46
language English (official); Chichewa
religion Christian 50%; Muslim 30%
literacy 52% male/31% female (1985 est)
GNP $1.1 bn (1984); $200 per head of population
chronology
1964 Nyasaland achieved independence, within the Commonwealth, as Malawi.
1966 Became a one-party republic, with Hastings Banda as president.
1971 Banda was made president for life.
1977 Banda started a programme of moderate liberalization, releasing some political detainees and allowing greater freedom of the press.
1986–89 Influx of over 650,000 refugees from Mozambique.

Malabo port and capital of Equatorial Guinea, on the island of Bioko; population (1983) 15,253. It was founded in the 1820s by the British as *Port Clarence*. Under Spanish rule it was known as *Santa Isabel* (until 1973).

Malacca or *Melaka* state of W Peninsular Malaysia; capital Malacca; area 1,700 sq km/656 sq mi; population (1980) 465,000 (about 70% Chinese). Products include rubber, tin, and wire. The town originated in the 13th century as a fishing village frequented by pirates, and later developed into a trading port. Portuguese from 1511, then Dutch from 1641, it was ceded to Britain 1824, becoming part of the Straits Settlements.

Malacca, Strait of channel between Sumatra and the Malay Peninsula; length 965 km/600 mi; narrows to less than 38 km/24 mi wide. It carries all shipping between the Indian Ocean and the South China Sea.

Málaga industrial seaport (sugar refining, distilling, brewing, olive-oil pressing, shipbuilding) and holiday resort in Andalusia, Spain; capital of Málaga province on the Mediterranean; population (1986) 595,000. Founded by the Phoenicians and taken by the Moors 711, Málaga was capital of the Moorish kingdom of Malaga from the 13th century until captured 1487 by Ferdinand and Isabella.

Malagasy Republic former name (1958–75) of ◊Madagascar.

Malatya capital of a province of the same name in E central Turkey, lying W of the river Euphrates; population (1985) 251,000.

Malawi country in SE Africa, bordered N and NE by Tanzania, E, S, and W by Mozambique, and W by Zambia.

Malawi, Lake or *Lake Nyasa* African lake, bordered by Malawi, Tanzania, and Mozambique, formed in a section of the Great ◊Rift Valley. It is about 500 m/1,650 ft above sea level and 560 km/350 mi long, with an area of 37,000 sq km/14,280 sq mi. It is intermittently drained to the south by the river Shiré into the Zambezi.

Malay Peninsula southern projection of the continent of Asia, lying between the Strait of Malacca,

Malaysia

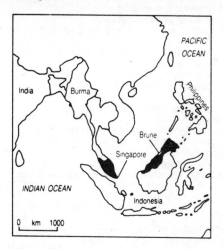

PACIFIC
OCEAN

India   Burma

Philippines

Brune

Singapore

INDIAN OCEAN

Indonesia

0   km   1000

area 329,759 sq km/127,287
sq mi
capital Kuala Lumpur
towns Kuching in Sarawak and Kota Kinabalu
in Sabah
physical comprises W Malaysia (the nine
Malay states – Perlis, Kedah, Johore, Selangor,
Perak, Negri Sembilan, Kelantan, Trengganu,
Pahang – plus Penang and Malacca); and E
Malaysia (Sarawak and Sabah); 75% of the
area tropical jungle; a central mountain range;
swamps in the E
head of state Rajah Azlan Muhibuddin Shah
(sultan of Perak) from 1989
head of government Mahathir bin Mohamad
from 1981
political system liberal democracy
political parties New United Malay's National

Organization (UMNO Baru) Malay-orientated
nationalist; Malaysian Chinese Association
(MCA), Chinese-orientated conservative;
Gerakan, Chinese-orientated left-of-centre;
Malaysian Indian Congress (MIC),
Indian-orientated; Democratic Action Party
(DAP), left-of-centre multi-racial, though Chinese
dominated; Pan-Malayan Islamic Party (PAS),
Islamic; Semangat '46, moderate, multi-racial.
exports pineapples, palm oil, rubber, timber,
petroleum (Sarawak), bauxite
currency ringgit (4.60 = £1 Feb 1990)
population (1988) 16,968,000 (Malaysian
47%, Chinese 32%, Indian 8%, and indigenous
peoples – Dayaks, Ibans – of E Malaysia 10%);
annual growth rate 2.5%
life expectancy men 65, women 69
language Malay (official, usually written in
Arabic characters); in Sarawak English is also
official
religion Muslim (official)
literacy 81% male/66% female (1985 est)
GNP $29.7 bn (1983); $714 per head of
population
chronology
1963 Formation of federation of Malaysia.
1965 Secession of Singapore from federation.
1969 Anti-Chinese riots in Kuala Lumpur.
1971 Launch of Bumiputra 'new economic
policy'.
1981 Election of Dr Mahathir bin Mohamad as
prime minister.
1982 Mahathir bin Mohamad re-elected.
1986 Mahathir bin Mohamad re-elected.
1987 Arrest of opposition DAP leader as
Malay-Chinese relations deteriorate.
1988 Split in ruling UMNO party over Mahathir's
leadership style; new UMNO formed.
1989 Semangat '46 set up by former members
of UMNO including ex-premier Tunku Abdul
Rahman.

which divides it from Sumatra, and the China Sea.
The northern portion is partly in Burma, partly
in Thailand; the south forms part of ◊Malaysia.
The island of Singapore lies off its southern
extremity.
Malaysia country in SE Asia, comprising the Malay
Peninsula, bordered to the N by Thailand, and surrounded E, S, and W by the South China Sea; and
the states of Sabah and Sarawak in the northern
part of the island of Borneo (S Borneo is part of
Indonesia).
Maldives country comprising a group of 1,196
islands in the N Indian Ocean, about 640 km/
400 mi SW of Sri Lanka, only 203 of which are
inhabited.

Maldon English market town in Essex, at the mouth
of the river Chelmer; population (1981) 14,750.
It was the scene of a battle in which the East
Saxons were defeated by the Danes in 991, com-
memorated in the Anglo-Saxon poem *The Battle of
Maldon.*
Malé capital of the Maldives in the Indian Ocean;
population (1985) 38,000. It trades in copra,
breadfruit, and palm products.
Mali landlocked country in NW Africa, bordered to
the NE by Algeria, E by Niger, SE by Burkina
Faso, S by the Ivory Coast, SW by Senegal and
Guinea, and W and N by Mauritania.
Malines French name for ◊Mechelen, city in Bel-
gium.

Maldives
Republic of
(Divehi Jumhuriya)

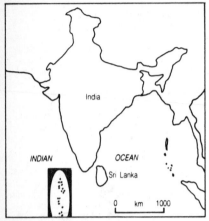

India

INDIAN   OCEAN

Sri Lanka

0   km   1000

area 298 sq km/115 sq mi
capital Malé
physical comprises 1,200 coral islands
grouped into 12 clusters of atolls, largely flat,
none bigger than 13 sq km/5 sq mi
features only about 200 of the islands are
inhabited
head of state and government Maumoon

Abdul Gayoom from 1978
political system authoritarian nationalism
political parties none; candidates elected
on the basis of personal influence and clan
loyalties
exports coconuts, copra, bonito (fish related to
tuna); tourism
currency Rufiya (16.00 = £1 Feb 1990)
population (1988) 200,000; annual growth
rate 3.2%
language Divehi (related to Sinhalese)
religion Islam
literacy 82% male/82% female (1977)
GNP $56 million (1983); $470 per head of
population
chronology
1953 Originally a sultanate, the Maldive Islands
became a republic within the Commonwealth.
1954 Sultanate restored.
1965 Achieved full independence outside the
Commonwealth.
1968 Sultan deposed and a republic reinstated
with Ibrahim Nasir as president.
1978 Nasir retired and was replaced by
Maumoon Abdul Gayoom.
1983 Gayoom re-elected.
1985 Rejoined the Commonwealth.
1988 Gayoom re-elected. Coup attempt by
mercenaries thought to have the backing of
former president Nasir was foiled by Indian
paratroops.

Mallorca Spanish form of ◊Majorca, an island in the Mediterranean.

Malmédy town in Liège, E Belgium 40 km/25 mi S of Aachen, in the region of Eupen et Malmédy.

Malmö industrial port (shipbuilding, engineering, textiles) in SW Sweden; population (1988) 231,000.

Malta island in the Mediterranean, S of Sicily, E of Tunisia, and N of Libya.

Maluku or *Moluccas* group of Indonesian islands
area 74,500 sq km/28,764 sq mi
capital Ambon, on Amboina
population (1980) 1,411,000
history as the Spice Islands, they were formerly part of the Netherlands East Indies, and the S Moluccas attempted secession from the newly created Indonesian republic from 1949; exiles continue agitation in the Netherlands.

Malvern English spa in Hereford and Worcester, on the E side of the *Malvern Hills*, which extend for about 16 km/10 mi, and have their high point in Worcester Beacon 425 m/1,395 ft; population (1981) 32,000.

Malvinas Argentinian name for the ◊Falkland Islands.

Mammoth Cave huge limestone cavern in Mammoth Cave National Park 1936, Kentucky, USA. The main cave is 6.5 km/4 mi long, and rises to a height of 38 m/125 ft; it is known for its stalactites and stalagmites. Indian councils were once held here.

Man. abbreviation for ◊*Manitoba.*

Managua capital and chief industrial city of Nicaragua, on the lake of the same name; population (1985) 682,000. It has twice been destroyed by earthquake and rebuilt, in 1931 and 1972; it was also badly damaged by civil war in the late 1970s.

Manama (Arabic *Al Manamah*) capital and free trade port of Bahrain, on Bahrain Island; handles oil and entrepôt trade; population (1988) 152,000.

Manaus capital of Amazonas, Brazil, on the Rio Negro, near its confluence with the Amazon; population (1980) 612,000. It can be reached by sea-going vessels, although 1,600 km/1,000 mi from the Atlantic. Formerly a centre of the rubber trade, it developed as a tourist centre in the 1970s.

Manawatu river in North Island, New Zealand, rising in the Ruahine Range. *Manawatu Plain* is a rich farming area, specializing in dairying and fat lamb production.

Mali

Republic of
(République du Mali)

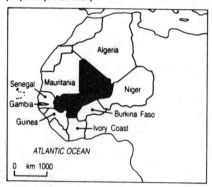

area 1,240,142 sq km/478,695 sq mi
capital Bamako
physical river Niger in S; savanna; part of the
Sahara in N
features the old town of Timbuktu
head of state and government Moussa Traoré
from 1968
political system one-party republic

political parties Malian People's Democratic
Union (UDPM), nationalist
exports cotton, groundnuts, livestock
currency CFA franc (replacing Mali franc 1984)
(485.00 = £1 Feb 1990)
population (1988) 7,784,000; annual growth
rate 2.8%
life expectancy men 40, women 44
language French (official), Bambara
religion Sunni Muslim 65%, animist 35%
literacy 23% male/11% female (1985 est)
GNP $1.1 bn (1983); $140 per head of
population
chronology
1959 With Senegal, formed the Federation
of Mali.
1960 Became the independent Republic of
Mali, with Mobido Keita as president.
1968 Keita replaced in an army coup by
Moussa Traoré.
1974 New constitution made Mali a one-party
state.
1976 New national party, the Malian People's
Democratic Union, announced.
1983 Agreement between Mali and Guinea
for eventual political and economic integration
signed.

Mancha see ◊La Mancha, former province of Spain.
Manche, La French name for the English ◊Channel.
It gives its name to a French *département*.
Manchester port in NW England, on the river Irwell,
50 km/31 mi E of Liverpool. It is a manufacturing
(textile machinery, chemicals, rubber, processed
foods) and financial centre; population (1985)
451,000. It is linked by the Manchester Ship
Canal, built 1894, to the river Mersey and the sea
features home of the Hallé Orchestra, the Royal
Northern College of Music, the Royal Exchange
(built 1869, now a theatre), a town hall (by Alfred
Waterhouse), and a Cotton Exchange (now a leisure centre)
history originally a Roman camp, Manchester is
mentioned in the Domesday Book, and already
by the 13th century was a centre for the wool
trade. Its damp climate made it ideal for cotton,
introduced in the 16th century, and in the 19th
century the Manchester area was a world centre
of manufacture, using cotton imported from North
America and India. After 1945 there was a sharp
decline, and many disused mills were refurbished
to provide alternative industrial uses.

Long a hub of Radical thought, Manchester has
always been a cultural and intellectual centre; it
was the original home of the *Guardian* (founded
as the *Manchester Guardian* 1821). Its pop-music
scene flourished in the 1980s.

Manchester, Greater former (1974–86) metropolitan county of NW England, replaced by a residuary body in 1986 which covers some of its former
functions
area 1,290 sq km/498 sq mi
towns administrative headquarters Manchester;
Bolton, Oldham, Rochdale, Salford, Stockport,
and Wigan
features Manchester Ship Canal links it with the
Mersey and the sea; Old Trafford cricket ground
at Stretford, and the football ground of Manchester
United
products industrial
population (1987) 2,580,000
famous people Anthony Burgess, John Dalton,
Gracie Fields, James Joule, Emmeline Pankhurst.
Mandalay chief town of Upper Myanmar, on the
river Irrawaddy, about 495 km/370 mi N of
Yangon; population (1983) 533,000.
Founded by King Mindon Min in 1857, it was
capital of Burma 1857–85, and has many pagodas,
temples, and monasteries.
Mangalore industrial port (textiles, timber, food-
processing) at the mouth of the Netravati River
in Karnataka, S India; population (1981) 306,000.
Manhattan an island 20 km/12.5 mi long and 4 km/
2.5 mi wide, lying between the Hudson and East
rivers and forming a borough of the city of
◊New York, USA; population (1980) 1,428,000.

Malta

Republic of
(Repubblika Ta'Malta)

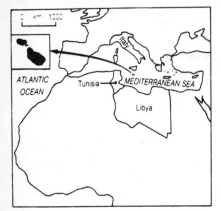

area 320 sq km/124 sq mi
capital Valletta
physical includes the island of Gozo
67 sq km/26 sq mi and Comino
2.5 sq km/1 sq mi
features large commercial dock facilities
head of state Vincent Tabone from 1989
head of government Edward Fenech Adami
from 1987
political system liberal democracy
political parties Malta Labour Party (MLP),
moderate, left-of-centre; Nationalist Party,
Christian, centrist, pro-European
exports vegetables, knitwear, handmade lace,
plastics, electronic equipment
currency Maltese pound (0.55 = £1 Feb 1990)
population (1987) 346,000; annual growth
rate 0.7%
life expectancy men 69, women 74
language Maltese (related to Arabic, with
Phoenician survivals and influenced by Italian)
religion Roman Catholic
literacy 86% male/82% female (1985 est)
GNP $1.04 bn (1983); $2,036 per head of
population
chronology
1942 Awarded the George Cross.
1955 Dom Mintoff of the Malta Labour Party
(MLP) became prime minister.
1956 Referendum approved proposal for
integration with the UK. Proposal opposed by
the Nationalist Party.
1958 MLP rejected the integration proposal.
1962 Nationalists elected, with Borg Olivier as
prime minister.
1964 Achieved full independence, within
the Commonwealth. Ten-year defence and
economic aid treaty with the UK signed.
1971 Mintoff re-elected. The 1964 treaty
declared invalid and negotiations began for the
leasing of the NATO base in Malta.
1972 Seven-year NATO agreement signed.
1974 Became a republic.
1984 Mintoff retired and was replaced by
Mifsud Bonnici as prime minister and MLP
leader.
1987 Edward Fenech Adami (Nationalist)
became prime minister.
1989 Vincent Tabone elected president.

It includes the Wall Street business centre and Broadway theatres.

Manila industrial port (textiles, tobacco, distilling, chemicals, shipbuilding) and capital of the Philippines, on the island of Luzon; population (1980) 1,630,000, metropolitan area (including ♢Quezon City) 5,926,000.

history Manila was founded 1571 by Spain, captured by the USA 1898, and in 1945 during World War II the old city to the south of the river Pasig was reduced to rubble in fighting between US and Japanese troops. It was replaced as capital by Quezon City 1948–76.

Manipur state of NE India
area 22,400 sq km/8,646 sq mi
capital Imphal
features Loktak Lake; original Indian home of polo

products grain, fruit, vegetables, sugar, textiles, cement
population (1981) 1,434,000
language Hindi
religion Hindu 70%
history administered from the state of Assam until 1947 when it became a Union Territory. It became a state 1972.

Man, Isle of island in the Irish Sea, a dependency of the British crown, but not part of the UK
area 570 sq km/220 sq mi
capital Douglas
towns Ramsey, Peel, Castletown
features Snaefell 620 m/2,035 ft; annual TT (Tourist Trophy) motorcycle races, gambling casinos, Britain's first free port, tax haven; tailless Manx cat; tourism, banking, and insurance are important
exports light engineering products

Maluku

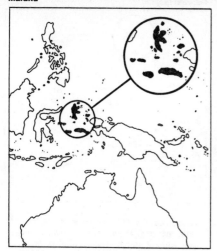

Manchester, Greater

currency the island produces its own coins and notes in UK currency denominations

population (1986) 64,000

language English (Manx, nearer to Scottish than Irish Gaelic, has been almost extinct since the 1970s)

government crown-appointed lieutenant-governor, a legislative council, and the representative House of Keys, which together make up the Court of Tynwald, passing laws subject to the royal assent. Laws passed at Westminster only affect the island if specifically so provided

history Norwegian until 1266, when the island was ceded to Scotland; it came under British administration 1765.

Manitoba prairie province of Canada

area 650,000 sq km/250,900 sq mi

capital Winnipeg

features lakes Winnipeg, Winnipegosis, and Manitoba (area 4,700 sq km/1,814 sq mi); 50% forested

exports grain, manufactured foods, beverages, machinery, furs, fish, nickel, zinc, copper, and the world's largest caesium deposits

population (1986) 1,071,000

history known as Red River settlement until it joined Canada 1870, it was the site of the Riel Rebellion 1885. The area of the province was extended 1881 and 1912.

Manitoba, Lake lake in Manitoba province, Canada, which drains into Lake Winnipeg to the NE through the river Dauphin; area 4,700 sq km/ 1,800 sq mi.

Manizales city in the Central Cordillera in W Colombia 2,150 m/7,000 ft above sea level, centre of a coffee-growing area; population (1985)

328,000. It is linked with Mariquita by the world's longest overhead cable transport system 72 km/ 45 mi.

Mannheim industrial city (heavy machinery, glass, earthenware, chemicals) on the Rhine in Baden-Württemberg, West Germany; population (1988) 295,000. The modern symphony orchestra, with its balance of instruments and the important role of the conductor, originated at Mannheim in the 18th century when the elector palatine assembled the finest players of his day.

Mansfield industrial town (textiles, shoes, machinery, chemicals, coal) in Nottinghamshire, England, on the river Maun, 22 km/14 mi N of Nottingham; population (1981) 59,000.

Manipur

INDIAN OCEAN

Manitoba

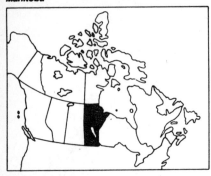

Mariana Islands

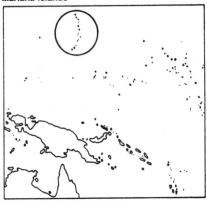

Manston RAF aerodrome in Kent, England, a major diversionary aerodrome for aircraft (civil or military) in distress.

Mansûra industrial town (cotton) and capital of Dakahlia province, NE Egypt, on the Damietta branch of the Nile; population (1983) 310,900. Mansûra was founded about 1220; St Louis IX, king of France, was imprisoned in the fortress while on a Crusade, 1250.

Mantua (Italian *Mantova*) capital of Mantua province, Lombardy, Italy, on an island of a lagoon of the river Mincio, SW of Verona; industry (chemicals, brewing, printing); population (1981) 60,866. The poet Virgil was born near Mantua, which dates from Roman times; it has Gothic palaces and a cathedral founded in the 12th century.

Maputo formerly (until 1975) *Lourenço Marques* capital of Mozambique, and Africa's second largest port, on Delagoa Bay; population (1986) 883,000. Linked by rail with Zimbabwe and South Africa, it is a major outlet for minerals, steel, textiles, processed foods, and furniture.

Maracaibo oil-exporting port in Venezuela, on the channel connecting Lake Maracaibo with the Gulf of Venezuela; population (1981) 889,000.

Maracaibo, Lake lake in a rich oil-producing region in NW Venezuela; area 14,000 sq km/5,400 sq mi.

Marburg manufacturing town (chemicals, machinery, pottery) in Hessen, West Germany, on the river Lahn, 80 km/50 mi N of Frankfurt-am-Main; population (1984) 77,300. The university 1527 was founded as a centre of Protestant teaching. Luther and Zwingli disputed on religion at Marburg in 1529.

Marche region of E central Italy consisting of the provinces of Ancona, Ascoli Piceno, Macerata, and Pesaro e Urbino; capital Ancona; area 9,700 sq km/3,744 sq mi; population (1988) 1,429,000.

marches the boundary areas of England with Wales, and England with Scotland. In the Middle Ages these troubled frontier regions were held by lords of the marches, sometimes called *marchiones* and later earls of March. The 1st Earl of March of the Welsh marches was Roger de Mortimer (*c*.1286–1330); of the Scottish marches, Patrick Dunbar (died 1285).

Margate town and seaside resort on the N coast of Kent, SE England; industry (textiles, scientific instruments); population (1981) 53,280. It has a fine promenade and sands.

Mari autonomous republic of the USSR, E of Gorky and W of the Urals
area 23,200 sq km/8,900 sq mi
capital Yoshkar-Ola
features the Volga flows through the SW; 60% is forested
products timber, paper; grain, flax, potatoes, fruit
population (1985) 725,000; about 43% are ethnic Mari
history the Mari were conquered by Russia in 1552. Mari was made an autonomous region 1920, an autonomous republic 1936.

Mariana Islands or *Marianas* archipelago in the NW Pacific, divided politically into ◊*Guam* and the *Northern Marianas*, a commonwealth in union with the USA of 16 mountainous islands, extending 560 km/350 mi north from Guam
area 480 sq km/185 sq mi
capital Garapan on Saipan
products sugar, coconuts, coffee
currency US dollar
population (1988) 21,000, mainly Micronesian
language 55% Chamorro, English
religion mainly Roman Catholic
government own constitutionally elected government
history sold to Germany by Spain 1899, the islands were mandated to Japan 1918, and taken by US Marines 1944–45 in World War II. They were under US trusteeship from 1947, and

Massachusetts

(1730–87) and Jeremiah Dixon (died 1777), English astronomers and surveyors who surveyed it 1763–67. It was popularly seen as dividing the North from the South.

Massachusetts New England state of the USA; nickname Bay State or Old Colony
area 21,500 sq km/8,299 sq mi
capital Boston
towns Worcester, Springfield, New Bedford, Brockton, Cambridge
features the two large Atlantic islands of Nantucket and Martha's Vineyard, former whaling centres; rivers Merrimac and Connecticut; University of Harvard 1636; Massachusetts Institute of Technology (MIT) 1861; Woods Hole Oceanographic Institute; Massachusetts Biotechnology Research Park to develop new products and processes; Norman Rockwell Museum at Stockbridge
products electronic and communications equipment, shoes, textiles, machine tools, building stone, cod
population (1985) 5,819,000
famous people Samuel Adams, Louisa May Alcott, Emily Dickinson, Emerson, Hawthorne, Poe, Revere, Thoreau, Whistler
history one of the original Thirteen Colonies, it was first settled 1620 by the Pilgrims at Plymouth, and became a state 1788.

Massawa chief port and naval base of Ethiopia, in Eritrea, on the Red Sea, with salt production and pearl fishing; population (1980) 33,000. It is one of the hottest inhabited spots in the world, the temperature reaching 100°F/37.8°C in May. Massawa was an Italian possession 1885–1941.

Massif Central mountainous plateau region of S central France; area 93,000 sq km/36,000 sq mi, highest peak Puy de Sancy 1,886 m/6,188 ft. It is a source of hydroelectricity.

Masulipatnam or *Manchilipatnam*, also *Bandar* Indian seaport (its name means fish town) in Andhra, at the mouth of the N branch of the river Kistna; population (1981) 138,500.

Masurian Lakes lakes in Poland (former East Prussia) which in 1914–15 were the scene of battles in which the Germans defeated the Russians.

Matabeleland the W portion of Zimbabwe between the Zambezi and Limpopo rivers, inhabited by the Ndebele people
area 181,605 sq km/70,118 sq mi
towns Bulawayo
features rich plains watered by tributaries of the Zambezi and Limpopo, with mineral resources
language Matabele
famous people Joshua Nkomo
history Matabeleland was granted to the British South Africa Company 1889 and occupied 1893 after attacks on white settlements in Mashonaland; in 1923 it was included in Southern Rhodesia. It is now divided into two administrative regions.

Matadi chief port of Zaïre on the river Zaïre, 115 km/70 mi from its mouth, linked by oil pipelines with Kinshasa; population (1984) 144,700.

Matanzas industrial port (tanning, textiles, sugar) in NW Cuba; population (1986) 105,400. Founded 1693, it became a major centre of coffee, tobacco, and sugar production.

Matlock spa town with warm springs, administrative headquarters of Derbyshire, England; population (1981) 21,000.

Mato Grosso (Portuguese 'dense forest') area of SW Brazil, now forming two states, with their capitals at Cuiaba and Campo Grande. The forests, now depleted, supplied rubber and rare timbers; diamonds and silver are mined.

Matsue city NW of Osaka on Honshu, Japan; population (1980) 135,500. It has remains of a magnificent castle, fine old tea houses, and the Izumo Grand Shrine (dating in its present form from 1744).

Matsuyama largest city on Shikoku, Japan; industries (agricultural machinery, textiles, chemicals); population (1984) 418,000. There is a feudal fortress 1634.

Matterhorn (French *le Cervin*, Italian *il Cervino*) mountain peak in the Alps on the Swiss-Italian border; 4,478 m/14,690 ft.
   It was first climbed in 1865 by English mountaineer Edward Whymper (1840–1911); four members of his party of seven were killed when the rope broke during the descent.

Mauna Loa active volcano rising to a height of 4,169 m/13,678 ft on the Pacific island of Hawaii; it has numerous craters, including the second largest active crater in the world.

Mauritania
Islamic Republic of
(République Islamique de Mauritanie)

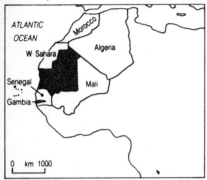

area 1,030,700 sq km/397,850 sq mi
capital Nouakchott
physical valley of river Senegal in south; the rest is arid
features includes part of the Sahara Desert
head of state and government Moaouia Ould Sidi Mohamed Taya from 1984
political system military republic
political parties no political parties allowed
exports iron ore, fish
currency ouguiya (142.25 = £1 Feb 1990)
population (1988) 1,894,000 (30% Arab Berber, 30% black Africans, 30% Haratine – descendants of black slaves, who remained slaves until 1980); annual growth rate 2.9%
life expectancy men 42, women 46
language Arabic (official), French
religion Sunni Muslim
literacy 2.9%
GDP $614 million (1984); $466 per head of population
chronology
1960 Achieved full independence, with Moktar Ould Daddah as president.
1975 Western Sahara ceded by Spain. Mauritania occupied the southern part and Morocco the rest. Polisario Front formed in Sahara to resist the occupation by Mauritania and Morocco.
1978 Daddah deposed in bloodless coup and replaced by Mohamed'Khouni Ould Haidalla. Peace agreed with Polisario Front.
1981 Diplomatic relations with Morocco broken.
1984 Haidalla overthrown by Moaouia Ould Sidi Mohamed Taya. Polisario regime formally recognized.
1985 Relations with Morocco restored.
1989 Violent clashes between Mauritanians and Senegalese in Nouakchott and Dakar following dispute over border grazing rights. Arab-dominated government expels thousands of Africans into N Senegal. Earlier, governments agreed to repatriate each other's citizens (about 250,000).

Mauritania country in NW Africa, bordered to the NE by Algeria, E and S by Mali, SW by Senegal, W by the Atlantic Ocean, and NW by Western Sahara.

Mauritius island in the Indian Ocean, E of Madagascar.

Mayagüez port in W Puerto Rico with needlework industry and a US agricultural experimental station; population (1980) 96,200.

Mayence French name for the West German city of ◊Mainz.

Mayenne *département* of W France in Pays-de-Loire region
area 5,212 sq km/2,033 sq mi
capital Laval
features river Mayenne
products iron, slate; paper
population (1982) 271,184.

Mayenne river in W France which gives its name to the *département* of Mayenne; length 200 km/ 125 mi. It rises in Orne, flows in a generally S direction through Mayenne and Maine-et-Loire, and joins the river Sarthe just above Angers to form the Maine.

Mayfair district of Westminster in London, England, vaguely defined as lying between Piccadilly and Oxford Street, and including Park Lane; formerly a fashionable residential district, but increasingly taken up by offices.

Maynooth village in Kildare, Republic of Ireland, with a Roman Catholic training college for priests; population (1981) 3,388.

Mayo county in Connacht province, Republic of Ireland
area 5,400 sq km/2,084 sq mi
towns administrative town Castlebar
features Lough Conn; wild Atlantic coast scenery; Achill Island; the village of Knock, where two women claimed a vision of the Virgin with two saints 1897, now a site of pilgrimage
products sheep and cattle farming; fishing
population (1986) 115,000.

Mayotte or *Mahore* island group of the ◊Comoros, off the E coast of Africa, a *collectivité territoriale* of France by its own wish. The two main islands are Grande Terre and Petite Terre.
area 374 sq km/144 sq mi

Mauritius
State of

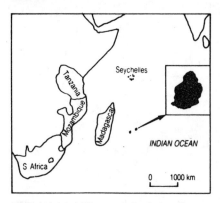

area 2,040 sq km/787 sq mi; the island of Rodrigues is part of Mauritius and there are several small island dependencies
capital Port Louis
physical a mountainous, volcanic island surrounded by coral reefs
features geologically part of Gondwanaland, it has unusual wildlife including flying fox and ostrich; it was the home of the dodo (extinct from about 1680)
head of state Elizabeth II represented by Veerasamy Ringadoo from 1986
head of government Aneerood Jugnauth from 1982

political system constitutional monarchy
political parties Mauritius Socialist Movement (MSM), moderate socialist-republican; Mauritius Labour Party (MLP), centrist Hindu-orientated; Mauritius Social Democratic Party (PMSD), conservative, Francophile; Mauritius Militant Movement (MMM), Marxist-republican.
exports sugar, knitted goods; tourism
currency Mauritius rupee (25.00 = £1 Feb 1990)
population (1987) 1,041,000; annual growth rate 1.9%
life expectancy men 64, women 69
language English (official); creole French
religion Hindu 45%, Christian 30%, Muslim 15%
literacy 89% male/77% female (1985 est)
GNP $957 million (1984); $1,240 per head of population
chronology
1968 Achieved full independence within the Commonwealth, with Seewoosagur Ramgoolam as prime minister.
1982 Aneerood Jugnauth prime minister.
1983 Jugnauth formed a new party, the Mauritius Socialist Movement, pledged to make Mauritius a republic within the Commonwealth, but Assembly refused. Ramgoolam appointed governor general. Jugnauth formed a new coalition government.
1985 Ramgoolam died, succeeded by Ringadoo.
1987 Jugnauth's coalition re-elected.

---

capital Dzaoudzi
products coffee, copra, vanilla, fishing
languages French, Swahili
population (1984) 59,000.
history a French colony 1843–1914, and later, with the Comoros, an overseas territory of France. In 1974, Mayotte voted to remain a French dependency.
Mbabane capital (since 1902) of Swaziland, 160 km/ 100 mi west of Maputo, in the Dalgeni Hills; population (1986) 38,000.
Mboma another spelling of ◊Boma, Zaïrean port.
ME abbreviation for ◊*Maine*.
Meath county in the province of Leinster, Republic of Ireland
area 2,340 sq km/903 sq mi
county town Trim
features Tara Hill, 155 m/509 ft high, was the site of a palace and coronation place of many kings of Ireland (abandoned in the 6th century) and St Patrick preached here.
products sheep, cattle

population (1986) 104,000.
Mecca (Arabic *Makkah*) city in Saudi Arabia and, as birthplace of Muhammad, the holiest city of the Islamic world; population (1974) 367,000. In the centre of Mecca is the Great Mosque, in whose courtyard is the

Mediterranean

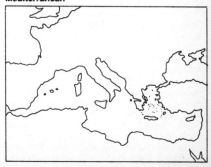

Kaaba, the shrine Muslims turn towards in prayer.

It also contains the well Zam-Zam, associated by tradition with the biblical characters Hagar and Ishmael. Most pilgrims come via the port of ◊Jiddah.

Mechelen (French *Malines*) industrial city (furniture, carpets, textiles) and market gardening centre in Antwerp province, N Belgium, which gave its name to Mechlin lace; population (1985) 76,120.

Medan seaport and economic centre of the island of Sumatra, Indonesia; population (1980) 1,379,000. It trades in rubber, tobacco, and palm oil.

Medellín industrial town (textiles, chemicals, engineering, coffee) in the Central Cordillera, Colombia, 1,538 m/5,048 ft above sea level; population (1985) 2,069,000. It has five universities. It is a centre of the Colombian drug trade, and there has been considerable violence since the late 1980s.

Medina (Arabic *Madinah*) Saudi Arabian city, about 355 km/220 mi N of Mecca; population (1974) 198,000. It is the second holiest city in the Islamic world, containing the tomb of Muhammad. It also contains the tombs of the caliphs or Muslim leaders Abu Bakr, Omar, and Fatima, Muhammad's daughter. The region produces grain and fruit.

Mediterranean inland sea separating Europe from N Africa, with Asia to the E; extreme length 3,700 km/2,300 mi; area 2,966,000 sq km/1,145,000 sq mi. It is linked to the Atlantic (at the Strait of Gibraltar), Red Sea, and Indian Ocean (by the Suez Canal), Black Sea (at the Dardanelles and Sea of Marmara). The main subdivisions are the Adriatic, Aegean, Ionian, and Tyrrhenian seas.

The Mediterranean is almost tideless, saltier and warmer than the Atlantic, and shallows from Sicily to Cape Bon (Africa) divide it into an E and W basin. It is endangered by human and industrial waste pollution; 100 million people live along the coast and it is regularly crossed by oil tankers. The Barcelona Convention 1976 to clean up the Mediterranean was signed by 17 countries and led to a ban on dumping of mercury, cadmium, persistent plastics, DDT, crude oil, and hydrocarbons.

Médoc French district bordering the Gironde in Aquitaine region, N of Bordeaux. It is famed for its wines, Margaux and St Julien being two of the best-known varieties. Lesparre and Pauillac are the chief towns.

Medway river of SE England, rising in Sussex and flowing through Kent and the *Medway towns* (Chatham, Gillingham, Rochester) to Sheerness, where it enters the Thames; about 96 km/60 mi long. In local tradition it divides the 'Men of Kent', who live to the E, from the 'Kentish Men', who live to the W.

Meerut industrial city (chemicals, soap, food processing) in Uttar Pradesh, N India; population

Meghalaya

INDIAN OCEAN

(1981) 538,000. The Indian Mutiny began here in 1857.

Meghalaya state of NE India
area 22,500 sq km/8,685 sq mi
capital Shillong
features mainly agricultural and comprises tribal hill districts
products potatoes, cotton, jute, fruit
minerals coal, limestone, white clay, corundum, sillimanite
population (1981) 1,328,000, mainly Khasi, Jaintia, and Garo
religion Hindu 70%
language various.

Meissen city in Dresden county, East Germany, on the river Elbe; known for Meissen or Dresden porcelain from 1710; population (1983) 38,908.

Mekele capital of Tigray region, N Ethiopia. Population (1984) 62,000.

Meknès (Spanish *Mequinez*) city in N Morocco, known for wine and carpetmaking; population (1981) 487,000. One of Morocco's four imperial cities, it was the capital until 1728, and is the site of the tomb of Sultan Moulay Ismail.

Mekong river rising as the Za Qu in Tibet and flowing to the South China Sea, through a vast delta (about 200,000 sq km/77,000 sq mi); length 4,425 km/2,750 mi. It is being developed for irrigation and hydroelectricity by Cambodia, Laos, Thailand, and Vietnam.

Melaka Malaysian form of ◊Malacca, state of peninsular Malaysia.

Melanesia islands in the SW Pacific between Micronesia to the north and Polynesia to the east, embracing all the islands from the New Britain archipelago to Fiji.

Melbourne capital of Victoria, Australia, near the mouth of the river Yarra; population (1986)

Mekong

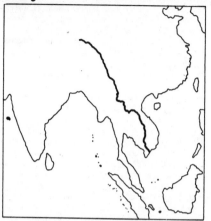

2,943,000. Industries include engineering, ship-building, electronics, chemicals, food processing, clothing, and textiles.

Founded 1835, it was named after Lord Melbourne 1837, grew in the wake of the gold rushes, and was the seat of the Australian government 1901–27. It is the country's second largest city, with three universities, and was the site of the 1956 Olympics.

Melilla port and military base on the NE coast of Morocco; area 14 sq km/5 sq mi; population (1986) 56,000. It was captured by Spain 1496 and is still under Spanish rule. Also administered from Melilla are three other Spanish possessions: Peñn ('rock') de Velez de la Gomera, Peñn d'Alhucemas, and the Chaffarine Islands.

Melos (modern Greek *Mílos*) Greek island in the Aegean, one of the Cyclades; area 155 sq km/

Melanesia

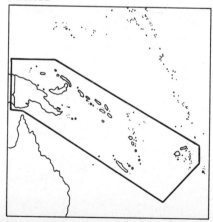

60 sq mi. The sculpture of *Venus de Milo* was discovered here 1820 (now in the Louvre). The capital is Plaka.

Melrose town in Borders region, Scotland. The heart of King Robert the Bruce is buried here and the ruins of Melrose Abbey 1136 are commemorated in verse by Sir Walter Scott.

Melton Mowbray market town in Leicestershire, England, on the river Eye; a hunting and horse-breeding centre known for pork pies and Stilton cheeses; population (1981) 29,500.

Memel German name for ◊Klaipeda, port in Lithuania, USSR.

Memphis industrial city (pharmaceuticals, food processing, cotton, timber, tobacco) on the Mississippi River, in Tennessee, USA; population (1986) 960,000. It has recording studios and record companies (Sun 1953–68, Stax 1960–75); Graceland, the home of Elvis Presley, is a museum.

Menai Strait channel of the Irish Sea, dividing Anglesey from the Welsh mainland; about 22 km/14 mi long, up to 3 km/2 mi wide. It is crossed by Telford's suspension bridge 1826 (reconstructed 1940) and Stephenson's tubular rail bridge 1850.

Menam another name for the ◊Chao Phraya river, Thailand.

Menderes (Turkish *Büyük Menderes*) river in European Turkey, about 400 km/250 mi long, rising near Afyonkarahisar and flowing along a winding course into the Aegean. The word 'meander' is derived from the ancient Greek name for the river.

Mendoza capital of the Argentine province of the same name; population (1980) 597,000. Founded 1561, it developed owing to its position on the Trans-Andean railway; it lies at the centre of a noted wine-producing area.

Menindee village and sheep centre on the Darling river in New South Wales, Australia. It is the centre of a scheme for conserving the waters of the Darling in *Menindee Lake* (155 sq km/60 sq mi) and other lakes nearby.

Menorca Spanish form of ◊Minorca, one of the Balearic Islands.

Menton (Italian *Mentone*) resort on the French Riviera, close to the Italian frontier; population (1982) 22,234. It belonged to the princes of Monaco from the 14th century until briefly independent 1848–60, when the citizens voted to merge with France.

Mequinez Spanish name for ◊Meknés, a town in Morocco.

Mérida capital of Yucatán state, Mexico, a centre of the sisal industry; population (1986) 580,000. It was founded 1542, and has a cathedral 1598. Its port on the Gulf of Mexico is Progreso.

Merionethshire former county of N Wales, included in the new county of Gwynedd 1974. Dolgellau was the administrative town.

Merseyside

Mersey river in NW England; length 112 km/
70 mi. Formed by the confluence of the Goyt
and Etherow rivers, it flows W to join the Irish Sea
at Liverpool Bay. It is linked to the Manchester
Ship Canal.

Merseyside former (1974–86) metropolitan county
of NW England, replaced by a residuary body in
1986 which covers some of its former functions
area 650 sq km/251 sq mi
towns administrative headquarters Liverpool;
Bootle, Birkenhead, St Helens, Wallasey, Southport
features river Mersey; Merseyside Innovation
Centre (MIC), linked with Liverpool University
and Polytechnic (with a science park); Prescot
Museum of clock and watch making; Speke Hall
(Tudor), and Croxteth Hall and Country Park (a
working country estate open to the public)
products chemicals, electrical goods, vehicles
population (1987) 1,457,000
famous people the Beatles

Mersin or **Içel** Turkish industrial free port (chrome,
copper, textiles, oil refining); population (1985)
314,000.

Merthyr Tydfil industrial town (light engineering,
electrical goods) in Mid Glamorgan, Wales,
UK; population (1982) 60,000. It was formerly a centre of the Welsh coal and steel
industries.

Merton borough of SW Greater London, including
the districts of Wimbledon, Merton, Mitcham, and
Morden
features part of Wimbledon Common (includes
Caesar's Camp – an Iron Age fort); All England
Tennis Club 1877
population (1982) 166,600

Mesa Verde (Spanish 'green table') a wooded clifftop
in Colorado, USA, with Pueblo dwellings, called
the Cliff Palace, built into its side. Dating from
about 1000 BC, with 200 rooms and 23 circular
ceremonial chambers (kivas), it had an estimated
population of about 400 people and was probably a
regional centre.

Meshed a variant spelling of ◊Mashhad, a town
in Iran.

Mesopotamia the land between the rivers Euphrates
and Tigris, part of modern Iraq. Here the civilizations of Sumer and Babylon flourished, and some
consider it the site of the earliest civilization.

Messina city and port in NE Sicily; population (1988)
271,000. It produces soap, olive oil, wine, and
pasta. Originally an ancient Greek settlement
(Zancle), it was taken first by Carthage and then by
Rome. It was rebuilt after an earthquake 1908.

Messina, Strait of channel in the central Mediterranean separating Sicily from mainland Italy;
in Greek legend a monster (Charybdis), who
devoured ships, lived in the whirlpool on the
Sicilian side, and another (Scylla), who devoured
sailors, in the rock on the Italian side. The classical
hero Odysseus passed safely between them.

metropolitan county in England, a group of six
counties (1974–86) established under the Local
Government Act 1972 in the major urban areas
outside London: Tyne and Wear, South Yorkshire,
Merseyside, West Midlands, Greater Manchester, and West Yorkshire. Their elected assemblies
were abolished 1986 when their areas of responsibility reverted to district councils.

Metz industrial city (shoes, metal goods, tobacco)
in Lorraine region, NE France, on the Moselle
river; population (1982) 186,000. Part of the Holy
Roman Empire 870–1552, it became one of the
great frontier fortresses of France, and was in
German hands 1871–1918.

Meurthe river rising in the Vosges mountains in NE
France and flowing in a NW direction to join the
Moselle at Frouard, near Nancy; length 163 km/
102 mi. It gives its name to the *département* of
Meurthe-et-Moselle.

Meuse (Dutch *Maas*) river flowing through France,
Belgium, and the Netherlands; length 900 km/
560 mi. It was a line of battle in both World Wars.

Mewar another name for ◊Udaipur, a city in Rajasthan, India.

Mexicali city in NW Mexico; population (1984)
500,000. It produces soap and cottonseed oil.
The availability of cheap labour attracts many US
companies (Hughes Aerospace, Rockwell International, and others).

Mexico country in Central America, bordered N by
the USA, E by the Gulf of Mexico, SE by Belize
and Guatemala, and SW and W by the Pacific
Ocean.

Mexico City (Spanish *Ciudad de México*) capital
and industrial (iron, steel, chemicals, textiles) and

Mexico
United States of
(Estados Unidos Mexicanos)

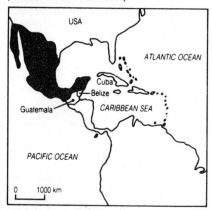

area 1,958,201 sq km/755,866 sq mi
capital Mexico City
towns Guadalajara, Monterrey; port Veracruz
physical partly arid central highlands flanked by Sierra Madre mountain ranges E and W; tropical coastal plains
features frontier of 2,000 miles with USA; resorts Acapulco, Mexicali, Tijuana; Baja California peninsula; volcanoes, such as Popocatepetl; archaeological sites of pre-Spanish period
head of state and government Carlos Salinas de Gortari from 1988

government federal democratic republic
political parties Institutional Revolutionary Party (PRI), moderate, left-wing; National Action Party (PAN), moderate Christian socialist
exports silver, gold, lead, uranium, oil, natural gas, traditional handicrafts, fish, shellfish
currency peso (free rate 4,109.63 = £1 Mar 1989)
population (1989) 88,087,000 (a minority are *criollos* of Spanish descent, 12% are American Indian, and the majority are of mixed descent; 50% of the total are under 20 years of age); annual growth rate 2.6%
life expectancy men 64, women 68
language Spanish (official); Indian languages include Nahuatl, Maya, and Mixtec
religion Roman Catholic
literacy 92% male/88% female (1985)
GNP $168 bn (1983); $1,800 per head of population
chronology
1821 Mexico achieved independence from Spain.
1846–48 Mexico at war with US.
1848 Maya Indian revolt suppressed.
1917 New constitution introduced, designed to establish permanent democracy.
1983–84 Financial crisis.
1985 Institutional Revolutionary Party (PRI) returned to power. Earthquake in Mexico City.
1986 IMF loan agreement signed to keep the country solvent until at least 1988.
1988 The PRI candidate, Carlos Salinas Gotari elected president.

cultural centre of Mexico, 2,255 m/7,400 ft above sea level on the southern edge of the central plateau; population (1986) 18,748,000. It is thought to be the most polluted city in the world.

Notable buildings include the 16th-century cathedral, the national palace, national library, Palace of Justice, and national university; the Ministry of Education has murals 1923–27 by Diego Rivera.

The city dates from about 1325, when the Aztec capital Tenochtitlán was begun on an island in Lake Texcoco. This city was levelled 1521 by the Spaniards, who in 1522 founded a new city on the site. Mexico City was the location of the 1968 Summer Olympics. In 1984, the explosion of a liquefied gas tank caused the deaths of over 450 people, and in 1985, over 2,000 were killed by a earthquake.

mezzogiorno (Italian 'midday') the hot, impoverished regions of S Italy.
MI abbreviation for ◊*Michigan*.
Miami city and port in Florida, USA; population (1984) 383,000. It is the hub of finance, trade, and

air transport for Latin America and the Caribbean. It is also a centre for oceanographic research, and a tourist resort for its beaches. There has been an influx of immigrants from Cuba, Haiti, Mexico, and South America since 1959.

Michigan state of the USA, bordered by the Great Lakes, Ohio, Indiana, Wisconsin, and Canada; nickname Great Lake State or Wolverine State

Michigan

Micronesia

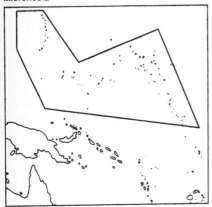

area 151,600 sq km/58,518 sq mi
capital Lansing
towns Detroit, Grand Rapids, Flint
features Lake Michigan; Porcupine Mountains;
Muskegon, Grand, St Joseph, and Kalamazoo rivers; over 50% forested
products cars, iron, cement, oil
population (1986) 9,145,000
famous people George Custer, Edna Ferber,
Henry Ford
history explored by the French from 1618, it
became British 1763, and a US state 1837.
In 1973, 97% of the population were contaminated by PBB (polybrominated biphenyl), a flame-retardant chemical inadvertently mixed with livestock feed.

Michigan, Lake lake in north central USA, one of the
Great Lakes; area 58,000 sq km/22,390 sq mi.
Chicago and Milwaukee are its main ports.
Lake Michigan is joined to Lake Huron by
the Straits of Mackinac. Green Bay is the
major inlet.

Micronesia islands in the Pacific Ocean lying N
of Melanesia, including the Federated States of
Micronesia, Belau, Kiribati, the Mariana and
Marshall Islands, Nauru, and Tuvalu.

Micronesia, Federated States of self-governing
island group (Kosrae, Ponape, Truk, and Yap) in
the W Pacific; capital Kolonia, on Ponape; area
700 sq km/270 sq mi; population (1988) 86,000.
It is part of the US Trust Territory. Purchased
by Germany from Spain 1898, they were occupied
1914 by Japan. They were captured by the USA
in World War II, and became part of the US Trust
Territory of the Pacific 1947. Micronesia became
internally self-governing from 1979, and in free
association with the USA from 1986 (there is US
control of military activities in return for economic
aid). The people are Micronesian and Polynesian,
and the main languages are Kosrean, Ponapean,

Trukese, and Yapese, although the official language is English.

Middelburg industrial town (engineering, tobacco,
furniture) in SW Netherlands, capital of Zeeland
and former ◊Hanseatic town ; population (1985)
38,930. Its town hall dates from the 15th century.

Middle East indeterminate area now usually taken
to include the Balkan States, Egypt, and SW Asia.
Until the 1940s, this area was generally called the
Near East, and the term Middle East referred to
the area from Iran to Burma.

Middle Range or *Middleback Range* mountain
range in the NE of Eyre Peninsula, South Australia, about 65 km/40 mi long, parallel with the
W coast of Spencer Gulf. Iron deposits are mined
at Iron Baron, Iron Knob, and Iron Monarch.

Middlesbrough industrial town and port on the
Tees, Cleveland, England, commercial and cultural
centre of the urban area formed by Stockton-on-
Tees, Redcar, Billingham, Thornaby, and Eston;
population (1983) 148,400. Formerly a centre of
heavy industry, it diversified its products in the
1960s. It is the birthplace of the navigator Captain
James Cook (1728–79).

Middlesex former English county, absorbed by
Greater London in 1965. Contained within the
Thames basin, it provided good agricultural
land before it was built over. It was settled in the 6th century by Saxons, and its
name comes from its position between the
kingdoms of the East and West Saxons. The
name is still used, as in Middlesex County
Cricket Club.

Mid Glamorgan county in S Wales
area 1,020 sq km/394 sq mi
towns administrative headquarters Cardiff; resort
Porthcawl; Aberdare, Merthyr Tydfil, Bridgend,
Pontypridd
features Caerphilly Castle, with its water
defences
products the north was formerly an important
coal (Rhondda) and iron and steel area; Royal Mint
at Llantrisant; agriculture in the south; Caerphilly
noted for mild cheese
population (1987) 535,000
language 8% Welsh, English.

Midi-Pyrénées region of SW France; area 45,300
sq km/17,486 sq mi; population (1986) 2,355,000.
Its capital is Toulouse, and it consists of the
départements of Ariège, Aveyron, Haute-Garonne,
Gers, Lot, Haute-Pyrénées, Tarn, and Tarn-et-
Garonne. Towns include Montauban, Cahors,
Rodez, and Lourdes. The region includes a
number of spa towns, winter resorts, and prehistoric caves.

Midlands area of England corresponding roughly
to the Anglo-Saxon kingdom of Mercia. *E Midlands* Derbyshire, Leicestershire, Northamptonshire, Nottinghamshire. *W Midlands* the former metropolitan county of ◊West Midlands

Mid Glamorgan

created from parts of Staffordshire, Warwick-shire, and Worcestershire; and (often included) *S Midlands* Bedfordshire, Buckinghamshire, and Oxfordshire.

In World War II, the E Midlands was worked for oil, and substantial finds were made in the 1980s; the oilbearing E Midlands Shelf extends into Yorkshire and Lincolnshire.

Midlothian former Scottish county S of the Firth of Forth, included 1975 in the region of Lothian; Edinburgh was the administrative headquarters.

Midway Islands two islands in the Pacific, 1,800 km/ 1,120 mi NW of Honolulu; area 5 sq km/2 sq mi; population (1980) 500. They were annexed by the USA 1867, and are now administered by the US Navy. The naval *Battle of Midway* 3–6 June 1942, between the USA and Japan, was the turning point in the Pacific in World War II.

Midwest or *Middle West* a large area of N central USA. It is loosely defined, but is generally taken to comprise the states of Ohio, Indiana, Illinois, Michigan, Iowa, Wisconsin, Minnesota, and sometimes Nebraska. It tends to be conservative socially and politically, and isolationist. Traditionally its economy is divided between agriculture and heavy industry.

Milan (Italian *Milano*) industrial city (aircraft, cars, locomotives, textiles), financial and cultural centre, capital of Lombardy, Italy; population (1988) 1,479,000.

features The Gothic cathedral, built about 1450, crowned with pinnacles, can hold 40,000 worshippers; the Brera art gallery; the convent with Leonardo da Vinci's *Last Supper* 1495–97; La Scala

opera house (Italian *Teatro alla Scala*) 1778; an annual trade fair.

history Settled by the Gauls in the 5th century BC, it was conquered by the Roman consul Marcellus 222 BC to become the Roman city of *Mediolanum*. Under Diocletian, in AD 286 Milan was capital of the Western empire. Destroyed by Attila the Hun 452, and again by the Goths 539, the city regained its power through the political importance of its bishops. It became an autonomous commune 1045; then followed a long struggle for supremacy in Lombardy.

The city was taken by Frederick I (Barbarossa) 1162; only in 1176 were his forces finally defeated, at the battle of Legnano. Milanese forces were again defeated by the emperor at the battle of Cortenuova 1237. In the Guelph-Ghibelline struggle the Visconti family emerged at the head of the Ghibelline faction; they gained power 1277, establishing a dynasty which lasted until 1450 when Francesco Sforza seized control and became duke. The Sforza court marked the highpoint of Milan as a cultural and artistic centre. Control of the city passed to Louis XII of France 1499, and in 1540 it was annexed by Spain, beginning a long decline. The city was ceded to Austria by the Treaty of Utrecht 1714, and in the 18th century began a period of intellectual enlightenment. Milan was in 1796 taken by Napoleon, who made it the capital of the Cisalpine Republic 1799, and in 1805 capital of the kingdom of Italy until 1814, when it reverted to the Austrians. In 1848, Milan rebelled unsuccessfully (the *Cinque Giornate/Five Days*), and in 1859 was joined to Piedmont.

Mildura town in NW Victoria, Australia, on the Murray River, with food-processing industries; population (1985) 16,500.

Mile End area of the East End of London, in the district of Stepney, now part of the London borough of Tower Hamlets. Mile End Green (now Stepney Green) was the scene of Richard II's meeting with the rebel peasants 1381, and in later centuries was the exercise ground of the London 'trained bands', or militia.

Milford Haven (Welsh *Aberdaugleddau*) seaport in Dyfed, SW Wales, on the estuary of the E and W Cleddau rivers; population (1985) 14,000. It has oil refineries, and a terminal for giant tankers linked by pipeline with Llandarcy, near Swansea.

Milton Keynes industrial (engineering, electronics) new town in Buckinghamshire, England; population (1983) 146,000. It was developed 1967 around the old village of the same name, following a grid design by Richard Llewelyn-Davies; it is the headquarters of the Open University.

Milwaukee industrial (meatpacking, brewing, engineering, textiles) port in Wisconsin, USA, on

Minnesota

Lake Michigan; population (1980) 1,207,000. It was founded by German immigrants in the 19th century.

Minas Gerais state in SE Brazil; major centre of the country's iron ore, coal, diamond and gold mining; area 587,172 sq km/226,794 sq mi; population (1980) 13,378,500; capital Belo Horizonte.

Mindanao the second largest island of the Philippines
area 94,627 sq km/36,526 sq mi
towns Davao, Zamboanga
physical mountainous, with rainforest
features in 1971, an isolated people, the Tasaday, were reputedly first seen by others (this may be a hoax). The active volcano Apo reaches 2,954 m/9,600 ft, and Mindanao is subject to severe earthquakes. There is a Muslim guerrilla resistance movement
products pineapples, coffee, rice, coconut, rubber, hemp, timber, nickel, gold, steel, chemicals, fertilizer
population (1980) 10,905,250.

Minden industrial town (tobacco, food processing) of North Rhine-Westphalia, West Germany, on the river Weser; population (1985) 80,000. The French were defeated here 1759 by an allied army from Britain, Hanover, and Brunswick, commanded by the duke of Brunswick.

Mindoro island of the Philippine Republic, S of Luzon
area 10,347 sq km 3,995 sq mi
towns Calapan
features Mount Halcon 2,590 m/8,500 ft
population (1980) 500,000.

Minhow former name 1934–43 for ◊Fuzhou, a town in SE China.

Minneapolis city in Minnesota, USA, forming with St Paul the Twin Cities area; population (1980) 371,000, metropolitan area 2,114,000.

The world's most powerful computers (Cray 2 supercomputer 1985) are built here, used for long-range weather forecasting, spacecraft design, code-breaking. The city centre is glass-covered against the difficult climate; there is an arts institute, symphony orchestra, Minnesota University, and Tyrone Guthrie theatre.

Minnesota state of the northern midwest USA; nickname North Star or Gopher State
area 218,700 sq km/84,418 sq mi
capital St Paul
towns Minneapolis, Duluth, Bloomington, Rochester
features sources of the Red, St Lawrence, and Mississippi rivers; Minnehaha Falls at Minneapolis; Mayo Clinic at Rochester
products cereals, potatoes, livestock, pulpwood, iron ore (60% of US output), farm and other machinery
population (1987) 4,246,000
famous people F Scott Fitzgerald, Sinclair Lewis, William and Charles Mayo, Prince
history the first Europeans to explore were French fur traders in the 17th century; part was ceded to Britain 1763, and part passed to the USA under the Louisiana Purchase 1803; it became a territory 1849 and a state 1858.

Minorca (Spanish *Menorca*) second largest of the ◊Balearic Islands in the Mediterranean
area 689 sq km/266 sq mi
towns Mahon, Ciudadela
products copper, lead, iron, tourism
population (1985) 55,500.

Minsk industrial city (machinery, textiles, leather; centre of the Soviet computer industry) and capital of the Byelorussian Republic, USSR; population (1987) 1,543,000.

Dating back to the 11th century and in turn held by Lithuania, Poland, Sweden, and Russia, Minsk was destroyed by Napoleon 1812 and the Germans 1944. Mass graves of over 30,000 victims of executions carried out by Stalin's security police 1937–41 were uncovered 1989 in the Kurapaty forest outside the city.

Miquelon Islands small group of islands off the S coast of Newfoundland which with St Pierre form a French overseas *département*. See ◊St Pierre and Miquelon
area 216 sq km/83 sq mi
products cod; silver fox and mink are bred
population (with St Pierre, 1982) 6,045.

Mirzapur city of Uttar Pradesh, Republic of India, on the river Ganges; a grain and cotton market, with

Mississippi

Mississippi and Missouri rivers

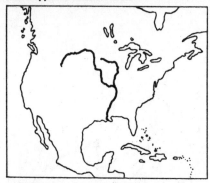

Missouri

bathing sites and temples on the river; population (1981) 127,785.

Miskolc industrial city (iron, steel, textiles, furniture, paper) in NE Hungary, on the river Sajo, 145 km/90 mi NE of Budapest; population (1988) 210,000.

Misr Egyptian name for ◊Egypt and for ◊Cairo.

Mississippi river in the USA, the main arm of the great river system draining the USA between the Appalachian and the Rocky mountains. The length of the Mississippi is 3,780 km/2,350 mi; of the Mississippi-Missouri 6,020 km/3,740 mi.

The Mississippi rises in the lake region of N Minnesota, with St Anthony Falls at Minneapolis. Below the tributaries Minnesota, Wisconsin, Des Moines, and Illinois, the confluence of the Missouri and Mississippi occurs at St Louis. The river turns at the Ohio junction, passing Memphis, and takes in the St Francis, Arkansas, Yazoo, and Red tributaries before reaching its delta on the Gulf of Mexico beyond New Orleans. In spring, warm air from the Gulf of Mexico collides with cold fronts from the north to create tornadoes along the Red River, a western tributary. The Spanish explorer Hernando de Soto reached a point on the Mississippi near present-day Memphis 1541.

Mississippi state of the S USA; nickname Magnolia State

area 123,600 sq km/47,710 sq mi

capital Jackson

towns Biloxi, Meridian, Hattiesburg

features Mississippi River; Vicksburg National Military Park (Civil War site)

products cotton, sweet potatoes, sugar, rice, canned sea food at Biloxi, timber, pulp, oil, natural gas, chemicals

population (1985) 2,657,000

famous people William Faulkner, Elvis Presley, Eudora Welty

history settled in turn by French, English, and Spanish until passing under US control 1798; statehood achieved 1817. After secession from

the Union during the Civil War, it was readmitted 1870.

Missolonghi (Greek *Mesolóngion*) town in W Central Greece and Eubrea region, on the N shore of the Gulf of Patras; population (1981) 10,200. It was several times under siege by the Turks in the wars of 1822–26 and it was here that the British poet Byron died.

Missouri state of the central USA; nickname Show Me State

area 180,600 sq km/69,712 sq mi

capital Jefferson City

towns St Louis, Kansas City, Springfield, Independence

features Mississippi and Missouri rivers; Pony Express Museum at St Joseph; birthplace of Jesse James; Mark Twain State Park; Harry S Truman Library at Independence

products meat and other processed food, aerospace and transport equipment, lead, clay, coal

population (1986) 5,066,000

famous people T S Eliot, Joseph Pulitzer, Mark Twain

history explored by de Soto 1541; acquired under the Louisiana Purchase; achieved statehood 1821.

Missouri River river in central USA, a tributary of the Mississippi, which it joins at St Louis; length 3,725 km/2,328 mi.

Mitilini modern Greek name of ◊Mytilene, town on the island of Lesvos.

Mitylene alternative spelling of ◊Mytilene, Greek city on the island of Lesvos.

Mizoram state of NE India

area 21,100 sq km/8,145 sq mi

capital Aizawl

products rice, hand-loom weaving

population (1981) 488,000

religion 84% Christian

history made a Union Territory 1972 from the Mizo Hills District of Assam. Rebels carried on a guerrilla war 1966–76, but in 1976 acknowledged Mizoram as an integral part of India. It became a state 1986.

Mmabatho or *Sun City* capital of Bophuthatswana, South Africa; population (1985) 28,000. It is a

Mizoram

INDIAN OCEAN

Moldavia

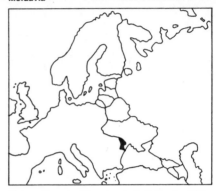

casino resort frequented by many white South Africans.

MN abbreviation for ◊*Minnesota*.

MO abbreviation for ◊*Missouri*.

Mobile industrial city (meat-packing, paper, cement, clothing, chemicals) and only seaport in Alabama, USA; population (1980) 443,500. Founded 1702 by the French a little to the north of the present city, Mobile was capital of the French colony of Louisiana until 1763. It was then British until 1780, and Spanish to 1813.

Mobutu Sese Seko Lake lake on the border of Uganda and Zaïre in the Great ◊Rift Valley; area 4,275 sq km/1,650 sq mi. The first European to see it was the British explorer Samuel Baker, who named it Lake Albert after the Prince Consort. It was renamed 1973 by Zaïre's president Mobutu after himself.

Moçambique the Portuguese name for ◊Mozambique.

Modena city in Emilia, Italy, capital of the province of Modena, 37 km/23 mi NW of Bologna; population (1988) 177,000. It has a 12th-century cathedral, a 17th-century ducal palace, and a university 1683, noted for its medical and legal faculties.

Mogadishu or *Mugdisho* capital and chief port of Somalia; population (1988) 1,000,000. It is a centre for oil refining, food processing, and uranium mining. It has mosques dating back to the 13th century, and a cathedral built 1925–28.

Mogilev industrial city (tractors, clothing, chemicals, furniture) in the Byelorussian Republic, USSR, on the Dneiper, 193 km/120 mi east of Minsk; population (1987) 359,000. It was annexed by Russia from Sweden 1772.

Mogok village in Burma, 114 km/71 mi NNE of Mandalay, known for its ruby and sapphire mines.

Mojave Desert arid region in S California, USA, part of the Great Basin; area 38,500 sq km/ 15,000 sq mi.

Mokha or *Mocha* seaport of N Yemen near the mouth of the Red Sea, once famed for its coffee exports. It has declined since the USSR built a new port near Hodeida. Population about 8,000.

Mold market town in Clwyd, Wales, on the river Alyn; population (1981) 8,555. It is the administrative headquarters of Clwyd and has two theatres.

Moldavia constituent republic of the Soviet Union from 1940

area 33,700 sq km/13,012 sq mi

capital Kishinev

features black earth region

products wine, tobacco, canned goods

population (1987) 4,185,000; 64% Moldavians (a branch of the Romanian people) Ukrainian 14%, Russian 13%, Gagauzi 4%, Jewish 2%

language Moldavian, allied to Romanian

religion Russian Orthodox

recent history formed from part of the former Moldavian Republic of the USSR (within Ukraine) and areas of Bessarabia ceded by Romania 1940, except the area bordering the Black Sea (added to the Ukraine). In 1988 a Democratic Movement for Perestroika was formed to campaign for reform. The Moldavian language was granted official status 1989, leading to conflict between Russian and Moldavian speakers in Kishniev. There were other violent clashes in 1989 as nationalist demonstrators called for the removal of hardline Moldavian leader Semyon Grossu (in office since 1980).

Moldavia former principality in Eastern Europe, on the river Danube, occupying an area divided today between the Soviet republic of Moldavia and modern Romania. It was independent between the 14th and 16th centuries, when it became part of the Ottoman Empire. In 1940 the E part, Bessarabia, became part of the Soviet Union, whereas the W part remained in Romania.

Monaco
Principality of

area 1.95 sq km/0.75 sq mi
capital Monaco-Ville
town Monte Carlo, noted for its film festival,

motor races, and casino
physical steep slope
features surrounded landward by French
territory, it is being expanded by filling in the
sea; aquarium and oceanographic centre
head of state Rainier III from 1949
head of government Jean Ausseil from 1986
government constitutional monarchy under
French protectorate
exports some light industry, but economy
depends on tourism and gambling
currency French franc (9.70 = £1 Feb 1990)
population (1989) 29,000; annual growth rate
−0.5%
language French
religion Roman Catholic
literacy 99% (1985)
chronology
1861 Became an independent state under
French protection.
1918 France given a veto over succession to
the throne.
1949 Prince Rainier III ascended the throne.

Molise mainly agricultural region of S central Italy, comprising the provinces of Campobasso and Isernia; area 4,400 sq km/1,698 sq mi; population (1988) 335,000. Its capital is Campobasso.

Molokai mountainous island of Hawaii State, USA, SE of Oahu
area 673 sq km/259 sq mi
features Kamakou 1,512 m/4,960 ft is the highest peak;
population (1980) 6,049
history the island is famous as the site of a leper colony organized 1873–89 by Belgian missionary Joseph De Veuster (Father Damien).

Molotov former name (1940–62) for the port of ◊Perm in USSR.

Moluccas another name for ◊Maluku, Indonesia.

Mombasa industrial port (oil refining, cement) in Kenya (serving also Uganda and Tanzania), built on Mombasa Island and adjacent mainland; population (1984) 481,000.

Mona Latin name for ◊Anglesey, island in Wales.

Monaco small sovereign state, forming an enclave in southern France, with the Mediterranean to the south.

Monadnock a mountain in New Hampshire, USA, 1,063 m/3,186 ft high. The term Monadnock is also used to mean any isolated hill or mountain.

Monaghan (Irish *Mhuineachain*) county of the NE Republic of Ireland, province of Ulster; area 1,290 sq km/498 sq mi; population (1986) 52,000. The county town is Monaghan. The county is low and rolling, and includes the rivers

Finn and Blackwater. Products include cereals, linen, potatoes, and cattle.

Monastir Turkish name for the town of ◊Bitolj in S Yugoslavia.

Monastir resort town on the Mediterranean coast of Tunisia, 18 km/11 mi S of Sousse. Summer residence of the president of Tunisia; birthplace of the former president, Habib Bourguiba.

Mönchengladbach industrial city (textiles, machinery, paper) in North Rhine-Westphalia, West Germany, on the river Niers near Düsseldorf; population (1988) 255,000. It is the NATO headquarters for N Europe.

Mongolia country in E Central Asia, bounded N by the USSR and S by China.

Mongolia, Inner (Chinese *Nei Mongol*) autonomous region of NE China from 1947
area 450,000 sq km/173,700 sq mi
capital Hohhot
features strategic frontier area with USSR; known for Mongol cattle herders, now becoming settled farmers
physical grassland and desert
products cereals under irrigation; coal; reserves of rare earth oxides europium, and yttrium at Bayan Obo
population (1986) 20,290,000.

Monmouth market town in Gwent, Wales; Henry V was born in the now ruined castle.

Monmouthshire former county of Wales, which in 1974 became, minus a small strip on the border with Mid Glamorgan, the new county of *Gwent*.

Mongolia
Mongolian People's Republic
(Bügd Nayramdakh Mongol Ard Uls)

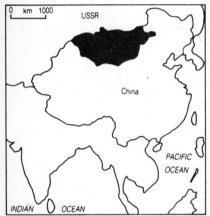

area 1,567,000 sq km/605,000 sq mi
capital Ulaanbaatar (formerly Ulan Bator)
towns Darkhan, Choybalsan
physical a high plateau with steppe (grasslands)
features Altai Mountains; salt lakes; part of Gobi Desert
head of state Jambyn Batmonh from 1984
head of government Dumagiin Sodnom from 1984

political system communism
exports meat and butter; varied minerals; furs
currency tugrik (5.71 = £1 Feb 1990)
population (1989) 2,093,000; annual growth rate 2.8%
life expectancy men 60, women 64
language Khalkha Mongolian (official), Chinese, Russian
religion formerly Tibetan Buddhist Lamaist, suppressed in the 1930s
literacy 93% male/85% female (1980 est)
GNP $1.8 bn (1983); $750 per head of population
chronology
1911 Outer Mongolia gained autonomy from China.
1915 Chinese sovereignty reasserted.
1921 Chinese rule finally overthrown with Soviet help.
1924 Mongolian People's Republic proclaimed.
1946 China recognized Mongolia's independence.
1966 20-year friendship, cooperation, and mutual-assistance pact signed with USSR. Deterioration in relations with China.
1984 Yumjaagiyn Tsedenbal, effective leader, deposed and replaced by Jambyn Batmonh.
1987 Soviet troop numbers reduced and Mongolia's external contacts broadened.
1989 Further major Soviet troop reductions.
1990 Democratization campaign launched by Mongolian Democratic Union; (Mar) entire politburo resigns following demands for reform

Monrovia capital and port of Liberia; population (1985) 500,000. Industries include rubber, cement, and petrol processing. It was founded 1821 for slaves repatriated from the USA. Originally called Christopolis, it was renamed after US president Monroe.

Mons (Flemish *Bergen*) industrial city (coalmining, textiles, sugar) and capital of the province of Hainaut, Belgium; population (1985) 90,500. The military headquarters of NATO is at nearby Chièvres-Casteau.

Montana state of the W USA on the Canadian border; nickname Treasure State
area 381,200 sq km/147,143 sq mi
capital Helena
towns Billings, Great Falls, Butte
features Missouri and Yellowstone rivers; Glacier National Park; Little Bighorn; Museum of the Plains Indian; the fourth largest state
physical mountainous forests in the west, rolling grasslands in the east
products wheat under irrigation, cattle, wool, copper, oil, natural gas

population (1986) 819,000
famous people Gary Cooper
history first settled 1809; influx of immigrants pursuing gold in the mid-19th century; became a state 1889.

Montauban industrial town (porcelain, textiles) in the Midi-Pyrénées region, SW France, on the river Tarn; population (1982) 53,147. The painter Ingres was born here.

Montana

Mont Blanc (Italian *Monte Bianco*) the highest mountain in the ◊Alps, between France and Italy; height 4,807 m/15,772 ft. It was first climbed 1786.

Mont Cenis pass in the Alps between Lyon, France, and Turin, Italy, at 2,082 m/6,831 ft.

Monte Bello Islands group of uninhabited islands in the Indian Ocean, off Western Australia, used by the UK for nuclear-weapons testing 1952; the largest of the group is Barrow Island.

Monte Carlo a town and resort in Monaco, known for its gambling; population (1982) 12,000.

Monte Cristo a small uninhabited island 40 km/25 mi to the S of Elba, in the Tyrrhenian Sea; its name supplied a title for Dumas' hero in *The Count of Monte Cristo*.

Montego Bay port and resort on the NW coast of Jamaica; population (1982) 70,200.

Montélimar town in Drôme district, France; noted for the nougat to which its name is given; population (1982) 30,213.

Montenegro (Serbo-Croat *Crna Gora*) constituent republic of Yugoslavia
area 13,800 sq km/5,327 sq mi
capital Titograd
town Cetinje
features smallest of the republics; Skadarsko Jezero (Lake Scutari) shared with Albania
physical mountainous
population (1986) 620,000, including 400,000 Montenegrins, 80,000 Muslims, and 40,000 Albanians
language Serbian variant of Serbo-Croat
religion Serbian Orthodox
history part of Serbia from the late 12th century, it became independent (under Venetian protection) after Serbia was defeated by the Turks 1389. It was forced to accept Turkish suzerainty in the late 15th century, but was never completely subdued by Turkey. It was ruled by bishop princes until 1851, when a monarchy was founded, and became a sovereign principality under the Treaty of Berlin 1878. Prince Nicholas took the title of king 1910. Montenegro participated in the Balkan Wars 1912 and 1913. It was overrun by Austria in World War I, and in 1918 voted after the deposition of King Nicholas to become part of the future Yugoslavia.

Monterey fishing port on Monterey Bay in California, USA, once the state capital; population (1980) 27,500. It is the setting for Steinbeck's novels *Cannery Row* 1945 and *Tortilla Flat* 1935 dealing with migrant fruit workers.

Monterrey industrial city (iron, steel, textiles, chemicals, food processing) in NE Mexico; population (1986) 2,335,000.

Montevideo capital and chief port (grain, meat products, hides) of Uruguay, on Río de la Plata; population (1985) 1,250,000. It was founded 1726.

Montgomery market town in Powys, Wales; population about 1,000.

Montgomery state capital of Alabama, USA; population (1980) 273,000. The *Montgomery Bus Boycott* 1955 began here when a black passenger, Rosa Parks, refused to give up her seat to a white. Led by Martin Luther King, it was a landmark in the civil-rights campaign. Alabama's bus-segregation laws were outlawed by the US Supreme Court 13 Nov 1953.

Montgomeryshire former county of N Wales, included in Powys 1974.

Montmartre district of Paris, France, dominated by the basilica of Sacre Coeur 1875. It is situated in the N of the city on a 120 m/400 ft high hill.

Montparnasse district of Paris, France, frequented by artists and writers. The Pasteur Institute is also here.

Montpellier industrial city (engineering, textiles, food processing, and a trade in wine and brandy), capital of Languedoc-Roussillon, France; population (1982) 221,000. It is the birthplace of the philosopher Auguste Comte.

Montreal inland port, industrial city (aircraft, chemicals, oil and petrochemicals, flour, sugar, brewing, meat packing) of Québec, Canada, on Montreal island at the junction of the Ottawa and St Lawrence rivers; population (1986) 2,921,000.
features Mont Réal (Mount Royal, 230 m/753 ft) overlooks the city; an artificial island in the St Lawrence (site of the international exhibition 1967); three universities; except for Paris, the world's largest French-speaking city
history Jacques Cartier reached the site 1535, Champlain established a trading post 1611, and the original Ville Marie (later renamed Montreal) was founded 1642 by Paul de Chomédy, Sieur de Maisonneuve (1612–76). It was the last town surrendered by France to Britain 1760. Nevertheless, when troops of the rebel Continental Congress occupied the city 1775–76, the citizens refused to be persuaded (even by a visit from Benjamin Franklin) to join the future USA in its revolt against Britain.

Montreux winter resort in W Switzerland on Lake Geneva; population (1980) 21,000. It is the site of the island rock fortress of Chillon, where François Bonivard (commemorated by the poet Byron), prior of the Abbey of St Victor, was imprisoned 1530–36 for his opposition to the Duke of Savoy. At the annual television festival (first held 1961), the premier award is the *Golden Rose of Montreux*.

Mont St Michel islet in NW France converted to a peninsula by an artificial causeway; noted for its Benedictine monastery, founded 708.

Montserrat volcanic island in the West Indies, one of the Leeward group, a British crown colony; capital Plymouth; area 110 sq km/42 sq mi; population (1985) 12,000. Practically all buildings were destroyed by Hurricane Hugo Sept 1989.

Montserrat produces cotton, cotton-seed, coconuts, citrus and other fruits, and vegetables. Its first European visitor was Christopher Columbus 1493, who named it after the mountain in Spain. It was first colonized by English and Irish settlers who moved from St Christopher 1632. The island became a British crown colony 1871.

Montserrat (Spanish *monte serrado* 'serrated mountain') mountain in NE Spain, height 1,240 m/ 4,070 ft, so called because its uneven outline resembles the edge of a saw.

Monza town in N Italy, known for its motor-racing circuit; population (1988) 123,000. Once the capital of the Lombards, it preserves the Iron Crown of Lombardy in the 13th-century cathedral. Umberto I was assassinated here.

Moonie town in SE Queensland, W of Brisbane, the site of Australia's first commercial oil strike; population (1961) approximately 100.

Moose Jaw town in S Saskatchewan, Canada, with grain elevators, extensive stockyards, petroleum refineries; population (1985) 35,500.

Moradabad trading city in Uttar Pradesh, India, on the Ramganga river; produces textiles and engraved brassware; population (1981) 348,000. It was founded 1625 by Rustam Khan, and the Great Mosque dates from 1631.

Moravia (Czech *Morava*) district of central Europe, from 1960 two regions of Czechoslovakia:
South Moravia (Czech *Jihomoravský*)
area 15,030 sq km/5,802 sq mi
capital Brno
population (1986) 2,075,000
North Moravia (Czech *Severomoravský*)
area 11,070 sq km/4,273 sq mi
capital Ostrava
population (1986) 1,957,000.
features (N and S) river Morava; 25% forested
products maize, grapes, wine in the south; wheat, barley, rye, flax, sugarbeet in the north; coal and iron
history part of the Avar territory since the 6th century; conquered by Charlemagne's Holy Roman Empire. In 874 the kingdom of Great Moravia was founded by the Slavic prince Sviatopluk, who ruled until 894. It was conquered by the Magyars 906, and became a fief of Bohemia 1029. It was passed to the Habsburgs 1526, and became an Austrian crown land 1849. It was incorporated in the new republic of Czechoslovakia 1918, forming a province until 1949.

Moray Firth North Sea inlet in Scotland, between Burghead (Grampian) and Tarbat Ness (Highland region), 38 km/15 mi wide at its entrance. The town of Inverness is situated at the head of the Firth.

Morayshire former county of NE Scotland, divided 1975 between Highland region (the SW section) and Grampian region (the NE); the county town was Elgin.

Morbihan, Gulf of seawater lake in Brittany, W France, linked by a channel with the Bay of Biscay; area 104 sq km/40 sq mi. Morbihan is a Breton word meaning 'little sea' and the gulf gives its name to a *département*.

Mordovia another name for ◊Mordvinia, republic of the USSR.

Mordvinia (or *Mordovia*) autonomous republic of central USSR
area 26,200 sq km/10,100 sq mi
capital Saransk
features river Sura on the E; forested in the W
products sugar beet, grains, potatoes; sheep and dairy farming; timber, furniture, and textiles
population (1986) 964,000
history Mordvinia was conquered by Russia during the 13th century. It was made an autonomous region 1930, and an Autonomous Soviet Socialist Republic 1934.

Morecambe town and resort in Lancashire, England, on Morecambe Bay, conjoined with the port of Heysham, which has a ferry service to Ireland; joint population (1982) 43,000.

Morecambe Bay inlet of the Irish Sea, between the Furness Peninsula (Cumbria) and Lancashire, England, with shallow sands. There are oil wells, and natural gas 50 km/30 mi offshore.

Morocco country in N Africa, bordered N and NW by the Mediterranean, E and SE by Algeria, and S by Western Sahara.

Moroni capital of the Comoros Republic, on Njazídja (Grand Comoro); population (1980) 20,000.

Moscow (Russian *Moskva*) capital of the USSR and of the Moskva region, on the Moskva river 640 km/400 mi SE of Leningrad; population (1987) 8,815,000. Its industries include machinery, electrical equipment, textiles, and chemicals
features The 12th-century Kremlin (Citadel), at the centre of the city, is a walled enclosure containing a number of historic buildings, including three cathedrals, one of them the burial place of the tsars; the Ivan Veliki tower 90 m/ 300 ft, a famine-relief work commissioned by Boris Godunov 1600; various palaces, including the former imperial palace, museums, and the Tsar Kolokol, the world's largest bell (200 tonnes) 1735. The walls of the Kremlin are crowned by 18 towers and have five gates. Red Square, used for political demonstrations and processions, contains St Basil's Cathedral, the state department store GUM, and Lenin's tomb. The headquarters of the KGB secret police, with Lubyanka Prison behind it, is in Dzerzhinsky Square; the underground railway was opened 1935. Institutions include Moscow University 1755 and People's Friendship University (for foreign students) 1953; the Academy

Morocco
Kingdom of (al-Mamlaka al-Maghrebia)

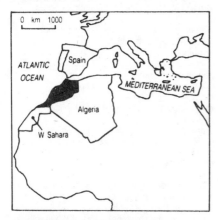

area 458,730 sq km/177,070 sq mi
capital Rabat
towns Marrakesh, Fez, Kenes; ports Casablanca, Tangier
physical mountain ranges NE–SW; plains in W
features Atlas Mountains; the towns Ceuta (from 1580), Melilla (from 1492), and three small coastal settlements are held by Spain; a tunnel across the Strait of Gibraltar to Spain was proposed 1985
head of state Hassan II from 1961
head of government Mohamed Karim Lamrani from 1984
government constitutional monarchy
political parties Constitutional Union (UC), right-wing; National Rally of Independents (RNI), royalist; Popular Movement (MP), moderate socialist; Istiqual, nationalist, right-of-centre; Socialist Union of Popular Forces (USFP), progressive socialist; National Democratic Party (PND), moderate, nationalist
economy dates, figs, cork, wood pulp, canned fish, phosphates, tourism
currency dirham (13.57 = £1 Feb 1990)
population (1989 est) 25,380,000; annual growth rate 2.5%
life expectancy men 57, women 60
language Arabic (official) 75%, Berber 25%, French, Spanish
religion Sunni Muslim
literacy 45% male/22% female (1985 est)
GNP $15.6 bn (1983); $800 per head of population
chronology
1956 Achieved independence from France as the Sultanate of Morocco.
1957 Sultan restyled king of Morocco.
1961 Hassan II came to the throne.
1969 Former Spanish province of Ifni returned to Morocco.
1972 Major revision of the constitution.
1975 Western Sahara ceded by Spain to Morocco and Mauritania.
1976 Guerrilla war in the Sahara by the Polisario Front. Sahrawi Arab Democratic Republic (SADR) established in Algiers. Diplomatic relations with Algeria broken.
1979 Mauritania signed a peace treaty with Polisario.
1983 Peace formula for the Sahara proposed by the Organization of African Unity (OAU) but not accepted by Morocco.
1984 Hassan signed an agreement for cooperation and mutual defence with Libya.
1987 Ceasefire agreed with Polisario but fighting continued.
1988 Diplomatic relations with Algeria restored.
1989 Diplomatic relations with Syria restored.

---

of Sciences, which moved from Leningrad 1934; Tretyakov Gallery of Russian Art 1856; Bolshoi Theatre 1780 for opera and ballet; Moscow Art Theatre 1898; Moscow State Circus. Moscow is the seat of the patriarch of the Russian Orthodox Church. On the city outskirts is Star City (Zvezdnoy Gorodok), the Soviet space centre.

Moscow is the largest industrial centre of the USSR, linked with Stavropol by oil pipeline 480 km/300 mi, built 1957.

history Moscow, founded as the city-state of Muscovy 1127, was destroyed by the Mongols during the 13th century, but rebuilt 1294 by Prince Daniel (died 1303) as the capital of his principality. During the 14th century, it was under the rule of Alexander Nevski, Ivan I

(1304–41), and Dmitri Donskai (1350–89), and became the foremost political power in Russia, and its religious capital. It was burned in 1571 by the khan of the Crimea, and ravaged by fire in 1739, 1748, and 1753; in 1812 it was burned by its own citizens to save it from Napoleon's troops, or perhaps by accident. It became capital of the Russian Soviet Federated Social Republic (RSFSR) 1918, and of the Union of Soviet Socialist Republics (USSR) 1922. In World War II Hitler's troops were within 20 mi of Moscow on the NW by Nov 1941, but the stubborn Russian defence and severe winter weather forced their withdrawal in Dec.

Moselle or *Mosel* a river in W Europe some 515 km/320 mi long; it rises in the Vosges, France,

Mozambique

People's Republic of *(República Popular de Moçambique)*

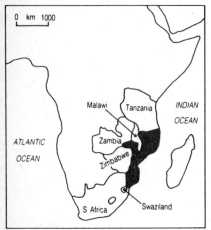

area 799,380 sq km/308,561 sq mi
capital and chief port Maputo
towns ports Beira, Nacala
physical mostly flat; mountains in W
features rivers Zambezi, Limpopo
head of state and government Joaquim Chissano from 1986

government one-party socialist republic
political parties National Front for the Liberation of Mozambique (Frelimo), Marxist-Leninist
exports sugar, cashews, tea, cotton, copra, sisal
currency metical (replaced escudo 1980) (1450.62 = £1 Sept 1987)
population (1989) 15,259,000 (mainly indigenous Bantu peoples; Portuguese 50,000); annual growth rate 2.8%
life expectancy men 44, women 46
language Portuguese (official)
religion animist 69%, Roman Catholic 21%, Muslim 10%
literacy 55% male/22% female (1985 est)
GDP $2.7 bn (1983); $220 per head of population
chronology
1962 Frelimo (liberation front) established.
1975 Full independence achieved as a socialist republic, with Samora Machel as president and Frelimo as the sole legal party.
1983 Re-establishment of good relations with Western powers.
1984 Nkomati Accord signed with South Africa.
1986 Machel killed in air crash, and succeeded by Joaquim Chissano.
1988 Tanzania announced complete withdrawal of its troops.
1989 Frelimo offered to abandon Marxist-Leninism; Chissano re-elected.

---

and is canalized from Thionville to its confluence with the ◊Rhine at Koblenz in Germany. It gives its name to the *département*s of Moselle and Meurthe-et-Moselle in France.

Mosi-oa-tunya the African name for the ◊Victoria Falls of the Zambezi River.

Moskva the Russian name for ◊Moscow, capital of the USSR.

Mosquito Coast the Caribbean coast of Honduras and Nicaragua, characterized by swamp, lagoons and tropical rainforest. A largely undeveloped territory occupied by Mosquito Indians, Garifunas and Zambos, many of whom speak English. Between 1823 and 1860 Britain maintained a protectorate over the Mosquito Coast which was ruled by a succession of 'Mosquito kings'.

Mostaganem industrial port (metal and cement) in NW Algeria, linked by pipeline with the natural-gas fields at Hassi Messaoud; population (1982) 169,500. It was founded in the 11th century.

Mostar industrial town (aluminium, tobacco) in Bosnia and Herzegovina, Yugoslavia, noted for its grapes and wines; population (1981) 110,000.

Mosul industrial city (cement, textiles) and oil centre in Iraq, on the right bank of the Tigris, opposite

the site of ancient Nineveh; population (1985) 571,000. Once it manufactured the light cotton fabric muslin, which was named after it.

Motherwell and Wishaw industrial town (Ravenscraig iron and steel works, coal mines) in Strathclyde, Scotland, SE of Glasgow; population (1981) 68,000. The two burghs were amalgamated in 1920.

Moulins capital of the *département* of Allier, Auvergne, central France; industries (cutlery, textiles, glass); population (1982) 25,500. Moulin was capital of the old province of Bourbonnais 1368–1527.

Moulmein port and capital of Mon state in SE Myanmar (Burma), on the Salween estuary; population (1983) 202,967.

Mount Isa mining town (copper, lead, silver, zinc) in NW Queensland, Australia; population (1984) 25,000.

Mount Lofty Range mountain range in SE South Australia; Mount Bryan 934 m/3,064 ft is the highest peak.

Mount Rushmore mountain in the Black Hills, South Dakota, USA; height 1,890 m/6,203 ft. On its granite face are carved giant portrait heads of presidents Washington, Jefferson, Lincoln, and

Theodore Roosevelt. The sculptor was Gutzon Borglum.

Mount St Helens volcanic mountain in Washington state, USA. When it erupted in 1980 after being quiescent since 1857, it devastated an area of 600 sq km /230 sq mi and its height was reduced from 2,950 m/9,682 ft to 2,560 m/8,402 ft.

Mount Vernon village in Virginia, USA, on the Potomac River, where George Washington lived 1752–99 and was buried on the family estate, now a national monument.

Mozambique country in SE Africa, bordered to the N by Zambia, Malawi, and Tanzania, E by the Indian Ocean, S by South Africa, and E by Swaziland and Zimbabwe.

MS abbreviation for ◊*Mississippi*.

MT abbreviation for ◊*Montana*.

Mtwara deepwater seaport in S Tanzania, on Mtwara Bay; population (1978) 48,500. It was opened 1954.

Mukalla seaport capital of the Hadhramaut coastal region of South Yemen; on the Gulf of Aden 480 km E of Aden; population(1984) 158,000.

Mukden former name of ◊Shenyang, city in China.

Mülheim an der Ruhr industrial city in North Rhine-Westphalia, West Germany, on the river Ruhr; population (1988) 170,000.

Mulhouse (German *Mülhausen*) industrial city (textiles, engineering, electrical goods) in Haut-Rhin *département*, Alsace, E France; population (1982) 221,000.

Mull second largest island of the Inner Hebrides, Strathclyde, Scotland; area 950 sq km/367 sq mi; population (1981) 2,600. It is mountainous, and is separated from the mainland by the Sound of Mull. There is only one town, Tobermory. The economy is based on fishing, forestry, tourism, and some livestock.

Mullingar county town of Westmeath, Republic of Ireland; population (1983) 7,000. It is a cattle market and trout-fishing centre.

Multan industrial city (textiles, precision instruments, chemicals, pottery, jewellery) in Punjab province, central Pakistan, 205 km/190 mi SW of Lahore; population (1981) 732,000. It trades in grain, fruit, cotton, and wool. It is on a site inhabited since the time of Alexander the Great.

Mulu mountainous region in N Borneo near the border with Sabah. Its limestone cave system, one of the largest in the world, was explored by a Royal Geographical Society Expedition 1978.

München German name of ◊Munich, city in West Germany.

Munich (German *München*) industrial city (brewing, printing, precision instruments, machinery, electrical goods, textiles), capital of Bavaria, West Germany, on the river Isar; population (1986) 1,269,400.

features Munich owes many of its buildings and art treasures to the kings Ludwig I and

Maximilian II of Bavaria. The cathedral is late 15th century. The Alte Pinakothek contains paintings by old masters, the Neue Pinakothek, modern paintings; there is the Bavarian National Museum, the Bavarian State Library, and the Deutsches Museum (science and technology). The university, founded at Ingolstadt 1472, was transferred to Munich 1826; to the NE at Garching there is a nuclear research centre.

history Dating from the 12th century, Munich became the residence of the dukes of Wittelsbach in the 13th century, and the capital of independent Bavaria. It was the scene of a revolution in Nov 1918, and, following a communist uprising, a Soviet republic was set up in Bavaria Apr–May 1919 with its capital in Munich; this was overthrown by the federal government. After the Hitler putsch of 1923, it became the centre of the Nazi movement, and the Munich Agreement of 1938 was signed there. When the 1972 Summer Olympics were held in Munich, a number of Israeli athletes were killed by guerrillas.

Munster southern province of Republic of Ireland, comprising the counties of Clare, Cork, Kerry, Limerick, North and South Tipperary, and Waterford; area 24,140 sq km/9,318 sq mi; population (1986) 1,019,000. It was a kingdom until the 12th century, and was settled in plantations by the English from 1586.

Münster industrial city (wire, cement, iron, brewing and distilling) in North Rhine-Westphalia, NW West Germany, formerly the capital of Westphalia; population (1988) 268,000. The Treaty of Westphalia was signed simultaneously here and at Osnabrück 1648, ending the Thirty Years' War. Its university was founded 1773. Badly damaged in World War II, its ancient buildings, including the 15th-century cathedral and town hall, have been restored or rebuilt.

Munternia Romanian name of ◊Wallachia, former province of Romania.

Murcia industrial city (silk, metal, glass, textiles, pharmaceuticals), capital of the Spanish province of Murcia, on the river Segura; population (1986) 310,000. Murcia was founded 825 on the site of a Roman colony by 'Abd-ar-Rahman II, caliph of Cordoba. It has a university and 14th-century cathedral.

Murcia autonomous region of SE Spain; area 11,300 sq km/4,362 sq mi; population (1986) 1,014,000. It includes the cities Murcia and Cartagena, and produces esparto grass, lead, zinc, iron, and fruit.

Murmansk seaport in NW USSR, on the Barents Sea; population (1987) 432,000. It is the largest city in the Arctic, the USSR's most important fishing port, and base of the icebreakers that keep the Northeast Passage open. It is the centre of Soviet Lapland and the only port on the Soviet Arctic coast that is in use all year round. After the entry of the USSR into World War II in 1941,

Myanmar, Union of
Socialist Republic of the Union of *(Pyidaungsu Socialist Thammada Myanma Naingngandaw;* formerly **Burma)**

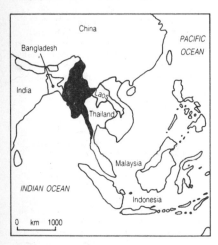

area 676,577 sq km/261,159 sq mi
capital and chief port Yangon (formerly Rangoon)
towns Mandalay, Karbe
physical over half is forested; rivers Irrawaddy and Chindwin; mountains in N, W, and E
head of state and government General Saw Maung from 1988
government military republic
political parties National Unity Party,

military-socialist ruling party; National League for Democracy (NLD), pluralist opposition grouping
exports rice, rubber, jute, teak, jade, rubies, sapphires
currency kyat (10.77 = £1 Feb 1990)
population (1989) 39,893,000; annual growth rate 1.9%
life expectancy men 56, women 59
language Burmese
religion Hinayana Buddhist; religious centre Pagan
literacy 76% male/66% female (1980 est)
GDP $6.5 bn (1983); $174 per head of population
chronology
1886 United as province of British India.
1937 Became crown colony in the British Commonwealth.
1942–45 Occupied by Japan.
1948 Granted independence from Britain. Left the Commonwealth.
1962 Gen Ne Win assumed power in army coup.
1973–74 Adoption of presidential-style 'civilian' constitution.
1975 Formation of opposition National Democratic Front.
1988 Government resigned after violent demonstrations. Two changes of regime later, Gen Saw Maung seized power in a military coup in Sept with over 1,000 killed.
1989 Martial law declared; arrest of thousands of people, including advocates of democracy and human rights.

---

supplies from the UK and later from the USA were unloaded there.

Murray principal river of Australia, 2,575 km/1,600 mi long. It rises in the Australian Alps near Mount Kosciusko and flows west, forming the boundary between New South Wales and Victoria, and reaches the sea at Encounter Bay, South Australia. With its main tributary, the Darling, it is 3,750 km/2,330 mi long.

Its other tributaries include the Lachlan and the Murrumbidgee. The Dartmouth Dam 1979 in the Great Dividing Range supplies hydroelectric power and has drought-proofed the Murray river system, but irrigation (for grapes, citrus and stone fruits) and navigation schemes have led to soil salinization.

Murrumbidgee river of New South Wales, Australia; length 1,690 km/1,050 mi. It rises in the Australian Alps, flows N to the Burrinjuck

reservoir, and then W to meet the river ◊Murray.

Muscat (Arabic *Masqat*) capital of Oman, E Arabia, adjoining the port of Matrah, which has a deepwater harbour; combined population (1982) 80,000. It produces natural gas and chemicals.

Muscat and Oman the former name of ◊Oman, country in the Middle East.

Musgrave Ranges Australian mountain ranges on the border between South Australia and the Northern Territory; the highest peak is Mount Woodruffe 1,525 m/5,000 ft. The area is an Aboriginal reserve.

Mustique an island in the Caribbean, part of ◊St Vincent and the Grenadines.

Mutare formerly (until 1982) *Umtali* industrial town (vehicle assembly, engineering, tobacco, textiles, paper) in E Zimbabwe, chief town of Manicaland province; population (1982) 69,621.

Myanmar formerly (until 1989) *Burma* country in SE Asia, bordered by India to the NW, China to the NE, Laos and Thailand to the SE, and the Bay of Bengal to the SW.

Mysore or *Maisur* industrial city (engineering, silk) in ◊Karnataka, some 130 km/80 mi SW of Banga-lore, India; population (1981) 476,000.

Mytilene (modern Greek *Mitilíni*) port, capital of the Greek island of Lesvos (to which the name Mytilene is sometimes applied) and a centre of sponge fishing; population (1981) 24,000.

Nablus market town on the West Bank of the river Jordan, N of Jerusalem, the largest Palestinian town, after E Jerusalem, in Israeli occupation; population (1971) 64,000. Formerly Shechem, it was the ancient capital of Samaria, and a few Samaritans remain. The British field marshal Allenby's defeat of the Turks here 1918 completed the conquest of Palestine.

Nacala seaport in Nampula province, N Mozambique; a major outlet for minerals. It is linked by rail with Malawi.

Naemen Flemish form of ◊Namur, city in Belgium.

Nafud desert area in Saudi Arabia to the south of the Syrian Desert.

Nagaland state of NE India, bordering Myanmar (Burma) on the east
area 16,721 sq km/6,456 sq mi
capital Kohima
products rice, tea, coffee, paper, sugar
population (1981) 775,000
history formerly part of Assam, it was seized by Britain from Burma 1826. The British sent 18 expeditions against the Naga peoples in the north 1832–87. After India attained independence 1947, there was Naga guerrilla activity against the Indian government; the state of Nagaland was established 1963 in response to demands for self-government, but fighting continued sporadically.

Nagasaki industrial port (coal, iron, shipbuilding) on Kyushu island, Japan; population (1987) 447,000. An atom bomb was dropped on it 9 Aug 1945.

Nagasaki was the only Japanese port open to European trade from the 16th century until other ports were opened 1859. Three days after ◊Hiroshima, the second atom bomb was dropped. Of Nagasaki's population of 212,000, 73,884 were killed and 76,796 injured, not counting the long-term victims of radiation.

Nagorno-Karabakh autonomous region (*oblast*) of the Soviet republic of ◊Azerbaijan; population (1987) 180,000 (76% Armenian, 23% Azeri), the Christian Armenians forming an enclave within the predominantly Shi'ite Muslim Azerbaijan. Since Feb 1988 the region has been the site of ethnic conflicts between the two groups and the subject of violent disputes between Azerbaijan and the neighbouring republic of Armenia
area 4,400 sq km/1,700 sq mi
capital Stepanakert
history an autonomous protectorate after the Russian revolution in 1917, Nagorno-Karabakh was annexed in 1923 to Azerbaijan against the wishes of the local population. Armenians in Nagorno-Karabakh felt discriminated against by the Azerbaijan republic. Inter-ethnic violence was provoked in 1988 by the local council voting to transfer the region's administrative control to Armenia, and in response the area was placed under direct rule from Moscow Jan–Nov 1989. During autumn 1989 the inter-republic conflict escalated, with Azerbaijan first imposing an economic blockade on Armenia, and then descending into civil war and threatening secession from the USSR, which resulted in 20,000 Soviet troops being sent to the republic in Jan 1990. The Armenian parliament had voted to annex Nagorno-Karabakh in Dec, and there were attacks on Armenians in Baku, the capital of Azerbaijan. There have been large-scale cross-border migrations of Armenians from Azerbaijan and Azeris from Armenia, involving over 300,000 people. Between 1988 and Jan 1990 some 170 people were killed in clashes.

Nagoya industrial seaport (cars, textiles, clocks) on Honshu island, Japan; population (1987)

Nagaland

INDIAN OCEAN

2,091,000. It has a shogun fortress 1610, and a noted Shinto shrine, *Atsuta Jingu.*

Nagpur industrial city (textiles, metals) in Maharashtra, India; population (1981) 1,298,000. The university was founded 1923.

Naha chief port on Okinawa island, Japan; population (1984) 304,000.

Nairnshire former county of Scotland, bounded on the north by the Moray Firth, included 1975 in the Highland region. The county town was Nairn.

Nairobi capital of Kenya, in the central highlands at 1,660 m/5,450 ft; population (1985) 1,100,000. It has light industry and food processing, and is the headquarters of the United Nations Environment Programme (UNEP). Nairobi was founded 1899, its university 1970. It has the International Louis Leakey Institute for African Prehistory 1977, and the International Primate Research Institute is nearby.

Najaf a holy city near the Euphrates in Iraq, 144 km/90 mi south of Baghdad.

Nakhichevan autonomous republic forming part of Azerbaijan Republic, USSR, even though it is entirely outside the Azerbaijan boundary, being separated from it by the Armenian Republic; area 5,500 sq km/2,120 sq mi; Its capital is Nakhichevan; population 278,000.

history Taken by Russia in 1828, it was annexed to the Azerbaijan Republic in 1924. The Muslim Azeris maintain strong links with Iran to the south. Tension between Armenians and Azeris broke out into open conflict in 1989.

Nakhodka pacific port in E Siberia, USSR, on the sea of Japan, E of Vladivostok; population (1985) 150,000. US-caught fish, especially pollock, is processed by Soviet factory ships in a joint venture.

Nakuru, Lake a salt lake in the Great Rift Valley, Kenya.

Namaqualand or *Namaland* near-desert area on the SW coast of Africa divided between Namibia and South Africa.

Great Namaqualand is in Namibia, north of the Orange River, area 388,500 sq km/150,000 sq mi; sparsely populated by the Nama, a Hottentot people;

Little Namaqualand is in Cape Province, South Africa, south of the Orange River, area 52,000 sq km/20,000 sq mi; copper and diamonds are mined here.

Namib Desert a coastal desert region in Namibia, between the Kalahari Desert and the Atlantic Ocean. Its sand dunes are among the tallest in the world, reaching heights of 370 m/1,200 ft.

Namibia former name (until 1968) *South West Africa* country bordered on the S by South Africa, on the E by Botswana, on the N by Angola and Zambia, and on the W by the Atlantic Ocean.

Nampo formerly (to 1947) *Chinnampo* city on the west coast of North Korea, 40 km/25 mi SW of Pyongan; population (1984) 691,000.

Namur (Flemish *Namen*) industrial city (cutlery, porcelain, paper, iron, steel), capital of the province of Namur, in S Belgium, at the confluence of the Sambre and Meuse rivers; population (1988) 103,000. It was a strategic location during both world wars. The province of Namur has an area of 3,700 sq km/1,428 sq mi, and a population (1987) of 415,000.

Nanaimo coal-mining centre of British Columbia, Canada, on the E coast of Vancouver Island; population (1985) 50,500.

Nanchang industrial (textiles, glass, porcelain, soap) capital of Jiangxi province, China, about 260 km/160 mi SE of Wuhan; population (1986) 1,120,000. It is an important road and rail junction. It was originally a walled city built in the 12th century. The first Chinese Communist rising took place here 1 Aug 1927.

Nancy capital of the *département* of Meurthe-et-Moselle and of the region of Lorraine, France, on the Meurthe 280 km/175 mi E of Paris; population (1982) 307,000. Nancy dates from the 11th century.

Nanda Devi peak in the Himalayas, Uttar Pradesh, N India; height 7,817 m/25,645 ft. Until Kanchenjunga was absorbed into India, Nanda Devi was the country's highest mountain.

Nanga Parbat peak in the Himalayan Karakoram mountains of Kashmir; height 8,126 m/26,660 ft.

Nanjing formerly *Nanking* capital of Jiangsu province, China, 270 km/165 mi NW of Shanghai; centre of industry (engineering, shipbuilding, oil refining), commerce, and communications; population (1986) 2,250,000. The bridge 1968 over the Chang Jiang river is the longest in China at 6,705 m/22,000 ft.

The city dates from the 2nd century BC, perhaps earlier. It received the name Nanjing ('southern capital') under the Ming dynasty (1368–1644), and was the capital of China 1368–1403, 1928–37, and 1946–49. Its university was founded 1888.

Nanking former name of ◊Nanjing, city in China.

Nanning industrial river port, capital of Guangxi autonomous region, China, on the You Jiang; population (1982) 866,000. It was an important supply town during the Vietnam war and the Sino-Vietnamese confrontation 1979.

Nantes industrial port in W France on the Loire, capital of Pays de la Loire region; industries (oil, sugar refining, textiles, soap, tobacco); population (1982) 465,000. It has a cathedral 1434–1884 and a castle founded 938. It is the birthplace of the writer Jules Verne.

Nantucket island and resort in Massachusetts, USA, S of Cape Cod, 120 sq km/46 sq mi. In the 18th–19th centuries, Nantucket was a whaling port.

Namibia
formerly **South West Africa**

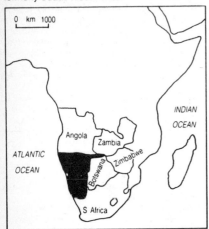

area 824,300 sq km/318,262 sq mi
capital Windhoek
physical mainly desert; includes the enclave of Walvis Bay (area 1,120 sq km/432 sq mi) currently administered by South Africa
head of state and government Sam Nujoma from 1990
government democratic republic
political parties South West African People's Organization of Namibia (SWAPO), socialist Ovambo-orientated; Democratic Turnhalle Alliance (DTA), moderate, multi-racial coalition; United Democratic Front (UDF), disaffected ex-SWAPO members; National Christian Action (ACN), white conservative
exports diamonds, uranium
currency South African rand (4.33 = Feb 1990)

population (1988) 1,288,000 (85% black African, 6% European). There are 300,000 displaced families, 50,000 refugees, and 75,000 in SWAPO camps in exile
life expectancy black 40, white 69
language Afrikaans, German, English
religion 51% Lutheran, 19% Roman Catholic, 6% Dutch Reformed Church, 6% Anglican
literacy 38%
GDP $1,247m (1985); $1,084 per head of population
chronology
1884 German and British colonies established.
1915 German colony seized by South Africa.
1920 Administered by South Africa, under League of Nations mandate, as British South Africa (SWA).
1946 Full incorporation in South Africa refused by United Nations (UN).
1958 South West African People's Organization (SWAPO) set up to seek racial equality and full independence.
1966 South Africa's apartheid laws extended to the country.
1968 Redesignated Namibia by UN.
1978 UN Security Council Resolution 435 for the granting of full sovereignty accepted by South Africa and then rescinded.
1988 Peace talks between South Africa, Angola, and Cuba led to agreement on full independence for Namibia.
1989 Unexpected incursion by SWAPO guerrillas from Angola into Namibia threatened agreed timetable for independence from South Africa.
1990 Liberal multi-party 'independence' constitution adopted; Sam Nujoma elected president.

Napa capital of Napa country, California, USA; population (1980) 50,900; centre of the notable wine-producing *Napa Valley* situated to the NE of San Francisco.

Napier wool port in Hawke Bay on the E coast of North Island, New Zealand; population (1986) 52,000.

Naples (Italian *Napoli*) industrial port (shipbuilding, cars, textiles, paper, food processing) and capital of Campania, Italy, on the Tyrrhenian Sea; population (1988) 1,201,000. To the south is the Isle of Capri, and behind the city is Mount Vesuvius, with the ruins of Pompeii at its foot.

Naples is the third largest city of Italy, and as a port second in importance only to Genoa. Buildings include the royal palace, the San Carlo Opera House, the Castel Nuovo 1283, and the university 1224.

The city began as the Greek colony Neapolis in the 6th century BC and was taken over by Romans 326 BC; it became part of the Kingdom of the Two Sicilies 1140 and capital of the Kingdom of Naples 1282.

Napoli Italian form of ◊Naples, city in Italy.

Nara city in Japan, in the S of Honshu island, the capital of the country AD 710–94; population (1984) 316,000. It was the birthplace of Japanese art and literature and has ancient wooden temples.

Narbonne city in Aude *département*, S France; population (1983) 39,246. It was the chief town of S Gaul in Roman times and a port in medieval times.

Narmada River a river that rises in the Maikala range in Madhya Pradesh state, central India,

Nauru
Republic of

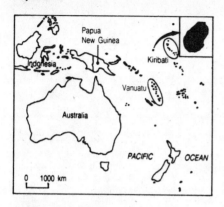

area 21 sq km/8 sq mi
capital Yaren
physical island country in W Pacific
features plateau circled by coral cliffs and
sandy beach
head of state and government Hammer
DeRoburt from 1987
political system liberal democracy
exports phosphates

currency Australian dollar (2.23 = £1 Feb
1990)
population (1989) 8,100 (mainly Polynesian;
Chinese 8%, European 8%); annual growth
rate 3.1%
language Nauruan (official), English
religion Protestant 45%
literacy 99%
GDP $155 million (1981); $21,400 per head of
population
chronology
1888 Annexed by Germany.
1920 Administered by Australia, New Zealand,
and UK until independence, except 1942–45,
when it was occupied by Japan.
1968 Full independence achieved, with 'special
member' Commonwealth status. Hammer
DeRoburt elected president.
1976 Bernard Dowiyogo elected president.
1978 DeRoburt returned to power.
1986 DeRoburt briefly replaced as president by
Kenneth Adeang.
1987 DeRoburt returned to power; Adeang
established the Democratic Party of Nauru.
1989 DeRoburt defeated on no confidance
motion and replaced by Kensas Aroi, who
later resigned and was succeeded by Bernard
Dowiyogo.

and flows 1,245 km/778 mi WSW to the Gulf of
Khambat, an inlet of the Arabian Sea. Forming
the traditional boundary between Hindustan and
Deccan, the Narmada is a holy river of the Hindus. India's Narmada Valley Project is one of the
largest and most controversial river development
projects in the world. Between 1990 and 2040 it is
planned to build 30 major dams, 135 medium-sized
dams and 3,000 smaller dams in a scheme that will
involve moving 1 million of the valley's population
of 20 million people.

Narragansett Bay Atlantic inlet, Rhode Island,
USA. Running inland for 45 km/28 mi, it encloses
a number of islands.

Narvik seaport in Nordland county, N Norway, on
Ofot Fjord, exporting iron ore from Swedish
mines; population (1980) 19,500. To secure this
ore supply Germany seized Narvik in Apr 1940.
British, French, Polish, and Norwegian forces
recaptured the port but had to abandon it on 10
Jun to cope with the worsening Allied situation
elsewhere in Europe.

Nashville port on the Cumberland river and capital
of Tennessee, USA; population (1986) 931,000.
It is a banking and commercial centre, and has
large printing, music-publishing, and recording
industries. Most of the Bibles in the USA are

printed here, and it is the hub of the country-music
business.
  Nashville dates from 1778, and the Confederate
army was defeated here in 1864 in the American
Civil War.

Nassau capital and port of the Bahamas, on New
Providence island; population (1980) 135,000.
English settlers founded it 1629.

Natal province of South Africa, NE of Cape Province, bounded on the E by the Indian Ocean
area 91,785 sq km/35,429 sq mi
capital Pietermaritzburg
towns Durban
physical slopes from the Drakensberg to a fertile
subtropical coastal plain
products sugar cane, black wattle (*Acacia
mollissima*), maize, fruits, vegetables, tobacco,
coal
population (1985) 2,145,000
history called Natal because Vasco da Gama
reached it Christmas Day 1497; part of the British
Cape Colony 1843–56, when it was made into a
separate colony; Zululand was annexed to Natal
1897, and the districts of Vrijheid, Utrecht, and
part of Wakkerstroom were transferred from the
Transvaal to Natal 1903; the colony became a part
of the Union of South Africa 1910.

Natal industrial (textiles, salt refining) seaport in Brazil, capital of the state of Rio Grande do Norte; population (1980) 376,500. Natal was founded 1599 and became a city 1822.

Natchez trading centre in Mississippi, USA, on the bluffs above the Mississippi River; population (1980) 22,000. It has many houses of the pre-American Civil War period, and was important in the heyday of steamboat traffic.

Natron, Lake a salt and soda lake in the Great Rift Valley, Kenya.

Natural Bridge a village in Virginia, USA, 185 km/ 115 mi W of Richmond. The nearby Cedar Creek is straddled by an arch of limestone 66 m/215 ft high and 27 m/90 ft wide.

Nauru island country in the SW Pacific, in Polynesia, W of Kiribati.

Navarre (Spanish *Navarra*) autonomous mountain region of N Spain
area 10,400 sq km/4,014 sq mi
capital Pamplona
features Monte Adi 1,503 m/4,933 ft; rivers Ebro and its tributary the Arga
population (1986) 513,000
history part of the medieval kingdom of Navarre. Estella, to the SW, where Don Carlos was proclaimed king 1833, was a centre of agitation by the Carlists.

Naxos an island of Greece, the largest of the Cyclades, area 453 sq km/175 sq mi. Known since early times for its wine, it was a centre for the worship of Bacchus, who, according to Greek mythology, found the deserted Ariadne on its shore and married her.

Nazareth town in Galilee, N Israel, SE of Haifa; population (1981) 64,000. According to the New Testament, it was the boyhood home of Jesus.

Nazca town south of Lima, Peru, near a plateau which has geometric linear markings interspersed with giant outlines of birds and animals. The markings were made by American Indians, possibly in the 6th century AD, and their function is thought to be ritual rather than astronomical.

Naze, the headland on the coast of Essex, England, S of the port of Harwich; also the English name for *Lindesnes*, a cape in S Norway.

NB abbreviation for ◊*New Brunswick*; ◊*Nebraska*.

NC abbreviation for ◊*North Carolina*.

ND abbreviation for ◊*North Dakota*.

N'djamena capital of Chad, at the confluence of the Chari and Logone rivers, on the Cameroon border; population (1985) 511,700.
Founded 1900 by the French at the junction of caravan routes, it was used 1903–12 as a military centre against the kingdoms of central Sudan. Its name until 1973 was Fort Lamy.

Ndola mining centre and chief city of the Copperbelt province of central Zambia; population (1987) 418,000.

Nebraska

Neagh, Lough lake in Northern Ireland, 25 km/ 15 mi W of Belfast; area 396 sq km/153 sq mi. It is the largest lake in the British Isles.

Near East term used until the 1940s to describe the area of the Balkan states, Egypt and SW Asia, now known as the ◊Middle East.

Neath town in West Glamorgan, Wales, near the mouth of the river Neath; population (1984) 26,000. The Roman fort of Nidum was discovered nearby 1949; there are also remains of a Norman castle and abbey.

Nebraska plains state of the central USA; nickname Cornhusker State
area 200,400 sq km/77,354 sq mi
capital Lincoln
towns Omaha, Grand Island, North Platte
features Rocky Mountain foothills; tributaries of the Missouri; Boys' Town for the homeless near Omaha; the ranch of Buffalo Bill
products cereals, livestock, processed foods, fertilizers, oil, natural gas
population (1987) 1,594,000
famous people Fred Astaire, Willa Cather, Henry Fonda, Gerald Ford, Harold Lloyd, Malcolm X
history ceded to Spain by France 1763, retroceded to France 1801, and part of the Louisiana Purchase 1803. It was first settled 1847, became a territory 1854, and a state 1867.

Needles, the a group of rocks in the sea near the Isle of ◊Wight, S England.

Negev desert in S Israel which tapers to the port of Eilat. It is fertile under irrigation, and minerals include oil and copper.

Negri Sembilan state of S Peninsular Malaysia; area 6,646 sq km/2,565 sq mi; population (1980) 574,000. It is mainly mountainous; products include rice and rubber. The capital is Seremban.

Nejd region of central Arabia consisting chiefly of desert; area about 2,720,000 sq km/800,000 sq mi. It forms part of the kingdom of Saudi Arabia, and is inhabited by Bedouins. The capital is Riyadh.

Nepal landlocked country in the Himalayan mountain range, bounded to the N by Tibet, to the E by Sikkim, and to the S and W by India.

Nepál
(Sri Nepala Sarkar)

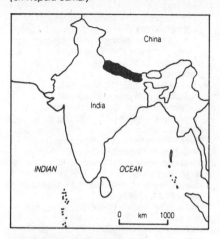

China

India

INDIAN   OCEAN

0   km   1000

area 147,181 sq km/56,812 sq mi
capital Katmandu
physical descends from the Himalaya
mountain range in the N to the river Ganges
plain in the S
features Mt Everest, Mt Kangchenjunga
head of state King Birendra Bir Bikram Shah
Dev from 1972
head of government Marich Man Singh
Shrestha from 1986
government constitutional monarchy
political parties banned from 1961; four
opposition parties function unofficially:
the Communist Party of Nepál (CPN),
Marxist-Leninist-Maoist; the Nepáli Congress
Party (NCP), left-of-centre; the United Liberation

Torchbearers and the Democratic Front, radical
republican
exports jute, rice, timber
currency Nepálese rupee (48.31 = £1 Feb
1990)
population (1989) 18,760,000 (mainly known
by the name of the predominant clan, the
Gurkhas; the Sherpas are a Buddhist minority
of NE Nepál); annual growth rate 2.3%
life expectancy men 47, women 45
language Nepáli
religion Hindu, with Buddhist minority
literacy 39% male/12% female (1985 est)
GNP $2.6 bn (1983); $140 per head of
population
chronology
1768 Nepál emerged as unified kingdom.
1815–16 Anglo-Nepáli 'Gurkha War'; Nepál
became a British-dependent 'buffer state'
1846–1951 Ruled by the Rana family.
1923 Independence from Britain recognized
1951 Monarchy restored.
1959 Constitution created elected legislature.
1960–61 Parliament dissolved by king and
political parties banned.
1980 Constitutional referendum held following
popular agitation.
1981 Direct elections held to national assembly
1983 Overthrow of monarch-supported prime
minister.
1986 New assembly elections returned a
majority opposed to *panchayat* system.
1988 Strict curbs placed on opposition activity,
with more than 100 supporters of banned
opposition party arrested and tight censorship
imposed.
1989 Border blockade imposed by India in
treaty dispute.

Ness, Loch see ◊Loch Ness.
Netherlands, the country in W Europe on the North
Sea, bounded to the E by West Germany and to the
S by Belgium.
Netherlands Antilles two groups of Caribbean
islands, part of the Netherlands with full internal autonomy, comprising ◊Curaçao and Bonaire
off the coast of Venezuela (Aruba is considered
separately), and St Eustatius, Saba, and the S part
of St Maarten in the Leeward Islands, 800 km/500
mi NE.
area 797 sq km/308 sq mi
capital Willemstad on Curaçao
products oil from Venezuela is refined here;
tourism
language Dutch (official), Papiamento, English
population (1983) 193,000.

Netherlands East Indies former name of ◊Indonesia
(1798–1945).
Netzahualcóyotl Mexican city lying to the south of
Lake Texcoco, forming a suburb to the NE of
Mexico City; population (1980) 1,341,200.
Neubrandenburg county in East Germany; capital
Neubrandenburg; area 10,950 sq km/4,227 sq mi;
population (1986) 619,000.
Neuchâtel (German *Neuenburg*) capital of
Neuchâtel canton in NW Switzerland, on
Lake Neuchâtel, W of Berne; population (1980)
34,500. It has a Horological (clock) Research
Laboratory.
Neusiedler See (Hungarian *Fertö Tó*) shallow lake
in E Austria and NW Hungary, SE of Vienna;
area 152 sq km/60 sq mi; the only steppe lake in
Europe.

Netherlands
Kingdom of the
(Koninkrijk der Nederlanden), popularly referred to as **Holland**

area 41,900 sq km/16,178 sq mi
capital Amsterdam
towns The Hague (seat of government); chief port Rotterdam
physical almost completely flat; rivers Rhine, Schelde *(Scheldt)*, Maas; Frisian Islands
territories Aruba, Netherlands Antilles
features land reclamation has turned the former Zuider Zee inlet into the freshwater ijsselmeer
head of state Queen Beatrix Wilhelmina

Armgard from 1980
head of government Rudolph Lubbers from 1982
government constitutional monarchy
political parties Christian Democratic Appeal (CDA), Christian, right-of-centre; Labour party (PVdA), moderate, left-of-centre; People's Party for Freedom and Democracy (VVD), free enterprise, centrist
exports dairy products, flower bulbs, vegetables, petrochemicals, electronics
currency guilder (3.21 = £1 Feb 1990)
population (1988) 14,715,000 (including 300,000 of Dutch-Indonesian origin absorbed 1949–64 from former colonial possessions); annual growth rate 0.5%
life expectancy men 73, women 80
language Dutch
religion Roman Catholic 35%, Protestant 28%
literacy 99% (1985)
GNP $122.4 bn (1984); $9,175 per head of population
chronology
1940–45 Occupied by Germany during World War II.
1947 Joined Benelux Union.
1948 Queen Juliana succeeded Queen Wilhelmina to the throne.
1949 Founder member of NATO.
1958 Joined European Community.
1980 Queen Juliana abdicated in favour of her daughter Beatrix.
1981 Opposition to Cruise missiles averted their being sited on Dutch soil.
1989 Prime minister Lubbers resigned over ecological issue. General election and new Lubbers-led coalition.

Neuss industrial city in North Rhine-Westphalia, West Germany; population (1988) 144,000.

Nevada state of the W USA; nickname Sagebrush, Silver, or Battleborn State
area 286,400 sq km/110,550 sq mi
capital Carson City
towns Las Vegas, Reno
physical Mojave Desert, Lake Tahoe, mountains and plateaus alternating with valleys
features legal gambling; Nuclear Rocket Development Station at Jackass Flats NW of Las Vegas: fallout from nuclear tests in the 1950s may have caused subsequent deaths, including that of John Wayne, who was filming there
products mercury, barite, gold, copper, oil, gaming machines
population (1987) 1,053,000
history ceded to the USA after the Mexican War 1848; first permanent settlement 1858; discovery of silver the same year led to rapid population growth; became a state 1864; huge water projects and military installations 20th century.

Nevers industrial town in Burgundy, central France, at the meeting of the Loire and Nièvre rivers; capital of the former province of Nivernais and the modern *département* of Nièvre; population (1982) 44,800.

New Amsterdam town in Guyana, on the Berbice, founded by the Dutch; population (1980) 25,000. Also a former name (1624–64) of ◊New York.

Newark largest city (industrial and commercial) of New Jersey, USA; industries (electrical equipment, machinery, chemicals, paints, canned meats); population (1980) 1,963,000. The city dates from 1666, when a settlement called Milford was made on the site.

Newark market town in Nottinghamshire, England; population (1981) 24,000. It has the ruins of a 12th-century castle in which King John died.

Netherlands Antilles

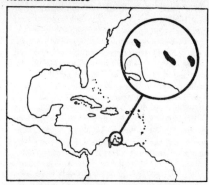

Nevada

New Britain largest island in the ◊Bismarck Archipelago, part of Papua New Guinea; capital Rabaul; population (1985) 253,000.

New Brunswick maritime province of E Canada
area 73,400 sq km/28,332 sq mi
capital Fredericton
towns Saint John, Moncton
features Grand Lake, St John River; Bay of Fundy
products cereals; wood, paper; fish; lead, zinc, copper, oil and natural gas
population (1986) 710,000, 37% French-speaking
history first reached by Europeans (Cartier) 1534; explored by Champlain 1604; remained a French colony as part of Nova Scotia until ceded to England 1713; after American Revolution, many United Empire Loyalists settled there, and it became a province 1784; one of the original provinces of Confederation 1867.

Newbury market town in Berkshire, England; population (1981) 26,000. It has a racecourse and training stables, and electronics industries. Nearby are ◊Aldermaston and Harwell with nuclear research establishments, and RAF ◊Greenham Common.

New Caledonia island group in the S Pacific, a French overseas territory between Australia and the Fiji Islands
area 18,576 sq km/7,170 sq mi
capital Nouméa
physical fertile, surrounded by a barrier reef
products nickel (the world's third largest producer), chrome, iron
currency CFP franc
population (1983) 145,300, 43% Kanak (Melanesian), 37% European, 8% Wallisian, 5% Vietnamese and Indonesian, 4% Polynesian
language French (official)
religion Roman Catholic 60%, Protestant 30%
history New Caledonia was visited by Captain Cook 1774, and became French 1853. A general strike to gain local control of nickel mines 1974 was defeated. In 1981 the French socialist government

promised moves towards independence. The 1985 elections resulted in control of most regions by Kanaks, but not the majority of seats. In 1986 the French conservative government reversed the reforms. The Kanaks boycotted a referendum Sept 1987 and a majority were in favour of remaining a French dependency. In 1989 the leader of the Socialist National Liberation front (the most prominent separatist group), Jean-Marie Tjibaou, was murdered.

Newcastle industrial port (iron, steel, chemicals, textiles, ships) in New South Wales, Australia; population (1986) 429,000. The nearby coalmines were discovered 1796. A penal settlement was founded 1804.

Newcastle-under-Lyme industrial town (coal, bricks and tiles, clothing) in Staffordshire, England; population (1981) 120,100. Keele University is nearby.

Newcastle-upon-Tyne industrial port (coal, shipbuilding, marine and electrical engineering, chemicals, metals), commercial and cultural centre in Tyne and Wear, NE England, administrative headquarters of Tyne and Wear and Northumberland; population (1981) 278,000.
features Parts are preserved of a castle built by Henry II 1172–77 on the site of an older castle; the cathedral is chiefly 14th century; there is a 12th-century church, and the Guildhall 1658. Newcastle is connected with the neighbouring town of

New Brunswick

Newfoundland and Labrador

Gateshead by several bridges. The headquarters of the Ministry of Social Security is here.

history Chiefly known as a coaling centre, Newcastle first began to trade in coal in the 13th century. In 1826 ironworks were established by George Stephenson, and the first engine used on the Stockton and Darlington railway was made in Newcastle.

New Delhi city in the Union Territory of Delhi, designed by Lutyens; capital of India since 1912; population (1981) 273,000.

New England region of NE USA, comprising the states of Maine, New Hampshire, Vermont, Massachusetts, Rhode Island, and Connecticut, originally settled by Pilgrims and Puritans from England. It is a geographic region rather than a political entity. The area is still heavily forested and the economy relies on tourism as well as industry.

New England district of N New South Wales, Australia, especially the tableland area of Glen Innes and Armidale.

New Forest ancient forest in S England: see under ◊Hampshire.

Newfoundland and Labrador Canadian province on Atlantic Ocean

area 405,700 sq km/156,600 sq mi

capital St John's

towns Corner Brook, Gander

physical Newfoundland island and ◊Labrador on the mainland on the other side of the Straits of Belle Isle; rocky

features Grand Banks section of the continental shelf rich in cod; home of the Newfoundland and Labrador dogs

products newsprint, fish products, hydroelectric power, iron, copper, zinc, uranium, offshore oil

population (1986) 568,000

history colonized by Vikings about 1000 AD. The English, under the Italian navigator Caboto, reached Newfoundland 1497. It was the first English colony, established 1583. France also made settlements and British sovereignty was not

recognized until 1713; internal self-government 1855; France retained the offshore islands of St Pierre and Miquelon. In 1934, as Newfoundland had fallen into financial difficulties, administration was vested in a governor and a special commission. A 1948 referendum favoured federation with Canada and the province joined Canada 1949.

New Guinea island in the SW Pacific, N of Australia, comprising Papua New Guinea and Irian Jaya (administered by Indonesia); area 775,213 sq km/ 229,232 sq mi; population (1980) 1,174,000. Part of the Dutch East Indies from 1828, it was ceded by the UN to Indonesia 1963. Its tropical rainforest and the 0.5 million hunter-gatherers who inhabit it are under threat from logging companies and resettlement schemes. The inhabitants' resistance to an enforced Indonesian way of life has been brutally put down; villages have been bombed and strafed from the air.

Newham borough of E Greater London, N of the Thames, includes East and West Ham

features former residents include Dick Turpin and Gerard Manley Hopkins; former Royal Victoria and Albert and King George V docks

population (1984) 209,400.

New Hampshire state of the NE USA; nickname Granite State

area 24,000 sq km/9,264 sq mi

capital Concord

towns Manchester, Nashua

features White Mountains; Mount Monadnock 1,063 m/3,489 ft; the state's early primary elections: no president has ever come to office without succeeding here

products electrical machinery, gravel, apples, maple syrup, livestock

population (1987) 1,057,000

famous people Mary Baker Eddy, Robert Frost

New Hampshire

New Jersey

history first settled 1623, it was the first colony to declare its independence of Britain. It became a state 1788, one of the original Thirteen States.

Newhaven port in E Sussex, SE England, with container facilities and cross-Channel services to Dieppe, France; population (1985) 11,000.

New Haven port town in Connecticut, USA, on Long Island Sound; population (1980) 418,000. *Yale University*, third oldest in the USA, was founded here 1701 and named after Elihu Yale (1648–1721), an early benefactor.

New Hebrides former name (until 1980) of ◊Vanuatu.

New Jersey state of NE USA; nickname Garden State
area 20,200 sq km/7,797 sq mi
capital Trenton
towns Newark, Jersey City, Paterson, Elizabeth
features coastal resorts, including Atlantic City; Princeton University 1746; Walt Whitman's house in Camden
products asparagus, fruit, potatoes, tomatoes, poultry, chemicals, metal goods, electrical machinery, clothing
population (1985) 7,562,000
famous people Aaron Burr, James Fenimore Cooper, Stephen Crane, Thomas Edison, Alexander Hamilton, Thomas Paine, Paul Robeson, Frank Sinatra, Bruce Springsteen
history colonized in the 17th century by the Dutch, it was ceded to England 1664, and became a state 1787, one of the original Thirteen States.

New London naval base and yachting centre of SE Connecticut, USA; on Long Island Sound at the mouth of the river Thames.

Newlyn seaport near Penzance, Cornwall, England, which gives its name to the Newlyn School of artists 1880–90, including Stanhope

Forbes (1857–1947). The Ordnance Survey relates heights in the UK to mean sea level here.

Newmarket town in Suffolk, E England, centre for horse racing since James I's reign, notably the One Thousand and Two Thousand Guineas, the Cambridgeshire, the Jockey Club Stakes and the Cesarewitch. It is the headquarters of the Jockey Club, and a bookmaker who is 'warned off Newmarket Heath' is banned from all British racecourses. The National Horseracing Museum 1983 is here.

New Mexico state of the SW USA; nickname Land of Enchantment
area 315,000 sq km/121,590 sq mi
capital Santa Fé
towns Albuquerque, Las Cruces, Roswell
physical more than 75% of the area is over 1,200 m/3,900 ft above sea level; plains, mountains, caverns
features Great Plains and Rocky Mountains; Rio Grande; Carlsbad Caverns, the largest known; Los Alamos atomic and space research centre; White Sands Missile Range (also used by Space Shuttle); Kiowa Ranch, site of D H Lawrence's Utopian colony in the Sangre de Christos mountains
products uranium, oil, natural gas, cotton, cereals, vegetables
population (1987) 1,500,000
famous people Kit Carson
history explored by Spain in the 16th century; most of it was ceded to the USA by Mexico 1848, and it became a state 1912.

New Orleans commercial and industrial city (banking, oil refining, rockets) and Mississippi river port in Louisiana, USA; population (1980) 557,500. It is the traditional birthplace of jazz.

Founded by the French in 1718, it still has a distinctive French Quarter and Mardi Gras celebrations. The Saturn rockets for Apollo spacecraft are built here. Dixieland jazz exponents still play at Preservation Hall. The Superdome sports palace is among the world's largest enclosed stadiums, and is adaptable to various games and expected audience size.

New Mexico

New Plymouth port on the W coast of North Island, New Zealand; population (1983) 36,500. It lies at the centre of a dairy-farming region; Taranaki gas fields are nearby.

Newport river port, capital of the Isle of Wight, England; population (1981) 23,500. Charles I was imprisoned in nearby Carisbrooke Castle.

Newport seaport in Gwent (administrative headquarters), Wales, on the river Usk, NW of Bristol; population (1983) 130,200. There is a steelworks at nearby Llanwern, and a high-tech complex at Cleppa Park. The Newport Transporter Bridge was built 1906.

Newport News industrial city (engineering, shipbuilding) and port of SE Virginia, USA, at the mouth of the river James; population (1980) 144,903.

New Rochelle residential suburb of New York on Long Island Sound; population (1980) 70,800.

New South Wales state of SE Australia
area 801,600 sq km/309,418 sq mi
capital Sydney
towns Newcastle, Wollongong, Broken Hill
physical Great Dividing Range (including Blue Mountains) and part of the Australian Alps (including Snowy Mountains and Mount Kosciusko); Murray, Darling, Murrumbidgee river system irrigates the Riverina district
features a major radio telescope at Parkes, and Siding Spring Mountain 859 m/2,817 ft, NW of Sydney, has telescopes that can observe the central sector of our galaxy. Canberra forms an enclave within the state, and New South Wales administers the dependency of ◊Lord Howe Island
products cereals, fruit, sugar, tobacco, wool, meat, hides and skins, gold, silver, copper, tin, zinc, coal; hydroelectric power from the Snowy river
population (1987) 5,570,000; 60% living in Sydney
history convict settlement 1788–1850, and opened to free settlement by 1819; received self-government 1856; became a state of the Commonwealth of Australia 1901. Since 1973 there has been decentralization to counteract the pull of Sydney, and the New England and Riverina districts have separatist movements. It was called New Wales by James Cook, who landed at Botany Bay 1770 and thought that the coastline resembled that of Wales.

New World the Americas, so called by Europeans who reached them later than other continents. The term is used as an adjective to describe animals and plants that live in the western hemisphere.

New York state of the NE USA; nickname Empire State
area 127,200 sq km/49,099 sq mi
capital Albany

New South Wales

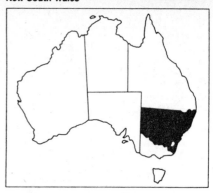

towns New York, Buffalo, Rochester, Yonkers, Syracuse
physical Adirondack and Catskill mountains; Lake Placid; bordering on lakes Erie and Ontario; Hudson river; Niagara Falls; ◊Long Island
features West Point, site of the US Military Academy 1802; National Baseball Hall of Fame, Cooperstown; racing at Saratoga Springs; Corning Museum of Glass 1951, reputedly the world's finest collection, including a portrait head of Amenhotep II of the 15th century BC; Washington Irving's home at Philipsburg Manor; Fenimore House commemorating J F Cooper, Cooperstown; home of F D Roosevelt at Hyde Park, and the Roosevelt Library; home of Theodore Roosevelt; the Adirondacks are noted for their scenery and sporting facilities; Seneca and Cayuga lakes
products clothing, printing, Steuben glass, titanium concentrate, cereals, apples, maple syrup, poultry, meat, dairy products, wine
population (1985) 17,783,000
famous people Henry and William James, Herman Melville, Walt Whitman
history explored by Champlain and Hudson 1609, colonized by the Dutch from 1614,

New York

New Zealand

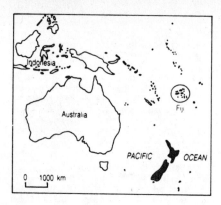

area 268,000 sq km/103,448 sq mi
capital Wellington
towns Hamilton, Palmerston North, Christchurch, Dunedin; ports Wellington, Auckland
physical comprises North Island, South Island, Stewart Island, Chatham Islands, and minor islands; mainly mountainous
overseas territories Tokelau (three atolls transferred 1926 from the former Gilbert and Ellice Islands colony); Niue Island (one of the Cook Islands, but separately administered from 1903: chief town Alafi); Cook Islands are internally self-governing, but share common citizenship with New Zealand; Ross Dependency is in Antarctica
features on North Island are Ruapehu, at 2,797 m/9,180 ft the highest of three active volcanoes, the geysers and hot springs of the Rotorua district, Lake Taupo (616 sq km/238 sq mi), source of Waikato River, and NE of the lake, Kaingaroa state forest, one of the world's largest planted forests. On South Island are the Southern Alps and Canterbury Plains, noted for sheep
head of state Elizabeth II from 1952 represented by Paul Reeves from 1985
head of government Geoffrey Palmer from 1989
government constitutional monarchy
political parties Labour Party, moderate, left-of-centre; New Zealand National Party, free enterprise, centre-right
exports lamb, beef, wool, leather, dairy products and other processed foods; kiwi fruit became a major export crop in the 1980s; seeds and breeding stock; timber, paper, pulp, light aircraft
currency New Zealand dollar (2.88 = £1 Feb 1990)
population (1989) 3,397,000 (including 270,000 Maoris and 60,000 other Polynesians; the whites are chiefly of British descent); annual growth rate 0.9%
life expectancy men 71, women 77
language English (official); Maori (the Lange government pledged to give it official status)
religion Protestant 50%, Roman Catholic 15%
literacy 99% (1984)
GNP $21.4 bn (1984); $7,916 per head of population
chronology
1947 Full independence within the Commonwealth confirmed by New Zealand parliament.
1972 National Party government replaced Labour Party, with Norman Kirk as prime minister.
1974 Kirk died and was replaced by Wallace Rowling.
1975 National Party returned, with Robert Muldoon as prime minister.
1984 Labour Party returned under David Lange.
1985 Non-nuclear defence policy created disagreements with France and the US.
1987 National Party declared support for the Labour government's non-nuclear policy. Lange re-elected. New Zealand officially became a 'friendly' rather than 'allied' country to the US because of its non-nuclear defence policy.
1988 Free-trade agreement with Australia signed.
1989 Lange resigned over economic row with finance minister, and was replaced by Geoffrey Palmer.

and annexed by the English 1664. The first constitution was adopted 1777, when New York became one of the original Thirteen States.

New York largest city in the USA, industrial port (printing, publishing, clothing), cultural and commercial centre in New York State, at the junction of the Hudson and East rivers; comprises the boroughs of the Bronx, Brooklyn, Manhattan, Queens, and Staten Island; population (1980) 9,081,000.

features The Statue of Liberty stands on Liberty Island (called Bedloe's Island until 1956) in the inner harbour. Skyscrapers include the World Trade Center (412 m/1,350 ft), the Empire State Building (381 m/1,250 ft), and the Art Deco

New Zealand

	Area sq km
North Island	114,688
South Island	150,460
Stewart Island	1,735
Chatham Islands	963
Minor Islands	320
	268,675

Island Territories:

Niue Island	260
Tokelau Islands	10
Cook Islands	230
Ross Dependency	453,250

Chrysler Building. St Patrick's Cathedral is 19th-century Gothic. There are a number of notable art galleries, among them the Frick Collection, the Metropolitan Museum of Art (with a medieval crafts department, the Cloisters), the Museum of Modern Art, and the Guggenheim, designed by Frank Lloyd Wright. Columbia University 1754 is the best known of a number of institutions of higher education. Central Park is the largest park.

history The Italian navigator Giovanni da Verrazano (? 1485–? 1528) reached New York Bay 1524, and Henry Hudson explored it 1609. The Dutch established a settlement on Manhattan 1613, named New Amsterdam from 1626; this was captured by the English in 1664 and renamed New York. During the War of Independence, British troops occupied New York 1776–84; it was the capital of the USA 1785–89. The five boroughs were linked 1898 to give the city its present extent.

New Zealand country in the S Pacific, SE of Australia.

NF abbreviation for ◊*Newfoundland*.

Ngorongoro Crater crater in the Tanzanian section of the African Great ◊Rift Valley, noted for its large numbers of wildebeests, gazelle, and zebra.

NH abbreviation for ◊*New Hampshire*.

Nicaragua
Republic of
(República de Nicaragua)

area 127,849 sq km/49,350 sq mi
capital Managua
towns chief port Corinto
physical volcanic mountain ranges; lakes Nicaragua and Managua
features largest state of Central America and most thinly populated
head of state and government from Apr 1990 Violeta Barios de Chamorro
political system emergent democracy
political parties Sandanista National Liberation Front (FSLN), Marxist-Leninist; Democratic Conservative Party (PCD), centrist; National Opposition Union (UNO), loose, US-backed coalition;
exports coffee, cotton, sugar
currency cordoba (68313.15 = £1 Feb 1990)
population (1989) 3,692,000 (70% mestizo, 15% Spanish descent, 10% Indian or black); annual growth rate 3.3%
life expectancy men 59, women 61
language Spanish (official)
religion Roman Catholic
literacy 61% male/60% female (1980 est)
GDP $3.4 bn (1983); $804 per head of population
chronology
1838 Achieved full independence.
1962 Sandinista National Liberation Front (FSLN) formed to fight Somoza regime.
1979 Somoza government ousted by FSLN.
1982 Subversive activity against the government promoted by the US. State of emergency declared.
1984 The US mined Nicaraguan harbours.
1985 Denunciation of Sandinista government by US president Reagan. FSLN, led by Daniel Ortega Saavedra, won big victory in assembly elections.
1987 Central American peace agreement co-signed by Nicaraguan leaders.
1988 Peace agreement failed. Nicaragua held talks with Contra rebel leaders. Hurricane left 180,000 people homeless.
1989 Demobilization of rebels and release of former Somozan supporters; cease-fire ended.
1990 FSLN defeated by UNO, a US-backed coalition; Violeta Chamorro president from Apr.

Niger
Republic of
(République du Niger)

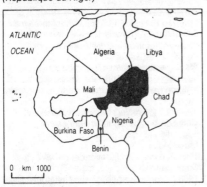

ATLANTIC
OCEAN
Algeria   Libya
Mali
Chad
Nigeria
Burkina Faso
Benin
0   km   1000

area 1,186,408 sq km/457,953 sq mi
capital Niamey
physical mountains in centre; arid except in S
(savanna) and SW (river Niger)
features part of the Sahara Desert and subject
to Sahel droughts

head of state and government Ali Seybou
from 1987
government military republic
political parties banned from 1974
exports groundnuts, livestock, gum arabic, tin,
uranium
currency CFA franc (485.00 = £1 Feb 1990)
population (1989) 7,444,000; annual growth
rate 2.8%
life expectancy men 41, women 44
language French (official), Hausa, Djerma
religion Sunni Muslim 85%, animist 15%
literacy 19% male/9% female (1985 est)
GDP $2.3 bn (1982); $475 per head of
population
chronology
1960 Achieved full independence from France
with Hamani Diori elected president.
1974 Diori ousted in an army coup led by Seyni
Kountché.
1977 Cooperation agreement signed with
France.
1987 Kountché died and was replaced by the
army commander-in-chief Ali Seybou.

Niagara Falls two waterfalls on the Niagara River, on the Canada–USA border, separated by Goat Island. The *American Falls* are 51 m/167 ft high, 330 m/1,080 ft wide; *Horseshoe Falls*, in Canada, are 49 m/160 ft high, 790 m/2,600 ft across.

On the west bank of the river is *Niagara Falls*, a city in Ontario, Canada; population (1986) 72,000, metropolitan area of Niagara Falls–St Catharines 343,000; on the east bank is *Niagara Falls*, New York State, USA; population (1980) 71,000. They have hydroelectric generating plants and tourism.

Niamey river port and capital of Niger; population (1983) 399,000. It produces textiles, chemicals, pharmaceuticals, and foodstuffs.

Nicaragua country in Central America, between the Pacific Ocean and the Caribbean, bounded N by Honduras and S by Costa Rica.

Nicaragua, Lake lake in Nicaragua, the largest in Central America; area 8,250 sq km/3,185 sq mi.

Nice city on the French Riviera; population (1982) 449,500. Founded in the 3rd century BC, it repeatedly changed hands between France and the Duchy of Savoy from the 14th to the 19th century. In 1860 it was finally transferred to France.

There is an annual Battle of Flowers, and chocolate and perfume are made. Chapels in the nearby village of Vence have been decorated by Chagall and Matisse, and Nice has a Chagall museum.

Nicobar Islands group of Indian islands, part of the Union Territory of ◊Andaman and Nicobar Islands.

Nicosia capital of Cyprus, with leather, textile, and pottery industries; population (1987) 165,000.

Nicosia was the residence of Lusignan kings of Cyprus 1192–1475. The Venetians, who took Cyprus 1489, surrounded Nicosia with a high wall which still exists; it fell to the Turks 1571. It was again partly taken by the Turks in the invasion 1974. The Greek and Turkish sectors are separated by the Attila Line.

Niederösterreich German name for the federal state of ◊Lower Austria.

Niedersachsen German name for the region of ◊Lower Saxony, West Germany.

Nièvre river in central France, rising near Varzy and flowing 40 km/25 mi south to join the Loire at Nevers; it gives its name to a *département*.

Niger third longest river in Africa, 4,185 km/2,600 mi from the highlands bordering Sierra Leone and Guinea NE through Mali, then SE through Niger and Nigeria to an inland delta on the Gulf of Guinea. Its flow has been badly affected by the expansion of the Sahara Desert. It is sluggish and frequently floods its banks. It was explored by Mungo Park 1795–96.

Niger landlocked country in W Africa, bounded to the N by Nigeria and Libya, to the E by Chad, to the S by Nigeria and Benin, and to the W by Burkina Faso and Mali.

Nigeria country in W Africa on the Gulf of Guinea, bounded to the N by Niger, to the E by Chad and Cameroon, and to the W by Benin.

Nigeria
Federal Republic of

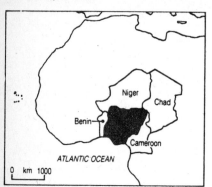

ATLANTIC OCEAN

0   km   1000

area 923,773 sq km/356,576 sq mi
capital Abuja; chief port Lagos
towns administrative headquarters Abuja;
Ibadan, Ogbomosho, Kano; ports Port
Harcourt, Warri, Calabar
physical the arid north becomes savanna and
farther south tropical rainforest, with mangrove
swamps along the coast; river Niger
features harmattan (a dry wind from the
Sahara); rich artistic heritage, for example
Benin bronzes
head of state and government Ibrahim
Babangida from 1985
government military republic
political parties Social Democratic Party
(SDP), left-of-centre; National Republican
Convention (NRC), right-of-centre

exports petroleum (richest African country in
oil resources), cocoa, groundnuts, palm oil,
cotton, rubber, tin
currency naira (13.33 = £1 Feb 1990)
population (1989) 115,152,000 (of three main
ethnic groups, Yoruba in the W, Ibo in the E,
and Hausa-Fulani in the N); annual growth
rate 3.3%
life expectancy men 47, women 50
language English (official), Hausa, Ibo, Yoruba
religion Sunni Muslim in the north, Christian in
the south
literacy 54% male/31% female (1985 est)
GDP $65 bn (1983); $750 per head of
population
chronology
1960 Achieved full independence within the
Commonwealth.
1963 Became a republic, with Nnamdi Azikiwe
as president.
1966 Military coup, followed by a counter-coup
led by Gen Yakubu Gowon. Slaughter of many
members of the Ibo tribe in the north.
1967 Conflict about oil revenues leads to
declaration of an independent state of Biafra
and outbreak of civil war.
1970 Surrender of Biafra and end of civil war.
1975 Gowon ousted in military coup; a second
coup puts Gen Obasanjo in power.
1979 Shehu Shagari becomes civilian
president.
1983 Shagari's government overthrown in coup
by Maj-Gen Buhari.
1985 Buhari replaced in a bloodless coup led
by Maj-Gen Ibrahim Babangida.
1989 Two new parties approved.

Niigata industrial port (textiles, metals, oil refining, chemicals) in Chubu region, Honshu island, Japan; population (1984) 459,000.

Nijmegen industrial city (brewery, electrical engineering, leather, tobacco) in E Netherlands, on the river Waal; population (1988) 241,000. The Roman Noviomagus, Nijmegen was a free city of the Holy Roman Empire and a member of the Hanseatic League.

Nikolayev port (with shipyards) and naval base on the Black Sea, in Ukraine, USSR; population (1987) 501,000.

Nile river in Africa, the world's longest, 6,695 km/ 4,160 mi. The Blue Nile rises in Lake Tana, Ethiopia, the White Nile at Lake Victoria, and they join at Khartoum, Sudan. It enters the Mediterranean at a vast delta in N Egypt.

Its remotest headstream is the Luvironza, in Burundi. The Nile proper begins on leaving Lake Victoria above ◊Owen Falls. From Lake Victoria it flows over rocky country, and there are many cataracts and rapids, including the Murchison Falls, until it enters Lake Mobutu (Albert). From here it flows across flat country and in places spreads out to form lakes. At Lake No it is joined by the Bahr el Ghazal, and from this point to Khartoum it is called the White Nile. At Khartoum it is joined by the Blue Nile, which rises in the Ethiopian highlands, and 320 km/200 mi below Khartoum it is joined by the Atbara. From Khartoum to ◊Aswan there are six cataracts. The Nile is navigable to the second cataract, a distance of 1,545 km/960 mi. The delta of the Nile is 190 km/120 mi wide. From 1982 Nile water has been piped beneath the Suez Canal to irrigate ◊Sinai. The water level behind the Aswan Dam fell from 170 m/558 ft (1979) to 150 m/492 ft (1988), threatening Egypt's hydroelectric power generation.

Nîmes capital of Gard *département*, Languedoc-Roussillon, S France; population (1982) 132,500.

Roman remains include an amphitheatre dating from the 2nd century AD and the Pont du Gard (aqueduct). The city gives its name to the cloth known as denim (de Nîmes); it is the birthplace of the writer Alphonse Daudet.

Ningbo port (formerly Ningpo) and special economic zone in Zhejiang province, E China; industries (fishing, shipbuilding, high-tech); population (1984) 615,600. Already a centre of foreign trade under the Tang dynasty (618–907), it was one of the original treaty ports 1842.

Ningpo former name for ◊Ningbo, port in China.

Ningxia or *Ningxia Hui* autonomous region (formerly Ninghsia-Hui) of NW China
area 170,000 sq km/65,620 sq mi
capital Yinchuan
physical desert plateau
products cereals and rice under irrigation; coal
population (1986) 4,240,000, including many Muslims and nomadic herders.

Nippon English transliteration of the Japanese name for ◊Japan.

Niterci resort city in Brazil on the E shore of Guanabara Bay, linked by bridge with Rio de Janeiro; population (1980) 382,700.

Niue coral island in the S Pacific, W of the Cook Islands; overseas territory of New Zealand
area 260 sq km/100 sq mi
towns port Alofi
products coconuts, passion fruit, honey
population (1988) 2,200
history inhabited by warriors who stopped Capt Cook from landing 1774; British protectorate 1900; annexed by New Zealand 1901; attained self-government in free association with New Zealand (with which there is common citizenship) 1974.

Nizhni-Novgorod former name (until 1932) of the city of ◊Gorky in central USSR.

Nile

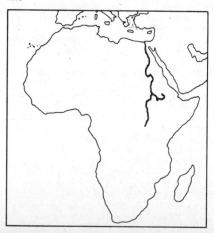

Norfolk

NJ abbreviation for ◊*New Jersey*.

NM abbreviation for ◊*New Mexico*.

Nord-Pas-de-Calais region of N France; area 12,400 sq km/4,786 sq mi; population (1986) 3,923,000. Its capital is Lille, and it consists of the *département*s of Nord and Pas-de-Calais.
      Pas-de-Calais is the French term for the Strait of Dover.

Nore, the sandbank at the mouth of the river Thames, England; site of the first lightship 1732.

Norfolk county on E coast of England
area 5,360 sq km/2,069 sq mi
towns administrative headquarters Norwich; King's Lynn, and resorts Great Yarmouth, Cromer, and Hunstanton
physical rivers Ouse, Yare, Bure, Waveney; the ◊Broads; Halvergate Marshes wildlife area
features traditional reed thatching; Grime's Graves (Neolithic flint mines); shrine of Our Lady of Walsingham, a medieval and modern centre of pilgrimage; Blickling Hall (Jacobean); residence of Elizabeth II at Sandringham (built 1869–71)
products cereals, turnips, sugar beet, turkeys, geese, offshore natural gas
population (1987) 736,000
famous people Fanny Burney, John Sell Cotman, John Crome ('Old Crome'), Rider Haggard, Thomas Paine.

Norfolk seaport in SE Virginia, USA, on the river Elizabeth, headquarters of the US Atlantic fleet; industries (shipbuilding, chemicals, motor vehicles); population (1980) 267,000.

Norfolk Island Pacific island territory of Australia, S of New Caledonia
area 40 sq km/15 sq mi

products citrus fruit, bananas; tourism is important

population (1986) 2,000

history reached by Cook 1774, settled 1856 by descendants of the mutineers of the *Bounty* from ◊Pitcairn Island; Australian territory from 1914, largely self-governing from 1979.

Norilsk world's most northerly industrial city (nickel, cobalt, platinum, selenium, tellurium, gold, silver) in Siberia, USSR; population (1987) 181,000. The permafrost is 30 m/1,000 ft deep, and the winter temperature may be −55°C.

Normandy two regions of NW France: ◊Haute-Normandie and ◊Basse-Normandie. Its main towns are Alençon, Bayeux, Dieppe, Deauville, Lisieux, Le Havre, and Cherbourg. It was named after the Viking Northmen (Normans), the people who conquered the area in the 9th century. As a French duchy it reached its peak under William the Conqueror and was noted for its centres of learning established by Lanfranc and St Anselm. Normandy was united with England 1100–35. England and France fought over it during the Hundred Years' War, England finally losing it 1449 to Charles VII. In World War II the Normandy beaches were the site of the Allied invasion on D-day, 6 June 1944. Features of Normandy include the painter Monet's restored home and garden at Giverny, Mont St Michel, Château Miromesnil, the birthplace of de Maupassant, Victor Hugo's house at Villequier, and Calvados apple brandy.

Northallerton market town, administrative headquarters of N Yorkshire, England; industries (tanning and flour milling); population (1985) 13,800.

North America third largest of the continents (including Central America), over twice the size of Europe

area 24,000,000 sq km/9,500,000 sq mi

largest cities (population over 1 million) Mexico City, New York, Chicago, Toronto, Los Angeles, Montreal, Guadalajara, Monterrey, Philadelphia, Houston, Guatemala City, Vancouver, Detroit

physical mountain belts to the E (Appalachians) and W (see ◊Cordilleras), the latter including the Rocky Mountains and the Sierra Madre; coastal plain on the Gulf of Mexico, into which the Mississippi river system drains from the central Great Plains; the St Lawrence and the Great Lakes form a rough crescent (with the Great Bear and Great Slave lakes, and lakes Athabasca and Winnipeg) around the exposed rock of the great Canadian/Laurentian Shield, into which Hudson Bay breaks from the north

population (1981) 345 million; the aboriginal American Indian, Inuit, and Aleut peoples are now a minority within a population predominantly of European immigrant origin. Many Africans were brought in as part of the slave trade

language predominantly English, Spanish, French

Northamptonshire

features climatic range is wide from arctic in Alaska and N Canada (only above freezing Jun–Sept) to the tropical in Central America, and much of the W of USA is arid. There are also great extremes within the range, owing to the vast size of the land mass

exports the immensity of the US home market makes it less dependent on exports, and the USA's industrial and technological strength automatically tends to exert a pull on Canada, Mexico, and Central America. The continent is unique in being dominated in this way by a single power, which also exerts great influence over the general world economy

religion predominantly Christian, Jewish.

Northampton county town of Northamptonshire, England; population (1984) 163,000. Boots and shoes (of which there is a museum) are still made, but engineering has superseded them as the chief industry; there is also food processing and brewing.

Northamptonshire county in central England

area 2,370 sq km/915 sq mi

towns administrative headquarters Northampton; Kettering

features river Nene; Canons Ashby, Tudor house, home of the Drydens for 400 years; churches with broached spires

products cereals, cattle

population (1987) 562,000

famous people John Dryden.

Northants abbreviation for ◊*Northamptonshire*.

North Brabant (Dutch *Noord-Brabant*) southern province of the Netherlands, lying between the Maas (Meuse) and Belgium: area 4,940 sq km/1,907 sq mi; population (1988) 2,156,000. The

North Carolina

North Dakota

capital is 's-Hertogenbosch. Former heathland is now under mixed farming. Towns such as Breda, Tilburg, and Eindhoven are centres of brewing, engineering, microelectronics, and textile manufacture.

North Cape (Norwegian *Nordkapp*) a cape in the Norwegian county of Finnmark; the most northerly point of Europe.

North Carolina state of the USA; nickname Tar Heel or Old North State
area 136,400 sq km/52,650 sq mi
capital Raleigh
towns Charlotte, Greensboro, Winston-Salem
features Appalachian Mountains (including Blue Ridge and Great Smoky Mountains); site of Fort Raleigh on Roanoke Island; Wright Brothers National Memorial at Kitty Hawk; the Research Triangle established 1956 (Duke University, University of North Carolina, and North Carolina State University) for high-tech industries
products tobacco, maize, soybeans, livestock, poultry, dairy products, textiles, clothing, furniture, computers, mica, feldspar, bricks
population (1986) 6,331,000
famous people Billy Graham, O Henry
history Walter Raleigh sent out 108 colonists from Plymouth 1585 under his cousin Richard Grenville, who established the first English settlement in the New World on Roanoke Island; the survivors were taken home by Drake 1586. Further attempts failed there until 1663. It was one of the original Thirteen States 1789.

Northd abbreviation for ◊*Northumberland*.

North Dakota prairie state of the N USA; nickname Sioux or Flickertail State
area 183,100 sq km/70,677 sq mi
capital Bismarck
towns Fargo, Grand Forks, Minot
features fertile Red River Valley, Missouri Plateau; Badlands, so called because the pioneers had great difficulty in crossing them (including Theodore Roosevelt's Elkhorn Ranch)
products cereals, meat products, farm equipment, oil, coal
population (1984) 686,000
famous people Maxwell Anderson, Louis L'Amour

history acquired by the USA partly in the Louisiana Purchase 1803 and partly by treaty with Britain 1813; it became a state 1889.

Northeast Frontier Agency former name (until 1972) for ◊Arunachal Pradesh, territory of India.

North-East India area of India (Meghalaya, Assam, Mizoram, Tripura, Manipur, and Nagaland, and Arunachal Pradesh) linked with the rest of India only by a narrow corridor. There is opposition to immigration from Bangladesh and the rest of India, and demand for secession.

Northeast Passage sea route from the N Atlantic, around Asia, to the N Pacific, pioneered by Nordenskjöld 1878–79, and developed by the USSR in settling N Siberia from 1935. The USSR owns offshore islands, and claims it as an internal waterway; the USA claims that it is international.

Northern Areas districts N of Azad Kashmir, directly administered by Pakistan but not merged with it. India and Azad Kashmir each claim them as part of disputed Kashmir. They include Baltistan, Gilgit and Skardu, and Hunza (an independent principality for 900 years until 1974).

Northern Ireland see ◊Ireland, Northern.

Northern Rhodesia former name (until 1964) of ◊Zambia.

Northern Territory territory of Australia
area 1,346,200 sq km/519,633 sq mi
capital and chief port Darwin
towns Alice Springs
features mainly within the tropics, though with wide range of temperature; very low rainfall, but artesian bores are used; Macdonnell Ranges (Mt Zeil 1,510 m/4,956 ft); ◊Cocos and ◊Christmas Islands were included in the territory 1984
exports beef cattle, prawns, bauxite (Gove), gold and copper (Tennant Creek), uranium (Ranger)
population (1987) 157,000
government there is an administrator and legislative assembly, and the territory is also represented in the federal parliament
history originally part of New South Wales, it was annexed 1863 to South Australia, but 1911–78 (when self-government was achieved) was under the control of the Commonwealth of Australia government. Mineral discoveries on

Northern Territory

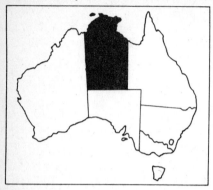

Northumberland

land occupied by Aborigines led to a royalty agreement 1979.

North Holland (Dutch *Noord-Holland*) low-lying coastal province of the Netherlands occupying the peninsula jutting northwards between the North Sea and the IJsselmeer; area 2,670 sq km/1,031 sq mi; population (1988) 2,353,000. Most of it is below sea level, protected from the sea by a series of sand dunes and artificial dykes. The capital is Haarlem; other towns are Amsterdam, Hilversum, Den Helder, and the cheese centres Alkmaar and Edam. Famous for its bulbfields, the province also produces grain and vegetables.

North Korea see ◊Korea, North.

North Ossetian area of the Caucasus, USSR; see also ◊Ossetia.

North Pole the north point where an imaginary line penetrates the Earth's surface by the axis about which it revolves; see also ◊Arctic.

North Rhine-Westphalia (German *Nordrhein-Westfalen*) administrative *Land* of West Germany

area 34,100 sq km/13,163 sq mi

capital Düsseldorf

towns Cologne, Essen, Dortmund, Duisburg, Bochum, Wuppertal, Bielefeld, Bonn, Gelsenkirchen, Münster, Mönchengladbach

features valley of the Rhine; Ruhr industrial district

products iron, steel, coal, lignite, electrical goods, fertilizers, synthetic textiles

population (1988) 16,700,000

religion Roman Catholic 53%, Protestant 42%

history see ◊Westphalia.

North Sea sea to the E of Britain and bounded by the coasts of Belgium, the Netherlands, Germany, Denmark, and Norway; area 523,000 sq km/ 202,000 sq mi; average depth 55 m/180 ft, greatest depth 660 m/2,165 ft. In the northeast it joins the Norwegian Sea, and in the south it

meets the Strait of Dover. It has fisheries, oil, and gas. In 1987, Britain dumped more than 4,700 tonnes of sewage sludge into the North Sea.

North Uist an island of the Outer Hebrides, Scotland. Lochmaddy is the main port of entry. It produces tweeds and seaweed, and crofting is practised.

Northumberland county in N England

area 5,030 sq km/1,942 sq mi

towns administrative headquarters Newcastle-upon-Tyne; Berwick-upon-Tweed, Hexham

features Cheviot Hills, rivers Tweed and upper Tyne of Northumberland National Park in the W; ◊Holy Island; ◊Farne Islands; part of Hadrian's Wall and Housestead's Fort; Alnwick and Bamburgh castles; Thomas Bewick museum; large moorland areas are used for military manoeuvres

products sheep

population (1986) 301,000

famous people Thomas Bewick, Bobby Charlton.

North-West Frontier Province province of Pakistan; capital Peshawar; area 74,500 sq km/ 28,757 sq mi; population (1985) 12,287,000. It was a province of British India 1901–47. It includes the strategic Khyber Pass, the site of constant struggle between the British Raj and the Pathan warriors. In the 1980s it has had to accommodate a stream of refugees from neighbouring Afghanistan.

Northwest Passage Atlantic–Pacific sea route around the north of Canada. Canada, which owns offshore islands, claims it as an internal waterway; the USA insists that it is an international waterway, and sent an icebreaker through without permission 1985.

Northwest Territories

Early explorers included the Englishmen Martin Frobisher and, later, John Franklin, whose failure to return 1847 led to the organization of 39 expeditions in the next ten years. R McClune explored the passage 1850–53 though he did not cover the whole route by sea. The polar explorer Amundsen was the first European to sail through.

Northwest Territories territory of Canada
area 3,426,300 sq km/1,322,552 sq mi
capital Yellowknife
physical extends to the North Pole, to Hudson's Bay in the east, and in the west to the edge of the Canadian Shield
features Mackenzie River; Great Slave Lake and Great Bear Lake; Miles Canyon
products oil and natural gas, zinc, lead, gold, tungsten, silver
population (1986) 52,000, over 50% native peoples (Indian, Inuit)
history the area was the northern part of Rupert's Land, bought by the Canadian government from the Hudson's Bay Company 1869. An act of 1952 placed the Northwest Territories under a commissioner acting in Ottawa under the Ministry of Northern Affairs and Natural Resources.

North Yorkshire county in NE England
area 8,320 sq km/3,212 sq mi
towns administrative headquarters Northallerton; York and the resorts of Harrogate, Scarborough, and Whitby
features England's largest county; including part of the Pennines, the Vale of York, and the Cleveland Hills and North Yorkshire Moors, which form a national park (within the park are Fylingdales radar station to give early warning—four minutes—of nuclear attack, and Rievaulx abbey); Yorkshire Dales National Park (including Swaledale, Wensleydale, and Bolton Abbey in Wharfedale); rivers Derwent and Ouse; Fountains Abbey near Rippon, with Studley Royal Gardens attached; Castle Howard; York Minster

North Yorkshire

products cereals, wool and meat from sheep, dairy products, coal, electrical goods
population (1987) 706,000
famous people Alcuin, W H Auden.

Norway country in NW Europe, on the Scandinavian peninsula, bounded E by Sweden and NE by Finland and the USSR.

Norwegian Sea part of the ◊Arctic Ocean.

Norwich cathedral city in Norfolk, E England; population (1986) 121,600. Industries include shoes, clothing, chemicals, confectionery, engineering, and printing.

It has a Norman castle with a collection of paintings by the Norwich school (Cotman and Crome); 15th-century Guildhall, medieval churches, Tudor houses, Georgian Assembly House. The Sainsbury Laboratory 1987, in association with the John Innes Institute, was founded to study the molecular causes of disease.

Nottingham industrial city (engineering, coal-mining, cycles, textiles, knitwear, pharmaceuticals, tobacco, lace, electronics) and administrative headquarters of Nottinghamshire, England; population (1981) 217,080.

Features include the university 1881, the Playhouse (opened 1963), and the recently refurbished Theatre Royal. Nearby are Newstead Abbey, home of Byron, and D H Lawrence's home at Eastwood.

Nottinghamshire county in central England
area 2,160 sq km/834 sq mi
towns administrative headquarters Nottingham; Mansfield, Worksop
features river Trent; the remaining areas of Sherwood Forest (home of Robin Hood), formerly a royal hunting ground, are included in

Norway
Kingdom of
(Kongeriket Norge)

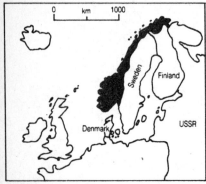

area 387,000 sq km/149,421 sq mi (includes Svalbard and Jan Mayen)
capital Oslo
towns Bergen, Trondheim
physical mountainous; forests cover 25% of area; extends north of Arctic Circle
territories dependencies in the Arctic (Svalbard and Jan Mayen) and in Antarctica (Bouvet and Peter I Island, and Queen Maud Land)
features beautiful fjords, including Hardanger and Sogne, the longest 185 km/115 mi and deepest 1,245 m/4,086 ft; glaciers in N; midnight sun and northern lights; great resources of hydroelectric power
head of state Olaf V from 1957
head of government Jan P Syse from 1989
government constitutional monarchy

political parties Norwegian Labour Party (DNA), moderate, left-of-centre; Conservative Party, progressive, right-of-centre; Christian People's Party (KrF), Christian, centre-left; Centre Party (SP), left-of-centre, rural-orientated
exports petrochemicals from North Sea oil and gas, paper, wood pulp, furniture, iron ore and other minerals, high-tech goods, sports goods, fish
currency krone (11.01 = £1 Feb 1990)
population (1989) 4,204,000; annual growth rate 0.3%
life expectancy men 73, women 80
language Riksmal (formal Dano-Norwegian) and Landsmal (based on the local dialects of Norway)
religion Evangelical Lutheran (endowed by state)
literacy 100% (1984)
GNP $56 bn (1982); $12,432 per head of population
chronology
1814 Independent from Denmark.
1905 Links with Sweden ended.
1940–45 Occupied by Germany.
1949 Joined NATO.
1952 Joined Nordic Council.
1957 King Haakon VII succeeded by his son, Olaf V.
1960 Joined EFTA.
1972 Accepted into membership of the European Community but application withdrawn after a referendum.
1988 Prime minister Gro Harlem Brundtland awarded Third World Prize.
1989 Brundtland defeated in elections. Jan P Syse became prime minister.

---

the 'Dukeries'; Cresswell Crags (remains of prehistoric humans); D H Lawrence commemorative walk from Eastwood (where he lived) to Old Brinsley Colliery
products cereals, cattle, sheep, light engineering, footwear, limestone, ironstone, oil
population (1987) 1,008,000
famous people D H Lawrence, Alan Sillitoe
history In World War II Nottinghamshire produced the only oil out of U-boat reach, and drilling revived in the 1980s.
Notts abbreviation for ◊*Nottinghamshire.*
Nouakchott capital of Mauritania; population (1985) 500,000. Products include salt, cement, and insecticides.
Noumaa a port on the SW coast of New Caledonia; population (1983) 60,100.
Nova Lisboa former name (1928–73) for ◊Huambo, in Angola.

Nova Scotia province of E Canada
area 55,500 sq km/21,423 sq mi
capital and chief port Halifax
towns Dartmouth, Sydney
features Cabot Trail (Cape Breton Island), Alexander Graham Bell Museum, Fortress Louisbourg; Strait of Canso Superport is the largest deepwater harbour on the Atlantic coast of the continent
products coal, gypsum, dairy products, poultry, fruit, forest products, fish products (including scallop and lobster)
population (1986) 873,000
history Nova Scotia was visited by the navigator Caboto 1497. A French settlement was established 1604, but expelled 1613 by English colonists from Virginia. The name of the colony was changed from *Acadia* to Nova Scotia 1621. England and France contended for possession of

Nottinghamshire

the territory until Nova Scotia (which then included present-day New Brunswick and Prince Edward Island) was ceded to Britain 1713; Cape Breton Island remained French until 1763. Nova Scotia was one of the four original provinces of the dominion of Canada.

Novaya Zemlya Arctic island group off the NE of the USSR; area 81,279 sq km/31,394 sq mi; population, a few Samoyed. It is rich in birds, seals, and walrus.

Novgorod industrial (chemicals, engineering, clothing, brewing) city on the Volkhov River, NW USSR, a major trading city in medieval times; population (1987) 228,000.

Novgorod was the original capital of the Russian state, founded at the invitation of the people of the city by the Viking (Varangian) chieftain Rurik 862. The Viking merchants who went there quickly became fully assimilated into the native Slav population. In 912, the capital of the principality moved to Kiev, but this did little to harm Novgorod. It developed a strong municipal government run by the leaders of the craft guilds and, until the 13th century, flourished as a major commercial centre (with a monopoly on the Russian fur trade) for trade with Scandinavia, the Byzantine empire and the Muslim world. It became one of the principal members of the Hanseatic League, but its economy had already started to decline. This was hastened during the 15th-century rule of the boyars, nobles who had seized power from the guilds 1416. It came under the control of Ivan the Great III 1478, and was sacked by Ivan the Terrible 1570.

Novi Sad industrial and commercial (pottery and cotton) city, capital of the autonomous province of

Nova Scotia

Vojvodina, Yugoslavia on the river Danube; population (1981) 257,700. Products include leather, textiles, and tobacco.

Novokuznetsk industrial city (steel, aluminium, chemicals) in the Kuzbas, S central USSR; population (1987) 589,000. It was called Stalinsk 1932–61.

Novorossiisk USSR Black Sea port and industrial (cement, metallurgy, food processing) city; population (1987) 179,000.

Novosibirsk industrial city (engineering, textiles, chemicals, food processing) in W Siberia, USSR, on the river Ob; population (1987) 1,423,000. Winter lasts eight months here.

At *Akademgorodok* ('Science City'), population 25,000, advanced research is carried on into Siberia's local problems.

Nowa Huta an industrial suburb of Krakow, on the Vistula River. The centre of Poland's steel industry.

NS abbreviation for ◊*Nova Scotia*.

NSW abbreviation for ◊*New South Wales*.

Nubia former African country now divided between Egypt and Sudan; it gives its name to the *Nubian Desert* S of Lake Nasser.

Ancient Egypt, which was briefly ruled by Nubian kings in the 8th–7th century BC, knew the N as Wawat and the S as Kush, with the dividing line roughly at Dongola. Egyptian building work in the area included temples at Abu Simbel, Philae, and a defensive chain of forts which established the lines of development of medieval fortification. Nubia's capital about 600 BC–350 AD was Meroe, near Khartoum. About 250–550 AD most of Nubia was occupied by the x-group people, of whom little is known; their royal mound tombs (mistaken by earlier investigations for natural mounds created by wind erosion) were excavated in the 1930s by W B Emery, and many horses and attendants were found to have been slaughtered to accompany the richly jewelled dead.

Nukua'lofa capital and port of Tonga on Tongatapu; population (1986) 29,000.

Nullarbor Plain arid coastal plateau area divided between W and S Australia; there is a network of caves beneath it. Atom-bomb experiments were carried out in the 1950s at Maralinga, an area in the NE bordering on the Great Victoria Desert.

Nuneaton market town in Warwickshire, England, on the river Anker, NE of Coventry; industries (ceramics, tiles and bricks); population (1984) 72,000.

Nuremberg (German *Nürnberg*) industrial city (electrical and other machinery, precision instruments, textiles, toys) in Bavaria, West Germany; population (1988) 467,000. From 1933 the Nuremberg rallies were held here, and in 1945 the Nuremberg trials of war criminals.

Created an imperial city 1219, it has an 11th–16th-century fortress and many medieval buildings (restored after destruction of 75% of the city in World War II), including the home of the 16th-century composer Hans Sachs, where the Meistersingers met. The artist Dürer was born here.

Nusa Tenggara volcanic archipelago in Indonesia, also known as the *Lesser Sunda Islands*, including ◊Bali, ◊Lombok, and ◊Timor; area 73,144 sq km/28,241 sq mi. The islands form two provinces of Indonesia: *Nusu Tenggara Barat*, population (1980) 2,724,500; and *Nusu Tenggara Timur*, population (1980) 2,737,000.

Nuuk Greenlandic for ◊Godthaab, capital of Greenland.

NV abbreviation for ◊*Nevada*.

NY abbreviation for ◊*New York*.

Nyasa former name for Lake ◊Malawi.

Nyasaland former name (until 1964) for ◊Malawi.

Nyíregyháza market town in E Hungary; population (1988) 119,000. It trades in tobacco and vegetables.

NZ abbreviation for ◊*New Zealand*.

Oahu island of Hawaii, USA, in the N Pacific
area 1,525 sq km/589 sq mi
towns state capital Honolulu
physical formed by two extinct volcanoes
features Waikiki beach; Pearl Harbor naval base
products sugar, pineapples; tourism is important
population (1980) 762,000.

Oakland industrial port (vehicles, textiles, chemicals, food processing, shipbuilding) in California, USA, on the E coast of San Francisco Bay; population (1980) 339,300. It is linked by bridge (1936) with San Francisco.

Oak Ridge town in Tennessee, E USA, on the river Clinch, noted for the Oak Ridge National Laboratory 1943 which manufactures plutonium for nuclear weapons; population (1980) 27,600.

Oaxaca capital of a state of the same name in the Sierra Madre del Sur mountain range, central Mexico; population (1980) 157,300; former home town of presidents Benito Juárez and Porfirio Diaz; industries include food processing, textiles, and handicrafts.

Ob river in Asiatic USSR, flowing 3,380 km/2,100 mi from the Altai mountains through the W Siberian Plain to the Gulf of Ob in the Arctic Ocean. With its main tributary, the *Irtysh*, it is 5,600 km/3,480 mi. Although frozen for half the year, and subject to flooding, it is a major transportation route. Novosobirsk and Barnaul are the main ports.

Oban seaport and resort in Strathclyde, W Scotland; population (1981) 8,000.

Obeid, El see ◊El Obeid, city in Sudan.

Oberammergau a town in Bavaria, West Germany, 72 km/45 mi SW of Munich. A passion play is performed here every ten years. Population (1980) 5,000.

Oberhausen industrial (metals, machinery, plastics, chemicals) and coalmining city in the Ruhr valley, North Rhine–Westphalia, West Germany; population (1988) 222,000.

Oberösterreich German name for the federal state of ◊Upper Austria.

Occitanie area of S France; see ◊Languedoc-Roussillon.

Oceania the islands of the S Pacific (Micronesia, ◊Melanesia, ◊Polynesia). The term is sometimes taken to include ◊Australasia and the ◊Malay archipelago, in which case it is considered as one of the seven continents.

Ocean Island another name for ◊Banaba, island in Kiribati.

Ocussi Ambeno port on the N coast of Indonesian West Timor, until 1975 an exclave of the Portuguese colony of East Timor. The port is an outlet for rice, copra, and sandalwood.

Odense industrial port on the island of Fyn, Denmark; population (1988) 174,000. Industries include shipbuilding, electrical goods, glass, and textiles. It is the birthplace of Hans Christian Andersen.

Oder (Polish *Odra*) European river flowing N from Czechoslovakia to the Baltic Sea (the river Neisse is a tributary); length 885 km/550 mi.

Oder–Neisse Line provisional border between Poland and East Germany agreed at the Potsdam Conference in 1945 at the end of World War II, named after the two rivers that form the frontier.

Odessa seaport in Ukraine, USSR, on the Black Sea, capital of Odessa region; population (1987) 1,141,000. Products include chemicals, pharmaceuticals, and machinery. Odessa was founded by Catherine II 1795 near the site of an ancient Greek settlement. Occupied by Germany 1941–44, Odessa suffered severe damage under the Soviet scorched-earth policy and from German destruction.

Offaly county of the Republic of Ireland, in the province of Leinster, between Galway on the west and Kildare on the east; area 2,000 sq km/772 sq mi; population (1986) 60,000.

Towns include the county town of Tullamore. Features include the rivers Shannon (along the W boundary), Brosna, Clodagh, and Broughill; the Slieve Bloom mountains in the SE.

Offa's Dyke a defensive earthwork along the Welsh border, of which there are remains from the mouth of the river Dee to that of the river Severn. It represents the boundary secured by the 8th-century king Offa's wars with Wales.

Offenbach am Main city in Hessen, West Germany; population (1988) 107,000. It faces Frankfurt on the other side of the river Main.

Ogaden region in Harar province, SE Ethiopia, that borders on Somalia. It is a desert plateau, rising to 1,000 m/3,000 ft, inhabited mainly by Somali nomads practising arid farming. A claim to the area was made by Somalia in the 1960s, resulting in guerrilla fighting that has continued intermittently. Civilian rule of the area returned to Ethiopia in Sept 1987.

Ogallala Aquifer the largest source of groundwater in the USA, stretching from southern South Dakota to NW Texas. The over-exploitation of this water resource has resulted in the loss of over 18% of the irrigated farmland of Oklahoma and Texas in the period 1940–90.

Ogbomosho city and commercial centre in W Nigeria, 80 km/50 mi NE of Ibadan; population (1981) 590,600.

Ogun a state of SW Nigeria; population (1982) 2,473,300; area 16,762 sq km/6,474 sq mi; capital Abeokuta.

OH abbreviation for ◊*Ohio*.

Ohio state of the midwest USA; nickname Buckeye State
area 107,100 sq km/41,341 sq mi
capital Columbus
towns Cleveland, Cincinnati, Dayton, Akron, Toledo, Youngstown, Canton
features Ohio River; Serpent Mound, a 1.3 m/4 ft embankment, 405 m/1,330 ft long, and about 5 m/18 ft across (built by Hopewell Indians about 1st–2nd century BC);
products coal, cereals, livestock, machinery, chemicals, steel
population (1986) 10,752,000
famous people Thomas Edison, John Glenn, Paul Newman, Gen Sherman, Orville Wright; six presidents (Garfield, Grant, Harding, Harrison, Hayes, and McKinley)
history ceded to Britain by France 1763; first settled by Europeans 1788; state 1803.

Ohio River river in the USA, 1,580 km/980 mi long; it is formed by the union of the Allegheny and Monongahela at Pittsburgh, Pennsylvania, and flows SW until it joins the river Mississippi at Cairo, Illinois.

Ohrid, Lake a lake on the frontier between Albania and Yugoslavia; area 350 sq km/135 sq mi.

Oise European river which rises in the Ardennes plateau, Belgium, and flows through France in a generally SW direction for 300 km/186 mi to join

the Seine about 65 km/40 mi below Paris. It gives its name to a French *département* in Picardie.

OK abbreviation for ◊*Oklahoma*.

Okavango Swamp marshy area in NW Botswana, fed by the *Okavango River*, which rises in Angola and flows SE about 1,600 km/1,000 mi.

Okayama industrial port (textiles, cotton) in W Honshu, Japan; population (1987) 570,000. It has three Buddhist temples.

Okeechobee lake in the N Everglades, Florida, USA; 65 km/40 mi long and 40 km/25 mi wide. The largest lake in southern USA.

Okefenokee swamp in SE Georgia and NE Florida, USA, rich in alligators, bears, deer, and birds. Much of its 1,700 sq km/660 sq mi forms a natural wildlife refuge.

Okhotsk, Sea of arm of the N Pacific between the Kamchatka Peninsula and Sakhalin, and bordered southward by the Kurile Island; area 937,000 sq km/361,700 sq mi. Free of ice only in summer, it is often fogbound.

Okinawa largest of the Japanese ◊Ryukyu Islands in the W Pacific
area 2,250 sq km/869 sq mi
capital Naha
population (1986) 1,190,000
history captured by the USA in the **Battle of Okinawa** 1 Apr–21 June 1945 with 47,000 US casualties (12,000 dead) and 60,000 Japanese (only a few hundred survived as prisoners); the island was returned to Japan 1972.

Oklahoma state of the south central USA; nickname Sooner State
area 181,100 sq km/69,905 sq mi
capital Oklahoma City
towns Tulsa, Lawton, Norman, Enid
features Arkansas, Red, and Canadian rivers; Wichita and Ozark ranges; the Oklahoma panhandle is part of the Dust Bowl; the high plains have Indian reservations (Cherokee, Chickasaw, Choctaw, Creek, and Seminole)
products cereals, peanuts, cotton, livestock, oil, natural gas, helium, machinery and other metal products
population (1986) 3,305,000
famous people Woody Guthrie, Will Rogers

Ohio

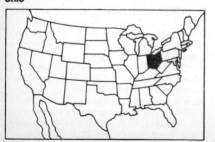

Oklahoma

Oman
Sultanate of
formerly known as
Muscat and Oman

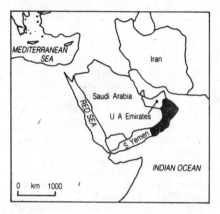

area 272,000 sq km/105,000 sq mi
capital Muscat
towns Salalah
physical mountains and a high arid plateau;
fertile coastal strip
features Jebel Akhdar highlands; Kuria
Muria islands; Masirah Island is used in aerial
reconnaissance of the Arabian Sea and Indian
Ocean
head of state and government Qaboos bin
Said from 1970
political system absolute monarchy
exports oil, dates, silverware
currency Omani rial (0.64 = £1 Feb 1990)
population (1989) 1,389,000; annual growth
rate 4.7%
life expectancy men 51, women 54
language Arabic
religion Sunni Muslim
literacy 20% (1983)
GNP $7 bn (1983); $2,400 per head of
population
chronology
1951 The Sultanate of Muscat and Oman
achieved full independence. Treaty of
friendship with Britain signed.
1970 After 38 years' rule, Sultan Said bin
Taimur replaced in coup by his son Qaboos bin
Said. Name changed to Sultanate of Oman.
1975 Left-wing rebels in the south defeated.
1982 Memorandum of Understanding with
the UK signed, providing for consultation on
international issues.

---

history the region was acquired with the
Louisiana Purchase 1803. Part of the present
state formed the Territory of Oklahoma from
1890, and was thrown open to settlers with
lotteries and other hurried distribution of land.
Together with what remained of Indian Territory,
it became a state 1907.
Oklahoma City industrial city (oil refining, machinery, aircraft, telephone equipment), capital of
Oklahoma, USA, on the Canadian River; population (1984) 443,500.
Oldenburg industrial city in Lower Saxony, West
Germany, on the river Hunte; population (1988)
139,000. It is linked by river and canal to the Ems
and Wieser rivers.
Oldham industrial city in Greater Manchester, England; population (1981) 107,800. Industries include
textiles and textile machinery, plastics, electrical
goods, and electronic equipment.
Old Sarum Iron Age hill-fort site near ◊Salisbury,
England.
Olduvai Gorge deep cleft in the Serengeti steppe,
Tanzania, where prehistoric stone tools were
found in the 1930s and 1958–59 Pleistocene
remains of prehumans and gigantic animals. The
gorge has given its name to the *Olduvai culture*,
a simple stone-tool culture of prehistoric hominids,
dating from 2–0.5 million years ago.

The Pleistocene remains included sheep the
size of a carthorse, pigs as big as a rhinoceros,
and a gorilla-sized baboon. The skull of an early
hominid (1.75 million years old) *Australopithecus
boisei* (its huge teeth earned it the nickname
'Nutcracker Man') was also found here, as well
as remains of *Homo habilis* and primitive types of
Homo erectus.
Old World the continents of the eastern hemisphere, so called because they were familiar
to Europeans before the Americas. Used as an
adjective to describe animals and plants that live
in the eastern hemisphere.
Olmos a small town on the edge of the Sechura
Desert, NW Peru. It gives its name to the large
Olmos Project which began in 1926 in an attempt
to irrigate the desert plain and increase cotton and
sugar-cane production.
Olney small town in Buckinghamshire, England,
where every Shrove Tuesday local women run a
pancake race.
Olomouc industrial city in central Czechoslovakia,
at the confluence of the Bystrice and Morava rivers; population (1986) 106,000. Industries include
sugar refining, brewing, and metal goods.
Olsztyn formerly *Allenstein* industrial town in
NE Poland at the centre of the Masurian
Lakes region; population (1985) 147,000. It

was founded 1334 and was formerly in East Prussia.

Olympus (Greek *Olimbos*) several mountains in Greece and elsewhere, the most famous being *Mount Olympus* in N Thessaly, Greece, 2,918 m/9,577 ft high. In ancient Greece it was considered the home of the gods.

Omagh county town of Tyrone, Northern Ireland, on the river Strule, 48 km/30 mi S of Londonderry; population (1981) 14,625.

Omaha city in E Nebraska, USA, on the Missouri; population (1980) 314,000. It is a livestock-market centre, with food-processing and meat-packing industries.

Oman country on the Arabian peninsula, bounded to the W by the United Arab Emirates, Saudi Arabia, and South Yemen, and to the E by the Arabian Sea.

Omdurman city in Sudan, on the White Nile, a suburb of Khartoum; population (1983) 526,000. It was the residence of the Sudanese sheik known as the Mahdi 1884–98. The Battle of Omdurman 1898 was a victory for British troops under Kitchener over the forces of the Mahdi.

Omsk industrial city (agricultural and other machinery, food processing, sawmills, oil refining) in the USSR, capital of Omsk region, W Siberia; population (1987) 1,134,000. The refineries are linked with Tuimazy in Bashkiria by a 1,600 km/1,000 mi pipeline.

Onega, Lake second largest lake in Europe, NE of Leningrad, partly in Karelia, USSR; area 9,600 sq km/3,710 sq mi. The *Onega canal*, along its south shore, is part of the Mariinsk system linking Leningrad with the river Volga.

Oneida small town in New York State, USA, named after the Oneida people (a nation of the Iroquois confederacy). It became known from 1848 for the *Oneida Community*, a religious sect which practised a form of 'complex marriage' until its dissolution 1879.

Ont. abbreviation for ◊*Ontario*.

Ontario province of central Canada
area 1,068,600 sq km/412,480 sq mi
capital Toronto
towns Hamilton, Ottawa (federal capital), London, Windsor, Kitchener, St Catharines, Oshawa, Thunder Bay, Sudbury
features Black Creek Pioneer Village; ◊Niagara Falls; richest, chief manufacturing, most populated, and leading cultural province of English-speaking Canada
products nickel, iron, gold, forest products, motor vehicles, iron, steel, paper, chemicals, copper, uranium
population (1986) 9,114,000
history first explored by the French in the 17th century, it came under British control 1763 (Treaty of Paris). An attempt 1841 to form a merged province with French-speaking Québec

Ontario

failed, and Ontario became a separate province of Canada 1867.

Ontario, Lake smallest and easternmost of the Great Lakes, on the US-Canadian border; area 19,200 sq km/7,400 sq mi. It is connected to Lake Erie by the Welland Canal and the Niagara River, and drains into the St Lawrence River. Its main port is Toronto.

Oostende Flemish form, meaning 'east end', of ◊Ostend.

Opole industrial town in S Poland, on the river Oder; population (1983) 121,900. It is an agricultural centre; other occupations include textiles, chemicals, and cement.

Oporto alternative form of ◊Porto in Portugal.

OR abbreviation for ◊*Oregon*.

Oradea or *Oradea-Mare* industrial city in Romania, on the river Koös; population (1983) 206,200. Industries include agricultural machinery, chemicals, non-ferrous metallurgy, leather goods, printing, glass, textiles, clothing, and brewing.
history Created seat of a bishopric by St Ladislas in 1083; destroyed by the Turks in 1241 and rebuilt. Many of its buildings date from the reign of Maria Theresa in the 18th century. It was ceded by Hungary to Romania in 1919, and held by Hungary 1940–45.

Oran (Arabic *Wahran*) seaport in Algeria; population (1984) 663,500. Products include iron, textiles, footwear, and processed food. University 1967; the port trades in grain, wool, vegetables and exports grass.
history Oran was part of the Ottoman Empire except 1509–1708 and 1732–91 under Spanish rule. It was occupied by France in 1831. After the surrender of France to Germany in 1940, the French warships in the naval base of Mers-el-Kebir nearby were put out of action by the British navy to prevent them from falling into German hands.

Orange town in France, N of Avignon; population (1982) 27,500. It has the remains of a Roman theatre and arch. It was a medieval principality from which came the royal house of Orange.

Orange town in New South Wales, Australia, 200 km/125 mi NW of Sydney; population (1984) 32,000. There is a woollen-textile industry based on local sheep flocks, and fruit is grown.

Orange County metropolitan area of S California, USA; area 2,075 sq km/801 sq mi; it adjoins Los Angeles County; population (1980) 1,932,700. Industries include aerospace and electronics. Oranges and strawberries are grown, Disneyland is here, and Santa Ana is the chief town.

Orange Free State province of the Republic of South Africa
area 127,993 sq km/49,405 sq mi
capital Bloemfontein
features plain of the High Veld; Lesotho forms an enclave on the Natal–Cape Province border
products grain, wool, cattle, gold, oil from coal, cement, pharmaceuticals
population (1987) 1,863,000 (1,525,000 ethnic Africans)
history original settlements from 1810 were complemented by the Great Trek, and the state was recognized by Britain as independent 1854. Following the South African or Boer War 1899–1902, it was annexed by Britain until it entered the union as a province 1910.

Orange River river in South Africa, rising on the Mont aux Sources in Lesotho and flowing W to the Atlantic; length 2,100 km/1,300 mi. It runs along the S boundary of the Orange Free State, and was named 1779 after William of Orange. Water from the Orange is diverted via the Orange–Fish River Tunnel 1975 to irrigate the semi-arid E Cape Province.

Orasul Stalin name 1948–56 of the Romanian town ◊Brașov.

Oregon state of the NW USA, on the Pacific; nickname Beaver State
area 251,500 sq km/97,079 sq mi
capital Salem
towns Portland, Eugene
features fertile Willamette river valley; Columbia and Snake rivers; Crater Lake, deepest in the USA (589 m/1,933 ft); Coast and Cascade mountain ranges, the latter including Mount St Helens
products wheat, livestock, timber, gold, silver, nickel, electronics
population (1987) 2,690,000
famous people Linus Pauling
history settled 1811 by the Pacific Fur Company, Oregon Territory included Washington until 1853. Oregon became a state 1859. The Oregon Trail (3,200 km/2,000 mi from Independence, Missouri, to the Columbia River) was the pioneer route across the USA 1841–60.

Orel industrial city in the USSR, capital of Orel region, on the river Oka 320 km/200 mi SSW of Moscow; population (1987) 335,000. Industries

Oregon

include engineering, textiles, and foodstuffs. It is the birthplace of the writer Ivan Turgenev.

Orenburg city in S central USSR, on the Ural river; population (1987) 537,000. It is a trading and mining centre and capital of Orenburg region. It dates from the early 18th century and was called *Chkalov* 1938–57 in honour of a long-distance flyer.

Orense town in NW Galicia, Spain, on the river Miño population (1986) 102,000. It produces textiles, furniture, food products, and metal goods.

Öresund strait between Sweden and Denmark; in English called the ◊Sound.

Orinoco river in N South America, flowing for about 2,400 km/1,500 mi through Venezuela and forming for about 320 km/200 mi the boundary with Colombia; tributaries include the Guaviare, Meta, Apure, Ventuari, Caura, and Caroni. It is navigable by large steamers for 1,125 km/700 mi from its Atlantic delta; rapids obstruct the upper river.

Orissa state of NE India
area 155,800 sq km/60,139 sq mi
capital Bhubaneswar
towns Cuttack, Rourkela

Orissa

INDIAN OCEAN

features mainly agricultural; Chilka lake with fisheries and game; temple of Jangannath or Juggernaut at Puri

products rice, wheat, oilseed, sugar, timber, chromite, dolomite, graphite, iron

population (1981) 26,272,000

language Oriya (official)

religion Hindu 90%

history administered by the British 1803–1912 as a subdivision of Bengal, it joined with Bihor to become a province; in 1936 Orissa became a separate province and 1948–49 its area was almost doubled before its designation as a state 1950.

Orizaba industrial city and resort in Veracruz state, Mexico; population (1980) 115,000. Industries include brewing, paper, and textiles. An earthquake in 1973 severely damaged it.

Orizaba Spanish name for ◊Citlaltépetl, mountain in Mexico.

Orkney Islands island group off the NE coast of Scotland

area 970 sq km/375 sq mi

towns administrative headquarters Kirkwall, on Mainland (Pomona)

features comprises about 90 islands and islets, low-lying and treeless; population, long falling, has in recent years risen as their remoteness from the modern world attracts new settlers; mild climate owing to the Gulf Stream; Skara Brae, a remarkably well-preserved Neolithic village on Mainland; Scapa Flow, between Mainland and Hoy, was a naval base in both world wars, and the German fleet scuttled itself here 21 June 1919

products fishing and farming, wind power (Burgar Hill has the world's most productive wind generator, with blades 60 m/197 ft diameter)

population (1987) 19,000

history Harold I (Fairhair) of Norway conquered the islands 876; they were pledged to James III of Scotland 1468 for the dowry of Margaret of Denmark, and annexed by Scotland (the dowry unpaid) 1472.

Orkneys, South islands in the British Antarctic Territory; see ◊South Orkneys.

Orlando industrial city in Florida, USA; population (1986) 148,000. Kennedy Space Center and Disney World are nearby. The city was named 1857 after Orlando Reeves, a soldier killed in a clash with Indians.

Orléans industrial city of France, on the river Loire; 115 km/70 mi SW of Paris; population (1982) 220,500. It is capital of Loiret *département*. Industries include engineering and food processing. Orléans, of pre-Roman origin and formerly the capital of the old province of Orléanais, is associated with Joan of Arc, who liberated it from English rule in 1429.

Orly a suburb of Paris in the *département* of Val-de-Marne; population (1982) 17,000. There is an international airport.

Orkney

Ormuz alternative name for ◊Hormuz, Iranian island.

Orne French river rising E of Sées and flowing NW, then NE to the English Channel below Caen; 152 km/94 mi long. A ship canal runs alongside it from Caen to the sea at Ouistreham. The Orne gives its name to a *département* in Normandy; population (1982) 295,500.

Orontes (Arabic *'Asi*) river flowing through Lebanon, Syria, and Turkey to the Mediterranean, and used mainly for irrigation; length 400 km/250 mi.

Orsk industrial city in the USSR, at the junction of the Or and Ural rivers; population (1987) 273,000. Industries include mining, oil refining, locomotives, and aluminium. Its refineries are fed by a pipeline from Guriev. The town was originally a fortress.

Orvieto town in Umbria, Italy, NE of Lake Bolsena, population (1981) 22,800. Built on the site of **Volsinii**, an Etruscan town destroyed by the Romans 280 BC, Orvieto has many Etruscan remains. The name is from Latin *Urbs Vetus*, 'old town'.

Osaka industrial port (iron, steel, shipbuilding, chemicals, textiles) on Honshu island; population (1987) 2,546,000, metropolitan area 8,000,000. It is the oldest city of Japan, and was at times the seat of government in the 4th–8th centuries.

Lying on a plain sheltered by hills and opening on to Osaka bay, Osaka is honeycombed with waterways. It is a tourist centre for Kyoto and the Seto Inland Sea, and linked with Tokyo by fast electric train 200 kph/124 mph. An underground shopping and leisure centre 1951 has been used as a model for others throughout Japan. It was a mercantile centre in the 18th century, and in the 20th century set the pace for Japan's revolution based on light industries. University 1931.

Oshogbo city and trading centre on the river Niger, in W Nigeria, 200 km/125 mi NE of Lagos; population (1986) 405,000. Industries include cotton and brewing.

Osijek (German *Esseg*) industrial port in Croatia, Yugoslavia, on the river Drava; population (1981) 158,800. Industries include textiles, chemicals, and electrical goods.

Oslo capital and industrial port (textiles, engineering, timber) of Norway; population (1988) 454,000. The first recorded settlement was made in the 11th century by Harald III, but after a fire 1624, it was entirely replanned by Christian IV and renamed *Christiania* 1624–1924.

The port is built at the head of Oslo fjord, which is kept open in winter by icebreakers. There is a Viking museum, 13th-century Akershus Castle, a 17th-century cathedral, and the National Gallery includes many paintings by Munch.

Osnabrück industrial city in Lower Saxony, West Germany; 115 km/71 mi west of Hanover; population (1988) 154,000. Industries include engineering, iron, steel, textiles, clothing, paper, and food processing. Before World War II, Osnabrück had some noted examples of Gothic and Renaissance architecture.

Osnabrück bishopric was founded by Charlemagne 783. The Treaty of Westphalia was signed at Osnabrück and Münster 1648, ending the Thirty Years' War. A type of rough fabric, *osnaburg*, was originally made here.

Ossa mountain in Thessaly, Greece; height 1,978 m/6,490 ft. Two of Poseidon's giant sons were said to have tried to dislodge the gods from Olympus by piling nearby Mount Pelion on top of Ossa to scale the great mountain.

Ossa, Mount the highest peak on the island of Tasmania, Australia; height 1,617 m/5,305 ft.

Ossetia region of SW USSR, in the Caucasus, on the border of the republic of Georgia. It is inhabited mainly by the Ossets, who speak the Iranian language Ossetic, and who were conquered by the Russians in 1802. Some live in the *North Ossetian* autonomous republic of the SW USSR; area 8,000 sq km/3,088 sq mi; population (1985) 613,000; capital Ordzhonikidze. The rest live in the *South Ossetian* autonomous region of the Georgian republic, population (1984) 98,000; capital Tshkinvali.

It has been the scene of Osset-Georgian inter-ethnic conflict from 1989. The Ossets have demanded that South Ossetia be upgraded to an autonomous republic as a preliminary to reunification with North Ossetia.

Ostend Flemish *Oostende* seaport and pleasure resort in W Flanders, Belgium; 108 km/67 mi NW of Brussels; population (1985) 69,000. There are large docks, and the Belgian fishing fleet has its headquarters here. Ferry links to Dover and Folkestone, England.

Ostrava industrial city (iron works, furnaces, coal, chemicals) in Czechoslovakia, capital of Severomoravsky region, NE of Brno; population (1984) 324,000.

Oswestry market town in Shropshire, England; population (1981) 12,400. Industries include agricultural machinery and plastics. It is named after St Oswald, killed here in 642.

Otago a peninsula and coastal plain on South Island, New Zealand, constituting a district; area 64,230 sq km/ 25,220 sq mi; chief cities include Dunedin and Invercargill.

Otaru fishing port on W coast of Hokkaido, Japan, with paper mills; processes fish and makes sake; population (1984) 179,000.

Otranto seaport in Puglia, Italy, on the *Strait of Otranto*; population (1981) 5,000. It has Greek and Roman remains, a ruined castle (the inspiration for Horace Walpole's novel *The Castle of Otranto* 1764), and a castle begun 1080. The port is linked by ferry with Corfu.

Ottawa capital of Canada, in E Ontario, on the hills overlooking the Ottawa River, and divided by the Rideau Canal into the Upper (western) and Lower (eastern) Town; population (1986) 301,000, metropolitan area (with adjoining Hull, Québec) 819,000. Industries include timber, pulp and paper, engineering, food processing, and publishing.

features National Museum, National Art Gallery, Observatory, Rideau Hall (the governor-general's residence), and the National Arts Centre 1969 (with an orchestra and English/French theatre).

history It was founded 1826–32 as *Bytown*, in honour of John By (1781–1836) whose army engineers were building the Rideau Canal. It was renamed 1854 after the Outaouac Indians. In 1858 it was chosen by Queen Victoria as the country's capital.

Ötztal Alps a range of the Alps in Italy and Austria, rising to 3,774 m/12,382 ft at Wildspitze, Austria's second highest peak.

Ouagadougou capital and industrial centre of Burkina Faso; population (1985) 442,000. Products include textiles, vegetable oil, and soap.

Oudenaarde small town in E Flanders, W Belgium, on the Scheldt, 28 km/18 mi SSW of Ghent; population (1982) 27,200. It is noted for its tapestries and carpet-weaving. Oudenaarde was the site of the victory by the British, Dutch, and Austrians over the French in 1708 during the War of Spanish Succession.

Oudh region of N India, now part of Uttar Pradesh. An independent kingdom before it fell under Mogul rule, Oudh regained independence 1732–1856, when it was annexed by Britain. Its capital was Lucknow, centre of the Indian Mutiny 1857–58.

Oxfordshire

In 1877 it was joined with Agra, from 1902 as the United Provinces of Agra and Oudh, renamed Uttar Pradesh 1950.

Ouessant French form of ◊Ushant, an island W of Brittany.

Oujda industrial and commercial city (lead and coalmining) in N Morocco, near the border with Algeria; population (1982) 471,000. It trades in wool, grain, and fruit.

Oulu (Swedish *Uleåborg*) industrial port (saw mills, tanneries, shipyards) in W Finland, on the Gulf of Bothnia; population (1986) 97,900. It was originally a Swedish fortress 1375.

Ouse name of several British rivers:

The *Great Ouse* rises in Northamptonshire and winds its way across 250 km/160 mi to enter the Wash north of King's Lynn. A huge sluice across the Great Ouse, near King's Lynn, was built as part of extensive flood-control works 1959.

The *Little Ouse* flows for 38 km/24 mi along part of the Norfolk/Suffolk border and is a tributary of the Great Ouse.

The Yorkshire *Ouse* is formed by the junction of the Ure and Swale near Boroughbridge, and joins the Trent to form the Humber.

The Sussex *Ouse* rises between Horsham and Cuckfield, and flows through the S Downs to enter the English Channel at Newhaven.

Ovamboland region of N Namibia stretching along the Namibia-Angola frontier; the scene of conflict between SWAPO guerrillas and South Africa forces in the 1970s and 1980s.

Ovens River river in Victoria, Australia, a tributary of the Murray.

Overijssel province of the E central Netherlands; capital Zwolle; area 3,340 sq km/1,289 sq mi; population (1988) 1,010,000. It is generally flat, and contains the rivers Ijssel and Vecht. Products include sheep, cattle, and dairy products.

Oviedo industrial city (textiles, metal goods, pharmaceuticals, matches, chocolate, sugar) and capital of Asturias region, Spain, 25 km/16 mi south of the Bay of Biscay; population (1986) 191,000.

Owen Falls waterfall in Uganda on the White Nile, 4 km/2.5 mi below the point at which the river leaves Lake Victoria. A dam, built 1949–60, provides hydroelectricity for Uganda and Kenya, and helps to control the flood waters.

Oxfordshire county in S central England
area 2,610 sq km/1,007 sq mi
towns administrative headquarters Oxford; Abingdon, Banbury, Henley-on-Thames, Witney, Woodstock
features river Thames and tributaries; Cotswolds and Chiltern Hills; Vale of the White Horse (chalk hill figure 114 m/374 ft long); Oxford University; Europe's major fusion project JET (Joint European Torus) is being built at the UK Atomic Energy Authority's fusion laboratories at Culham
products cereals, cars, paper, bricks, cement
population (1987) 578,000
famous people Flora Thompson.

Oxus ancient name of ◊Amu Darya, river in USSR.

Ozark Mountains area in USA (shared by Arkansas, Illinois, Kansas, Mississippi, Oklahoma) of ridges, valleys, and streams, highest point only 700 m/2,300 ft; area 130,000 sq km/50,000 sq mi.

PA abbreviation for ◊*Pennsylvania*.

Paarl a town on the Great Berg River, Cape Province, South Africa; population (1980) 71,300. It is the centre of a noted wine-producing area, 50 km/31 mi NE of Cape Town. Nelson Mandela served the last days of his imprisonment at the Victor Vester prison near here.

Pacaraima, Sierra mountain range along the Brazil–Venezuela frontier, extending into Guyana; length 620 km/385 mi. Highest point is **Mount Roraima**, a plateau about 50 sq km/20 sq mi, 2,629 m/8,625 ft above sea level, surrounded by 300 m/1,000 ft cliffs, at the conjunction of the three countries. Formed 300 million years ago, it has a largely unique fauna and flora, because of its isolation, consisting only of grasses, bushes, flowers, insects, and small amphibians.

Pacific islands United Nations trust territory in the W Pacific comprising over 2,000 islands and atolls, under Japanese mandate 1919–47, and administered by the USA 1947–80, when all its members, the ◊Carolines, ◊Marianas (except ◊Guam), and ◊Marshall Islands, became independent.

Padang port on the W coast of Sumatra, Indonesia; population (1980) 481,000. The Dutch secured trading rights here 1663. The port trades in copra, coffee, and rubber.

Paderborn market town in North Rhine-Westphalia, West Germany; population (1988) 110,000. Industries include leather goods, metal products, and precision instruments. It was the seat of a bishopric in Charlemagne's time, and later became a member of the Hanseatic League.

Padua (Italian *Padova*) city in N Italy, 45 km/28 mi W of Venice; population (1988) 224,000. The astronomer Galileo taught at the university, founded 1222. The 13th-century Palazzo della Ragione, the basilica of S Antonio, and the botanical garden 1545 are notable. It is the birthplace of the historian Livy and the painter Andrea Mantegna.

Pagalu former name (1973–79) of ◊Annobón, island in Equatorial Guinea.

Pago Pago chief port of American Samoa on the island of Tutuila; population (1980) 3,060. Formerly a naval coaling station, it was acquired by the USA under a commercial treaty with the local king 1872.

Pahang state of E Peninsular Malaysia; capital Kuantan; area 36,000 sq km/13,896 sq mi; population (1980) 799,000. It is mountainous and forested, and produces rubber, tin, gold, and timber. There is a port at Tanjung Gelang. Pahang is ruled by a sultan.

Pahsien another name for ◊Chongqing, port in SW China.

Pakistan country in S Asia, stretching from the Himalayas to the Arabian Sea, bounded to the W by Iran, to the NW by Afghanistan, to the NE by China, and to the E by India.

Palau former name (until 1981) of the Republic of ◊Belau.

Paldiski small, ice-free port in Estonia, a Soviet naval base 40 km/25 mi W of Tallinn at the entrance to the Gulf of Finland.

Palembang oil-refining city in Indonesia, capital of S Sumatra province; population (1980) 786,000. Palembang was the capital of a sultanate when the Dutch established a trading station there 1616.

Palermo capital and seaport of Sicily; population (1988) 729,000. Industries include shipbuilding, steel, glass, and chemicals. It was founded by the Phoenicians in the 8th century BC.

Palestine (also called the *Holy Land* because of its links with Judaism, Christianity, and Islam) the area between the Mediterranean and the river Jordan, with Lebanon to the north and Sinai to the south. It was in ancient times dominated in turn by Egypt, Assyria, Babylonia, Persia, Macedonia, the Ptolemies, the Seleucids, and the Roman and Byzantine empires. Today it forms part of Israel. The Palestinian people (about 500,000 in the West Bank, E Jerusalem, and the Gaza Strip; 1,200,000 in Jordan; 1,200,000 in Israel; 300,000 in Lebanon; and 100,000 in the USA) are descendants of the people of Canaan, an empire of the 3rd millennium BC.

AD 636 Conquest by the Muslim Arabs, which made it a target for the Crusades (see also ◊Jerusalem).

1516 Conquest by the Ottoman Turks.

1880-1914 Jewish immigration increased sharply as a result of pogroms in Russia and Poland.

1897 At the first Zionist Congress Jews called for a homeland in Palestine.

Pakistan
Islamic Republic of

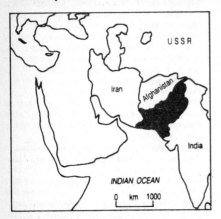

area 796,100 sq km/307,295 sq mi; one-third of Kashmir is under Pakistani control
capital Islamabad
towns Karachi (largest city and port), Lahore
physical fertile plains; Indus river; Himalaya mountains in the N
features the 'five rivers' (Indus, Jhelum, Chenab, Ravi and Sutlej) feed one of the world's largest irrigation systems; K2; Khyber Pass; sites of the Indus Valley civilization
head of state Ghulam Ishaq Khan from 1988
head of government Benazir Bhutto from 1988
government emergent democracy
political parties Pakistan People's Party (PPP), moderate, Islamic, socialist; Islamic Democratic Alliance (IJI), including the Pakistan Muslim League (PML), Islamic conservative; Mohajir National Movement (MQM), Sind-based Mohajir settlers

exports cotton textiles, rice, leather, carpets
currency Pakistan rupee (36.20 = £1 Feb 1990)
population (1989) 110,358,000 (66% Punjabi, 13% Sindhi); annual growth rate 3.1%
life expectancy men 51, women 49
language Urdu and English (official); Punjabi
religion Sunni Muslim 75%, Shi'ite Muslim 20%, Hindu 4%
literacy 40% male/19% female (1985 est)
GDP $35 bn (1983); $280 per head of population
chronology
1947 Pakistan formed following partition of India.
1956 Proclaimed a republic.
1958 Military rule imposed by Gen Ayub Khan.
1969 Power transferred to Gen Yahya Khan.
1971 Secession of East Pakistan (Bangladesh). After civil war, power was transferred to Zulfiqar Ali Bhutto.
1977 Bhutto overthrown in military coup by Gen Zia ul-haq. Martial law imposed.
1979 Bhutto executed.
1981 Opposition Movement for Restoration of Democracy formed. Islamization process pushed forward.
1985 Non-party elections held, amended constitution adopted, martial law and ban on political parties lifted.
1986 Agitation for free elections launched by Benazir Bhutto, daughter of Zulfiqar Ali Bhutto
1988 Zia introduced Islamic legal code, the *Shariah*. He was killed in a military air crash in Aug, and Benazir Bhutto was elected prime minister in Nov.
1989 Pakistan rejoined the Commonwealth.
1990 Army mobilized in support of Muslim separatists in Indian Kashmir (Apr).

1917–18 Turks driven out by the British field marshal Allenby in World War I.
1909 Tel Aviv, the first all-Jewish town in Palestine, was built.
1922 Britain received Palestine as a League of Nations mandate (incorporating the Balfour Declaration) to administer both historic Palestine and lands across the river Jordan which were recognized 1923 as the Hashimite Kingdom of Jordan.
1929 and *1936–38* Arab revolts fuelled by Jewish immigration (300,000 during 1920–39).
1937 Peel Commission report; Pan-Arab Congress Sept.
1938 Woodhead Commission.
1939 British plan for Palestine.

1939–45 Both Arab and Jewish Palestinians served in the Allied forces in World War II.
1947 Following Jewish guerrilla activities, prompted by restriction of Jewish immigration, Britain put the question before the United Nations, which voted for partition.
1948 15 May (eight hours before Britain's renunciation of the mandate was due) a Jewish state of ◊Israel was proclaimed. A series of Arab-Israeli Wars (1948–49, 1956, 1967, 1973, 1982) resulted in the total loss of the Palestinian state, and the displacement of large numbers of Palestinian Arabs.
1964 The Palestine Liberation Organization (PLO) was formed and a guerrilla war was waged against the Jewish state.

1974 The PLO became the first nongovernmental delegation to be admitted to a plenary session of the United Nations General Assembly.

1979 Egypt and Israel signed a peace treaty that recognized the need to negotiate full autonomy for the Palestinian Arabs of the Israeli-occupied Gaza Strip and the West Bank.

1987 A prolonged Palestinian uprising (*intifada*) in the Israeli-occupied territories was sparked off by an incident in which four Arabs were killed.

1989 Israeli prime minister Yitzhak Shamir proposed Palestinian elections in the West Bank/ Gaza Strip.

Palk Strait a channel separating SE India from the island of Sri Lanka; 53 km/33 mi at its widest point.

Palma, La one of the ◊Canary Islands, Spain
area 730 sq km/282 sq mi
capital Santa Cruz de la Palma
features forested
products wine, fruit, honey, silk; tourism is important
population (1981) 77,000.

Palma (Spanish *Palma de Mallorca*) industrial port (textiles, cement, paper, pottery), resort, and capital of the Balearic Islands, Spain, on Majorca; population (1986) 321,000. Palma was founded 276 BC as a Roman colony.

Palmas, Las port in the Canary Islands; see ◊Las Palmas.

Palm Beach winter resort in Florida, USA, on an island between Lake Worth and the Atlantic; population (1980) 9,730.

Palmerston North town on the SW coast of North Island, New Zealand; industries (textiles, dairy produce, electrical goods); population (1986) 67,400.

Palm Springs resort and spa in S California, USA, about 160 km/100 mi E of Los Angeles; population (1980) 32,300.

Palmyra coral atoll 1,600 km/1,000 mi SW of Hawaii, in the Line Islands, S Pacific, purchased by the USA from a Hawaiian family 1979 for the storage of highly radioactive nuclear waste from 1986.

Palo Alto city in California, USA, situated SE of San Francisco at the centre of the high-tech region known as Silicon Valley; site of Stanford University.

Pamirs central Asian plateau mainly in the USSR, but extending into China and Afghanistan, traversed by mountain ranges. Its highest peak is Mount Communism (Kommunizma Pik 7,495 m/ 24,600 ft) in the Akademiya Nauk range, the highest mountain in the USSR.

Pampas flat, treeless Argentinian plains, lying between the Andes and the Atlantic, and rising gradually from the coast to the lower slopes of the mountains. The E Pampas contain large cattle ranches and the flax- and grain-growing

area of Argentina; the W Pampas are arid and unproductive.

Pamplona industrial city (wine, leather, shoes, textiles) in Navarre, N Spain, on the Arga river; population (1986) 184,000. A pre-Roman town, it was rebuilt by Pompey 68 BC, captured by the Visigoths 476, sacked by Charlemagne 778, became the capital of Navarre, and was taken by Wellington in the Peninsular War 1813. An annual running of bulls takes place in the streets every July.

Panama country in Central America, on a narrow isthmus between the Caribbean and the Pacific Ocean, bounded to the W by Costa Rica and to the E by Colombia.

Panama Canal canal across the Panama isthmus in Central America, connecting the Pacific and Atlantic oceans; length 80 km/50 mi, with 12 locks. Built by the USA 1904–14 after an unsuccessful attempt by the French, it was formally opened 1920. The *Panama Canal Zone* was acquired 'in perpetuity' by the USA 1903, comprising land extending about 5 km/3 mi on either side of the canal. The zone passed to Panama 1979, and control of the canal itself was ceded to Panama by the USA in Jan 1990 under the terms of the Panama Canal Treaty 1977.

Panama City capital of the Republic of Panama, near the Pacific end of the Panama Canal; population (1980) 386,000. Products include chemicals, plastics, and clothing. An earlier Panama, to the NE, founded 1519, was destroyed 1671, and the city was founded on the present site 1673.

Pan-American Highway road linking the USA with Central and South America; length 25,300 km/ 15,700 mi. Starting from the US-Canadian frontier (where it links with the Alaska Highway), it runs through San Francisco, Los Angeles, and Mexico City to Panama City, then down the W side of South America to Valparaiso, Chile, where it crosses the Andes and goes to Buenos Aires, Argentina. The road was first planned 1923.

Panay one of the Philippine islands, lying between Mindoro and Negros
area 11,515 sq km/4,446 sq mi
capital Iloilo
features mountainous, 2,215 m/7,265 ft in Madiaás
products rice, sugar, pineapples, bananas, copra; copper
history seized by Spain 1569; occupied by Japan 1942–45.

Panipat town in Punjab, India; scene of three decisive battles: 1526, when Baber (1483–1530), great-grandson of Tamerlane, defeated the emperor of Delhi and founded the Mogul Empire; 1556, won by his descendant Akbar; 1761, when the Mahrattas were defeated by Ahmad Shah of Afghanistan.

Panama
Republic of
(República de Panamá)

area 77,100 sq km/29,768 sq mi
capital Panama City
towns Cristóbal, Balboa, Colón
physical mountain ranges; tropical rainforest
features Panama Canal; Barro Colorado Island
in Gatun Lake (the reservoir which supplies
the canal), a tropical forest reserve since 1923;
Smithsonian Tropical Research Institute
head of state and government Guillermo
Endara from 1989
government emergent democratic republic
political parties Democratic Revolutionary
Party (PRD), right-wing; Labour Party (PALA),
right-of-centre; Republican Party (PR), right-wing;
National Liberal Republican Movement
(MOLIRENA), left-of-centre; Authentic Panama
Party (PPA), centrist; Christian Democratic
Party (PDC), centre-left
exports bananas, petroleum products, copper
from one of the world's largest deposits,
shrimps
currency balboa (1.70 = £1 Feb 1990)
population (1989) 2,370,000; annual growth
rate 2.2%
life expectancy men 69, women 73
language Spanish
religion Roman Catholic
literacy 89% male/88% female (1985)
GDP $4.1 bn (1983); $1,116 per head of
population
chronology
1903 Became independent from Colombia.
1974 Agreement to negotiate a full transfer of
the Panama Canal from the US to Panama.
1977 US-Panama treaties transfer the canal
to Panama, with the US guaranteeing its
protection and an annual payment.
1984 Nicolas Ardito Barletta elected president,
but army commander-in-chief Gen Manuel
Noriega in effective control.
1985 Barletta resigned to be replaced by Eric
Arturo del Valle.
1987 Noriega resisted calls for his removal,
despite suspension of US military and
economic aid.
1988 Trying to dismiss Noriega, del Valle was
replaced by Manuel Solis Palma. Noriega,
charged with drug smuggling by a US federal
court, declared a state of emergency.
1989 Assembly elections declared invalid after
complaints of fraud. US invaded Panama and
Noriega eventually surrendered. Guillermo
Endara installed as president.

Panjshir Valley the valley of the river Panjshir
which rises in the Panjshir range to the N
of Kabul, E Afghanistan. It has been the
chief centre of Mujaheddin rebel resistance
against the Soviet-backed Najibullah government since 1979.

Pantanal a large area of swamp land in the Mato
Grosso of SW Brazil, occupying 220,000 sq km/
84,975 sq mi in the upper reaches of the Paraguay
river; one of the world's great wildlife ref-
uges; 1,370 sq km/530 sq mi were designated
as national park in 1981.

Pantelleria volcanic island in the Mediterranean,
100 km/62 mi SW of Sicily and part of that region
of Italy
area 115 sq km/45 sq mi
town Pantelleria
products sheep, fruit, olives, capers
population (1981) 7,800

history Pantelleria has drystone dwellings dating
from prehistoric times. The Romans called it
Cossyra and sent people into exile there. Strategically placed, the island has been much fought
over. It was strongly fortified by Mussolini in
World War II, and surrendered to the Allies 11
June 1943.

Papeete capital and port of French Polynesia
on the NW coast of Tahiti; population (1983)
79,000. Products include vanilla, copra, and
mother-of-pearl.

Paphos resort town on the SW coast of Cyprus;
population (1985) 23,200; capital of Cyprus in
Roman times and the legendary birthplace of
Aphrodite who rose out of the sea; archaeological remains include the 2,300-year-old underground 'Tombs of the Kings', the Roman villa
of Dionysos and the 7th-century Byzantine
castle.

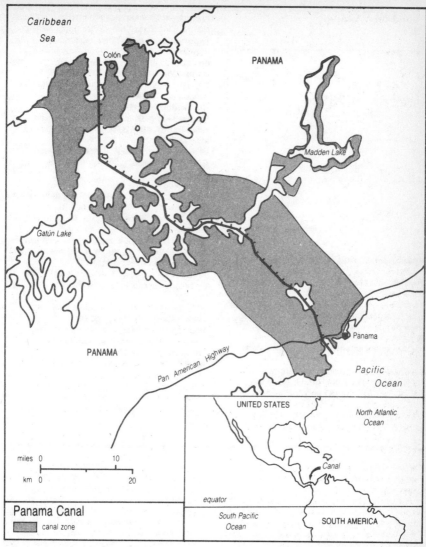

Panama Canal

▨ canal zone

Papua original name of the island of New Guinea, but latterly its SE section, now part of ◊Papua New Guinea.

Papua New Guinea country in the SW Pacific, comprising the E part of the island of New Guinea, the New Guinea islands, the Admiralty islands, and part of the Solomon islands.

Pará alternative name of the Brazilian port ◊Belém.

Paracels (Chinese **Xisha**/Vietnamese **Hoang Sa**) group of about 130 small islands in the S China Sea. Situated in an oil-bearing area, they were occupied by China following a skirmish with Vietnam 1974.

Paraguay landlocked country in South America, bounded to the NE by Brazil, to the S by Argentina, and to the NW by Bolivia.

Paramaribo port and capital of Suriname, South America, 24 km/15 mi from the sea on the river Surinam; population (1980) 193,000. Products include coffee, fruit, timber, and bauxite. It was founded by the French on an Indian village 1540,

Papua New Guinea

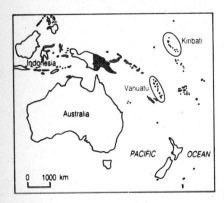

area 462,840 sq km/178,656 sq mi
capital Port Moresby (on E New Guinea)
physical mountains in centre; thickly forested
features wholly within the tropics, with annual
rainfall 100 cm/39 in; rare birds of paradise, the
world's largest butterfly, orchids
head of state Elizabeth II, represented by
Kingsford Dibela from 1983
head of government Rabbie Namaliu from
1988
government constitutional monarchy
political parties Papua New Guinea Party
(Pangu Pati: PP), urban- and coastal-orientated
nationalist; People's Democratic Movement
(PDM), 1985 breakaway from the PP; National
Party (NP), highlands-based; Melanesian
Alliance (MA), Bougainville-based autonomy;
People's Progress Party (PPP), conservative
exports copra, coconut oil, palm oil, tea,
copper
currency kina (1.64 = £1 Feb 1990)
population (1989) 3,613,000 (including
Papuans, Melanesians, Pygmies, and various
minorities); annual growth rate 2.6%
life expectancy men 51, women 53
language English (official); pidgin English
religion Protestant 33%, Roman Catholic 18%,
local faiths
literacy 55% male/36% female (1985 est)
GNP $2.5 bn (1983); $480 per head of
population
chronology
1883 Annexed by Queensland, became known
as the Australian Territory of Papua.
1884 NE New Guinea annexed by Germany; SE
claimed by Britain.
1914 NE New Guinea occupied by Australia.
1921–42 Held as a League of Nations mandate.
1942–45 Occupied by Japan.
1975 Achieved full independence, within the
Commonwealth, with Michael Somare as prime
minister.
1980 Julius Chan became prime minister.
1982 Somare returned to power.
1985 Somare challenged by deputy prime
minister, Paias Wingti, who later formed a
five-party coalition government.
1988 Wingti defeated on no-confidence
vote and replaced by Rabbie Namaliu, who
established a six-party coalition government.
1989 State of emergency imposed in
Bougainville in response to separatist violence.

made capital of British Surinam 1650, and placed
under Dutch rule 1816–1975.
Paraná river in South America, formed by the
confluence of the Rio Grande and Paranaiba; the
Paraguay joins it at Corrientes, and it flows into
the Rio de la Plata with the Uruguay; length 4,500
km/2,800 mi. It is used for hydroelectric power
by Argentina, Brazil, and Paraguay.
Paraná industrial port (flour mills, meat canneries)
and capital of Entre Rios province in E Argentina, on the Paraná river, 560 km/350 mi NW of
Buenos Aires; population (1980) 160,000.
Paris port and capital of France, on the river Seine;
département in the Ile de France region; area 105
sq km/40.5 sq mi; population (1982, metropolitan
area) 8,707,000. Products include metal, leather,
and luxury goods; chemicals, glass, and tobacco.
features The Seine is spanned by 32 bridges,
the oldest being the Pont Neuf 1578. Churches
include Notre Dame cathedral 1163–1250; the
Invalides, with the tomb of Napoleon; the Gothic
Saint-Chapelle; and the 19th-century basilica of
Sacré-Coeur, 125 m/410 ft high. Among notable
buildings are the Palais de Justice, the Hôtel
de Ville, the Luxembourg Palace and Gardens.
The former palace of the Louvre is one of
the world's most important art galleries; the
Orsay Museum 1986 has Impressionist and other
19th-century paintings; the Pompidou Centre
(Beaubourg) 1977 shows modern art. Other
landmarks are the Tuileries gardens, the Place
de la Concorde, the Eiffel Tower, and the avenue
Champs-Elysées leading to the Arc de Triomphe.
Central Paris was replanned in the 19th century
by Baron Haussmann. To the west is the Bois
de Boulogne; Montmartre is in the north of the
city; the university, founded about 1150, is on the
Left Bank.

Paraguay
Republic of
(República del Paraguay)

area 406,752 sq km/157,006 sq mi
capital Asunción
town port Concepción
physical mostly flat; divided by river Paraguay; river Paraná in the south
features Itaipú dam on border with Brazil; Gran Chaco plain with huge swamps
head of state and government Andrés Rodríguez from 1989
government military republic

political parties National Republican Association (Colorado Party), right-of-centre; Liberal Party (PL), right-of-centre; Radical Liberal Party (PLR), centrist
exports cotton, soya beans, timber, tung oil, maté
currency guaraní (2177.49 = £1 Feb 1990)
population (1989) 4,518,000 (95% of mixed Guaraní Indian-Spanish descent); annual growth rate 3.0%
life expectancy men 63, women 68
language Spanish (official), spoken by 6%; Guaraní 40%; remainder bilingual
religion Roman Catholic
literacy 91% male/85% female (1985 est)
GDP $5.6 bn (1983); $1,614 per head of population
chronology
1811 Independent from Spain.
1865–70 At war with Argentina, Brazil, and Uruguay. Much territory lost.
1932–35 Much territory won from Bolivia during the Chaco War.
1940–48 Gen Higino Morinigo president.
1948–54 Political instability with six different presidents.
1954 Gen Alfredo Stroessner seized power. He was subsequently re-elected seven times, despite increasing opposition and accusations of human-rights violations.
1989 Stroessner ousted in a coup led by Gen Andrés Rodríguez. Rodríguez and the Colorado Party won presidential and congressional elections.

---

history Paris, the Roman *Lucetia*, capital of the Parisii, a Gaulish people, was occupied by Julius Caesar 53 BC. The Merovingian king Clovis made it his capital in about AD 508, and the city became important under the Capetian kings 987–1328. Paris was occupied by the English 1420—36, and was beseiged by Henry IV 1590–94. The Bourbon kings did much to beautify the city. Napoleon I adorned it with new boulevards, bridges, and triumphal arches, as did Napoleon III. Paris was the centre of the revolutions of 1789–94, 1830, and 1848. It was besieged by Prussia 1870–71 and by government troops during the Commune (local socialist government) Mar–May 1871. During World War I it suffered from air raids and bombardment, and in World War II it was occupied by German troops June 1940–Aug 1944.

Paris-Plage resort in Nord-Pas-de-Calais region, N France, adjoining ◊Le Touquet.

Parma city in Emilia-Romagna, N Italy; industries (food processing, textiles, engineering); population (1988) 175,000. Founded by the Etruscans, it

was the capital of the duchy of Parma 1545–1860. It has given its name to Parmesan cheese.

Parnassus mountain in central Greece; height 2,457 m/8,064 ft, revered as the abode of Apollo and the Muses. Delphi lies on its southern flank.

Parramatta River inlet, W arm of Sydney Harbor, New South Wales, Australia. It is 24 km/15 mi long and is lined with industrial suburbs of Sydney: Balmain, Drummoyne, Concord, Parramatta, Ermington and Rydalmere, Ryde, and Hunter's Hill.

Pasadena city in SW California, USA, part of the ◊Los Angeles conurbation; population (1980) 118,500. On 1 Jan the East–West football game is held here in the 85,000-seat Rose Bowl. The California Institute of Technology (Caltech) owns the Hale Observatories (which include the Mount Palomar telescope) and is linked with the Jet Propulsion Laboratories.

Pas-de-Calais French name for the ◊Strait of Dover and of the French *département* bordering it, of which Arras is the capital and Calais the chief port. See also ◊Nord-Pas de Calais.

Passau town in SE Bavaria, West Germany, at the junction of the Inn and Ilz with the Danube. The Treaty of Passau 1552 between Maurice, elector of Saxony, and the future emperor Ferdinand I allowed the Lutherans full religious liberty after the Reformation.

Passchendaele village in W Flanders, Belgium, near Ypres. The Passchendaele ridge before Ypres was the object of a costly and unsuccessful British offensive in World War I, Jul–Nov 1917; British casualties numbered nearly 400,000.

Patagonia geographic area of South America, south of latitude 40° S, with sheep farming and coal and oil resources. Sighted by Magellan 1520, it was claimed by both Argentina and Chile until divided between them 1881.

Patiala city in E Punjab, India; industries (textile and metalwork); population (1981) 206,254.

Patmos Greek island in the Aegean, one of the Dodecanese; the chief town is Hora. St John is said to have written the New Testament Book of Revelation while in exile here.

Patna capital of Bihar state, India, on the Ganges; population (1981) 916,000. It has remains of a hall built by the emperor Asoka in the 3rd century BC.

Patras (Greek *Patrai*) industrial city (hydroelectric installations; textiles and paper) in the NW Peloponnese, Greece, on the Gulf of Patras; population (1981) 141,500. The ancient *Patrae*, it is the only one of the 12 cities of ◊Achaea to survive.

Pau industrial city (electrochemical and metallurgical) and resort, capital of Pyrenees-Atlantiques *département* in Aquitaine, SW France, near the Spanish border; population (1982) 131,500. It is the centre of the ◊Basque area of France, and there has been guerrilla activity.

Paysandú city in Uruguay, capital of Paysandú department, on the river Uruguay; population (1985) 74,000. Tinned meat is the main product. The city dates from 1772, and is linked by bridge 1976 with Puerto Colón in Argentina.

Pays de la Loire agricultural region of W France, comprising the *département*s of Loire-Atlantique, Maine-et-Loire, Mayenne, Sarthe, and Vendée; capital Nantes; area 32,100 sq km/12,391 sq mi; population (1986) 3,018,000. Industries include shipbuilding and wine.

Peace river formed in British Columbia, Canada, by the union at Finlay Forks of the Finlay and Parsnip rivers and flowing through the Rockies and across Alberta to join the river Slave just N of Lake Athabasca; length 1,600 km/1,000 mi.

Peak District tableland of the S Pennines in NW Derbyshire, England. It is a tourist region and a national park (1951). The highest point is Kinder Scout 636 m/2,088 ft.

Pechenga (Finnish *Petsamo*) ice-free fishing port in Murmansk, USSR, on the Barents Sea. Russia ceded Pechenga to Finland 1920 but recovered it under the 1947 peace treaty.

Pechora river in the USSR, rising in the N Urals. It carries coal, timber, and furs (Jun–Sept) to the Barents Sea 1,800 km/1,125 mi to the N.

Pécs city in SW Hungary, the centre of a coalmining area on the Yugoslavia frontier; population (1988) 182,000. Industries include metal, leather, and wine. The town dates from Roman times, and was under Turkish rule 1543–1686.

Peeblesshire former county of S Scotland, included from 1975 in Borders region; Peebles was the county town.

Peel fishing port in the Isle of Man, 19 km/12 mi NW of Douglas.

Pegu city in S Burma, on the river Pegu, NE of Rangoon; population (1983) 254,762. It was founded 573 AD and is noted for the Shwemawdaw pagoda.

Peiping name, meaning 'northern peace', 1928–49 of ◊Beijing in China.

Peipus, Lake (Estonian *Peipsi*, Russian *Chudskoye*) lake on the Estonian border in the USSR. Alexander Nevski defeated the Teutonic Knights on its frozen surface 1242.

Peking former name of ◊Beijing, capital of China.

Pelée, Mont volcano on the island of Martinique; height 1,258 m/4,428 ft. It destroyed the town of St Pierre during its eruption 1902.

Pelion mountain in Thessaly, Greece, near Mount ◊Ossa; height 1,548 m/5,079 ft. In Greek mythology it was the home of the centaurs.

Peloponnese (Greek *Peloponnesos*) peninsula forming the S part of Greece; area 21,549 sq km/8,318 sq mi; population (1981) 1,012,500. It is joined to the mainland by the narrow isthmus of Corinth, and is divided into the administrative areas of Argolis, Arcadia, Achaea, Elis, Corinth, Lakonia, and Messenia, representing its seven ancient states.

Pemba coral island in the Indian Ocean, 48 km/30 mi NE of Zanzibar, and forming with it part of Tanzania
area 984 sq km/380 sq mi
capital Chake Chake
products cloves, copra
population (1985) 257,000.

Pembroke seaport and engineering centre in Dyfed, Wales; population (1981) 15,600. Henry VII was born in Pembroke Castle.

Pembrokeshire former extreme SW county of Wales, which became part of Dyfed 1974; the county town was Haverfordwest.

Penang (Malay *Pulau Pinang*) state in W Peninsular Malaysia, formed of Penang Island, Province Wellesley, and the Dindings on the mainland; area 1,030 sq km/398 sq mi; capital Penang (George Town); population (1980)

Pennsylvania

955,000. Penang Island was bought by Britain from the ruler of Kedah 1785; Province Wellesley was acquired 1800.

Penarlag Welsh name of ◊Hawarden, town in Clwyd, Wales.

Pennines mountain system, 'the backbone of England', broken by a gap through which the river Aire flows to the E and the Ribble to the W; length (Scottish border to the Peaks in Derbyshire) 400 km/250 mi.

Pennsylvania state of NE USA; nickname Keystone State

area 117,400 sq km/45,316 sq mi

capital Harrisburg

towns Philadelphia, Pittsburgh, Erie, Allentown, Scranton

features Allegheny mountains; Ohio, Susquehanna, and Delaware rivers; University of Pennsylvania is one of the leading research campuses in the USA

products mushrooms, fruit, flowers, cereals, tobacco, meat, poultry, dairy products, anthracite, electrical equipment

population (1986) 11,889,000

famous people Marian Anderson, Maxwell Anderson, Stephen Foster, Benjamin Franklin, George C Marshall, Robert E Peary, Gertrude Stein, John Updike, Andy Warhol

history founded and named by William Penn 1682, following a land grant by Charles II. It was one of the original Thirteen States. There was a breakdown at the Three Mile Island nuclear reactor plant in Harrisburg 1979.

Pensacola port in NW Florida, USA, on the Gulf of Mexico, with a large naval air-training station; industries (chemicals, synthetic fibres, paper); population (1984) 60,500. Pensacola was founded by the Spanish 1696.

Pentland Firth the channel separating the Orkney Islands from N Scotland.

Penza industrial city (sawmills, bicycles, watches, calculating machines, textiles) in the USSR, capital of Penza region, 560 km/350 mi SE of Moscow, at the junction of the Penza and Sura rivers; population (1987) 540,000. It was founded as a fort 1663.

Penzance seaport for the Scilly Isles and resort in Cornwall, SW England, on Mount's Bay; population (1981) 19,500. It now incorporates the seaport of ◊Newlyn.

Peoria city in central Illinois, USA, on the river Illinois, a transport, mining, and agricultural centre; population (1980) 366,000. Fort Crève Coeur was built here by the French explorer La Salle 1680 and became a trading centre. The first US settlers arrived 1818 and the town was known as Fort Clark until 1825. In US comedy, Peoria is the epitome of a small town.

Perak state of W Peninsular Malaysia; capital Ipoh; area 21,000 sq km/8,106 sq mi; population (1980) 1,805,000. It produces tin and rubber. The government is a sultanate. The other important town is Taiping.

Pereira capital of Risaralda department, central Colombia, situated at an altitude of 1,463 m/4,800 ft, overlooking the fertile Cauca valley west of Bogota; population (1985) 390,000. Founded 1863, the city has developed into an important centre of the country's coffee and cattle industries.

Périgueux capital of Dordogne *département*, Aquitaine, France, on the river Isle, 127 km/79 mi ENE of Bordeaux; trading centre for wine and truffles; population (1982) 35,392. The Byzantine cathedral dates from 984.

Perim island in the strait of Bab-el-Mandeb, the S entrance to the Red Sea; part of South Yemen; area 13 sq km/5 sq mi.

Perlis border state of Peninsular Malaysia, NW Malaysia; capital Kangar; area 800 sq km/309 sq mi; population (1980) 148,000. It produced rubber, rice, coconuts, and tin. Perlis is ruled by a raja. It was transferred by Siam to Britain 1909.

Perm industrial city (shipbuilding, oil refining, aircraft, chemicals, sawmills), capital of Perm region, USSR, on the Kama near the Ural mountains; population (1987) 1,075,000. It was called Molotov 1940–57.

Pernambuco state of NE Brazil, on the Atlantic

area 98,281 sq km/37,946 sq mi

capital Recife (former name Pernambuco)

features highlands; the coast is low and humid

population (1985) 6,776,000.

Perpignan market town (olives, fruit, wine) and resort, capital of the Pyrénées-Orientales *département* of France, just off the Mediterranean coast, near the Spanish border; population (1982) 138,000. Overlooking Perpignan is the castle of the counts of Roussillon.

Persian Gulf or *Arabian Gulf* a large shallow inlet of the Arabian Sea; area 233,000 sq km/90,000 sq mi. It divides the Arabian peninsula from Iran, and is linked by the Strait of Hormuz and the Gulf of Oman to the Arabian Sea. Oilfields surround it in the Gulf States of Bahrain, Iran,

Peru
Republic of
(República del Perú)

area 1,285,200 sq km/496,093 sq mi
capital Lima, including port of Callao
towns Arequipa, Iquitos, Chiclayo
physical Andes mountains N–S cover 27%; Amazon river-basin jungle in NE
features Lake Titicaca; Peru Current; Atacama Desert; monuments of the Chimu and Inca civilizations
head of state and government Alan García Pérez from 1985
government democratic republic
political parties American Popular Revolutionary Alliance (APRA), moderate, left-wing; United Left (IU), left-wing
exports coffee, alpaca, llama and vicuna wool, fish meal, lead, copper, iron, oil
currency inti (21834.40 = £1 Feb 1990)
population (1989) 21,792,000 (46% American Indian, mainly Quechua and Aymara; 43% of mixed Spanish-American Indian descent); annual growth rate 2.6%
life expectancy men 57, women 61
language Spanish 68%, Quechua 27% (both official), Aymará 3%
religion Roman Catholic
literacy 91% male/78% female (1985 est)
GNP $18.6 bn (1983); $655 per head of population
chronology
1824 Achieved independence from Spain, the last South American country to do so.
1902 Boundary dispute with Bolivia settled.
1927 Boundary dispute with Colombia settled.
1942 Boundary dispute with Ecuador settled.
1948 Army coup, led by Gen Manuel Odria, installed a military government.
1963 Return to civilian rule, with Fernando Belaúnde Terry as president.
1968 Return of military government in a bloodless coup by Gen Juan Velasco Alvarado.
1975 Velasco replaced, in a bloodless coup, by Gen Morales Bermúdez.
1980 Return to civilian rule, with Fernando Belaúnde as president.
1981 Boundary dispute with Ecuador renewed.
1985 Belaúnde succeeded by Social Democrat Alan García Pérez.
1987 President García delayed the nationalization of Peru's banks after a vigorous campaign against the proposal.
1988 García under pressure to seek help from the International Monetary Fund.
1989 The International Development Bank suspended credit to Peru because it was six months behind in debt payments. The annual inflation rate to Apr was 4,329%.

Iraq, Kuwait, Oman, Qatar, Saudi Arabia, and the United Arab Emirates.

Perth industrial town in Tayside, E Scotland, on the river Tay; population (1981) 42,000. It was the capital of Scotland from the 12th century until James I of Scotland was assassinated here 1437.

Perth capital of Western Australia, with its port at nearby Fremantle on the Swan river; population (1986) 1,025,300. Products include textiles, cement, furniture, and vehicles. It was founded 1829, and is the commercial and cultural centre of the state.

Perthshire former inland county of central Scotland, of which the major part was included in Tayside 1975, the SW being included in Central region; Perth was the administrative headquarters.

Peru country in South America, on the Pacific, bounded to the N by Ecuador and Colombia, to the E by Brazil and Bolivia, and to the S by Chile.

Perugia capital of Umbria, Italy, 520 m/1,700 ft above the Tiber, about 137 km/85 mi north of Rome; population (1988) 148,000. Its industries include textiles, liqueurs, and chocolate. One of the 12 cities of Etruria, it surrendered to Rome 309 BC. There is a university 1276, municipal palace 1281, and a 15th-century cathedral.

Pescadores (Chinese *Penghu*) group of about 60 islands off Taiwan, of which they form a dependency; area 130 sq km/50 sq mi.

Pescara town in Abruzzi, E Italy, at the mouth of the Pescara river, on the Adriatic; population (1988) 131,000. Hydroelectric installations supply Rome with electricity. It is linked to Yugoslavia by ferry.

Peshawar capital of North-West Frontier Province, Pakistan, 18 km/11 mi E of the Khyber Pass; population (1981) 555,000. Products include textiles, leather, and copper.

Peterborough city in Cambridgeshire, England, noted for its 12th-century cathedral; population (1981) 115,400. It was designated a new town 1967. Nearby Flag Fen disclosed 1985 a well-preserved Bronze Age settlement of 660 BC.

Peterhead industrial seaport (fishing, shipbuilding, light engineering, whisky distilling, woollens) in Grampian, Scotland, 54 km/33 mi NE of Aberdeen; population (1981) 17,015. The Old Pretender landed here 1715. The harbour is used by service industries for North Sea oil.

Peter I Island uninhabited island in the Bellingshausen Sea, Antarctica, belonging to Norway since 1931; area 180 sq km/69 sq mi.

Peterlee new town in County Durham, England, established 1948; population (1981) 22,750. It was named after Peter Lee, first Labour chair of a county council.

Petra (Arabic *Wadi Musa*) ruined city carved out of the red rock at a site in modern Jordan, on the eastern slopes of the Wadi el Araba, 90 km/56 mi south of the Dead Sea. An Edomite stronghold and capital of the Nabataeans in the 2nd century, it was captured by the Roman emperor Trajan 106 AD and wrecked by the Arabs in the 7th century. It was forgotten in Europe until 1812 when the Swiss traveller J L Burckhardt came across it.

Petrograd name 1914–24 of ◊Leningrad, city in the USSR.

Petropavlovsk industrial city (flour, agricultural machinery, leather) in the Kazakh Republic, USSR, on the Ishim river, the Trans-Siberian railway, and the Transkazakh line, opened 1953; population (1987) 233,000. A former caravan station, it was founded as a Russian fortress 1782.

Petropavlovsk-Kamchatskiy Pacific seaport and Soviet naval base on the E coast of the Kamchatka peninsula, USSR; population (1987) 252,000.

Petrópolis hill resort in SE Brazil, founded by Pedro II; population (1980) 149,427.

Petrovsk former name (until 1921) of the Soviet port ◊Makhachkala.

Petrozavodsk industrial city (metal goods, cement, prefabricated houses, sawmills), capital of Karelia Republic, USSR, on the W shore of Lake Onega; population (1987) 264,000. Peter the Great established the township 1703 as an ironworking centre; it was named Petrozavodsk 1777.

Petsamo Finnish name of the Murmansk port ◊Pechenga.

Pevensey English village in Sussex, 8 km/5 mi NE of Eastbourne, the site of William the Conqueror's landing 1066. The walls remain of the Roman fortress of Anderida, later a Norman castle, and prepared against German invasion in World War II.

Pforzheim city in Baden-Württemberg, West Germany, 26 km/16 mi SE of Karlsruhe, with goldsmith industries; population (1988) 105,000. It was a Roman settlement, and the residence of the margraves of Baden 1300–1565.

Phil. abbreviation for ◊*Philadelphia*.

Philadelphia ('city of brotherly love') industrial city and port on the Delaware River in Pennsylvania, USA; population (1980) 1,688,000, metropolitan area 3,700,000. Products include refined oil, chemicals, textiles, processed food, printing and publishing. Founded 1682, it was the first capital of the USA 1790–1800.

Philae island in the Nile, Egypt, above the first rapids, famed for the beauty of its temple of Isis (founded about 350 BC and in use until the 6th century AD). In 1977 the temple was re-erected on the nearby island of Agilkia above the flooding caused by the Aswan Dam.

Philippeville former name (until 1962) of Algerian port of ◊Skikda.

Philippines country on an archipelago between the Pacific Ocean to the E and the South China Sea to the W.

Phnom Penh capital of Kampuchea, on the Mekong, 210 km/130 mi NW of Saigon; population (1981) 600,000. Industries include textiles and food-processing. On 17 Apr 1975 the entire population of the city was forcibly evacuated by the Khmer Rouge; survivors later returned.

Phoenicia ancient Greek name for the E Mediterranean seaboard of Lebanon and Syria, inhabited by a people of seafaring traders and artisans until conquered by Alexander the Great in 332 BC.

Phoenix capital of Arizona, USA; industrial city (steel, aluminium, electrical goods, food processing) and tourist centre on the Salt River; population (1986) 882,000.

Phoenix Islands group of eight islands in the South Pacific, included in Kiribati; total land area 18 sq km/11 sq mi. Drought has rendered them all uninhabitable.

Piacenza industrial city (agricultural machinery, textiles, pottery) in Emilia-Romagna, N Italy, on the Po, 65 km/40 mi SE of Milan; population (1988) 105,000. The Roman *Placentia*, Piacenza dates from 218 BC and has a 12th-century cathedral.

Picardie (English *Picardy*) region of N France, including Aisne, Oise, and Somme *départements*; area 19,400 sq km/7,488 sq mi; population (1986) 1,774,000. Industries include chemicals and

Philippines
Republic of the
(Republika ng Pilipinas)

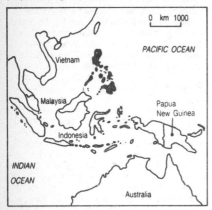

area 300,000 sq km/115,800 sq mi
capital Manila (on Luzon)
towns Quezon City
ports Cebu, Davao (on Mindanao) and Iloilu
physical comprises over 7,000 islands, with
volcanic mountain ranges traversing the
main chain N–S, and 50% of the area still
forested. The largest islands are Luzon
108,172 sq km/41,754 sq mi and **Mindanao**
94,227 sq km/36,372 sq mi; others include
Samar, Negros, Palawan, Panay, Mindoro,
Leyte, Cebu, and the Sulu group
features Luzon, is the site of Clark Field, US air
base used as a logistical base in the Vietnam
War, and Subic Bay, US naval base; Mindanao
has active volcano Apo (2,855 m/9,370 ft) and
mountainous rainforest
head of state and government Corazón
Aquino from 1986
government emergent democracy

political parties People's Power, including the
PDP-Laban Party and the Liberal Party, centrist
pro-Aquino; Nationalist Party, Union for National
Action (UNA), and Grand Alliance for Democra
cy (GAD), conservative oposition groupings;
Mindanao Alliance, Mindanao Island-based
decentralist body
exports sugar, copra and coconut oil, timber,
iron ore and copper concentrates
currency peso (37.00 = £1 Feb 1990)
population (1989) 61,971,000 (93%
Malaysian); annual growth rate 2.4%
life expectancy men 60, women 64
language Filipino (based on Malay dialect
Tagalog), but English and Spanish are
widespreadreligion Roman Catholic 84%,
Protestant 9%, Muslim 5%
literacy 86% male/85% female (1985 est)
GNP $16 bn (1984); $772 per head of
population
chronology
1542 Named the Philippines by Spanish
explorers.
1565 Conquered by Spain.
1898 Ceded to the US.
1335 Grant of internal self-government.
1942–45 Japanese occupation.
1946 Independence granted.
1965 Ferdinand Marcos elected president.
1983 Murder of Benigno Aquino.
1986 Overthrow of Marcos by Corazón
Aquino's People's Power movement.
1987 'Freedom constitution' adopted; People's
Power won majority in congressional elections.
Attempted right-wing coup suppressed.
Communist guerrillas active. Government in
rightward swing.
1988 Diluted land-reform act gave favourable
compensation to large estateholders.
1989 Failure of referendum on southern
autonomy; attempted coup foiled with US air
support.

---

metals. It was a major battlefield in World
War I.

Picton small port at the NE extremity of South
Island, New Zealand, with a ferry to Wellington,
North Island.

Piedmont (Italian *Piemonte*) region of N Italy,
bordering Switzerland on the north and France on
the west, and surrounded, except on the east, by
the Alps and the Apennines; area 25,400 sq km/
9,804 sq mi; population (1988) 4,377,000. Its
capital is Turin, and towns include Alessandria,
Asti, Vercelli, and Novara. It also includes the fertile Po river valley. Products include fruit, grain,
cattle, cars, and textiles. The movement for the

unification of Italy started in the 19th century in
Piedmont, under the house of Savoy.

Pietermaritzburg industrial city (footwear, furniture, aluminium, rubber, brewing), capital from
1842 of Natal, South Africa; population (1980)
179,000. Founded 1838 by Boer trekkers from
the Cape, it was named after their leaders,
Piet Retief and Gert Maritz, killed by the
Zulus.

Pikes Peak mountain in the Rampart range of
the Rocky Mountains, Colorado, USA; height
4,300 m/14,110 ft.

Pilsen German form of Czechoslovakian town of
◊Plzeň.

Pindus Mountains (Greek *Pindhos Oros*) range in N W Greece and Albania, between Epirus and Thessaly: highest point Smolikas 2,633 m/8,638 ft.

Piraeus port of both ancient and modern ◊Athens and main port of Greece, on the Gulf of Aegina; population (1981) 196,400. Constructed as the port of Athens about 493 BC, it was linked with that city by the Long Walls about 460 BC. After the destruction of Athens by Sulla 86 BC, Piraeus declined. Modern Piraeus is an industrial suburb of Athens.

Pisa city in Tuscany, Italy; population (1988) 104,000. The Leaning Tower is 55 m/180 ft high and about 5 m/16.5 ft out of perpendicular.

The Leaning Tower (under repair in 1990) has foundations only about 3 m/10 ft deep and is the campanile of Pisa's 11th–12th-century cathedral (with a pulpit by Giovanni Pisano); university 1338. Pisa was a maritime republic in the 11th–12th centuries. The scientist Galileo was born there.

Pistoia city in Tuscany, Italy, 16 km/10 mi NW of Florence; industries (steel, small arms, paper, pasta, olive oil); population (1982) 92,500. Pistoia was the site of the Roman rebel Catiline's defeat 62 BC. It is surrounded by walls (1302) and has a 12th-century cathedral.

Pitcairn Islands British colony in Polynesia, 5,300 km/3,300 mi NE of New Zealand

area 27 sq km/10 sq mi

capital Adamstown

features in the group are the uninhabited Henderson Islands, an unspoiled coral atoll with a rare ecology, and tiny Ducie and Oeno, annexed by Britain in 1902

exports fruit and souvenirs to passing ships

population (1982) 54

language English

government the governor is the British high commissioner in New Zealand

history the islands were first settled by nine mutineers from the *Bounty* together with some Tahitians, their occupation remaining unknown until 1808.

Pittsburgh industrial city (machinery and chemicals) and inland port, where the Allegheny and Monongahela join to form the Ohio River in Pennsylvania, USA; population (1980) 423,940, metropolitan area 2,264,000. Established by the French as Fort Duquesne 1750, the site was taken by the British 1758 and renamed Fort Pitt.

Piura capital of the department of the same name in the arid NW of Peru, situated on the Piura river, 160 km/100 mi SW of Punta Pariñas; population (1981) 186,000. It is the most westerly point in South America, and was founded 1532 by the conquistadors left behind by Pizarro. Cotton is grown in the surrounding area.

Plate, River English name of Río de ◊la Plata, estuary in South America.

Plenty, Bay of broad inlet on the NE coast of North Island, New Zealand, with the port of Tauranga. One of the first canoes bringing Maori immigrants landed here about 1350.

Pleven industrial town (textiles, machinery, ceramics) in N Bulgaria; population (1987) 134,000. In the Russo-Turkish War 1877, Pleven surrendered to the Russians after a siege of five months.

Ploeşti industrial city (textiles, paper, petrochemicals; oil centre) in SE Romania; population (1985) 234,000.

Plovdiv industrial city (textiles, chemicals, leather, tobacco) in Bulgaria, on the Maritsa; population (1987) 357,000. Conquered by Philip of Macedon in the 4th century BC, it was known as Philippopolis (Philip's city).

Plymouth city and seaport in Devon, England, at the mouth of the river Plym, with dockyard, barracks, and naval base at Devonport; population (1981) 244,000.

The city rises N from the Hoe headland where tradition has it that Drake played bowls before leaving to fight the Spanish Armada. John Hawkins, Drake, and the Pilgrims in *Mayflower* sailed from Plymouth Sound. The city centre was reconstructed after heavy bombing in World War II.

Plynlimon mountain in Powys, Wales, with three summits; the highest is 752 m/2,468 ft.

Plzeň (German *Pilsen*) industrial city (heavy machinery, cars, beer) in W Czechoslovakia, capital of Západočeský region; 84 km/52 mi SW of Prague; population (1984) 174,000.

Pnom Penh alternative form of ◊Phnom Penh, capital of Cambodia.

Po longest river in Italy, flowing from the Cottian Alps to the Adriatic; length 668 km/415 mi. Its valley is fertile and contains natural gas. The river is heavily polluted with nitrates, phosphates, and arsenic.

Pobeda, Pik highest peak in the ◊Tian Shan mountain range on the Soviet-Chinese border; at 7,439 m/24,406 ft, it is the second highest mountain in the USSR.

Podgorica former name (until 1946) of ◊Titograd, city in Yugoslavia.

Podolsk industrial city (oil refining, machinery, cables, cement, ceramics) in the USSR, 40 km/25 mi SW of Moscow; population (1987) 209,000.

Pointe-Noire chief port of the Congo, formerly (1950–58) the capital; population (1984) 297,000. Industries include oil refining and shipbuilding.

Poitiers capital of Poitou-Charentes, W France; population (1982) 103,200; products include chemicals and clothing. The Merovingian king Clovis

Poland
Polish Republic

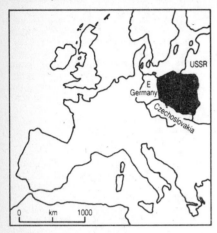

area 312,700 sq km/120,733 sq mi
capital Warsaw
towns Lódź, Kraków, Wroclaw, Poznań, Katowice, Bydgoszcz, Lublin; ports Gdánsk, Szczecin, Gdynia
physical comprises part of the great plain of Europe; Vistula, Oder, and Neisse rivers; Sudeten, Tatra, and Carpathian mountains
head of government Tadeusz Mazowieki from 1989
government socialist pluralist republic
political parties Social Democratic Party of the Polish Republic, the 1990 successor to the Polish United Worker's Party (PUWP), formerly Marxist-Leninist, now social democratic; Union of Social Democrats, radical breakaway from the PUWP formed 1990; Solidaårnosc (Solidarity) Parliamentary Club (OKP), anti-communist coalition
exports coal, softwood timber, chemicals, machinery, ships
currency zloty (16061 = £1 Feb 1990)
population (1989) 38,389,000; annual growth rate 0.9%
life expectancy men 67, women 75
language Polish, a member of the western branch of the Slavonic family
religion Roman Catholic 93%
literacy 99.3% male/98.3% female (1978)
GNP $110 bn (1984); $2,750 per head of population
chronology
1918 Poland revived as independent republic.
1939 German invasion and occupation.
1944 Germans driven out by Soviet force.
1945 Polish boundaries redrawn at Potsdam Conference.
1947 Communist people's republic proclaimed.
1956 Poznań riots. Gomulka installed as Polish United Workers' Party (PUWP) leader.
1970 Gomulka replaced by Gierek after Gdańsk riots.
1980 Emergence of Solidarity free trade union following Gdańsk disturbances.
1981 Imposition of martial law by Gen Jaruzelski.
1983 Ending of martial law.
1984 Amnesty for political prisoners.
1985 Zbigniew Messner became prime minister.
1987 Referendum on economic reform rejected.
1988 Solidarity strikes and demonstrations were called off after pay increases and government agreement to hold a church-state-union conference. Messner resigned and was replaced by the reformist Mieczyslaw Rakowski.
1989 Historic agreement to re-legalize Solidarity and introduce new socialist pluralist constitution following Church-state-union round table negotiations (Apr). Solidarity sweep board in national assembly elections (June). Zaruzelski elected president (July). 'Grand coalition' formed headed by Solidarity's Mazowiecki (Sept).
1990 PUWP dissolved and replaced by new Social Democrat Party and breakaway Union of Social Democrats (Jan).

---

defeated the Visigoths under Alaric here 507; Charles Martel stemmed the Saracen advance 732, and Edward the Black Prince defeated the French 1356.

Poitou-Charentes region of W central France, comprising the *départements* of Charente, Charente-Maritime, Deux-Sèvres, and Vienne; capital Poitiers; area 25,800 sq km/9,959 sq mi; population (1986) 1,584,000. The region is noted for the brandy produced at Cognac.

Poland country in E Europe, bounded to the E by the USSR, to the S by Czechoslovakia, and to the W by East Germany.

Poltava industrial city (machinery, foodstuffs, clothing) in Ukraine, USSR, capital of Poltava region, on the river Vorskla; population (1987) 309,000. Peter the Great defeated Charles XII of Sweden here 1709.

Polynesia those islands of Oceania E of 170° E latitude, including Hawaii, Kiribati, Tuvalu, Fiji,

Polynesia

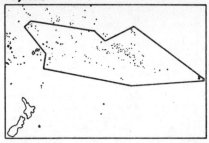

Tonga, Tokelau, Samoa, Cook Islands, and French Polynesia.

Pomerania (Polish *Pomorze*, German *Pommern*) region along the south shore of the Baltic Sea, including the island of Rügen, forming part of Poland and (west of the Oder–Neisse line) East Germany from 1945. The chief port is Gdańsk. It was formerly a province of Germany.

Pomfret an old form of ◊Pontefract, a town in Yorkshire, England.

Pommern German form of ◊Pomerania, former province of Germany.

Pomorze Polish form of ◊Pomerania, region of N Europe, now largely in Poland.

Ponce industrial port (textiles, sugar, rum) in S Puerto Rico, USA; population (1980) 189,000; named after the Spanish explorer Ponce de León.

Pondicherry Union Territory of SE India; area 480 sq km/185 sq mi; population (1981) 604,000. Its capital is Pondicherry, and products include rice, groundnuts, cotton, and sugar. Pondicherry was founded by France 1674 and changed hands several times between French, Dutch, and British before being returned to France 1814 at the close of the Napoleonic wars. Together with Karaikal, Yanam, and Mahé (on the Malabar Coast) it formed a French colony until 1954 when all were transferred to the government of India; since 1962 they have formed the Union Territory of Pondicherry. Languages spoken include·French, English, Tamil, Telegu, and Malayalam.

Ponta Delgada port, resort, and chief commercial centre of the Portuguese ◊Azores, on SãMiguel; population (1981) 22,200.

Pontefract town in Wakefield borough, W Yorkshire, N England, 34 km/21 mi SW of York; population (1981) 33,000. Produces coal and confectionery (liquorice Pontefract cakes). Features include the remains of the Norman castle where Richard II died.

Pontiac a motor-manufacturing city in Michigan, USA, 38 km/24 mi NW of Detroit; population (1980) 76,700.

Pontine Marshes formerly malarial marshes in Lazio region, Italy, near the coast 40 km/25 mi SE of Rome. They defied the attempts of the Romans to drain them, and it was not until 1926, under Mussolini's administration, that they were brought into cultivation. Products include cereals, fruit and vines, and sugar beet.

Pontypool industrial town in Torfaen district, Gwent, SE Wales, on the Afon Llwyd, 15 km/9 mi N of Newport; population (1981) 36,761. Products include coal, iron and steel goods, tinplate glass, synthetic textiles, and scientific instruments.

Pontypridd industrial town (coal mining, chain and cable works, light industry on the Treforest trading estate) in Taff-Ely district, Mid Glamorgan, S Wales; population (1981) 33,134.

Poole industrial town (chemicals, engineering, boatbuilding, confectionery, pottery from local clay) and yachting centre on Poole harbour, Dorset, S England, 8 km/5 mi west of Bournemouth; population (1984) 123,000.

The first Scout camp was held 1907 on Brownsea Island in the harbour, which is now owned by the National Trust. Furzey Island, also within the·harbour, is part of Wytch Farm, Britain's largest onshore oil development.

Pool Malebo lake on the border between the Congo and Zaïre, formed by a widening of the Zaïre river, 560 km/350 mi from its mouth.

Poona former spelling of ◊Pune, city in India.

Popocatépetl (Aztec 'smoking mountain') volcano in central Mexico, 50 km/30 mi SE of Mexico City; 5,340 m/17,526 ft. It last erupted 1920.

Pori Swedish *Björneborg* ice-free industrial port (nickel and copper refining, sawmills, paper, textiles) on the Gulf of Bothnia, SW Finland; population (1985) 79,000. A deepwater harbour was opened in 1985.

Port Adelaide industrial port (cement, chemicals) in South Australia, on Gulf St Vincent, 11 km/7 mi NW of Adelaide; population (1985) 37,000.

Port Arthur industrial deepwater port (oil refining, shipbuilding, brass, chemicals) in Texas, USA, 24 km/15 mi SE of Beaumont; population (1980) 61,000. Founded 1895, it gained importance with the discovery of petroleum near Beaumont in 1901.

Port Arthur former name (until 1905) of the port and naval base of Lüshun in NE China, now part of ◊Lüda.

Port Augusta port (trading in wool and grain) in South Australia, at the head of Spencer Gulf, NNW of Adelaide; population (1985) 17,000. Base for the Royal Flying Doctor Service.

Port-au-Prince capital and industrial port (sugar, rum, textiles, plastics) of Haiti; population (1982) 763,000.

Port Darwin port serving ◊Darwin, capital of Northern Territory, Australia.

Port Elizabeth industrial port (engineering, steel, food processing) in Cape province, South Africa, about 710 km/440 mi E of Cape Town on Algoa Bay; population (1980) 492,140.

Port Harcourt port (trading in coal, palm oil, and groundnuts) and capital of Rivers state in SE Nigeria, on the river Bonny in the Niger delta; population (1983) 296,200. It is also an industrial centre producing refined mineral oil, aluminium sheet, tyres, and paints.

Port Kelang Malaysian rubber port (Port Swettenham until 1971) on the Strait of Malacca, 40 km/25 mi SW of Kuala Lumpur. Population (1980) 192,080.

Portland industrial port (aluminium, paper, timber, lumber machinery, electronics) and capital of Multnomah County, NW Oregon, USA; on the Columbia River, 173 km/108 mi from the sea, at its confluence with the Willamette River; population (1980) 366,400.

Portland industrial port (shipbuilding) and largest city of Maine, USA, on Casco Bay, SE of Sebago Lake; population (1980) 61,500. Birthplace of the poet Longfellow.

Portland, Isle of rocky peninsula off Dorset, S England, joined to the mainland by the ◊Chesil Bank. Portland Castle was built by Henry VIII 1520; Portland harbour is a naval base; building stone is still quarried.

Port Louis capital of Mauritius, on the island's NW coast; population (1987) 139,000. Exports include sugar, textiles, watches, and electronic goods.

Port Mahón port serving ◊Mahón on the Spanish island of Minorca.

Portmeirion holiday resort in Gwynedd, Wales, built by the architect Clough Williams-Ellis in Italianate fantasy style; setting of the 1967 cult television series *The Prisoner*.

Port Moresby capital and port of Papua New Guinea on the S coast of New Guinea; population (1987) 152,000.

Porto (English *Oporto*) industrial city (textiles, leather, pottery) in Portugal, on the Douro, 5 km/3 mi from its mouth; population (1984) 327,000. It exports port. It is the second largest city in Portugal, and has a 12th-century cathedral.

Pôrto Alegre port and capital of Rio Grande do Sul state, S Brazil; population (1986) 2,705,000. It is a freshwater port for ocean-going vessels, and is Brazil's major commercial centre.

Port-of-Spain port and capital of Trinidad and Tobago, on Trinidad; population (1988) 58,000.

Porto Novo capital of Benin, W Africa; population (1982) 208,258. It was a former Portuguese centre for the slave and tobacco trade with Brazil, and became a French protectorate 1863.

Porto Rico name until 1932 of ◊Puerto Rico, US island in the Caribbean.

Port Phillip Bay inlet off Bass Strait, Victoria, Australia, on which Melbourne stands.

Port Pirie industrial port (smelting of ores from the Broken Hill mines, and chemicals) in S Australia; population (1985) 16,030.

Port Rashid port serving ◊Dubai in the United Arab Emirates.

Port Royal former capital of ◊Jamaica, at the entrance to Kingston harbour.

Port Said port in Egypt, on reclaimed land at the N end of the ◊Suez Canal; population (1983) 364,000. During the 1967 Arab-Israel war the city was damaged and the canal was blocked; Port Said was evacuated by 1969, but by 1975 had been largely reconstructed.

Portsmouth city and naval port in Hampshire, England, opposite the Isle of Wight; population (1981) 179,500.

Portsmouth port in Rockingham county, SE New Hampshire, USA, on the estuary of the river Piscataqua; population (1980) 26,000. The naval base on Seavy's Island specializes in submarine construction and maintenance. Founded in 1623, Portsmouth was the state capital 1679–1775. The treaty ending the Russo-Japanese War was signed here 1905.

Portsmouth port and independent city in SE Virginia, USA, on the Elizabeth River, seat of a US navy yard and training centre, population (1980) 104,577. It also makes textiles, chemicals, fertilizers, raises oysters, and trades in tobacco and cotton.

Port Sunlight a model village built 1888 by W H Lever (1851–1925) for workers at the Lever Brothers soap factory at Birkenhead near Liverpool, NW England. Designed for a population of 3,000, and covering an area of 320 ha/130 acres, it includes an art gallery, church, library, and social hall.

Port Swettenham former name of ◊Port Kelang, port in Peninsular Malaysia.

Port Talbot industrial port (tinplate and steel strip mill) in W Glamorgan, Wales; population (1981) 47,500.

Portugal country in SW Europe, on the Atlantic, bounded to the N and E by Spain.

Portugal: former colonies

Name	Colonized	Independent
Brazil	1532	1822
Uruguay	1533	1828
Mozambique	1505	1975
Angola	1941	1975

Portuguese East Africa former name of ◊Mozambique.

Portuguese Guinea former name of ◊Guinea-Bissau.

Portuguese West Africa former name of ◊Angola.

Posen German form of ◊Poznań, city in Poland.

Portugal
Republic of
(República Portuguesa)

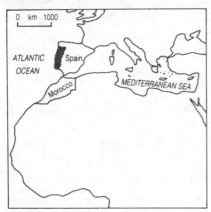

area 92,000 sq km/35,521 sq mi (including Azores and Madeira)
capital Lisbon
towns Coimbra, ports Porto, Setúbal
physical mountainous in the N, plains in the S
features rivers Minho, Douro, Tagus, Guadiana; Serra da Estrélla
head of state Mario Alberto Nobre Lopes Soares from 1986
head of government Cavaco Silva from 1985
government democratic republic
political parties Social Democratic Party (PSD), moderate, left-of-centre; Socialist Party (PS), progressive socialist; Democratic Renewal Party (PRD), centre-left; Democratic Social Centre Party (CDS) , moderate, left-of-centre
exports port wine, olive oil, resin, cork, sardines, textiles, pottery, pulpwood

currency escudo (251.45 = £1 Feb 1990)
population (1989) 10,240,000; annual growth rate 0.7%
life expectancy men 68, women 75
language Portuguese, one of the Romance languages, ultimately derived from Latin, but considerably influenced later by Arabic
religion Roman Catholic
literacy 89% male/80% female (1985)
GDP $19.4 bn (1984); $1,930 per head of population
chronology
1928–68 Military dictatorship under Antonio de Oliveira Salazar.
1968 Salazar succeeded by Marcello Caetano.
1974 Caetano removed in a military coup led by Gen Antonio Ribeiro de Spinola. Spinola was then replaced by Gen Fransisco da Costa Gomes.
1975 African colonies became independent.
1976 New constitution, providing for a gradual return to civilian rule, adopted. Minority government appointed, led by the Socialist Party leader Mario Soares.
1978 Soares resigned.
1980 Francisco Balsema formed a centre-party coalition after two and a half years of political instability.
1982 Draft of new constitution approved, reducing the powers of the presidency.
1983 Centre-left coalition government formed.
1985 Cavaco Silva became prime minister.
1986 Mario Soares elected first civilian president for 60 years. Portugal joined European Community.
1987 Soares re-elected with large majority.
1988 Portugal joined the Western European Union.
1989 Constitution amended to allow state undertakings to be denationalised.

Potchefstroom oldest town in the Transvaal, S Africa on the river Mooi, founded by Boers trekking from the Cape 1838. It is the centre of a large cattle-rearing area.

Potomac river in W Virginia, Virginia and Maryland states, USA, rising in the Allegheny mountains, and flowing SE through Washington, DC, into Chesapeake Bay. It is formed by the junction of the N Potomac, about 153 km/95 mi long, and S Potomac, about 209 km/130 mi long, and is itself 459 km/285 mi long.

Potosí town in SW Bolivia, on the Cerro de Potosí slopes at 4,020 m/13,189 ft; it is one of the highest towns in the world; population (1982) 103,000. Silver, tin, lead, and copper are mined here. It was

founded by Spaniards 1545; during the 17th and 18th centuries it was the chief silver-mining town and most important city in South America.

Potsdam capital of Potsdam county, East Germany, on the river Havel W of Berlin; population (1986) 140,000. Products include textiles, pharmaceuticals, and electrical goods. The New Palace 1763–70 and Sans Souci were both built by Frederick the Great, and Hitler's Third Reich was proclaimed in the garrison church 21 Mar 1933. The Potsdam Conference took place here. Potsdam county has an area of 12,570 sq km/ 4,852 sq mi, and a population of 1,120,000.

Potteries, the region of the Midlands, England, in the upper Trent basin of N Staffordshire. It covers

Powys

Prince Edward Island

and food processing. It became capital 1918.

Praha Czech name for ◊Prague.

Praia port and capital of the Republic of Cape Verde, on the island of Sa Tiago (Santiago); population (1980) 37,500. Industries include fishing and shipping.

prairie the central North American plain, formerly grass-covered, extending over most of the region between the Rockies on the west and the Great Lakes and Ohio River on the east.

Prato industrial town (woollens) in Tuscany, central Italy; population (1988) 165,000. The 12th-century cathedral has works of art by Donatello, Filippo Lippi, and Andrea della Robbia.

Pressburg German name of ◊Bratislava, city in Czechoslovakia.

Preston industrial seaport (textiles, chemicals, electrical goods, aircraft and shipbuilding), adminstrative headquarters of Lancashire, NW England, on the river Ribble 34 km/21 mi S of Lancaster; population (1983) 125,000. Cromwell defeated the Royalists at Preston in 1648; the birthplace of Richard Arkwright, inventor of cotton-spinning machinery.

Prestonpans town in Lothian region, E Scotland, where Prince Charles Edward Stuart's Jacobite forces defeated the English in 1745.

Prestwick town in Strathclyde, SW Scotland; population (1985) 13,532. Industries include engineering and aerospace engineering. The international airport is linked with a free port.

Pretoria administrative capital of the Republic of South Africa from 1910 and capital of Transvaal province from 1860; population (1985) 741,300. Industries include engineering, chemicals, iron, and steel. Founded 1855, it was named after Boer leader Andries Pretorius (1799–1853).

Pribilof Islands group of four islands in the Bering Sea, of volcanic origin, 320 km/200 mi SW of Bristol Bay, Alaska, USA. Named after Gerasim Pribylov who reached them in 1786, they were sold by Russia to the USA in 1867 with Alaska, of

the area around Stoke-on-Trent and includes the formerly separate towns of Burslem, Hanley, Longton, Fenton, and Tunstall. The Potteries is the centre of the china and earthenware industry, with the Wedgwood and Minton factories.

Poverty Bay inlet on the E coast of North Island, New Zealand, on which the port of Gisborne stands. Captain Cook made his first landing here 1769.

Powys county in central Wales
area 5,080 sq km/1,961 sq mi
towns administrative headquarters Llandrindod Wells
features Brecon Beacons National Park, Black mountains, rivers Wye and Severn, which both rise on Plynlimon (see ◊Dyfed); Lake Vyrnwy, artificial reservoir supplying Liverpool and Birmingham, and same size as Lake ◊Bala; alternative technology centre near Machynlleth
products agriculture, dairy cattle, sheep
population (1987) 113,000
language 20% Welsh, English.

Poznań (German *Posen*) industrial city (machinery, aircraft, beer) in W Poland; population (1985) 553,000. Settled by German immigrants 1253, it passed to Prussia 1793, but was restored to Poland 1919.

Pozzuoli port in Campania, S Italy, W of Naples; population (1981) 71,000. It is shaken by some 25 earthquakes a day, 60% of its buildings are uninhabitable, and an eventual major disaster seems inevitable.

Prague (Czech *Praha*) city and capital of Czechoslovakia on the river Vltava; population (1985) 1,190,000. Industries include cars and aircraft, chemicals, paper and printing, clothing, brewing,

which they form part. They were made a fur-seal reservation in 1868.

Primorye territory of the USSR in SE Siberia on the Sea of Japan; area 165,900 sq km/64,079 sq mi; population (1985) 2,136,000; capital Vladivostok. Timber and coal are produced.

Prince Edward Island province of E Canada
area 5,700 sq km/2,200 sq mi
capital Charlottetown
features named after Prince Edward of Kent, father of Queen Victoria; PEI National Park; Summerside Lobster Carnival
products potatoes, dairy products, lobsters, oysters, farm vehicles
population (1986) 127,000.
history first recorded visit by Cartier 1534, who called it Isle St-Jean; settled by French; taken by British 1758; annexed to Nova Scotia 1763; separate colony 1769; settled by Scottish 1803; joined Confederation 1873. In the late 1980s, there was controversy about whether to build a bridge to the mainland.

Prince Rupert fishing port at the mouth of the Skeena River in British Columbia, Canada, on Kaien Island, W side of Tsimpsean peninsula; population (1983) 16,786.

Princeton borough in Mercer County, W central New Jersey, USA, 80 km/50 mi SW of New York; population (1983) 12,035. The seat of Princeton University, founded 1746 at Elizabethtown and moved to Princeton 1756.

Princetown village on the W of Dartmoor, Devon, SW England, containing Dartmoor prison, opened 1809.

Prince William Sound a sound of the Gulf of Alaska, extending 200 km/125 mi NW from Kayak Island. In Mar 1989 the oil tanker *Exxon Valdez* ran aground here, spilling 12 million gallons of crude oil in what was reckoned to be the world's greatest oil-pollution disaster.

Pripet (Russian *Pripyat*) river in W Soviet Union, a tributary of the Dnieper, which it joins 80 km/50 mi above Kiev, Ukraine, after a course of about 800 km/500 mi. The *Pripet marshes* near Pinsk were of strategic importance in both world wars.

Priština capital of Kosovo autonomous province, S Serbia, Yugoslavia; population (1981) 216,000.

Prokopyevsk chief coalmining city of the Kuzbas, Siberia, USSR, on the river Aba; population (1987) 278,000.

Provence-Alpes-Côte d'Azur region of SE France, comprising the *départements* of Alpes-de-Haute-Provence, Hautes-Alpes, Alpes Maritimes, Bouches-du-Rhône, Var, and Vaucluse; area 31,400 sq km/12,120 sq mi; capital Marseille; population (1986) 4,059,000. The *Côte d'Azur*, on the Mediterranean, is a tourist centre. Provence was an independent kingdom in the 10th century, and the area still has its own language, Provençal.

Prussia

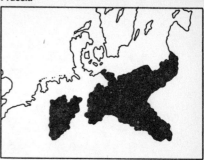

Providence industrial port (jewellery, silverware, textiles and textile machinery, watches, chemicals meat packing), capital of Rhode Island, USA, on the Providence River, 43 km/27 mi from the Atlantic; population (1980) 919,000. Providence was settled by Roger Williams 1636.

Prudhoe Bay a bay in N ◊Alaska. A pipeline links oil fields with the Gulf of Alaska to the S.

Prussia former N German state formed 1618 by the union of Brandenburg and the duchy of Prussia. It became a kingdom under Frederick I 1701 and underwent military expansion until in 1866 it comprised Siberia, East Frisia, West Prussia, parts of the Rhineland and Saxony, Schleswig, Holstein, Hanover, Nassau, Frankfurt-am-Main, and Hesse-Cassel, and became the head of the North German Confederation. It was subsumed in Hitler's Germany in 1933 and was abolished in 1946, its territories being divided among East and West Germany, Poland, and the USSR.

Prut a river that rises in the Carpathian Mountains of SW Ukraine, USSR, and flows 900 km/565 mi to meet the Danube at Reni, USSR. For part of its course it follows the E frontier of Romania.

Przemysl industrial city (timber, ceramics, flour milling, tanning, distilling, food processing, gas, engineering) in SE Poland; population (1981) 62,000.
history Founded in the 8th century, it belonged alternately to Poland and Kiev in the 10th–14th centuries. An Austrian territory 1722–1919, it was a frontier fortress besieged by Soviet troops Sept 1914–Mar 1915, and was occupied by the Germans June 1941–July 1944.

Pskov industrial city (food processing, leather) in USSR, on the Velikaya river, SW of Leningrad; population (1987) 202,000. Dating from 965, it was independent 1348–1510, when it became Russian.

Puebla (de Zaragoza) industrial city (textiles, sugar refining, metallurgy, hand-crafted pottery and tiles) and capital of Puebla state, S central Mexico; population (1986) 1,218,000. Founded 1535 as *Pueblo de los Angeles*, it was later

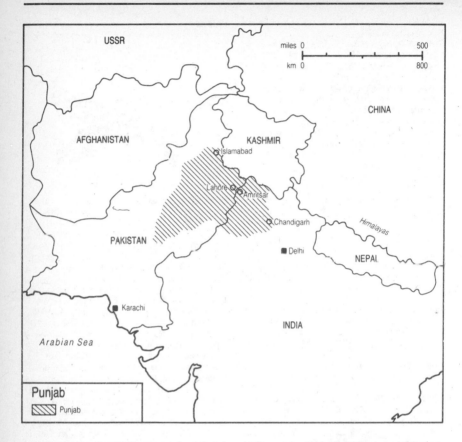

Punjab

⧄⧄ Punjab

renamed after Gen de Zaragoza, who defeated the French here 1862.

Puerto Rico Commonwealth of
area 9,000 sq km/3,475 sq mi
capital San Juan
towns ports Mayagüez, Ponce
features highest per capita income in Latin America
exports sugar, tobacco, rum, pineapples, textiles, plastics, chemicals, processed foods
currency US dollar
population (1980) 3,197,000, 67% urban
language Spanish and English (official)
religion Roman Catholic
government under the constitution of 1952, similar to that of the USA, with a governor elected for four years, and a legislative assembly with a senate and house of representatives
history visited 1493 by Columbus; annexed by Spain 1509; ceded to the USA after the Spanish-American War 1898; achieved Commonwealth status with local self-government 1952.

This was confirmed in preference to independence by a referendum 1967, but there is an independence movement, and another wishing incorporation as a state of the USA. The US Congress passed an act in 1989 to provide for a referendum for Puerto Ricans 1991 on whether to remain a commonwealth, become a US state, or go independent.

Puerto Sandino a major port on the Pacific W coast of Nicaragua, known as *Puerto Somoza* until 1979.

Puget Sound an inlet of the Pacific Ocean on the W coast of Washington State, USA.

Puglia (English *Apulia*) region of Italy, the south eastern 'heel'; area 19,300 sq km/7,450 sq mi; capital Bari, population (1988) 4,043,000. Products include wheat, grapes, almonds, olives, and vegetables. The main industrial centre is Taranto.

Pula commercial and naval port in W Croatia, Yugoslavia, on the Adriatic coast; population (1981) 77,278. A Roman naval base, *Colonia Pietas*

Punjab

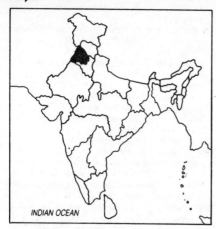

INDIAN OCEAN

Julia, it was seized by Venice in 1148, passed to Austria 1815, to Italy 1919, and Yugoslavia 1947. It has a Roman theatre, and a castle and cathedral constructed under Venetian rule. There is an annual film festival.

Pune formerly *Poona* city in Maharashtra, India; population (1985) 1,685,000. Products include chemicals, rice, sugar, cotton, paper, and jewellery.

Punjab (Sanskrit 'five rivers': the Indus tributaries Jhelum, Chnab, Ravi, Beas, and Sutlej) former state of British India, now divided between India and Pakistan. Punjab was annexed by Britain 1849, after the Sikh Wars 1845–46 and 1848–49, and formed into a province with its capital at Lahore. Under the British, W Punjab was extensively irrigated, and land was granted to Indians who had served in the British army.

Punjab state of NW India
area 50,400 sq km/19,454 sq miles
capital Chandigarh
towns Amritsar
features mainly agricultural, crops chiefly under irrigation; longest life expectancy rates in India (59 for women, 64 for men); Harappa has ruins from the Indus Valley civilization 2500–1600 BC
population (1981) 16,670,000
language Punjabi
religion Sikh 60%, Hindu 30%; there is friction between the two groups.

Punjab state of NE Pakistan
area 205,344 sq km/79,263 sq mi
capital Lahore
features wheat cultivation (by irrigation)
population (1981) 47,292,000
language Punjabi, Urdu
religion Muslim.

Punta Arenas (Spanish 'sandy point') former name *Magallanes* seaport (trading in meat, wool, and oil) in Chile, capital of Magallanes province, on Magellan Strait, most southerly town on the American mainland; population (1982) 99,000.

Purbeck, Isle of a peninsula in the county of Dorset, S England. Purbeck marble and china clay are obtained from the 'isle', which includes Corfe Castle and Swanage.

Puri town in Orissa, E India, with a statue of Jagganath or Vishnu, one of the three gods of Hinduism, dating from about 318, which is annually taken in procession on a large vehicle (hence the word 'juggernaut'). Devotees formerly threw themselves beneath its wheels.

Pusan or *Busan* chief industrial port of South Korea (textiles, rubber, salt, fishing); population (1985) 3,517,000. It was invaded by the Japanese 1592, and opened to foreign trade 1883.

Pushkin town NW of Leningrad, USSR; population 80,000. Founded by Peter the Great as *Tsarskoe Selo* ('tsar's village') 1708, it has a number of imperial summer palaces, restored after German troops devastated the town 1941–44. In the 1920s it was renamed *Detskoe Selo* ('children's village') but since 1937 it has been known as Pushkin, the poet having been educated at the school which is now a museum commemorating him.

Puy, Le see ◊Le Puy, town in France.

Pwllheli resort in Gwynedd, Wales; the Welsh National Party, Plaid Cymru, was founded here 1925.

Pylos port in SW Greece where the battle of Navarino was fought 1827.

Pyongyang capital and industrial city (coal, iron, steel, textiles, chemicals) of North Korea; population (1984) 2,640,000.

Pyrenees (French *Pyrénées*; Spanish *Pirineos*) mountain range in SW Europe between France and Spain; length about 435 km/270 mi; highest peak Aneto (French Néthon) 3,404 m/11,172 ft. Andorra is entirely within the range. Hydroelectric power has encouraged industrial development in the foothills.

Qatar country in the Middle East, occupying Qatar peninsula in the Arabian Gulf, bounded to the SW by Saudi Arabia and to the S by United Arab Emirates.

Qattara Depression tract of the Western Desert, Egypt, up to 125 m/400 ft below sea level. Its very soft sand makes it virtually impassable to vehicles, and it protected the left flank of the Allied armies before and during the battle of Alamein 1942. Area 20,000 sq km/7,500 sq mi.

Qingdao formerly *Tsingtao* industrial port and summer resort in Shandong province, E China; population (1984) 1,229,500. Industries include brewing.

Qinghai formerly *Tsinghai* province of NW China
area 721,000 sq km/278,306 sq mi
capital Xining
features mainly desert, with nomadic herders
products oil, livestock, medical products
population (1986) 4,120,000, including many Tibetans and other minorities.

Qisarya Mediterranean port north of Tel Aviv-Jaffa, Israel; there are underwater remains of Herod the Great's port of Caesarea.

Qld abbreviation for ◊*Queensland*.

Qom or *Qum* holy city of Shi'ite Muslims, in central Iran, 145 km/90 mi south of Tehran; population (1986) 551,000. The Islamic academy of Madresseh Faizieh 1920 became the headquarters of Ayatollah Khomeini.

Quai d'Orsay part of the left bank of the Seine in Paris, where the French Foreign Office and other government buildings are situated. The name has become synonymous with the Foreign Office itself.

Que. abbreviation for ◊*Québec*.

Québec capital and industrial port (textiles, leather, timber, paper, printing and publishing) of Québec province, on the St Lawrence River, Canada;

Qatar
State of
(Dawlat Qatar)

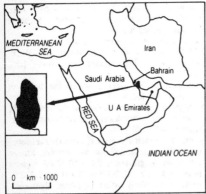

0   km   1000

area 11,400 sq km/4,402 sq mi
capital and chief port Doha
towns Dukhan, centre of oil production
physical mostly flat desert
features negligible rain and surface water, so that only 3% is fertile, but irrigation allows self-sufficiency in fruit and vegetables; rich oil discoveries since World War II
head of state and government Sheik Khalifa bin Hamad al-Thani from 1972
government absolute monarchy
political parties none
exports oil, natural gas, petrochemicals, fertilizers, iron, steel
currency riyal (6.1881 = £1 Feb 1990)
population (1989) 342,000 (half in Doha); annual growth rate 6.8%
life expectancy men 65, women 70
language Arabic
religion Sunni Muslim
literacy 60% (1985)
GNP $5.9 bn (1983); $35,000 per head of population
chronology
1970 Constitution adopted, confirming the emirate as an absolute monarchy.
1971 Achieved full independence. New treaty of friendship with the UK signed.
1972 Emir Sheik Ahmad replaced in a bloodless coup, by his cousin, Crown Prince Sheik Khalifa.

Québec

population (1986) 165,000, metropolitan area
603,000. It was founded 1608 by the French
explorer Champlain, and was a French colony
1608–1763. The British, under Gen Wolfe, captured Québec 1759 after a battle on the nearby
Plains of Abraham; both Wolfe and the French
commander Montcalm were killed. Québec is a
centre of French culture, and there are two universities, Laval 1663 (oldest in North America)
and Québec 1969. Its picturesque old town survives below the citadel about 110 m/360 ft above
the St Lawrence River.

Québec province of E Canada
area 1,540,700 sq km/594,710 sq mi
capital Québec
towns Montreal, Laval, Sherbrooke, Verdun,
Hull, Trois-Rivières
features immense water-power resources, for
example the James Bay project
products iron, copper, gold, zinc, cereals, potatoes, paper, textiles, fish, maple syrup (70% of
world's output)
population (1986) 6,540,000
language French is the only official language
since 1974, although 17% speak English. Language laws 1989 prohibit the use of English on
street signs
history known as New France 1534–1763; captured by the British, and became province of
Québec 1763–90, Lower Canada 1791–1846,
Canada East 1846–67; one of the original provinces 1867; nationalist feelings 1960s (despite
existing safeguards for Québec's French-derived
civil law, customs, religion, and language) led to
the foundation of the Parti Québecois by René
Lévesque 1968; uprising by FLQ separatists
1970; referendum on 'sovereignty-association'
(separation) defeated 1980; Robert Bourassa and
Liberals returned to power 1985, and enacted
restrictive English-language legislation.

Queen Charlotte Islands archipelago about 160 km/
100 mi off the coast of ◊British Columbia, W
Canada, of which it forms part; area 9,790 sq km/

3,780 sq mi; population 2,500. Graham and
Moresby are the largest of about 150 islands.
There are timber and fishing industries.

Queen Maud Land a region of Antarctica W of
Enderby Land, claimed by Norway since 1939.

Queens a borough and county at the W end of Long
Island, New York City, USA; population (1980)
1,891,300.

Queen's County former name (until 1920) of
◊Laois, county in the Republic of Ireland.

Queensland state in NE Australia
area 1,727,200 sq km/666,699 sq mi
capital Brisbane
towns Gold Coast-Tweed, Townsville, Sunshine
Coast, Toowoomba, Cairns
features Great Dividing Range, including Mount
Bartle Frere 1,657 m/5,438 ft; Great Barrier
Reef (collection of coral reefs and islands about
2,000 km/1,250 mi long off the E coast; City of
Gold Coast holiday area in the south, population
120,000; Mount Isa mining area
exports sugar, pineapples, beef, cotton, wool,
tobacco, copper, gold, silver, lead, zinc, coal,
nickel, bauxite, uranium, natural gas
population (1987) 2,650,000
history part of New South Wales until 1859, it
then became self-governing. In 1989 the ruling
National Party was defeated after 32 years in
power, and replaced by the Labour Party.

Queenstown former name (1849–1922) of ◊Cobh,
port in the Republic of Ireland.

Quemoy island off the SE coast of China,
and administered by Taiwan; area 130 sq km/
50 sq mi; Matsu 40 sq km/17 sq mi; population (1982) 57,847. When the islands were
shelled from the mainland in 1960, the
USA declared they would be defended if
attacked.

Quetta summer resort and capital of Baluchistan,
W Pakistan; population (1981) 281,000. Linked
to Shikarpur by a gas pipeline in 1982.

Queensland

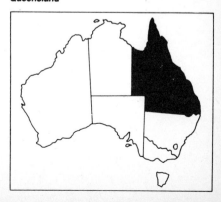

Quezon City former capital of the Philippines 1948–76, NE part of metropolitan ◊Manila, on Luzon Island; population (1980) 1,166,000. It was named after the Philippines' first president, Manuel Luis Quezon (1878–1944).

Qufu formerly *Chufu* town in Shandong province, China; population 27,000. It is the birthplace of Kong Zi (Confucius) and the site of the Great Temple of Confucius.

Quiberon peninsula and coastal town in Brittany, NW France; in 1759 the British admiral Hawke defeated a French fleet (under Conflans) in Quiberon Bay.

Quimper town in Brittany, NW France, on the river Odet; population (1982) 60,162; a centre for the manufacture of decorative pottery since the 16th century.

Quintana Roo state in SE Mexico, on the E of the ◊Yucatán peninsula, population (1980) 226,000. There are Maya remains at Tulum; Cancun is a major resort and free port.

Quito capital and industrial city (textiles, chemicals, leather, gold, silver) of Ecuador, about 3,000 m/9,850 ft above sea level; population (1982) 1,110,250. It was an ancient settlement, taken by the Incas about 1470 and by the Spanish 1534. It has a temperate climate all year round.

Qum a holy city of the Shia Muslims in Iran, 145 km/90 mi S of Tehran.

QwaQwa a black homeland of South Africa which achieved self-governing status in 1974; population (1985) 181,600.

Rajasthan

INDIAN OCEAN

Rabat capital of Morocco, industrial port (cotton textiles, carpets, leather goods) on the Atlantic coast, 177 km/110 mi W of Fez; population (1982) 519,000, Rabat-Salé 842,000. It is named after its original *ribat* or fortified monastery.

Rabaul largest port (trading in copra and cocoa) of Papua New Guinea, on the volcanic island of New Britain, SW Pacific; population (1980) 14,954. It was destroyed by British bombing after its occupation by the Japanese in 1942, but rebuilt.

Radium Hill mining site SW of Broken Hill, New South Wales, Australia, formerly a source of radium and uranium.

Radnorshire former border county of Wales, merged with Powys 1974. Presteign was the county town.

Radom industrial city (flour-milling, brewing, tobacco, leather, bicycles, machinery; iron works) in Poland, 96 km/60 mi S of Warsaw; population (1985) 214,000. Radom became Austrian 1795, Russian 1825, and was returned to Poland 1919.

Ragusa town in Sicily, Italy, 54 km/34 mi SW of Syracuse; textile industries; population (1981) 64,492. It stands over 450 m/1,500 ft above the river Ragusa, and there are ancient tombs in caves nearby.

Ragusa Italian name (to 1918) for the Yugoslavian town of ◊Dubrovnik. Its English name was *Arrogosa*, from which the word 'argosy' is derived, because of the town's fame for its trading fleets while under Turkish rule in the 16th century.

Rainier, Mount mountain in the ◊Cascade Range, Washington State, USA; 4,392 m/14,415 ft, crowned by 14 glaciers and carrying dense forests on its slopes. It is a quiescent volcano. Mount Rainier national park was dedicated 1899.

Rajasthan state of NW India
area 342,200 sq km/132,089 sq mi
capital Jaipur
features includes the larger part of the Thar Desert, where India's first nuclear test was carried out
products oilseed, cotton, sugar, asbestos, copper, textiles, cement, glass
population (1981) 34,103,000
language Rajasthani, Hindi
religion Hindu 90%, Muslim 3%
history formed 1948, enlarged 1956.

Rajshahi capital of Rajshahi region, W Bangladesh; population (1981) 254,000. It trades in timber and vegetable oil.

Raleigh industrial city (food processing, electrical machinery, textiles), capital of North Carolina, USA; population (1980) 148,000.

Raleigh, Fort site of the first English settlement in America, at the N end of Roanoke Island, North Carolina, USA, to which in 1585 Walter Raleigh sent 108 colonists from Plymouth, England, under his cousin Richard Grenville. In 1586 Francis Drake took the dissatisfied survivors back to England. The outline fortifications are preserved.

Ramat Gan industrial city (textiles, food processing) in W Israel, NE of Tel Aviv; population (1987) 116,000. It was established 1921.

Rambouillet town in the S of the forest of Rambouillet, SW of Paris, France; population (1985) 22,500. The former royal château is now the presidential summer residence. A breed of fine-woolled sheep is named after the town.

Ramsgate seaside resort and cross-Channel port in the Isle of Thanet, Kent, SE England; population (1981) 39,642. There is a maritime museum. The architect Pugin built a home there, and is buried in the church next door (St Augustine's).

Rance river in Brittany, NW France, flowing into the English Channel between Dinard and St Malo, where a dam built 1960–67 (with a lock for ships) uses the 13 m/44 ft tides to feed the world's first successful tidal power station.

Rand abbreviation for the ◊Witwatersrand, a mountain ridge in Transvaal, South Africa.

Rangoon former name (until 1989) of ◊Yangon, capital of Myanmar.

Rapallo port and winter resort in Liguria, NW Italy, 24 km/15 mi SE of Genoa on the Gulf of Rapallo; population (1981) 29,300. Treaties were signed here 1920 (settling the common frontiers of Italy and Yugoslavia) and 1922 (cancelling German and Russian counter-claims for indemnities for World War I).

Rapa Nui another name for ◊Easter Island, an island in the Pacific.

Ras el Khaimah or *Ra's al Khaymah* an emirate on the Persian Gulf; area 1,690 sq km/652 sq mi; population (1980) 73,700. Products include oil, pharmaceuticals and cement. It is one of the seven members of the ◊United Arab Emirates.

Rathlin island off the N Irish coast, in Antrim; St Columba founded a church there in the 6th century, and in 1306 Robert Bruce hid there after his defeat by the English at Methven.

Ratisbon English name for the West German city of ◊Regensburg.

Ravenna historical city and industrial port (petrochemical works) in Emilia-Romagna, Italy; population (1988) 136,000. It lies in a marshy plain and is known for its Byzantine churches with superb mosaics.

Ravenna was a Roman port and naval station, and capital of the W Roman emperors 404–93; of Theodoric the Great 493–526; and later of the Byzantine exarchs (bishops) 539–750. The British poet Byron lived for some months in Ravenna, home of Countess Guiccioli, during the years 1819–21.

Ravi river in the Indian subcontinent, a tributary of the ◊Indus. It rises in India, forms the boundary between India and Pakistan for some 95 km/70 mi, and enters Pakistan above Lahore, the chief town on its 725 km/450 mi course. It is an important source of water for the Punjab irrigation canal system.

Rawalpindi city in Punjab province, Pakistan, in the foothills of the Himalayas; population (1981) 928,400. Industries include oil refining, iron, chemicals, and furniture.

Reading industrial town (biscuits, electronics) on the river Thames, administrative headquarters of Berkshire, England; university 1892; population (1985) 138,000. An agricultural and horticultural centre. It was extensively rebuilt after World War II. Oscar Wilde spent two years in Reading jail.

Reading industrial city (textiles, special steels) in Pennsylvania, USA; population (1980) 78,686.

Recife industrial seaport (cotton textiles, sugar refining, fruit canning, flour milling) and naval base in Brazil, capital of Pernambuco state, at the mouth of the river Capibaribe; population (1980) 1,184,215. It was founded 1504.

Recklinghausen industrial town (coal, iron, chemicals, textiles, engineering) in North Rhine-Westphalia, West Germany, 24 km/15 mi NW of Dortmund; population (1988) 118,000. It is said to have been founded by Charlemagne.

Redbridge borough of NE Greater London, including Ilford, Wanstead, and Woodford, and parts of Chigwell and Dagenham
features part of Epping Forest; Hainault Forest
population (1981) 225,300.

Redditch industrial town (needles, fishing tackle, car and aircraft components, cycles, motorcycles, electrical equipment) in Hereford and Worcester, England; population (1981) 66,854. Developed from 1965 as a new town to take Birmingham's overspill.

Redoubt, Mount an active volcanic peak rising to 3,140 m/10,197 ft W of Cook inlet in S Alaska, USA. There have been recent eruptions in 1966 and 1989.

Red River western tributary of the ◊Mississippi, USA, so called because of the reddish soil sediment it carries. The stretch that forms the Texas–Oklahoma border is known as Tornado Alley because of the tornadoes caused by the collision in spring of warm air from the Gulf of Mexico with cold fronts from the north.

Red River river in N Vietnam, 500 km/310 mi long, which flows into the Gulf of Tonkin. Its extensive delta is a main centre of population.

Redruth town in Cornwall, England, part of the combined town of ◊Camborne-Redruth.

Red Sea submerged section of the Great ◊Rift Valley (2,000 km/1,200 mi long and up to 320 km/200 mi wide). Egypt, Sudan, and Ethiopia (in Africa) and Saudi Arabia (Asia) are on its shores.

Regensburg (English *Ratisbon*) city in Bavaria, West Germany, on the Danube at its confluence with the Regen, 100 km/63 mi NE of Munich; population (1988) 124,000. It has many medieval buildings, including a Gothic cathedral 1275–1530.

Regensburg stands on the site of a Celtic settlement dating from 500 BC It became the Roman *Castra Regina* AD 179, the capital of the Eastern Frankish Empire, a free city 1245, and seat of the German *Diet* (parliament) 16th century–1806. It was included in Bavaria 1810.

Reggio di Calabria industrial centre (farm machinery, olive oil, perfume) of Calabria, S Italy; population (1988) 179,000. It was founded by Greeks about 720 BC.

Reggio nell'Emilia chief town of the province of the same name in Emilia-Romagna region, N Italy; population (1987) 130,000. It was here in 1797 that the Congress of the cities of Emilia adopted the tricolour flag that was later to become the national flag of Italy.

Regina industrial city (oil refining, cement, steel, farm machinery, fertilizers), capital of Saskatchewan, Canada; population (1986) 175,000. It was founded 1882 as *Pile O'Bones*, and renamed in honour of Queen Victoria of England.

Rehoboth Gebeit a district of Namibia to the south of Windhoek; area 32,168 sq km/ 12,420 sq mi; chief town Rehoboth. The area is occupied by the Basters, a mixed race of European-Nama descent.

Reigate town in Surrey, England, at the foot of the North Downs; population (1981) 52,554. With Redhill it forms a residential suburb of London.

Reims (English *Rheims*) capital of Champagne-Ardenne region, France; population (1982) 199,000. It is the centre of the champagne industry, and has textile industries. It was known in Roman times as *Durocorturum*. From 987 all but six French kings were crowned here. Ceded to England 1420 under the Treaty of Troyes, it was retaken by Joan of Arc, who had Charles VII consecrated in the 13th-century cathedral. The German High Command formally surrendered here to Eisenhower 7 May 1945.

Remscheid industrial city in North Rhine-Westphalia, West Germany, where stainless-steel implements are manufactured; population (1988) 121,000.

Renfrew town on the Clyde, in Strathclyde, 8 km/ 5 mi NW of Glasgow, Scotland; population (1981) 21,396. It was formerly the county town of Renfrewshire.

Renfrewshire former county of W central Scotland, bordering the Firth of Clyde. It was merged with the region of Strathclyde in 1975. The county town was Renfrew.

Rennes industrial city (oil refining, chemicals, electronics, cars) and capital of Ille-et-Vilaine *département*, W France, at the confluence of the Ille and Vilaine, 56 km/35 mi SE of St Malo; population (1982) 234,000. It was the old capital of Brittany. Its university specializes in Breton culture. The second Dreyfus trial was held here 1899.

Reno city in Nevada, USA, known for gambling and easy divorces; population (1984) 112,000.

Réunion French island of the Mascarenes group, in the Indian Ocean, 650 km/400 mi E of Madagascar, and 180 km/110 mi SW of Mauritius
area 2,512 sq km/970 sq mi
capital St Denis
physical forested, rising in Piton de Neiges to 3,069 m/10,072 ft
features administers five uninhabited islands also claimed by Madagascar
products sugar, maize, vanilla, tobacco, rum
population (1987) 565,000

Réunion

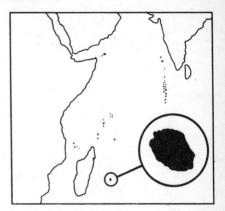

history the first European visitors were the Portuguese 1513; annexed by Louis XIII of France 1642; overseas *département* of France 1946; overseas region 1972.

Reus industrial city with an international airport in Catalonia, E Spain, 10 km/6 mi NW of Tarragona.

Reval former name of the Soviet port of ◊Tallinn.

Reykjavik capital (since 1918) and chief port of Iceland, on the SW coast; population (1988) 93,000. Fish processing is the main industry. Reykjavik is heated by underground mains fed by volcanic springs. It was a seat of Danish administration from 1801. Its university was founded 1911.

Rheims English version of ◊Reims, city in France.

Rheinland-Pfalz German name for the ◊Rhineland-Palatinate region, West Germany.

Rhine (German *Rhein*, French *Rhin*) European river rising in Switzerland and reaching the North Sea via West Germany and the Netherlands; length 1,320 km/820 mi. Tributaries include the Moselle and the Ruhr. The Rhine is linked with the Mediterranean by the Rhine-Rhône Waterway, and with the Black Sea by the Rhine-Main-Danube Waterway.

The *Lorelei* is a rock in the river in Rhineland-Palatinate, West Germany, with a remarkable echo; the German poet Brentano gave currency to the legend of a siren who lured sailors to death with her song, also subject of a poem by Heine.

Rhineland-Palatinate (German *Rheinland-Pfalz*) administrative region (German *Land*) of West Germany
area 19,800 sq km/7,643 sq mi
capital Mainz
towns Ludwigshafen, Koblenz, Trier, Worms

Rhine

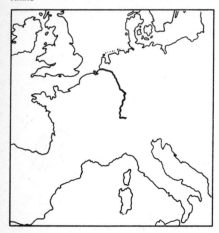

physical wooded mountain country, river valleys of Rhine and Moselle
products wine (75% of German output), tobacco, chemicals, machinery, leather goods, pottery
population (1988) 3,611,000
history formed 1946 of the Rhenish Palatinate and parts of Hessen, Rhine province, and Hessen-Nassau.

Rhode Island smallest state of the USA, in New England; nickname Little Rhody or the Ocean State
area 3,100 sq km/1,197 sq mi
capital Providence
towns Cranston, Woonsocket
features Narragansett Bay runs inland 45 km/28 mi
products apples, potatoes, poultry (especially Rhode Island Reds), dairy products, jewellery (30% of the workforce), textiles, silverware, machinery, rubber, plastics, electronics
population (1987) 986,000
history founded 1636 by Roger Williams, exiled from Massachusetts Bay colony for religious dissent; one of the original Thirteen States.

Rhodes (Greek *Rodhos*) Greek island, largest of the Dodecanese, in the E Aegean Sea
area 1,412 sq km/545 sq mi
capital Rhodes
products grapes, olives
population (1981) 88,000
history settled by Greeks about 1000 BC; the Colossus of Rhodes (fell 224 BC) was one of the Seven Wonders of the World; held by the Knights Hospitallers of St John 1306–1522; taken from Turkish rule by the Italian occupation 1912; ceded to Greece 1947.

Rhodesia former name of ◊Zambia (North Rhodesia) and ◊Zimbabwe (South Rhodesia).

Rhodope Mountains a range of mountains on the frontier between Greece and Bulgaria, rising to 2,925 m/9,497 ft at Musala.
Rhondda industrial town in Mid Glamorgan, Wales; population (1981) 81,725. Light industries have replaced coalmining, formerly the main source of employment.
Rhône river of S Europe; length 810 km/500 mi. It rises in Switzerland and flows through Lake Geneva to Lyons in France, where at its confluence with the Saône the upper limit of navigation is reached. The river turns due south, passes Vienne and Avignon, and takes in the Isère and other tributaries. Near Arles it divides into the *Grand* and *Petit Rhône*, flowing respectively SE and SW into the Mediterranean west of Marseille.
  Here it forms a two-armed delta; the area between the tributaries is the ◊Camargue, a desolate marsh. The Rhône is harnessed for hydroelectric power, the chief dam being at Genissiat in Ain *département*, constructed 1938–48. Between Vienne and Avignon it flows through a major wine-producing area.
Rhône-Alpes region of E France in the upper reaches of the Rhône; area 43,700 sq km/16,868 sq mi; population (1986) 5,154,000. It consists of the *département*s of Ain, Ardèche, Drôme, Isère, Loire, Rhône, Savoie, and Haute-Savoie. The chief town is Lyon. There are several notable wine-producing areas including Chenas, Fleurie, and Beaujolais. Industrial products include chemicals, textiles, and motor vehicles.
Rhyl seaside holiday resort in Clwyd, N Wales; population (1980) 23,000.
RI abbreviation for ◊*Rhode Island.*
Ribble river in N England; length 120 km/75 mi. From its source in the Pennine hills, N Yorkshire, it flows S and SW past Preston, Lancashire, to join the Irish Sea.

Rhode Island

Richborough (Roman *Rutupiae*) former port in Kent, England; now marooned in salt marshes, it was militarily reactivated in both world wars.

Richmond capital of Virginia, USA; population (1980) 219,000. It is the centre of the Virginian tobacco trade. It was the capital of the Confederacy 1861–65, and a museum commemorates the writer Edgar Allan Poe, who grew up here.

Richmond town in N Yorkshire, England; population (1971) 7,245. It has a theatre built 1788.

Richmond-upon-Thames borough of SW Greater London

features Hampton Garrick Villa; Old Court House (the architect Wren's last home), Faraday House; Hampton Court Palace and Bushy Park; *Kew* outhoused departments of the Public Record Office; Kew Palace (former royal residence), within the Royal Botanic Gardens.

Richmond gatehouse of former Richmond Palace, Richmond Hill and Richmond Park (including White Lodge, home of the Royal Ballet School); Ham House (17th century);

Teddington highest tidal point of the Thames; National Physical Laboratory;

Twickenham Kneller Hall (Royal Military School of Music); Marble Hill House (Palladian home of the Duchess of Suffolk, mistress of George II); Strawberry Hill (home of Horace Walpole); Twickenham Rugby Ground; Alexander Pope is buried in the church;

population (1981) 157,867.

Rif, Er mountain range about 290 km/180 mi long on the Mediterranean seaboard of Morocco.

Rift Valley, Great volcanic valley formed 10–20 million years ago by a crack in the Earth's crust, and running about 6,400 km/4,000 mi from the Jordan valley in Syria through the Red Sea to Mozambique in SE Africa. At some points its traces have been lost by erosion, but elsewhere, such as S Kenya, cliffs rise thousands of metres. It is marked by a series of lakes, including Lake Turkana (formerly Lake Rudolph) and volcanoes, such as Mount Kilimanjaro.

Riga capital and port of Latvian Republic, USSR; population (1987) 900,000. A member of the Hanseatic League from 1282, Riga has belonged in turn to Poland 1582, Sweden 1621, and Russia 1710. It was the capital of independent Latvia 1918–40, and was occupied by Germany 1941–44, before being annexed by the USSR.

Rigi mountain in central Switzerland, between Lakes Lauerz, Lucerne, and Zug; height 1,800 m/5,908 ft.

Rijeka industrial port (oil refining, distilling, paper, tobacco, chemicals) in NW Yugoslavia; population (1983) 193,044.

history It has changed hands many times, and after being seized by Gabriele d'Annunzio 1919, was annexed by Italy 1924 (Italian *Fiume*). It was ceded back to Yugoslavia 1949.

Rimini industrial port (pasta, footwear, textiles, furniture) and holiday resort in Emilia-Romagna, Italy; population (1988) 131,000.

Its name in Roman times was *Ariminum*, and it was the terminus of the Flaminian Way from Rome. In World War II it formed the eastern strongpoint of the German 'Gothic' defence line, and was badly damaged in the severe fighting Sept 1944, when it was taken by the Allies.

Rineanna the Irish name of Shannon Airport, County Clare.

Río de Janeiro port and resort in Brazil; population (1980) 5,091,000, metropolitan area 10,217,000. The name commemorates the arrival of Portuguese explorers 1 Jan 1502, but there is in fact no river. Sugar Loaf Mountain stands at the entrance to the harbour. It was the capital of Brazil 1822–1960.

Some colonial churches and other buildings survive; there are modern boulevards, including the Avenida Rio Branco, and Copacabana is a luxurious beachside suburb.

Rio de Oro former district in the south of the province of Spanish Sahara. See ◊Western Sahara.

Rio Grande river rising in the Rockies in S Colorado, USA, and flowing south to the Gulf of Mexico, where it is reduced to a trickle by irrigation demands on its upper reaches; length 3,050 km/1,900 mi. Its last 2,400 km/1,500 mi form the US-Mexican border.

Rio Grande do Norte state of NE Brazil; capital Natal; area 53,000 sq km/20,460 sq mi; population (1980) 1,900,750.

Riom town on the river Ambène, in the Puy-de-Dôme *département* of central France. In World War II, it was the scene Feb–Apr 1942 of the 'war guilt' trials of several prominent Frenchmen by the ◊Vichy government. The accused included the former prime ministers Blum and Daladier, and Gen Gamelin. The occasion turned into a wrangle over the reasons for French unpreparedness for war, and at the German dictator Hitler's instigation, the court was dissolved. The defendants remained in prison until released by the Allies 1945.

Río Muni the mainland portion of ◊Equatorial Guinea.

Río Negro river in South America, rising in E Colombia and joining the Amazon at Manáus, Brazil; length 2,250 km/1,400 mi.

Río Tinto town in Andalusia, Spain; population (1983) 8,400. Its copper mines, first exploited by the Phoenicians, are now almost worked out.

Ripon city and market town in N Yorkshire, England; population (1981) 11,952. There is a cathedral 1154–1520; and the nearby 12th-century ruins of Fountains Abbey are among the finest monastic ruins in Europe.

Riva del Garda town on Lake Garda, Italy, where the Prix Italia broadcasting festival has been held since 1948.

Riverina district of New South Wales, Australia, between the Lachlan and Murray rivers, through which runs the Murrumbidgee. On fertile land, artificially irrigated from the three rivers, wool, wheat, and fruit are produced.

Riverside city in California, USA, on the Santa Ana river east of Los Angeles; population (1980) 170,500. Founded 1870. It is the centre of a citrus-growing district and has a citrus research station: the seedless orange was developed at Riverside in 1873.

Riviera the Mediterranean coast of France and Italy from Marseille to La Spezia. The most exclusive section, with the finest climate, is the ◊Côte d'Azur, Menton–St Tropez, which includes Monaco. It has the highest property prices in the world.

Riyadh (Arabic *Ar Riyad*) capital of Saudi Arabia and of the Central Province, formerly the sultanate of Nejd, in an oasis, connected by rail with Damman on the Arabian Gulf; population (1986) 1,500,000. Outside the city are date gardens irrigated from deep wells. There is a large royal palace, and Islamic university 1950.

Roanoke industrial city (railway repairs, chemicals, steel goods, furniture, textiles) in Virginia, USA, on the Roanoke River; population (1980) 100,500. Founded in 1834 as *Big Lick*, it was a small village until 1881 when the repair shops of the Virginia Railway were set up here, after which it developed rapidly.

Robben Island a notorious prison island in Table Bay, Cape Town, South Africa.

Rochdale industrial town (textiles, machinery, asbestos) in Greater Manchester, England, on the river Roch 16 km/10 mi NE of Manchester; population (1981) 92,704. The so-called Rochdale Pioneers founded the first Co-operative Society in England, in Toad Lane, Rochdale, 1844. The popular singer Gracie Fields was born here and a theatre is named after her.

Rochefort industrial port (metal goods, machinery) in W France, SE of La Rochelle and 15 km/9 mi from the mouth of the Charente; population (1982) 27,716. The port dates from 1666 and it was from here that Napoleon embarked for Plymouth on the *Bellerophon* on his way to final exile in 1815.

Rochelle, La see ◊La Rochelle, port in W France.

Rochester industrial city (flour, Kodak films and cameras) in New York State, USA, on the Genesee River south of Lake Ontario; population (1980) 970,000. Its university was founded 1850.

Rochester commercial centre with dairy and food-processing industries in Minnesota, USA; population (1980) 57,890. The Mayo Clinic is here.

Rochester upon Medway city in Kent, England; population (1983, with Chatham and Strood) 146,200. There is a 12th-century Norman castle keep, a 12th–15th-century cathedral, and many timbered buildings. A Dickens centre 1982 commemorates the town's many links with the novelist. The first borstal was near Rochester.

Rockall British islet in the Atlantic, 24 m/80 ft across and 22 m/65 ft high, part of the Hatton-Rockall bank, and 370 km/230 mi west of North Uist in the Hebrides. The bank is part of a fragment of Greenland that broke away 60 million years ago. It is in a potentially rich oil/gas area. A party of British marines landed in 1955 formally to annex Rockall, but Denmark, Iceland, and Ireland challenge Britain's claims for mineral, oil, and fishing rights. The *Rockall Trough* between Rockall and Ireland, 250 km/155 mi wide and up to 3,000 m/10,000 ft deep, forms an ideal marine laboratory.

Rockhampton port in E Queensland, Australia; population (1984) 56,500.

Rocky Mountains largest North American mountain system. They extend from the junction with the Mexican plateau, northward through the west central states of the USA, through Canada to the Alaskan border. The highest mountain is Mount McKinley (6,194 m/20,320 ft).

Many large rivers rise in the Rocky Mountains, including the Missouri. The Rocky Mountain National Park 1915 in Colorado has more than 100 peaks over 3,350 m/11,000 ft; Mount Logan on the Canadian-Alaskan border is 6,050 m/19,850 ft. In the 1980s computer techniques enabled natural gas in large quantities to be located in the W Rockies.

Rodhos Greek name for the island of ◊Rhodes.

Roeselare (French *Roulers*) textile town in West Flanders province, NW Belgium; population (1985) 52,000. It was a major German base in World War I.

Roma town in SE Queensland, linked by rail and gas pipeline to Brisbane; population (1985) 6,500.

Romagna area of Italy on the Adriatic coast, under papal rule 1278–1860, and now part of the region of ◊Emilia-Romagna.

Romania country in SE Europe, on the Black Sea, bounded to the N and E by the USSR, to the S by Bulgaria, to the SW by Yugoslavia, and to the NW by Hungary.

Rome (Italian *Roma*) capital of Italy and of Lazio region, on the Tiber, 27 km/17 mi from the Tyrrhenian Sea; population (1988) 2,817,000. Rome has few industries but is an important cultural, road, and rail centre. A large section of the population finds employment in government offices. Remains of the ancient city include the Forum, Colosseum, and Pantheon.

history After the deposition of the last emperor Romulus Augustus 476, the papacy became the real ruler of Rome, and from the 8th century was recognized as such. As a result of the French Revolution, Rome temporarily became a republic 1798–99, and was annexed to the French Empire

Romania
Socialist Republic of
(Republica Socialistă România)

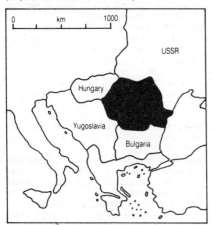

area 237,500 sq km/91,699 sq mi
capital Bucharest
towns Brasov, Timisoara, Cluj, Iasi; ports Galati, Constanta, Sulina
physical mountains surrounding a plateau, with river plains south and east
features Carpathian Mountains, Transylvanian Alps; river Danube; Black Sea coast; rich in mineral springs
head of state Ion Iliescu from 1989
head of government Petre Roman from 1989
government emergency
exports petroleum products and oilfield equipment, electrical goods, cars (largely to communist countries)
currency leu (35.36 = £1 Feb 1990)
population (1989) 23,155,000, including

2,000,000 Hungarians, 1,000,000 Gypsies, 250,000 Germans, and 30,000 Jews; annual growth rate 0.7%
life expectancy men 68, women 73
language Romanian, a Romance language descended from that of Roman settlers, though later modified by Slav influences
religion Romanian Orthodox (linked with Greek Orthodox)
literacy 97% male/94% female (1980 est)
GNP $45 bn (1984); $5,250 per head of population
chronology
1944 Pro-Nazi Antonescu government overthrown.
1945 Communist-dominated government appointed.
1947 Boundaries redrawn. King Michael abdicated and People's Republic proclaimed.
1949 New constitution adopted. Joined Comecon.
1952 New Soviet-style constitution.
1955 Romania joined Warsaw Pact.
1958 Soviet occupation forces removed.
1965 New constitution adopted.
1974 Ceauşescu created president.
1985–86 Winters of austerity and power cuts.
1987 Workers demonstrations against austerity programme.
1988–89 Relations with Hungary deteriorate over 'systematization programme', whereby villages were destroyed and their inhabitants urbanized.
1989 Bloody overthrow of Ceauşescu regime in 'Christmas Revolution' and power assumed by new military-dissident-reform–communist National Salvation Front, headed by Ion Iliescu. Ceauşescu tried and executed.

1808–14, until the pope returned on Napoleon's fall. During the 1848–49 revolution, a republic was established under Mazzini's leadership, but in spite of Garibaldi's defence was overthrown by French troops. In 1870 Rome became the capital of Italy, the pope retiring into the Vatican until 1929 when the Vatican City was recognized as a sovereign state. The occupation of Rome by the Fascists 1922 marked the beginning of Mussolini's rule, but in 1943 Rome was occupied by Germany, and then captured by the Allies 1944.

features East of the river are the seven hills on which it was originally built (Quirinal, Aventine, Caelian, Esquiline, Viminal, Palatine, and Capitol), to the west the popular quarter of Trastevere, the more modern residential quarters of the Prati, and the Vatican. Other features

are Castel Sant' Angelo (the mausoleum of the emperor Hadrian), and baths of Caracalla; Renaissance palaces include the Lateran, Quirinal (with the Trevi fountain nearby), Colonna, Borghese, Barberini, and Farnese. There are a number of churches of different periods; San Paolo was founded by the emperor Constantine on St Paul's grave. The house where the English poet Keats died is near the Piazza di Spagna, known for the Spanish Steps.

Romney Marsh a stretch of drained marshland on the Kent coast, SE England, between Hythe and Rye, used for sheep pasture. The seaward point is Dungeness. Romney Marsh was reclaimed in Roman times. *New Romney*, formed by the amalgamation of Romney, one of the Cinque Ports, with Littlestone and Greatstone, is now more than a mile from the sea; population (1981) 4,563.

Romsey market town in Hampshire, S England; population (1984) 13,150. The fine Norman church of Romsey Abbey (founded by Edward the Elder) survives, as does King John's Hunting Box of about 1206 (now a museum); nearby Broadlands was the seat of Earl Mountbatten and Lord Palmerston.

Roncesvalles village of N Spain, in the Pyrenees 8 km/5 mi S of the French border, the scene of the defeat of the rearguard of Charlemagne's army under Roland, who with the 12 peers of France was killed 778.

Rondônia a state in NW Brazil; known as the Federal Territory of Guaporé until 1956, it became a state in 1981; the centre of Amazonian tin and gold mining and of experiments in agricultural colonization; area 243,044 sq km/93,876 sq mi; population (1986) 776,000.

Roodepoort-Maraisburg goldmining town in Transvaal, South Africa, 15 km/9 mi W of Johannesburg, at an altitude of 1,745 m/5,725 ft; population (1980) 165,315. Leander Starr Jameson and his followers surrendered here in 1896 after an attempt to overthrow the government.

Roquefort-sur-Soulzon village in Aveyron *département*, France; population (1982) 880. It gives its name to a strong cheese made of sheep's and goats' milk and matured in caves.

Roraima, Mount plateau in the ◊Pacaraima range in South America, rising to 2,875 m/9,432 ft on the Brazil–Guyana–Venezuela frontier.

Rosario industrial river port (sugar refining, meat packing, maté processing) in Argentina, 280 km/175 mi NW of Buenos Aires, on the Paraná; population (1980) 955,000. It was founded 1725.

Roscoff a port on the Brittany coast of France with a ferry link to Plymouth in England; population (1982) 4,000.

Roscommon county of the Republic of Ireland in the province of Connacht
area 2,460 sq km/950 sq mi
towns county town Roscommon
physical bounded on the east by the river Shannon; lakes Gara, Key, Allen; rich pastures
features remains of a castle put up in the 13th century by English settlers. The name, originally Ros-Comain, means 'wood around a monastery'
population (1986) 55,000.

Roseau formerly *Charlotte Town* capital of ◊Dominica, West Indies; population (1981) 20,000.

Roseires a port at the head of navigation of the Blue Nile in Sudan. A hydroelectric scheme here provides the country with 70% of its electrical power.

Roskilde port at the S end of Roskilde Fjord, Zealand, Denmark; population (1981) 39,659; capital of the country from the 10th century until 1443.

Ross and Cromarty former county of Scotland. In 1975 Lewis, in the Outer ◊Hebrides, became part of the ◊Western Isles, and the mainland area was included in ◊Highland region. Dingwall was the administrative headquarters.

Ross Dependency all the Antarctic islands and territories between 160° E and 150° W longitude and south of 60° S latitude; it includes Edward VII Land, Ross Sea and its islands, and parts of Victoria Land
area 450,000 sq km/173,700 sq mi
features the *Ross Ice Shelf* or Barrier is a permanent layer of ice across the Ross Sea about 425 m/1,400 ft thick
population there are a few scientific bases with about 250 staff, 12 of whom are present during winter
history given to New Zealand 1923. It is probable that marine organisms beneath the ice shelf had been undisturbed from the Pleistocene period until drillings were made 1976.

Ross Island name of two islands in Antarctica:
Ross Island in Weddell Sea, discovered 1903 by the Swedish explorer Nordenskjöld, area about 3,885 sq km/1,500 sq mi;
Ross Island in Ross Sea, discovered 1841 by the British explorer James Ross, area about 6,475 sq km/2,500 sq mi, with the research stations Roos (New Zealand) and McMurdo (USA), and Mount Erebus 3,794 m/12,520 ft, the world's southernmost active volcano. Its lake of molten lava may provide a window on the magma beneath the earth's crust which fuels volcanoes.

Rosslare port in County Wexford, Republic of Ireland, 15 km/9 mi SE of Wexford; population (1980) 600; the Irish terminus of the steamer route from Fishguard from 1906. It was founded by the English 1210.

Ross Sea Antarctic inlet of the S Pacific. See also ◊Ross Dependency and ◊Ross Island.

Rostock industrial port (electronics, fish processing, ship repair) and capital of Rostock county, on the river Warnow, in East Germany, 13 km/8 mi south of the Baltic; population (1986) 246,000. Founded 1189, in the 14th century it became a powerful member of the Hanseatic League. Rostock county has an area of 7,080 sq km/2,733 sq mi, and a population of 903,000.

Rostov-on-Don industrial port (shipbuilding, tobacco, cars, locomotives, textiles) in SW USSR, capital of Rostov region, on the river Don, 23 km/14 mi E of the Sea of Azov; population (1987) 1,004,000. Rostov dates from 1761, and is linked by river and canal with Volgograd on the Volga.

Rosyth a naval base and dockyard used for nuclear submarine refits, in Fife, Scotland, built 1909 on the N shore of the Firth of Forth; population (1980) 6,500.

Rota naval base near ◊Cádiz, Spain.

Rothamsted an agricultural research centre in Hertfordshire, England, NW of St Albans.

Rothenburg town in Bavaria, West Germany, 65 km/40 mi west of Nuremberg; population (1978) 13,000. It is noted for its medieval buildings, churches, and walls.

Rotherham industrial town (pottery, glass, coal) in South Yorkshire, England, on the river Don, NE of Sheffield; population (1981) 81,988.

Rotorua town with medicinal hot springs and active volcanoes in North Island, New Zealand, near Lake Rotorua; population (1985) 52,000.

Rotterdam industrial port (brewing, distilling, ship-building, sugar and petroleum refining, margarine, tobacco) in the Netherlands and one of the foremost ocean cargo ports in the world, in the Rhine-Maas delta, linked by canal 1866–90 with the North Sea; population (1988) 1,036,000.

Rotterdam dates from the 12th century or earlier, but the centre was destroyed by German air attack 1940, and rebuilt; its notable art collections were saved. The philosopher Erasmus was born here. The university was founded 1973.

Roubaix town in Nord-Pay-de-Calais, N France, adjacent to Lille, population (1982) 102,000; important centre of French woollen textile production.

Rouen industrial port (cotton textiles, electronics, distilling, oil refining) on the Seine, capital of Haute-Normandie, NW France; population (1982) 380,000.

history Rouen was capital of ◊Normandy from 912. Lost by King John 1204, it returned briefly to English possession 1419–49; Joan of Arc was burned in the square 1431. The novelist Flaubert was born here, and the hospital where his father was chief surgeon is now a Flaubert museum.

Roulers French name of ◊Roeselare, town in Belgium.

Rovaniemi capital of Lappi province, N Finland, and chief town of Finnish Lapland, situated just S of the Arctic Circle; population (1986) 32,769. After World War II the town was rebuilt by the architect Alvar Aalto who laid out the main streets in the form of a reindeer's antlers.

Roxburgh former border county of Scotland, included in 1975 in Borders region. A mainly upland area, where sheep are raised, it includes the fringes of the Cheviot hills. Jedburgh was the county town.

RSFSR abbreviation for ◊*Russian Soviet Federal Socialist Republic*, the largest constituent republic of the USSR.

Ruahine mountain range in North Island, New Zealand.

Ruanda alternative spelling of ◊Rwanda, country in central Africa.

Ruapehu volcano in New Zealand, SW of Lake Taupo; the highest peak in North Island, 2,797 m/9,175 ft.

Rub' al Khali vast sandy desert in S Saudi Arabia; area 650,000 sq km/250,000 sq mi. The British explorer Bertram Thomas (1892–1950) was the first European to cross it 1930–31.

Rubicon a river in Emilia-Romagna region, Italy; rising NW of San Marino, it flows 40 km/25 mi NE to enter the Adriatic NW of Rimini. The Rubicon, when crossed by Julius Caesar, was the southern boundary of Cisalpine Gaul.

Ruda Śląska town in Silesia, Poland, with metallurgical industries, created 1959 by a merger of Ruda and Nowy Butom; population (1984) 163,000. Silesia's oldest mine is nearby.

Rudolf former name of Lake ◊Turkana in E Africa.

Rugby market town and railway junction in Warwickshire, England; population (1981) 59,500. Rugby School 1567 established its reputation under Thomas Arnold. Rugby football originated here.

Rügen island in the Baltic, part of Rostock county of East Germany; area 927 sq km/358 sq mi. It is a holiday centre, linked by causeway to the mainland; chief town Bergen, main port Sassnitz. As well as tourism there is agriculture and fishing. Rügen was annexed by Denmark 1168, Pomerania 1325, Sweden 1648, and Prussia 1815.

Ruhr river in West Germany; it rises in the Rothaargebirge and flows west to join the Rhine at Duisburg. The *Ruhr valley* (228 km/142 mi), a metropolitan industrial area (petrochemicals, cars; iron and steel at Duisburg and Dortmund) was formerly a coalmining centre.

The area was occupied by French and Belgian troops 1923–25 in an unsuccessful attempt to force Germany to pay reparations laid down in the Treaty of Versailles. During World War II the Ruhr district was severely bombed. Allied control of the area from 1945 came to an end with the setting-up of the European Coal and Steel Community 1952.

Rum or *Rhum* island of the Inner Hebrides, Highland region, Scotland, area 110 sq km/42 sq mi, a nature reserve from 1957. Haskeval is 741 m/2,432 ft high.

Rumania alternative spelling of ◊Romania.

Rum Jungle uranium-mining centre in the NW of Northern Territory, Australia.

Runcorn industrial town (chemicals) in Cheshire, England, 24 km/15 mi up the Mersey estuary from Liverpool; population (1983) 64,600. As a new town it has received Merseyside overspill from 1964.

Rupert's Land area of N Canada, of which Prince Rupert was the first governor. Granted to the Hudson's Bay Company 1670, it was later split among Québec, Ontario, Manitoba, and the Northwest Territories.

Ruse (Anglicized name *Rustchuk*) Danube port in Bulgaria, linked by rail and road bridge with Giurgiu in Romania; population (1987) 191,000.

Russia originally the name of the pre-revolutionary Russian Empire (until 1917), and now accurately

Russian Soviet Federal Socialist Republic

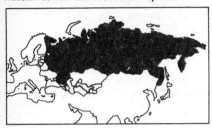

restricted to the ◊Russian Soviet Federal Socialist Republic only. It is incorrectly used to refer to the whole of the present ◊Union of Soviet Socialist Republics.

Russian Soviet Federal Socialist Republic (RSFSR; Russian *Rossiyskaya*) constituent republic of the USSR
area 17,075,000 sq km/6,592,658 sq mi
capital Moscow
towns Leningrad, Gorky, Rostov-on-Don, Volgograd
physical largest of the Soviet republics, it occupies about three-quarters of the USSR, and includes the fertile Black Earth district; extensive forests; the Ural Mountains with large mineral resources

features the heavily industrialized area around Moscow; Siberia; it includes 16 autonomous republics
products three-quarters of the agricultural and industrial output of the USSR
population (1987) 145,311,000; 83% Russian
language Great Russian
religion traditionally Russian Orthodox
recent history see ◊Union of Soviet Socialist Republics
Autonomous Soviet Socialist Republics (capitals in brackets)
Bashkir (Ufa); Buryat (Ulan-Udé); Checheno-Ingush (Grozny); Chuvash (Cheboksary); Dagestan (Makhachkala); Kabardino-Balkar (Nalchik); Kalmyk (Elista); Karelia (Petrozavodsk); Komi (Syktyvkar); Mari (Yoshkar-Ola); Mordovia (Saransk); North Ossetia (Ordzhonikidze); Tatar (Kazan); Tuva (Kizyl); Udmurt (Izhevsk); Yakut (Yakutsk).

Ruthenia or *Carpathian Ukraine* region of central Europe, on the south slopes of the Carpathian mountains, home of the Ruthenes or Russniaks. Dominated by Hungary from the 10th century, it was part of Austria-Hungary until World War I. Divided among Czechoslovakia, Poland, and Romania 1918, it was independent for a single day in 1938, immediately occupied by Hungary, captured by the USSR 1944,

Rwanda
Republic of
(Republika y'u Rwanda)

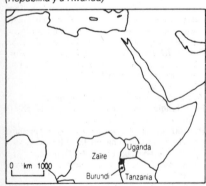

area 26,300 sq km/10,154 sq mi
capital Kigali
physical high savanna and hills, with volcanic mountains in NW
features part of lake Kivu; highest peak Mount Karisimbi 4,507 m/14,792 ft; Kagera river (whose headwaters are the source of the Nile) and National Park
head of state and government Juvenal

Habyarimana from 1973
government one-party military republic
political parties National Revolutionary Development (MRND), nationalistic, socialist
exports coffee, tea, pyrethrum, tin, tungsten
currency franc (129.48 = £1 Feb 1990)
population (1989) 7,276,000 (Hutu 90%, Tutsi 9%); annual growth rate 3.3%
life expectancy men 45, women 48
language Kinyarwanda (a Bantu language), French
religion Christian (mainly Catholic) 54%, animist 45%, Muslim 1%
literacy 61% male/33% female (1985 est)
GNP $1.7 bn (1984); $270 per head of population
chronology
1962 Rwanda achieved full independence as the Republic of Rwanda, with Gregoire Kayibanda as president.
1962–65 Tribal warfare between the Hutu and the Tutsi.
1972 Renewal of tribal fighting.
1973 Kayibanda ousted in a military coup led by Maj-Gen Juvenal Habyarimana.
1978 New constitution approved but Rwanda remained a military-controlled state.

and 1945–47 became incorporated into Ukraine Republic, USSR.

Rutland formerly the smallest English county, now part of ◊Leicestershire.

Ruwenzori a mountain range on the frontier between Zaire and Uganda, rising to 5,119 m/ 16,794 ft at Mount Stanley.

Rwanda landlocked country in central Africa, bounded to the N by Uganda, to the E by Tanzania, to the S by Burundi, and to the W by Zaïre.

Ryazan industrial city (agricultural machinery, leather, shoes) dating from the 13th century, capital of Ryazan region, USSR, on the river Oka near Moscow; population (1987) 508,000.

Rybinsk port and industrial city (engineering) on the Volga, NE of Moscow in the Russian Soviet Federal Socialist Republic; population (1987) 254,000. Between 1984 and 1988 it was named Andropov after a president of the USSR.

Ryde English resort on the NE coast of the Isle of Wight, on the Solent opposite Portsmouth, with which there is steamer and hovercraft connection.

Rye town in East Sussex, England, noted for its literary associations; population (1985) 4,490. It was formerly a flourishing port (and one of the Cinque Ports), but silt washed down by the river Rother has left it 3 km/2 mi inland. The novelist Henry James lived here; another writer, E F Benson (who was mayor of Rye 1934–37), later lived in James' house.

Ryukyu Islands southernmost island group of Japan, stretching towards Taiwan and including Okinawa, Miyako, and Ishigaki

area 2,254 sq km/870 sq mi

capital Naha on Okinawa

features 73 islands, some uninhabited; subject to typhoons

products sugar, pineapples, fish

population (1985) 1,179,000

history originally an independent kingdom; ruled by China from the late 14th century until seized by Japan 1609 and controlled by the Satsuma feudal lords until 1868, when the Japanese government took over. Chinese claims to the islands were relinquished 1895. In World War II the islands were taken by USA 1945 (see under ◊Okinawa); northernmost group, Oshima, restored to Japan 1953, the rest 1972.

SA abbreviation for ◊*South Africa*; ◊*South Australia*.

Saar (French *Sarre*) river in W Europe; it rises in the Vosges mountains, in France, and flows 240 km/149 mi N to join the Moselle river in West Germany. Its valley is noted for vineyards.

Saarbrücken city on the Saar, West Germany; population (1988) 184,000. It is situated on a large coalfield, and is an industrial centre (engineering, optical equipment). It has been the capital of Saarland since 1919.

Saarland (French *Sarre*) *Land* (state) of West Germany, crossed NW–S by the river Saar. Saarland is one-third forest.
area 2,570 sq km/992 sq mi
capital Saarbrücken
products former flourishing coal and steel industries survive only by government subsidy; cereals and other crops; cattle, pigs, poultry
population (1988) 1,034,000
history in 1919, the Saar district was administered by France under the auspices of the League of Nations; a plebiscite returned it to Germany 1935; Hitler gave it the name Saarbrücken; part of the French zone of occupation 1945; economic union with France 1947; returned to Germany 1957; it is the smallest and poorest of the West German *Länder*.

Sabah self-governing state of the federation of Malaysia, occupying NE Borneo, forming (with Sarawak) East Malaysia; area 73,613 sq km/28,415 sq mi; population (1984) 1,177,000, of which the Kadazans form the largest ethnic group at 30%; also included are 250,000 immigrants from Indonesia and the Philippines. Its capital is Kota Kinabalu (formerly Jesselton), and its exports include hardwoods (quarter of the world's supplies), rubber, fish, cocoa, palm oil, copper, copra, and hemp. It is chiefly mountainous (highest peak Mount Kinabalu 4,098 m/13,450 ft) and forested. The languages are Malay (official) and English, the religions Sunni Muslim and Christian (the Kadazans, among whom there is unrest about increasing Muslim dominance). Its government consists of a constitutional head of state with a chief minister, cabinet, and legislative assembly. In 1877–78 the Sultan of Sulu made concessions to the North Borneo Company, which was eventually consolidated with Labuan as a British colony 1946, and became the state of Sabah within Malaysia 1963. The Philippines have advanced territorial claims on Sabah 1962 and 1968 on the grounds that the original cession by the Sultan was illegal, Spain having then been sovereign in the area.

Sachsen German form of ◊Saxony, former kingdom and state of Germany.

Sacramento industrial port and capital (since 1854) of California, USA, 130 km/80 mi NE of San Francisco; population (1980) 276,000, metropolitan area 796,000. It stands on the Sacramento River, which flows 615 km/382 mi through Sacramento Valley to San Francisco Bay. Industries include the manufacture of detergents and jet aircraft, and food processing, especially almonds, peaches, and pears. It was founded as *Fort Sutter* 1848 on land bought by John Sutter 1839. Its old town has been restored.

Safi Atlantic port in Tensift province, NW Morocco; population (1981) 256,000. It exports phosphates and has fertilizer plants, sardine factories, and boat-building yards.

Sagamihara city on the island of Honshu, Japan, with a large silkworm industry; population (1987) 489,000.

Sagarmatha Nepalese name for Mount ◊Everest, 'the Goddess of the Universe', and the official name of the 1,240 sq km/476 sq mi Himalayan national park established 1976.

Saguenay river in Québec, Canada, used for hydroelectric power as it flows from Lac St Jean SE to the St Lawrence estuary; length 765 km/475 mi.

Sahara the largest desert in the world, occupying 5,500,000 sq km/2,123,000 sq mi of N Africa from the Atlantic to the Nile, covering W Egypt, part of W Sudan, large parts of Mauritania, Mali, Niger, and Chad, and southern parts of Morocco, Algeria, Tunisia, and Libya. Small areas in Algeria and Tunisia are below sea level, but it is mainly a plateau with a central mountain system, including the Ahaggar Mountains in Algeria, the Aïr Massif in Niger and the Tibesti Massif in Chad, of which the highest peak is Emi Koussi 3,415 m/11,208 ft. The area of the Sahara has expanded by 650,000 sq km/251,000 sq mi in the last half century, but reafforestation is being attempted in certain areas.

St Christopher (St Kitts)-Nevis

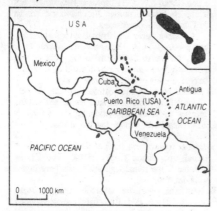

area 267 sq km/103 sq mi
capital Basseterre (on St Kitts)
towns Nevis (chief town of Nevis)
physical two islands in the Lesser Antilles
features St Kitts was the first of the British West Indian islands to be colonized
head of state Elizabeth II from 1983 represented by Clement Athelston Arrindell
head of government Kennedy Alphonse Simmonds from 1980
government federal constitutional monarchy

political parties People's Action Movement (PAM), centre-right; Nevis Reformation Party (NRP), Nevis-separatist; Labour Party, moderate, left-of-centre
exports sugar, molasses, cotton; tourism is important
currency East Caribbean dollar (4.59 = £1 Feb 1990)
population (1989) 40,000; annual growth rate 2.3%
language English
religion Christian
literacy 90% (1984)
GNP $40 million (1983)
chronology
1967 St Christopher, Nevis, and Anguilla were granted internal self-government, within the Commonwealth, with Robert Bradshaw, Labour Party leader, as prime minister.
1971 Anguilla left the federation.
1978 Bradshaw died and was succeeded by Paul Southwell.
1979 Southwell died and was succeeded by Lee L Moore.
1980 Coalition government led by Kennedy Simmonds.
1983 St Christopher-Nevis achieved full independence within the Commonwealth.
1984 Coalition government re-elected.
1989 Prime minister Simmonds won a third successive term.

Oases punctuate the caravan routes, now modern roads. Resources include oil and gas in the north. Satellite observations have established a pattern of dried-up rivers below the surface, which existed two million years ago. Cave paintings confirm that 4,000 years ago running rivers and animal life existed.

Sahel marginal area to the south of the Sahara, from Senegal to Somalia, where the desert has extended because of a population explosion, poor agricultural practice, destruction of scrub, and climatic change.

Saida ancient *Sidon* port in Lebanon; population (1980) 24,740. It stands at the end of the Trans-Arabian oil pipeline from Saudi Arabia. Sidon was the chief city of Phoenicia, a bitter rival of Tyre about 1400–701 BC, when it was conquered by Sennacherib. Later a Roman city, it was taken by the Arabs AD 637, and fought over during the Crusades.

Saigon former name (until 1976) of ◊Ho Chi Minh City, Vietnam.

St Albans city in Hertfordshire, England, on the river Ver, 40 km/25 mi NW of London; population (1981) 51,000. The cathedral was founded 793 in honour of St Alban; nearby are the ruins of the Roman city of *Verulamium* on Watling Street.

St Andrews town in Fife, Scotland, on the coast 19 km/12 mi SE of Dundee; population (1981) 11,400. The university (1411) is the oldest in Scotland, and the Royal and Ancient Club (1754) is the ruling body for most of the world's golf, with a golf museum.

St Augustine port and holiday resort in Florida, USA; population (1980) 12,000. Founded by the Spanish 1565, it was burned by the English sea captain Drake 1586, and ceded to the USA 1821. It includes the oldest house (late 16th century) and oldest masonry fort, Castillo de San Marcos (1672), in the USA.

St Austell market town in Cornwall, England, 22 km/14 mi NE of Truro; population (1981) 36,500 (with Fowey, with which it is administered). It is the centre of the China clay area which supplies the Staffordshire potteries.

St Bernard Passes the *Great* and *Little St Bernard Passes*, passes through the ◊Alps.

St Christopher (St Kitts)-Nevis country in the West Indies, in the Leeward Islands.

St-Cloud town in the Ile de France region, France; population about 29,000. The château, linked with Marie Antoinette and Napoleon, was demolished 1781, but the park remains. It is the site of the ◊Sèvres porcelain factory.

St David's (Welsh *Tyddewi*) small city in Dyfed, Wales. Its cathedral, founded by St David, was rebuilt 1180–1522.

St-Denis industrial town, a northern suburb of Paris, France; population (1983) 96,000. Abelard was a monk at the famous 12th-century Gothic abbey, which contains many tombs of French kings.

St Elias Mountains mountain range on Alaska-Canada border; Mount Logan 6,050 m/19,850 ft, Canada's highest mountain, is its highest peak.

St-Étienne city in S central France, capital of Loire *département*, Rhônes-Alpes region; population (1982) 317,000. Industries include the manufacture of aircraft engines, electronics, and chemicals, and it is the site of a school of mining, established 1816.

St Gallen (German *Sankt Gallen*) town in NE Switzerland; population (1987) 126,000. Industries include natural and synthetic textiles. It was founded in the 7th century by the Irish missionary St Gall, and the Benedictine abbey library has many medieval manuscripts.

St George's port and capital of Grenada; population (1981) 4,800, urban area 29,000.

St George's Channel stretch of water between SW Wales and SE Ireland, linking the Irish Sea with the Atlantic. It is 160 km/100 mi long and 80–150 km/50–90 mi wide. It is also the name of a channel between New Britain and New Ireland, Papua New Guinea.

St Gotthard Pass a pass through the Swiss ◊Alps, at an altitude of 2,000 m/6,500 ft.

St Helena

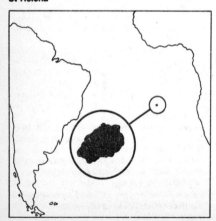

St Helena island in the S Atlantic, 1,900 km/1,200 mi W of Africa, area 122 sq km/47 sq mi; population (1985) 5,900. Its capital is Jamestown, and it exports fish and timber. Ascension and Tristan da Cunha are dependencies.

St Helena became a British possession 1673, and a colony 1834. Napoleon died in exile here 1821. Native to St Helena is the giant earwig *Labidura herculeana*, up to 8 cm/3 in long, the largest species of earwig in the world.

St Helens town in Merseyside, England, 19 km/12 mi NE of Liverpool, and connected to the Mersey by canal; population (1981) 99,000. It is an important centre for the manufacture of sheet glass.

St Helier resort and capital of Jersey, Channel Islands; population (1981) 25,700. The 'States of Jersey', the island legislature, sits here in the *salle des états*.

St Ives fishing port and resort in Cornwall; population (1981) 10,000. Its artists' colony, founded by W Sickert and James Whistler, later included Naum Gabo, Barbara Hepworth (a museum and sculpture gardens commemorate her), and Ben Nicholson.

St John largest city of New Brunswick, Canada, on the Saint John River; population (1986) 121,000. It is a fishing port, and has shipbuilding, timber, fish processing, and textiles industries. Founded by the French as *Saint-Jean* 1635, it was taken by the British 1758.

St John's capital and chief port of Newfoundland, Canada; population (1986) 96,000, urban area 162,000. It was founded by Humphrey Gilbert 1582. Marconi's first transatlantic radio message was received on Signal Hill 1901. The main industry is codfish-processing. Memorial University was founded 1925.

St John's port and capital of Antigua and Barbuda, on Antigua; population (1982) 30,000.

St John's Wood residential suburb of NW London. It is the site of Lord's cricket ground, headquarters of the Marylebone Cricket Club (MCC).

St Kilda three mountainous islands, the most westerly of the Outer Hebrides, 200 km/124 mi west of the Scottish mainland; area 16 sq km/6 sq mi. They were populated from prehistory until 1930, and are now a nature reserve.

St Kitts-Nevis contracted form of ◊St Christopher-Nevis.

St Lawrence River river in E North America. From ports on the ◊Great Lakes, it forms, with linking canals (which also give great hydroelectric capacity to the river), the *St Lawrence Seaway* for ocean-going ships, ending in the *Gulf of St Lawrence*. It is 1,050 km/650 mi long, and is ice-bound for four months annually.

St Leonards seaside town near ◊Hastings, England.

St Lucia

area 617 sq km/238 sq mi
capital Castries
physical mountainous; mainly tropical forest
features volcanic in origin; second largest of
the Windward group
head of state Elizabeth II from 1979
represented by Vincent Floissac from 1987
head of government John G M Compton
from 1982
government constitutional monarchy

political parties United Worker's Party (UWP),
moderate, left-of-centre; St Lucia Labour Party
(SLP), moderate, left-of-centre;
Progressive Labour Party (PLP), moderate,
left-of-centre
exports bananas, cocoa, copra; tourism is
important
currency East Caribbean dollar (4.59 = £1 Feb
1990)
population (1989) 128,000; annual growth
rate 1.2%
language English
religion Roman Catholic 90%
literacy 78% (1984)
GNP $133 million (1982); $698 per head of
population
chronology
1967 Granted internal self-government as a
West Indies associated state.
1979 Achieved full independence within the
Commonwealth, with John Compton, leader
of the United Workers' Party (UWP), as prime
minister. Allan Louisy, leader of the Saint Lucia
Labour Party (SLP), replaced Compton as
prime minister.
1981 Louisy resigned and was replaced by
Winston Cenac.
1982 Compton returned to power at the head of
a UWP government.
1987 Compton re-elected with reduced majority.

St-Lô market town in Normandy, France, on the
river Vire; population (1982) 24,800. In World
War II it was almost entirely destroyed 10–18
Jul 1944, when US forces captured it from the
Germans.

St Louis city in Missouri, USA, on the Mississippi
River; population (1980) 453,000, metropolitan
area 2,356,000. Its industries include aerospace
equipment, aircraft, vehicles, chemicals, electrical
goods, steel, and beer.

Founded as a French trading post 1764, it
passed to the USA 1803 under the Louisiana
Purchase. The Gateway Arch 1965 is a memorial
by Eliel Saarinen to the pioneers of the West.

Saint Lucia country in the West Indies, one of the
Windward Islands.

St-Malo seaport and resort in the Ille-et-Vilaine
département, W France, on the Rance estuary;
population (1985) 47,500. It took its name from
the Welshman Maclou who was bishop there
about 640.

St Michael's Mount island in Mount's Bay, Cornwall,
England, linked to the mainland by a causeway.

St-Nazaire industrial seaport in Pays de la Loire
region, France; population (1982) 130,000. It
stands at the mouth of the river Loire, and in

World War II was used as a German submarine
base. Industries include shipbuilding, engineering,
and food canning.

St-Omer town in Pas-de-Calais *département*, France,
42 km/26 mi SE of Calais; population (1985)
15,500. In World War I, it was the site of
British general headquarters 1914–16.

St Paul capital and industrial city of Minnesota,
USA, adjacent to ◊Minneapolis; population (1980)
270,000. Industries include electronics, publishing
and printing, petrochemicals, cosmetics, and
meat-packing.

St Peter Port only town of Guernsey, Channel
Islands; population 16,000.

St Petersburg former name of the city of ◊Leningrad,
USSR.

St Petersburg seaside resort and industrial city
(space technology), W Florida, USA; population
(1986) 243,000. It is across Tampa Bay from
◊Tampa.

St Pierre and Miquelon territorial collectivity of
France, eight small islands off the south coast of
Newfoundland, Canada
area St Pierre group 26 sq km/10 sq mi; Miquelon-
Langlade group 216 sq km/83 sq mi
capital St Pierre

St Vincent and the Grenadines

area 388 sq km/150 sq mi, including Northern Grenadines 43 sq km/17 sq mi
capital Kingstown
physical volcanic mountains, thickly forested
features Mustique, one of the Grenadines, is an exclusive holiday resort
head of state Elizabeth II from 1979

represented by Joseph Lambert Eustace from 1985
head of government James Mitchell from 1984
government constitutional monarchy
political parties New Democratic Party (NDP), moderate, left-of-centre; St Vincent Labour Party (SVLP), moderate, left-of-centre
exports bananas, tarros, sweet potatoes, arrowroot, copra
currency Eastern Caribbean dollar (4.59 = £1 Feb 1990)
population (1987) 113,000; annual growth rate –4%
language English
religion Christian (47% Anglican, 28% Methodist, 13% Roman Catholic)
literacy 85% (1981)
GNP $90 million (1983); $250 per head of population
chronology
1969 Granted internal self-government.
1979 Achieved full independence within the Commonwealth, with Milton Cato as prime minister.
1984 James Mitchell replaced Cato as prime minister.
1989 Mitchell decisively re-elected.

features the last surviving remnant of France's North American empire
products fish
currency French franc
population (1987) 6,300
language French
religion Roman Catholic
government French-appointed commissioner and elected local council; one representative in the National Assembly in France
history settled 17th century by Breton and Basque fishermen; French territory 1816–1976; overseas département until 1985; violent protests 1989 when France tried to impose its claim to a 200-mile fishing zone around the islands; Canada maintains that there is only a 12-mile zone.

St-Quentin town on the river Somme, Picardie, N France; population (1985) 69,000. It was the site of a Prussian defeat of the French 1871, and was almost obliterated in World War I. It is linked by canal to the industrial centres of Belgium and Germany. Its traditional textile production has been replaced by chemicals and metalworks.

St-Tropez fishing port on the French Côte d'Azur; population (1985) 6,250. It became popular as a resort in the 1960s.

St Vincent cape of the Algarve region of SW Portugal off which England defeated the French and Spanish fleets 1797.

St Vincent and the Grenadines country in the Windward Islands, West Indies.

St Vincent Gulf inlet of the Southern Ocean on which Adelaide, South Australia, stands. It is named after Admiral John Jervis, 1st Earl of St Vincent (1735–1823).

Sakai city on the island of Honshu, Japan; population (1987) 808,000. Industries include engineering, aluminium, and chemicals.

Sakhalin (Japanese Karafuto) island in the Pacific, north of Japan, which since 1947 forms with the ♭Kurils a region of the USSR; capital Yuzhno-Sakhalinsk (Japanese Toyohara); area 74,000 sq km/28,564 sq mi; population (1981) 650,000, including aboriginal Ainu and Gilyaks. There are two parallel mountain ranges, rising to over 1,525 m/5,000 ft, which extend throughout its length, 965 km/600 mi. The economy is based on dairy farming, leguminous crops, oats, barley, and sugar beet. In the milder south, there is also timber, rice, wheat, fish, and some oil and coal. The island was settled by both Russians and Japanese from the 17th century. In 1875 the south was ceded by Japan to Russia, but Japan regained it 1905, only to cede it again 1945. It has a missile base.

Sakkara or Saqqara a village in Egypt, 16 km/10 mi south of Cairo, with 20 pyramids, of which the oldest (third dynasty) is the 'Step Pyramid' designed by Imhotep, whose own tomb here was the nucleus of the Aesklepieion, a centre of healing in the ancient world.

Salado two rivers of Argentina, both rising in the Andes, and about 1,600 km/1,000 mi long. *Salado del Norte* or *Juramento* flows from the Andes to join the Paraná; the *Salado del Sud* or *Desaguadero* joins the Colorado and flows into the Atlantic south of Bahía Blanca.

Salamanca city in Castilla-León, W Spain, on the river Tormes, 260 km/162 mi NW of Madrid; population (1986) 167,000. It produces pharmaceuticals and wool. Its university was founded about 1230. It has a superbly designed square, the Plaza Mayor.

Salamis island off Piraeus, the port of Athens, Greece; area 101 sq km/39 sq mi; population (1981) 19,000. The town of Salamis, on the W coast, is a naval station.

Salang Highway the main N–S route between Kabul, capital of Afghanistan, and the Soviet frontier; length 422 km/264 mi. The high-altitude *Salang Pass* and *Salang Tunnel* cross a natural break in the Hindu Kush mountains about 100 km/60 mi N of Kabul. This supply route was a major target of the Mujaheddin resistance fighters during the Soviet occupation of Aghanistan.

Sale residential suburb of Manchester, England; population (1981) 57,824.

Sale town in Victoria, Australia, linked by canal via the Gippsland Lake to Bass Strait; population (1981) 13,000. It has benefited from the Strait deposits of oil and natural gas, and the brown coal to the south. The town was named after the British general Sir Robert Sale (1782–1845).

Salem industrial city (iron mining, and textiles) in Tamil Nadu, India; population (1981) 515,000.

Salem city and manufacturing centre in Massachusetts, USA, 24 km/15 mi NE of Boston; population (1980) 38,300. It was the site of witch trials 1692, which ended in the execution of 19 people.

Salem city in NW Oregon, USA, settled about 1840 and made state capital 1859; population (1980) 89,200. There are food-processing and high-tech industries.

Salerno port in Campania, SW Italy, 48 km/30 mi SE of Naples; population (1988) 154,000. It was founded by the Romans about 194 BC, destroyed by Charlemagne, and sacked by Holy Roman Emperor Henry VI 1194. The temple ruins of the ancient Greek city of ◊*Paestum*, with some of the earliest Greek paintings known, are nearby. The university (1150–1817, revived 1944) and Salerno's medical school have been famous since medieval times.

Salford industrial city in Greater Manchester, England, on the river Irwell; population (1981) 98,000. Industries include engineering, electrical goods, textiles, and chemicals.

Salisbury city in Wiltshire, England, 135 km/84 mi SW of London; population (1981) 35,355. The cathedral of St Mary, built 1220–66, is an example of Early English architecture; its decorated spire 123 m/404 ft is the highest in England. The cathedral library contains one of only four copies of the *Magna Carta*. Salisbury is an agricultural centre, and industries include brewing and carpet manufacture. Another name for it is *New Sarum*, Sarum being a medieval Latin corruption of the ancient Romano-British name *Sorbiodonum*. *Old Sarum*, on a 90 m/300 ft hill to the north, was deserted when New Sarum was founded 1220, but was later again inhabited; it was brought within the town boundary 1953.

Salisbury former name (until 1980) of ◊Harare, capital of Zimbabwe.

Salisbury Plain a 775 sq km/300 sq mi area of open downland between Salisbury and Devizes in Wiltshire, England. It rises to 235 m/770 ft in Westbury Down, and includes Stonehenge. For many years it has been a military training area.

Salonika English name for ◊Thessaloniki, a port in Greece.

Salop abbreviation and former official name (1972–80) for ◊Shropshire, county in England.

Salt Lake City capital of Utah, USA, on the river Jordan, 18 km/11 mi SE of the Great Salt Lake; population (1982) 164,000. Founded 1847, it is the headquarters of the Mormon Church. Mining, construction, and other industries are being replaced by high technology.

Salton Sea brine lake in SE California, USA, area 650 sq km/250 sq mi, accidentally created in the early 20th century during irrigation works from the Colorado River. It is used to generate electricity by solar ponds.

Salvador port and naval base in Bahia state, NE Brazil, on the inner side of a peninsula separating Todos Santos Bay from the Atlantic; population (1985) 2,126,000. Products include cocoa, tobacco, and sugar. Founded 1510, it was the capital of Brazil 1549–1763.

Salvador, El republic in Central America; see ◊El Salvador.

Salween river rising in E Tibet and flowing 2,800 km/1,740 mi through Myanmar to the Andaman Sea; it has many rapids.

Salzburg capital of the state of Salzburg, W Austria, on the river Salzach, in W Austria; population (1981) 139,400. The city is dominated by the Hohensalzburg fortress. It is the seat of an archbishopric founded by St Boniface about 700 and has a 17th-century cathedral. Industries include stock rearing, dairy farming, forestry, and tourism. Birthplace of Mozart; there are music festivals.

Salzburg federal province of Austria; area 7,200 sq km/2,779 sq mi; population (1987) 462,000. Its capital is Salzburg.

Salzgitter city in Lower Saxony, West Germany; population (1988) 105,000.

Samara name until 1935 of ◊Kuibyshev, a port in the USSR.

Samarkand city in Uzbek Republic, USSR, capital of Samarkand region, near the river Zerafshan, 217 km/135 mi E of Bukhara; population (1987) 388,000. It was the capital of the empire of the 14th-century Mongol ruler Tamerlane, and was once an important city on the Silk Road. Tamerlane is buried here, and the splendours of his city have been restored. It was occupied by the Russians in 1868 but remained a centre of Muslim culture until the Russian Revolution. Industries include cotton-ginning and silk manufacture, and engineering.

Samarra ancient town in Iraq, on the river Tigris, 105 km/65 mi NW of Baghdad; population (1970) 62,000. Founded 836 by the Abbasid Caliph Motassim, it was the Abbasid capital until 876, and is a place of pilgrimage for Shi'ite Muslims.

Samoa volcanic island chain in the SW Pacific. It is divided into Western ◊Samoa and American ◊Samoa.

Samoa, American group of islands 4,200 km/2,610 miles south of Hawaii, an unincorporated territory of the USA.
area 200 sq km/77 sq mi
capital Fagatogo on Tutuila
features five volcanic islands, including Tutuila, Tau, and Swain's Island, and two coral atolls. National park (1988) includes prehistoric village of Saua, virgin rainforest, flying foxes
exports canned tuna, handicrafts
currency US dollar
population (1981) 34,000
language Samoan and English
religion Christian
government as a non-self-governing territory of the USA, under Governor A P Lutali, it is administered by the US Department of the Interior
history the islands were acquired by the United States Dec 1899 by agreement with Britain and Germany under the Treaty of Berlin. A constitution was adopted 1960 and revised 1967.

Samoa, Western country in the SW Pacific, in Polynesia, NE of Fiji.

Samos Greek island in the Aegean Sea, about 1.5 km/1 mi off the W coast of Turkey; area 476 sq km/184 sq mi; capital Limén Vathéos; population (1981) 31,600. Mountainous but fertile, it produces wine and olive oil. The mathematician Pythagoras was born here. The modern town of Teganion is on the site of the ancient city of Samos, which was destroyed by Darius I of Persia.

Samsun Black Sea port and capital of a province of the same name in N Turkey; situated at the mouth of the Murat river in a tobacco-growing area; site of the ancient city of Amisus; population (1985) 280,000.

San'a capital of North Yemen, SW Arabia, 320 km/200 mi north of Aden; population (1986) 427,000.

A walled city, with fine mosques and traditional architecture, it is rapidly being modernized.

San Andreas fault a geological fault line stretching for 1,125 km/700 mi in a NW–SE direction through the state of California, USA.
Two sections of the Earth's crust meet at the San Andreas fault and friction is created as the coastal Pacific plate moves NW, rubbing against the American continental plate which is moving slowly SE. The relative movement is only about 5 cm/2 in per year, which means that Los Angeles will reach San Francisco's latitude in 10 million years' time. The friction caused by this tectonic movement gives rise to periodic earthquakes.

San Antonio city in S Texas, USA; population (1980) 1,070,000. A commercial and financial centre, industries include aircraft maintenance, oil refining, and meat packing. Founded 1718, it grew up round the site of the Alamo fort.

San Bernardino city in California, USA, 80 km/50 mi E of Los Angeles; population (1980) 119,000, metropolitan area 703,000. It was founded 1851 by Mormons.

San Cristóbal capital of Tachira state, W Venezuela, near the Colombian border; population (1981) 199,000. It was founded by the Spanish 1561, and stands on the ◊Pan-American Highway.

Sandhurst small town in Berkshire, England. The Royal Military Academy (for which the name Sandhurst is often used) is nearby.

San Diego city and military and naval base in California, USA; population (1980) 1,704,000. Industries include bio-medical technology, aircraft missiles, and fish canning. ◊Tijuana adjoins San Diego across the Mexican border.

Sandwich resort and market town in Kent, England; population (1981) 4,184. It has many medieval buildings, and was one of the Cinque Ports, but recession of the sea has left the harbour useless since the 16th century.

Sandwich Islands former name of ◊Hawaii, a group of islands in the Pacific.

San Francisco chief Pacific port of the USA, in California; population (1982) 691,637, metropolitan area of San Francisco and Oakland 3,192,000. The city stands on a peninsula, south of the Golden Gate 1937, the world's second longest single-span bridge, 1,280 m/4,200 ft. The strait gives access to San Francisco Bay. Industries include meat-packing, fruit canning, printing and publishing, and the manufacture of metal goods.
history In 1578 Sir Francis Drake's flagship, the *Golden Hind*, stopped near San Francisco on its voyage round the world. San Francisco was occupied in 1846 during the war with Mexico, and in 1906 was almost destroyed by an earthquake which killed 452 people. It was the site of the drawing-up of the United Nations Charter in 1945, and of the signing of the peace treaty between the Western Allies and Japan in 1951.

Samoa, Western
Independent State of
(Samoa i Sisifo)

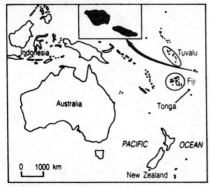

area 2,830 sq km/1,093 sq mi
capital Apia on Upolu
physical comprises islands of Savai'i and
Upolu, with two smaller islands and islets;
mountain ranges on the main islands
features huge lava flows on Savai'i have cut
down the area available for agriculture
head of state King Malietoa Tanumafili II
from 1962
head of government Tofilau Eti Alesana
from 1988
government liberal democracy
political parties Human Rights Protection Party
(HRPP), led by Tofilau Eti Alesana; the Va'ai

Kolone Group (VKG); Christian Democratic
Party (CDP), led by Tupuola Taisi Efi. All the
parties are personality-based groupings
exports copra, bananas, cocoa; tourism is
important
currency taia (3.88 = £1 Feb 1990)
population (1989) 169,000; annual growth
rate 1.1%
language English and Samoan (official)
religion Christian
literacy 90% (1983)
GDP $65 million (1978); $400 per head of
population
chronology
1959 Local government elected.
1961 Referendum favoured independence.
1962 Achieved full independence within the
Commonwealth, with Fiame Mata'afa Mulinu'u
as prime minister.
1975 Mata'afa died and was succeeded by
Tupuola Taisi Efi, the first non-royal prime
minister.
1982 Va'ai Kolone became prime minister,
but was replaced the same year by Tupuola
Efi. When the assembly failed to approve his
budget, Tupuola Efi resigned and was replaced
by Tofilau Eti Alesana.
1985 At the end of the year Tofilau Eti resigned
over his budget proposals and the head of
state refused to call a general election, inviting
Va'ai Kolombe to return to lead the government.
1988 Elections produced a hung parliament,
with first Tupuola Efi as prime minister and then
Tofilau Eti.

San José capital of Costa Rica; population (1984)
245,370. Products include coffee, cocoa, and
sugar cane. Founded in 1737, and capital since
1823.

San José city in Santa Clara Valley, California, USA;
population (1980) 1,244,000. Industries include
aerospace research and development, electronics,
flowers, fruit canning, and wine making. It was the
first capital of California 1849–51.

San Juan capital of Puerto Rico; population (1980)
434,850. It is a port and industrial city. Products
include sugar, rum, and cigars.

San Luis Potosí silver-mining city and capital of
San Luis Potosí state, central Mexico; population
(1986) 602,000. Founded 1586 as a Franciscan
mission, it was the colonial administrative headquarters and has fine buildings of the period.

San Marino landlocked country within N central
Italy.

San Pedro Sula main industrial and commercial city
in NW Honduras, the second largest city in the
country; population (1986) 400,000. It trades in

bananas, coffee, sugar, and timber, and manufactures textiles, plastics, furniture, and cement.

San Salvador capital of El Salvador 48 km/30 mi
from the Pacific, at the foot of San Salvador volcano 2,548 m/8,360 ft; population (1984) 453,000.
Industries include food processing and textiles.
Since its foundation 1525, it has suffered from
several earthquakes.

San Sebastián port and resort in the Basque
Country, Spain; population (1986) 180,000. It
was formerly the summer residence of the Spanish court.

Santa Ana commercial city in NW El Salvador,
the second largest city in the country; population
(1980) 205,000. It trades in coffee and sugar.

Santa Barbara town in S California, USA; population (1980) 74,414. It is the site of a campus
of the University of California. The Santa Ynez
mountains are to the north. Vandenburg air force
base is 80 km/50 mi to the northwest.

Santa Cruz de la Sierra capital of Santa Cruz
department in E Bolivia, the second largest city

San Marino
Most Serene Republic of
(Repubblica di San Marino)

area 60 sq km/23 sq mi
capital San Marino
physical on the slope of Mount Titano

features completely surrounded by Italian territory; one of the world's smallest states
head of state and government two captains-regent, elected for a six-month period
government direct democracy
political parties San Marino Christian Democrat Party (PDCS), right-of-centre; San Marino Communist Party (PCS), moderate Euro-communist; Socialist Unity Party (PSU) and Socialist Party (PSS), both left-of-centre
exports wine, ceramics, paint, chemicals
currency Italian lira (2,116 = £1 Feb 1990)
population (1989) 23,000; annual growth rate 3%
language Italian
religion Roman Catholic
literacy 97% (1985)
chronology
1862 Treaty with Italy signed, recognizing its independence and providing for its protection.
1947–86 Governed by a series of left-wing and centre-left coalitions.
1986 Formation of Communist and Christian Democrat 'grand coalition'.

in the country; population (1982) 377,000. Sugar cane and cattle were the chief base of local industry until newly discovered oil and natural gas led to phenomenal growth.

Santa Cruz de Tenerife capital of Tenerife and of the Canary Islands; population (1986) 211,000. It is a fuelling port and cable centre. Industry also includes oil refining, pharmaceuticals, and trade in fruit. Santa Cruz was bombarded by the British admirals Blake 1657 and Nelson 1797 – the action in which he lost his arm.

Santa Fé capital of New Mexico, USA, on the river Santa Fé, 65 km/40 mi west of Las Vegas; population (1980) 48,935, many Spanish-speaking. A number of buildings date from the Spanish period, including a palace 1609–10; the cathedral 1869 is on the site of a monastery built 1622. Santa Fé is noted for American Indian jewellery and textiles; its chief industry is tourism. It is the oldest state capital in the USA.

Santa Fé capital of Santa Fé province, Argentina, on the Salado river 153 km/95 mi north of Rosario; population (1980) 287,000. It has shipyards and exports timber, cattle, and wool. It was founded 1573, and the 1853 constitution was adopted here.

Santander port on the Bay of Biscay, Cantabria, Spain; population (1986) 189,000. Industries include chemicals, textiles, vehicles, and shipyards. It was sacked by the French marshal Soult 1808, and was largely rebuilt after a fire 1941. Palaeolithic cave wall paintings of bison, wild boar, and deer

were discovered at the nearby *Altamira* site 1879.

Santiago capital of Chile; population (1987) 4,858,000. Industries include textiles, chemicals, and food processing. It was founded 1541, and is famous for its broad avenues.

Santiago de Compostela city in Galicia, Spain; population (1986) 104,000. The 11th-century cathedral was reputedly built over the grave of Sant Iago el Mayor (St James the Great), patron saint of Spain, and was one of the most popular places for medieval pilgrimage.

Santiago de Cuba port on the S coast of Cuba; population (1986) 359,000. Industries include sugar, rum, and cigars.

Santiago de los Caballeros second largest city in the Dominican Republic; population (1982) 395,000. It is a trading and processing centre.

Santo Domingo capital and chief sea port of the Dominican Republic; population (1982) 1,600,000. Founded in 1496 by Bartolomeo, brother of Christopher Columbus, it is the oldest colonial city in the Americas. Its cathedral was built 1515–40.

Santos coffee-exporting port in SE Brazil, 72 km/45 mi SE of São Paulo; population (1980) 411,000. The footballer Pelé played here for many years.

Saône river in E France, rising in the Vosges mountains and flowing 480 km/300 mi to join the Rhône at Lyon.

São Paulo city in Brazil, 72 km/44 mi NW of its port Santos; population (1980) 7,034,000, metropolitan area 15,280,000. It is 900 m/3,000 ft above sea

São Tomé e Príncipe
Democratic Republic of

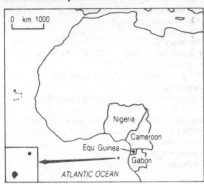

area 1,000 sq km/386 sq mi
capital São Tomé
physical comprises the two main islands and
several smaller ones, all of volcanic origin;
thickly forested and fertile
head of state and government Manuel Pinto
da Costa from 1975

government one-party socialist republic
political parties Movement for the Liberation of
São Tomé and Príncipe (MLSTP), nationalistic
socialist
exports cocoa, copra, coffee, palm oil and
kernels
currency dobra (180.01 = £1 Feb 1989)
population (1989) 114,000; annual growth
rate 2.5%
language Portuguese
religion Roman Catholic
literacy 73% male/42% female (1981)
GNP $31 million (1983); $261 per head of
population
chronology
1471 Discovered by Portuguese.
1522–1973 A province of Portugal.
1973 Granted internal self-government.
1975 Achieved full independence, with Manuel
Pinto da Costa as president.
1984 Formally declared itself a nonaligned
state.
1987 President now popularly elected.
1988 Unsuccessful coup attempt against Pinto
da Costa.

---

level, and 2°S of the tropic of Capricorn. It is South
America's leading industrial city, producing electronics, steel, and chemicals, has meat-packing
plants, and is the centre of Brazil's coffee trade.
It originated as a Jesuit mission in 1554.

São Tomé port and capital of São Tomé e Príncipe,
on São Tomé island, Gulf of Guinea; population
(1984) 35,000.

São Tomé e Príncipe country in the Gulf of Guinea,
off the coast of W Africa.

Sapporo capital of Hokkaido, Japan; population
(1987) 1,555,000. Industries include rubber and
food processing. It is a winter sports centre, and
was the site of the 1972 Winter Olympics. Giant
figures are sculpted in ice at the annual snow
festival. The university was founded in 1918.

Saragossa English spelling of ◊Zaragoza, city in
Aragon, Spain.

Sarajevo capital of Bosnia and Herzegovina,
Yugoslavia; population (1982) 449,000. Indus-
tries include engineering, brewing, chemicals,
carpets, and ceramics. A Bosnian, Gavrilo
Princip, assassinated Archduke Francis Ferdinand
here 1914, thereby precipitating World War
I. It was the site of the 1984 Winter
Olympics.

Saratoga Springs city and spa in New York State,
USA, population (1980) 23,906. In 1777 the British general John Burgoyne was defeated in two
engagements nearby during the War of American
Independence.

Saratov industrial port (chemicals, oil refining) on
the river Volga in central USSR; population (1987)
918,000. It was established in the 1590s as a fortress to protect the Volga trade route.

Sarawak state of Malaysia, on the NW corner
of the island of Borneo; capital Kuching; area
124,400 sq km/48,018 sq mi; population (1986)
1,550,000. It has a tropical climate, and produces
timber, oil, rice, pepper, rubber, and coconuts.
Sarawak was granted by the Sultan of Brunei
to James Brooke 1841, who became 'Rajah of

Sardinia

Saudi Arabia
Kingdom of
(al-Mamlaka al-'Arabiya as-Sa'udiya)

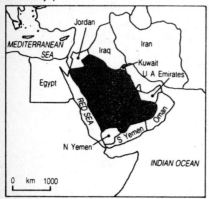

area 2,200,518 sq km/849,400 sq mi
capital Riyadh
towns Mecca, Medina; ports Jidda, Dammam
physical desert, sloping to the Persian Gulf from a height of 2,750 m/9,000 ft in the W
features Nafud desert in the N, and the Rub'al Khali (Empty Quarter) in the S, area 650,000 sq km/250,000 sq mi

head of state and government King Fahd Ibn Abdul Aziz from 1982
government absolute monarchy
political parties none
exports oil
currency rial (6.37 = £1 Feb 1990)
population (1989) 12,678,000 (16% nomadic); annual growth rate 4.2%
life expectancy men 59, women 63
language Arabic
religion Sunni Muslim, with a Shi'ite minority in the E
literacy 34% male/12% female (1980 est)
GDP $110.5 bn (1983); $11,500 per head of population
chronology
1926–32 Territories united and kingdom established.
1953 King ibn-Saud died and was succeeded by his eldest son, Saud.
1964 King Saud forced to abdicate and was succeeded by his brother Faisal.
1975 King Faisal assassinated by a nephew and succeeded by his half-brother Khalid.
1982 King Khalid died suddenly of a heart attack and was succeeded by his brother Crown Prince Fahd, who had effectively been ruling the country for some years because of King Khalid's ill health.

Sarawak'. It was a British protectorate from 1888 until captured by the Japanese in World War II. It was a Crown Colony 1946–63, when it became part of Malaysia.

Sardinia (Italian *Sardegna*) mountainous island, special autonomous region of Italy; area 24,100 sq km/9,303 sq mi; population (1988) 1,651,000. Its capital is Cagliari, and it exports cork and petrochemicals. It is the second largest Mediterranean island, and includes Costa Smeralda (Emerald Coast) tourist area in the northeast and *nuraghi* (fortified Bronze Age dwellings). After centuries of foreign rule, it became linked 1720 with Piedmont, and this dual kingdom became the basis of a united Italy 1861.

Sargasso Sea part of the N Atlantic (between 40° and 80° W and 25° and 30° N) left static by circling ocean currents, and covered with floating weed *Sargassum natans*.

Sark one of the ◊Channel Islands, 10 km/6 mi E of Guernsey; area 5 sq km/2 sq mi; there is no town or village. It is divided into Great and Little Sark, linked by an isthmus, and is of great natural beauty. The Seigneurie of Sark was established by Elizabeth I, the ruler being known as Seigneur/Dame, and has its own parliament, the Chief Pleas. There is no

income tax and cars are forbidden; immigration is controlled.

Sarum former settlement from which the modern city of ◊Salisbury, Wiltshire, England, developed.

Sasebo seaport and naval base on the W coast of Kyushu, Japan; population (1985) 251,000.

Sask. abbreviation for ◊Saskatchewan.

Saskatchewan province of W Canada
area 652,300 sq km/251,788 sq mi
capital Regina
towns Saskatoon, Moose Jaw, Prince Albert
physical prairies in the south; to the north forests, lakes and subarctic tundra
products more than 60% of Canada's wheat; oil, natural gas, uranium, zinc, potash (world's largest reserves), copper, the only western reserves of helium outside the USA
population (1986) 1,010,000.
history French trading posts established about 1750; owned by Hudson's Bay Company, first permanent settlement 1774; ceded to Canadian government 1870 as part of Northwest Territories; became a province 1905.

Saskatoon city in Saskatchewan, Canada; population (1986) 201,000. Industries include cement, oil refining, chemicals, and metal goods. The university was founded 1907.

Sassari capital of the province of the same name, in the NW corner of Sardinia, Italy; population (1987) 121,000. Every May the town is the scene of the Sardinian Cavalcade, the greatest festival on the island.

Saudi Arabia country on the Arabian peninsula, stretching from the Red Sea to the Arabian Gulf, bounded to the N by Jordan, Iraq, and Kuwait, to the E by Qatar and United Arab Emirates, to the SE by Oman, and to the S by North and South Yemen.

Sault Ste Marie twin industrial ports on the Canadian-US border, one in Ontario and one in Michigan; population (1981) 82,902 and (1980) 14,448 respectively. They stand at the falls (French *sault*) in St Mary's River, which links lakes Superior and Huron. The falls are bypassed by canals. Industries include steel, pulp, and agricultural trade.

Saumur town in Maine-et-Loire *département*, France, on the river Loire; population (1985) 34,000. The area is famous for its sparkling wines. The cavalry school, founded 1768, has since 1942 also been a training school for the French armed forces.

Savannah city and port of Georgia, USA, 29 km/ 18 mi from the mouth of the Savannah river; population (1980) 226,000. Founded 1733, Savannah was the first city in the USA to be laid out in geometrically regular blocks. It exports cotton, and produces cottonseed oil, fertilizers, and machinery. The *Savannah*, the first steam-powered ship to cross the Atlantic, was built here; most of the 25-day journey, in 1819, was made under sail. The first nuclear-powered merchant ship, launched by the USA 1959, was given the same name.

Sayan Mountains range in the SE USSR, on the Mongolian border; the highest peak is Munku Sardik 3,489 m/11,451 ft. The mountains have coal, gold, silver, graphite, and lead resources.

SC abbreviation for ◊*South Carolina*.

Scafell Pike highest mountain in England, 978 m/ 3,210 ft. It is in Cumbria in the Lake District and is separated from Scafell 964 m/3,164 ft by a ridge called Mickledore. The summit of Scafell Pike was presented to the National Trust by the third Lord Leconfield, as a war memorial, in 1919.

Scandinavia peninsula in NW Europe, comprising Norway and Sweden; politically and culturally it also includes Denmark and Finland.

Scapa Flow expanse of sea in the Orkney Islands, Scotland, until 1957 a base of the Royal Navy. It was the main base of the Grand Fleet during World War I, and in 1919 was the scene of the scuttling of 71 surrendered German warships.

Scarborough spa and holiday resort in N Yorkshire, England; population (1985) 50,000. A ruined Norman castle overlooks the town, which is a touring centre for the Yorkshire Moors.

Schaffhausen town in N Switzerland; population (1980) 34,250. Industries include the manufacture of watches, chemicals, and textiles. The Rhine falls here in a series of cascades 60 m/197 ft high.

Scheldt (Dutch *Schelde*, French *Escaut*) river rising in Aisne *département*, N France, and flowing 400 km/250 mi to join the North Sea south of Walcheren, in the Netherlands. Antwerp is the chief town on the Scheldt.

Schenectady industrial city on the river Mohawk, New York State, USA; population (1980) 67,972. It dates from 1662, and produces electrical goods.

Scheveningen seaside resort and northern suburb of The ◊Hague, Netherlands. There is a ferry link with Great Yarmouth, England.

Schiedam port in Zuid-Holland province, SW Netherlands, on the river Meuse, 5 km/3 mi west of Rotterdam; population (1987) 69,350. It is famous for its gin.

Schleswig-Holstein *Land* (state) of West Germany
area 15,700 sq km/6,060 sq mi
capital Kiel
towns Lübeck, Flensburg, Schleswig
features river Elbe, Kiel Canal, Heligoland
products shipbuilding, mechanical and electrical engineering, food processing
population (1988) 2,613,000
religion Protestant 87%; Catholic 6%
history Schleswig (Danish *Slesvig*) and Holstein were two duchies held by the kings of Denmark from 1460, but were not part of the kingdom; a number of the inhabitants were German, and Holstein was a member of the Confederation of the Rhine formed 1815. Possession of the duchies had long been disputed by Prussia, and when Frederick VII of Denmark died without an heir 1863, Prussia, supported by Austria, fought and defeated the Danes 1864, and in 1866 annexed the two duchies. A plebiscite held 1920 gave the northern part of Schleswig to Denmark, which made it the province of Haderslev and Aabenraa; the rest, with Holstein, remained part of Germany.

Schwarzwald German name for the ◊Black Forest, coniferous forest in West Germany.

Schwerin capital of Schwerin county, East Germany; population (1986) 128,000. Industries include the manufacture of machinery and chemicals. It was formerly the capital of Mecklenburg and earlier of Mecklenburg-Schwerin. Schwerin county has an area of 8,670 sq km/3,347 sq mi, and a population of 592,000.

Schwyz capital of Schwyz canton, Switzerland; population (1980) 12,100. Schwyz was one of the three original cantons of the Swiss Confederation 1291, which gave its name to the whole country about 1450.

Scilly Islands group of 140 islands and islets lying 40 km/25 mi SW of Land's End, England; administered by the Duchy of Cornwall; area 16 sq km/ 6.3 sq mi; population (1981) 1,850. The five inhabited islands are **St Mary's**, the largest, on which is Hugh Town, capital of the Scillies; **Tresco**, the second largest, with subtropical gardens; **St Martin's**, noted for beautiful shells; **St Agnes**, and **Bryher**.

Products incluse vegetables and flowers and tourism is important. The islands have remains of Bronze Age settlements. The numerous wreck sites off the islands include many of Sir Cloudesley Shovell's fleet in 1707. The Isles of Scilly are an important birdwatching centre with breeding sea birds in the summer and rare migrants in the spring and autumn.

Scone village in Tayside, Scotland, N of Perth. Most of the Scottish kings were crowned in its former ancient palace on the Stone of Destiny (now in the Coronation Chair at Westminster, London).

Scotland the northernmost part of Great Britain, formerly an independent country, now part of the United Kingdom

area 78,470 sq km/30,297 sq mi

capital Edinburgh

towns Glasgow, Dundee, Aberdeen

features the Highlands in the north (see ◊Grampian Mountains); central Lowlands, including valleys of the Clyde and Forth, with most of the country's population and industries; Southern Uplands (including the Lammermuir Hills); and islands of the Orkneys, Shetlands, and Western Isles

industry electronics, aero and marine engines, oil, natural gas, chemicals, textiles, clothing, printing, paper, food processing, tourism

currency pound sterling

population (1987) 5,113,000

language English; Gaelic spoken by 1.3%, mainly in the Highlands

Scotland: regions

Regions	Administrative headquarters	Area sq km
Borders	Newtown St Boswells	4,662
Central	Stirling	2,590
Dumfries and Galloway	Dumfries	6,475
Fife	Glenrothes	1,308
Grampian	Aberdeen	8,550
Highland	Inverness	26,136
Lothian	Edinburgh	1,756
Strathclyde	Glasgow	13,856
Tayside	Dundee	7,668
Island Authorities:		
Orkney	Kirkwall	974
Shetland	Berwick	1,427
Western Islands	Stornoway	2,901
		78,303

religion Presbyterian (Church of Scotland), Roman Catholic

famous people Robert Bruce, Walter Scott, Robert Burns, Robert Louis Stevenson, Adam Smith

government Scotland sends members to the UK Parliament at Westminster. Local government is on similar lines to that of England, but there is a differing legal system.

Scranton industrial city on the Lackawanna River, Pennsylvania, USA; population (1980) 88,117; Scranton-Wilkes-Barre metropolitan area (1980) 728,000. Anthracite is mined nearby.

Scunthorpe industrial town in Humberside, England, 39 km/24 mi W of Grimsby; population (1981) 66,047. It has one of Europe's largest iron and steel works, which has been greatly expanded with EEC help.

SD abbreviation for ◊*South Dakota.*

Seaham seaport in Durham, England, 8 km/5 mi south of Sunderland; population (1983) 23,000. Coal mines and engineering were developed from the 19th century. The poet Byron married Anne Isabella Milbanke at Seaham Hall nearby.

Seattle port (grain, timber, fruit, fish) of the state of Washington, USA, situated between Puget Sound and Lake Washington; population (1980) 493,846, metropolitan area (with Everett) 1,601,000. It is a centre for the manufacture of jet aircraft (Boeing), and also has shipbuilding, food processing, and paper industries. There are two universities, Washington (1861) and Seattle (1891). First settled 1851, as the nearest port for Alaska, Seattle grew in the late 19th century under the impetus of the gold rush. It is named after the Indian Sealth.

Sebastopol alternative spelling of ◊Sevastopol, port in the USSR.

Secunderabad northern suburb of Hyderabad city, Andhra Pradesh, India, separated from the rest of the city by the Hussain Sagar lake; population (1981) 144,287. Formerly a separate town, it was founded as a British army cantonment, with a parade ground where 7,000 troops could be exercised. It was by experiments at Secunderabad that Ronald Ross established that malaria is carried by the anopheles mosquito.

Sedan town on the river Meuse, in Ardennes *département*, NE France; population (1982) 24,535. Industries include textiles and dyestuffs; the town's prosperity dates from the 16th–17th centuries, when it was a Huguenot centre. In 1870 Sedan was the scene of Napoleon III's surrender to Germany during the Franco-Prussian War. It was the focal point of the German advance into France 1940.

Seeland German form of ◊Sjælland, the main island of Denmark.

Segovia town in Castilla-León, central Spain; population (1981) 50,760. Thread, fertilizer, and chemicals are produced. It has a Roman aqueduct with 118 arches in current use, and the Moorish alcázar (fortress) was the palace of the monarchs of Castile. Isabella of Castile was crowned here 1474.

Seikan Tunnel the world's largest underwater tunnel, opened 1988, linking the Japanese islands of Hokkaido and Honshu which are separated by the Tsungaru Strait; length 51.7 km/32.3 mi.

Seine French river rising on the Langres plateau NW of Dijon, and flowing 774 km/472 mi in a NW direction to join the English Channel near Le Havre, passing through Paris and Rouen.

Sekondi-Takoradi seaport of Ghana; population (1982) 123,700. The old port was founded by the Dutch. Takoradi has an artificial harbour, opened 1928. Railway engineering, boat building, and cigarette manufacture are important.

Selangor state of the Federation of Malaysia; area 7,956 sq km/3,071 sq mi; population (1980) 1,516,000. It was under British protection from 1874, and was a Federated State 1895–1946. The capital was transferred to Shah Alam from Kuala Lumpur 1973. Klang is the seat of the sultan and a centre for rubber-growing and tin-mining, and Port Klang (formerly Port Keland and, in 1971, Port Swettenham) exports tin.

Selbourne village in Hampshire, England, 8 km/5 mi SE of Alton. Gilbert White, author of *The Natural History of Selbourne* 1789, was born here. The Selbourne Society (founded 1885) promotes the study of wildlife.

Selby town on the river Ouse, North Yorkshire, England; population (1981) 10,726. The nearby Selby coalfield, discovered 1967, consists of 2,000 million tonnes of pure coal.

Selkirkshire former inland county of Scotland, included in the Borders region 1975.

Sellafield formerly *Windscale* site of a nuclear power station on the coast of Cumbria, NW England, near Whitehaven. There is also a plant for reprocessing spent nuclear fuel. In 1957, fire destroyed the core of a reactor, releasing large quantities of lethal radioactive fumes into the atmosphere.

Semarang port in N Java, Indonesia; population (1980) 1,027,000. There is a shipbuilding industry and exports include coffee, teak, sugar, tobacco, kapok, and petroleum from nearby oilfields.

Semipalatinsk town in Kazakh Republic, USSR, on the river Irtysh; population (1987) 330,000. It was founded 1718 as a Russian frontier post, and moved to its present site 1776. Industries include meat-packing, tanning, and flour-milling, and the region produces nickel and chromium. The Kvzyl Kum atomic-weapon-testing ground is nearby.

Sendai city in Tojoku region, NE Honshu, Japan; population (1987) 686,000. Industries include metal goods (a Metal Museum was established 1975), textiles, pottery, and food processing.

Senegal country in W Africa, on the Atlantic, bounded to the N by Mauritania, to the E by Mali, to the S by Guinea and Guinea-Bissau, and enclosing Gambia on three sides.

Senegal River river in W Africa, formed by the confluence of the Bafing and the Bakhoy and flowing 1,125 km/700 mi NW and W to join the Atlantic near St Louis, Senegal. In 1968 the Organization of Riparian States of the River Senegal (Guinea, Mali, Mauretania, and Senegal) was formed to develop the river valley, including a dam for hydroelectric power and irrigation at Joina Falls in Mali; its headquarters is in Dakar. The river gives its name to the Republic of Senegal.

Sennar town about 260 km/160 mi SE of Khartoum, on the Blue Nile, Sudan Republic; population (1972) 10,000. Nearby is the Sennar Dam 1926, part of the Gezira irrigation scheme.

Sens town in Yonne *département*, Burgundy, France; population (1982) 26,961. Its 12th–16th-century cathedral is one of the earliest in the Gothic style in France.

Seoul or *Sŏul* capital of South Korea, near the Han river, and with its chief port at Inchon; population (1985) 9,646,000. Industries include engineering, textiles, and food processing. It was the capital of Korea 1392–1910, and has a 14th-century palace and four universities. It was the site of the 1988 Summer Olympics.

Serang alternative form of ◊Ceram, an Indonesian island.

Serbia (Serbo-Croat *Srbija*) constituent republic of Yugoslavia, which includes Kosovo and Vojvodina
area 88,400 sq km/34,122 sq mi
capital Belgrade
features includes the autonomous provinces of ◊*Kosovo*, capital Priština, of which the predominantly Albanian population demands unification with Albania; and ◊*Vojvodina*, capital Novi Sad, largest town Subotica, with a predominantly Serbian population.
physical fertile Danube plains in the north, and mountainous in the south
population (1986) 9,660,000
language the Serbian variant of Serbo-Croat, sometimes written in Cyrillic script
religion Serbian Orthodox
history the Serbs settled in the Balkans 7th century, and became Christians 9th century. They were united as one kingdom about 1169, and under Stephen Dushan (1331–55) founded an empire covering most of the Balkans. After their defeat at Kosovo 1389 they came under the domination of the Turks, who annexed Serbia 1459. Uprisings 1804–16, led by Kara George and Milosh Obrenovich, forced the Turks to recognize Serbia as an autonomous prinicipality under Milosh. The assassination of Kara George on Obrenovich's orders gave rise to a long feud between the two houses. After a war with

Turkey 1876–78, Serbia became an independent kingdom. On the assassination of the last Obrenovich 1903 the Karageorgevich dynasty came to the throne. The two Balkan Wars 1912–13 greatly enlarged Serbia's territory at the expense of Turkey and Bulgaria. Serbia's designs on Bosnia and Herzegovina, backed by Russia, led to friction with Austria, culminating in the outbreak of war 1914. Serbia was completely overrun 1915–16, and was occupied until 1918, when it became the nucleus of the new kingdom of the Serbs, Croats, and Slovenes, later ◊Yugoslavia. There is still rivalry between Croats and Serbs. Slobodan Milosevic was elected president May 1989.

Seringapatam town in Karnataka, India, on an island in the Cauvery. It was the capital of Mysore State 1610–1799, when it was taken from the Sultan of Mysore, Tipu Sahib, by the British general Cornwallis.

Sète town on the Mediterranean coast of France, in Hérault *département*, SW of Montpellier; population (1982) 40,466. It is a seaport, and handles fish, wine, brandy, and chemicals. It was founded 1666 as an outlet to the Canal du Midi.

Seto Naikai a narrow body of water almost enclosed by the islands of Honshu, Shikoku, and Kyushu. It is both a transport artery and a national park (1934) with 3,000 islands.

Sevastopol or *Sebastopol* port, resort, and fortress in the Crimea, Ukraine Republic, USSR; population (1987) 350,000. It is the base of the Soviet Black Sea fleet, and also has shipyards and a wine-making industry. Founded by Catherine II 1784, it was successfully besieged by the English and French in the Crimean War (Oct 1854–Sept 1855), and in World War II by the Germans (Nov 1941–July 1942), but was retaken by the Soviets 1944.

Senegal
Republic of
(République du Sénégal)

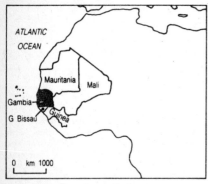

area 196,200 sq km/75,753 sq mi
capital and chief port Dakar
towns Thies, Kaolack
physical plains; swamp and tropical forest in SW
features river Senegal; The Gambia forms an enclave within Senegal
head of state and government Abdou Diouf from 1981
government emergent socialist deomocratic republic
political parties Senegalese Socialist Party (PS), democratic socialist; Senegalese Democratic Party (PDS), left-of-centre
exports groundnuts, cotton, fish, phosphates
currency CFA franc (485.00 = £1 Feb 1990)
population (1989) 7,704,000; annual growth rate 2.6%

life expectancy men 42, women 45
language French (official)
religion Muslim 80%, Christian 10% (chiefly Roman Catholic), animist 10%
literacy 37% male/19% female (1985 est)
GNP $2.7 bn (1983); $342 per head of population
chronology
1659 Became a French colony.
1854–65 Interior occupied.
1902 Became a territory of French West Africa.
1959 Formed the Federation of Mali with French Sudan.
1960 Achieved full independence, but withdrew from the federation. Léopold Sedar Senghor, leader of the Sengalese Progressive Union (UPS), became president.
1966 UPS declared the only legal party.
1974 Pluralist system re-established.
1976 UPS reconstituted as the Sengalese Socialist Party (PS). Prime Minister Abdou Diouf nominated as Senghor's successor.
1980 Senghor resigned and was succeeded by Diouf. Troops sent to defend The Gambia.
1981 Military help again sent to The Gambia.
1982 Confederation of Senegambia came into effect.
1983 Diouf re-elected. Post of prime minister abolished.
1988 Diouf decisively re-elected.
1989 Violent clashes between Senegalese and Mauritanians in Dakar and Nouakchott, killing more than 450 people. Over 50,000 people repatriated from both countries June. Senegambia federation abandoned.

Seychelles

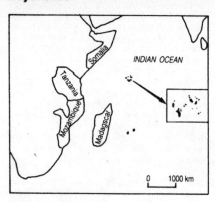

INDIAN OCEAN

0   1000 km

area 453 sq km/175 sq mi
capital Victoria on Mahé
physical comprises two distinct island groups, one concentrated, the other widely scattered, totalling over 100 islands and islets
features the unique 'double coconut'
head of state and government France-Albert René from 1977
government one-party socialist republic
political parties Seychelles People's Progressive Front (SPPF), nationalistic socialist
exports copra, cinnamon; tourism is important
currency Seychelles rupee (9.21 = £1 Feb 1990)
population (1989) 70,000; annual growth rate 0.6%
language creole, spoken by 95%, English and French (all official)
religion Christian (Roman Catholic 90%)
literacy 60% (1983)
GDP $143 million (1982); $1,030 per head of population
chronology
1970 Constitutional conference in London on future status of Seychelles. James Mancham, leader of the Seychelles Democratic Party (SDP), argued for full independence, while France-Albert René, leader of the Seychelles People's United Party (SPUP), favoured full integration with the UK.
1975 Internal self-government granted.
1976 Full independence achieved as a republic within the Commonwealth, with Mancham as president.
1977 René ousted Mancham in an armed coup and took over the presidency.
1979 New constitution adopted, making the SPUP, restyled the Seychelles People's Progressive Front (SPPF), the only legal party.
1981 Attempted coup by South African mercenaries thwarted.
1984 René re-elected.
1987 Coup attempt foiled.
1989 René re-elected.

Sevenoaks town in Kent, England. It lies 32 km/20 mi SE of London, population (1980) 19,000. Nearby are the 17th-century houses of Knole and Chevening. Its seven oaks were blown down in a hurricane 1987, and subsequent attempts to replant them have been foiled by vandals.

Severn river of Wales and England, rising on the NE side of Plynlimmon, N Wales, and flowing some 338 km/210 mi through Shrewsbury, Worcester, and Gloucester to the Bristol Channel. The *Severn bore* is a tidal wave up to 2 m/6 ft high.

S England and S Wales are linked near Chepstow by a rail tunnel 1873–85 and road bridge 1966. A barrage has been proposed (seaward of Cardiff and Weston-super-Mare) which would be the world's largest tidal power-generating project; it would be 16 km/10 mi across, and would produce 5% of the UK's electricity. It would also improve dock developments in Cardiff and Bristol.

Seveso town in Lombardy, Italy, site of a factory manufacturing the herbicide hexachlorophene. In 1976 one of the by-products escaped in a cloud which contaminated the area, resulting in severe chlorance and deformed births.

Seville (Spanish *Sevilla*) city in Andalucia, Spain, on the Guadalquivir river, 96 km/60 mi north of Cádiz, population (1986) 668,000. Industries include machinery, spirits, porcelain, pharmaceuticals, silk, and tobacco.

Formerly the centre of a Moorish kingdom, it has a 12th-century Alcázar palace, a 15th–16th-century Gothic cathedral, and a university 1502. Seville was the birthplace of the artists Murillo and Velázquez.

Sèvre two French rivers from which the *département* of Deux Sèvres takes its name. The *Sèvre Nantaise* joins the Loire at Nantes; the *Sèvre Niortaise* flows into the Bay of Biscay.

Sèvres town in the Île de France region of France; now a Paris suburb, population about 21,000. The state porcelain factory was established in the park of ◊St-Cloud 1756, and it is also the site of a national museum of ceramics.

Seychelles country in the Indian Ocean, off E Africa, N of Madagascar.

Sfax (Arabic *Safaqis*) port and second largest city in Tunisia; population (1984) 232,000. It is the capital of Sfax district, on the Gulf of Gabès, and lies about 240 km/150 mi SE of Tunis.

Industries include leather, soap, and carpets; there are also salt works and phosphate workings nearby. Exports include phosphates, olive oil, dates, almonds, esparto grass, and sponges.

SFSR abbreviation for *Soviet Federal Socialist Republic*.

's Gravenhage Dutch name for The ◊Hague.

Shaanxi formerly *Shensi* province of NW China
area 195,800 sq km/75,579 sq mi
capital Xian
physical mountains; Huang He valley, one of the earliest settled areas of China
products iron, steel, mining, textiles, fruit, tea, rice, wheat
population (1986) 30,430,000

Shaba formerly (until 1972) *Katanga* region of Zaïre; area 496,965 sq km/191,828 sq mi; population (1984) 3,874,000. Its main town is Lubumbashi, formerly Elisabethville.

Shache alternative name for ◊Yarkand, a city in China.

Shaftesbury market town and agricultural centre in Dorset, England, 30 km/19 mi SW of Salisbury; population (1985) 6,000. King Alfred is said to have founded an abbey on the site 880; Canute died at Shaftesbury 1035.

Shakhty town in the Donbas region of the Russian Soviet Federal Socialist Republic, 80 km/50 mi NE of Rostov; population (1987) 225,000. Industries include anthracite mining, stone quarrying, textiles, leather, and metal goods. It was known as Aleksandrovsk Grushevskii until 1921.

Shandong formerly *Shantung* province of NE China
area 153,300 sq km/59,174 sq mi
capital Jinan
towns ports Yantai, Weihai, Qingdao, Shigiusuo
features crossed by the Huang He river and the ◊Grand Canal; Shandong Peninsula
products cereals, cotton, wild silk, varied minerals
population (1986) 77,760,000.

Shanghai port on the Huang-pu and Wusong rivers, Jiangsu province, China, 24 km/15 mi from the Chang Jiang estuary; population (1986) 6,980,000, the largest city in China. The municipality of Shanghai has an area of 5,800 sq km/2,239 sq mi and a population of 12,320,000. Industries include textiles, paper, chemicals, steel, agricultural machinery, precision instruments, shipbuilding, flour and vegetable-oil milling, and oil refining. It handles about 50% of China's imports and exports.

Shanghai is reckoned to be the most heavily populated area in the world with an average of 6 sq m/65 sq ft of living space and 2.2 sq m/2.6 sq yd of road per person.
features Famous buildings include the Jade Buddha Temple 1882; the former home of the revolutionary Sun Yat-sen; the house where the First National Congress of the Communist Party of China met secretly in 1921; and

the house, museum, and tomb of the writer Lu Xun.
history Shanghai was a city from 1360, but became important only after 1842, when the treaty of Nanking opened it to foreign trade. The international settlement then developed, which remained the commercial centre of the city after the departure of European interests 1943–46.

Shannon longest river in Ireland, rising in County Cavan and flowing 386 km/240 mi through Loughs Allen and Ree and past Athlone, to reach the Atlantic through a wide estuary below Limerick. It is also the major source of electric power in the republic, with hydroelectric installations at and above Ardnacrusha, 5 km/3 mi N of Limerick.

Shansi former name for the Chinese province of ◊Shanxi.

Shantou formerly *Swatow* port and industrial city in SE China; population (1970) 400,000. It was opened as a special foreign trade area 1979.

Shantung former name for the Chinese province of ◊Shandong.

Shanxi formerly *Shansi* province of NE China
area 157,100 sq km/60,641 sq mi
capital Taiyuan
features a drought-ridden plateau, partly surrounded by the Great Wall; the province saw the outbreak of the Boxer Rising
products coal, iron, fruit
population (1986) 26,550,000.

Sharjah or *Shariqah* third largest of the seven member states of the ◊United Arab Emirates, situated on the Arabian Gulf NE of Dubai; area 2,600 sq km/1,004 sq mi; population (1985) 269,000. Since 1952 it has included the small state of Kalba. In 1974 oil was discovered offshore. Industries include ship repair, cement, paint, and metal products.

Sharon coastal plain in Israel between Haifa and Tel Aviv, and a sub-district of Central district; area 348 sq km/134 sq mi; population (1983) 190,400. It has been noted since ancient times for its fertility.

Sharpeville black township in South Africa, 65 km/40 mi S of Johannesburg and N of Vereeniging; 69 people were killed here when police fired on a crowd of demonstrators on 21 Mar 1960, during a campaign launched by the Pan-Africanist Congress against the pass laws (laws requiring nonwhite South Africans to carry identity papers).

On the anniversary in 1985, during funerals of protesters against unemployment who had been killed, 19 people were shot by the police at Langa near Port Elizabeth.

Shasta, Mount dormant volcano rising to a height of 4,317 m/14,162 ft in the Cascade Range, N California, USA.

Shatt-al-Arab (Persian *Arvand*) the waterway formed by the confluence of the rivers ◊Euphrates and ◊Tigris; length 190 km/120 mi to the Persian

Shetland Islands

Gulf. Basra, Khorramshahr, and Abadan stand on it. Its lower reaches form a border of disputed demarcation between Iran and Iraq. In 1975, the two countries agreed on the deepest water line as the frontier, but Iraq repudiated this 1980; the dispute was a factor in the Iran-Iraq war 1980–88.

Sheba ancient name for modern South ◊Yemen (Sha'abijah). It was once renowned for gold and spices. According to the Old Testament, its queen visited Solomon; the former Ethiopian royal house traced its descent from their union.

Sheerness seaport and resort on the Isle of Sheppey, Kent, England; population (1981) 11,250. Situated at the confluence of the Thames and Medway, it was originally a fortress 1660, and was briefly held by the Dutch admiral de Ruyter 1667. It was a royal dockyard until 1960.

Sheffield industrial city on the Don river, South Yorkshire, England; population (1986) 538,700. From the 12th century, iron smelting was the chief industry, and by the 14th century Sheffield cutlery, silverware, and plate were famous. During the Industrial Revolution the iron and steel industries developed rapidly. It now produces alloys and special steels, cutlery of all kinds, permanent magnets, drills, and precision tools. Other industries include electroplating, type-founding, and the manufacture of optical glass.

The parish church of St Peter and St Paul (14th–15th centuries) is the cathedral of Sheffield bishopric established 1914. Mary Queen of Scots was imprisoned at Sheffield 1570–84, part of the time in the Norman castle, which was captured by the Parliamentarians 1644 and subsequently

destroyed. There are two art galleries; Cutlers' Hall; Ruskin museum, opened 1877 and revived 1985; and a theatre, the Crucible 1971; there is also a university 1905 and a polytechnic 1969. The city is a touring centre for the Peak District. The headquarters of the National Union of Mineworkers are in Sheffield.

Shenandoah river in Virginia, USA, a tributary of the Potomac, which it joins at Harper's Ferry. The Union general Sheridan laid waste the Shenandoah valley in the American Civil War.

Shensi former name for the Chinese province of ◊Shanxi.

Shenyang industrial city and capital of Liaoning province, China; population (1986) 4,200,000. It was the capital of the Manchu emperors 1644–1912.

Their tombs are nearby. Historically known as Mukden, it was taken from Russian occupation by the Japanese in the Battle of Mukden 20 Feb–10 Mar 1905, and was again taken by the Japanese 1931.

Shenzen a Special Economic Zone established in 1980 opposite Hong Kong on the coast of Guangdong province, S China. Its status provided much of the driving force of its spectacular development in the 1980s when its population rose from 20,000 in 1980 to 600,000 in 1989. Part of the population is 'rotated' newcomers from other provinces who return to their homes after a few years learning foreign business techniques.

Sheppey island off the N coast of Kent, England; area 80 sq km/31 sq mi; population about 27,000. Situated at the mouth of the river Medway, it is linked with the mainland by Kingsferry road and rail bridge over the Swale, completed 1960. The resort and port of Sheerness is here.

's-Hertogenbosch (French *Bois-le-Duc*) capital of North Brabant, Netherlands, on the river Meuse, 45 km/28 mi SE of Utrecht; population (1988) 193,000. It has a Gothic cathedral, and was the birthplace of the painter Hieronymus Bosch.

Sherwood Forest a hilly stretch of parkland in W Nottinghamshire, England, area about 520 sq km/200 sq mi. Formerly a royal forest, it is associated with the legendary outlaw Robin Hood.

Shetland Islands islands off N coast of Scotland
area 1,400 sq km/541 sq mi
towns administrative headquarters Lerwick, on Mainland, largest of 19 inhabited islands
physical comprise over 100 islands; Muckle Flugga (latitude 60° 51   N) is the most northerly of the British Isles
products Europe's largest oil port is Sullom Voe, Mainland; processed fish, handknits from Fair Isle and Unst, miniature ponies
population (1987) 22,000
language the dialect is derived from Norse, the islands having been a Norse dependency from the 8th century until 1472.

Shropshire

Shihchiachuang former name for the city of ◊Shijiazhuang in China.

Shijiazhuang formerly *Shihchiachuang* city and major railway junction in Hebei province, China; population (1986) 1,160,000. Industries include textiles, chemicals, printing, and light engineering.

Shikoku smallest of the four main islands of Japan, S of Honshu, E of Kyushu; area 18,800 sq km/ 7,257 sq mi; population (1986) 4,226,000; chief town Matsuyama. Products include rice, wheat, soya, sugar cane, orchard fruits, salt, and copper.

It has a mild climate and annual rainfall in the south can reach 266 cm/105 in. The highest point is Mount Ishizuchi (1,980 m/6,498 ft). A suspension bridge links Shikoku to Awajishima Island over the Naruto whirlpool in the ◊Seto Naikai (Inland Sea).

Shillelagh village in County Wicklow, Republic of Ireland, which gives its name to a rough cudgel of oak or blackthorn. The district was once covered by the Shillelagh Wood, which supplied oak roofing for St Patrick's cathedral in Dublin.

Shillong capital of Meghalaya state, NE India; population (1981) 109,244. It was the former capital of Assam.

Shimonoseki seaport in the extreme SW of Honshu, Japan; population (1985) 269,000. It was opened to foreign trade 1890. The first of the Sino-Japanese Wars ended with a treaty signed at Shimonoseki 1895. Industries include fishing, shipbuilding, engineering, textiles, and chemicals.

Shiraz ancient walled city of S Iran, the capital of Fars province; population (1986) 848,000. It is

noted for wines, carpets, and silverwork, and for its many mosques.

Shiré Highlands an upland area of S Malawi, E of the Shiré River; height up to 1,750 m/5,800 ft. Tea and tobacco are grown there.

Shizuoka town in Chubo region, Honshu, Japan; population (1985) ,468,000. Industries include metal and food processing, and especially tea.

Shkodër (Italian *Scutari*) town on the Bojana, NW Albania, SE of Lake Shkodër, 19 km/12 mi from the Adriatic; population (1983) 71,000. Industries include woollens and cement. During World War I it was occupied by Austria 1916–18; and during World War II by Italy.

Sholapur town in Maharashtra state, India; population (1981) 514,860. Industries include textiles, leather goods, and chemicals.

Shreveport port on the Red River, Louisiana, USA; population (1980) 205,800. Industries include oil, natural gas, steel, telephone equipment, glass, and timber. It was founded 1836, and named after Henry Shreeve, a riverboat captain who cleared a giant log jam.

Shrewsbury market town on the river Severn, Shropshire, England; population (1985) 87,300. It is the administrative headquarters of the county. To the east is the site of the Roman city of Viroconium (larger than Pompeii). In the 5th century, as Pengwern, Shrewsbury was capital of the kingdom of Powys, which later became part of Mercia. In the battle of Shrewsbury 1403, Henry IV defeated the rebels led by Hotspur (Sir Henry Percy).

Shropshire county in W England
area 3,490 sq km/1,347 sq mi
towns administrative headquarters Shrewsbury; Telford, Oswestry, Ludlow
features on the Welsh border, it is bisected NW to SE by the Severn; the name is sometimes abbreviated to *Salop*, and was officially so known from 1974 until local protest reversed the decision 1980; Ellesmere is the largest of several lakes in the SW; and the Clee Hills rise to about 610 m/ 1,800 ft in the SW; Ironbridge Gorge open-air museum of industrial archaeology includes the Iron Bridge 1779
products chiefly agricultural: sheep and cattle
population (1987) 397,000.

Siachen Glacier Himalayan glacier at an altitude of 5,236 m/17,000 ft in the Karakoram mountains of N Kashmir. Occupied by Indian forces 1984, the glacier has been the focal point of a territorial dispute between India and Pakistan since independence 1947. Three wars in 1947, 1965, and 1971 resulted in the establishment of a temporary boundary between the two countries through the province of Jammu and Kashmir, but the accords failed to define a frontier in the farthest reaches of N Kashmir. Pakistan responded to the 1984

Indian action by sending troops to the heights of the nearby Baltoro Glacier.

Sialkot city in Punjab province, E Pakistan; population (1981) 302,000. Industries include the manufacture of surgical and sports goods, metalware, carpets, textiles, and leather goods.

Sian former name of ◊Xian, China.

Siberia Asiatic region of the USSR, extending from the Urals to the Pacific

area 12,050,000 sq km/4,650,000 sq mi

towns Novosibirsk, Omsk, Krasnoyarsk, Irkutsk

features long and extremely cold winters

products hydroelectric power from rivers Lena, Ob, and Yenisei; forestry; mineral resources, including gold, diamonds, oil, natural gas, iron, copper, nickel, cobalt

history overrun by Russia in the 17th century, it was used from the 18th to exile political and criminal prisoners. The first *Trans-Siberian Railway* 1892–1905 from Leningrad (via Omsk, Novosibirsk, Irkutsk and Khabarovsk) to Vladivostok, approximately 8,700 km/5,400 mi, began to open it up. A popular front was formed 1988, campaigning for ecological and political reforms.

Sichuan formerly *Szechwan* province of central China

area 569,000 sq km/219,634 sq mi

capital Chengdu

towns Chongqing

features surrounded by mountains, it was the headquarters of the Nationalist government 1937–45, and China's nuclear research centres are here; it is China's most populous administrative area

products rice, coal, oil, natural gas

population (1986) 103,200,000.

Sicily (Italian *Sicilia*) largest Mediterranean island, an autonomous region of Italy; area 25,700 sq km/ 9,920 sq mi; population (1988) 5,141,000. Its capital is Palermo, and towns include the ports of Catania, Messina, Syracuse, and Marsala. It exports Marsala wine, olives, citrus, refined oil and petrochemicals, pharmaceuticals, potash, asphalt, and marble. The autonomous region of Sicily also includes the islands of ◊Lipari, Egadi, Ustica, and ◊Pantelleria. Etna, 3,323 m/10,906 ft high, is the highest volcano in Europe; its last major eruption was in 1971. Conquered by most of the major powers of the ancient world, it flourished under the Greeks who colonized it during the 8th–5th centuries BC. It was invaded by Carthage, and became part of the Roman empire 241 BC–476 AD. In the Middle Ages it was ruled successively by the Arabs; by the Normans 1059–1194, who established the *Kingdom of the Two Sicilies* (that is, Sicily and the southern part of Italy); by the German emperors; and then by the Angevins, until the popular revolt known as the *Sicilian Vespers* 1282. Spanish rule was invited and continued in varying forms, with a temporary displacement of

the Spanish Bourbons by Napoleon, until Garibaldi's invasion 1860 resulted in the two Sicilies being united with Italy 1861.

Sidi Barrâni coastal settlement in Egypt, about 370 km/230 mi W of Alexandria, the scene of much fighting 1940–42 during World War II.

Sidi-Bel-Abbès trading city in Algeria; population (1983) 187,000. Because of its strategic position, it was the headquarters of the French Foreign Legion until 1962.

Sidon alternative name for ◊Saida, Lebanon.

Siegen city in North Rhine-Westphalia, West Germany; population (1988) 107,000.

Siena city in Tuscany, Italy; population (1985) 60,670. Founded by the Etruscans, it has medieval architecture by Pisano and Donatello, including a 13th-century Gothic cathedral, and many examples of the Sienese school of painting which flourished in the 13th–16th centuries. The *Palio* ('banner', in reference to the prize) is a horse race in the main square, held annually since the Middle Ages.

Sierra Leone country in W Africa, on the Atlantic, bounded to the N and E by Guinea and to the SE by Liberia.

Sierra Madre chief mountain system of Mexico, consisting of three ranges, enclosing the central plateau of the country; highest point Pico de Orizaba 5,700 m/18,700 ft. The Sierra Madre del Sur ('of the south') runs along the SW Pacific coast.

Sierra Nevada mountain range of S Spain; highest point Mulhacén 3,481 m/11,425 ft.

Sierra Nevada mountain range in E California, USA; highest point Mount Whitney 4,418 m/ 14,500 ft. It includes the King's Canyon, Sequoia, and Yosemite Valley national parks.

Si-Kiang former name of ◊Xi Jiang, Chinese river.

Sikkim or *Denjong* state of NE India; formerly a protected state, it was absorbed by India 1975, the monarchy being abolished. China does not recognize India's sovereignty.

area 7,300 sq km/2,818 mi

capital Gangtok

features Mount Kangchenjunga; wildlife including birds, butterflies, and orchids

products rice, grain, tea, fruit, soyabeans, carpets, cigarettes, lead, zinc, copper

population (1981) 316,000

language Bhutia, Lepecha, Khaskura (Nepáli) (all official)

religion Mahayana Buddhism, Hinduism.

Silicon Valley nickname given to Santa Clara County, California, USA, since the 1950s; it is the site of many high-technology electronics firms, whose properity is based on the silicon chip.

Simferopol city in the Crimea, Ukraine, USSR; population (1987) 338,000. Industries include the manufacture of soap and tobacco. It is on the site

Sierra Leone
Republic of

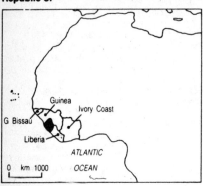

area 73,300 sq km/28,301 sq mi
capital Freetown
towns Bo, Kenema, Makeni
physical mountains in east; hills and forest;
coastal mangrove swamps
features hot and humid climate
(3,500 mm/138 in rainfall annually)
head of state and government Joseph Saidu
Momoh from 1985
government one-party republic
political parties All People's Congress (APC),
moderate socialist
exports palm kernels, cocoa, coffee, ginger,
diamonds, bauxite, rutile
currency leone (200.89 = £1 Feb 1990)
population (1989) 4,318,000; annual growth
rate 1.8%
life expectancy men 33, women 36
language English (official); local languages
religion Muslim 60%, animist 30%
literacy 38% male/21% female (1985 est)
GNP $1.2 bn (1983); $176 per head of
population
chronology
1961 Achieved full independence as a constitutional monarchy within the Commonwealth,
with Milton Margai, leader of the Sierra Leone
People's Party (SLPP), as prime minister.
1964 Milton succeeded by his half-brother
Albert Margai.
1967 General election results disputed by
the army, who set up a National Reformation
Council and forced the governor general to
leave.
1968 Another army revolt made Siaka Stevens,
leader of the All-People's Congress (APC),
prime minister.
1971 New constitution adopted, making Sierra
Leone a republic, with Stevens as president.
1978 APC declared the only legal party.
Stevens sworn in for another seven-year term.
1985 Stevens retired at the age of 80 and was
succeeded by Maj-Gen Joseph Momoh.
1989 Attempted coup against Momoh foiled.

of the Tatar town of Ak-Mechet, conquered by
the Russians 1783 and renamed.

Simla capital of Himachal Pradesh state, India,
2,300 m/7,500 ft above sea level, population
(1980) 70,604. It was the summer administrative
capital of British India 1864–1947.

Simplon (Italian *Sempione*) Alpine pass Switzerland–Italy. The road was built by Napoleon
1800–05, and the Simplon Tunnel 1906, 19.8 km/
12.3 mi, is one of Europe's longest.

Simpson Desert desert area in Australia, chiefly
in Northern Territory; area 145,000 sq km/
56,000 sq mi. It was named after a president
of the South Australian Geographical Society who
financed its exploration.

Sinai Egyptian peninsula, at the head of the Red
Sea; area 65,000 sq km/25,000 sq mi. Resources
include oil, natural gas, manganese, and coal; irrigation water from the Nile is carried under the
Suez Canal.
   Sinai was occupied by Israel 1967–82. After
the Battle of Sinai 1973, Israel began a gradual withdrawal from the area, under the dis-
engagement agreement 1975, and the Camp
David peace treaty 1979, and restored the
whole of Sinai to Egyptian control by Apr
1982.

Sinai, Mount (Arab *Gebel Mûsa*) mountain near
the tip of the Sinai Peninsula, height 2,285 m/
7,500 ft. In the Old Testament, this is allegedly where Moses received the Ten Com-
mandments from Jehovah. Egypt established a
religious complex (Jewish-Muslim-Christian) at
Mount Sinai 1979.

Sind province of SE Pakistan, mainly in the Indus
delta
area 140,914 sq km/54,393 sq mi
capital and chief seaport Karachi
population (1981) 19,029,000
language 60% Sindi; others include Urdu, Punjabi,
Baluchi, Puhsto
features Sukkur Barrage, which enables water
form the Indus river to be used for irrigation
history annexed 1843, it became a province of
British India, and part of Pakistan on independence. There is agitation for its creation as a
separate state, Sindhudesh.

Singapore country in SE Asia, off the tip of the
Malay Peninsula.

Sikkim

INDIAN OCEAN

Singapore City capital of Singapore, on the SE coast of the island of Singapore; population (1980) 2,413,945. It is an important oil-refining centre and port.

Sing Sing name until 1901 of the village of *Ossining*, New York, with a state prison of that name from 1825 (rebuilt 1930).

Sining former name of the city of ◊Xining, Tsinghai province, W central China.

Sinuiju capital of North Pyongan province, near the mouth of the Yalu river, North Korea; population (1984) 754,000. It was founded 1910.

Sioux Falls largest city in South Dakota, USA; population (1980) 81,343. Its industry (electrical goods and agricultural machinery) is powered by the Big Sioux River over the Sioux Falls 30 m/100 ft.

Sirte, Gulf of gulf off the coast of Libya, on which Benghazi stands. Access to the gulf waters has been a cause of dispute between Libya and the USA.

Six Counties the six counties that form Northern Ireland, namely Antrim, Armagh, Down, Fermanagh, Londonderry, and Tyrone.

Sjælland or *Zealand* the main island of Denmark, on which Copenhagen is situated; area 7,000 sq km/2,700 sq mi; population (1970) 2,130,000. It is low-lying with an irregular coastline. The chief industry is dairy farming.

Skagerrak arm of the North Sea between the S coast of Norway and the N coast of Denmark. In May 1916 it was the scene of the Battle of Jutland.

Skåne or *Scania* area of S Sweden. It is a densely populated and fertile agricultural region, comprising the counties of Malmöhus and Kristianstad. Malmö and Hälsingborg are important centres. It was under Danish rule until ceded to Sweden 1658.

Skegness holiday resort on the coast of Lincolnshire, England; population (1985) 14,553. It was the site of the first Butlin holiday camp.

Skelmersdale town in Lancashire, England, west of Wigan; population (1985) 41,800. It was developed as a 'new town' from 1962, with many light industries, including electronics, engineering, and textiles.

Skiddaw mountain (930 m/3,052 ft) in Cumbria, England, in the Lake District, north of Keswick.

Skikda trading port in Algeria; population (1983) 141,000. Products include wine, citrus, and vegetables. It was founded by the French 1838 as *Philippeville*, and renamed after independence 1962.

Skipton industrial (engineering) town in North Yorkshire, England; population (1981) 13,246.

Skopje capital and industrial city of Macedonia, Yugoslavia; population (1981) 506,547. Industries include iron, steel, chromium mining, and food processing.

It stands on the site of an ancient town destroyed by earthquake in the 5th century, and was taken in the 13th century by the Serbian king Milutin, who made it his capital. Again destroyed by earthquake 1963, Skopje was rebuilt on a safer nearby site. It is an Islamic centre.

Skye largest island of the Inner Hebrides, Scotland; area 1,740 sq km/672 sq mi; population (1981) 8,000. It is separated from the mainland by the Sound of Sleat. The chief port is Portree. The economy is based on crofting, tourism, and livestock. Bonnie Prince Charlie (Charles Edward Stuart) took refuge here after the Battle of Culloden.

Skyros or *Skiros* Greek island, one of the ◊Sporades; area 209 sq km/81 sq mi. It is noted for its furniture and weaving. Rupert Brooke is buried here.

Sligo county in the province of Connacht, Republic of Ireland, situated on the Atlantic coast of NW Ireland; area 1,800 sq km/695 sq mi; population (1986) 56,000. The county town is Sligo; there is livestock and dairy farming.

Slough industrial town (pharmaceuticals, electronics, engineering) in Berkshire, England, near Windsor; population (1981) 97,000. Also chocolate manufacture – the Mars bar. The home of astronomer William Herschel is a museum.

Slovenia or *Slovenija* constituent republic of NW Yugoslavia
area 20,300 sq km/7,836 sq mi
capital Ljubljana
physical mountainous; rivers Sava and Drava
features the wealthiest republic: contains 7% of the population of Yugoslavia, but produces 15% of Yugoslavia's GNP
products grain, sugarbeet, livestock, timber, cotton and woollen textiles, steel, vehicles

Singapore
Republic of

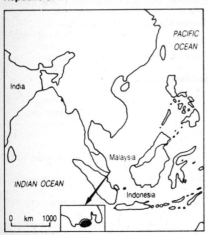

PACIFIC OCEAN

India

Malaysia

INDIAN OCEAN

Indonesia

0   km   1000

area 620 sq km/239 sq mi
capital Singapore City in the south of the island, a major world port and financial centre, founded by Stamford Raffles
physical comprises Singapore Island, which is low and flat, and 57 small islands
features Singapore Island is joined to the mainland by a causeway across the Strait of Johore; temperature ranges only 24°–31°C/75°–88°F
head of state Wee Kim Wee from 1985
head of government Lee Kuan Yew from 1959
government liberal democratic republic

political parties People's Action Party (PAP) conservative; Worker's Party (WP), socialist; Singapore Democratic Party (SDP), liberal pluralist
exports electronics, petroleum products, rubber, machinery, vehicles
currency Singapore dollar (3.16 = £1 Feb 1990)
population (1989) 2,668,000 (Chinese 75%, Malay 14%, Tamil 7%); annual growth rate 1.2%
life expectancy men 69, women 75
language Malay, Chinese, Tamil, and English (all official)
religion Buddhist, Taoist, Muslim, Hindu, Christian
literacy 93% male/79% female (1985 est)
GNP $17.9 bn (1984); $6,526 per head of population
chronology
1819 Singapore leased to British East India Company.
1858 Placed under Crown rule.
1942 Invaded and occupied by Japan.
1945 Japanese removed by British forces.
1959 Independence granted from Britain; Lee Kuan Yew became prime minister.
1963 Joined new Federation of Malaysia.
1965 Left federation to become independent republic.
1984 Opposition made advances in parliamentary elections.
1986 Opposition leader convicted of perjury, debarred from standing for election.
1988 The ruling conservative party elected to all but one of the available assembly seats.

---

population (1986) 1,930,000, including 1,710,000 Slovenes
language Slovene, resembling Serbo-Croat, written in Roman characters
religion Roman Catholic
history settled by the Slovenes 6th century; until 1918 it was the Austrian province of *Carniola*; an autonomous republic of Yugoslavia 1946. In Sept 1989 it voted to give itself the right to secede from Yugoslavia and to prevent the Yugoslavian government from interfering with Slovenian affairs.

Smithfield site of a meat market from 1868 and poultry and provision market from 1889 in the City of London, England. Formerly an open space, it was the scene of the murder of Wat Tyler, leader of the Peasants Revolt, 1381, and the execution of many Protestant martyrs in the 16th century. The annual Bartholomew Fair was held here 1614–1855.

Smolensk city on the river Dnieper, W USSR; population (1987) 338,000. Industries include textiles, distilling, and flour milling. It was founded 882 as the chief town of a Slavic tribe, and captured by Napoleon 1812. The Germans took the city 1941, and it was liberated by the Soviets 1943. Nearby is ◊*Katyn Forest*.

Smyrna former name (until 1922) of the Turkish port of ◊Izmir.

Snaefell highest mountain in the Isle of ◊Man, 620 m/2,035 ft.

Snake tributary of the Columbia River, in NW USA; length 1,670 km/1,038 mi. It flows 65 km/40 mi through Hell's Canyon, one of the deepest gorges in the world.

Snowdon highest mountain in Wales, 1,085 m/3,560 ft above sea level. It consists of a cluster of five peaks. At the foot of Snowdon are the Llanberis, Aberglaslyn, and Rhyd-ddu passes. A rack railway ascends to the summit from

Solomon Islands

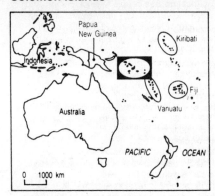

Papua
New Guinea
Kiribati
Indonesia
Fiji
Australia
Vanuatu
PACIFIC   OCEAN
0   1000 km

area 27,600 sq km/10,656
sq mi
capital Honiara on Guadalcanal
physical comprises all but the northernmost
islands (which belong to Papua New Guinea) of
a Melanesian archipelago that stretches nearly
1,500 km/900 mi. The largest is Guadalcanal
(area 6,500 sq km/2,510 sq mi); others are
Malaita, San Cristobal, New Georgia, Santa
Isabel, Choiseul; mainly mountainous and
forested
features rivers ideal for hydroelectric power
head of state Elizabeth II, represented by
George Lepping from 1988
head of government Solomon Mamaloni
from 1989

government constitutional monarchy
political parties People's Alliance Party (PAP),
centre-left; Solomon Islands United Party
(SIUPA), right-of-centre
exports palm oil, copra, rice, timber
currency Solomon Island dollar (4.11 = £1 Feb
1990)
population (1989) 314,000 (the majority
Melanesian); annual growth rate 3.9%
language English (official)
religion Christian
literacy 13% (1980)
GDP $160 million (1983); $628 per head of
population
chronology
1978 Achieved full independence within the
Commonwealth, with Peter Kenilorea as prime
minister.
1981 Solomon Mamaloni replaced Kenilorea as
prime minister.
1984 Kenilorea returned to power, heading a
coalition government.
1986 Kenilorea resigned after allegations of
corruption, and was replaced by his deputy,
Ezekiel Alebua.
1988 Kenilorea back as deputy prime minister.
The Solomon Islands joined Vanuatu and
Papua New Guinea to form the Spearhead
Group, aiming to preserve Melanesian cultural
traditions and secure independence for the
French territory of New Caledonia.
1989 Solomon Mamaloni (People's Action
Party) returned as prime minister and formed
PAP-dominated coalition.

Llanberis. Snowdonia, the surrounding mountain
system, was made a national park 1951.
Snowy Mountains range in the Australian Alps,
chiefly in New South Wales, near which Snowy
River rises; both river and mountains are known
for a hydroelectric and irrigation system.
Sochi seaside resort in the USSR, on the Black Sea;
population (1987) 317,000. In 1976 it became the
world's first 'no smoking' city.
Society Islands (French *Archipel de la Société*)
an archipelago in ◊French Polynesia, divided
into Windward Islands and Leeward Islands;
area 1,685 sq km/650 sq mi; population (1983)
142,000. The administrative headquarters is
Papeete on ◊Tahiti. The *Windward Islands*
(French *Îles du Vent*) have an area of
1,200 sq km/460 sq mi, and a population (1983)
123,000. They comprise Tahiti, Moorea (area
132 sq km/51 sq mi; population 7,000), Maio
(or Tubuai Manu; 9 sq km/3.5 sq mi; population
200), and the smaller Tetiaroa and Mehetia. The
Leeward Islands (French *Îles sous le Vent*)

have an area of 404 sq km/156 sq mi, and a
population of 19,000. They comprise the volcanic islands of Raiatea (including the main town
of Uturoa), Huahine, Bora-Bora, Maupiti, Tahaa,
and four small atolls. Claimed by France 1768, the
group became a French protectorate 1843, and a
colony 1880.
Socotra Yemeni island in the Indian Ocean; capital
Tamridah; area 3,500 sq km/1,351 sq mi. Under
British protection from 1886, it became part of
South Yemen 1967, and is used as a military base
by the USSR.
Sofia or *Sofiya* capital of Bulgaria since 1878; population (1987) 1,129,000. Industries include textiles, rubber, machinery, and electrical equipment.
It lies at the foot of the Vitosha Mountains.
Sogne Fjord longest and deepest fjord in Norway,
185 km/115 mi long and 1,245 m/4,080 ft deep.
Soho district of London, England, which houses the
offices of publishing, film, and recording companies; restaurants; nightclubs; and a decreasing
number of sexshops.

Somalia
Democratic Republic of
(Jamhuriyadda Dimugradiga Somaliya)

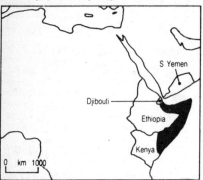

area 637,700 sq km/246,220 sq mi
capital Mogadishu
towns Hargeisa, Kismayu; port Berbera
physical mainly flat, with hills in the north
features many of the people are nomadic raisers of livestock
head of state and government Mohamed Siad Barre from 1969
government one-party socialist republic
political parties Somali Revolutionary Socialist Party (SRSP), nationalistic socialist

exports livestock, skins, hides, bananas
currency Somali shilling (698.02 = £1 Feb 1990)
population (1989) 8,552,000 (including 1 million refugees from W Somalia); annual growth rate 4.1%
life expectancy men 39, women 43
language Somali (national language), Arabic (also official), Italian, English
religion Sunni Muslim
literacy 18% male/6% female (1985 est)
GNP $1.2 bn (1983); less than $500 per head of population
chronology
1960 Achieved full independence.
1963 Border dispute with Kenya, diplomatic relations with the UK broken.
1968 Diplomatic relations with the UK restored.
1969 Following the assassination of the president, the army seized power. Maj-Gen Mohamed Siad Barre suspended the constitution and set up a Supreme Revolutionary Council.
1978 Defeated in eight-month war with Ethiopia.
1979 New constitution for a socialist one-party state adopted.
1987 Barre re-elected.
1989 Dissatisfaction with government and increased guerrilla activity in the N.

Soissons market town in Picardie region, N France; population (1982) 32,000. The chief industry is metallurgy. In 486 Clovis defeated the Gallo-Romans here, ending their rule in France.

Sokoto trading centre and capital of Sokoto state, NW Nigeria; population (1983) 148,000.

Sokoto state in Nigeria, established 1976; capital Sokoto; area 102,500 sq km/39,565 sq mi; population (1984) 7,609,000. It was a Fula sultanate from the 16th century until occupied by the British 1903.

Solent, the channel between the coast of Hampshire, England, and the Isle of ◊Wight. It is now a yachting centre.

Solingen city in North Rhine-Westphalia, West Germany; population (1988) 158,000. It was once famous for swords, and today produces high-quality steel for razor blades and cutlery.

Solomon Islands country in the W Pacific, E of New Guinea, comprising many hundreds of islands, the largest of which is Guadalcanal.

Solway Firth inlet of the Irish Sea, formed by the estuaries of the Eden and the Esk, at the western end of the border between England and Scotland.

Somalia country in the Horn of Africa, on the Indian Ocean.

Somaliland region of Somali-speaking peoples in E Africa including the former British Somaliland Protectorate (established 1887) and Italian Somaliland (made a colony 1927, conquered by Britain 1941 and administered by Britain until 1950), which both became independent 1960 as the Somali Democratic Republic, the official name for ◊Somalia; and former French Somaliland, which was established 1892, became known as the Territory of the Afars and Issas 1967, and became independent as ◊Djibouti 1977.

Somerset county in SW England
area 3,451 sq km/1,365 sq mi
towns administrative headquarters Taunton; Wells, Bridgewater, Glastonbury, Yeovil
features rivers Avon, Parret, and Exe; marshy coastline on the Bristol Channel; Mendip Hills (including Cheddar Gorge and Wookey Hole, a series of limestone caves where Old Stone Age flint implements and bones of extinct animals have been found); Quantock Hills; Exmoor
products dairy products, cider
poulation (1986) 450,800
famous people Henry Fielding

Somme river in N France, on which Amiens and Abbeville stand; length 240 km/150 mi. It rises in

Aisne *département* and flows west through Somme *département* to the English Channel.

Soochow former name for the Chinese city of ◊Suzhou.

Sorrento town on the Gulf of Naples, SW Italy; population (1981) 17,301. It has been a resort since Roman times.

Sosnowiec chief city of the Darowa coal region in the Upper Silesian province of Katowice, S Poland; population (1985) 255,000.

Sound, the strait dividing SW Sweden from Denmark and linking the ◊Kattegat and the Baltic; length 113 km/70 mi; width 5 km/3 mi–60 km/37 mi.

South, the historically, in the USA, the states south of the ◊Mason-Dixon line, with an agrarian economy based on plantations worked by slaves, which seceded from the Union at the beginning of the US Civil War, becoming the Confederacy. The term is now loosely applied in a geographic and cultural sense, with Texas often regarded as part of the Southwest rather than the South.

South Africa country on the S tip of Africa, bounded to the N by Namibia, Botswana, and Zimbabwe, and to the NE by Swaziland and Mozambique.

South America fourth largest of the continents, nearly twice as large as Europe
area 17,854,000 sq km/6,893,429 sq mi
largest cities (over 3.5 million inhabitants) Buenos Aires, SaPaulo, Rio de Janeiro, Bogotá, Santiago, Lima, Caracas
features Andes in the west, Brazilian and Guiana highlands; central plains from the Orinoco basin to Patagonia; Parana-Paraguay-Uruguay system

Somerset

flowing to form the La Plata estuary; Amazon river basin, with its remaining great forests, with their rich fauna and flora
exports coffee, cocoa, sugar, bananas, oranges, wine, meat and fish products, cotton, wool, handicrafts, minerals incuding oil, silver, iron ore, copper
population (1985) 263,300,000, originally American Indians, who survive chiefly in Bolivia, Peru, and Ecuador, and are increasing in number; in addition there are many mestizo (people of mixed Spanish or Portuguese and Indian ancestry) elsewhere; many people originally from Europe, largely Spanish, Italian, and Portuguese; and many of African descent, originally imported as slaves
language many American Indian languages, Spanish; Portuguese is the chief language in Brazil
religion Roman Catholic; American Indian beliefs
history since the American Indian cultures:
16th century arrival of Europeans, with the Spanish (Pizarro) and Portuguese conquest; the American Indians were mainly killed, assimilated, or, where considered unsuitable for slave labour, replaced by imported slaves from Africa.
18th century revolt of Túpac Amarú.
19th century Napoleon's toppling of the Spanish throne opened the way for the liberation of its colonies (led by Bolívar and San Martín). Brazil became peacefully independent. Large-scale European immigration took place (Hispanic, Italian, and German). Interstate wars took a heavy toll, for example, the Paraguay War (see under ◊Paraguay) and Pacific War.
20th century rapid industrialization and high population growth. In the 1980s heavy indebtedness incurred to fund economic expansion led to an inability to meet interest payments in the world slump.
1946–55 Perón president in Argentina.
1970–73 elected socialist regime under Salvador Allende in Chile, overthrown by military backed by the US Central Intelligence Agency.
1982 Falklands War between the UK and Argentina.

Southampton port in Hampshire, England; population (1981) 204,604. Industries include engineering, chemicals, plastics, flour-milling, and tobacco; it is also a passenger and container port.
The *Mayflower* set sail from here en route to North America 1620, as did the *Titanic* on its fateful maiden voyage 1912. There is a university, established 1952.

South Arabia, Federation of former grouping (1959–67) of Arab emirates and sheikdoms, joined by ◊Aden 1963. The western part of the area was claimed by ◊Yemen, and sporadic fighting and terrorism from 1964 led to British

South Africa
Republic of (Afrikaans
Republiek van Suid-Afrika)

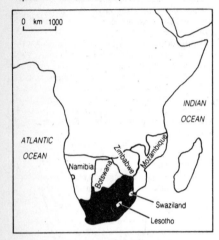

area 1,223,181 sq km/433,678 sq mi
capital Cape Town (legislative), Pretoria
(administrative)
towns Johannesburg, Bloemfontein; ports
Cape Town, Durban, Port Elizabeth, East
London
physical a plateau
territories Prince Edward Island in the
Antarctic
features Drakensberg Mountains, Table
Mountain; Limpopo and Orange rivers; the Veld
and the Karroo; part of Kalahari Desert; Kruger
National Park, largest in the world
head of state and government F W de Klerk
from 1989
government racialist, nationalist republic
political parties White: National Party (NP),
right-of-centre, racialist; Conservative Party of
South Africa (CPSA), extreme-right, racialist;
Democratic Party (DP), left-of-centre, multi-racial.
Coloureds: Labour Party of South Africa,
left-of-centre; People's Congress Party,
right-of-centre. Indian: National People's Party,
right-of-centre; Solidarity Party, left-of-centre.
Black: African National Congress (ANC),
left-wing, anti-apartheid
exports maize, sugar, fruit; wool; gold,
platinum (world's largest producer), diamonds
currency rand (commercial rate 4.33 = £1 Feb
1990)
population (1989) 35,625,000 (68% black, of
whom the largest nations are the Zulu, Xhosa,
Sotho, and Tswana, 18% white, 10% of mixed

ancestry, and 3% Asiatic); annual growth
rate 2.5%
life expectancy men 55, women 55
language Afrikaans and English (both official);
various Bantu languages
religion Christian; largest denomination is
the Nederduits Gereformeerde Kerk/Dutch
Reformed Church. Congregations are
segregated
literacy 81% male/81% female (1980 est),
ranging from 98% whites to 50% blacks
GNP $76.8 bn (1983); $1,296 per head of
population
chronology
1910 Union of South Africa formed from two
British colonies and two Boer republics.
1912 African National Congress (ANC) formed.
1948 Apartheid system of racial discrimination
initiated by Daniel Malan.
1955 Freedom Charter adopted by African
National Congress (ANC).
1958 Malan succeeded as prime minister by
Hendrik Verwoerd.
1960 ANC banned.
1961 South Africa withdrew from the
Commonwealth and became a republic.
1962 ANC leader Nelson Mandela jailed.
1964 Mandela, Walter Sisulu, Govan Mbeki,
and five other ANC leaders sentenced to life
imprisonment.
1966 Verwoerd assassinated and succeeded
by B J Vorster.
1976 Soweto uprising.
1977 Death in custody of Pan African Congress
activist Steve Biko.
1978 Vorster resigned and was replaced by
Pieter W Botha.
1984 New constitution adopted, giving
segregated representation to coloureds
and Asians and making Botha president.
Nonaggression pact with Mozambique signed
but not observed.
1985 Growth of violence in black townships.
1986 Commonwealth agreed on limited
sanctions. US Congress voted to impose
sanctions. Several multinational companies
announced closure of their South African
operations.
1987 The government formally acknowledged
the presence of its military forces in Angola.
1988 Peace agreement with Angola and Cuba,
recognising independence for Namibia.
1989 Botha gave up NP leadership and state
presidency. Democratic Party (DP) launched.
F W de Klerk became president. Walter Sisulu
and other ANC activists released
1990 Nelson Mandela released. ANC legalized.

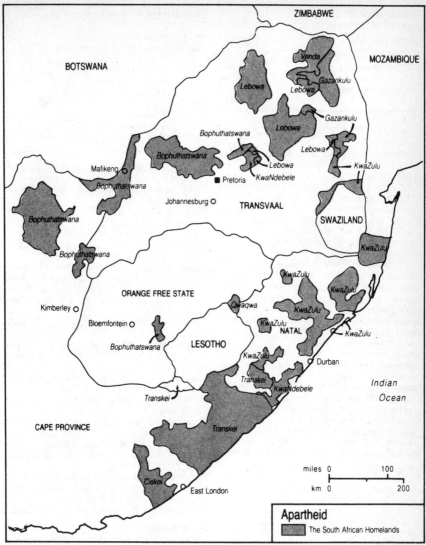

Apartheid

The South African Homelands

withdrawal 1967, and the proclamation of the Republic of South Yemen.

South Australia state of the Commonwealth of Australia

area 984,000 sq km/379,824 sq mi

capital and chief port Adelaide

towns Whyalla, Mount Gambier

features Murray Valley irrigated area, including wine-growing Barossa Valley; Lakes ◊Eyre and ◊Torrens; Mount Lofty, Musgrave and Flinders Ranges; parts of the ◊Nullarbor Plain, and Great Victoria and Simpson deserts; experimental rocket range in the arid north at Woomera; and at Maralinga British nuclear tests were made 1963 in which Aborigines were said to have died

products meat and wool (80% of area cattle and sheep grazing), wines and spirits, dried and canned fruit, iron (Middleback Range), coal (Leigh Creek), copper, uranium (Roxby Downs), oil and natural gas in the NE, lead, zinc, iron, opals, household and electrical goods, vehicles

South Africa: territorial divisions

Provinces and Capital	Area sq km
Cape of Good Hope *Cape Town*	721,000
Natal *Pietermaritzburg*	86,965
Transvaal *Pretoria*	286,064
Orange Free State *Bloemfontein*	129,152
	1,223,181

population (1987) 1,388,000, including 13,300 Aborigines

history possibly known to the Dutch in the 16th century; surveyed by Tasman 1644; first European settlement 1834; province 1836; state 1901.

South Bank an area of London south of the river Thames, the site of the Festival of Britain 1951, and now a cultural centre. Buildings include the Royal Festival Hall 1951 (Robert Matthew and Leslie Martin) and the National Theatre 1976 (Denys Lasdun), all connected by a series of walkways.

South Bend city on the St Joseph River, N Indiana, USA; population (1980) 110,000. Industries include the manufacture of agricultural machinery, cars, and aircraft equipment.

South Carolina state of the SE USA; nickname Palmetto State

area 80,600 sq km/31,112 sq mi

capital Columbia

towns Charleston, Greenville-Spartanburg

physical large areas of woodland; subtropical climate in coastal areas

products tobacco, cotton, fruit, soybeans, meat, textiles, clothing, paper, woodpulp, furniture, bricks, chemicals, machinery

population (1988) 3,493,000

famous people John C Calhoun

history first Spanish settlers 1526; Charles I gave the area (known as Carolina) to Robert

South Australia

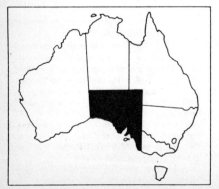

South Carolina

Heath (1575–1649), attorney general 1629; Declaration of Independence, one of the original Thirteen States 1776; joined the Confederacy 1860; readmitted to Union 1868.

South Dakota state of the USA; nickname Coyote or Sunshine State

area 199,800 sq km/77,123 sq mi

capital Pierre

towns Sioux Falls, Rapid City, Aberdeen

physical Great Plains; Black Hills (which include granite Mount Rushmore, on whose face giant relief portrait heads of former presidents Washington, Jefferson, Lincoln, and T Roosevelt are carved); Badlands

products cereals, livestock, gold (greatest USA producer)

population (1986) 708,000

famous people Crazy Horse, Sitting Bull, Ernest O Lawrence

history claimed by French 18th century; first white settlements 1794; state 1889.

South East Cape most southerly point of Australia, in Tasmania.

Southend-on-Sea resort in Essex, England; population (1981) 157,100. Industries include light engineering and boat-building. The shallow water of the Thames estuary enabled the building of a pier 2 km/1.25 mi long.

Southern and Antarctic Territories French overseas territory created 1955. It comprises the islands of *St Paul* and *Amsterdam* (67 sq km/26 sq mi); the *Kerguelen* and *Crozet* Islands

South Dakota

South Glamorgan

(7,515 sq km/2,901 sq mi); and *Adélie Land* on Antarctica itself (432,000 sq km/165,500 sq mi). All are uninhabited, except for research stations.

South Georgia island in the S Atlantic, a British crown colony administered with the South Sandwich Islands; area 3,757 sq km/1,450 sq mi. South Georgia lies 1,300 km/800 mi SE of the Falkland Islands, of which it was a dependency until 1985. The British Antarctic Survey has a station on nearby Bird Island.

South Georgia was visited by Captain James Cook 1775. The explorer Edward Shackleton is buried there. The chief settlement, Grytviken, was established as a whaling station 1904 and abandoned 1966; it was reoccupied by a small military garrison after the Falklands War 1982.

South Glamorgan county in S Wales
area 420 sq km/162 sq mi
towns administrative headquarters Cardiff; Barry, Penarth
features fertile Vale of Glamorgan; Welsh Folk Museum at St Fagans, near Cardiff
products dairy farming, industry (steel, plastics, engineering) in the Cardiff area
population (1987) 400,000
language 6% Welsh; English.

South Holland (Dutch *Zuid-Holland*) low-lying coastal province of the Netherlands; area 2,910 sq km/1,123 sq mi; population (1988) 3,208,000. The capital is The Hague. Noted for its bulbfields and glasshouses, the province also includes part of the Randstadt conurbation with major ports at Rotterdam and the Hook of Holland. Dairy cattle are reared; there are petroleum refineries at Rotterdam, and distilleries at Schiedam.

South Korea see ◊Korea, South.

Southland Plain plain on S South Island, New Zealand, on which Invercargill stands. It is an agricultural area with sheep and dairy farming.

South Orkney Islands group of barren, uninhabited islands in ◊British Antarctic Territory, SE of Cape Horn; area 622 sq km/240 sq mi. They were discovered by the naval explorer Capt George Powell 1821. Argentina, which lays claim to the islands, maintained a scientific station there 1976–82.

South Sandwich Islands actively volcanic uninhabited British Dependent Territory; area 337 sq km/130 sq mi. Along with South Georgia, 750 km/470 mi to the NW, it is administered from the Falkland Islands. They were claimed by Capt Cook 1775, and annexed by the UK 1908 and 1917. They were first formally claimed by Argentina 1948. In Dec 1976, 50 Argentine 'scientists' landed on Southern Thule, and were removed June 1982. There is an ice-free port off Cumberland Bay.

South Shetland Islands archipelago of 12 uninhabited islands in the South Atlantic, forming part of ◊British Antarctic Territory; area 4,622 sq km/1,785 sq mi.

South Shields manufacturing port in Tyne and Wear, England, on the Tyne estuary, east of Gateshead; population (1981) 87,000. Products include electrical goods, cables, and chemicals.

South Uist an island in the Outer Hebrides, Scotland, separated from North Uist by the island of Benbecula. There is a guided-missile range here.

Southwark borough of S London, England; population (1986) 215,000. It is the site of the Globe Theatre (built on Bankside 1599 by Burbage, Shakespeare, and others, and burned down 1613); the 12th-century Southwark Cathedral; the George Inn (last galleried inn in London); the Imperial War Museum; Dulwich College and Picture Gallery, and the Horniman Museum.

South West Africa former name (until 1968) of ◊Namibia.

South Yorkshire metropolitan county of England, created 1976, originally administered by an elected council; its powers reverted to district councils from 1986
area 1,560 sq km/602 sq mi
towns administrative headquarters Barnsley; Sheffield, Doncaster
features river Don; part of Peak District National Park
products all the main towns are metal-working centres; coal, dairy, sheep, arable farming
population (1987) 1,296,000.

Sovetsk town in Kaliningrad region, USSR. In 1807 Napoleon signed peace treaties with Prussia and Russia here. Until 1945 it was known as *Tilsit*, and was part of East Prussia.

Soviet Central Asia formerly *Turkestan* an area of the USSR consisting of ◊Kazakstan, ◊Uzbekistan, ◊Tadzhikistan, ◊Turkmenistan, and ◊Kirghizia constituent republics.

South Yorkshire

These were conquered by Russia as recently as 1866–73, and until 1917 were divided into the Khanate of Khiva, the Emirate of Bokhara, and the Governor-Generalship of Turkestan. The Soviet government became firmly established 1919, and in 1920, the Khan of Khiva and the Emir of Bokhara were overthrown, and People's Republics set up. Turkestan became an Autonomous Soviet Socialist Republic (ASSR) 1921. Boundaries were redistributed 1925 along nationalist lines, and Uzbekistan, Tadzhikistan, and Turkmenistan became republics of the USSR, along with Bokhara and Khiva. The area populated by Kazakhs were united with Kazakhstan, which became a Union Republic 1936, the same year as Kirghizia. Shortfalls in agricultural production led to the establishment in 1962 of a Central Asian Bureau to strengthen centralized control by the Party Praesidium in Moscow. These republics are the home of the majority of Soviet Muslims, and strong nationalist sentiment persists.

Soviet Far East geographical, not administrative, division of Asiatic USSR, on the Pacific coast. It includes the Amur, Lower Amur, Kamchatka, and Sakhalin regions, and Khabarovsk and Maritime territories.

Soviet Union alternative name for the ◊Union of Soviet Socialist Republics (USSR).

Soweto (*South West Township*) racially segregated urban settlement in South Africa, SW of Johannesburg; population (1983) 915,872. It has experienced civil unrest over the years due to the apartheid regime.

It began as a shanty town in the 1930s, and is now the largest black city in South Africa, but until 1976 its population could have status only as temporary residents, serving as a workforce for Johannesburg. There were serious riots in June 1976, sparked by a ruling that Afrikaans be used in African schools there. Reforms followed but riots flared up again in 1985, and continued into the late 1980s.

Spa town in Liège province, Belgium; population (1982) 9,600. Famous since the 14th century for its mineral springs, it has given its name to similar centres elsewhere.

Spain country in SW Europe, on the Iberian Peninsula between the Atlantic and the Mediterranean, bounded to the N by France and to the W by Portugal.

Spalato Italian name for ◊Split, a port in Yugoslavia.

Spalding market town on the river Welland, in Lincolnshire, England; population (1981) 18,000. The bulb farms are famous and there is a flower festival in May.

Spanish Guinea former name of the Republic of ◊Equatorial Guinea.

Spanish Main term often used to describe the Caribbean in the 16th–17th centuries, but more properly the South American mainland between the river Orinoco and Panama.

Spanish Sahara former name for the ◊Western Sahara.

Spanish Town town in Middlesex county, Jamaica; population (1982) 89,000. Founded by Diego Columbus about 1525, it was the capital of Jamaica 1535–1871.

Spey river in Highland and Grampian regions, Scotland, rising SE of Fort Augustus, and flowing 172 km/107 mi to the Moray Firth between Lossiemouth and Buckie. It has salmon fisheries at its mouth.

Speyer (English *Spires*) ancient city on the Rhine, in Rhineland-Palatinate, West Germany, 26 km/

Spain: territorial divisions

	Area in sq km
Andalusia	87,268
Aragón	47,669
Asturias	10,565
Basque	17,682
Castilla la Nueva	72,363
Castilla la Vieja	49,976
Catalonia	31,930
Extremadura	41,602
Galicia	29,434
Murcia	26,175
Léon	54,594
Valencia	23,305
Balearic Islands	5,014
Canary Islands	7,273
	504,750

Spain
(España)

area 499,700 sq km/192,884 sq mi
capital Madrid
towns Bilbao, Valencia, Zaragoza, Murcia; ports Barcelona, Seville, Málaga
physical a central plateau with mountain ranges; lowlands in the south
features includes Balearic and Canary Islands, and Ceuta and Melilla on N African coast; rivers Ebro, Douro, Tagus, Guadiana, Guadalquivir; Iberian Plateau (Meseta); Pyrenees, Cantabrian Mountains, Andalusian Mountains, Sierra Nevada
head of state Juan Carlos I from 1975
head of government Felipe González Marquez from 1982
government constitutional monarchy
political parties Socialist Worker's Party (PSOE), democratic socialist; Popular Alliance (AP), centre-right; Christian Democrats (DC), centrist; Liberal Party (PL), left-of-centre

exports citrus, grapes, pomegranates, vegetables, wine (especially sherry), olive oil, tinned fruit and fish, iron ore, cork, cars and other vehicles, leather goods, ceramics
currency peseta (183.95 = £1 Feb 1990)
population (1989) 39,784,000; annual growth rate 0.6%
life expectancy men 71, women 78
language Spanish (Castilian, official), but regional languages are recognized within their own boundaries (Basque, Catalan,. Galician, Valencian, and Majorcan are the chief examples)
religion Roman Catholic (there are restrictions on the practice of Protestantism)
literacy 97% male/92% female (1985 est)
GDP $160.4 bn (1984); $5,500 per head of population
chronology
1947 Gen Franco announced there would be a return to the monarchy after his death, with Prince Juan Carlos as his successor.
1975 Franco died and was succeeded by King Juan Carlos I as head of state.
1978 New constitution adopted, with Adolfo Suárez, leader of the Democratic Centre Party, as prime minister.
1981 Suárez resigned and was succeeded by his deputy, Calvo-Sotelo. Attempted military coup thwarted.
1982 Socialist Workers' Party (PSOE), led by Felipe González, won a sweeping electoral victory. Basque separatist organization (ETA) stepped up its guerrilla campaign.
1985 ETA's campaign spread to holiday resorts.
1986 Referendum confirmed NATO membership. Spain joined the European Community.
1988 Spain joined the Western European Union. PSOE lost seats, holding only parity after general election.
1989 Talks between government and ETA collapsed and truce ended.

---

16 mi south of Mannheim; population (1983) 43,000. It was at the *Diet of Spires* 1529 that Protestantism received its name.

Spice Islands former name of the ◊Moluccas, a group of islands in the Malay Archipelago.

Spires English name for the German city of ◊Speyer.

Spitalfields district in the Greater London borough of ◊Tower Hamlets. It was once the home of Huguenot silk weavers.

Spithead a roadstead between the mainland of England and the Isle of ◊Wight. The name is

often applied to the entire eastern area of the ◊Solent.

Spitsbergen the main island in the Norwegian archipelago of ◊Svalbard.

Split (Italian *Spalato*) port in Yugoslavia, on the Adriatic; population (1981) 236,000. Industries include engineering, cement, and textiles, and it is also a tourist resort. The Roman emperor Diocletian retired here in 305.

Spokane city on the Spokane River, E Washington, USA; population (1980) 341,000. It is situated in a mining, timber, and rich agricultural

Sri Lanka
Democratic Socialist Republic of
(former name **Ceylon**)
*Prajathanrika Samajawadi
Janarajaya Sri Lanka*

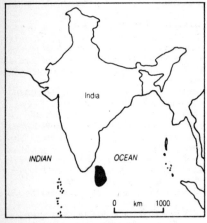

area 65,600 sq km/25,328 sq mi
capital and chief port Colombo
towns Kandy; ports Jaffna, Galle, Negombo, Trincomalee
physical flat in the N and around the coast; hills and mountains in the S
features Adam's Peak; ruined cities of Anuradhapura, Polonnaruwa
head of state Ranasinghe Premadsa from 1989
head of government Dingiri Banda Wijetunge from 1989
government liberal democratic republic
political parties United National Party (UNP), right-of-centre; Sri Lanka Freedom Party (SLFP), left-of-centre; Tamil United Liberation Front (TULF), Tamil autonomy; Eelam People's

Revolutionary Liberation Front (EPLRF), Indian-backed Tamil-secessionist *Tamil Tigers*; People's Liberation Front (JVP), Sinhala-extremist organization, banned from 1983
exports tea, rubber, coconut products, plumbago, sapphires, rubies, precious stones
currency Sri Lanka rupee (67.80 = £1 Feb 1990)
population (1989) 17,541,000 (including 2,500,000 Tamils); annual growth rate 1.8%
life expectancy men 67, women 70
language Sinhalese (official, but English and Tamil are national languages)
religion Buddhist 67% (official), Hindu 18%
literacy 91% male/83% female (1985 est)
GNP $5.3 bn (1984); $340 per head of population
chronology
1948 Independence from Britain achieved (as Ceylon).
1956 Sinhalese established as official language.
1959 Assassination of Prime Minister Solomon Bandaranaike.
1972 Socialist Republic of Sri Lanka proclaimed.
1978 Presidential constitution adopted by new Jayawardene government.
1983 Tamil guerrilla violence escalated; state of emergency imposed.
1987 Violence continued despite ceasefire policed by Indian troops.
1988 Left-wing guerrilla campaign against the Indo-Sri Lankan peace pact. Prime Minister Premadasa elected president amid allegations of fraud.
1989 Premadasa became president; Wijetunge, prime minister. Leaders of the TULF and JVP assassinated. India agreed to withdraw troops by April 1990.

area, and is the seat of Gonzaga University 1887.

Spoleto town in Umbria, central Italy; population (1985) 37,000. There is an annual opera and drama festival established by Gian Carlo Menotti. It was a papal possession 1220–1860, and has Roman remains and medieval churches.

Sporades Greek island group in the Aegean Sea. The chief island of the *Northern Sporades* is ◊Skyros. The *Southern Sporades* are more usually referred to as the ◊Dodecanese.

Springfield capital and agricultural and mining centre of Illinois, USA; population (1980) 176,000. President Abraham Lincoln was born and is buried here.

Springfield city in Massachusetts, USA; population

(1980) 531,000. It was the site (1794–1968) of the US arsenal and armoury, known for the Springfield rifle.

Springfield city and agricultural centre in Missouri, USA; population (1980) 133,000. Industries include engineering and textiles.

Springs city in Transvaal, South Africa, 40 km/25 mi east of Johannesburg; population (1980) 154,000. It is a mining centre, producing gold, coal, and uranium.

Sri Lanka island in the Indian Ocean, off the SE coast of India.

Srinagar summer capital of the state of Jammu and Kashmir, India; population (1981) 520,000. It is a beautiful resort, intersected by waterways, and has carpet, papier mâché, and leather industries.

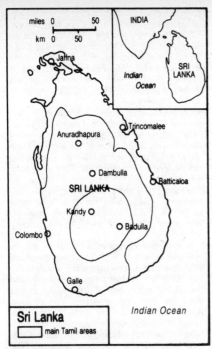

miles 0 — 50
km 0 — 50

INDIA

Indian Ocean

SRI LANKA

Jaffna

Trincomalee

Anuradhapura

Dambulla

SRI LANKA

Batticaloa

Kandy

Badulla

Colombo

Galle

Indian Ocean

Sri Lanka
☐ main Tamil areas

The university of Jammu and Kashmir was established 1948.

SSR abbreviation for *Soviet Socialist Republic*.

Staffa uninhabited island in the Inner Hebrides, west of Mull. It has a rugged coastline and many caves, including ◊Fingal's Cave.

Staffordshire county in W central England
area 2,720 sq km/1,050 sq mi
towns administrative headquarters Stafford; Stoke-on-Trent
features largely flat, comprising the Vale of Trent and its tributaries; Cannock Chase; Keele University 1962; Staffordshire bull terriers
products coal in north; china and earthenware in the Potteries and the upper Trent basin
population (1987) 1,028,000
famous people Peter de Wint.

Staffs abbreviation for ◊*Staffordshire*.

Stalin former name 1949–56 of the port of ◊Varna, Bulgaria.

Stalingrad name (1925–1961) of the Soviet city of ◊Volgograd.

Stalinsk former name (1932–61) of ◊Novokuznetsk, city in USSR.

Stamboul the old part of the Turkish city of Istanbul, the area formerly occupied by ◊Byzantium.

Stanley town on E Falkland, capital of the ◊Falkland Islands; population (1986) 1,200. After changing its name only once between 1843 and 1982, it was renamed five times in the space of six weeks during the Falklands War in Apr–June 1982.

Stanley Falls former name (until 1972) of ◊Boyoma Falls, on the Zaïre river.

Stanley Pool former name (until 1972) of ◊Pool Malebo, on the Zaïre river.

Stanleyville former name (until 1966) of the Zaïrean port of ◊Kisangani.

Stansted site of London's third airport, in Essex, England.

Staten Island island in New York harbour, part of New York City, USA, constituting the borough of Richmond; area 155 sq km/60 sq mi; population (1980) 352,500.

Stavanger seaport and capital of Rogaland county, SW Norway, population (1988) 96,000. It has fish-canning, oil, and shipbuilding industries.

Stavropol a territory of the Russian Soviet Federal Socialist Republic, lying N of the Caucasus mountains; area 80,600 sq km/31,128 sq mi; population (1985) 2,715,000. The capital is Stavropol. Irrigated land produces grain but sheep are also reared. There are natural gas deposits.

Stavropol formerly (1935–43) *Voroshilovsk* town SE of Rostov, in the N Caucasus, USSR; population (1987) 306,000. Founded 1777 as a fortress town, it is now a market centre for an agricultural area, and makes agricultural machinery, textiles, and food products.

Stębark Polish name (since 1945) for the village of ◊Tannenberg, formerly in East Prussia, now part of Poland.

Steep Point the most westerly extremity of Australia, in Western Australia, NW of the Murchison River.

Staffordshire

Strathclyde

Steiermark German name for ◊Styria, province of Austria.

Stellenbosch town in Cape Province, South Africa; population (1985) 43,000. It is the centre of a wine-producing district. It was founded 1679, and is the oldest European settlement in South Africa after Cape Town.

Stepney district of London, now part of the borough of ◊Tower Hamlets, north of the Thames, and east of the City of London.

Sterea Ellas-Evvoia the region of central Greece and Euboea, occupying the southern part of the Greek mainland between the Ionian and Aegean seas and including the island of Euboea; population (1981) 1,099,800; area 24,391 km2/9,421 sq mi. Chief city is Athens.

Stettin German name for the Polish city of ◊Szczecin.

Stevenage town in Hertfordshire, England, 45 km/ 28 mi north of London; population (1981) 74,000. Dating from medieval times, in 1946 Stevenage was the first place chosen for development as a new town.

Stewart Island volcanic island divided from South Island, New Zealand, by the Foveaux Strait; area 1,750 sq km/676 sq mi; population (1981) 600. Industries include farming, fishing, and granite quarrying. Oban is the main settlement (called Halfmoon Bay until the early 1940s).

Stilton village in Cambridgeshire, England, 10 km/ 6 mi SW of Peterborough. It gives its name to a cheese brought here in coaching days for transport to London, and still made at and around Melton Mowbray.

Stirling administrative headquarters of Central region, Scotland, on the river Forth; population (1981) 39,000. Industries include the manufacture of agricultural machinery, textiles, and carpets. The castle, which guarded a key crossing of the river, predates the 12th century, and was long a Scottish royal residence. Wallace won a victory at Stirling bridge 1297. Edward II of England (in raising a Scottish siege of the town) went into battle at Bannockburn 1314, and was defeated by Robert I (the Bruce).

Stirlingshire former county of Scotland. In 1975 most of it was merged with Central region, but a SW section, including Kilsyth, went to Strathclyde. The area lay between the Firth of Forth and Loch Lomond, and included the Lennox hills and the fringe of the Highlands. The county town was Stirling.

Stockholm capital and industrial port of Sweden; population (1988) 667,000. It is built on a number of islands. Industries include engineering, brewing, electrical goods, paper, textiles, and pottery.

A network of bridges links the islands and the mainland; an underground railway was completed 1957. The 18th-century royal palace stands on the site of the 13th-century fortress which defended the trading settlements of Lake Mälar, around which the town first developed. The old town is well preserved and has a church 1264. The town hall was designed by Ragnar Östberg 1923. Most of Sweden's educational institutions are in Stockholm (including the Nobel Institute). The warship *Wasa* (built for King Gustavus Adolphus) sank in the harbour 1628, was raised 1961 and is preserved in a museum.

Stockport town in Greater Manchester, England; population (1981) 137,000. The Tame and Goyt rivers join here to form the Mersey. Industries include electronics, chemicals, engineering, and still some cotton textiles.

Stockton industrial river port (agricultural machinery, food processing) on the San Joaquin in California, USA; population (1980) 149,779.

Stockton-on-Tees town and port on the river Tees, Cleveland, NE England; population (1981) 155,000. There are shipbuilding, steel, and chemical industries, and it was the starting point for the world's first passenger railway 1825. It has the oldest railway-station building in the world, and there are many Georgian buildings.

Stoke-on-Trent city in Staffordshire, England, on the river Trent; population (1981) 253,000. It is the heart of the Potteries, and a major ceramic centre. Other industries include steel, chemicals, engineering machinery, paper, rubber, and coal.

Stoke was formed 1910 from Burslem, Hanley, Longton, Stoke-on-Trent, Fenton, and Tunstall. The ceramics factories of Minton and Wedgwood are here; the Gladstone Pottery Museum is the only working pottery museum.

Stornoway port on the island of Lewis in the Outer

Sudan
Democratic Republic of
(Jamhuryat es-Sudan)

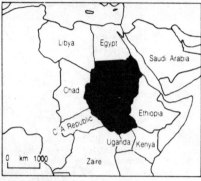

area 2,505,800 sq km/967,489 sq mi
capital Khartoum
towns Omdurman, Juba, Wadi Medani,
al-Obeid, Kassala, Atbara, al-Qadarif, Kosti; chief
port Port Sudan
physical fertile valley of the river Nile separates
Libyan Desert in west from high rocky Nubian
Desert in east
features Sudd swamp; largest country in Africa
head of state and government Gen Omar
Hasan Ahmed el-Bashir from 1989
government military republic
political parties New National Umma Party
(NNUP), Islamic, nationalist; Democratic
Unionist Party (DUP), moderate, nationalist;
National Islamic Front, Islamic nationalist
exports cotton, gum arabic, sesame,
groundnuts, durra
currency Sudanese pound (19.49 = £1 Feb
1990)
population (1989) 25,008,000 (70% of whom
are Muslim, Arab-speaking, and in the N;
speakers of African languages in the S); annual
growth rate 2.9%
life expectancy men 47, women 49
language 51% Arabic (official); 6% Darfurian;
18% Nilotic (Dinka and Nuer); 5% Nilo-Hamitic;
5% Sudanic

religion Sunni Muslim in the north, animist in
the south, with a Christian minority
literacy 38% male/14% female (1981 est)
GNP $27.3 bn (1983); $361 per head of
population
chronology
1955 Civil war between the Muslim N and
non-Muslim S.
1956 Sudan achieved independence as a
republic.
1958 Military coup replaced the civilian
government with a Supreme Council of the
Armed Forces.
1964 Civilian rule reinstated.
1969 Coup led by Col Gaafar Mohammed
Nimeri established a Revolutionary Command
Council (RCC) and the country's name
changed to the Democratic Republic of Sudan.
1970 Agreement in principle on union with
Egypt.
1971 New constitution adopted, Nimeri
confirmed as president, and the Sudanese
Socialist Union (SSU) declared to be the only
legal party.
1972 Proposed Federation of Arab
Republics, comprising Sudan, Egypt, and
Syria, abandoned. Addis Ababa conference
proposed autonomy for southern provinces.
1974 National assembly established.
1983 Nimeri re-elected amid growing opposition
to his social, economic, and religious policies.
Sharia (Islamic law) introduced.
1985 Nimeri deposed in a bloodless coup led
by Gen Swar al-Dahab, who set up a transitional
military council. State of emergency declared.
1986 More than 40 political parties fought the
general election and a coalition government
was formed.
1987 Virtual civil war with Sudan People's
Liberation Movement (SPLM).
1988 Al-Mahdi formed a new coalition. Another
flare-up of civil war between N and S created
tens of thousands of refugees. Floods made 1.5
million people homeless. Peace pact signed
with Sudan People's Liberation Movement.
1989 Sadiq Al-Mahdi overthrown in coup led by
Gen Omar Hasan Ahmed el-Bashir.

Hebrides, Scotland; population (1981) 8,660. It
is the administrative centre for the Western
Isles. The economy is based on fishing, tourism, tweeds, and offshore oil. Stornoway was
founded by James VI of Scotland (James I of
England).
Stourbridge market town in West Midlands, England, on the Stour river, SW of Birmingham;

population (1981) 55,000. Industries include the
manufacture of glass and bricks.
Straits Settlements former province of the East
India Company 1826–58, and British crown colony
1867–1946: it comprised Singapore, Malacca,
Penang, Cocos Islands, Christmas Island, and
Labuan.
Stranraer port in Dumfries and Galloway region,

Suez Canal

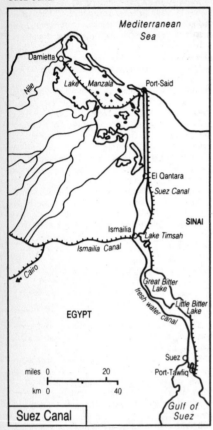

Suffolk

an earlier building 1877–79 which burned down 1926. Shakespeare's birthplace contains relics of his life and times. His grave is in the parish church; his wife Anne Hathaway's cottage is nearby.

Strathclyde region of Scotland
area 13,900 sq km/5,367 sq mi
towns administrative headquarters Glasgow; Paisley, Greenock, Kilmarnock, Clydebank, Hamilton, Coatbridge, Prestwick
features includes some of Inner Hebrides; river Clyde; part of Loch Lomond; Glencoe, site of the massacre of the Macdonald clan; Breadalbane; the islands of Arran, Bute, and Mull
products dairy, pig, and poultry products, shipbuilding, engineering, coal from Ayr and Lanark, oil-related services
population (1987) 2,333,000, half the population of Scotland
famous people David Livingstone, William Burrell.

Stretford town in Greater ◊Manchester, England; population (1981) 48,000. It includes the Old Trafford cricket ground. There are engineering, chemical, and textile industries.

Stromboli Italian island in the Tyrrhenian Sea, one of the ◊Lipari Islands; area 12 sq km/5 sq mi. It has an active volcano, 926 m/3,039 ft high. The island produces Malmsey wine and capers.

Stuttgart capital of Baden-Württemberg, West Germany; population (1988) 565,000. Industries include publishing and the manufacture of vehicles and electrical goods. It is the headquarters of US European Command (Eucom). Hegel was born here.

Scotland; population (1981) 10,800. There is a ferry service to Larne in Northern Ireland.

Strasbourg city on the river Ill, in Bas-Rhin *département*, capital of Alsace, France; population (1982) 373,000. Industries include car manufacture, tobacco, printing and publishing, and preserves. The Council of Europe meets here, and sessions of the European Parliament alternate between Strasbourg and Luxembourg. Seized by France 1681, it was surrendered to Germany 1870–1919 and 1940–44. It has a 13th-century cathedral.

Stratford port and industrial town in SW Ontario, Canada; population (1981) 26,000. It is the site of a Shakespeare festival.

Stratford-upon-Avon market town on the river Avon, in Warwickshire, England; population (1981) 21,000. It is the birthplace of William Shakespeare.

The Royal Shakespeare Theatre 1932 replaced

Styria (German *Steiermark*) alpine province of SE Austria; area 16,400 sq km/6,330 sq mi; population (1987) 1,181,000. Its capital is Graz, and its industries include iron, steel, lignite, vehicles, electrical goods, and engineering. An independent state from 1056 until it passed to the Habsburgs in the 13th century, it was annexed by Germany 1938.

Subotica largest town in Vojvodina, NW Serbia, Yugoslavia; population (1981) 155,000. Industries include chemicals and electrical machinery.

Suceava capital of Suceava county, N Romania; population (1985) 93,000. Industries include textiles and lumber. It was a former centre of pilgrimage and capital of Moldavia 1388–1564.

Sucre legal capital and judicial seat of Bolivia; population (1985) 87,000. It stands on the central plateau at an altitude of 2,840 m/9,320 ft.

history The city was founded 1538, its cathedral dates from 1553, and the University of San Francisco Xavier 1624 is probably the oldest in South America. The first revolt against Spanish rule in South America began here 25 May 1809.

Sudan country in NE Africa, S of Egypt, with a Red Sea coast; it is the largest country in Africa.

Sudbury city in Ontario, Canada; population (1986) 149,000. A buried meteorite there yields 90% of the world's nickel.

Sudetenland mountainous region of N Czechoslovakia, annexed by Germany under the Munich Agreement 1938; returned to Czechoslovakia 1945.

Suez (Arabic *El Suweis*) port at the Red Sea terminus of the ◊Suez Canal; population (1985) 254,000. Industries include oil refining and the manufacture of fertilizers. It was reconstructed after the Arab-Israeli War 1973.

Suez Canal artificial waterway, 160 km/100 mi long, from Port Said to Suez, linking the Mediterranean and Red seas, separating Africa from Asia, and providing the shortest sea route from

---

Suriname
Republic of

area 163,800 sq km/63,243 sq mi
capital Paramaribo
physical hilly and forested, with flat coast
features river Surinam
head of state and government Ramsewak Shankar from 1988
government democratic republic
political parties Party for National Unity and Solidarity (KTPI)*, Indonesian, left-of-centre; Suriname National Party (NPS)*, Creole, left-of-centre; Progressive Reform Party (VHP)*, Indian, left-of-centre; National Democratic Party (NDP), nationalist, left-of-centre

*members of Front for Democracy and Development (FDD)
exports bauxite, rice, citrus, timber
currency Suriname guilder (3.30 = £1 Feb 1990)
population (1989) 400,000 (Creole, Chinese, Hindu, and Indonesian peoples); annual growth rate 1.1%
life expectancy men 66, women 71
language Dutch, English (both official)
religion Christian 35%, Hindu 25%, Muslim 17%
literacy 90% male/90% female (1985)
GNP $1.2 bn (1983); $2,600 per head of population
chronology
1954 Granted internal self-government as Dutch Guiana.
1975 Achieved full independence with Dr Johan Ferrier as president and Henck Arron as prime minister. About 40% of the population, especially those of East Indian origin, emigrated to the Netherlands.
1980 Arron's government overthrown in an army coup but Ferrier refused to recognize the military regime and appointed Dr Henk Chin A Sen to lead a civilian administration. Army replaced Ferrier with Dr Chin A Sen.
1982 Army, led by Lt-Col Desi Bouterse, seized power, setting up a Revolutionary People's Front.
1985 Ban on political activities lifted.
1987 New constitution approved.
1988 Ramsewak Shankar elected president.

Europe eastwards. It was opened 1869, nationalized 1956, blocked by Egypt during the Arab-Israeli war 1967, and not reopened until 1975.

The French Suez Canal Company was formed 1858 to execute the scheme of Ferdinand de Lesseps. The canal was opened 1869, and in 1875 British prime minister Disraeli acquired a major shareholding for Britain from the khedive of Egypt. The 1888 Convention of Constantinople opened it to all nations. The Suez Canal was admininstered by a company with offices in Paris controlled by a council of 33 (ten of them British) until 1956 when it was forcibly nationalized by President Nasser of Egypt. The new Damietta port complex on the Mediterranean at the mouth of the canal was inaugurated July 1986. The port is designed to handle 16 million tons of cargo.

Suffolk county of E England
area 3,800 sq km/1,467 sq mi
towns administrative headquarters Ipswich; Bury St Edmunds, Lowestoft, Felixstowe
physical low undulating surface and flat coastline; rivers Waveney, Alde, Deben, Orwell, Stour; part of the Norfolk Broads
features Minsmere marshland bird reserve, near Aldeburgh; site of Sutton Hoo (7th-century ship-burial); site of Sizewell B, planned as the first of Britain's pressurized-water nuclear reactor (PWR) plants (approved 1987).
products cereals, sugar beet, working horses (Suffolk punches), fertilizers, agricultural machinery
population (1987) 635,000
famous people Constable, Gainsborough, Elizabeth Garrett Anderson, Benjamin Britten, George Crabbe.

Suhl county in East Germany; area 3,860 sq km/
Surrey

1,490 sq mi; population (1986) 549,000. Its capital is Suhl. It is dominated by the Thuringian forest.

Sukkur or *Sakhar* port in Sind province, Pakistan, on the Indus; population (1981) 191,000. The Sukkur-Lloyd Barrage 1928–32 lies to the west.

Sulawesi (formerly *Celebes*) island in E Indonesia, one of the Sunda Islands; area (with dependent islands) 190,000 sq km/73,000 sq mi; population (1980) 10,410,000. It is mountainous and forested, and produces copra and nickel.

Sulu Archipelago group of about 870 islands off SW Mindanao in the Philippines, between the Sulawesi and Sulu seas; area 2,700 sq km/1,042 sq mi; population (1980) 361,000. The capital is Jolo, on the island (the largest) of the same name. Until 1940 the islands were an autonomous sultanate.

Sumatra or *Sumatera* second largest island of Indonesia, one of the Sunda Islands; area 473,600 sq km/182,800 sq mi; population (1980) 28,016,000. East of a longitudinal volcanic mountain range is a wide plain; both are heavily forested. Products include rubber, rice, tobacco, tea, timber, tin, and petroleum.

Northern Sumatra is rapidly being industrialized, and the Asakan river (rising in Lake Toba) was dammed for power 1974. The main towns are Palembang, Padang, and Benkuelen.

history A Hindu empire was founded in the 8th century, but Islam was introduced by Arab traders from the 13th century, and by the 16th century was adopted throughout the island.

Sunbelt popular name given to a region of the USA, south of Washington DC, between the Pacific and Atlantic coasts, because of its climate.

Sunbury-on-Thames market town and boating centre in Surrey, NE England, on the river Thames; population (1981) 39,000.

Sun City alternative name for ◊Mmabatho, resort in Bophuthatswana, South Africa.

Sunda Islands islands west of the Moluccas, in the Malay Archipelago, the greater number belonging to Indonesia. They are so named because they lie largely on the Indonesian extension of the Sunda continental shelf. The *Greater Sundas* include Borneo, Java (including the small island of Madura), Sumatra, Sulawesi, and Belitung. The *Lesser Sundas* (Indonesian *Nusa Tenggara*) are all Indonesian, and include Bali, Lombok, Flores, Sumba, Sumbawa, and Timor.

Sunderland port in Tyne and Wear, England; population (1981) 196,150. Industries were formerly only coalmining and shipbuilding, but have now diversified to electronics, glass, and furniture. There is a polytechnic and a civic theatre, the Sunderland Empire.

Sundsvall port in E Sweden; population (1986) 93,000. It has oil, timber, and wood-pulp industries.

Sungari river in Manchuria, NE China, which

Swaziland
Kingdom of

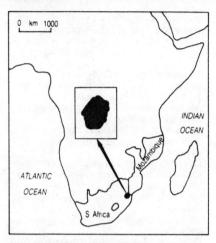

area 17,400 sq km/6,716 sq mi
capital Mbabane
physical central valley; mountains in W
features landlocked enclave between South Africa and Mozambique
head of state and government King Mswati III from 1986
government near-absolute monarchy
political parties Imbokodvo National Movement (INM), nationalistic monarchist
exports sugar, citrus, timber, asbestos, iron ore
currency lilangeni (4.33 = £1 Feb 1990)

population (1989) 757,000; annual growth rate 3%
life expectancy men 47, women 50
language Swazi 90%, English (both official)
religion Christian, both Protestant and Catholic; animist
literacy 70% male/66% female (1985 est)
GNP $610 million (1983); $790 per head of population
chronology
1967 Achieved internal self-government.
1968 Achieved full independence from Britain, within the Commonwealth, as the Kingdom of Swaziland, with King Sobhuza II as head of state.
1973 The king suspended the constitution and assumed absolute powers.
1978 New constitution adopted.
1982 King Sobhuza died and his place was taken by one of his wives, Dzeliewe, until his son, Prince Makhosetive, reached the age of 21.
1983 Queen Dzeliewe ousted by another wife, Ntombi.
1984 After a royal power struggle, it was announced that the crown prince would become king at the age of 18.
1986 Crown prince formally invested as King Mswati III.
1987 A power struggle developed between the advisory council Liqoqo and Queen Ntombi over the accession of the king. Mswati dissolved parliament and a new government was elected with Sotsha Dlamini as prime minister.

---

joins the Amur on the Siberian frontier; length 1,300 km/800 mi.

Superior, Lake largest of the ◊Great Lakes, and the second largest lake in the world; area 83,300 sq km/32,200 sq mi.

Sur or **Soûr** Arabic name for the Lebanese port of ◊Tyre.

Surabaya port on the island of Java, Indonesia; population (1980) 2,028,000. It has oil refineries and shipyards, and is a naval base.

Surat city in Gujarat, W India, at the mouth of the Tapti; population (1981) 913,000. The chief industry is textiles. The first East India Company trading post in India was established here 1612.

Suriname country on the northern coast of South America, on the Atlantic coast, between Guyana and French Guiana.

Surrey county in S England
area 1,660 sq km/641 sq mi
towns administrative headquarters Kingston upon Thames; Guildford, Woking

features rivers Thames, Mole, and Wey; Box and Leith Hills; North Downs; Runnymede, Thameside site of the signing of Magna Carta; Yehudi Menuhin School; Kew Palace and Royal Botanic Gardens
products market garden vegetables, agricultural products, service industries
population (1987) 1,000,000
famous people John Galsworthy.

Surtsey a volcanic island 20 km/12 mi SW of Heimaey in the Westman islands of Iceland. The island was created following an underwater volcanic eruption Nov 1963.

Susa (French **Sousse**) port and commercial centre in NE Tunisia; population (1984) 83,500. It was founded by the Phoenicians, and has Roman ruins.

Susquehanna river rising in central New York State, USA, and flowing 715 km/444 mi to Chesapeake Bay. It is used for hydroelectric power. On the strength of its musical name, Samuel Coleridge

Sweden
Kingdom of
(Konungariket Sverige)

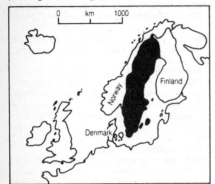

area 450,000 sq km/173,745 sq mi
capital Stockholm
towns Göteborg, Malmö, Uppsala, Norrköping, Västera
physical mountains in the NW; plains in the south; much of the land is forested
features many lakes, for example Väner, Vätter, Mälar, Hjälmar; islands of Öland and Gotland; large herds of wild elk
head of state Carl XVI Gustaf from 1973
head of government Ingvar Carlsson from 1986
government constitutional monarchy
political parties Social Democratic Labour party (SAP), moderate, left-of-centre; Moderate Party, right-of-centre; Liberal Party, centre-left; Centre Party, centrist; Christian Democratic Party, Christian, centrist; Left (Communist) Party, European, Marxist
exports aircraft, cars, domestic equipment, ballbearings, drills, missiles, electronics, petrochemicals, textiles, furnishings, ornamental glass
currency krona (10.44 = £1 Feb 1990)
population (1989) 8,371,000 (including 1,200,000 postwar immigrants from Finland, Turkey, Yugoslavia, Greece); annual growth rate 0.1%
life expectancy men 73, women 79
language Swedish, one of the Scandinavian division of Germanic languages
religion Christian (Evangelical Lutheran)
literacy 99% (1984)
GNP $88 bn (1983); $14,821 per head of population
chronology
12th century United as an independent nation.
1397–1520 Under Danish rule.
1914–45 Neutral in both World Wars.
1951–76 Social Democratic Labour Party (SAP) in power.
1969 Olof Palme became SAP leader and prime minister.
1971 Constitution amended, creating a single-chamber parliament.
1975 Monarch's constitutional powers reduced.
1976 Thorbjörn Fälldin, leader of the Centre Party, became prime minister, heading centre-right coalition.
1982 SAP, led by Palme, returned to power.
1985 SAP won the largest number of seats in parliament and formed a minority government, with communist support.
1986 Olof Palme murdered in Stockholm. Ingvar Carlsson became prime minister and SAP party leader.
1988 SAP re-elected with reduced majority; Green Party increased its vote dramatically.
1990 SAP government resigned.

---

planned to establish a Pantisocratic (communal) settlement here with his fellow poet Robert Southey.

Sussex former county of England, on the south coast, now divided into ◊East Sussex and ◊West Sussex.

According to tradition, the Saxon Ella landed here 477, defeated the inhabitants, and founded the kingdom of the South Saxons which was absorbed by Wessex 825.

Sutherlandshire former county of Scotland, with deep sea lochs and mountains in the west, Ben More Assynt rising to 999 m/3,279 ft. In 1975 it was merged with Highland Region. Dornoch was the administrative headquarters.

Sutlej river in Pakistan, a tributary of the river ◊Indus; length 1,370 km/851 mi.

Sutton borough of S Greater London; population (1981) 168,000. It was the site of Nonsuch Palace built by Henry VIII, which was demolished in the 17th century.

Sutton Coldfield a residential part of the West Midlands conurbation around ◊Birmingham, England; population (1981) 103,000.

Sutton-in-Ashfield town in Nottinghamshire, England; population (1981) 41,000. It has coal, hosiery, and plastics industries.

Suva capital and industrial port of Fiji, on Viti Levu; population (1981) 68,000. It produces soap and coconut oil.

Suzhou formerly *Soochow* and *Wuhsien* 1912–49 city on the Grand Canal, in Jiangsu province, China; population (1983) 670,000. It has embroidery and jade-carving traditions, and Shizilin and Zhuozheng

Switzerland
Swiss Confederation (German
Schweiz, French *Suisse*, Italian,
Svizzera)

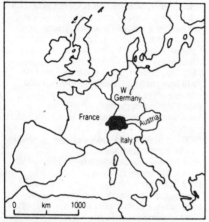

area 41,300 sq km/15,946 sq mi
capital Bern
towns Zürich, Geneva, Lausanne; river port
Basel
physical most mountainous country in Europe
(Alps and Jura Mountains)
features winter sports area of the upper valley
of the river Inn (Engadine); lakes Maggiore,
Lučerne, Geneva, Constance
head of state and government Arnold Koller

from 1990
government federal democratic republic
political parties Radical Democratic Party
(FDP), radical, centre-left; Social Democratic
party (SPS), moderate, left-of-centre; Christian
Democratic Party (PDC), Christian, moderate,
centrist; People's Party (SVP), centre-left; Liberal
Party (PLS), federalist, centre-left; Green Party,
ecological
exports electrical goods, chemicals, pharmaceuticals, watches, precision instruments,
confectionery, banking, insurance; tourism is
important
currency Swiss franc (2.53 = £1 Feb 1990)
population (1989) 6,485,000; annual growth
rate 0.2%
life expectancy men 73, women 80
language German 65%, French 18%, Italian
10%, Romansch 1%
religion Roman Catholic 50%, Protestant 48%
literacy 99% (1985)
GNP $93.7 bn (1984); $14,408 per head of
population
chronology
1648 Became independent of the Holy Roman
Empire.
1798–1815 Helvetic Republic established by
French Revolutionary armies.
1847 Civil war resulted in greater centralization.
1971 Women given the vote in federal
elections.
1984 First female cabinet minister appointed.
1986 Referendum rejected a proposal for
membership of United Nations.

---

gardens. The city dates from about 1000 BC, and
the name Suzhou from the 7th century AD; it was
reputedly visited by the Venetian Marco Polo.
Svalbard Norwegian archipelago in the Arctic
Ocean. The main island is Spitsbergen; other
islands include North East Land, Edge Island,
Barents Island, and Prince Charles Foreland.
area 62,000 sq km/23,938 sq mi
towns Long Year City on Spitsbergen
features weather and research stations. Wildlife
includes walrus and polar bear; fossil palms show
that it was in the tropics 40 million years ago
products coal, phosphates, asbestos, iron ore,
and galena are mined by the USSR and Norway
population (1982) 4,000, including 1,450 Nor-
wegians and 2,500 Russians
history under the *Svalbard Treaty* 1925, Norway has sovereignty, but allows free scientific and
economic access to others.
Sverdlovsk formerly *Ekaterinburg* (until 1924)
industrial town in W USSR, in the E foothills of
the Urals; population (1987) 1,331,000. Industries

include copper, iron, platinum, engineering, and
chemicals. Tsar Nicholas II and his family were
murdered here 1918.
Swanage town on the Isle of Purbeck, Dorset,
England.
Swansea (Welsh *Abertawe*) port and administra-
tive headquarters of West Glamorgan, S Wales,
at the mouth of the river Tawe where it meets
the Bristol Channel; population (1981) 168,000.
It has oil refineries and metallurgical industries,
and is the vehicle-licensing centre of the UK.
Swatow another name for the Chinese port of
◊Shantou.
Swaziland country in SE Africa, bounded by
Mozambique and the Transvaal province of South
Africa.
Sweden country in N Europe on the Baltic Sea,
bounded to the W by Norway and to the NE by
Finland.
Swindon town in Wiltshire, 124 km/77 mi west
of London, England; population (1981) 91,000.
Since 1841 the site of the British Rail Engineering

Syria
Syrian Arab Republic
(al-Jamhuriya al-Arabya as-Suriya)

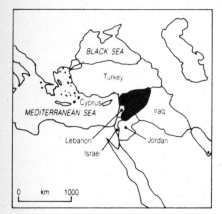

area 185,200 sq km/71,506 sq mi
capital Damascus
towns Aleppo, Homs, Hama; chief port Latakia
physical mountains alternate with fertile plains
and desert areas; river Euphrates
features Mount Hermon, Golan Heights;
crusader castles (Krak des Chevaliers);
Phoenician city sites (Ugarit)
head of state and government Hafez al-Assad
from 1971
government socialist republic
political parties National Progressive Front
(NPF), pro-Arab, socialist; Communist Action
Party, socialist
exports cotton, cereals, oil, phosphates
currency Syrian pound (official rate 35.75 = £1
Feb 1990)
population (1989) 12,210,000; annual growth
rate 3.5%

life expectancy men 61, women 64
language Arabic (official) 89%, Kurdish 6%,
Armenian 3%
religion Sunni Muslim, but the ruling minority is
Alawite, an Islamic sect; also Druse, again an
Islamic sect
literacy 76% male/43% female (1985 est)
GNP $16.5 bn (1983); $702 per head of
population
chronology
1946 Achieved full independence from France.
1958 Merged with Egypt to form the United
Arab Republic (UAR).
1961 UAR disintegrated.
1967 Six-Day War resulted in the loss of territory
to Israel.
1970–71 Syria supported Palestinian guerrillas
against Jordanian troops.
1971 Following a bloodless coup, Hafez
al-Assad became president.
1973 Israel consolidated its control of the Golan
Heights after the Yom Kippur War.
1976 Substantial numbers of troops committed
to the civil war in Lebanon.
1978 Assad re-elected.
1981–82 Further military engagements in
Lebanon.
1982 Islamic militant uprising suppressed;
5,000 dead.
1984 Presidents Assad and Gemayel approved
a plan for government of national unity in
Lebanon.
1985 Assad secured the release of US
hostages held in an aircraft hijacked by an
extremist Shi'ite group. Assad re-elected.
1987 Improved relations with US and attempts
to secure the release of western hostages in
Lebanon.
1989 Diplomatic relations with Morocco
restored. Continued fighting in Lebanon.

Works, it has diversified since 1950 into heavy
engineering, electronics, and electrical manufacture.

Switzerland landlocked country in W Europe,
bounded to the N by West Germany, to the
E by Austria, to the S by Italy, and to the W
by France.

Sydney capital and port of New South Wales,
Australia; population (1986) 3,431,000. Industries include engineering, oil refining, electronics, scientific equipment, chemicals, clothing, and
furniture. It is a financial centre, and has three
universities. The 19th-century Museun of Applied
Arts and Sciences is the most poular museum in
Australia.
history Originally a British penal colony 1788,

rapid development followed the discovery of gold
in the surrounding area. The main streets still
follow the lines of the original wagon tracks,
and the Regency Bligh House survives. Modern landmarks are the harbour bridge (single
span 503.5 m/1,652 ft) 1923–32; Opera House
1959–73; Centre Point Tower 1980.

Sydney Harbor or *Port Jackson* an inlet of the
Pacific Ocean on the E coast of New South Wales,
Australia. It is 12 km/8 mi long and 2.4 km/1.5 mi
wide at its mouth, with many coves, including the
Parramatta River.

Syktyvkar capital of Komi Republic, USSR; population (1987) 224,000. Industries include timber,
paper, and tanning. It was founded 1740 as a
Russian colony.

Sylhet capital of Sylhet region, NE Bangladesh; population (1981) 168,000. It is a tea-growing centre, and also produces rice, jute, and sugar. There is natural gas nearby. It is the former capital of a Hindu kingdom, and was conquered by Muslims in the 14th century. In the 1971 civil war, which led to the establishment of Bangladesh, it was the scene of heavy fighting.

Syracuse industrial city on Lake Onondaga, in New York State, USA; population (1980) 170,000. Industries include the manufacture of electrical and other machinery, paper, and food processing. There are canal links with the ◊Great Lakes, and the Hudson and St Lawrence rivers. Syracuse was founded 1805 on the site of an Iroquois Indian capital.

Syracuse (Italian *Siracusa*) industrial port (chemicals, salt) in E Sicily; population (1988) 124,000. It has a cathedral and remains of temples, aqueducts, catacombs, and an amphitheatre. Founded 734 BC by the Corinthians, it became a centre of Greek culture, especially under the elder and younger Dionysius. After a three-year siege it was taken by Rome 212 BC. In 878 it was destroyed by the Arabs, and the rebuilt town came under Norman rule in the 11th century.

Syria country in W Asia, on the Mediterranean, bounded to the N by Turkey, to the E by Iraq, to the S by Jordan, and to the SW by Israel and Lebanon.

Szczecin (German *Stettin*) industrial (shipbuilding, fish processing, synthetic fibres, tools, iron) port on the river Oder, in NW Poland; population (1989) 391,000.

A Hanseatic port from 1278, it was Swedish 1648–1720, when it was taken by Prussia. It was Germany's chief Baltic port until captured by the Russians 1945, and came under Polish adminis- tration. Catherine the Great of Russia was born here.

Szechwan alternative spelling for the central Chinese province of ◊Sichuan.

Szeged port on river Tisza, and capital of Csongrad county, S Hungary; population (1988) 188,000. The chief industry is textiles, and the port trades in timber and salt.

Székesfehérvár industrial city in W central Hungary; population (1988) 113,000. It is a market centre for wine, tobacco, and fruit, and manufactures metal products.

T

Tabah or *Taba* small area of disputed territory, 1 km long, between Eilat (Israel) to the E and the Sinai Desert (Egypt) to the W on the Red Sea. Under an Anglo-Egyptian-Turkish agreement 1906, the border ran through Tabah; under a British survey of 1915 headed by T E Lawrence (who made 'adjustments' allegedly under British government orders) it runs to the east. Taken by Israel 1967, it was returned to Egypt 1989.

Table Bay inlet on the SW coast of the Cape of Good Hope, South Africa, on which Cape Town stands. It is overlooked by Table Mountain (highest point Maclear's Beacon 1,087 m/3,568 ft), the cloud often above it being known as the 'tablecloth'.

Tabora trading centre in W Tanzania; population (1978) 67,400. It was founded about 1820 by Arab traders of slaves and ivory.

Tabriz city in NW Iran; population (1986) 972,000. Industries include metal casting, carpets, cotton, and silk textiles.

Tacna city in S Peru; population (1988) 138,000. It is undergoing industrial development. In 1880 Chile defeated a combined Peruvian-Bolivian army nearby, and occupied Tacna until 1929.

Tacoma port in Washington State, USA, on Puget Sound, 40 km/25 mi south of Seattle; population (1980) 483,000. Founded 1868, it developed after being chosen as the terminus of the North Pacific Railroad 1873.

Tadzhikistan constituent republic of the S central USSR from 1929, part of Soviet Central Asia
area 143,100 sq km/55,251 sq mi
capital Dushanbe
features few areas are below 3,500 m/11,000 ft; includes ◊Communism Peak; health resorts and mineral springs

products fruit, cereals, cotton, cattle, sheep, silks, carpets, coal, lead, zinc, chemicals, oil, gas
population (1987) 4,807,000; 59% Tadzhik, 23% Uzbek, 11% Russian or Ukrainian
language Tadzhik, similar to Farsi (Persian)
religion Sunni Muslim
recent history formed 1924 from the Tadzhik areas of Bokhara and Turkestan. It experienced a devastating earthquake Jan 1989 (274 people died) and ethnic conflict 1989–90. In Dushanbe, 18 were killed in Feb 1990 in rioting against Communist Party headquarters after claims that Christian Armenians from ◊Azerbaijan were being provided with housing before Tadzhiks.

Taegu largest inland city of South Korea after Seoul; population (1985) 2,031,000.

Taejon capital of South Chungchong province, central South Korea; population (1985) 866,000. Korea's tallest standing Buddha and oldest wooden building are found NE of the city at Popchusa in the Mount Songnisan National Park.

Taganrog port in the NE corner of the Sea of Azov, S USSR, west of Rostov; population (1987) 295,000. Industries include iron, steel, metal goods, aircraft, machinery, and shoes. A museum commemorates the playwright Chekhov, who was born here.

Tagus (Spanish *Tajo*, Portuguese *Tejo*) river rising in Aragon, Spain, and reaching the Atlantic at Lisbon, Portugal; length 1,007 km/626 mi. At Lisbon it is crossed by the April 25 (formerly Salazar) Bridge, so named in honour of the 1974 revolution. The *Tagus-Segura* irrigation scheme serves the rainless Murcia/Alicante region for early fruit and vegetable growing.

Tahiti largest of the Society Islands, in ◊French Polynesia; area 1,042 sq km/402 sq mi; population (1983) 116,000. Its capital is Papeete. Tahiti

Tadzhikistan

Taiwan
Republic of China
(Chung Hua Min Kuo)

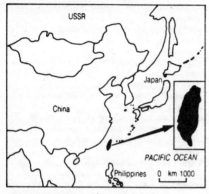

area 36,179 sq km/13,965 sq mi
capital Taipei
towns ports Keelung, Kaohsiung
physical island (formerly Formosa) off the coast of the People's Republic of China; mountainous, with lowlands in the W
features Penghu (Pescadores), Jinmen (Quemoy), and Mazu (Matsu) islands
head of state Lee Teng-hui from 1988
head of government Lee Huan from 1989
government system emergent democracy
political parties Nationalist Party of China (Kuomintang: KMT), anti-communist, Chinese nationalist; Democratic Progressive Party (DPP), centrist-pluralist, though internally highly-factionalized, pro-self determination grouping;

Workers party (Kungtang), left-of-centre.
exports with US aid, Taiwan is highly industrialized: textiles, petrochemicals, steel, plastics, electronics
currency Taiwan dollar (44.50 = £1 Mar 1990)
population (1989) 20,283,000 (89% Taiwanese, 11% mainlanders whose dominance causes resentment); annual growth rate 1.4%
language Mandarin Chinese
religion officially atheist, but traditional religions are Taoist, Confucian, and Buddhist
literacy 89% (1983)
GNP $56.6 bn (1984); $3,000 per head of population
chronology
1683 Taiwan (Formosa) annexed by China.
1895 Ceded to Japan.
1945 Recovered by China.
1949 Flight of Nationalist government to Taiwan after Chinese revolution.
1954 US-Taiwanese mutual defence treaty.
1971 Expulsion from United Nations.
1972 Commencement of legislature elections.
1975 President Chiang Kai-shek died and was replaced as Kuomintang leader by his son, Chiang Ching-kuo.
1979 US severed diplomatic relations and annulled security pact.
1986 Formation of first opposition party to the Nationalist Kuomintang.
1987 Martial law lifted.
1988 President Chiang Ching-kuo died and was replaced by Taiwanese-born Lee Teng-hui.
1989 Kuomintang win in first free assembly elections.

was visited by Capt James Cook 1769 and by Bligh of the *Bounty* 1788. It came under French control 1843 and became a colony 1880. It has attracted artists such as Gauguin, and modern tourists.

Taipei (mainland spelling *Taibei*) capital and commercial centre of Taiwan; population (1987) 2,640,000. Industries include electronics, plastics, textiles, and machinery. The National Palace Museum 1965 houses the world's greatest collection of Chinese art, taken there from the mainland 1948.

Taiwan country in SE Asia, officially the Republic of China, occupying the island of Taiwan between the E China Sea and the S China Sea.

Taiyuan capital of Shanxi province, NE China; population (1986) 1,880,000. Industries include iron, steel, agricultural machinery, and textiles. It is a walled city, founded in the 5th century AD,

on the river Fen He, and is the seat of Shanxi university.

Ta'iz third largest city of North Yemen; situated in the south of the country at the centre of a coffee-growing region, population (1980) 119,500. Cotton, leather, and jewellery are also produced.

Tajo Spanish name for the river ◊Tagus.

Takao Japanese name for ◊Kaohsiung, a city on the W coast of Taiwan.

Takoradi port in Ghana, administered with ◊Sekondi.

Talavera de la Reina town in Castilla-Léon, central Spain, on the Tagus, 120 km/75 mi SW of Madrid; population (1970) 46,000. It produces soap, pharmaceuticals, and textiles. Spanish and British forces defeated the French here in the Peninsular War 1809.

Talcahuano port and chief naval base in Biobio region, Chile; population (1987) 231,000. Industries include oil refining and timber.

Talien part of the port of ◊Lüda, China.

Tallahassee capital of Florida, USA; population (1980) 82,000. It is an agricultural and lumbering centre. The explorer De Soto found an Indian settlement here 1539. It has many pre–Civil War mansions.

Tallinn (German *Reval*) naval port and capital of Estonian Republic, NW USSR; population (1987) 478,000. Industries include electrical and oil drilling machinery, textiles, and paper. Founded 1219, it was a member of the Hanseatic League, passed to Sweden 1561, and to Russia 1750. Vyshgorod castle (13th century) and other medieval buildings remain. It is a yachting centre.

Tamale town in NE Ghana; population (1982) 227,000. It is a commercial centre, dealing in rice, cotton, and peanuts.

Tamar river rising in N Cornwall, England, and flowing to Plymouth Sound; for most of its 97 km/ 60 mi length it forms the Devon-Cornwall border.

Tamar river flowing into Bass Strait, Tasmania, formed by the union of the N and S Esk; length 65 km/40 mi.

Tamatave former name (until 1979) for ◊Toamasina, the chief port of Madagascar.

Tambov city in W central USSR; population (1987) 305,000. Industries include engineering, flour milling, and the manufacture of rubber and synthetic chemicals.

Tamil Nadu state of SE India; former name to 1968 *Madras State*
area 130,100 sq km/50,219 sq mi
capital Madras
products mainly industrial (cotton, textiles, silk, electrical machinery, tractors, rubber, sugar refining)
population (1981) 48,297,000
language Tamil
history the present state was formed 1956. Tamil Nadu comprises part of the former British Madras presidency (later province) formed from areas taken from France and Tipu Sahib, the sultan of Mysore, in the 18th century, which became a state of the Republic of India 1950. The NE was detached to form Andhra Pradesh 1953; other areas went to Kerala and Mysore (now Karnataka) 1956, and the Laccadive Islands (now Lakshadweep) became a separate Union Territory.

Tampa port and resort in W Florida, USA; population (1986) 279,000. Industries include fruit and vegetable canning, shipbuilding, and the manufacture of fertilizers, clothing, and cigars.

Tampere (Swedish *Tammerfors*) city in SW Finland; population (1988) 171,000, metropolitan area 258,000. It is the second largest city in Finland. Industries include textiles, paper, footwear, and turbines.

Tampico port on the Rio Pánuco, 10 km/6 mi from the Gulf of Mexico, in Tamaulipas state, Mexico;

population (1980) 268,000. Industries include oil refining and fishing.

Tamworth town in Staffordshire, England, on the Tame, NE of Birmingham; population (1981) 64,000. Industries include engineering, paper, and clothing.

Tamworth dairying centre with furniture industry in New South Wales, Australia, on the river Peel; population (1984) 34,000.

Tana lake in Ethiopia, 1,800 m/5,900 ft above sea level; area 3,600 sq km/1,390 sq mi. It is the source of the Blue Nile.

Tananarive former name for ◊Antananarivo, the capital of Madagascar.

Tanga seaport and capital of Tanga region, NE Tanzania, on the Indian Ocean; population (1978) 103,000. The port trades in sisal, fruit, cocoa, tea, and fish.

Tanganyika former British colony in E Africa, which now forms the mainland of ◊Tanzania.

Tanganyika, Lake lake 772 m/2,534 ft above sea level in the Great Rift Valley, E Africa, with Zaïre to the west, Zambia to the south, and Tanzania and Burundi to the east. It is about 645 km/ 400 mi long, with an area of about 31,000 sq km/ 12,000 sq mi, and is the deepest lake in Africa (1,435 m/4,710 ft). The mountains around its shores rise to about 2,700 m/8,860 ft. The chief ports are Bujumbura (Burundi), Kigoma (Tanzania), and Kalé mié (Zaïre).

Tangier or *Tangiers* or *Tanger* port in N Morocco, on the Strait of Gibraltar; population (1982) 436,227. It was an important Phoenician trading centre in the 15th century BC. It was captured by the Portuguese 1471, passed to England 1662 as part of the dowry of Catherine of Braganza, but was abandoned 1684 and later became a lair of Barbary pirates. From 1923, Tangier and a small surrounding enclave became an international zone, which was administered by Spain 1940–45. In 1956 it was transferred to independent Morocco, and became a free port 1962.

Tangshan industrial city in Hebei province, China; population (1986) 1,390,000. Almost destroyed by an earthquake 1976, with 200,000 killed, it was rebuilt on a new site, coal seams being opened up under the old city.

Tannu-Tuva former independent republic in NE Asia; see ◊Tuva.

Tanzania country in E Africa, on the Indian Ocean, bounded to the N by Uganda and Kenya, to the S by Mozambique, Malawi, and Zambia, and to the W by Zaïre, Burundi, and Rwanda.

Taormina coastal resort in E Sicily, at the foot of Mount Etna; population (1985) 9,000. It has an ancient Greek theatre.

Tara Hill ancient religious and political centre in County Meath, S Ireland. The site of a palace and coronation place of many Irish kings, abandoned in the 6th century. St Patrick preached here.

Tanzania
United Republic of
(Jamhuri ya Muungano wa Tanzania)

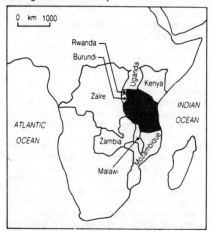

area 945,000 sq km/364,865 sq mi
capital Dodoma
towns chief port Dar es Salaam
physical a central plateau with lakes in the west and coastal plains
features comprises the islands of Zanzibar and nearby Pemba; Mount Kilimanjaro, called 'shining mountain', because of snow and glaciers which crown it (Kibo, an extinct volcano and its highest peak, is the highest mountain in Africa 5,895 m/19,347 ft); parts of Lakes Victoria and Tanganyika; Serengeti National Park, and the Olduvai Gorge; Ngorongoro Crater 14.5 km/9 mi across and 762 m/2,500 ft deep
head of state and government Ali Hassan Mwinyi from 1985
government system one-party socialist republic
political parties Revolutionary Party of Tanzania (CCM), African, socialist.
exports coffee, cotton, sisal, cloves from Zanzibar, tea, tobacco
currency Tanzanian shilling (327.80 = £1 Mar 1990)
population (1989) 24,746,000; annual growth rate 3.5%
life expectancy men 49, women 53
language Kiswahili, English (both official)
religion Muslim 35%, Christian 35%, traditional 30%
literacy 78% male/70% female (1978)
GNP $4.9 bn (1983); $225 per head of population
chronology
1961 Tanganyika achieved full independence, within the Commonwealth, with Julius Nyerere as prime minister.
1962 Tanganyika became a republic with Nyerere as president.
1964 Tanganyika and Zanzibar became the United Republic of Tanzania with Nyerere as president.
1967 East African Community (EAC) formed. Arusha Declaration.
1977 Revolutionary Party of Tanzania (CCM) proclaimed the only legal party. EAC dissolved.
1979 Tanzanian troops sent to Uganda to help overthrow the president, Idi Amin.
1984 Nyerere announced his retirement but stayed on as CCM leader. Prime Minister Edward Sokoine killed in a road accident.
1985 Ali Hassan Mwinyi elected president.

Taranaki peninsula in North Island, New Zealand, dominated by Mount ◊Egmont; volcanic soil makes it a rich dairy-farming area, noted for cheese.

Taranto naval base and port in Puglia region, SE Italy; population (1988) 245,000. An important commercial centre, its steelworks are part of the new industrial complex of S Italy. It was the site of the ancient Greek *Tarentum*, founded in the 8th century BC by Sparta, and was captured by the Romans 272 BC.

Tarawa port and capital of Kiribati; population (1985) 21,000.

Tarbes capital of Hautes-Pyrénées *département*, SW France, a tourist centre for the Pyrenees; population (1983) 55,000. It belonged to England 1360–1406.

Taree town in a dairying area of NE New South Wales, Australia; population (1981) 16,000.

Tarim Basin (Chinese *Tarim Pendi*) internal drainage area in Xinjiang Uygur province, NW China, between the Tien Shan and Kunlun Mountains; area about 900,000 sq km/350,000 sq mi. It is crossed by the Tarim He river, and includes the lake of Lop Nur. The Taklimakan desert lies to the south of the Tarim He.

Tarn river in SW France, rising in the Cévennes and flowing 350 km/217 mi to the Garonne. It cuts the limestone plateaux in picturesque gorges.

Tarragona port in Catalonia, Spain; population (1986) 110,000. Industries include petrochemicals, pharmaceuticals, and electrical goods. It has a cathedral and Roman remains, including an aqueduct and amphitheatre.

Tarrasa town in Catalonia, NE Spain; industries include textiles and fertilizers; population (1986) 160,000.

Tasmania

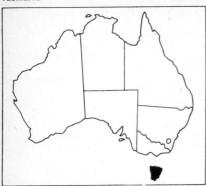

Tarsus city in Içel province, SE Turkey, on the river Pamuk; population (1980) 121,000. Formerly the capital of the Roman province of Cilicia, and the birthplace of St Paul.

Tartu city in Estonian Republic, USSR; industries include engineering and food processing; population (1981) 107,000. Once a stronghold of the Teutonic Knights, it was taken by Russia 1558, and then held by Sweden and Poland, but has been under Russian control since 1704.

Tas. abbreviation for ◊*Tasmania*.

Tashkent capital of Uzbekistan, S central USSR; population (1987) 2,124,000. Industries include the manufacture of mining machinery, chemicals, textiles, and leather goods. Founded in the 7th century, it was taken by the Turks in the 12th century, and captured by Tamerlane 1361. In 1865 it was taken by the Russians. It was severely damaged by an earthquake 1966.

A temporary truce between Pakistan and India over ◊Kashmir was established at the Declaration of Tashkent 1966.

Tasmania island off the S coast of Australia, a state of the Commonwealth of Australia
area 67,800 sq km/26,171 sq mi
capital Hobart
towns chief port Launceston
features an island state (including small islands in the Bass Strait, and Macquarie Island); Franklin river, a wilderness area saved from a hydroelectric scheme 1983, which also has a prehistoric site; unique fauna include Tasmanian devil, Tasmanian 'tiger'
products wool, dairy products, apples and other fruit, timber, iron, tin, coal, copper, silver
population (1987) 448,000
history the first European to visit Tasmania was Abel Tasman 1642; it joined the Australian Commonwealth as a state 1901. The last of the Tasmanian Aboriginals died 1876.

Tasman Sea the part of the ◊Pacific Ocean between SE Australia and NW New Zealand. It is named after the Dutch explorer Abel Tasman.

Tatar Autonomous Republic administrative region of W central USSR
capital Kazan
area 68,000 sq km/26,250 sq mi
population (1986) 3,537,000
products oil, chemicals, textiles, timber
history territory of Volga-Kama Bulgar state 10th–13th centuries; conquered by Mongols until 15th century; conquered by Russia 1552; became an autonomous republic 1920.

Tatra Mountains range in central Europe, extending for about 65 km/40 mi along the Polish-Czechoslovakian border; the highest part of the central ◊Carpathians.

Taunton market town and administrative headquarters of Somerset, England; population (1985) 56,000. The Elizabethan hall survives, in which Judge Jeffreys held the Bloody Assizes 1685 after the Duke of Monmouth's rebellion.

Taunus Mountains mountain range in Hessen, West Germany, noted for its mineral spas.

Taupo largest lake in New Zealand, in a volcanic area of hot springs; area 620 sq km/239 sq mi. It is the source of the Waikato river.

Tauranga port in North Island, New Zealand; exports (citrus fruit, dairy produce, timber); population (1986) 59,000.

Taurus Mountains (Turkish *Toros Dağlari*) mountain range in S Turkey, forming the southern edge of the Anatolian plateau, and rising to over 3,656 m/12,000 ft.

Tavistock market town 24 km/15 mi N of Plymouth, Devon, England; population (1981) 9,000.

Tay the longest river in Scotland; length 189 km/118 mi. Rising in NW Central region, it flows NE through Loch Tay, then E and SE past Perth to the Firth of Tay, crossed at Dundee by the Tay Bridge, before joining the North Sea. The Tay has important salmon fisheries; its main tributaries are the Tummel, Isla, and Earn.

Tayside region of Scotland
area 7,700 sq km/2,973 sq mi
towns administrative headquarters Dundee; Perth, Arbroath, Forfar
features river Tay; ◊Grampian Mountains; Lochs Tay and Rannoch; Ochil and Sidlaw Hills; vales of the North and South Esk
products beef and dairy products, soft fruit from the fertile Carse of Gowrie (SW of Dundee)
population (1987) 394,000
famous people James Barrie.

Tbilisi formerly *Tiflis* capital of the Georgian Republic, SW USSR; population (1987) 1,194,000. Industries include textiles, machinery, ceramics, and tobacco. Dating from the 5th century AD, it is a centre of Georgian culture, with fine medieval churches. Anti-Russian demonstrations were

Tayside

Tennessee

sugar, printing, and publishing. Tel Aviv was founded 1909 as a Jewish residential area in the Arab town of Jaffa, with which it was combined 1949; their ports were superseded 1965 by Ashdod to the south.

Tema port in Ghana; population (1982) 324,000. It has the largest artificial harbour in Africa, opened 1962, as well as oil refineries and a fishing industry.

Temuco market town and capital of Araucanía region, Chile; population (1987) 218,000.

Tenerife largest of the ◊Canary Islands, Spain; area 2,060 sq km/795 sq mi; population (1981) 557,000. *Santa Cruz* is the main town, and *Pico de Teide* is an active volcano.

Tennessee state of the E central USA; nickname Volunteer State

area 109,200 sq km/42,151 sq mi

capital Nashville

towns Memphis, Knoxville, Chattanooga, Clarksville

features Tennessee Valley Authority; Great Smoky Mountains National Park; Grand Old Opry, Nashville; research centres include Oak Ridge and the Arnold Engineering Development Centre for aircraft

products cereals, cotton, tobacco, timber, coal, zinc, pyrites, phosphates, iron, steel, chemicals

population (1987) 4,855,000

famous people Davy Crockett, David Farragut, W C Handy, Bessie Smith

history first settled 1757, it became a state 1796.

Teplice industrial (peat- and lignite-mining, glass, porcelain, cement, paper) city and spa in Czechoslovakia; population (1984) 54,000.

Terengganu alternate spelling of ◊Trengganu, state in Peninsular Malaysia.

Terni industrial city in the valley of the Nera river, Umbria region, central Italy; population (1987) 111,000. The nearby Marmore Falls, the highest in Italy, were created by the Romans in order to drain the Rieti marshes.

Terre Adélie French name for ◊Adélie Land, Antarctica.

quashed here by troops 1981 and 1989, the latter following rejected demands for autonomy from Abkhazia enclave, resulting in 19 or more deaths from poison gas (containing chloroacetophenone) and 100 injured.

Teddington part of Twickenham, in the Greater London borough of ◊Richmond upon Thames; site of the National Physical Laboratory, established 1900.

Tees river flowing from the Pennines in Cumbria, England, to the North Sea via Tees Bay in ◊Cleveland; length 130 km/80 mi.

Teesside industrial area at the mouth of the river Tees, Cleveland, NE England; population (1981) 382,700. Industries include high-technology, capital-intensive steelmaking, chemicals, an oilfuel terminal, and the main North Sea natural-gas terminal. Middlesbrough is a major port.

Tegucigalpa capital of Honduras, population (1986) 605,000. It has textile and food-processing industries. It was founded 1524 as a gold and silver mining centre.

Tehran capital of Iran; population (1986) 6,043,000. Industries include textiles, chemicals, engineering, and tobacco. It was founded in the 12th century, and made the capital 1788 by Muhammad Shah. Much of the city was rebuilt in the 1920s and 1930s. Tehran is the site of the Gulistan Palace (the former royal residence).

Teignmouth port and resort in S Devon, England, at the mouth of the Teign; population (1985) 14,000.

Tejo Portuguese name for the river ◊Tagus.

Tel Aviv officially *Tel Aviv-Jaffa* city in Israel, on the Mediterranean Sea; population (1987) 320,000. Industries include textiles, chemicals,

Texas

Terre Haute city in W Indiana, USA, on the Wabash; industries (plastics, chemicals, glass); population (1980) 61,000.

Tethys Sea sea which once separated ◊Laurasia from ◊Gondwanaland; roughly corresponding to the present-day Mediterranean.

Tetuán or **Tétouan** town in NE Morocco, near the Mediterranean coast, 64 km/40 mi SE of Tangier; population (1982) 372,000. Products include textiles, leather, and soap. It was settled by Moorish exiles from Spain in the 16th century.

Texas state of the SW USA; nickname Lone Star State
area 691,200 sq km/266,803 sq mi
capital Austin
towns Houston, Dallas-Fort Worth, San Antonio, El Paso, Corpus Christi, Lubbock
features Rio Grande del Norte and Red rivers; arid Staked Plains, reclaimed by irrigation; the Great Plains
products rice, cotton, sorghum, peanuts, pecans, vegetables, fruit, meat products, oil (one third of the needs of the USA), natural gas, asphalt, graphite, sulphur, salt, helium, chemicals, oil products, processed food, machinery, transport equipment
population (1985) 16,370,000
famous people James Bowie, Buddy Holly, Sam Houston, Howard Hughes, Lyndon Johnson, Janis Joplin, Katherine Ann Porter
history settled by the Spanish 1682; part of Mexico 1821–36; Santa Anna massacred the Alamo garrison 1836, but was defeated by Sam Houston at San Jacinto the same year; Texas became an independent republic 1836–45, with Houston as president; in 1845 it became a state of the USA.

Texas is the only state in the USA to have previously been an independent republic.

Texel or **Tessel** largest and most westerly of the ◊Frisian Islands, in North Holland province, the Netherlands; area 190 sq km/73 sq mi. Den Burg is the chief settlement.

Thailand country in SE Asia on the Gulf of Siam, bounded to the E by Laos and Kampuchea, to the S by Malaysia, and to the W by Myanmar (Burma).

Thames river in SE England; length 338 km/210 mi. It rises in the Cotswolds above Cirencester, and is tidal as far as Teddington. Below London there is protection from flooding by means of the Thames barrier. The headstreams unite at Lechlade. Tributaries from the north are the Windrush, Evenlode, Cherwell, Thame, Colne, Lea, and Roding; and from the south, Kennet, Loddon, Wey, Mole, Darent, and Medway. Above Oxford it is sometimes poetically called *Isis*.

Thames, Firth of inlet between Auckland and the Coromandel Peninsula, New Zealand.

Thanet, Isle of NE corner of Kent, England, bounded by the North Sea and the river Stour. It was an island until the 16th century, and includes the coastal resorts of Broadstairs, Margate, and Ramsgate.

Thar Desert or **Indian Desert** desert on the borders of ◊Rajasthan and Pakistan; area about 250,000 sq km/96,500 sq mi.

Thessaloniki (English *Salonika*) port in Macedonia, NE Greece, at the head of the Gulf of Thessaloniki, the second largest city of Greece; population (1981) 706,200. Industries include textiles, shipbuilding, chemicals, brewing, and tanning. It was founded from Corinth by the Romans 315 BC as *Thessalonica* (to whose inhabitants St Paul addressed two epistles), captured by the Saracens 904 AD, by the Turks 1430, and restored to Greece 1912.

Thessaly (Greek *Thessalia*) region of E central Greece, on the Aegean; area 13,904 sq km/5,367 sq mi; population (1981) 695,650. It is a major area of cereal production. It was an independent state in ancient Greece, and later formed part of the Roman province of ◊Macedonia. It was Turkish from the 14th century until incorporated in Greece 1881.

Thetford market town in Norfolk, England; population (1982) 19,000. It is the birthplace of Thomas Paine.

Thetford Mines site of the world's largest asbestos deposits, 80 km/50 mi S of Québec, Canada; discovered 1876.

Thimbu or **Thimphu** capital since 1962 of the Himalayan state of Bhutan; population (1982) 15,000.

Thousand Islands group of about 1,500 islands on the border between Canada and the USA in the upper St Lawrence River.

Thrace (Greek *Thráki*) ancient empire (6000 BC–300 AD) in the Balkans, SE Europe, formed by parts of Greece and Bulgaria. It was held successively by the Greeks, Persians, Macedonians, and Romans.

The area was divided 1923 into western Thrace (the Greek province of Thráki) and eastern Thrace (European Turkey). However, the heart of the ancient Thracian Empire was Bulgaria, where since 1945 there have been tomb finds of gold and silver dishes,

Thailand
Kingdom of
(Prathet Thai or *Muang-Thai)*

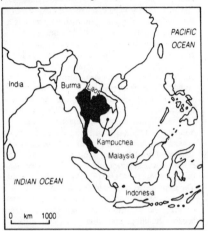

area 513,100 sq km/198,108 sq mi
capital and chief port Bangkok
towns Chiangmai
physical central valley flanked by highlands;
tropical rainforest
features rivers Chao Phraya, Mekong,
Salween; tools and weapons from the Bronze
Age
head of state King Bhumibol Adulyadej
from 1946
head of government Chatichai Choonhavan
from 1988
government system emergent democracy
political parties Thai Ntion (Chart Thai)
conservative, pro-business; Democratic Party
(Prachipat) right-of-centre, pro-monarchist; Social
Action Party (Kij Sangkhom) right-of-centre; Citi-

zen's Party (Rassadorn) conservative; Solidarity
Party (Ekkaparb), right-of-centre opposition force
formed through mergers in 1989; Thai Citizens'
party (Prachakorn Thai) far-right, monarchist;
the Righteous Force (Palang Dharma), a
Bangkok-based anti-corruption, Buddhist
grouping
exports rice, sugar, rubber, teak, tin (fifth
largest producer), rubies, sapphires
currency baht (43.20 = £1 Mar 1990)
population (1989) 55,017,000 (Thai 75%,
Chinese 14%); annual growth rate 2%
life expectancy men 61, women 65
language Thai and Chinese (both official)
religion Buddhist
literacy 94% male/88% female (1985 est)
GNP $42 bn (1985); $828 per head of
population
chronology
1782 Siam absolutist dynasty commenced.
1896 Anglo-French agreement recognized Siam
as independent buffer state.
1932 Constitutional monarchy established.
1939 Name of Thailand adopted.
1941–44 Japanese occupation.
1947 Military seized power in coup.
1972 Withdrawal of Thai troops from South
Vietnam.
1973 Military government overthrown.
1976 Military reassumed control.
1980 Gen Prem Tinsulanonda assumed power.
1983 Civilian government formed but martial
law maintained.
1988 Prime Minister Prem resigned and
was replaced by the conservative Chatichai
Choonhavan.
1989 Thai pirates continued to murder, pillage,
and kidnap Vietnamese 'boat people' on the
high seas.

---

drinking vessels, and jewellery with animal designs. The legend of Orpheus and the cult of Dionysus were both derived by the Greeks from Thrace. The area was conquered by Persia 6th–5th centuries BC and by Macedon 4th–2nd centuries BC. From 46 AD it was a Roman province, then part of the Byzantine Empire, and Turkish from the 15th century until 1878; it was then subject to constant dispute until after World War I.

Three Mile Island an island in the Shenandoah River near Harrisburg, Pennsylvania. The site of a nuclear power station which was put out of action following a major accident in Mar 1979. Opposition to nuclear power in the USA was reinforced after this accident and safety standards reassessed.

Three Rivers English name for the Canadian port of ◊Trois-Rivières.

Thule Greek and Roman name for the most northerly land known. It was applied to the Shetlands, the Orkneys, and Iceland, and by later writers to Scandinavia.

Thunder Bay city and port on Lake Superior, Ontario, Canada, formed by the union of Port Arthur and its twin city of Fort William to the south; industries include shipbuilding, timber, paper, wood pulp, and export of wheat; population (1986) 122,000.

Thuringia former state of central Germany 1919–46; capital Weimar. The area includes the

Thuringian Forest. Thuringia was a *Land* until 1952, when it became the East German counties of Erfurt, Gera, and Suhl.

Thursday Island island in Torres Strait, Queensland, Australia; area 4 sq km/1.5 sq mi; chief centre Port Kennedy. It is a centre of the pearl-fishing industry.

Thurso port in Highland region, Scotland. It is the mainland terminus of the steamer service to the Orkneys, and the experimental atomic station of Dounreay lies to the west.

Tianjin formerly *Tientsin* port and industrial and commercial city in Hubei province, central China; population (1986) 5,380,000. The special municipality of Tianjin has an area of 4,000 sq km/1,544 sq mi, and a population of 8,190,000. Its handmade silk and wool carpets are renowned. Dagan oilfield is nearby. Tianjin was opened to foreign trade 1860, and occupied by the Japanese 1937.

Tian Shan (Chinese *Tien Shan*) mountain system on the Soviet-Chinese border. *Pik Pobedy* on the Xinjiang–Kirghizia border is the highest peak at 7,439 m/24,415 ft.

The British climber Chris Bonington led the expedition that first reached the summit of Kongur Shan 1981.

Tiber (Italian *Tevere*) river in Italy on which Rome stands; length from the Apennines to the Tyrrhenian Sea 400 km/250 mi.

Tiberias, Lake or *Sea of Galilee* lake in N Israel, 210 m/689 ft below sea level, into which the ◊Jordan flows; area 170 sq km/66 sq mi. The first Israeli kibbutz (cooperative settlement) was founded nearby 1909.

Tibesti Mountains range in the central Sahara, N Chad; highest peak *Emi Koussi* 3,415 m/11,208 ft.

Tibet autonomous region of SW China (Pinyin form *Xizang*)
area 1,221,600 sq km/471,538 sq mi
capital Lhasa
features Tibet occupies a barren plateau bounded S and SW by the Himalayas and N by the Kunlun Mountains, traversed W–E by the Bukamagna, Karakoram, and other ranges, and having an average elevation of 4,000–4,500 m/13,000–15,000 ft. The Sutlej, Brahmaputra, and Indus rivers rise in Tibet, which has numerous lakes, many of which are salty. The yak is the most important domestic animal
government Tibet is an autonomous region of China, with its own People's Government and People's Congress. The controlling force in Tibet is the Communist Party of China, represented locally by First Secretary Wu Jinghua from 1985
products wool, borax, salt, horn, musk, herbs, furs, gold, iron pyrites, lapis lazuli, mercury, textiles, chemicals, agricultural machinery

population (1986) 2,030,000; many Chinese have settled in Tibet
religion traditionally Lamaist (a form of Mahayana Buddhism)
history Tibet was an independent kingdom from the 5th century AD. It came under nominal Chinese suzerainty about 1700. Independence was regained after a revolt 1912. China regained control 1951 when the historic ruler and religious leader, the Dalai Lama, was driven from the country and the monks (who formed 25% of the population) were forced out of the monasteries. Between 1951 and 1959 the Chinese People's Liberation Army (PLA) controlled Tibet, although the Dalai Lama returned as nominal spiritual and temporal head of state. In 1959 a Tibetan uprising spread from bordering regions to Lhasa and was supported by the Tibet local government. The rebellion was suppressed by the PLA, prompting the Dalai Lama and 9,000 Tibetans to flee to India. The Chinese proceeded to dissolve the Tibet local government, abolish serfdom, collectivize agriculture, and suppress Lamaism. In 1965 Tibet became an autonomous region of China. Chinese rule continued to be resented, however, and the economy languished.

From 1979, the leadership in Beijing adopted a more liberal and pragmatic policy towards Tibet. Traditional agriculture, livestock, and trading practices were restored (under the 1980 slogan 'relax, relax, and relax again'), a number of older political leaders and rebels were rehabilitated or pardoned, and the promotion of local Tibetan cadres was encouraged. In addition, a more tolerant attitude towards Lamaism has been adopted (temples damaged during the 1965–68 Cultural Revolution are being repaired) and attempts, thus far unsuccessful, have been made to persuade the Dalai Lama to return from exile.

Pro-independence demonstrations erupted in Lhasa in Sept–Oct 1987, repeatedly throughout 1988, and in March 1989 and were forcibly suppressed by Chinese troops. In May and Oct 1988 peacefully demonstrating monks and civilians were shot by police. In 1989 many anti-China demonstrators were shot and all foreigners were expelled. These clashes exhibit the continuing strength of nationalist feeling. The country is one of immense strategic importance to China, being the site of 50,000–100,000 troops and a major nuclear missile base at Nagchuka.

Tien Shan Chinese form of ◊Tian Shan, a mountain system of central Asia.

Tientsin former name for ◊Tianjin, an industrial city in NE China.

Tierra del Fuego island group divided between Chile and Argentina. It is separated from the mainland of South America by the Strait of Magellan, and Cape Horn is at the southernmost point. Ushuaia, Argentina is the chief town, and the world's most southerly town. Industries include oil and sheep farming.

To the south of the main island is **Beagle Channel** (named after the ship of Charles Darwin's voyage) with three islands at the east end, finally awarded 1985 to Chile rather than Argentina.

Tiflis former name (until 1936) of the city of ◊Tbilisi in the USSR.

Tigray or **Tigré** region in the northern highlands of Ethiopia; area 65,900 sq km/25,444 sq mi. Chief town is Mekele. The region had an estimated population of 2.4 million in 1984, at a time when drought and famine were driving large numbers of people to fertile land in the south or into neighbouring Sudan. Since 1978 a guerrilla group known as the Tigray People's Liberation Front has been fighting for regional autonomy.

Tigris (Arabic **Shatt Dijla**) river flowing through Turkey and Iraq (see also ◊Mesopotamia), joining the ◊Euphrates above Basra, where it forms the ◊Shatt-al-Arab; length 1,600 km/1,000 mi.

Tijuana city and resort in NW Mexico; population (1980) 461,257; noted for horse races and casinos. ◊San Diego adjoins it across the US border.

Tilbury port in Essex, on the N bank of the Thames; population (1981) 12,000. Greatly extended 1976, it became London's largest container port. It dates from Roman times.

Tilsit former name (until 1945) of the Soviet town of ◊Sovetsk.

Timaru industrial port and resort in South Island, New Zealand; industries include flour milling, deep freezing, pottery, and brewing; population (1983) 29,000.

Timbuktu or **Tombouctou** town in Mali; population (1976) 20,500. A camel caravan centre from the 11th century on the fringe of the Sahara, since 1960 it has been surrounded by the southward movement of the desert, and the former canal link with the Niger is dry. Products include salt.

Timişoara capital of Timiş county, W Romania; population (1985) 319,000. The revolt against the Ceauşescu regime began here in Dec 1989 when a crowd of demonstrators prevented the arrest and deportation of Laszlo Tokes, a popular Protestant minister who was actively promoting the rights of ethnic Hungarians. This soon led to full-scale pro-democracy rallies.

Timor largest and most easterly of the Sunda Islands, part of Indonesia; area 33,610 sq km/12,973 sq mi. **West Timor** (capital Kupang) was formerly Dutch and was included in Indonesian independence. **East Timor** (capital Dili) was an overseas province of Portugal until it was annexed by Indonesia 1975. Guerrilla warfare by local people seeking independence continues. Since 1975 over 500,000 have been killed or have resettled in West Timor, according to Amnesty International. Products include coffee, maize, rice, and coconuts.

Tindouf a Saharan oasis in the Aïn-Sefra region of Algeria, crossed by the Agadir–Dakar desert route. There are large iron deposits in the area; the oasis is a base for exiled Polisario guerrillas of the Western Sahara.

Tintagel village resort on the coast of N Cornwall, England. There are castle ruins, and legend has it that King Arthur was born and held court here.

Tipperary county in the Republic of Ireland, province of Munster, divided into north and south regions. **North Tipperary**: administrative headquarters Nenagh; area 2,000 sq km/772 sq mi; population (1986) 59,000. **South Tipperary**: administrative headquarters Clonmel; area 2,260 sq km/872 sq mi; population (1986) 77,000. It includes part of the Golden Vale, a dairy-farming region.

Tirana or **Tiranë** capital (since 1920) of Albania; population (1983) 206,000. Industries include metallurgy, cotton textiles, soap, and cigarettes. It was founded in the early 17th century by Turks when part of the Ottoman Empire. Though now mainly modern, some older districts and mosques have been preserved.

Tîrgu Mureş city in Transylvania, Romania, on the river Mureş; population (1978) 137,000. Comprising approximately equal numbers of ethnic Hungarians and Romanians, the city was the scene of rioting between the two groups following Hungarian demands for greater autonomy in 1990; six people were killed.

Tirol federal province of Austria; area 12,600 sq km/4,864 sq mi; population (1987) 610,000. Its capital is Innsbruck, and it produces diesel engines, optical instruments, and hydroelectric power. Tirol was formerly a province (from 1363) of the Austrian Empire, divided 1919 between Austria and Italy (see ◊Trentino-Alto Adige).

Tiruchirapalli formerly **Trichinopoly** 'three-headed demon' city in Tamil Nadu, India; chief industries (cotton textiles, cigars, and gold and silver filigree); population (1981) 362,000. It is a place of pilgrimage, and was the capital of Tamil kingdoms during the 10th–17th centuries.

Tisza tributary of the river Danube, rising in the USSR and flowing through Hungary to Yugoslavia; length 967 km/601 mi.

Titicaca lake in the Andes, 3,810 m/12,500 ft above sea level; area 8,300 sq km/3,200 sq mi, the largest lake in South America. It is divided between Bolivia (port at Guaqui) and Peru (ports at Puno and Huancane). It has huge edible frogs.

Titograd formerly (until 1948) **Podgorica** capital of Montenegro, Yugoslavia; population (1981) 132,300. Industries include metal working, furniture making, and tobacco. It was damaged in

Togo

Republic of
(République Togolaise)

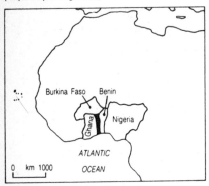

Burkina Faso   Benin

Ghana   Nigeria

ATLANTIC

0   km 1000   OCEAN

area 56,800 sq km/21,930 sq mi
capital Lomé
physical two savanna plains, divided by a
range of hills NE–SW
features rich mineral deposits (phosphates,
bauxite, marble, iron ore, limestone); dry plains,
forest, and arable land
head of state and of government Etienne
Gnassingbe Eyadema from 1967
government system one-party socialist

republic
political parties Assembly of the Tongolese
People (RPT), nationalist, socialist
exports cocoa, coffee, coconuts, copra,
phosphate, bauxite
currency CFA franc (485.00 = £1 Mar 1990)
population (1986) 3,423,000; annual growth
rate 3%
life expectancy men 49, women 52
language French (official), many local
languages
religion traditional 60%, Muslim 20%, Christian
20%
literacy 53% male/28% female (1985 est)
GNP $790 million (1983); $348 per head of
population
chronology
1960 Achieved full independence as the
Republic of Togo with Sylvanus Olympio as
head of state.
1963 Olympio killed in a military coup. Nicolas
Grunitzky became president.
1967 Grunitzky replaced by Lt-Gen Etienne
Gnassingbe Eyadema in a bloodless coup.
1973 The Assembly of Togolese People (RPT)
formed as the only legal political party.
1979 Eyadema returned in election.
1986 Attempted coup failed.

World War II, and after rebuilding was renamed
in honour of Marshal Tito. It was the birthplace
of the Roman emperor Diocletian.

Tivoli town NE of Rome, Italy; population (1981)
52,000. It has remains of Hadrian's villa, with gardens; and the Villa d'Este with Renaissance gardens laid out 1549 for Cardinal Ippolito d'Este.

Tlemcen (Roman *Pomaria*) town in NW Algeria;
population (1983) 146,000. Carpets and leather
goods are made, and there is a 12th-century Great
Mosque.

TN abbreviation for ◊*Tennessee*.

Tobago island in the West Indies; part of the republic of ◊Trinidad and Tobago.

Tobolsk river port and lumber centre at the confluence of the Tobol and Irtysh rivers in N Tyumen,
W Siberia, USSR; population (1985) 75,000. It
was founded by Cossacks 1587; Tsar Nicholas II
was exiled here 1917.

Tobruk Libyan port; population (1984) 94,000.
Occupied by Italy 1911, it was taken by Britain
1941, and unsuccessfully besieged by Axis forces
Apr–Dec 1941. It was captured by Germany June
1942 after the retreat of the main British force
to Egypt, and this precipitated the replacement
of Auchinleck by Montgomery as British commander.

Togliatti or *Tolyatti*, formerly *Stavropol* port on
the river Volga, W central USSR; industries
include engineering and food processing; population (1987) 627,000. The city was relocated in the
1950s after a flood and renamed after the Italian
Communist Palmiro Togliatti.

Togo country in W Africa, bounded to the W by
Ghana, to the E by Benin, and to the N by
Burkina Faso.

Tohoku mountainous region of N Honshu island,
Japan; population (1986) 9,737,000; area
66,971 sq km/25,867 sq mi. Timber, fruit, fish,
and livestock are produced. Chief city is Sendai.
It is linked to the island of Hokkaido by the Seikan
tunnel, the world's longest underwater tunnel.

Tokelau formerly *Union Islands* overseas territory of New Zealand, 480 km/300 mi north of
Western Samoa, comprising three coral atolls:
Atafu, Fakaofo, and Nukunonu; area 10 sq km/
4 sq mi; population (19860) 1,700. The islands
belong to the Polynesian group. Their resources
are small and until 1975 many of the inhabitants
settled in New Zealand, which has administered
them since 1926 when they were separated from
the British Gilbert and Ellice Islands colony.

Tokyo capital of Japan, on Honshu Island; population (1987) 8,209,000, the metropolitan area of

Tonga
Kingdom of
(Pule'anga Fakatu'i 'o Tonga)
or **Friendly Islands**

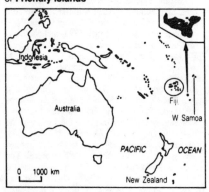

area 750 sq km/290 sq mi
capital Nuku'alofa on Tongatapu
physical comprises three groups of islands in the SW Pacific, mostly coral formations, but the western are actively volcanic

features fewer than one-third of the islands are inhabited
head of state and of government King Taufa'ahau Tupou IV from 1965
political system absolute monarchy
political parties none
currency Tongan dollar or pa'anga (2.08 = £1 Mar 1989)
population (1988) 95,000; annual growth rate 2.4%
language Tongan and English
religion Wesleyan 47%, Roman Catholic 14%, Free Church of Tonga 14%, Mormon 9%, Church of Tonga 9%
literacy 93% (1985)
GNP $80 million (1983); $430 per head of population
chronology
1831 Tongan dynasty founded by Prince Taufa'ahau Tupou
1900 Became a British protectorate
1965 Death of Queen Salote. She was succeeded by her son, Prince Tupout'a, who took the title King Tupou IV.
1970 Achieved full independence within the Commonwealth.

Tokyo-to over 12,000,000. The Sumida river delta separates the city from its suburb of Honjo. It is Japan's main cultural and industrial centre (engineering, chemicals, textiles, electrical goods). Founded in the 16th century as *Yedo* (or *Edo*), it was renamed when the emperor moved his court there from Kyoto 1868. An earthquake 1923 killed 58,000 people. The city was severely damaged by Allied bombing in World War II. The subsequent rebuilding has made it into one of the world's most modern cities.

Features include the Imperial Palace, National Diet (parliament), National Theatre, Tokyo University 1877, and the National Athletic Stadium.

Toledo city on the river Tagus, Castilla–La Mancha, central Spain; population (1982) 62,000. It was the capital of the Visigoth kingdom 534–711, then became a Moorish city, and was the Castilian capital 1085–1560.

In the 12th century, Toledo had a flourishing steel industry, and a school of translators, run by Archbishop Raymond (1125–1151), writing Latin versions of Arabic philosophical works. The painter El Greco worked here from about 1575 (his house and garden are preserved), and the local landscape is the setting of Cervantes' novel *Don Quixote*.

Toledo port on Lake Erie, Ohio, USA, at the mouth of the Maumee River; industries include food processing and the manufacture of vehicles,

electrical goods, and glass; population (1980) 355,000.

Tomsk city on the river Tom, W central Siberia; industries (synthetic fibres, timber, distilling, plastics, electrical motors); population (1987) 489,000. It was formerly a gold-mining town and the administrative centre of much of Siberia.

Tonga country in the SW Pacific, in ◊Polynesia.

Tongariro volcanic peak at the centre of North Island, New Zealand. Sacred to the Maori, the mountain was presented to the government by chief Te Heuheu Tukino IV 1887. It was New Zealand's first national park and the fourth to be designated in the world.

Tonkin or *Tongking* former region of Vietnam, on the China Sea; area 103,500 sq km/39,951 sq mi. Under Chinese rule from 111 BC, Tonkin became independent 939 AD, and remained self-governing until the 19th century. A part of French Indochina 1885–1946, capital Hanoi, it was part of North Vietnam from 1954, and was merged with Vietnam after the Vietnam War.

Tonkin, Gulf of part of the South China Sea, with oil resources. China and Vietnam disagree over their territorial boundaries in the area.

Tonle Sap or *Great Lake* lake on a tributary of the ◊Mekong river, W Cambodia; area 2,600 sq km/ 1,000 sq mi to 6,500 sq km/ 2,500 sq mi at the height of the monsoon. During the June–Nov wet season it acts as a natural flood reservoir.

Toowoomba town and commercial and industrial (coal-mining, iron-working, engineering, clothing) centre in the Darling Downs, SE Queensland, Australia; population (1987) 79,000.

Topeka capital of Kansas, USA; population (1980) 119,000. It is a major centre for psychiatric research and agricultural trade, with engineering and textile industries.

Torbay district in S Devon, England; population (1981) 116,000. It was created 1968 by the union of the seaside resorts of Paignton, Torquay, and Brixham.

Torgau town in Leipzig county, East Germany; population 20,000. In 1760, during the Seven Years' War Frederick II of Prussia defeated the Austrians nearby, and in World War II the US and Soviet forces first met here.

Torino Italian name for the city of ◊Turin.

Torness site of an advanced gas-cooled nuclear reactor 7 km/4.5 mi SW of Dunbar, East Lothian, Scotland. It started to generate power 1987.

Toronto port on Lake Ontario, capital of Ontario, Canada; metropolitan population (1985) 3,427,000. It is Canada's main industrial and commercial centre (banking, shipbuilding, cars, farm machinery, food processing, publishing), and also a cultural centre, with theatres and a film industry. A French fort was established 1749, and the site became the provincial capital (then named York) 1793; it was renamed Toronto (North American Indian 'place of meeting') 1834, when incorporated as a city.

Torquay resort in S Devon, England, part of the district of ◊Torbay.

Torrens salt lake 8 m/25 ft below sea level in E South Australia; area 5,800 sq km/2,239 sq mi. It is reduced to a marsh in dry weather.

Torreón industrial and agricultural city in Coahuila state, N Mexico, on the river Nazas at an altitude of 1,127 m/3,700 ft; population (1986) 730,000. Before the arrival of the railway 1907 Torreón was the largest of the Laguna cotton district tri-cities (with Gómez Palacio and Ciudad Lerdo). Since then it has developed as a major thoroughfare and commercial centre.

Torres Strait channel separating New Guinea from Australia, with scattered reefs; width 130 km/80 mi. The first European to sail through it was the Spanish navigator Luis Vaez de Torres 1606.

Tortuga island off the N coast of ◊Haiti; area 180 sq km/69 sq mi. It was a pirate lair during the 17th century.

Toruń (German **Thorn**) industrial (electronics, fertilizers, synthetic fibres) river port in N Poland, on the Vistula; population (1982) 183,000. It was founded by the Teutonic Knights 1230, and is the birthplace of the astronomer Copernicus.

Toscana Italian name for the region of ◊Tuscany.

Tottenham district of the Greater London borough of ◊Haringey.

Toulon port and capital of Var *département*, SE France, on the Mediterranean Sea, 48 km/30 mi SE of Marseille; population (1983) 410,000. It is the chief Mediterranean naval station of France. Industries include oil refining, chemicals, furniture, and clothing. Toulon was the Roman *Telo Martius*, and was made a port by Henry IV. It was occupied by the British 1793, and Napoleon first distinguished himself in driving them out. In World War II the French fleet was scuttled here to avoid its passing to German control.

Toulouse capital of Haute-Garonne *département*, S France, on the river Garonne SE of Bordeaux; population (1982) 541,000. The chief industries are textiles and aircraft construction (Concorde was built here). Toulouse was the capital of the Visigoths and later of Aquitaine 781–843. The university was founded 1229 to combat heresy. Toulouse has a 12th–13th century cathedral. The Duke of Wellington repulsed the French marshal Soult at Toulouse 1814 in the Peninsular War.

Touraine former province of W central France, now part of the *départements* of Indre-et-Loire and Vienne; capital Tours.

Tourcoing town in Nord *département*, France, part of metropolitan Lille; population (1983) 102,000. It is situated near the Belgian border, and has been a textile centre since the 12th century.

Tournai (Flemish **Doornik**) town in Hainaut province, Belgium, on the Scheldt; population (1983) 67,000. Industries include carpets, cement, and leather. It stands on the site of a Roman relay post, and has an 11th-century Romanesque cathedral.

Tours industrial (chemicals, textiles, machinery) city and capital of the Indre-et-Loire *département*, W central France, on the the Loire; population (1982) 263,000. It has a 13th–15th century cathedral. An ancient city, and former capital of Touraine, it was the site of the French defeat of the Arabs 732 under Charles Martel. Tours became the French capital for four days during World War II.

Tower Hamlets borough of E Greater London; population (1984) 146,000. It includes the Tower of London, and the World Trade Centre in former St Katharine's Dock; *Isle of Dogs* bounded on three sides by the Thames, including the former India and Millwall Docks. Redevelopment includes Billingsgate fish market, removed here 1982, and the Docklands railway, linking the isle with the City; *Limehouse district*; *Spitalfields district*; *Bethnal Green* has a Museum of Childhood; *Wapping* has replaced Fleet Street as the centre of the newspaper industry.

Townsville port on Cleveland Bay, N Queensland, Australia; population (1987) 108,000. It is the centre of a mining and agricultural area, and exports meat, wool, sugar, and minerals, including gold and silver.

Trabzon formerly *Trebizond* port on the Black Sea, NE Turkey, 355 km/220 mi SW of Batum; population (1985) 156,000. Its exports include fruit, tobacco, and hides.

Trail mining centre in British Columbia, Canada, on the Columbia River; population (1981) 10,000. It has lead, zinc, and copper industries.

Trans-Amazonian Highway or *Transamazonica* initiated as part of the Brazilian National Integration Programme (PIN) in 1970, the Trans-Amazonian Highway was designed to enhance national security, aid the development of the north of Brazil and act as a safety valve for the overpopulated coastal regions. The highway links Recife in the east with the provinces of Rondonia, Amazonas, and Acre in the west.

Transcaucasia region of the USSR south of the Caucasus. It includes Armenia, Azerbaijan, and ◊Georgia, which formed the *Transcaucasian Republic* 1922, broken up 1936 when each became a separate republic of the USSR.

Transjordan former name (1923–49) of the Hashemite kingdom of ◊Jordan.

Transkei largest of South Africa's Bantu Homelands, extending NE from the Great Kei River, on the coast of Cape Province, to the border of Natal; area 43,808 sq km/16,910 sq mi; population (1985) 3,000,000, including small white and Asian minorities. It became self-governing 1963, and achieved full 'independence' 1976. Its capital is Umtata, and it has a port at Mnganzana. It is one of the two homelands of the Xhosa people (the other is ◊Ciskei), and products include livestock, coffee, tea, sugar, maize, and sorghum. Its government consists of a president (paramount chief Tutor Nyangelizwe Vulinolela Ndamase from 1986) and single-chamber national assembly.

Trans-Siberian Railway railway line connecting the cities of European Russia with Omsk, Novosibirsk, Irkutsk, and Khabarovsk, and terminating at Vladivostok on the Pacific. It was built 1891–1905; from Leningrad to Vladivostok is about 8,700 km/ 5,400 mi. A 3,102 km/1,928 mi northern line was completed 1984 after ten years' work.

Transvaal province of NE South Africa, bordering Zimbabwe in the N; area 262,499 sq km/ 101,325 sq mi; population (1985) 7,532,000. Its capital is Pretoria, and towns include Johannesburg, Germiston, Brakpan, Springs, Benoni, Krugersdorp, and Roodepoort. Products include diamonds, coal, iron ore, copper, lead, tin, manganese, meat, maize, tobacco, and fruit. The main rivers are the Vaal and Limpopo with their tributaries. Swaziland forms an enclave on the Natal border. It was settled by *Voortrekkers*, Boers who left Cape Colony in the Great Trek from 1831. Independence was recognized by Britain 1852, until the settlers' difficulties with the conquered Zulus led to British annexation 1877. It was made a British colony after the South African War 1899–1902, and in 1910 became a province of the Union of South Africa.

Transylvania mountainous area of central and NW Romania, bounded to the S by the Transylvanian Alps (an extension of the ◊Carpathians), formerly a province, with its capital at Cluj. It was part of Hungary from about 1000 until its people voted to unite with Romania 1918. It is the home of the vampire legends.

Trapani port and naval base in NW Sicily, about 48 km/30 mi north of Marsala; population (1981) 72,000. It trades in wine, salt, and fish.

Transylvania

Trinidad and Tobago
Republic of

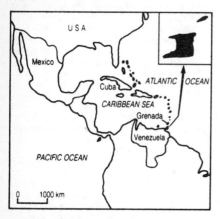

area Trinidad 4,800 sq km/1,853 sq mi and Tobago 300 sq km/116 sq mi
capital Port of Spain
towns San Fernando
physical comprises the two main islands, and some smaller ones; Trinidad has coastal swamps, and hills E–W
features Pitch Lake is a self-renewing source of asphalt and was used by the 16th-century explorer Walter Raleigh when repairing his ships
head of state Noor Hassanali from 1987
head of government Arthur Robinson from 1986

government system democratic republic
political parties National Alliance for Reconstruction (NAR) , nationalistic, left-of-centre; People's National Movement (PNM), nationalistic, moderate, centrist.
exports angostura bitters, asphalt, natural gas, oil
currency Trinidad and Tobago dollar (7.23 = £1 Mar 1990)
population (1988) 1,261,000 (equally divided between those of African and E Indian descent), 1.2 million on Trinidad; annual growth rate 1.6%
life expectancy men 66, women 71
language English (official), Hindi, French, Spanish
religion Roman Catholic 33%, Protestant 14%, Hindu 25%, Muslim 6%
literacy 97% male/95% female (1985 est)
GNP $6.8 bn (1983); $6,800 per head of population
chronology
1956 The People's National Movement (PNM) founded.
1959 Granted internal self-government, with PNM leader Eric Williams as chief minister.
1967 Achieved full independence, within the Commonwealth, with Williams as prime minister.
1976 Became a republic, with Ellis Clarke as president and Williams as prime minister.
1981 Williams died and was succeeded by George Chambers, with Arthur Robinson as leader of the opposition.
1986 Arthur Robinson became prime minister.
1987 Noor Hassanali became president.

Trebizond former English name of ◊Trabzon, a city in Turkey.

Trengganu or *Terengganu* state of E Peninsular Malaysia; capital Kuala Trengganu; area 13,000 sq km/5,018 sq mi; population (1980) 541,000. Its exports include copra, black pepper, tin, and tungsten; there are also fishing and offshore oil industries.

Trent third longest river of England; length 275 km/170 mi. Rising in the S Pennines, it flows first south and then NE through the Midlands to the Humber. It is navigable by barge for nearly 160 km/100 mi.

Trentino–Alto Adige autonomous region of N Italy, comprising the provinces of Bolzano and Trentó; capital Trento; chief towns Trento in the Italian-speaking southern area, and Bolzano-Bozen in the northern German-speaking area of South ◊Tirol (the region was Austrian until ceded to Italy 1919); area 13,600 sq km/5,250 sq mi; population (1988) 882,000.

Trento capital of Trentino–Alto Adige region, Italy, on the Adige River; population (1988) 101,000. Industries include the manufacture of electrical goods and chemicals. The Council of Trent was held here 1545–63.

Trenton capital of New Jersey, USA, on the Delaware River; population (1980) 92,000. It has metalworking and ceramics industries. It was first settled by Quakers 1679; George Washington defeated the British here 1776.

Trèves the French name for ◊Trier, a city in West Germany.

Treviso city in Veneto, NE Italy; population (1981) 88,000. Its industries include the manufacture of machinery and ceramics. The 11th-century cathedral has an altarpiece by Titian.

Trichinopoly former name for ◊Tiruchirapalli, a city in India.

Trier (French *Trèves*) city in Rhineland-Palatinate, West Germany; population (1984) 95,000. Once

Tripura

INDIAN OCEAN

the capital of the Treveri, a Celto-Germanic tribe, it became known as *Augusta Treverorum* under the Roman emperor Augustus about 15 BC, and was the capital of an ecclesiastical principality during the 14th–18th centuries. Karl Marx was born here.

Trieste port on the Adriatic, opposite Venice, in Friuli-Venezia-Giulia, Italy; population (1988) 237,000, including a large Slovene minority. It is the site of the International Centre for Theoretical Physics, established 1964.

Trieste was under Austrian rule from 1382 (apart from Napoleonic occupation 1809–14) until transferred to Italy 1918. It was claimed after World War II by Yugoslavia, and the city and surrounding territory were divided 1954 between Italy and Yugoslavia.

Triglav mountain in the Julian Alps, rising to 2,863 m/9,393 ft. It is the highest peak in Yugoslavia.

Trincomalee port in NE Sri Lanka; population (1981) 45,000. It was an early Tamil settlement, and a British naval base until 1957.

Trinidad town in Beni region, N Bolivia, near the river Mamoré, 400 km/250 mi NE of La Paz; population (1980) 36,000. It is built on an artificial earth mound, above flood-level, the work of a little-known early American Indian people.

Trinidad and Tobago country in the West Indies, off the coast of Venezuela.

Tripoli (Arabic *Tarabolus esh-sham*) port in N Lebanon, 65 km/40 mi NE of Beirut; population (1980) 175,000. It stands on the site of the Phoenician city of Oea.

Tripoli (Arabic *Tarabolus al-Gharb*) capital and chief port of Libya, on the Mediterranean; population (1980) 980,000. Products include olive oil, fruit, fish, and textiles.

history Tripoli was founded about the 7th century BC by Phoenicians from Oea (now Tripoli in Lebanon). It was an important base for Axis powers during World War II. In 1986 it was bombed by the US Air Force in response to perceived international guerrilla activity.

Tripolitania former province of Libya, stretching from Cyrenaica in the east to Tunisia in the west. Italy captured it from Turkey 1912, and the British captured it from Italy 1942, and controlled it until the formation of the newly independent United Kingdom of Libya 1951. In 1963 Tripolitania was subdivided into administrative divisions.

Tripura state of NE India since 1972, formerly a princely state, between Bangladesh and Assam.
area 10,500 sq km/4,053 sq mi
capital Agartala
products rice, cotton, tea, sugar cane; steel, jute
features agriculture on a shifting system in the jungle, now being superseded by modern methods
population (1981) 2,060,000
language Bengali
religion Hindu

Tristan da Cunha group of islands in the S Atlantic, part of the British dependency of St Helena
area 110 sq km/42 sq mi
features comprises four islands: Tristan, Gough, Inaccessible, and Nightingale. Tristan consists of a single volcano 2,060 m/6,761 ft; it is an important meteorological and radio station
government administrator, plus island council, as a dependency of ◊St Helena
exports crawfish
currency pound sterling
population (1982) 325
language English
history the first European to visit the then uninhabited islands was the Portuguese admiral after whom they are named, in 1506; they were annexed by Britain 1816. Believed to be extinct, the Tristan volcano erupted 1961 and the population were evacuated, but in 1963 they chose to return.

Trivandrum capital of Kerala, SW India; population (1981) 483,000. It has chemical, textile, and rubber industries. Formerly the capital of the princely state of Travancore, it has many palaces, an old fort, and a shrine.

Trois-Rivières port on the St Lawrence River, Québec, Canada; population (1986) 129,000. The chief industry is the production of newsprint.

Tromsø fishing port and the largest town in NW Norway, on Tromsø island; population (1988) 49,000.

Trondheim fishing port in Norway; population (1988) 136,000. It has canning, textile, margarine, and soap industries. It was the medieval capital of Norway, and Norwegian kings are crowned in the cathedral.

Trossachs woodland glen between lochs Katrine and Achray in Central Region, Scotland, 3 km/2 mi long. Featured in the novels of Walter Scott, it has become a favoured tourist spot.

Trowbridge market town in Wiltshire, England; population (1981) 23,000. Its industries include dairy produce, bacon, ham, and wool.

Troyes industrial (textiles and food processing) town in Champagne-Ardenne, NE France; population (1982) 65,000. The *Treaty of Troyes* 1420 granted the French crown to Henry V of England.

Trucial States former name (until 1971) of the ◊United Arab Emirates. It derives from the agreements made with Britain 1820 to ensure a truce in the area, and to suppress piracy and slavery.

Trujillo city in NW Peru, with its port at Salaverry; population (1988) 491,000. Industries include engineering, copper, sugar milling, and vehicle assembly.

Truong Sa one of the ◊Spratly Islands, in the South China Sea.

Truro city in Cornwall, England, and administrative headquarters of the county; population (1982) 16,000. Truro was the traditional meeting place of the *Stannary* (see ◊Cornwall); the nearby tin mines flourished briefly in the early 1980s.

Tsaritsyn a former name (until 1925) of ◊Volgograd, a city in the USSR.

Tsavo one of the world's largest national parks, established 1948, comprising East and West Tsavo. It occupies 20,821 sq km/8,036 sq mi of SE Kenya.

Tsinan another name for ◊Jinan, capital of Shandong province, E China.

Tsingtao another name for ◊Qingdao, a port in E China.

Tsumeb the principal mining centre (diamonds, copper, lead, zinc) of N Namibia, NW of Grootfontein; population 13,500.

Tsushima Japanese island between Korea and Japan in Tsushima Strait; area 702 sq km/271 sq mi. The Russian fleet was destroyed by the Japanese here 1905 in the Russo-Japanese War. The chief setlement is Izuhara.

Tuamotu Archipelago two parallel ranges of 78 atolls, part of ◊French Polynesia; area 690 sq km/266 sq mi; population (1983) 11,800, including the ◊Gambier Islands to the east. The atolls stretch 2,100 km/1,300 mi north and east of the Society Islands. The administrative headquarters is Apataki. The largest atoll is Rangiroa, and the most important Hao; they produce pearl shell and copra. Mururoa and Fangataufa atolls to the southeast have been a French nuclear test site since 1966. Spanish explorers landed 1606, and the islands were annexed by France 1881.

Tübingen town in Baden-Württemberg, West Germany, on the Neckar river, 30 km/19 m S of Stuttgart; population (1985) 75,000. Industries include paper, textiles, and surgical instruments. It was capital of the French zone of occupation after World War II.

Tubuai Islands or *Austral Islands* chain of volcanic islands and reefs 1,300 km/800 mi long, in ◊French Polynesia, south of the Society Islands; area 148 sq km/57 sq mi; population (1983) 6,300. The main settlement is Mataura on Tubuai. They were visited by Capt Cook 1777, and annexed by France 1880.

Tucson town and resort in the Sonora Desert in SE Arizona, USA; population (1986) 384,000. It stands 760 m/2,500 ft above sea level, and the Santa Catalina Mountains to the NE rise to about 2,750 m/9,000 ft. Industries include aircraft, electronics, and copper smelting.

Tucumán or *San Miguel de Tucumán* capital of Tucumán province, NW Argentina, on the Rio Sali, in the foothills of the Andes; population (1980) 497,000. Industries include sugar mills and distilleries. Founded 1565, Tucumán was the site of the signing of the Argentine declaration of independence from Spain 1816.

Tula city in W central USSR, on the river Upa, 193 km/121 mi south of Moscow; population (1987) 538,000. Industries include engineering and metallurgy. Site of the government ordnance factory, founded 1712 by Peter the Great.

Tula de Allende town in Mexico, near the site of the ancient Toltec Indian capital.

Tunbridge Wells, Royal spa town in Kent, SE England, with iron-rich springs discovered 1606; population (1985) 98,500. There is an expanding light industrial estate. The shopping parade, or *Pantiles* (paved with tiles in the reign of Queen Anne) was a fashionable resort; 'Royal' since 1909.

Tunbs, the two islands in the Strait of Hormuz, formerly held by Ras al Khaimah, and annexed from other Gulf states by Iran 1971; their return to their former owners was an Iraqi aim in the Iran–Iraq War.

Tunis capital and chief port of Tunisia; population (1984) 597,000. Industries include chemicals and textiles. Founded by the Arabs, it was occupied by the French 1881, and by the Axis powers 1942–43. The ruins of ancient ◊Carthage are to the NE.

Tunisia country in N Africa, on the Mediterranean, bounded to the SE by Libya and to the W by Algeria.

Turin (Italian *Torino*) capital of Piedmont, NW Italy, on the river Po; population (1988) 1,025,000. Industries include iron, steel, cars, silk and other textiles, fashion goods, chocolate, and wine. It was the first capital of united Italy 1861–64.

Turkana, Lake formerly *Lake Rudolf* lake in the Great Rift Valley, 375 m/1,230 ft above sea level, with its northernmost end in Ethiopia and the rest in Kenya; area 9,000 sq km/3,475 sq mi. It is

Tunisia
Republic of
(al-Jumhuriya at-Tunisiya)

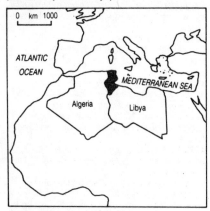

area 154,500 sq km/59,652 sq mi
capital and chief port Tunis
towns ports Sfax, Sousse, Bizerta
physical arable and forested land in the N
changes to desert in the S
features fertile island of Jerba, linked to the
mainland by a causeway, and identified with
the island of the lotus-eaters; Shott el Jerid salt
lakes; holy city of Kairouan, ruins of Carthage
head of state and of government Zine el
Abdin Ben Ali from 1987

political system emergent democratic republic
political parties Constitutional Democratic
Rally (RDC), nationalistic, moderate, socialist
exports oil, phosphates, iron ore
currency dinar (1.53 = £1 Mar 1990)
population (1989) 7,930,000; annual growth
rate 2%
life expectancy men 60, women 61
language Arabic (official), French
religion Sunni Muslim, with a politically active
fundamentalist opposition to the government;
Jewish and Christian minorities
literacy 68% male/41% female (1985 est)
GNP $8.8 bn (1983); $844 per head of
population
chronology
1955 Granted internal self-government.
1956 Achieved full independence as a
monarchy, with Habib Bourguiba as prime
minister.
1957 Became a republic with Bourguiba as
president.
1975 Bourguiba made president for life.
1985 Diplomatic relations with Libya severed.
1987 In Oct Bourguiba removed Prime Minister
Rashed Sfar and appointed Zine el Abdin Ben
Ali. In Nov Ben Ali had Bourguiba declared
incompetent and seized power.
1988 Constitutional changes towards
democracy announced. Diplomatic relations
with Libya restored.
1989 Government party, RCD, won all
assembly seats in general election.

---

saline, and shrinking by evaporation. Its shores
were an early human hunting ground, and valuable
remains have been found which are accurately dat-
able because of undisturbed stratification.

Turkestan the area of central Asia divided among
USSR (Kazakh, Kirghiz, Tadzhik, Turkmen, and
Uzbek republics), Afghanistan, and China (part of
Xinjiang Uygur).

Turkey country between the Black Sea and the
Mediterranean, bounded to the E by the USSR
and Iran, to the S by Iraq and Syria.

Turkmenistan constituent republic of the USSR
from 1924, part of Soviet Central Asia
area 488,100 sq km/188,455 sq mi
capital Ashkhabad
features Kara Kum 'Black Sands' desert, which
occupies most of the republic, area about
310,800 sq km/120,000 sq mi (on its edge is
Altyn Depe, 'golden hill', site of a ruined city with a
ziggurat excavated from 1967); river Amu Darya
products silk, sheep, astrakhan fur, carpets, oil,
chemicals
population (1987) 3,361,000; 69% Turkmenian,
13% Russian, 9% Uzbek, 3% Kazakh

language West Turkic, closely related to Turkish
religion Sunni Muslim.

Turks and Caicos Islands a British crown colony
in the West Indies, the SE archipelago of the
Bahamas
area 430 sq km/166 sq mi
capital Cockburn Town on Grand Turk
features a group of 30 islands, of which six are
inhabited. The largest is the uninhabited *Grand
Caicos*; others include *Grand Turk* (population
3,100), *South Caicos* (1,400), *Middle Caicos*
(400), *North Caicos* (1,300), *Providenciales*
(1,000), and *Salt Cay* (300); since 1982 the Turks
and Caicos have developed as a tax haven
exports crayfish and conch (flesh and shell)
currency US dollar
population (1980) 7,500, 90% of African descent
language English, French Creole
religion Christian
government governor, with executive and legislative councils (chief minister from 1985 Nathaniel
Francis, Progressive National Party)
history secured by Britain 1766 against French
and Spanish claims, the islands were a Jamaican

Turkey
Republic of
(Türkiye Cumhuriyeti)

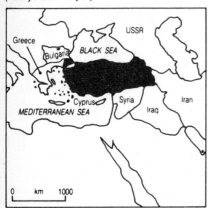

area 779,500 sq km/300,965 sq mi
capital Ankara
towns ports Istanbul and Izmir
physical central plateau surrounded by mountains
features Bosporus and Dardanelles; Taurus Mountains in SW (highest peak Kaldi Dağ, 3,734 m/12,255 ft); in E the sources of the Euphrates and Tigris. Archaeological sites include Catal Hüyük, Ephesus, and Troy; the rock villages of Cappadocia, and historic towns (Antioch, Iskenderun, Tarsus)
head of state Turgot Ozal from 1989
head of government Vildirim Akbulut from 1989
government system democratic republic
political parties Motherland Party (ANAP), Islamic, nationalist, right-of-centre; Social Democratic Populist Party (SDPP), moderate, left-of-centre; True Path Party (TPP), centre-right
exports cotton, yarn, hazelnuts, citrus, tobacco, dried fruit, chromium ores
currency Turkish lira (4040.52 = £1 Mar 1990)

population (1989) 55,377,000 (85% Turkish, 12% Kurdish); annual growth rate 2.1%
life expectancy men 60, women 63
language Turkish (official; related to Mongolian, but written in the Western Latin script), Kurdish Arabic
religion Sunni Muslim
literacy 86% male/62% female (1985)
GNP $58 bn (1983); $1,000 per head of population
chronology
1919–22 Turkish War of Independence provoked by Greek occupation of Izmir. Mustafa Kemal (Atatürk), leader of nationalist congress, defeated Italian, French, and Greek forces.
1923 Treaty of Lausanne established Turkey as independent republic under Kemal. Westernization began.
1950 First free elections; Adnan Menderes became prime minister.
1960 Menderes executed after military coup by Gen Cemal Gürsel.
1965 Suleyman Demirel became prime minister.
1971 Army forced Demirel to resign.
1973 Civilian rule returned under Bulent Ecevit.
1974 Turkish troops sent to protect the Turkish community in Cyprus.
1975 Demirel returned at the head of a right-wing coalition.
1978 Ecevit returned, in the face of economic difficulties and factional violence.
1979 Demeril returned. Violence grew.
1980 Army took over and Bulent Ulusu became prime minister. Harsh repression of political activists attracted international criticism.
1982 New constitution adopted.
1983 Ban on political activity lifted. Turgut Ozal became prime minister.
1987 Ozal maintained his majority in general election.
1988 Improved relations and talks with Greece.
1989 Turgot Ozal elected president; Turkey's application for EC membership refused

---

dependency 1873–1962, and in 1976 attained internal self-government. The chief minister, Norman Saunders, resigned 1985 after his arrest in Miami on drugs charges, of which he was convicted.

Turku (Swedish *Åbo*) port in SW Finland, near the mouth of the river Aura, on the Gulf of Bothnia; population (1988) 262,000. Industries include shipbuilding, engineering, textiles, and food processing. It was the capital of Finland until 1812.

Tuscany (Italian *Toscana*) region of central Italy; area 23,000 sq km/8,878 sq mi; population (1988) 3,568,000. Its capital is Florence, and towns include Pisa, Livorno, and Siena. The area is mainly agricultural, with many vineyards, especially in the Chianti hills; it also has lignite and iron mines, and marble quarries. The Tuscan dialect has been adopted as the standard form of Italian. Tuscany was formerly the Roman *Etruria*, and inhabited by Etruscans around 500 BC. In medieval times the area was divided into small states,

Turkmenistan

united under Florentine rule during the 15th–16th
centuries. It became part of united Italy 1861.

Tuva (Russian *Tuvinskaya*) autonomous republic
of the USSR, NW of Mongolian People's Republic,
of which it was part until 1911
capital Kyzyl
area 170,500 sq km/65,813 sq mi
population (1986) 284,000
features good pasture; gold, asbestos, cobalt

history declared a Russian protectorate 1914,
after the 1917 revolution it became the independent Tannu-Tuva republic 1920, until incorporated
in the USSR as an autonomous region 1944. It was
made the Tuva Autonomous Republic 1961.

Tuvalu country in the SW Pacific, on the former
Ellice Islands; part of Polynesia.

Tver former name (until 1932) of ◊Kalinin, a city in
the USSR.

Tweed river rising in SW Borders region, Scotland,
and entering the North Sea at Berwick-upon-
Tweed, Northumberland; length 156 km/97 mi.

Twickenham district in the Greater London borough of ◊Richmond-upon-Thames.

TX abbreviation for ◊*Texas*.

Tyburn stream in London, England (now underground) near which (at the junction of Oxford
Street and Edgware Rd) Tyburn gallows stood
from the 12th century until 1783.

Tyne river of NE England formed by the union of
the N Tyne (rising in the Cheviot Hills) and S Tyne
(rising in Cumbria) near Hexham, Northumberland, and reaching the North Sea at Tynemouth;
length 72 km/45 mi. Kielder Water (1980) in the
N Tyne Valley is Europe's largest artificial lake,
12 km/7.5 mi long and 0.8 km/0.5 mi wide, and
supplies the industries of Tyneside, Wearside, and
Teesside.

Tyne and Wear metropolitan county in NE England, created 1974, originally administered by an

---

Tuvalu
South West Pacific State of

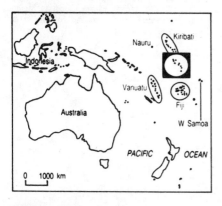

area 25 sq km/9.5 sq mi
capital Funafuti
physical low coral atolls in Polynesia
features the name means 'cluster of eight'
islands (there are actually nine, but one is very
small)

head of state Elizabeth II from 1978
represented by Tupua Leupena from 1986
head of government Bikenibeu Paeniu
from 1989
government system liberal democracy
political parties none, members are elected to
parliament as independents.
exports phosphates, copra, handicrafts,
stamps
currency Australian dollar (2.23 = £1 Mar
1990)
population (1989) 9,000 (mainly Polynesian);
annual growth rate 3.4%
language Tuvaluan and English
religion Christian, chiefly Protestant
literacy 96% (1979)
GDP (1983) $711 per head of population
chronology
1978 Achieved full independence within the
Commonwealth with Toaripi Lauti as prime
minister.
1981 Dr Tomasi Puapua replaced Lauti as
premier
1986 Islanders rejected proposal for republican
status.
1989 Bikenibeu Paeniu elected new prime
minister

Tyne and Wear

elected metropolitan council; its powers reverted to district councils 1986.

area 540 sq km/208 sq mi

towns administrative headquarters Newcastle-upon-Tyne; South Shields, Gateshead, Sunderland

features bisected by the rivers Tyne and Wear; includes part of Hadrian's Wall; Newcastle and Gateshead are linked with each other and with the coast on both sides by the Tyne and Wear Metro (a light railway using existing suburban lines, extending 54 km/34 mi beneath both cities)

products once a centre of heavy industry, it is now being redeveloped and diversified

population (1987) 1,136,000

famous people Thomas Bewick, Robert Stephenson, Harry Patterson/'Jack Higgins'.

Tynemouth port and resort in Tyne and Wear, England; population (1985) 9,442.

Tyre Arabic *Sur* or *Soûr* town in SW Lebanon, about 80 km/50 mi south of Beirut, formerly a port until its harbour silted up; population about 14,000. It stands on the site of the ancient city of the same name, a seaport of ◊Phoenicia.

Built on the mainland and two small islands, the city was a commercial centre, known for its purple dye. Besieged and captured by Alexander the Great 333–332 BC, it came under Roman rule 64 BC and was taken by the Arabs 638 AD. The Crusaders captured it 1124, and it never recovered from the destruction it suffered when retaken by the Arabs 1291. In the 1970s it became a Palestinian guerrilla stronghold, and was shelled by Israel 1979.

Tyrol a variant spelling of ◊Tirol, state of Austria.

Tyrone county of Northern Ireland

area 3,160 sq km/1,220 sq mi

towns county town Omagh; Dungannon, Strabane, Cookstown

features rivers Derg, Blackwater, and Foyle; Lough Neagh

products mainly agricultural

population (1981) 144,000.

Tyumen oldest town in Siberia, central USSR (founded 1586), on the river Nitsa; population (1987) 456,000. Industries include oil refining, machine tools, and chemicals.

Tywi or *Towy* river in Dyfed, SW Wales; length 108 km/68 mi. It rises in the Cambrian Mountains of central Wales, flowing SW to enter Camarthen Bay.

Ubangi-Shari former name for the ◊Central African Republic.

Udaipur or *Mecvar* industrial city (cotton, grain) in Rajasthan, India, capital of the former princely state of Udaipur; population (1981) 232,588. It was founded 1568, has several palaces (two on islands in a lake) and the Jagannath Hindu temple 1640.

Udine industrial city (chemicals, textiles), NE of Venice, Italy; population (1984) 101,000. Udine was the capital of Friuli in the 13th century, and passed to Venice 1420.

Udmurt (Russian *Udmurtskaya*) autonomous republic (administrative unit) in the W Ural foothills, central USSR
area 42,100 sq km/16,200 sq mi
capital Izhevsk
products timber, flax, potatoes, peat, quartz
population (1985) 1,559,000; Udmurt 33%, Tatar 7%, Russian 58%
history conquered in the 15th–16th centuries; constituted the Votyak Autonomous Region 1920; name changed to Udmurt 1932; autonomous republic 1934.

Ufa industrial city (engineering, oil refining, petrochemicals, distilling, timber) and capital of the Republic of Bashkir, central USSR, on the river Bielaia, in the W Urals; population (1987) 1,092,000. It was founded by Russia 1574 as a fortress.

Uganda landlocked country in E Africa, bounded to the N by Sudan, to the E by Kenya, to the S by Tanzania and Rwanda, and to the W by Zaïre.

Uist two small islands in the Outer ◊Hebrides, Scotland: North Uist and South Uist.

Ujiji port on Lake Tanganyika, Tanzania, where the journalist H M Stanley found the explorer Livingstone 1871; population (1970) 17,000. It was originally an Arab trading post for slaves and ivory.

Ujung Pandang formerly (until 1973) *Macassar* or *Makassar* chief port (trading in coffee, rubber, copra, and spices) on Sulawesi, Indonesia, with fishing and food-processing industries; population (1980) 709,000. Established by the Dutch 1607.

UK abbreviation for ◊*United Kingdom*.

Ukraine constituent republic of the SE USSR from 1923
area 603,700 sq km/233,089 sq mi
capital Kiev
towns Kharkov, Donetsk, Odessa, Dniepropetrovsk, Lvov, Zaporozhe, Krivoi Rog
physical Russian plain, Carpathian and Crimean Mountains; rivers Dnieper (with the Dnieper dam 1932), Donetz, and Bug
products grain; 60% of Soviet coal reserves; oil and other minerals
population (1987) 51,201,000; Ukrainian 74%, Russian 21%, Russian-speaking Jews 2%. Some 1.5 million émigrés live in the USA, 750,000 in Canada
language Ukrainian (Slavonic), with a literature that goes back to the Middle Ages; noted writers are Ivan Kotlyarevsky (1769–1838) and Taras Shevchenko (1814–1861)
religion traditionally Ukrainian Orthodox
history a state by the 9th century; under Polish rule from the 14th; Russia absorbed E Ukraine 1667, the rest 1793, from Austrian rule; proclaimed itself a people's republic 1918; from 1920, one of the republics of the USSR; overrun by Germans in World War II. In the famine of 1932–33 more than 7.5 million people died. Radioactive contamination from the ◊Chernobyl nuclear accident 1986 caused widespread damage, giving rise to a popular environmentalist movement. Nationalist and pro-reform demonstrations have increased; the People's Movement of the Ukraine (Rukh) was established in June 1989.

Ukraine

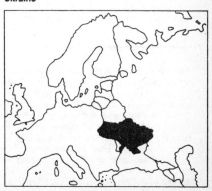

Uganda
Republic of

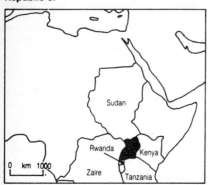

area 236,600 sq km/91,350 sq mi
capital Kampala
towns Jingar, M'Bale, Entebbe
physical plateau with mountains in W; forest and grassland; arid in N
features Ruwenzori Range; national parks with wildlife (chimpanzees, some of Africa's largest crocodiles, and Nile perch to 70 kg/160 lb); Owen Falls on the White Nile where it leaves Lake Victoria
head of state and government Yoweri Museveni from 1986
government emergent democratic republic
political parties National Resistance Movement (NRM), left-of-centre; Democratic Party (DP), centre-left; Conservative Party (CP), centre-right; Uganda People's Congress (UPC), left-of-centre; Uganda Freedom Movement (UFM), left-of-centre
exports coffee, cotton, tea, copper
currency Uganda new shilling (648.98 = £1 Mar 1990)
population (1987) 15,500,000 (the largest ethnic group is the Baganda, from whom the name of the country comes; others include the

Langi and Acholi, and there are a few surviving Pygmies); annual growth rate 3.3%
life expectancy men 47, women 51
language English (official); Swahili is a lingua franca
religion Christian 50%, animist 45%, Muslim 5%
literacy 70% male/45% female (1985 est)
GNP $6.2 bn (1984); $400 per head of population
chronology
1962 Achieved independence within the Commonwealth, with Milton Obote as prime minister.
1963 Proclaimed a federal republic with King Mutesa II as president.
1966 King Mutesa ousted in a coup led by Obote, who ended the federal status and became executive president.
1969 All opposition parties banned after an assassination attempt on Obote.
1971 Obote overthrown in an army coup led by Maj-Gen Idi Amin, who established a ruthlessly dictatorial regime, expelling nearly 49,000 Ugandan Asians. Up to 300,000 opponents of the regime are said to have been killed.
1978 After heavy fighting, Amin was forced to leave the country. A provisional government was set up with Yusuf Lule as president. Lule was replaced by Godfrey Binaisa.
1978–79 Fighting with Tanzanian troops.
1980 Binaisa overthrown by the army. Elections held and Milton Obote returned to power.
1985 After years of opposition, mainly by the National Resistance Army (NRA), and uncontrolled indiscipline in the regular army, Obote was ousted by Brig Basilio Okello, who entered a power-sharing agreement with the NRA leader, Yoweri Museveni.
1986 Agreement ended and Museveni became president, heading a broad-based coalition government.

There have also been demonstrations calling for the relegalization of the Ukranian Uniate Catholic Church, which was proscribed by Stalin in 1946 and forcibly merged with the Russian Orthodox Church, and strikes by miners during 1989 in the Donbas coalfield. In Jan 1990 millions of Ukranians formed a 300-mile-long human chain linking the cities of Kiev and Lvov to commemorate the territory's unification, in 1918, as an independent republic.

Ulaanbaatar or *Ulan Bator*, until 1924 *Urga* capital of the Mongolian Republic, a trading centre

producing carpets, textiles, vodka; population (1988) 500,000.
Ulan Bator alternative name of ◊Ulaanbaatar, capital of Mongolia.
Ulan-Ude formerly (until 1934) *Verkhne-Udinsk* industrial city (sawmills, cars, glass) and capital of the republic of Buryat in SE USSR, on the river Ibla and the Trans-Siberian railway; population (1987) 351,000. It was founded as a Cossack settlement in the 1660s.
Uleåborg Swedish name for the Finnish port of ◊Oulu.

397

Union of Soviet Socialist Republics
(USSR);
Soyuz Sovyetskikh Sotsialisticheskikh Respublik)

area 22,274,500 sq km/8,600,184 sq mi
capital Moscow
towns Kiev, Tashkent, Kharkov, Gorky, Novosibirsk, Minsk, Sverdlovsk, Kuibyshev, Chelyabinsk, Dnepropetrovsk, Tbilisi; ports Leningrad, Odessa, Baku, Archangel, Murmansk, Vladivostok, Vostochny, Rostov
physical Ural Mountains separate the European from the Asian plain; Caucasus Mountains are in the S between the Black Sea and the Caspian Sea, and there are mountain ranges in the S and E of the Asiatic part
head of state Mikhail Gorbachev from 1988
head of government Nikolai Ryzhkov from 1985 (premier); Mikhail Gorbachev from 1985 (head of Communist Party)
government communism
political parties the Communist Party of the Soviet Union; nationalist 'Popular Fronts' now operate at the republic level; a conservative Russian United Workers' Front established 1989; pluralist, intelligentsia-led Democratic Union in Moscow from May 1988
exports cotton, timber, iron, steel, non-ferrous metals, electrical equipment, machinery, arms, oil and natural gas and their products, asbestos, gold, manganese
currency rouble (1.0176 = £1 Mar 1990, but this is not a commercial rate)
population (1988) 284,500,000 (two-thirds living in towns, and of 125 different nationalities; 52% Russian, 17% Ukrainian); annual growth rate 1%
life expectancy men 67, women 75
language Slavic (Russian, Ukrainian, Byelorussian, Polish), Altaic (Turkish, Mongolian, and others), Uralian, Caucasian
religion the largest Christian denomination is the Orthodox Church (30 million), but the largest religious sect is Sunni Muslim (40 million), Jews 2,500,000
literacy 99% (1985)

GNP $734 bn (1984); $2,600 per head of population
chronology
1917 Revolution: provisional democratic government established in Mar by Mensheviks. Communist takeover in Nov by Bolsheviks under Lenin.
1922 Soviet Union established.
1924 Death of Lenin.
1928 Stalin emerged as absolute ruler after ousting Trotsky.
1930s Purges of Stalin's opponents.
1939 Nonaggression pact signed with Germany.
1941–45 Great Patriotic War against Germany.
1953 Death of Stalin. Removal of Beria.
1955 Creation of Warsaw Pact.
1957–58 Ousting of 'anti-party' group and Bulganin.
1960 Sino-Soviet rift.
1962 Cuban missile crisis.
1964 Khrushchev ousted by new 'collective leadership'.
1968 Invasion of Czechoslovakia.
1969 Sino-Soviet border war.
1972 Salt I arms-limitation agreement with USA.
1977 Brezhnev elected president.
1979 Salt II. Soviet invasion of Afghanistan.
1982 Deaths of Suslov and Brezhnev. Andropov new Communist Party leader.
1984 Chernenko succeeded Andropov.
1985 Gorbachev succeeded Chernenko and introduced wide-ranging reforms. Gromyko appointed president.
1986 Chernobyl nuclear disaster.
1987 USSR and USA agreed to scrap intermediate-range nuclear missiles. Boris Yeltsin, Moscow party chief, dismissed
1988 Nationalist challenges in Kazakhstan, Baltic republics, Armenia, and Azerbaijan. Earthquake killed 100,000 in Armenia. Gorbachev replaced Gromyko as head of state.
1989 Troop withdrawal from Afghanistan completed.General election held, with candidate choice for new congress of People's Deputies. 20 killed in nationalist riots in Georgia. 74 members of CPSU Central Committee (mostly conservatives) removed, a quarter of the total. Gorbachev elected by CUPD as state president. Abandoning 'Brezhnev Doctrine' Gorbachev allowed overthrow of conservative communist regimes in Eastern Europe. Relations with China normalized (first time since 1960s).
1990 Troops sent to Azerbaijan during civil war with Armenia. CPSU Central Committee agrees end to one-party rule.

United Arab Emirates

(UAE) federation of the emirates
of **Abu Dhabi, Ajman, Dubai,
Fujairah, Sharjah, Umm al
Qaiwain, Ras al Khaimah**

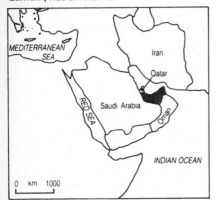

0 km 1000

total area 83,657 sq km/32,292 sq mi
capital Abu Dhabi
towns chief port Dubai
physical mainly desert; mountains in E
features linked by their dependence on oil
revenues
head of state and of government Zayed Bin

Sultan al-Nahayan from 1971
government absolutism
political parties no recognisable political
parties
exports oil, natural gas
currency UAE dirham (1.00 = £1 Mar 1990)
population (1986) 1,770,000 (10% are
nomadic); annual growth rate 6.1%
life expectancy men 65, women 70
language Arabic (official); Farsi, Hindi and
Urdu are spoken by immigrant oilfield workers
from Iran, India, and Pakistan
religion Muslim 90%, Christian, Hindu
literacy 56% (1985)
GNP $25 bn (1983); $23,000 per head of
population
chronology
1952 Trucial Council established.
1971 Federation of Arab Emirates came into
being but was later dissolved. Six of the Trucial
States formed the United Arab Emirates,
with the ruler of Abu Dhabi, Sheik Zayed, as
president.
1972 The seventh state joined.
1976 Sheik Zayed threatened to relinquish
presidency unless progress towards
centralization became more rapid.
1985 Diplomatic and economic links with the
USSR and China established.
1987 Diplomatic relations with Egypt restored.

Ulm industrial city (vehicles, agricultural machinery, precision instruments, textiles) in Baden-Württemberg, West Germany, on the river Danube; population (1988) 101,000. Its Gothic cathedral with the highest stone spire ever built (161 m/528 ft) escaped damage in World War II when two-thirds of Ulm was destroyed. It was a free imperial city from the 14th century to 1802. Albert Einstein was born here.

Ulsan industrial city (vehicles, shipbuilding, oil refining, petrochemicals) in South Kyongsang province, SE South Korea; population (1985) 551,000.

Ulster former kingdom in Northern Ireland, annexed by England 1461, from Jacobean times a centre of English, and later Scottish, settlement on land confiscated from its owners; divided 1921 into Northern Ireland (counties Antrim, Armagh, Down, Fermanagh, Londonderry, and Tyrone) and Cavan, Donegal, and Monaghan in the Republic of Ireland.

Ulundi capital of the 'homeland' KwaZulu in Natal, South Africa.

Umbria mountainous region of Italy in the central Apennines; including the provinces of Perugia and Terni; area 8,500 sq km/3,281 sq mi; population (1988) 818,000. Its capital is Perugia, and it

includes the river Tiber. Industry includes wine, grain, olives, tobacco, textiles, chemicals, and metalworking. This is the home of the Umbrian school of artists, including Raphael.

Umm al Qaiwain one of the ◊United Arab Emirates.

Umtali former name (until 1982) for the town of ◊Mutare in Zimbabwe.

Umtata capital of the South African Bantu homeland of Transkei; population (1976) 25,000.

Ungava district in N Québec and Labrador, Canada, E of Hudson Bay; area 351,780 sq mi/911,110 sq km. It has large deposits of iron-ore.

Union of Soviet Socialist Republics (USSR) country in N Asia and E Europe, stretching from the Baltic Sea and the Black Sea to the Arctic and Pacific oceans.

USSR: Constituent Republics

Republic	Capital	Area in sq km	Date of joining USSR
Armenia	Yerevan	29,800	1936**
Azerbaijan	Baku	86,600	1936**
Byelorussia	Minsk	207,600	1922
Estonia	Tallinn	45,100	1940
Georgia	Tbilisi	69,700	1936**

Kazakhstan	Alma-Ata	2,717,300	1936*
Kirghizia	Frunze	198,500	1936*
Latvia	Riga	63,700	1940
Lithuania	Vilnius	65,200	1940
Moldavia	Kishinev	33,700	1940
RSFSR	Moscow	17,075,000	1922
Tadzhikistan	Dushanbe	143,100	1929*
Turkmenistan	Ashkhabad	488,100	1924*
Ukraine	Kiev	603,700	1922
Uzbekistan	Tashkent	447,400	1924*
Total		*22,274,500*	

* Formerly autonomous republics within the USSR
** Formerly part of the Trans-Caucasian Soviet Socialist Republic which joined the USSR 1922.

United Arab Emirates federation in SW Asia, on the Arabian Gulf, bounded to the SW by Saudi Arabia and to the SE by Oman.

United Arab Republic union formed 1958, broken 1961, between ◊Egypt and ◊Syria. Egypt continued to use the name after the breach until 1971.

United Kingdom country in NW Europe off the coast of France, consisting of England, Scotland, Wales, and Northern Ireland.

United Provinces of Agra and Oudh former province of British India which formed the major part of the state of ◊Uttar Pradesh; see also ◊Agra, ◊Oudh.

United States of America (USA) country in North America, extending from the Atlantic to the Pacific, bounded by Canada to the N and Mexico to the S, and including the outlying states of Alaska and Hawaii.

United States of America

State	Capital	Area sq km	Date of joining the Union
Alabama	Montgomery	134,700	1819
Alaska	Juneau	1,531,100	1959
Arizona	Phoenix	294,100	1912
Arkansas	Little Rock	137,800	1836
California	Sacramento	411,100	1850
Colorado	Denver	269,700	1876
Connecticut	Hartford	13,000	1788
Delaware	Dover	5,300	1787
Florida	Tallahassee	152,000	1845
Georgia	Atlanta	152,600	1788
Hawaii	Honolulu	16,800	1959
Idaho	Boise	216,500	1890
Illinois	Springfield	146,100	1818
Indiana	Indianapolis	93,700	1816
Iowa	Des Moines	145,800	1846
Kansas	Topeka	213,200	1861
Kentucky	Frankfort	104,700	1792
Louisiana	Baton Rouge	135,900	1812

Maine	Augusta	86,200	1820
Maryland	Annapolis	31,600	1788
Massachusetts	Boston	21,500	1788
Michigan	Lansing	151,600	1837
Minnesota	St Paul	218,700	1858
Mississippi	Jackson	123,600	1817
Missouri	Jefferson City	180,600	1821
Montana	Helena	381,200	1889
Nebraska	Lincoln	200,400	1867
Nevada	Carson City	286,400	1864
New Hampshire	Concord	24,000	1788
New Jersey	Trenton	20,200	1787
New Mexico	Santa Fé	315,000	1912
New York	Albany	127,200	1788
North Carolina	Raleigh	136,400	1789
North Dakota	Bismarck	183,100	1889
Ohio	Columbus	107,100	1803
Oklahoma	Oklahoma City	181,100	1907
Oregon	Salem	251,500	1859
Pennsylvania	Harrisburg	117,400	1787
Rhode Island	Providence	3,100	1790
South Carolina	Columbia	80,600	1788
South Dakota	Pierre	199,800	1889
Tennessee	Nashville	109,200	1796
Texas	Austin	691,200	1845
Utah	Salt Lake City	219,900	1896
Vermont	Montpelier	24,900	1791
Virginia	Richmond	105,600	1788
Washington	Olympia	176,700	1889
West Virginia	Charleston	62,900	1863
Wisconsin	Madison	145,500	1848
Wyoming	Cheyenne	253,400	1890
District of Columbia	Washington	180	
Total		9,391,880	

Upington town in Transvaal, South Africa, 800 km/500 mi W of Pretoria. In Nov 1985 it was the scene of a demonstration against high rents that resulted in the death of a police officer and the subsequent arrest of 25 people. The 'Upington 25', as they came to be known, were later found guilty of murder under the law of common purpose.

Upper Austria (German *Oberösterreich*) mountainous federal province of Austria, drained by the Danube; area 12,000 sq km/4,632 sq mi; population (1987) 1,294,000. Its capital is Linz. In addition to wine, sugar-beet and grain, there are reserves of oil. Manufactured products include textiles, chemicals, and metal goods.

Upper Volta former name (until 1984) of ◊Burkina Faso.

Uppsala city in Sweden, NW of Stockholm; population (1988) 160,000. Industries include engineering and pharmaceuticals. The botanist Linnaeus lived here. The university was founded in 1477; there are a Gothic cathedral and Viking relics.

Ural Mountains (Russian *Ural'skiy Khrebet*) mountain system running from the Arctic to the Caspian Sea, traditionally separating Europe from

United Kingdom
of Great Britain and Northern Ireland (UK)

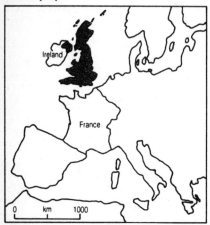

area 243,363 sq km/93,938 sq mi
capital London
towns Birmingham, Glasgow, Leeds, Sheffield. Liverpool, Manchester, Edinburgh, Bradford, Bristol, Belfast, Newcastle-upon-Tyne, Cardiff
physical rolling landscape, becoming increasingly mountainous towards the north, with the Grampian Mountains in Scotland and Snowdon in Wales; rivers Thames and Severn
head of state Elizabeth II from 1952
head of government Margaret Thatcher from 1979
government liberal democracy
political parties Conservative and Unionist Party, right-of centre; Labour Party, moderate, left-of-centre; Social and Liberal Democrats, centre-left; Social Democratic Party (SDP) centrist; Scottish National Party (SNP), Scottish nationalist; Plaid Cymru (Welsh Nationalist Party), Welsh nationalist; Official Ulster Unionist Party (OUP), Northern Ireland moderate right-of-centre; Democratic Unionist Party (DUP), Northern Ireland, right-of-centre; Social Democratic Labour Party (SDLP), Northern Ireland, moderate, left-of-centre; Ulster People's Unionist Party (UPUP), Northern Ireland, militant right-of-centre; Sinn Fein, Northern Ireland, pro-united Ireland; Green Party, ecological
exports cereals, rape, sugar beet, potatoes, meat and meat products, poultry, dairy products, electronic and telecommunications equipment, engineering equipment and scientific instruments, North Sea oil and gas, chemicals, film and television programmes; tourism
currency pound sterling

population (1985) 56,620,000; annual growth rate 0.1%
religion mainly Christian (Church of England and other Protestant sects with Roman Catholic minority); Jewish, Muslim, Hindu minorities
language English, Welsh, Gaelic
literacy 99% (1984)
GNP $505 bn (1983); $7,216 per head of population
chronology
1707 Act of Union between England and Scotland under Queen Anne.
1783 Loss of the American colonies.
1801 Act of Ireland united Britain and Ireland.
1832 Great Reform Bill became law, shifting political power from upper to middle class.
1867 Second Reform Bill extended franchise.
1906 Liberal victory; programme of social reform.
1920 Home Rule Act incorporated the NE of Ireland (Ulster) into the United Kingdom of Great Britain and Northern Ireland.
1921 Ireland, except for Ulster, became a dominion (Irish Free State, later Eire, 1937).
1924 First Labour government led by Ramsay MacDonald.
1926 General Strike.
1931 National government; unemployment reached 3 million.
1940 Winston Churchill became head of coalition government.
1945 Labour government under Clement Attlee; birth of welfare state.
1951 Conservatives defeated Labour.
1956 Suez crisis.
1964 Labour victory under Harold Wilson.
1970 Conservatives under Edward Heath defeated Labour.
1972 Parliament prorogued in Northern Ireland; direct rule from Westminster began.
1973 UK joined European Community.
1974 Three-day week, coal strike; Wilson replaced Heath.
1976 James Callaghan replaced Wilson as prime minister.
1979 Victory for Conservatives under Margaret Thatcher.
1981 Formation of Social Democratic Party (SDP). Riots in inner cities.
1982 Unemployment over 3 million. Falklands War.
1984–85 Coal strike, the longest in British history.
1987 Thatcher re-elected for third term.
1988 Liberals and most of SDP merged
1989 The Green Party polled 2 million votes in the European election
1990 Riots as Poll Tax introduced in England.

United States of America (USA)

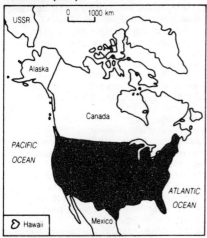

area 9,391,900 sq km/3,626,213 sq mi
capital Washington DC
towns New York, Los Angeles, Chicago, Philadelphia, Detroit, San Francisco, Washington, Dallas, San Diego, San Antonio, Houston, Boston, Baltimore, Phoenix, Indianapolis, Memphis: all metropolitan areas over 2 million population
physical includes almost every kind of topography and vegetation; mountain ranges parallel with E and W coasts, and the Rocky Mountains separate rivers emptying into the Pacific from those flowing into the Gulf of Mexico; Great Lakes in N; rivers Hudson, Mississippi, Missouri, Colorado, Columbia
head of state and of government George Bush from 1989
government liberal democracy
political parties Democratic Party, liberal, centre; Republican Party, centre-right
currency US dollar (1.70 = £1 Mar 1990)
population (1985) 238,740,000 (ethnic minorities include 26,500,000 black, about 20,000,000 Hispanic, and 1,000,000 American Indians, of whom 50% concentrated in Arizona, California, New Mexico, North Carolina, Oklahoma); annual growth rate 0.9%
life expectancy men 71, women 78
language English; largest minority language Spanish
religion 73 million Protestant, 50 million Roman Catholic, 6 million Jewish, 4 million Eastern Orthodox
literacy 99% (1985)
GNP $3,855 bn (1983); $13,451 per head of population

chronology
1776 Declaration of Independence.
1787 US constitution drawn up.
1789 Washington elected as first president.
1803 Louisiana Purchase.
1812–14 War of 1812 with England,
1841 First wagon train left Missouri with emigrants for California.
1846–48 Mexican War resulted in cession to US of Arizona, California, Colorado (part), Nevada, New Mexico, Texas, and Utah.
1848 California gold rush.
1861–65 Civil War between North and South.
1865 Slavery abolished. Lincoln assassinated.
1867 Alaska bought from Russia.
1890 Battle of Wounded Knee, last major battle between American Indians and US troops.
1898 War with Spain ended with the Spanish cession of Philippines, Puerto Rico, and Guam; it was agreed that Cuba be independent.
1898 Hawaii annexed.
1929 Wall Street stock-market crash.
1933 F D Roosevelt's New Deal to alleviate the Depression put into force.
1941 The Japanese attack on Pearl Harbor precipitated US entry into World War II.
1950–53 US involvement in Korean war. McCarthy anti-communist investigations.
1952 Gen Eisenhower elected president.
1960 J F Kennedy elected president.
1961 Bay of Pigs abortive CIA-backed invasion of Cuba.
1963 Assassination of Kennedy. Johnson assumed the presidency.
1964–73 US involvement in Vietnam War.
1968 Nixon elected president.
1973–74 Watergate scandal.
1974 Nixon resigned as president; replaced by Gerald Ford
1975 Final US withdrawal from Vietnam.
1976 Carter elected president.
1979 US-Chinese diplomatic relations normalized.
1979–80 Iranian hostage crisis.
1980 Reagan elected president. Republicans gained Senate majority.
1986 Republicans lost Senate majority. Scandal over secret US arms sales to Iran and subsidies to Contra guerrillas in Nicaragua.
1987 INF treaty with USSR. Wall Street stock-market crash.
1988 Vice president Bush elected president. Democrats retained control over both houses of Congress. US becomes world's largest debtor nation, owing $532 billion.
1989 US troops overthrow Noriega regime in Panama.
1990 Widespread cuts in defence expenditure proposed.

Uruguay
Oriental Republic of
*(República
Oriental del Uruguay)*

Brazil

PACIFIC
OCEAN

ATLANTIC
OCEAN

Argentina

0   1000 km

area 176,200 sq km/68,031 sq mi
capital Montevideo
physical grassy plains (pampas)
features smallest of the South American
republics; rivers Negro and Uruguay
head of state and of government Luis Lacalle
Herrera from 1989
government democratic republic
political parties Colorado Party (PC),
progressive, centre-left; National (Blanco) Party
(PN), traditionalist, right-of-centre; Amplio Front
(FA), moderate, left-wing

exports meat and meat products, leather, wool,
textiles
currency nuevo peso (1487.75 = £1 Mar 1990)
population (1988) 3,080,000 (mainly of
Spanish and Italian descent, also mestizo,
mulatto, and black); annual growth rate 0.7%
life expectancy men 67, women 74
language Spanish
religion Roman Catholic 60%
literacy 95% male/95% female (1980 est)
GNP $7.3 bn (1983); $1,665 per head of
population
chronology
1958 Blanco Party in power.
1966 Colorado Party elected. President Jorge
Pacheco Areco outlawed left-wing parties.
Tupamaro guerrilla activity began.
1971 The Colorado Party returned, with Juan
Maria Bordaberry Arocena as president.
1973 Having crushed the Tupamaros, the
military seized effective control, leaving
Bordaberry as a figurehead.
1976 Bordaberry deposed by the army and Dr
Méndez Manfredini became president.
1980 World's highest proportion of political
prisoners (1 in 50 citizens). Some 350,000
political exiles.
1984 Violent anti-government protests after ten
years of repressive rule.
1985 Agreement reached between the
army and political leaders for a return to
constitutional government. Colorado Party
narrowly won the general election and Dr Julio
Maria Sanguinetti became president.
1986 A government of national accord
established under President Sanguinetti's
leadership.
1989 Luis Lacalle elected president.

Asia. The highest peak is Naradnaya 1,894 m/
6,214 ft. It has vast mineral wealth.

The middle Urals is one of the most impor-
tant industrial regions of the USSR. Perm,
Chelyabinsk, Sverdlovsk, Magnitogorsk, and
Zlatoust are important industrial centres.

Urga former name (until 1924) of ◊Ulaanbaatar, the
capital of Mongolia.

Uruguay country in South America, on the Atlantic,
bounded N by Brazil and W by Argentina.

Urumchi former name for the city of ◊Urumqi,
China.

Urumqi formerly *Urumchi* industrial city and capital of Xinjiang Uygur autonomous region, China,
at the N foot of the Tyan Shan mountains; population (1986) 1,147,000. It produces cotton textiles,
cement, chemicals, iron, and steel.

US or *USA* abbreviation for ◊*United States*.

Ushant French *Ouessant* French island 18 km/
11 mi west of Brittany, off which the British
admiral R Howe defeated the French navy 1794
on 'the Glorious First of June'.

Ushuaia southernmost town in the world, at the tip of
Tierra del Fuego, Argentina, less than 1,000 km/
620 mi from Antarctica; population (1980) 11,000.
It is a free port and naval base.

Usküb Turkish name of ◊Skopje, a city in Yugoslavia.

Usküdar suburb of Istanbul, Turkey; formerly a
separate town, which under the name *Scutari*
was the site of the hospital set up by Florence
Nightingale during the Crimean War.

USSR abbreviation of ◊Union of Soviet Socialist
Republics.

Ussuri river in E Asia, tributary of the Amur. Rising
north of Vladivostok and joining the Amur south of

Utah

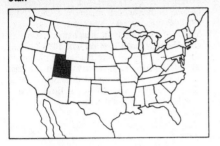

Uttar Pradesh

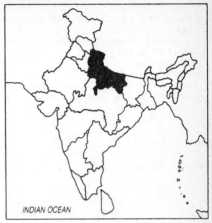

INDIAN OCEAN

Khabarovsk, it forms part of the border between the Chinese province of Heilongjiang and the USSR. There were military clashes 1968–69 over the sovereignty of Damansky Island (Chenpao).

Ust-Kamenogorsk river port and chief centre of the nuclear industry in the USSR, situated in the Altai mountains, on the river Irtysh; population (1987) 321,000.

Utah state of the W USA; nickname Beehive State
area 219,900 sq km/84,881 sq mi
capital Salt Lake City
towns Provo, Ogden
physical Colorado Plateau to the east; mountains in centre; Great Basin to the west; Great Salt Lake
features Great American Desert; Colorado rivers system; Dinosaur National Monument; Rainbow Bridge
products wool, gold, silver, uranium, coal, salt, steel
population (1985) 1,645,000
famous people Brigham Young
history part of the area ceded by Mexico 1848; developed by Mormons, still the largest religious sect in the state; territory 1850, but not admitted to statehood until 1896 because of Mormon reluctance to relinquish plural marriage.

Utica industrial city (textiles, firearms) in central New York State, USA; population (1980) 75,500. The first Woolworth store was opened here 1879.

Utrecht a province of the Netherlands lying SE of Amsterdam Netherlands, on the Kromme Rijn (crooked Rhine); area 1,330 sq km/513 sq mi; population (1988) 965,000. In rural areas livestock farming predominates. Manufactured products include textiles, chemicals, fertilizers, and electrical goods. The capital is Utrecht, which forms the NE corner of the Randstad conurbation; population (1988) 522,000. It has a Gothic cathedral, and a university 1636.

Uttar Pradesh state of N India
area 294,400 sq km/113,638 sq mi
capital Lucknow

towns Kanpur, Varanasi, Agra, Allahabad, Meerut
features most populous state; Himalayan peak Nanda Devi 7,817 m/25,655 ft
population (1981) 110,858,000
famous people Indira Gandhi, Ravi Shankar
language Hindi
religion Hindu 80%, Muslim 15%
history formerly the heart of the Mogul Empire, and generating point of the Indian Mutiny 1857 and subsequent opposition to British rule; see also the ◊United Provinces of ◊Agra and ◊Oudh.

Uzbekistan constituent republic of the SE USSR, part of Soviet Central Asia
area 447,400 sq km/172,741 sq mi
capital Tashkent
towns Samarkand

Uzbekistan

physical oases in the deserts; rivers Amu Darya and Syr Darya; Fergana Valley

products rice, dried fruit, vines (all grown by irrigation), cotton, silk

population (1987) 19,026,000; 69% Uzbek, 11% Russian, 4% Tadzhik, 4% Tatar

language Uzbek

religion Sunni Muslim

history part of Turkestan, it was conquered by Russia 1865–76. The Tashkent soviet gradually extended its power 1917–24 and Uzbekistan became a constituent republic of the USSR 1925. Some 160,000 Mesketian Turks were forcibly transported from their native Georgia to Uzbekistan by Stalin 1944. In June 1989 Tashlak, Yaipan, and Fergana were the scenes of riots in which Mesketian Turks were attacked. At least 70 were killed and 850 wounded. In Sept 1989 an Uzbek nationalist organization, the Birlik ('Unity') People's Movement, was formed.

Vaal river in South Africa, the chief tributary of the Orange. It rises in the Drakensberg and for much of its course of 1,200 km/750 mi it separates Transvaal from Orange Free State.

Vadodara formerly *Baroda*, until l976 industrial city (metal goods, chemicals, textiles) and rail junction in Gujarat, India; population (1981) 744,881.

Vaduz capital of the European principality of Liechtenstein; population (1984) 5,000. Industries include engineering and agricultural trade.

Valdai Hills small forested plateau between Leningrad and Moscow, where the Volga and W Dvina rivers rise. The Viking founders of the Russian state used it as a river route centre to reach the Baltic, Black, Caspian, and White seas. From the 15th century it was dominated by Moscow.

Valdivia industrial port (shipbuilding, leather, beer, soap) and resort in Chile; population (1983) 115,500. It was founded 1552 by the Spanish conquistador Pedro de Valdivia (*c.*1500–54), conqueror of Chile.

Valence market town and capital of Drôme *département*; SE France, on the Rhône; population (1982) 68,100. Industries include electrical goods and components for aerospace. It is of pre-Roman origin, and has a Romanesque cathedral consecrated 1095.

Valencia industrial city (textiles, leather, sugar) and agricultural centre in Carabobo state, N Venezuela, on the Cabriales River; population (1981) 624,000. It is 478 m/1,569 ft above sea level, and was founded 1555.

Valencia industrial city (wine, fruit, chemicals, textiles, ship repair) in Valencia region, E Spain; population (1986) 739,000. The Valencian Community, consisting of Alicante, Castellón, and Valencia, has an area of 23,300 sq km/8,994 sq mi, and a population of 3,772,000.

Valencia was ruled by the mercenary El Cid 1094–99, after he recaptured it from the Moors. There is a cathedral of the 13th–15th centuries, and a university 1500.

Valenciennes industrial town in Nord *département*, NE France, near the Belgian border, once known for its lace; population (1982) 349,500. It became French in 1678.

Valladolid industrial town (food processing, vehicles, textiles, engineering), capital of Valladolid province, Spain; population (1986) 341,000.

It was capital of Castile and Leon in the 14th–15th centuries, then of Spain until 1560. Ferdinand and Isabella were married at Valladolid 1469. The home of the writer Cervantes is preserved, and Columbus died here. It has a university 1346 and a cathedral 1595.

Valle d'Aosta autonomous region of NW Italy; area 3,300 sq km/1,274 sq mi; population (1988) 114,000, many of whom are French-speaking. It produces wine and livestock. Its capital is Aosta.

Valletta capital and port of Malta; population (1987) 9,000, but the urban harbour area is 101,000.

It was founded 1566 by the Knights of St John of Jerusalem, and named after their grand master Jean de la Valette (1494–1568), who fended off a Turkish siege May–Sept 1565. The 16th-century palace of the grand masters survives. Malta was formerly a British naval base, and was under heavy attack in World War II.

Valona Italian form of ◊Vlorë, port in Albania.

Valparaiso industrial port in Chile, capital of Valparaiso province, on the Pacific; population (1987) 279,000. Industries include sugar refining, textiles, and chemicals. Founded 1536, it was occupied by the English naval adventurers Drake 1578 and Hawkins 1595, pillaged by the Dutch 1600, and bombarded by Spain 1866; it has also suffered from earthquakes.

Van city in Turkey on a site on *Lake Van* that has been inhabited for more than 3,000 years; population (1985) 121,000. It is a commercial centre for a fruit and grain producing area.

Vancouver industrial city (oil refining, engineering, shipbuilding, aircraft, timber, pulp and paper, textiles, fisheries) in Canada, its chief Pacific seaport, on the mainland of British Columbia; population (1986) 1,381,000.

It is situated on Burrard Inlet, at the mouth of the Fraser River. The site was taken possession of by George Vancouver for Britain 1792. It was settled by 1875, under the name of Granville, and was renamed when it became a city 1886, having been reached by the Canadian Pacific Railroad.

Vancouver Island island off the W coast of Canada, part of British Columbia
area 32,136 sq km/12,404 sq mi
towns Victoria, Nanaimo, naval base Esquimalt

Vanuatu
Republic of

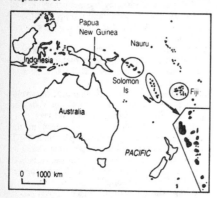

area 14,800 sq km/5,714 sq mi
capital Vila on Efate
physical comprises about 70 islands, including Espiritu Santo, Malekala, and Efate; densely forested
features three active volcanoes
head of state Fred Timakata from 1989
head of government Walter Lini from 1980

government democratic republic
political parties Vanuaaki Pati (VP: 'Party of Our Land'), Melanesian socialist; Union of Moderate Parties (UMP), Francophone opposition grouping
exports copra, fish, coffee; tourism is important
currency vatu (192.50 = £1 Mar 1990)
population (1988) 149,400 (90% Melanesian); annual growth rate 23.6%
language Bislama 82%, English, French, all official
religion Presbyterian 40%, Roman Catholic 16%, Anglican 14%, animist 15%
chronology
1975 Representative assembly established.
1978 Government of national unity formed, with Father Gerard Leymang as chief minister.
1980 Revolt on the island of Espiritu Santo delayed independence but it was achieved, within the Commonwealth, with George Sokomanu as president and Father Walter Lini as prime minister.
1988 An attempt by Sokomanu to unseat Lini led to Sokomanou's arrest for treason.
1989 Sokomanu sentenced to six years' imprisonment and succeeded as president by Fred Timakata.

---

products coal, timber, fish
history Vancouver Island was visited by the British explorer Cook 1778, and was surveyed 1792 by Capt George Vancouver.
Vänern, Lake largest lake in Sweden, area 5,550 sq km/2,140 sq mi.
Vannin, Ellan Gaelic name for ◊Isle of Man.
Vanuatu country comprising a group of islands in the S Pacific, part of Melanesia.
Var river in S France, rising in the Maritime Alps and flowing generally SSE for 134 km/84 mi into the Mediterranean near Nice. It gives its name to a *département* in the Provence-Alpes-Côte d'Azur region.
Varanasi or *Benares* holy city of the Hindus in Uttar Pradesh, India, on the Ganges; population (1981) 794,000. There are 1,500 golden shrines, and a 5 km/3 mi frontage to the Ganges with sacred stairways (ghats) for purification by bathing. At the burning ghats, the ashes of the dead are scattered on the river to ensure a favourable reincarnation. There are two universities 1916 and 1957.
Varna port in Bulgaria, on an inlet of the Black Sea; population (1987) 306,000. Industries include shipbuilding and the manufacture of chemicals. Varna was a Greek colony in the 6th century BC, and part of the Ottoman Empire 1391–1878; renamed *Stalin* 1949–56.

Vatican City State sovereign area in central Rome, Italy.
Vaucluse mountain range in SE France, part of the Provence Alps, E of Avignon, rising to 1,242 m/4,075 ft. It gives its name to a *département*. The Italian poet Petrarch lived in the Vale of Vaucluse 1337–53.
Venda Black National State from 1979, near Zimbabwe border, in South Africa
area 6,500 sq km/2,510 sq mi
capital Thohoyandou
towns MaKearela
features homeland of the Vhavenda people
government executive president (paramount chief P R Mphephu in office from Sept 1979) and national assembly
products coal, copper, graphite, construction stone
population (1980) 343,500
language Luvenda, English.
Vendée river in W France which rises near the village of La Châtaigneraie and flows 72 km/45 mi to join the Sèvre Niortaise 11 km/7 mi E of the Bay of Biscay.
Vendée, La *département* in W France. A peasant rising against the Revolutionary government (the War of the Vendée) began there in 1793 and spread to the other areas of France, lasting until 1795.

Vatican City State
(Stato della Città del Vaticano)

area 0.4 sq km/109 acres
physical forms an enclave in the heart of
Rome, Italy
features Vatican Palace, official residence of
the pope; the basilica and square of St Peter's;
also includes a number of churches in and near
Rome, and the pope's summer villa at Castel
Gandolfo
head of state and government John Paul II
from 1978
government absolute Catholic
currency issues its own coinage, which
circulates together with that of Italy
population (1985) 1,000
language Italian
religion Roman Catholic
chronology
1947 New Italian constitution confirmed the
sovereignty of the Vatican City State.
1978 John Paul II became the first non-Italian
pope for more than 400 years.
1985 New concordat signed under which
Roman Catholicism ceased to be the state
religion.

Venetia Roman name of that part of NE Italy which
later became the republic of Venice, including the
◊Veneto region.

Veneto region of NE Italy, comprising the
provinces of Belluno, Padova (Padua), Treviso, Rovigo, Venezia (Venice), and Vicenza;
area 18,400 sq km/7,102 sq mi; population (1988)
4,375,000. Its capital is Venice, and towns include
Padua, Verona, and Vicenza. Veneta forms part
of the N Italian plain, with the delta of the Po; it
includes part of the Alps and Dolomites, and Lake
Garda Products include cereals, fruit, vegetables,
wine, chemicals, shipbuilding, and textiles.

Venezia Italian form of ◊Venice, city, port, and naval
base on the Adriatic.

Venezuela country in northern South America, on
the Caribbean Sea, bounded E by Guyana, S by
Brazil, and W by Colombia.

Venice (Italian *Venezia*) city, port, and naval base,
capital of Veneto, Italy, on the Adriatic; population
(1988) 328,000. The old city is built on piles on
low-lying islands. Apart from tourism, industries
include glass, jewellery, textiles, and lace. Venice
was an independent trading republic from the 10th
century, ruled by a doge, or chief magistrate, and
was one of the centres of the Italian Renaissance.

It is now connected with the mainland and
its industrial suburb, Mestre, by road and rail
viaduct. The Grand Canal divides the city and
is crossed by the Rialto bridge; transport is by
traditional gondola or *vaporetto* (water bus).

St Mark's Square has the 11th-century Byzantine cathedral of San Marco, the 9th–16th century campanile (rebuilt 1902), and the 14th–15th

century Gothic Doge's Palace (linked to the for-
mer state prison by the 17th-century Bridge of
Sighs). The nearby Lido is a bathing resort.
The *Venetian School* of artists includes the
Bellinis, Carpaccio, Giorgione, Titian, Tintoretto,
and Veronese.

Venice was founded in the 5th century by refugees from mainland cities sacked by the Huns, and
became a wealthy independent trading republic
in the 10th century, stretching by the mid-15th
century to the Alps and including Crete. It was
governed by an aristocratic oligarchy, the Council
of Ten, and a senate, which appointed the doge, or
chief magistrate, 697–1797. Venice helped defeat

Vermont

Venezuela
Republic of
(República de Venezuela)

area 912,100 sq km/352,162 sq mi
capital Caracas
towns Barquisimeto, Valencia; port Maracaibo
physical valleys and delta of river Orinoco flanked by mountains
features Lake Maracaibo, Angel Falls; unique flora and fauna; annual rainfall over 7,600 mm/300 in
head of state and of government Carlos Andrés Pérez from 1988
government federal democratic republic
political parties Democratic Action Party (AD), moderate, left-of-centre; Christian Social Party (COPEI), Christian centre-right ; Movement towards Socialism (MAS), left-of-centre
exports coffee, cocoa, timber, oil, aluminium,

iron ore, petrochemicals
currency bolívar (74.16 = £1 Mar 1990)
population (1988) 18,770,000 (70% mestizos, 32,000 American Indians); annual growth rate 2.8%
life expectancy men 66, women 72
religion Roman Catholic
language Spanish (official), Indian languages 2%
literacy 84% male/78% female (1980 est)
GNP $70.8 bn (1983); $4,716 per head of population
chronology
1961 New constitution adopted, with Rómulo Betancourt as president.
1964 Dr Raúl Leoni became president.
1969 Dr Rafael Caldera became president.
1974 Carlos Andrés Pérez Rodríguez became president.
1979 Dr Luis Herrera became president.
1984 Dr Jaime Lusinchi became president. He tried to solve the nation's economic problems through a social pact between the government, trade unions, and business, and by rescheduling the national debt.
1987 Widespread social unrest triggered by inflation; student demonstrators shot by police.
1988 Andrés Pérez elected president. Venezuela suspends payments on foreign debts, which had increased due to the drop in oil prices since the 1970s.
1989 Economic austerity programme enforced by $4.3 billion loan from International Monetary Fund. Price rises triggered riots in which 300 people were killed; martial law declared in Feb. General strike in May.

---

the Ottoman Empire in the naval battle of Lepanto 1571, but was overthrown by Napoleon 1797. It passed to Austria 1815, but finally became part of the kingdom of Italy 1866.

Vent, Iles du French name for the Windward Islands, part of the ◊Society Islands in ◊French Polynesia. The Leeward Islands are known as the *Iles sous le Vent.*

Veracruz port (trading in coffee, tobacco, and vanilla) in E Mexico, on the Gulf of Mexico; population (1980) 305,456. Products include chemicals, sisal, and textiles. It was founded by the Spanish conquistador Cortés as *Villa Nueva de la Vera Cruz* (new town of the true cross) on a nearby site 1519, and transferred to its present site 1599.

Vermont state of the USA in New England; nickname Green Mountain State
area 24,900 sq km/9,611 sq mi

capital Montpelier
towns Burlington, Rutland
features noted for brilliant foliage in the autumn, and winter sports; Green Mountains; Lake Champlain
products apples, maple syrup, dairy products, china clay, asbestos, granite, marble, slate, business machines, furniture, paper
population (1986) 541,000
history explored by Champlain from 1609; settled 1724; state 1791. The *Green Mountain Boys* were irregulars who fought to keep Vermont from New York interference.

Verona industrial city (printing, paper, plastics, furniture, pasta) in Veneto, Italy, on the Adige; population (1988) 259,000. It trades in fruit and vegetables. It has Roman ruins, including an amphitheatre, and a 12th-century cathedral.

Victoria

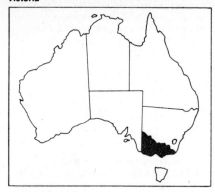

Versailles city in N France, capital of Les Yvelines *département*, on the outskirts of Paris; population (1982) 95,240. It grew up around the palace of Louis XV. Within the palace park are two small châteaux, Le Grand and Le Petit Trianon, built for Louis XIV (by J-H Mansart) and Louis XV (by J A Gabriel 1698–1782) respectively.

Vesuvius (Italian *Vesuvio*) active volcano SE of Naples, Italy; height 1,277 m/4,190 ft. In 79 BC it destroyed the cities of Pompeii, Herculaneum, and Oplonti.

VI abbreviation for *Virgin Islands*; *Vancouver Island*.

Viborg industrial town (brewing, engineering, textiles, tobacco) in Jutland, Denmark; population (1981) 28,700. It is also the Swedish name for ◊Vyborg, port and naval base in the USSR.

Vicenza city in Veneto region, NE Italy, capital of Veneto province, manufacturing textiles and musical instruments; population (1988) 110,000. It has a 13th-century cathedral and many buildings by Palladio, including the Teatro Olimpico 1583.

Vichy town in central France, on the river Allier in Allier *département*; population 33,000. It is a health resort with thermal springs, known to the Romans. During World War II it was the seat of Marshal Pétain's government 1940–44, which collaborated with the Nazis, and the term *Vichy France* refers to that part of France ruled by his puppet dictatorship and not occupied by German troops until Nov 1942.

Victoria state of SE Australia
area 227,600 sq km/87,854 sq mi
capital Melbourne
towns Geelong, Ballarat, Bendigo
physical part of the Great Dividing Range runs E–W and includes the larger part of the Australian Alps; Gippsland lakes, shallow lagoons on the coast; the mallee shrub region
products sheep, beef cattle, dairy products, tobacco, wheat; vines for wine and dried fruit, orchard fruits, vegetables, gold, brown coal (Latrobe Valley), oil and natural gas in Bass Strait
population (1987) 4,184,000; 70% live in the Melbourne area
history annexed for Britain by Cook 1770; settled in the 1830s; after being part of New South Wales, it became a separate colony 1851, named after the queen; became a state 1901.

Victoria industrial port (shipbuilding, chemicals, clothing, furniture) on Vancouver Island, capital of British Columbia, Canada; population (1986) 256,000. It was founded as Fort Victoria 1843 by the Hudson's Bay Company. Its university was founded 1964.

Victoria port and capital of the Seychelles, on Mahé island; population (1985) 23,000.

Victoria district of ◊Hong Kong, rising to 554 m/ 1,800 ft at Victoria Park.

Victoria Falls or *Mosi-oa-tunya* waterfall on the river Zambezi, on the Zambia–Zimbabwe border. The river is 1,700 m/5,580 ft wide, and drops 120 m/400 ft to flow through a 30 m/100 ft wide gorge. The falls were named after Queen Victoria by the Scottish explorer Livingstone in 1855.

Victoria, Lake or *Victoria Nyanza* largest lake in Africa, over 69,400 sq km/26,800 sq mi (410 km/ 255 mi long) on the equator at an altitude of 1,136 m/3,728 ft. It lies between Uganda, Kenya, and Tanzania, and is a source of the Nile. The British explorer Speke named it after Queen Victoria 1858.

Vienna (German *Wien*) capital of Austria, on the river Danube at the foot of the Wiener Wald (Vienna Woods); population (1986) 1,481,000. Industries include engineering and the production of electrical goods and precision instruments. The United Nations city 1979 houses the United Nations Industrial Development Organization (UNIDO) and the International Atomic Energy Agency (IAEA).
features Much Renaissance and baroque architecture; the Hofburg (former imperial palace), the 18th-century royal palaces of Schönbrunn and Belvedere, with formal gardens; the Steiner house 1910 by Adolf Loos; several notable collections of paintings; Vienna is known for its · theatre and opera; the psychoanalyst Freud's home is a museum; university 1365.
history Vienna was the capital of the Austro-Hungarian Empire 1278–1918 and the commercial centre of E Europe. The old city walls were replaced by a wide street, the Ringstrasse, 1860. After much destruction in World War II the city was divided into US, British, French, and Soviet occupation zones 1945–55. Vienna is associated with Haydn, Mozart, Beethoven, Schubert, Strauss waltzes, and the development of atonal music; with the Vienna Sezession group of painters; the philosophical Vienna Circle; and psychoanalysis originated here.

Vietnam
Socialist Republic of
(Công Hòa Xà
Hôi Chu Nghía Việt Nam)

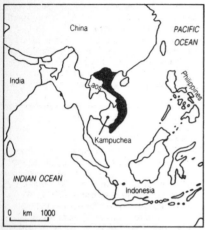

area 329,600 sq km/127,260 sq mi
capital Hanoi .
towns ports Ho Chi Minh City (formerly Saigon), Da Nang, and Haiphong
physical Red River and Mekong deltas, where cultivation and population are concentrated; some tropical rainforest; the rest is barren and mountainous
head of state Vo Chi Cong from 1987
head of government Do Muoi from 1988
government communism
exports rice, rubber, coal, iron, apatite
currency dong (7661.25 = £1 Mar 1990)

population (1989) 64,000,000 (750,000 refugees, the majority ethnic Chinese, left the country 1975–79, some settling in SW China, others fleeing by sea – the 'boat people' – to Hong Kong and elsewhere); annual growth rate 2%
life expectancy men 57, women 61
language Vietnamese, of uncertain origin but tonal like Chinese and Thai
religion traditionally Buddhist and Taoist
literacy 78% (1978)
GNP $9.8 bn (1983); $189 per head of population
chronology
1945 Japanese removed from Vietnam.
1946 Commencement of Vietminh war against French.
1954 France defeated at Dien Bien Phu. Vietnam divided along 17th parallel.
1964 USA entered Vietnam War.
1973 Paris ceasefire agreement.
1975 Saigon captured by North Vietnam.
1976 Socialist Republic of Vietnam proclaimed.
1978 Admission into Comecon. Invasion of Kampuchea (Cambodia).
1979 Sino-Vietnamese border war.
1986 Retirement of old-guard leaders.
1987–88 Over 10,000 political prisoners released.
1988–89 Troop withdrawals from Cambodia continued.
1989 'Boat people' leaving Vietnam continuing to be murdered and robbed on the high seas by Thai pirates. Troop withdrawal from Cambodia completed.
1990 Inflation reduced to 25%, but unemployment over 20%.

Vientiane capital and chief port of Laos on the Mekong river; population (1985) 377,000.
Vietnam country in SE Asia, on the South China Sea, bounded N by China and W by Cambodia and Laos.

Virginia

Vigo industrial port (oil refining, leather, paper, distilling) and naval station on Vigo bay, Galicia, NW Spain; population (1986) 264,000.
Viipuri Finnish name of ◊Vyborg, port and naval base in the USSR.
Vila or *Port-Vila* port and capital of Vanuatu, on the SW of Efate island; population (1988) 15,000.
Vilnius capital of Lithuanian Republic, USSR; population (1987) 566,000. Industries include engineering, and the manufacture of textiles, chemicals, and foodstuffs.

From a 10th-century settlement, Vilnius became the Lithuanian capital 1323 and a centre of Polish and Jewish culture. It was then Polish from 1386 until the Russian annexation 1795. Claimed by both Poland and Lithuania after World War I, it was given to Poland 1921, occupied by the USSR 1939, and immediately transferred to Lithuania. Its university was founded 1578.

Virgin Islands

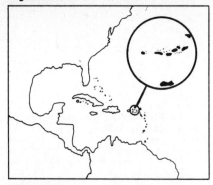

Vinson Massif highest point in ◊Antarctica, rising to 5,140 m/16,863 ft in the Ellsworth Mountains.

Virginia state of the S USA; nickname Old Dominion
area 105,600 sq km/40,762 sq mi
capital Richmond
towns Norfolk, Virginia Beach, Newport News, Hampton, Chesapeake, Portsmouth
features Blue Ridge mountains, which include the Shenandoah National Park; Arlington National Cemetery; Mount Vernon, the village where George Washington lived 1752–99; Monticello (Thomas Jefferson's home at Charlottesville); Stratford Hall (Robert E Lee's birthplace at Lexington)
products sweet potatoes, corn, tobacco, apples, peanuts, coal, furniture, paper, chemicals, processed food, textiles
population (1986) 5,787,000
famous people Richard E Byrd, Patrick Henry, Meriwether Lewis and William Clark, Edgar Allan Poe, Booker T Washington
history named in honour of Elizabeth I; Jamestown first permanent English settlement in the New World 1607; took a leading part in the American Revolution, and was one of the original Thirteen States; joined the Confederacy in the Civil War.

Virgin Islands group of about 100 small islands, northernmost of the Leeward Islands in the Antilles, West Indies. Tourism is the main industry.

They comprise the *US Virgin Islands* St Thomas (with the capital, Charlotte Amalie), St Croix, St John, and about 50 small islets; area 350 sq km/135 sq mi; population (1985) 111,000; and the *British Virgin Islands* Tortola (with the capital, Road Town), Virgin Gorda, Anegada, Jost van Dykes, and about 40 islets; area 150 sq km/58 sq mi; population (1987) 13,250.

The US Virgin Islands were purchased from Denmark 1917, and form an 'unincorporated territory'. The British Virgin Islands were taken over from the Dutch by British settlers 1666, and have partial internal self-government.

Vistula (Polish *Wisla*) river in Poland, which rises in the Carpathians and runs SE to the Baltic at Gdańsk; length 1,090 km/677 mi. It is heavily polluted, carrying into the Baltic every year large quantities of industrial and agricultural waste, including phosphorus, oil, nitrogen, mercury, cadmium, and zinc.

Vitebsk industrial city (glass, textiles, machine tools, shoes) in NE Byelorussia, USSR, on the Dvina River; population (1987) 347,000. Vitebsk dates from the 10th century and has been Lithuanian, Russian, and Polish.

Vitoria capital of Alava province, in the Basque country, N Spain; population (1986) 208,000. Products include motor vehicles, agricultural machinery, and furniture.

Vittorio Veneto industrial town (motorcycles, agricultural machinery, furniture, paper, textiles) in Veneto, NE Italy, which gives its name to the final victory of Italy and Britain over Austria Oct 1918; population (1981) 30,000.

Vizcaya Basque form of ◊Biscay, a bay in the Atlantic off France and Spain. Also the name of one of the three Spanish Basque provinces.

Vladivostok port (naval and commercial) in E USSR at the Amur Bay on the Pacific coast; population (1987) 615,000. It is kept open by icebreakers during winter. Industries include shipbuilding, and the manufacture of precision instruments.

It was established 1860 as a military port. It is the administrative centre of the Far East Science Centre 1969, with subsidiaries at Petropavlovsk, Khabarovsk, and Magadan.

Vlissingen Dutch form of ◊Flushing, a port in SW Netherlands.

Vlorë port and capital of Vlorë province, SW Albania, population (1980) 58,000. A Turkish possession from 1464, it was the site of the declaration of independence by Albania 1912.

Vojvodina autonomous area in N Serbia, Yugoslavia; area 21,500 sq km/8,299 sq mi; population (1986) 2,050,000, including 1,110,000 Serbs and 390,000 Hungarians. Its capital is Novi Sad.

Volga longest river in Europe; 3,685 km/2,290 mi, 3,540 km/2,200 mi of which are navigable. It drains most of the central and eastern parts of European USSR, rises in the Valdai plateau and flows into the Caspian Sea 88 km/55 mi below Astrakhan.

The Soviet Union is going ahead with controversial schemes for diverting water from north-flowing rivers, east and west of the Urals, to irrigate the croplands of central Asia. Diversion of water into the south-flowing Volga from the Sukhona river and surrounding lakes is due for completion 1990. A canal stretching 2,400 km/1,500 mi from the river Ob to Amu Darya is still in the planning stage.

Volgograd industrial city (metal goods, machinery, sawmills, oil refining) in SW USSR, on the river Volga; population (1987) 988,000. It was called *Tsaritsyn* until 1925 and *Stalingrad* 1925–61. Its successful defence 1942–43 against Germany was a turning point in World War II.

Volta main river in Ghana, about 1,600 km/1,000 mi long, with two main upper branches, the Black and White Volta. It has been dammed to provide power.

Volta, Upper name until 1984 of ◊Burkina Faso.

Vorarlberg ('in front of the Arlberg') alpine federal province of W Austria draining into the Rhine and Lake Constance; area 2,600 sq km/1,004 sq mi; population (1987) 314,000. Its capital is Bregenz. Industries include forestry and dairy farming.

Voronezh industrial city (chemicals, construction machinery, electrical equipment) and capital of the Voronezh region of the USSR, S of Moscow on the Voronezh river; population (1987) 872,000. There has been a town on the site since the 11th century.

Voroshilovgrad former name (1935–58 and 1970–89) of ◊Lugansk in Ukraine, USSR.

Vosges mountain range in E France, rising in the Ballon de Guebwiller to 1,422 m/4,667 ft and forming the W edge of the Rhine rift valley.

VT abbreviation for ◊*Vermont*.

Vyborg (Finnish *Viipuri*) port (trading in timber and wood products) and naval base in E Karelia, USSR, on the Gulf of Finland, 112 km/70 mi NW of Leningrad; population (1973) 51,000. Products inlcude electrical equipment and agricultural machinery. Founded by the Swedes 1293, it was Finnish 1918–40.

US Air Force administration since 1972; area 8 sq km/3 sq mi; population (1980) 300. It was discovered by Captain William Wake 1841, annexed by the USA 1898, and uninhabited until 1935 when it was made an air staging point, with a garrison. It was occupied by Japan 1941–45.

Walachia alternative spelling of ◊Wallachia, part of Romania.

Walcheren island in Zeeland province, Netherlands, in the estuary of the Scheldt
area 200 sq km/80 sq mi
capital Middelburg
towns Flushing (Vlissingen)
features flat and for the most part below sea level
products dairy, sugar-beet, and root vegetables
history a British force seized Walcheren in 1809; after 7,000 of the garrison of 15,000 had died of malaria, the remainder were withdrawn. It was flooded by deliberate breaching of the dykes to drive out the Germans 1944–45, and in 1953 by abnormally high tides.

Wales: counties

County	Administrative Headquarters	Area sq km
Clwyd	Mold	2,420
Dyfed	Carmarthen	5,770
Gwent	Cwmbran	1,380
Gwynedd	Caernarvon	3,870
Mid Glamorgan	Cardiff	1,020
Powys	Llandrindod Wells	5,080
South Glamorgan	Cardiff	420
West Glamorgan	Swansea	820
Total		20,780

Wales (Welsh *Cymru*) Principality of; constituent part of the United Kingdom, in the west between the Bristol Channel and the Irish Sea
area 20,780 sq km/8,021 sq mi
capital Cardiff
towns Swansea
features Snowdonia mountains (Snowdon 1,085 m/ 3,561 ft, the highest point in England and Wales) in the NW and in the SE the Black Mountain, Brecon Beacons, and Black Forest ranges; rivers Severn, Wye, Usk, and Dee
exports traditional industries (coal and steel) have declined, but varied modern and high-technology ventures are being developed; Wales has the largest concentration of Japanese-owned plant in the UK. It also has the highest density of sheep in the world and a dairy industry; tourism is important
currency pound sterling
population (1987) 2,836,000
language Welsh 19% (1981), English
religion Nonconformist Protestant denominations; Roman Catholic minority
government returns 38 members to the UK Parliament.

WA abbreviation for ◊*Washington* (state); ◊*Western Australia*.

Waddenzee European estuarine area (tidal flats, salt marshes, islands, and inlets) N of the Netherlands and West Germany, and W of Denmark; area 10,000 sq km/4,000 sq mi. It is the nursery for the North Sea fisheries, but the ecology is threatened by tourism and other development.

Wadi Halfa frontier town in Sudan, NE Africa, on Lake Nuba (the Sudanese section of Lake Nasser, formed by the Nile dam at Aswan, Egypt, which partly flooded the archaeological sites here).

Wagga Wagga agricultural town in SE New South Wales, Australia; population (1985) 49,500.

Waikato river on North Island, New Zealand, 355 km/220 mi long; Waikato is also the name of the dairy area the river traverses, chief town Hamilton.

Wairarapa area of North Island, New Zealand, round *Lake Wairarapa*, specializing in lamb and dairy farming; population (1986) 39,600. The chief market centre is Masterton.

Wairau river in N South Island, New Zealand, flowing 170 km/105 m NE to Cook Strait.

Waitaki river in SE South Island, New Zealand, which flows 215 km/135 mi to the Pacific. The Benmore hydroelectric installation has created an artificial lake.

Wakefield industrial city (chemicals, machine tools), administrative headquarters of West Yorkshire, England, on the river Calder, S of Leeds; population (1981) 310,200. The Lancastrians defeated the Yorkists here 1460, during the Wars of the Roses.

Wake Islands a small Pacific atoll comprising three islands 3,700 km/2,300 mi west of Hawaii, under

Wallis and Futuna two island groups in the SW Pacific, an overseas territory of France; area 367 sq km/143 sq mi; population (1983) 12,400. They produce copra, yams, and bananas. Discovered by European sailors in the 18th century, the islands became a French protectorate 1842, and an overseas territory 1961.

Wallsend town in Tyne and Wear, NE England, on the river Tyne at the E end of Hadrian's Wall; population (1981) 45,000. Industries include shipbuilding, engineering, and coalmining.

Wall Street street in Manhattan, New York, on which the stock exchange is situated, and a synonym for stock dealing in the USA. It is so called from a stockade erected 1653.

Walsall industrial town (castings, tubes, electrical equipment, leather goods) in West Midlands, England, 13 km/8 mi NW of Birmingham; population (1981) 179,000.

Walvis Bay chief port of Namibia, SW Africa; population (1980) 26,000. It has a fishing industry with allied trades. It has been a detached part of Cape Province, area 1,100 sq km/425 sq mi, from 1884, but administered with Namibia from 1922.

Wanganui port (textiles, clothing) in SW North Island, New Zealand, at the mouth of the Wanganui river; population (1986) 41,000.

Wankie name until 1982 of ◊Hwange, a town and national park in Zimbabwe.

Wapping district of the Greater London borough of Tower Hamlets; situated between the Thames and the former London Docks. It replaced Fleet Street as the centre of the UK newspaper industry.

Warrington industrial town (metal goods, chemicals, brewing) in Cheshire, NW England, on the river Mersey; population (1985) 178,000. An important trading centre since Roman times, it was designated a 'new town' 1968.

Warrnambool port near the mouth of Hopkins river, SW Victoria, Australia; population (1981) 22,000. A tourist centre, it also manufactures textiles and dairy products.

Warrumbungle Range mountain range of volcanic origin in New South Wales, Australia. Siding Spring Mountain 859 m/2,819 ft is the site of an observatory; the Breadknife is a 90 m/300 ft high rock only 150 cm/5 ft wide; the highest point is Mount Exmouth 1,228 m/4,030 ft. The name is Aboriginal and means 'broken-up small mountains'.

Warsaw (Polish *Warszawa*) capital of Poland, on the river Vistula; population (1985) 1,649,000. Industries include engineering, food processing, printing, clothing, and pharmaceuticals.

Founded in the 13th century, it replaced Kraków as capital 1595. Its university was founded 1818. It was taken by the Germans 27 Sept 1939 and 250,000 Poles were killed during

Warwickshire

two months of street fighting that started 1 Aug 1944. It was finally liberated 17 Jan 1945. The old city was virtually destroyed in World War II but has been reconstructed. Marie Curie was born here.

Warwick market town, administrative headquarters of Warwickshire, England; population (1981) 22,000. Industries include carpets and engineering. Founded 914, it has many fine medieval buildings including a 14th-century castle.

Warwickshire county in central England
area 1,980 sq km/764 sq mi
towns administrative headquarters Warwick; Leamington, Nuneaton, Rugby, Stratford-upon-Avon
features Kenilworth and Warwick castles; remains of the 'Forest of Arden' (portrayed by Shakespeare in *As You Like It*); site of the Battle of Edgehill
products mainly agricultural, engineering, textiles
population (1987) 484,000
famous people George Eliot, William Shakespeare.

Washington state of the NW USA; nickname Evergreen State
area 176,700 sq km/68,206 sq mi
capital Olympia
towns Seattle, Spokane, Tacoma
features Columbia River; Olympic (Olympic Mountains) National Park, and Mount Rainier (Cascade Range) National Park
products apples, cereals, livestock, processed food, timber, chemicals, cement, zinc, uranium, lead, gold, silver, aircraft, ships, road vehicles
population (1987) 4,481,000, including 61,000 Indians, mainly of the Yakima people
famous people Bing Crosby, Jimi Hendrix, Frances Farmer

Washington

history settled from 1811, it became a state 1889. Labour disputes occurred here in the 1910s, brutally suppressed by the authorities.

Washington town on the river Wear, Tyne and Wear, NE England, designated a 'new town' 1964; population (1985) 56,000. Industries include textiles, electronics, and car assembly.

Washington DC (District of Columbia) national capital of the USA, on the Potomac River

area 180 sq km/69 sq mi

capital the District of Columbia covers only the area of the city of Washington

features it was designed by a French engineer, Pierre L'Enfant (1754–1825). Among buildings of architectural note are the Capitol, the Pentagon, the White House, and the Lincoln Memorial. The National Gallery has a good collection of paintings; libraries include the Library of Congress, the National Archives, and the Folger Shakespeare Library. The Smithsonian Institute is here

population (1983) 623,000 (metropolitan area, extending outside the District of Columbia, 3 million)

history the District of Columbia, initially land ceded from Maryland and Virginia, was established by Act of Congress 1790–91, and was first used as the seat of Congress 1800. The right to vote in national elections was not granted to residents until 1961.

Wash, the bay of the North Sea between Norfolk and Lincolnshire, England. King John lost his baggage and treasure in crossing it 1216.

Waterbury city in W Connecticut, USA, on the Naugatuck River; population (1980) 103,000. Products include clocks, watches, brass and copper ware, and plastics. It was founded 1674.

Waterford county in Munster province, Republic of Ireland; area 1,840 sq km/710 sq mi; population (1986) 91,000. The county town is Waterford. The county includes the rivers Suir and Blackwater, and the Comeragh and Monavallagh mountain ranges in the north and centre. Products include cattle, beer, whiskey, and glassware.

Waterford port and county town of County Waterford, SE Republic of Ireland, on the Suir;

population (1986) 41,000. Handmade Waterford crystal glass (34% lead content instead of the normal 24%) was made here until 1851 and again from 1951.

Watford industrial town (printing, engineering, and electronics) in Hertfordshire, SE England; dormitory town for London; population (1986) 77,000.

Waziristan mountainous territory in Pakistan, on the border with Afghanistan, inhabited by Waziris and Mahsuds.

Weald, the area between the North and South Downs, England, once thickly wooded, and forming part of Kent, Sussex, Surrey, and Hampshire. Now an agricultural area, it produces fruit, hops, and vegetables. In the Middle Ages, its timber and iron ore made it the industrial heart of England, and its oaks were used in shipbuilding. The name often refers only to the area of Kent SW of the greensand ridge running from Hythe to Westerham.

Wear river in NE England; length 107 km/67 mi. From its source in the Pennines it flows E past Durham to meet the North Sea at Sunderland.

Weddell Sea an arm of the S Atlantic Ocean that cuts into the Antarctic continent SE of Cape Horn; area 8,000,000 sq km/3,000,000 sq mi. Much of it is covered with thick pack ice for most of the year. It is named after the British explorer James Weddell.

Weihai commercial port (textiles, rubber articles, matches, soap, vegetable oils) in Shandong, China; population about 220,000. It was leased to Britain 1898–1930, during which time it was a naval and coaling station; occupied by Japan 1938–45.

Weimar town in SW East Germany, on the river Elm; population (1980) 64,000. Products include farm machinery and textiles. It was the capital of the grand duchy of Saxe-Weimar 1815–1918; in 1919 the German National Assembly drew up the constitution of the new Weimar Republic here. The writers Goethe, Schiller, and Herder, and the composer Liszt lived in the town; the former concentration camp of Buchenwald is nearby.

Welland Ship Canal Canadian waterway, part of the ◊St Lawrence Seaway, linking Lake Erie to Lake Ontario.

Wellington capital and industrial port (woollen textiles, chemicals, soap, footwear, bricks) of New Zealand in North Island on Cook Strait; population (1987) 351,000. The city was founded 1840, and became the seat of government 1865.

Founded 1840 by Edward Gibbon Wakefield as the first settlement of the New Zealand Company, it has been the seat of government since 1865. Victoria University was founded 1897. A new assembly hall (designed by the British architect Basil Spence and popularly called 'the beehive' because of its shape) was opened 1977 alongside the original parliament building.

West Bengal

INDIAN OCEAN

Wells market town in Somerset, SW England; population (1981) 8,500. Industries include printing and the manufacture of animal foodstuffs. The 12th–13th century cathedral, built near the site of a Saxon church, has a west front with 386 carved figures. Wells was made the seat of a bishopric about 900 (Bath and Wells from 1244) and has a bishop's palace.

Welwyn Garden City industrial town (chemicals, electrical engineering, clothing, food) in Hertfordshire, England, 32 km/20 mi north of London; population (1981) 41,000. It was founded as a garden city 1919–20 by Ebenezer Howard, and designated a 'new town' 1948.

Wembley district of the Greater London borough of Brent. Wembley Stadium, opened 1924, has been the scene of the British Empire Exhibition, the annual Football Association Cup final, the 1948 Olympic Games, the Live Aid concert 1985, and many other concerts. A conference centre was opened 1977.

Wenchow former name of Chinese town ◊Wenzhou.

Wenzhou industrial port (textiles, medicine) in Zhejiang, SE China; population (1984) 519,000. It was opened to foreign trade 1877 and is now a special economic zone.

Wesermünde name until 1947 of ◊Bremerhaven, a port in West Germany.

West Bank the area (5,879 sq km/2,270 sq mi) on the west bank of the river Jordan; population (1988) 866,000. The West Bank was taken by the Jordanian army 1948 at the end of the Arab-Israeli war which resulted in the creation of Israel, and was captured by Israel during the Six-Day War 5–10 June 1967. The continuing Israeli occupation has created tensions with the Arab population, especially as a result of Jewish Israeli settlements in the area.

West Bengal state of NE India
area 87,900 sq km/33,929 sq mi
capital Calcutta
towns Asansol, Durgarpur
physical occupies the W part of the vast alluvial plain created by the Ganges and Brahmaputra, with the Hooghly river; annual rainfall in excess of 250 cm/100 in
products rice, jute, tea, coal, iron, steel, cars, locomotives, aluminium, fertilizers
population (1981) 54,486,000
history created 1947 from the former British province of Bengal, with later territories added: Cooch Behar 1950, Chandernagore 1954, and part of Bihar 1956.

West Bromwich industrial town (metalworking, springs, tubes) in West Midlands, England, NW of Birmingham; population (1981) 155,000.

Western Australia state of Australia
area 2,525,500 sq km/974,843 sq mi
capital Perth
towns main port Fremantle, Bunbury, Geraldton, Kalgoorlie-Boulder, Albany
features largest state in Australia; Monte Bello Islands; rivers Fitzroy, Fortescue, Gascoyne, Murchison, and Swan; NW coast subject to hurricanes ('willy-willies'); Lasseter's Reef
products wheat, fresh and dried fruit, meat and dairy products; natural gas (NW shelf) and oil (Canning Basin), iron (the Pilbara), copper, nickel, uranium, gold, diamonds
population (1987) 1,478,000
history a short-lived convict settlement at King George Sound 1826; Captain James Stirling (1791–1865) founded the modern state at Perth 1829; self-government 1890; state 1901.

Western Isles island area of Scotland, comprising the Outer Hebrides (Lewis, Harris, North and South Uist, and Barra); unofficially the Inner and Outer Hebrides generally
area 2,900 sq km/1,120 sq mi

Western Australia

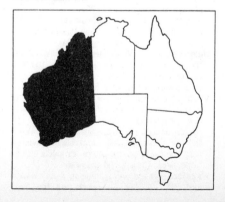

Western Isles

towns administrative headquarters Stornoway on Lewis
features divided from the mainland by the Minch; Callanish monolithic circles of the Stone Age on Lewis
products Harris tweed, sheep, fish, cattle
population (1987) 31,000.
Western Provinces in Canada, the provinces of ◊Alberta, ◊British Columbia, ◊Manitoba, and ◊Saskatchewan.
Western Sahara formerly ***Spanish Sahara*** disputed territory in NW Africa bounded to the N by Morocco, to the W and S by Mauritania, and to the E by the Atlantic Ocean
area 266,800 sq km/103,011 sq mi
capital La'Youn (Arabic ***El Aaiún***)
towns phosphate mining town of Bou Craa
features electrically monitored fortified wall enclosing the phosphate area
exports phosphates
currency dirham
population (1988) 181,400; another estimated 165,000 live in refugee camps near Tindouf, SW Algeria. Ethnic composition: Sawrawis (traditionally nomadic herders)
language Arabic
religion Sunni Muslim
government administered by Morocco
history this 1,000-km-long Saharan coastal region, which during the 19th century separated French-dominated Morocco and Mauritania, was designated a Spanish 'sphere of influence' in 1884 because it lies opposite the Spanish-ruled Canary Islands. On securing its independence in 1956, Morocco laid claim to and invaded this 'Spanish Sahara' territory, but was repulsed. Moroccan

interest was rekindled from 1965, following the discovery of rich phosphate resources at Bou-Craa, and within Spanish Sahara a pro-independence nationalist movement developed, spearheaded by the Popular Front for the Liberation of Saguia al Hamra and Rio de Oro (Polisario), which was established in 1973. After the death of the Spanish ruler Franco, Spain withdrew and the territory was partitioned between Morocco and Mauritania. Polisario rejected this partition, declared their own independent Saharan Arab Democratic Republic (SADR), and proceeded to wage a guerrilla war, securing indirect support from Algeria and, later, Libya. By 1979 they had succeeded in their struggle against Mauritania, who withdrew from their southern sector and concluded a peace agreement with Polisario, and in 1982 the SADR was accepted as a full member of the Organization of African Unity. By the end of 1989, 70 countries had granted diplomatic recognition to the SADR.

Morocco, who occupied the Mauritanian-evacuated zone, still retained control over the bulk of the territory, including the key towns and phosphate mines, which they protected with an 2,500-km-long 'electronic defensive wall'. From the mid-1980s this wall was gradually extended outwards as Libya and Algeria reduced their support for Polisario and drew closer to Morocco. In 1988, Morocco and the Polisario Front agreed to United Nations–sponsored plans for a cease-fire and a referendum in Western Sahara, based on 1974 voting rolls, to decide the territory's future. However, divisions persisted during 1989–90 over the terms of the referendum and sporadic fighting continued.

Western Samoa see ◊Samoa, Western.
West Germany see ◊Germany, West.
West Glamorgan county in SW Wales
area 820 sq km/317 sq mi
towns administrative headquarters Swansea; Port Talbot, Neath
features Gower Peninsula
products tinplate, copper, steel, chemicals
population (1987) 363,000
language 16% Welsh, English.
West Indies archipelago of about 1,200 islands, dividing the Atlantic from the Gulf of Mexico and the Caribbean. The islands are divided into:
Bahamas
Greater Antilles Cuba, Hispaniola (Haiti, Dominican Republic), Jamaica, Puerto Rico
Lesser Antilles Aruba, Netherlands Antilles, Trinidad and Tobago, the Windward Islands (Grenada, Barbados, St Vincent, St Lucia, Martinique, Dominica, Guadeloupe), the Leeward Islands (Montserrat, Antigua, St Christopher (St Kitts)-Nevis, Barbuda, Anguilla, St Martin, British and US Virgin Islands), and many smaller islands.

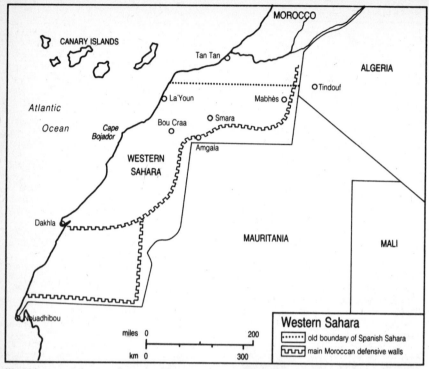

MOROCCO

CANARY ISLANDS

Tan Tan

ALGERIA

○Tindouf

○La'Youn   Mabhès○

Atlantic

○Smara

Bou Craa ○

Ocean   *Cape Bojador*

Amgala

WESTERN
SAHARA

Dakhla ○

MAURITANIA   MALI

○Nouadhibou

miles 0 ——— 200
km 0 ——— 300

Western Sahara

······· old boundary of Spanish Sahara
⊔⊔⊔⊔ main Moroccan defensive walls

West Irian former name for ◊Irian Jaya.

West Lothian former county of central Scotland, bordering the S shore of the Firth of Forth; from 1975 included (except for the Bo'ness area, which went to Central region) in Lothian region. Linlithgow was the administrative headquarters.

Westman Islands small group of islands off the south coast of Iceland. In 1973 volcanic eruption caused the population of 5,200 to be temporarily evacuated, and added 2.5 sq km/1 sq mi to the islands' area. Heimaey is one of Iceland's chief fishing ports.

Westmeath inland county of Leinster province, Republic of Ireland
area 1,760 sq km/679 sq mi
town county town Mullingar
physical rivers Shannon, Inny, and Brosna; lakes Ree, Sheelin, and Ennell
products agricultural and dairy products, limestone, textiles
population (1986) 63,000.

West Midlands metropolitan county in central England, created 1974, originally administered by an elected council; its powers reverted to district councils from 1986
area 900 sq km/347 sq mi
towns administrative headquarters Birmingham

features created 1974 from the area around and including Birmingham, and comprising Wolverhampton, Walsall, Dudley, West Bromwich, Smethwick, Coventry
products manufacturing industrial goods
population (1987) 2,624,000
famous people Philip Larkin.

Westminster, City of borough of central Greater London, on the north bank of the Thames between Kensington and the City of London; population (1986) 176,000. It encompasses Bayswater, Belgravia, Mayfair, Paddington, Pimlico, Soho, St John's Wood, and Westminster.
Bayswater residential and hotel area north of Kensington Gardens
Belgravia bounded to the north by Knightsbridge, has squares laid out 1825–30 by Thomas Cubitt
Mayfair between Oxford Street and Piccadilly, includes Park Lane and Grosvenor Square (with the US embassy)
Paddington with Little Venice on the Grand Union Canal
Pimlico with the Tate Gallery (Turner collection, British, and modern art)
Soho with many restaurants, a Chinese community around Gerrard Street, and formerly known for strip clubs and sex shops

West Glamorgan

West Midlands

St John's Wood has Lord's cricket ground and the studios at 11 Abbey Road where the Beatles recorded their music

Westminster encompasses Buckingham Palace (royal residence), Green Park, St James's Park and St James's Palace (16th century), Marlborough House, Westminster Abbey, Westminster Hall (1097–1401), the Houses of Parliament with Big Ben, Whitehall (government offices), Downing Street (homes of the prime minister at number 10 and the chancellor of the Exchequer at number 11), Hyde Park with the Albert Memorial opposite the Royal Albert Hall, Trafalgar Square with the National Gallery and National Portrait Gallery.

Westmorland former county in the Lake District, England, part of Cumbria from 1974.

Weston-super-Mare seaside resort and town in Avon, SW England, on the Bristol Channel; population (1984) 170,000. Industries include plastics, and engineering.

West Sussex county on the S coast of England
area 2,020 sq km/780 sq mi
towns administrative headquarters Chichester; Crawley, Horsham, Haywards Heath; resorts Worthing, Littlehampton, Bognor Regis; port Shoreham
physical the Weald, South Downs; rivers Arun, West Rother, Adur
features Arundel and Bramber castles; Goodwood, Petworth House (17th century), and Wakehurst Place, where the Royal Botanic Gardens, Kew, has additional grounds.
population (1987) 700,000.

West Virginia state of the E USA; nickname Mountain State

area 62,900 sq km/24,279 sq mi
capital Charleston
towns Huntington, Wheeling
physical Allegheny Mountains; Ohio River
features port of Harper's Ferry, restored as when John Brown seized the US armoury 1859
products fruit, poultry, dairy and meat products, timber, coal, natural gas, oil, chemicals, synthetic fibres, plastics, steel, glass, pottery
population (1986) 1,919,000
famous people Pearl Buck, Thomas 'Stonewall' Jackson

West Sussex

West Virginia

West Yorkshire

history mound builders 6th century; explorers and fur traders 1670s; German settlements 1730s; industrial development early 19th century; on the secession of Virginia from the Union 1862, West Virginians dissented, and formed a new state 1863; industrial expansion accompanied by labour strife in the early 20th century.

West Yorkshire metropolitan county in NE England, created 1976, originally administered by an elected metropolitan council; its powers reverted to district councils from 1986
area 2,040 sq km/787 sq mi
towns administrative headquarters Wakefield; Leeds, Bradford, Halifax, Huddersfield
features Ilkley Moor, Haworth Moor, Haworth Parsonage; part of the Peak District National Park
products coal, woollen textiles
population (1987) 2,052,000
famous people the Brontës, David Hockney, Henry Moore, J B Priestley.

Wexford seaport and county town of Wexford, Republic of Ireland; population (1981) 15,000. Products include textiles, cheese, and agricultural machinery. It was founded by the Danes in the 9th century, and devastated by Cromwell 1649.

Wexford county in the Republic of Ireland, province of Leinster
area 2,350 sq km/907 sq mi
towns county town Wexford; Rosslare
products fish, livestock, oats, barley, potatoes
population (1986) 102,000.

Weymouth seaport and resort in Dorset, S England; population (1981) 46,000. It is linked by ferry to France and the Channel Islands. Weymouth, dating from the 10th century, was the first place in England to suffer from the Black Death 1348, and was popularized as a bathing resort by George III.

Whipsnade a zoo in Bedfordshire, England, 5 km/3 mi S of Dunstable, opened 1931, where wild animals and birds are bred and exhibited in conditions resembling their natural state.

Whitby port and resort in N Yorkshire, England, on the North Sea coast; population (1981) 14,000.

Industries include boatbuilding, fishing, and plastics. Remains of a Benedictine abbey built 1078 survive on the site of the original foundation by St Hilda 657, which was destroyed by the Danes 867. Captain Cook's ship *Resolution* was built in Whitby, where he had served his apprenticeship, and he sailed from here on his voyage to the Pacific in 1768.

Whitehall street in central London, between Trafalgar Square and the Houses of Parliament, with many government offices and the Cenotaph war memorial.

Whitehaven town and port in Cumbria, NW England, on the Irish sea coast; population (1981) 27,000. Indstries include chemicals and printing. Britain's first nuclear power station was sited at Calder Hall to the SE, where there is also a plant for reprocessing spent nuclear fuel at ◊Sellafield.

Whitehorse capital of Yukon Territory, Canada; population (1986) 20,000. Whitehorse is on the NW Highway. It replaced Dawson as capital in 1953.

White Russia English translation of ◊Byelorussia, republic of the USSR.

White Sea (Russian *Beloye More*) gulf of the Arctic Ocean, on which the port of Archangel stands. There is a Soviet warship construction base, including nuclear submarines, at Severodvinsk. The North Dvina and Onega rivers flow into it, and there are canal links with the Baltic, Black, and Caspian seas.

Whitstable resort in Kent, SE England, at the mouth of the river Swale, noted for its oysters; population (1985) 27,000.

Whyalla port and industrial city (iron and steel) in South Australia; population (1985) 30,000.

WI abbreviation for ◊*West Indies*; ◊*Wisconsin*.

Wichita industrial city (oil refining, aircraft, motor vehicles) in S Kansas, USA; population (1980) 280,000. It was settled 1864 and named after an Indian tribe.

Wick fishing port and industrial town (shipping, distilleries, North Sea oil) in NE Scotland, in the Highland region; population about 8,000. Air services to the Orkneys and Shetlands operate from here.

Wicklow county in the Republic of Ireland, province of Leinster
area 2,030 sq km/784 sq mi
towns county town Wicklow
physical Wicklow Mountains; rivers Slane and Liffey.
features the village of Shillelagh gave its name to rough cudgels of oak or blackthorn made there
population (1986) 94,000.

Wicklow port and county town of County Wicklow, Republic of Ireland; population (1981) 5,000.

Wien German name for ◊Vienna, capital of Austria.

Wiesbaden spa town and capital of Hessen, West Germany, on the Rhine 20 km/12 mi west of Frankfurt; population (1988) 267,000. Products include cement, plastics, wines and spirits; most of the German sparkling wine cellars are in this area. Wiesbaden was the capital of the former duchy of Nassau 12th century–1866.

Wigan industrial town (food processing, engineering, paper) in Greater Manchester, NW England; population (1981) 80,000. The *Wigan Alps* are a recreation area with ski slopes and water sports created from industrial dereliction including colliery spoil heaps.

Wight, Isle of island and county in S England
area 380 sq km/147 sq mi
towns administrative headquarters Newport; resorts Ryde, Sandown, Shanklin, Ventnor
features the *Needles* a group of pointed chalk rocks up to 30 m/100 ft high in the sea to the west; the *Solent* the sea channel between Hampshire and the island (including the anchorage of *Spithead* opposite Portsmouth, used for naval reviews); *Cowes*, venue of Regatta Week and headquarters of the Royal Yacht Squadron; Osborne House, near Cowes, a home of Queen Victoria, for whom it was built 1845; Farringford, home of Tennyson, near Freshwater
economy agriculture, tourism
population (1987) 127,000
history called *Vectis* ('separate division') by the Romans, who conquered it AD 43. Charles I was imprisoned 1647–48 in Carisbrooke Castle, now ruined.

Wigtown former county of SW Scotland extending to the Irish Sea, merged 1975 in Dumfries and Galloway. The administrative headquarters was Wigtown.

Wilhelmshaven North Sea industrial port, resort, and naval base in Lower Saxony, West Germany, on Jade Bay; population (1983) 99,000. Products include chemicals, textiles, and machinery.

Williamsburg historic city in Virginia, USA; population (1980) 10,000. Founded in 1632, capital of the colony of Virginia 1699–1779, much of it has been restored to its 18th-century appearance. The College of William and Mary 1693 is one of the oldest in the USA.

Wilmington industrial port and city (chemicals, textiles, shipbuilding, iron and steel goods, headquarters of Du Pont enterprises) in Delaware, USA; population (1980) 70,000. Founded by Swedish settlers as *Fort Christina* 1638; taken and renamed by the British in the 1730s.

Wilton market town in Wiltshire, S England, outside Salisbury; population (1981) 4,000. It has manufactured carpets since the 16th century. Wilton House, the seat of the earls of Pembroke, was built from designs by Holbein and Inigo Jones, and is associated with Sir Philip Sidney and Shakespeare.

Wilts abbreviation for ◊*Wiltshire*.

Wiltshire county in SW England
area 3,480 sq km/1,343 sq mi
towns administrative headquarters Trowbridge; Salisbury, Swindon, Wilton
physical Marlborough Downs, Savernake Forest; rivers Kennet and Salisbury and Bristol Avons; Salisbury Plain, including Stonehenge
features Salisbury Plain has been used as a military training area since Napoleonic times; Longleat House (Marquess of Bath), Wilton House (Earl of Pembroke), and Stourhead with 18th-century gardens

Wiltshire

products wheat, cattle, carpets, rubber, engineering
population (1987) 551,000.

Wimbledon district of the Greater London borough of Merton, headquarters of the All-England Lawn Tennis and Croquet Club where international matches have been held since 1877.

Winchester cathedral city and administrative headquarters of Hampshire, on the river Itchen; population (1984) 93,000. Tourism is important and there is also light industry. Originally a Roman town, Winchester was the capital of Wessex. Winchester Cathedral is the longest medieval church in Europe and was remodelled from Norman-Romanesque to Perpendicular Gothic under the patronage of William of Wykeham (founder of Winchester College 1382), who is buried there, as are Saxon kings, St Swithun, and the writers Izaac Walton and Jane Austen. A medieval 'reconstruction' of Arthur's Round Table is preserved in the 13th-century hall (all that survives) of the castle.

Windermere largest lake in England, in Cumbria, 17 km/10.5 mi long and 1.6 km/1 mi wide.

Windhoek capital of Namibia; population (1988) 115,000. It is just north of the tropic of Capricorn, 290 km/180 mi from the W coast.

Windscale former name of ◊Sellafield, nuclear plant in Cumbria, England.

Windsor industrial lake port (car engines, pharmaceuticals, iron and steel goods, paint, and bricks) in Ontario, SE Canada, opposite Detroit, USA; population (1986) 254,000. It was founded as a Hudson Bay Company post 1853.

Windsor town in Berkshire, S England, on the river Thames; population (1981) 28,000. It is the site of Windsor Castle, Eton College (public school) 1540, and has a 17th-century guildhall designed by Christopher Wren.

Windward Islands islands in the path of the prevailing wind, notably:
West Indies see under ◊Antilles
◊***Cape Verde Islands***
◊***French Polynesia*** (Tahiti, Moorea, and Makatea).

Winnipeg capital and industrial city (sawmills, textiles, meat packing) in Manitoba, Canada, on the Red River, south of Lake Winnipeg; population (1986) 623,000. Established as Winnipeg 1873 on the site of earlier forts, the city expanded with the arrival of the Canadian Pacific Railroad 1881.

Winnipeg, Lake lake in S Manitoba, Canada, draining much of the Canadian prairies; area 24,500 sq km/9,460 sq mi.

Winterthur Swiss town and spa NE of Zürich; population (1987) 108,000. Manufacturing includes engines and textiles.

Wisconsin state of the north central USA; nickname Badger State
area 145,500 sq km/56,163 sq mi
capital Madison

Wisconsin

towns Milwaukee, Green Bay, Racine
features Great Lakes
products premier dairying state, cereals, coal, iron, zinc, lead, agricultural machinery, precision instruments, plumbing equipment
population (1988) 4,816,000
famous people Edna Ferber, Harry Houdini, Joseph McCarthy, Spencer Tracy, Orson Welles, Thornton Wilder, Frank Lloyd Wright
history originally settled by the French; passed to Britain 1763; became American 1783; state 1848.

Witten city in North Rhine-Westphalia, West Germany; population (1988) 102,000.

Wittenberg town in East Germany, on the river Elbe, SW of Berlin, long known for its university (1502, but transferred to Halle 1815); population (1981) 54,000. Luther preached in the Stadtkirche (in which he is buried), nailed his 95 theses to the door of the Schlosskirche 1517, and taught philosophy at the university. The artists Lucas Cranach, father and son, lived here.

Witwatersrand or ***the Rand*** the economic heartland of S Transvaal, South Africa. Its mountain ridge, which stretches nearly 100 km/62 mi, produces over half the world's gold. Gold was first found there in 1857. The chief city of the region is Johannesburg. Forming a watershed between the Vaal and the Olifant rivers, the Rand comprises a series of parallel ranges which extend 100 km/60 mi E–W and rise to 1,525–1,830 m/5,000–6,000 ft above sea level. Gold occurs in reefs that are mined at depths of up to 3,050 m/10,000 ft.

Wolfsburg town NE of Brunswick in West Germany, chosen 1938 as the Volkswagen (Hitler's 'People's Car') factory site; population (1988) 122,000.

Wollongong industrial city (iron, steel) in New South Wales, Australia, 65 km/40 mi south of Sydney; population (1985, with Port Kembla) 238,000.

Wolverhampton industrial city (metalworking, chemicals, tyres, aircraft, commercial vehicles) in West Midlands, England, 20 km/12 mi NW of Birmingham; population (1984) 254,000.

Woolwich London district cut through by the Thames, the northern section being in the borough of Newham and the southern in Greenwich. There is a ferry here and a flood barrier 1984. The Royal Arsenal, an ordnance depot from 1518, was closed down 1967.

Woomera town in South Australia, site of a rocket range from 1946; population (1984) 1,800.

Worcester cathedral city with industries (gloves, shoes, Worcester sauce; Royal Worcester porcelain from 1751) in Hereford and Worcester, W central England, administrative headquarters of the county, on the river Severn; population (1985) 76,000. The cathedral dates from the 13th–14th centuries. The birthplace of the composer Elgar at nearby Broadheath is a museum. At the *Battle of Worcester* 1651 Cromwell defeated Charles I.

Worcester industrial port (textiles, engineering, printing) in central Massachusetts, USA, on the Blackstone River; population (1980) 373,000. It was founded 1713.

Worcestershire former Midland county of England, merged 1974 with Herefordshire in the new county of Hereford and Worcester, except for a small projection in the north, which went to West Midlands. Worcester was the county town.

Worcs abbreviation for ◊*Worcestershire*.

Worksop market and industrial town (coal, glass, chemicals, engineering) in Nottinghamshire, central England, on the river Ryton; population (1981) 37,000. Mary Queen of Scots was imprisoned at Worksop Manor (burned 1761).

Worms industrial town in Rhineland-Palatinate, West Germany, on the Rhine; population (1984) 73,000. Liebfraumilch wine is produced here. The Protestant reformer Luther appeared before the *Diet* (Assembly) *of Worms* 1521, and was declared an outlaw by the Roman Catholic Church.

Worthing seaside resort in West Sussex, England, at the foot of the South Downs; population (1984) 94,000. Industries include electronics, engineering, plastics, and furniture. There are traces of prehistoric and Roman occupation in the vicinity.

Wounded Knee site on the Oglala Sioux Reservation, South Dakota, USA, of a confrontation between the US Army and American Indians. Sitting Bull was killed, supposedly resisting arrest, on 15 Dec 1890, and on 29 Dec a group of Indians involved with him in the Ghost Dance Movement (aimed at resumption of Indian control of North America with the aid of the spirits of dead braves) were surrounded and 153 killed.

In 1973 the militant American Indian Movement, in the siege of Wounded Knee 27 Feb–8 May, held hostages and demanded a government investigation of the Indian treaties.

Wrexham town in Clwyd, NE Wales, 19 km/12 mi SW of Chester; population (1983) 40,000. Industries include coal, electronics, and pharmaceuticals. Seat of the Roman Catholic bishopric of Menevia (Wales). Elihu Yale, benefactor of Yale university, died in Wrexham and is buried in the 15th-century church of St Giles.

Wroclaw industrial river port in Poland, on the river Oder; population (1985) 636,000. Under the German name of Breslau, it was the capital of former German Silesia. Industries include shipbuilding, engineering, textiles, and electronics.

Wuchang former city in China; amalgamated with ◊Wuhan.

Wuhan river port and capital of Hubei province, China, at the confluence of the Han and Chang Jiang, formed 1950 as one of China's greatest industrial areas by the amalgamation of Hankou, Hanyang, and Wuchang; population (1986) 3,400,000. It produces iron, steel, machine tools, textiles, and fertilizer.

A centre of revolt in both the Taiping Rebellion 1851–65 and the 1911 revolution, it had an anti-Mao revolt 1967 during the Cultural Revolution.

Wuhsien another name for ◊Suzhou, a city in China.

Wuppertal industrial town in North Rhine-Westphalia, West Germany, 32 km/20 mi east of Düsseldorf; population (1988) 374,000. Industries include textiles, plastics, brewing, and electronics. It was formed 1929 (named 1931) by uniting Elberfeld (13th century) and Barmen (11th century).

Württemberg former kingdom in SW Germany, 1805–1918, which joined the German Reich in 1870. Its capital was Stuttgart. Divided in 1946 between the administrative West German *Länder* of Württemberg-Baden and Württemberg-Hohenzollern, from 1952 it was part of the *Land* of ◊Baden-Württemberg.

Würzburg industrial town (engineering, printing, wine, brewing) in NW Bavaria, West Germany; population (1988) 127,000. The bishop's palace was decorated by Tiepolo.

WV abbreviation for ◊*West Virginia*.

WY abbreviation for ◊*Wyoming*.

Wye river in Wales and England; length 208 km/130 mi. It rises on Plynlimmon, NE Dyfed, flowing SE and E through Powys, and Hereford and Worcester, then follows the

Wyoming

Gwent/Gloucestershire border before joining the river Severn S of Chepstow. Other rivers of the same name in the UK are found in Buckinghamshire (15 km/9 mi) and Derbyshire (32 km/20 mi).

Wyoming state of W USA; nickname Equality State

area 253,400 sq km/97,812 sq mi

capital Cheyenne

towns Casper, Laramie

features Rocky Mountains; Yellowstone (including the geyser Old Faithful) and Grand Teton national parks

products oil, natural gas, tin, sodium salts, coal, phosphates, sulphur, uranium, sheep, beef

population (1988) 477,000

famous people Buffalo Bill Cody

history part of the Louisiana Purchase; first settled by whites 1834; granted women the vote 1869; state 1890.

Xiamen formerly *Amoy* port on Ku Lang island in Fujian province, SE China; population (1984) 533,000. Industries include textiles, food products, and electronics. It was one of the original five treaty ports used for trade under foreign control 1842–1943 and a special export-trade zone from 1979.

Xian industrial city and capital of Shaanxi province, China; population (1986) 2,330,000. It produces chemicals, electrical equipment, and fertilizers.

It was the capital of China under the Zhou dynasty (1126–255 BC); under the Han dynasty (206 BC–AD 220), when it was called *Changan* (long peace); under the Tang dynasty 618–906, as *Siking* ('western capital'); the Manchus called it *Sian* ('western peace'), now spelled Xian; it reverted to Changan 1913–32; was Siking 1932–43; and again Sian from 1943. It was here that the imperial court retired after the Boxer rising 1900.

Its treasures include the 600-year-old Ming wall; the pottery soldiers buried to protect the tomb of the first Qin emperor Shi Huangdi; Big Wild Goose Pagoda, one of the oldest in China; and the Great Mosque 742.

Xi Jiang (formerly *Si-Kiang*) river in China, which rises in Yunnan and flows into the South China Sea; length 1,900 km/1,200 mi. Guangzhou lies on the N arm of its delta, and Hong Kong island at its mouth. The name means West River.

Xingú river rising in the Mato Grosso, Brazil, and flowing 1,932 km/1,200 mi to the Amazon delta.

Xingu river (Amazon tributary) and region in Pará, Brazil. In 1989 Xingú Indians protested at the creation of a huge, intrusive lake for the Babaquara and Kararao dams of the Altamira complex.

Xining formerly *Sining* industrial city, capital of Qinghai province, China; population (1982) 873,000.

Xinjiang Uygur formerly *Sinkiang Uighur* autonomous region of NW China
area 1,646,800 sq km/635,665 sq mi
capital Urumqi
features largest of Chinese administrative areas; Junggar Pendi (Dzungarian Basin) and Tarim Pendi (Tarim Basin, which includes ◊Lop Nor, China's nuclear testing ground, though the research centres were moved to the central province of Sichuan 1972) separated by the Tyan Shan mountains
products cereals, cotton, fruit in valleys and oases; uranium, coal, iron, copper, tin, oil
population (1986) 13,840,000
religion 50% Muslim
history under Manchu rule from the 18th century; large sections ceded to Russia 1864 and 1881; China has raised the question of their return and regards the 480 km/300 mi frontier between Xinjiang Uygur and Soviet Tadzikistan as undemarcated.

Xizang Chinese name for ◊Tibet, an autonomous region of SW China from 1965.

Xochimilco lake about 11 km/7 mi SE of Mexico City, Mexico, noted for its floating gardens, all that remains of an ancient water-based agricultural system.

Yakut (Russian *Yakutskaya*) autonomous republic in NE USSR
area 3,103,000 sq km/1,197,760 sq mi
capital Yakutsk
features Yakut is one of world's coldest inhabited places; river Lena
products furs; gold, natural gas, some agriculture in the south
population (1986) 1,009,000; Yakuts 37%, Russians 50%
history the nomadic Yakuts were conquered by Russia 17th century; Yakut became a Soviet republic 1922.

Yakutsk capital of Yakut republic, USSR, on the river Lena; population (1987) 184,000. Industries include timber, tanning, and brick-making. It is the coldest point of the Arctic in NE Siberia, and has an institute for studying the permanently frozen soil area (permafrost).

Yalu river forming the N boundary between North Korea and Jilin and Liaoning provinces (Manchuria) in China; length 790 km/491 mi. It is only navigable near the mouth and is frozen from Nov to Mar.

Yamal Peninsula peninsula in NW Siberia, USSR, with gas reserves estimated at 6 trillion cubic metres; supplies are piped to W Europe.

Yamoussoukro capital designate of Ivory Coast (Côte d'Ivoire); population (1986) 120,000. The economy is based on tourism and agricultural trade.

Yamuna alternative name for the ◊Jumna River in India.

Yan'an formerly *Yenan* industrial city in Shaanxi province, central China; population (1984) 254,000. The Long March ended here Jan 1937, and it was the communist headquarters 1936–47 (the caves in which Mao lived are preserved).

Yangon former name until 1989 *Rangoon* capital and chief port of Myanmar (Burma), on the Yangon River, 32 km/20 mi from the Indian Ocean; population (1983) 2,459,000. Products include timber, oil, and rice. The city *Dagon* was founded on the site AD 746; it was given the name Rangoon (meaning 'end of conflict') by King Alaungpaya 1755.

Yangtze-Kiang former name for ◊Chang Jiang, greatest Chinese river.

Yangzhou formerly *Yangchow* canal port in Jiangsu province, E China, on the Yangtze river; population (1984) 382,000. It is noted for its gardens and pavilions and is an artistic centre for crafts, jade carving, and printing.

Yantai formerly *Chefoo* ice-free port in Shandong province, E China; population (1984) 700,000. A special economic zone; industries include tourism, wine, and fishing.

Yaoundé capital of Cameroon, 210 km/130 mi E of the port of Douala; population (1984) 552,000. Industry includes tourism, oil refining, and cigarette manufacturing. Established by the Germans as a military port 1899, it became capital of French Cameroon 1921.

Yarkand or *Shache* walled city in Xinjiang Uygur region of China, in an oasis of the Tarim basin, on the caravan route to India and W USSR; a centre of Islamic culture; population (1985) 100,000.

Yarmouth or *Great Yarmouth* holiday resort and port in Norfolk, England; at the mouth of the river Yare; population (1981) 55,000. Formerly a fishing town, it is now a leading base for North Sea oil and gas, and a container port.

Yaroslavl industrial city (textiles, rubber, paints, commercial vehicles) in the USSR, capital of Yaroslavl region, on the Volga 250 km/155 mi NE of Moscow; population (1987) 634,000.

Yazd or *Yezd* silk-weaving town in central Iran, in an oasis on a trade route; population (1986) 231,000.

Yellowknife capital of Northwest Territories, Canada, on the north shore of Great Slave Lake; population (1984) 11,000. It was founded 1935 when gold was discovered in the area, and became the capital 1967.

Yellow River English name for the ◊Huang He river, China.

Yellow Sea gulf of the Pacific Ocean between China and Korea; area 466,200 sq km/180,000 sq mi. It receives the Huang He (Yellow River) and Chang Jiang.

Yellowstone National Park largest US nature reserve, established 1872, on a broad plateau in the Rocky Mountains, Wyoming. 1 million of its 2.2 million acres have been destroyed by fire since July 1988.

Yemen, North
Yemen Arab Republic *(al Jamhuriya al Arabiya al Yamaniya)*

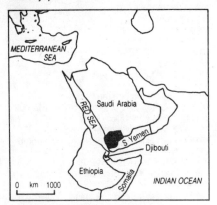

area 195,000 sq km/75,290 sq mi
capital San'a
towns Ta'iz, and chief port Hodeida
physical hot moist coastal plain, rising to plateau
features known in classical times as *Arabia felix* because of its fertility
head of state and of government Ali Abdullah Saleh from 1978
goverment system authoritarian republic
political parties no recognizable parties
exports cotton, coffee, grapes
currency rial (16.59 = £1 Mar 1990)
population (1989) 6,937,000; annual growth rate 2.7%
life expectancy men 47, women 50
language Arabic
religion Sunni Muslim 50%, Shi'ite Muslim 50%
literacy 27% male/3% female (1985 est)
GNP $3.9 bn (1983); $475 per head of population
chronology
1962 North Yemen declared the Arab Republic of Yemen (YAR), with Abdullah al-Sallal as president. Civil war broke out between royalists and republicans.
1967 Civil war ended with the republicans victorious. Sallal deposed and replaced by a Republican Council.
1971–72 War between South Yemen and YAR. Both sides finally agreed to a union but the agreement was not kept.
1974 Ibrahim al-Hamadi seized power and a Military Command Council was set up.
1977 Hamadi assassinated and replaced by Ahmed ibn Hussein al-Ghashmi.
1978 Constituent People's Assembly appointed and the Military Command Council dissolved. Ghashmi killed by an envoy from South Yemen and succeeded by Ali Abdullah Saleh. War broke out again between the two Yemens.
1979 Ceasefire agreed with, again, a commitment to a future union.
1983 Saleh elected president for a further five-year term.
1984 Joint committee on foreign policy for the two Yemens met in Aden.
1988 President Saleh re-elected.
1989 Draft constitution for single Yemen state published.
1990 Border with South Yemen opened.

Yemen two countries (North Yemen and South Yemen) between which union was agreed 1979, and unification was proclaimed in May 1990, with a 30-month period of implementation. The capital of the new Republic of Yemen will be Sama'a. A democratic system of government is promised; a presidential council will oversee the process of unification; president Lt-Gen Ali Abdullah Saleh.

Yemen, North country in SW Asia, on the Red Sea, bounded to the N by Saudi Arabia and to the S by South Yemen.

Yemen, South country in SW Asia, on the Arabian Sea, bounded to the N by Saudi Arabia, to the E by Oman, and to the NW by North Yemen.

Yenan former name for city of ◊Yan'an in Chinese province of Shaanxi.

Yenisei river in Asiatic USSR, rising in Tuva region and flowing across the Siberian plain into the Arctic Ocean; length 4,100 km/2,550 mi.

Yerevan industrial city (tractor parts, machine tools, chemicals, bricks, bicycles, wine, fruit canning), capital of Armenian Republic, USSR, a few miles north of the Turkish border; population (1987) 1,168,000. It was founded 7th century, and was alternately Turkish and Persian from the 15th century until ceded to Russia 1828. Its university was founded 1921. The city has seen mounting inter-ethnic violence and Armenian nationalist demonstrations since 1988, fanned by the ◊Nagorno-Karabakh dispute.

Yezd another name for the Iranian town of ◊Yazd.

Yezo another name for ◊Hokkaido, most northerly of the four main islands of Japan.

Yichang port at the head of navigation of the Chang Jiang, Hubei province, China; population (1982) 175,000.

Yinchuan capital of Ningxia autonomous region, NW China; population (1984) 383,000.

Yemen, South

People's Democratic Republic of Yemen
(Jumhuriyah al-Yemen al Dimuqratiyah al Sha'abiyah)

area 336,900 sq km/130,077 sq mi
capital Aden
physical desert and mountains; very hot and dry
features it includes the islands of Perim (in the strait of Bab-el-Mandeb, at the southern entrance to the Red Sea), Socotra, and Kamaran; Aden is used by the USSR as a naval base
head of state and government Haydar Abu Bakr al-Attas from 1986
government system one-party socialist republic
political parties Yemen Socialist Party (YSP), Marxist-Leninist
exports cotton goods, coffee
currency Yemeni dinar (0.58=£1 Mar 1990)
population (1989) 2,488,000; annual growth rate 2.8%
life expectancy men 47, women 50
language Arabic
religion Sunni Muslim 91%
literacy 39% (1980)
GNP $1 bn (1983); $310 per head of population
chronology
1967 People's Republic of Southern Yemen founded.
1970 Country renamed the People's Democratic Republic of Yemen (PDRY), led by the Marxist National Front Party (NF).
1971–72 War with North Yemen.
1978 North Yemen president killed by a bomb carried by a PDRY envoy. Yemen Socialist Party (YSP) formed as a 'Marxist-Leninist vanguard party'. War between North and South Yemen.
1979 Ceasefire agreed and the two Yemens agreed to move towards eventual union.
1983 Joint Yemen council established.
1985 Ali Nasser Muhammad elected president but was deposed after his personal guards killed three of his party opponents.
1986 Hayder Abu Bakr al-Attas became president and secretary general of the YPS Politburo.
1987 Discussions with North Yemen about possible merger.
1989 Draft constitution for unified state published.
1990 Border with North Yemen opened.

Yogyakarta city in Java, Indonesia, capital 1945–49; population (1980) 399,000. The Buddhist pyramid shrine to the NW at Borobudur (122 m/400 ft square) was built AD 750–850.

Yokohama Japanese port on Tokyo Bay; population (1987) 3,072,000. Industries include ship-building, oil refining, engineering, textiles, glass, and clothing.

In 1859, it was the first Japanese port opened to foreign trade. From then it grew rapidly from a small fishing village to the chief centre of trade with Europe and the USA. Almost destroyed in an earthquake 1923, it was again rebuilt after World War II.

Yokosuka Japanese seaport and naval base (1884) on Tokyo Bay, south of Yokohama; population (1984) 428,000.

Yonkers city in Westchester county, New York, USA, on the Hudson; population (1980) 204,000. It was a Dutch settlement from about 1650.

Yonne French river, 290 km/180 mi long, rising in central France and flowing north into the Seine;

it gives its name to a *département* in Burgundy region.

York cathedral and industrial city (railway rolling stock, scientific instruments, sugar, chocolate, and glass) in North Yorkshire, N England; population (1985) 102,000.

features The Gothic York Minster contains medieval stained glass. Much of the 14th-century city wall survives, with four gates or 'bars', as well as the medieval shambles (slaughterhouse). Jorvik Viking Centre opened 1984 after excavation of site at Coppergate, containing wooden remains of Viking houses. Also notable are 17th–18th-century domestic architecture; the Theatre Royal, site of a theatre since 1765; Castle Museum; National Railway Museum and the 19th-century railway station; university 1963.

history York was a British city, traditionally the capital of the north of England, before becoming from AD 71 the Roman fortress of *Eboracum*, and the first bishop of York (Paulinus) was consecrated 627 in the wooden church which first

Yugoslavia
Socialist Federal Republic of
(Socijalistička Federativna Republika Jugoslavija)

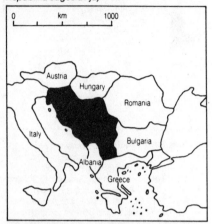

area 255,800 sq km/98,739 sq mi
capital Belgrade
towns Zagreb, Skopje, Ljubljana; ports Split, Rijeka
physical mountainous; river Danube plains in north and east
features constituent republics of Bosnia and Herzegovina, Croatia, Macedonia, Montenegro, Serbia (including the autonomous provinces of Kosovo and Vojvodina), and Slovenia; scenic Dalmatian coast and Dinaric Alps; Lake Shkodër
head of state Janez Drovsek from 1988
head of government Ante Markovic from 1989
government system communism
political parties League of Communists of Yugoslavia (SKJ), Marxist-Leninist-Titoist; new competing parties are beginning to emerge in Croatia and Slovenia
exports machinery, electrical goods, chemicals

currency dinar (19.91=£1 Mar 1989)
population (1989) 23,753,000 (Serbs 36%, Croats 20%, Muslims 9%, Slovenes 8%, Albanians 8%, Macedonians 6%, Montenegrins 3%, Hungarians 2%, 5.5% declared themselves to be 'Yugoslavs'); annual growth rate 0.8%
life expectancy men 68, women 74
language individual national languages have equality, but Serbo-Croat is the most widespread
religion Orthodox (Serbs), Roman Catholic (Croats), Muslim (50% in Bosnia)
literacy 97% male/86% female (1985 est)
GNP $46.3 bn (1984); $3,109 per head of population
chronology
1917–18 Creation of Kingdom of the Serbs, Croats, and Slovenes.
1929 Name of Yugoslavia adopted.
1941 Invasion by Germany.
1945 Communist federal republic formed under leadership of Tito.
1948 Split with USSR.
1953 Self-management principle enshrined in constitution.
1961 Formation of Nonaligned Movement under Yugoslavia's leadership.
1974 New constitution adopted.
1980 Death of Tito. Collective leadership assumed power.
1987 Threat to use the army to curb unrest.
1988 Economic difficulties: 1,800 strikes, inflation over 250%, almost 20% unemployment. Ethnic unrest in Montenegro and Vojvodina led to party reshuffles and the resignation of the government.
1989 A reformist Croatian, Ante Markovic, became prime minister. 29 died in ethnic riots in Kosovo province and state of emergency imposed. Inflation rate over 1,000%
1990 Communist Party voted to end monopoly of power (Jan). Multi-party systems established in Slovenia and Croatia.

---

preceded York Minster. Paulinus baptized King Edwin there 627 and York was created an archbishopric 732. In the 10th century it was a Viking settlement. Its commercial prosperity depended on the wool trade in the Middle Ages. An active Quaker element in the 18th and 19th centuries included the Rowntree family that founded the chocolate factory.

Yorks. abbreviation for ◊*Yorkshire*.

Yorkshire county in NE England on the North Sea, formerly divided into north, east, and west ridings (thirds), but in 1974 reorganized to form a number of new counties: the major part of *Cleveland*

and *Humberside*; *North Yorkshire, South Yorkshire,* and *West Yorkshire.* Small outlying areas also went to Durham, Cumbria, Lancashire, and Greater Manchester. South and West Yorkshire are both former metropolitan counties.

Yosemite area in the Sierra Nevada, E California, USA, a national park from 1890. It includes Yosemite Gorge, Yosemite Falls, 762 m/2,500 ft in three leaps, and many others, and groves of giant sequoias.

Youngstown industrial city (iron and steel) in E Ohio, USA, on the river Mahoning; population (1980) 116,000.

Ysselmeer alternative spelling of ◊IJsselmeer, lake in the Netherlands.

Yucatán peninsula in Central America, divided between Mexico, Belize, and Guatemala; area 180,000 sq km/70,000 sq mi. Tropical crops are grown. It is inhabited by Maya Indians and contains the remains of their civilization. There are ruins at Chichén Itzá and Uxmal. The Mexican state of Yucatán has an area of 38,402 sq km/14,823 sq mi, and a population (1980) of 1,035,000. Its capital is Mérida.

Yugoslavia country in SE Europe, on the Adriatic Sea, bounded W by Italy, N by Austria and Hungary, E by Romania and Bulgaria, and S by Greece and Albania.

Yugoslavia: Constituent Republics

Republic	Capital	Area sq km
Bosnia and Herzegovina	Sarajevo	51,100
Croatia	Zagreb	56,500
Macedonia	Skopje	25,700
Montenegro	Titograd	13,800
Serbia	Belgrade	88,400
Kosovo	Pristina	10,900
Vojvodina	Novi Sad	21,500
Slovenia	Ljubljana	20,300
Total		255,800

Yukon territory of NW Canada

area 483,500 sq km/186,631 sq mi

towns capital Whitehorse; Dawson City

features named after its chief river, the Yukon; includes the highest point in Canada, Mount Logan 6,050 m/19,850 ft

products oil, natural gas, gold, silver, coal

population (1986) 24,000

history settlement dates from the gold rush 1896–1910, when 30,000 people moved to the

Yukon

Klondike river valley (silver is now worked there); became separate from Northwest Territories 1898, with Dawson City as the original capital.

Yukon River river in North America, 3,185 km/ 1,979 mi long, flowing from Lake Tagish in the Yukon Territory, NW Canada, into Alaska where it empties into the Bering Sea in a great delta.

Yungning former name 1913–45 for Chinese port of ◊Nanning.

Yunnan province of SW China, adjoining Burma, Laos, and Vietnam

area 436,200 sq km/168,373 sq mi

capital Kunming

physical Chang Jiang, Salween, and Mekong rivers; crossed by the Burma Road; mountainous and well forested

products rice, tea, timber, wheat, cotton, rubber, tin, copper, lead, zinc, coal, salt.

population (1986) 34,560,000.

Yuzovka former name (1872–1924) for the town of ◊Dometsk, Ukraine, USSR, named after the Welshman John Hughes who established a metallurgical factory there in the 1870s.

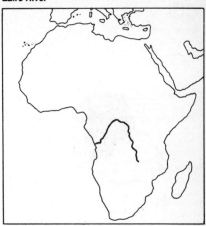

Zaïre River

Zaandam industrial port (timber, paper) in North Holland province, Netherlands, on the Zaan, NW of Amsterdam, since 1974 included in the municipality of ◊Zaanstad.

Zaanstad industrial town in W Netherlands which includes the port of ◊Zaandam; population (1988) 129,000.

Zabrze industrial city (coalmining, iron, chemicals) in Silesia, S Poland, formerly the German town of Hindenburg; population (1985) 198,000.

Zadar (Italian *Zara*) port and resort in Croatia, W Yugoslavia; population (1981) 116,000. It was alternately held and lost by the Venetian republic from the 12th century until its seizure by Austria 1813. It was the capital of Dalmatia 1815–1918, and part of Italy 1920–47, when it became part of Yugoslavia. The city was sacked by the army of the Fourth Crusade 1202, which led to the Crusade being excommunicated by Pope Innocent III.

Zagorsk town 70 km/45 mi NE of Moscow, USSR; population (1983) 111,000. The Trinity Monastery of St Sergius 1337, surrounded by a fortified wall, has a large collection of medieval Russian architecture and art.

Zagreb industrial city (leather, linen, carpets, paper, and electrical goods), capital of Croatia, Yugoslavia, on the Sava river; population (1981) 1,174,512. Zagreb was a Roman city (*Aemona*) and has a Gothic cathedral. Its university was founded 1874.

Zaïre country in central Africa.

Zaïre River formerly (until 1971) *Congo* second longest river in Africa, rising near the Zambia–Zaïre border (and known as the *Lualaba River* in the upper reaches) and flowing 4,500 km/2,800 mi to the Atlantic, running in a great curve which crosses the Equator twice, and discharging a volume of water second only to the Amazon.

The chief tributaries are the Ubangi, Sangha, and Kasai.

Navigation is interrupted by dangerous rapids up to 160 km/100 mi long, notably from the Zambian border to Bukama; below Kongolo, where the gorge known as the Gates of Hell is located; above Kisangani, where the Stanley Falls are situated; and between Kinshasa and Matadi.

Boma is a large port on the estuary; Matadi is a port 80 km/50 mi from the Atlantic, for ocean-going ships; and at Pool Malebo (formerly Stanley Pool), a widening of the river 560 km/350 mi from its mouth which encloses the marshy island of Bamu, are Brazzaville on the western shore and Kinshasa on the southwestern. The Inga dam supplies Matadi and Kinshasa with electricity.

history The mouth of the Zaïre was seen by the Portuguese navigator Diego Cal 482, but the vast extent of its system became known to Europeans only with the explorations of Livingstone and Stanley. Its navigation from source to mouth was completed by the expedition 1974 led by English explorer John Blashford-Snell (1936–   ), supported by President Mobutu.

Zákinthos or *Zante* most southerly of the ◊Ionian Islands, Greece; area 410 sq km/158 sq mi; population (1981) 30,000. Products include olives, currants, grapes, and carpets.

Zambezi river in central and SE Africa; length 2,650 km/1,650 mi from NW Zambia through Mozambique to the Indian Ocean, with a wide delta near Chinde. Major tributaries include the Kafue in Zambia.

It is interrupted by rapids, and includes on the Zimbabwe–Zambia border the Victoria Falls (Mosi-oa-tunya) and Kariba Dam, which forms the reservoir of Lake Kariba with large fisheries.

Zambia landlocked country in central Africa.

Zaïre

Republic of
(République du Zaïre)

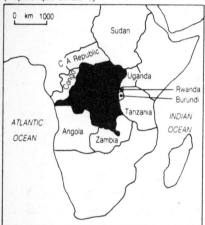

area 2,344,900 sq km/905,366 sq mi
capital Kinshasa
towns Lubumbashi, Kananga, Kisangani; ports
Matadi, Boma
physical Zaïre river·basin has tropical
rainforest and savanna; mountains in east
and west
features lakes Tanganyika, Mobutu Sésé Séko,
and Edward; Ruwenzori mountains
head of state and of government Mobuto
Sésé Séko Kuku Ngbendu wa Zabanga

from 1965
government system one-party socialist
republic
political parties Popular Movement of the
Revolution (MPR), African socialist.
exports palm oil, coffee, tea, rubber, timber,
copper, cobalt (80% of world output), zinc,
cadmium, industrial diamonds
currency zaïre (804.05 = £1 Mar 1989)
population (1988) 33,991,000; annual grow;h
rate 2.9%
life expectancy men 48, women 52
language French (official), Swahili, Lincala
religion 70% Christian, 10% Muslim
literacy 79% male/45% female (1985 est)
GNP $5 bn (1983); $127 per head of population
chronology
1960 Achieved full independence as the
Republic of the Congo. Civil war roke out
between the central government and Katanga
province.
1963 Katanga war ended.
1967 New constitution adopted.
1970 Col Mobutu elected president.
1971 Country became the Republic of Zaïre,
with the Popular Movement of the Revolution
(MPR) the only legal political party.
1974 Foreign-owned businesses and plantations
seized by Mobutu and given in political
patronage.
1977 Original owners of confiscated properties
invited back. Mobutu re-elected.
1984 Mobutu re-elected.
1988 Potential rift with Belgium avoided.

Zante Italian name for the Ionian island of ◊Zákinthos,
Greece.

Zanzibar island region of Tanzania
area 1,658 sq km/640 sq mi (80 km/50 mi long)
towns Zanzibar
products cloves, copra
population (1985) 571,000
history Arab traders settled in the 7th century,
and Zanzibar became a sultanate; under British
protection 1890–1963; together with the island
of Pemba, some nearby islets, and a strip of
mainland territory, it became a republic; merged
with Tanganyika as Tanzania 1964.

Zaporozhye formerly (until 1921) *Aleksandrovsk*
industrial city (steel, chemicals, aluminium goods,
pig iron, magnesium) in Ukraine, USSR, on the
Dnieper, capital of Zaporozhye region and site of
the Dnieper Dam; population (1987) 875,000. It
was occupied by Germany 1941–43.

Zara Italian name for ◊Zadar, port on the Adriatic
coast of Yugoslavia.

Zaragoza (English *Saragossa*) industrial city in
Aragon, Spain; population (1986) 596,000. It

produces iron, steel, chemicals, plastics, canned
food, and electrical goods. The medieval city walls
and bridges over the Ebro survive, and there is a
15th-century university.
history Founded as *Salduba* in pre-Roman days,
it took its present name from Roman conqueror Caesar Augustus; later it was captured by Visigoths and Moors, and was
taken in 1118 by Alfonso the Warrior, King
of Navarre and Aragon, after a nine-month
siege. It remained capital of Aragon until the
end of the 15th century. From June 1808 to
Feb 1809, in the Peninsular War, it resisted
a French siege. Maria Augustin, known as
the 'Maid of Zaragoza' (died 1859), became
a national hero for her part in the defence;
her story is told in Byron's *Childe Harold*
1812–18.

Zealand another name for ◊Sjælland, main island of
Denmark, and for ◊Zeeland, SW province of the
Netherlands.

Zeebrugge small Belgian ferry port on the North
Sea, linked to Bruges by 14 km/9 mi canal (built

Zambia
Republic of

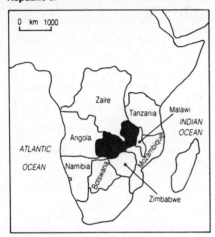

0 km 1000

Zaïre

Tanzania   Malawi
           INDIAN
           OCEAN
Angola

ATLANTIC
OCEAN   Namibia

Zimbabwe

Mozambique

Botswana

area 752,600 sq km/290,579 sq mi
capital Lusaka
towns Kitwe, Ndola, Kabwe, Chipata,
Livingstone
physical a forested plateau cut through
by rivers
features Zambezi River, Kariba Dam; Luangwa
Valley national park has one of the greatest
concentrations of animal life in Africa
head of state and government Kenneth

Kaunda from 1964
government system one-party socialist
republic
political parties United National Independence
Party (UNIP), African socialist
exports copper, emeralds, tobacco
currency kwacha (40.50 = £1 Mar 1989)
population (1989) 7,770,000; annual growth
rate 3.3%
life expectancy men 50, women 53
language English (official); the majority speak
Bantu languages
religion mainly animist, 21% Roman Catholic,
also Protestant, Hindu, and Muslim minorities
literacy 84% male/67% female (1985 est)
GNP $2.6 bn (1984); $570 per head of
population
chronology
1964 Achieved full independence, within the
Commonwealth, as the Republic of Zambia,
with Kenneth Kaunda as president.
1972 United Independence Party (UNIP)
declared the only legal party.
1976 Support for the Patriotic Front in Rhodesia
declared.
1980 Unsuccessful coup against President
Kaunda.
1985 Kaunda elected chair of the Front Line
States.
1987 Kaunda elected chair of the Organization
of African Unity (OAU).
1988 Kaunda re-elected unopposed for sixth
term.

1896–1907). In Mar 1987 it was the scene of a
disaster in which over 180 passengers lost their
lives when the car ferry *Herald of Free Enterprise*
put to sea from Zeebrugge with its car loading
doors not properly closed.

Zeeland province of the SW Netherlands; capital
Middelburg; area 1,790 sq km/691 sq mi; population (1988) 356,000. It includes the estuary of
the Scheldt and the island of Walcheren and North
and South Beveland. Most of Zeeland is below
sea level.

Zelenograd city 145 km/90 mi NE of Moscow,
USSR, where much of the Soviet microelectronics industry is concentrated.

Zermatt tourist centre in the Valais canton, Switzerland, at the foot of the Matterhorn; population
(1985) 3,700.

Zetland official form until 1974 of ◊Shetland, islands
of N Scotland.

Zhangjiakou formerly *Changchiakow* historic
town and trade centre in Hebei province, China,
160 km/100 mi NW of Beijing, on the Great Wall;
population (1980) 1,100,000. Zhangjiakou is on
the border of Inner Mongolia (its Mongolian

name is Kalgan, 'gate') and on the road and
railway to Ulaanbaatar in Mongolia. It developed under the Manchu dynasty, and was
the centre of the tea trade from China to
Russia.

Zhdanov former name (1948–89) of ◊Mariupol, in
Ukraine, USSR.

Zhejiang formerly *Chekiang* province of SE China
area 101,800 sq km/39,295 sq mi
capital Hangzhou
features smallest of the Chinese provinces, it
was the base of the Song dynasty 12th–13th centuries; it is densely populated
products rice, cotton, sugar, jute, maize; timber
on the uplands
population (1986) 40,700,000.

Zhengzhou formerly *Chengchow* industrial city
(light engineering, cotton textiles, foods), capital
of Henan province (from 1954), China, on the
Huang Ho; population (1986) 1,590,000.

In the 1970s the earliest city yet found in China,
from 1500 BC, was excavated near the walls of
Zhengzhou. The Shaolin temple, where the martial art of kung fu originated, is nearby.

Zimbabwe
Republic of

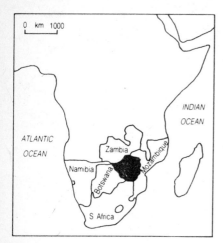

area 390,300 sq km/150,695 sq mi
capital Harare
towns Bulawayo, Gweru, Kwekwe, Mutare, Hwange
physical a high plateau with mountains in the east
features Hwange National Park, part of Kalahari Desert
head of state and government Robert Mugabe from 1987
government system effectively one party socialist republic
political parties Zimbabwe African National Union-Patriotic Front (ZANU-PF), African socialist.
exports tobacco, citrus, tea, coffee, gold, silver
currency Zimbabwe dollar (3.92 = £1 Mar 1989)
population (1989) 9,987,000 (Shona 80%, Ndbele, of Zulu descent, 19%; before independence there were some 275,000 whites, in 1985 about 100,000); annual growth rate 3.5%
life expectancy men 54, women 58
language English (official); Shona, Ndbele, Nyanja
religion Christian
literacy 81% male/67% female (1985 est)
GDP $5 bn (1983); $640 per head of population
chronology
1961 Zimbabwe African People's Union (ZAPU) formed, with Joshua Nkomo as leader.
1962 ZAPU declared illegal.
1963 Zimbabawe African National Union (ZANU) formed, with Robert Mugabe as secretary general.
1964 Ian Smith became prime minister. Nkomo and Mugabe imprisoned.
1965 ZANU banned. Smith declared unilateral independence.
1966–68 Abortive talks between Smith and UK prime minister Harold Wilson.
1974 Nkomo and Mugabe released.
1975 Geneva conference agreed a date for constitutional independence.
1979 Smith produced a new constitution and established a government with Bishop Abel Muzorewa as prime minister. New government denounced by Nkomo and Mugabe. Conference in London agreed independence arrangements (Lancaster House Agreement).
1980 Full independence achieved, with Robert Mugabe as prime minister.
1981 Rift between Mugabe and Nkomo.
1982 NЯomo dismissed from the cabinet and left the country temporarily.
1984 ZANU-People's Front (PF) Party Congress agreed to create a one-party state at some time in the future.
1985 Relations between Mugabe and Nkomo improved.
1986 Joint ZANU-PF rally held amid plans for merger.
1987 White-roll seats in the assembly were abolished. President Banana retired and Mugabe combined the posts of head of state and prime minister with the title executive president.
1988 Nkomo returned to the cabinet and appointed vice-president.
1989 Opposition party, the Zimbabwe Unity Movement, formed by Edgar Tekere. ZANU and ZAPU formally merged.
1990 Mugabe and ZANU-PF re-elected.

Zhitomir capital of Zhitomir region in Ukraine, USSR, west of Kiev; population (1987) 287,000. It is a timber and grain centre, and has furniture factories. Zhitomir dates from the 13th century.

Zhonghua Renmin Gonghe Guo Chinese for People's Republic of ◊China.

Zian another spelling of ◊Xian, city in China.

Zimbabwe landlocked country in central Africa.

Zlatoust industrial city (metallurgy) in Chelyabinsk region, USSR, in the S Urals; population (1987) 206,000. It was founded 1754 as an iron and copper-working settlement, destroyed 1774 by a peasant rising, but developed as an armaments centre from the time of Napoleon's invasion of Russia.

Zomba former capital of Malawi, 32 km/20 mi W of Lake Shirwa; population (1985) 53,000. It was replaced by Lilongwe as capital 1975, but remains the university town.

Zuider Zee former sea inlet in Holland, cut off from the North Sea by the closing of a dyke in 1932, much of which has been reclaimed as land. The remaining lake is called the ◊IJsselmeer.

Zululand region in Natal, South Africa, largely corresponding to the Black National State KwaZulu. It was formerly a province, annexed to Natal 1897.

Zürich financial centre and industrial city (machinery, electrical goods, textiles) on Lake Zürich, capital of Zürich canton, the largest city in Switzerland; population (1987) 840,000. The university was refounded 1833.

Zutphen town in Gelderland province, Netherlands; population (1987) 31,000.

Zwickau coalmining and industrial town in Karl-Marx-Stadt county, East Germany, on the Mulde; population (1986) 121,000. It is the birthplace of the composer Robert Schumann.

Zwolle capital of Overijssel province, Netherlands, a market town with brewing, distilling, butter making, and other industries; population (1988) 91,000.